Books on the Analytic Hierarchy Process Available from RWS Publications

Analytical Planning: The Organization of Systems, Thomas L. Saaty and Kevin P. Kearns, 208 pp., paperback edition, 1991.

Decision Making for Leaders, Thomas L. Saaty, paperback, 291 pp., 1990.

Multicriteria Decision Making: The Analytic Hierarchy Process, Thomas L. Saaty, paperback, 502 pp., extended edition, paperback, 1991.

The Logic of Priorities: Applications in Business, Energy, Health, and Transportation, Thomas L. Saaty and Luis G. Vargas, paperback, 299 pp., paperback edition, 1991.

Books on the Analytic Hierarchy Process Available from other Publishers

Marketing Decisions Using Expert Choice, R.F. Dyer, E.A. Forman, E.H. Forman, G. Jouflas, workbook, 201 pp., 1988, Expert Choice, Inc., Pittsburgh, Pennsylvania.

An Analytic Approach to Marketing Decisions, Robert F. Dyer & Ernest H. Forman, 367 pp., 1991, Prentice Hall, Inc.

The Analytic Hierarchy Process: Applications and Studies, Bruce L. Golden, Patrick T. Harker and Edward A. Wasil,(Eds.), 1989, Springer-Verlag, New York.

Conflict Resolution: The Analytic Hierarchy Approach, Thomas L. Saaty and Joyce M. Alexander, 1989, Praeger, New York.

Thinking with Models, Thomas L. Saaty and Joyce M. Alexander, 181 pp., 1981, Pergamon Press, Inc.

Prediction, Projection, and Forecasting, Thomas L. Saaty and Luis G. Vargas, 253 pp., 1991, Kluwer Academic Publishers.

To Order RWS Publications' Books: Call, Write or Fax

RWS PUBLICATIONS
Decision Making Using the AHP
4922 Ellsworth Avenue
Pittsburgh, PA 15213 USA

Phone: (412) 621-4492   FAX: (412) 682-3844

Analytical Planning

The Organization of Systems

The first part of the book is a distillation of the philosophy, ideology, and practices of systems science and planning. The authors suggest that the systems approach is a necessary but not sufficient condition of holistic problem solving. In order to have a meaningful impact on planning in the public and private sectors, the theory and philosophy of the systems approach must be operationalized in a practical and useable framework for practitioners. The Analytic Hierarchy Process, developed by Thomas L. Saaty, is introduced as a systems approach to systems problems.

Part two introduces planning as a unique form of decision making with illustrations of some prominent philosophical and methodological approaches. The Analytical Hierarchy Process is applied to many problems of strategic planning, benefit/cost analysis, and resource allocation.

Analytical Planning is ideal for advanced undergraduates or graduate students in the social and behavioral sciences, management science, operations research, and schools of business and public administration. It will also be a useful reference for practitioners with an interest in planning in many different contexts.

Analytical Planning
The Organization of Systems

by

THOMAS L. SAATY

and

KEVIN P. KEARNS

Volume IV

The Analytic Hierarchy Process Series

To Order RWS Publications' Books: Call, Write or Fax

RWS PUBLICATIONS
Decision Making Using the AHP
4922 Ellsworth Avenue
Pittsburgh, PA 15213 USA

Phone (412) 621-4492   FAX (412) 682-3844

First edition 1985 by Pergamon Press, Oxford under the title:

Analytical Planning
The Organization of Systems
under the ISBN 0-08-032599-8

Copyright © 1985 T.L. Saaty and K.P. Kearns

Reprinted in paperback, 1991, by RWS Publications

ISBN 0-9620317-4-7

RWS Publications
Decision Making using the AHP
4922 Ellsworth Avenue
Pittsburgh, PA 15213
Phone: (412) 621-4492
FAX: (412) 682-3844

Preface

This book is about a new methodological approach to planning. The Analytic Hierarchy Process has been applied to planning for at least 10 years beginning with the Sudan Transport Study, followed by another application to one of the largest beer industries in Mexico. Since that time, the process has been used widely in several countries to set priorities, carry out cost-benefit analysis and allocate resources. Recent applications have been made by several organizations to the nuclear energy field. The Nuclear Regulatory Commission has used the method as has the Canadian National Research Council to allocate resources to research areas. More recently, the AHP has been used in systems design. In Israel, Professor Ami Arbel has worked with the aircraft industry to design a new airplane. He found it helpful to deal with trading off intangible factors and also tangible ones for which no formula is available to relate them analytically.

A large number of applications to planning have been made by managers in Pittsburgh industries ranging from banking to steel and to the development of energy resources. We have applied it in the municipal area to induce cooperation and coordinate services under a common purpose. This variety has led us to write a book about it.

We decided to include in this book a discussion of complexity and systems to make it clear that the methodology used in planning cannot be simplistic without losing some major elements in a planning problem. Our conclusion is that the structure of the problem can be as complex as one desires, to include the relevant actors, objectives, criteria and alternatives, but the analysis must be simple and uniform. The approach should not defy the capabilities of the average person to understand what is going on and participate in the inputs and in the interpretation of the outputs.

For space limitations, we have worked out some examples in detail and given references to a large number of other applications.

Our complex society, with its myriad problems, can no longer be taken a little at a time. It must be approached as a whole; related issues must be looked at simultaneously rather than sequentially. Systems and planning are two fundamental concepts that are intertwined: it is impossible to think of one without the other. We plan within a system, for no system comes about by chance. It must be designed with considerable forethought. Some systems develop and evolve in response to needs. The food system is one example; a biological system is another. It takes such systems long periods of time to find the correct response. Often the response does not work well. Most systems, in fact, disintegrate and vanish. If the needs are those of sick or hungry people, compassion demands that we design responses quickly rather than wait for things simply to happen. Our human spirit rebels when we stand by to see an undesirable outcome beyond our control materialize. Selective inattention and wishful thinking too often result in undesirable outcomes.

In complex environments, things do not automatically work themselves out. We must plan in order to be better equipped to respond. Our world society with 4.8 billion inhabitants, 6 billion in twenty more years, will not get simpler. It cannot rely on statistics for solutions. We need to plan our future with a clear and definite sense of purpose, and we must learn to do it successfully.

The book is organized according to a conceptual framework which links the concepts of systems and planning and suggests a methodological tool for integrating the two.

Part I presents the basic ideas behind complexity, systems, hierarchies and prioritization.

Part II of the book introduces planning as a unique form of decision making with illustrations of some prominent philosophical and methodological approaches. In particular, we discuss some shortcomings of traditional approaches to planning and illustrate how the systems approach addresses these shortcomings.

This book is intended as an introduction to the subject designed for both researchers and practitioners. Those impatient with the philosophy of systems but are interested in planning may read Chapter 3 along with Part II.

Contents

PART I. Systems and Complexity

Chapter 1 Complexity   3

  1. Introduction   3
  2. Complexity   4
  3. Examples of Complex Problems   5
  4. Need for a Broader World View   7
     References   8
     Suggested Readings   9
     Books on Systems Theory   9
     Journals   11

Chapter 2 Systems   12

  1. The Rationale for Systems Thinking   12
  2. Causal Explanation—How Reductionism Works   13
  3. Systems Theory Past and Present   15
  4. The Conceptual Value of Systems Theory   17
     References   18
     Suggested Readings   18

Chapter 3 The Analytic Hierarchy Process   19

  1. Introduction   19
  2. The Principle of Identity and Decomposition   20
  3. The Principle of Discrimination and Comparative Judgments   22
  4. Synthesis of Priorities   30
  5. A Summary of Steps in the AHP   38
  6. Hierarchies as Representations of Complexity   39
  7. Some Justification for the 1–9 Scale   44
  8. Group Judgments and Variable Judgments   46
  9. Measuring Performance   46
  10. Additional Applications of the AHP   47
  11. Comments on Dependence   52
  12. Comparison with Other Methods   56
  13. Conclusion   60
     References   61
     Suggested Readings   62

Chapter 4 Systems Characteristics and the Analytic Hierarchy Process   63

  1. Introduction   63
  2. Purpose   63
  3. Functions   69
  4. Flows   70
  5. Structures   72

Contents

6. Characterization of Open Systems — 74
7. Prerequisites for an Effective Systems Methodology — 79
8. The Object of Systems Study: Design and Control — 81
9. On Designing Adaptive Systems — 84
   References — 85
   Suggested Readings — 86

PART II. Strategic Planning

Chapter 5 Current Theories of Planning — 89

1. Introduction: To Plan or Not to Plan? — 89
2. Ways of Thinking about Planning — 90
3. A Definition of Planning — 95
4. Philosophies of Planning — 98
5. Conclusion — 126
   References — 127
   Suggested Readings — 129

Chapter 6 Strategic Planning — 133

1. Introduction — 133
2. The Planning Process — 134
3. The Forward-Backward Planning Process — 134
4. Rationale for the Forward-Backward Planning Process — 136
5. Combining the Forward and Backward Processes — 136
6. Summary of Forward-Backward Analysis — 139
7. Forward Planning Example: Future of Higher Education in the United States (1985–2000) — 140
8. Backward Planning Example with Program Selection and Allocation of Resources for Commercial Power Generation Engineering — 151
9. Forward-Backward Planning for a Consumer Products Manufacturer — 154
10. Risk and Uncertainty — 165
11. The Future of Synthetic Transportation Fuels — 167
12. Conclusion — 175
    References — 176
    Suggested Readings — 177

Chapter 7 Benefit-Cost Analysis and Resource Allocation — 178

1. Introduction — 178
2. Benefit-Cost Analysis: Traditional and AHP Approaches — 179
3. Resource Allocation — 186
4. Conclusion — 198
   References — 199
   Suggested Readings — 199
   Other Books on Benefit-Cost Analysis and Resource Allocation — 200

Author Index — 201

Subject Index — 205

PART I
Systems and Complexity

This part includes four chapters on systems and complexity and on the Analytic Hierarchy Process as a systems *approach to* systems *problems. Chapter 1 deals with complexity and interaction, Chapter 2 with systems, Chapter 3 with the methodology and Chapter 4 with systems characteristics and how they are reflected in the methodology.*

CHAPTER 1
Complexity

1. Introduction

A striking feature of our world environment is the increasing complexity and interdependence of its parts. The myriad problems that occur in our daily lives are interwoven in a fabric whose features cannot be described simply by the colors of its constituent threads.

These problems, whether social, political, or economic, do not exist in isolation. They cannot be factored out of the whole, each explained on its own and the set of explanations thrown together to explain the whole. Indeed, we might even question that problems fall into specialized "social," "political," or "economic" classes. All but the very trivial issues in any of these spheres of activity are related to corresponding problems in the other spheres. Adding to our dilemma is the continually changing nature of this interdependence. Interdependence is affected by changes in population, resources, cartels, technology and the like.

The environment in which problems occur is itself not a static entity. It is *dynamic* as it is always changing by being drawn on, dumped in, explored and manipulated. The environment changes as its problems and their solutions change; it changes in physical and conceptual *space* as the relations among the parts are altered by technological advances and filtered through highly personal interpretive structures. It also changes in time, as events markedly affect it.

Complexity is many things acting together. This concept lies at the heart of general systems theory, the topic of our inquiry. Our finite, partly emotional, partly logical minds, which are our windows for seeing the world, have complexities of their own. These internal complexities must themselves be understood because we believe that our construction of reality is relative to our physical and behavioral make-up.

In this chapter we explore the nature of complexity itself and some of the current problems facing society. Systems ideas have been applied in a diversity of real life problems ranging from food distribution to medicine. Still the practical value of systems thinking in such areas, has been questioned and criticized. We intend to examine some of what has been said.

What we need are sensible ways to deal with our problems. The approach given here facilitates the use of creativity and experience to structure complex

4   Analytical Planning

problems and pursue their solution within an accessible and systematic framework.

2. Complexity

Complexity has been defined as a large number of things that interact in a nonsimple way (Simon, 1965). Some would argue that quantity is not a requirement for complexity. A single thing like a knot in a rope can, of itself, be complex. However, we must distinguish between the complex and the difficult. The knot has a single solution that may be difficult but whose purpose is clear: to free the rope. A complex problem usually has many possible solutions, and these solutions can serve many purposes. For example, the design or modification of an integrated urban transportation system will require consideration of air, land and, possibly, water facilities. The objective would be to develop and maintain an appropriate *mix* of these that would complement each other. There would be several, perhaps many, such mixes, any one of which might effectively address the problem.

Complexity is *interaction* and, more importantly, *interdependence*—that is, the behavior of one or several elements affects the behavior of other elements. For example, the economy depends on energy and other resources, the availability of energy depends on politics, politics depends on power, and power depends on military strength and economic stability. Note that these interdependencies are symmetrical: politics depends on the economy, but the economy also depends on politics. What results is a complex network of symmetric relations with varying *intensity*. It is through *differentiation* that the degree of exclusiveness of the elements becomes apparent in the complex framework in which they occur. By differentiation we mean that the social and/or functional roles of the interacting elements are clearly different; they unfold in a unique and discernible pattern. Complexity depends not only on the interdependence but also on the *number* of interacting components. (See also Weaver, 1948.) Therefore a defensible framework for dealing with complexity depends on the new properties produced from the *synergy* of interaction of interdependent parts. Such properties are not in the parts and are frequently attributable to new elements or clusters that are a result of interactions of existing elements.

Our interpretation and understanding of complexity depends on our culture, language, previous experience, professional training and the logic we use to piece together the parts of the puzzle. This subjectivity presents a higher-order dilemma that dispels any latent suspicion that there is an objective interpretation of reality that transcends our senses and cognition. It seems that our best hope is to make do with what we have in the only way we know how by setting our priorities and pursuing their fulfillment to the best of our ability. Few of our answers are likely to remain unchanged forever.

The people (called actors) who decide what action to take to solve complex problems and those affected by the decision (called stakeholders) usually have different interests and conflicting goals. There may be no consensus (within these two groups or between them) on desired ends or on strategies designed to achieve these ends. Thus, the selection of goals and also the selection of the means to achieve them require debate and compromise. Participants may approach the decision process with different assumptions about environmental constraints and the internal constraints of the system itself. These assumptions shape their perceptions, determine their definitions of the problem, and condition their responses to it. Precisely because conflicting goals result from alternative judgments and judgments are value-laden, we must attempt to bring to the surface, draw out, and examine values and special interests in complex decision problems.

Another difficulty one encounters in understanding complexity is what we discussed earlier, that is, the linkage of its many problems in what is called the *problematique*. The solution of the set as a whole cannot be derived by dividing it into small problems, solving these, and synthesizing an overall solution to the larger problem. Complex problems never exist in isolation and seldom are characterized by one-way causal relations. Rather, complexity links problems together and forms a pattern of mutual interaction and multiple causality. The precise nature of the pattern may not be clearly understood. Too often we discover that problems are linked only after we have implemented "solutions," which to our dismay, generate second-order problems.

3. Examples of Complex Problems

A host of interdependent domestic and international problems graphically illustrate that our world is much more than a mere collection of isolated and autonomous elements. Here are a few brief examples.

Consider the availability of venture capital which is an important factor in a robust economy. Also consider the availability of new sources of energy. The availability of money to explore and develop alternative energy sources depends on economic policies such as tax breaks for certain investments, lower interest rates on loans, and sufficient rewards for success. Such measures could encourage excess money to float in the direction of new energy development. The ultimate outcome would be intensified competition in the energy market and lower oil prices. In turn, lower oil prices would help slow down the rate of inflation, thus contributing to robustness of the economy.

Patterns of food production and distribution are also linked to issues of international economic development. Third World nations often are frustrated in their attempts to industrialize their economies. The reason is, in part, that they must export many of their most precious raw materials and natural resources in order to obtain favorable trade relations with the industrialized nations for their food producing potential.

Shifting the emphasis of food production from the cultivation of currently

6 *Analytical Planning*

arable regions to the cultivation of unused land, as some have suggested, only worsens the interrelated energy problems. Rendering new land productive requires a greater investment of energy per acre.

In addition, preparing new land for cultivation frequently entails deforestation which can upset the ecological balance. Also expanding the productive capacity of currently used land can result in severe soil erosion. In the long run, once rich farmland may be transformed into a barren desert. It appears that both supply and demand for food has effects on the ecology and on expenditure for energy.

Another example is the nuclear arms race. Issues of disarmament involve more than the obvious concerns of national security and real or imagined risk. Military spending has a significant impact on the infrastructure of industries and activities that supply transportation, communication, and central power—the base of any modern economic system. A dramatic shift in the pattern of military spending is likely to have immediate and far-reaching effects on any economic system of which it has become an integral component. Reduced military spending would not only put many people out of work; it would also constrain research activities that often lead to products with peacetime as well as war-time uses. This problem which is affected by tangible and intangible forces is considered a high priority problem as it affects the survival of mankind.

The economy presents yet another example of complexity. Our frequent failure to accurately predict fluctuations in the economy suggests that the complexity inherent in socio-economic behavior may exceed the limits of our intellectual capabilities. Even with the use of sophisticated economic theories and models, we find that we are unable to cope with the complex network of interrelations. We have difficulty predicting the short-term, year-to-year or even month-to-month, state of the economy. Long term predictions of several years or more amount to little more than educated guesswork. Symptoms occur in one sector of the economy as a result of events in another sector. For example, productivity is related to capital investment, which in turn is related to interest rates, credit availability, and tax incentives. The state of the economy is also related to labor mobility patterns, which in turn are related to a host of local and regional issues such as employment opportunities, cost of living, and general quality of life. Finally, the state of the economy is, to a large extent, determined by intangibles such as confidence in the policies of elected leaders. If there is widespread trust and confidence in the economic policies formulated by government leaders, then economic growth becomes, in effect, a self-fulfilling prophecy. The reverse is also true. This economic vitality may be as much a state of mind as a state of being.

The circular patterns of the economy and its subjective, intangible elements make it difficult to identify points of intervention that offer the potential for producing desired effects. We have come to realize that actions taken now are not likely to produce immediate results; and the results ultimately produced may be manifestations of the multiple intervening forces that are not easily isolated or clearly understood today.

4. Need for a Broader World View

Complexity and interdependence play a prominent role in all the examples above.

Addressing these problems requires an approach which enables us to use a variety of relevant information including both "hard" data, such as quantifiable information, and "soft" data derived from intuition, experience, values, judgments and imaginative guesswork. In this way we might extend our analysis to include possible outcomes that may otherwise have escaped notice.

Our conceptualization of "knowledge" should include subjective observations and interpretations as well as "objective" assessments of reality. This is partly because there is knowledge other than that derived from repeated experimentation and scientific proof. With respect to the systems that touch our lives, such as the community in which we live or the organizations in which we work, we "know" things about phenomena which we have never rigorously analyzed and we draw conclusions which we have never proved in a scientific manner. In any event it may not always be possible to define the most objective approach.

Finally we have seen new interpretations of much of our basic knowledge as new information is made available. Newtonian physics no longer enjoys the status developed over two centuries and even the theory of relativity may come under revision because of new findings. Scientific knowledge is dynamic, and undergoes revolutions (Kuhn, 1970) as old theories are replaced or substantially modified. Objectivity is relative to the degree of knowledge we possess. It follows that our view of the real world is still largely a matter of cultural understanding and interpretation. In recent years scientists are learning to take seriously processes of cognition that deviate from the norms of the classical scientific method. LeShan and Margenau (1982) in a remarkable book liken the theory of relativity to van Gogh's sky as an ingenious product of imagination and culture rather than of greater and greater success to fathom an "ultimate truth." Still there are many scientists living today who would tend to dismiss as "personal opinion" knowledge claims that are not derived from a scientific process that includes rules and procedures.

We must pause to draw attention to the fact that the scientific method has not adapted well to human affairs. The fields of Operations Research and Management Science have developed a variety of models and techniques to deal with complexity mechanistically. Their greatest failure has been in the human area of learning and adaptability, politics, and conflict resolution. Classical problem solving requires that a problem be solved in advance or

8   Analytical Planning

better, prevented from happening. As a result one simulates data for use in the model before the problem occurs. But no problem occurs exactly as people perceive it. This is especially true of conflicts. One may attempt to prevent conflicts from occurring but once they have occurred, a different procedure is needed to diffuse or stop them. The real situation is that problems are solved (if at all) when they occur and the more lasting a problem is the more it is that it needs to be solved in process. In that case the information obtained has greater value and repetition giving a better idea about what sort of new information might be needed.

Still there are complex problems whose solutions are far too costly or practically impossible to obtain. For such problems it may be cheaper and more desirable to redesign the system in which they arise. To do this requires a considerable investment in intellectual and material resources and a political ability to pursuade people to accept change.

The systems approach would be somewhat better suited for problem solving were it in a better position to utilize joint use of the deductive and inductive methods of science. The first to understand what is likely to happen and the second how best to control situations so that the likely outcome can be steered towards what is desired. We turn to the study of systems in Chapter 2.

References

Bertalanffy, Ludwig von (1968) *General Systems Theory*, New York: George Braziller.
Bertalanffy, Ludwig von (1972) The History and Status of General Systems Theory, *In Trends in General Systems Theory*, George Klir (ed.), New York; Wiley, pp. 21–41.
Boulding, Kenneth E. (1968) General Systems Theory: The Skeleton of Science, in *Modern Systems Research for the Behavioral Scientist*, Walter Buckley (ed.) Chicago: Aldine, pp. 3–10.
Blauberg, Igor, V. N. Sardovsky and E. G. Yudin (1977) *Systems Theory: Philosophical and Methodological Problems*, Moscow: Progress Press.
Churchman, C. West, R. L. Ackoff and E. L. Arnoff (1957) *Introduction to Operations Research*, New York: John Wiley and Sons.
Ellul, Jacques (1964) *The Technological Society*, New York: Alfred A. Knopf.
Kuhn, Thomas (1970) *The Structure of Scientific Revolutions*, Chicago: Aldine.
LeShan, Lawrence and Henry Margenau (1982) *Einstein's Space and van Gogh's Sky*, New York: McMillan.
Mitroff, Ian and James Emshoff (1979) On Strategic Assumption-making: A Dialectic Approach to Policy and Planning, *Academy of Management Review*, 4, pp. 1–12.
Odum, Howard T. (1971) *Environment, Power and Society*, New York: Wiley Interscience.
Saaty, Thomas L. (1980) *The Analytic Hierarchy Process*, New York: McGraw-Hill.
Shannon, Claude and Warren Weaver (1964 (c) 1948) *The Mathematical Theory of Communication*, Urbana: University of Illinois Press.
Simon, Herbert A. (1965) The Architecture of Complexity, in *Yearbook of the Society for General Systems Research*, Ludwig von Bertalanffy and Anatol Rappoport (eds.) 10, pp. 63–76.
Watson, James D. (1968) *The Double Helix*, New York: Signet.
Weaver, Warren (1948) Science and Complexity, *American Scientist*, 36, pp. 536–544.
Wiener, Norbert (1948) *Cybernetics*, Cambridge: Technology Press.
Wilson, Edward O. (1975) *Sociobiology: The New Synthesis*, Cambridge, MA: Harvard University Press.

Suggested Readings

Ellul, Jaques, *The Technological Society*, New York: Alfred A. Knopf, 1964.
  Ellul's thesis is that rapid advances in scientific methods and technological innovations will soon come to dominate the human processes that created them. Rationalism, scientism and the endless search for optimally efficient systems have become obsessions of man which have permeated and dehumanized every realm of his activities from the production of children's toys to strategies of nuclear warfare. In Ellul's view, man has become a slave of his means and consequently has lost sight of the ends for which the means were invented. Unless we take immediate steps to once again control our technology, we will gradually lose confidence in our own innate judgment while becoming more and more devoted to and, indeed, enslaved by the power of rationalism. When rational methods take precedence over human judgment, our capacity to think and reason independently of "science" will gradually whither and die.

Mitroff, Ian and Fransico Sagasti, Epistemology as General Systems Theory: An Approach to the Design of Complex Decision Making Experiments, *Philosophy of the Social Sciences*, 3 (1973) pp. 117–134.
  This article is an example of the post-positive approach to problem definition and problem structuring. Problems are not objective conditions determined by facts but rather are subjectively mediated and interpreted in terms of the values, interests, and world views of the observer. Ill-structured problems are actually interdependent systems of problems in which multiple decision makers in a pluralistic environment consider unlimited alternatives whose outcomes are either unknown or very uncertain. Most problems confronting society are ill-structured problems which require that systems thinkers impose parts of themselves on the problem in order to define it. This mode of problem structuring requires creativity and acknowledgement of the roles of values, interests, and subjective judgment.

Books on Systems Theory

Ackoff, R. L., *Redesigning the Future: A Systems Approach to Societal Problems*, New York: Wiley, 1974.
Ackoff, R. L. and Emery, *On Purposeful Systems*, Chicago: Aldine, 1972.
Ashby, W. R., *An Introduction to Cybernetics*, New York: Wiley, 1963.
Baker, Frank (editor), *Organizational Systems: General Systems Approaches to Complex Organizations*, Irwin, 1973.
Banathy, Bela, *A Systems View of Education*, Fearon, 1973.
Beckett, J. A., *Management Dynamics: One New Synthesis*, New York: McGraw-Hill, 1971.
Beer, S., *Brain of the Firm: A Development in Management Cybernetics*, Herder and Herder, 1972.
Beishon, John and Peters, Geoff eds. *Systems Behavior*, New York: Harper Row, 1973.
Benton, J. B., *Managing the Organizational Decision Process*, Lexington: Lexington Books, 1973.
Berlinski, D., *On Systems Analysis: An Essay Concerning the Limitations of Some Mathematical Methods in the Social, Political, and Biological Sciences*, Cambridge: MIT Press, 1976.
Berrien, F., A General Systems Approach to Organizations, in *Handbook of Industrial and Organizational Psych.*, M. Dunnette, ed., Chicago: Rand McNally, 1976.
Bertalanffy, Ludwig von, *General Systems Theory*, New York: George Braziller, 1968.
Bertalanffy, Ludwig von, *Perspectives on General Systems Theory: Scientific and Philosophical Studies*, New York: George Braziller, 1975.
Boguslow, Robert, *The New Utopians, A Study of System Design and Social Change*, Englewood Cliffs: Prentice-Hall, 1965.
Bossel, S., Klacko and N. Muller (editors), *Systems Theory in the Social Sciences: Stochastic and Control Systems, Fuzzy Analysis, Simulation, Behavioral Models*, Basez, Birkhauser, 1976.
Brauers, W. K., *Systems Analysis, Planning and Decision Models*: with special reference to national defense. New York: Elsevier, 1976.
Buckley, Walter Frederick, *Modern Systems Research for Behavioral Scientist; a Source Book*, Chicago: Aldine, 1968.
Buckley, Walter Frederick, *Sociology and Modern System Theory*, Englewood Cliffs: Prentice-Hall, 1967.
Buckley, Walter Frederick, (editor) *Scientist*, Chicago: Aldine, 1968.

10   Analytical Planning

Buckley, Walter Frederick, *Sociology and Modern System Theory*, Englewood Cliffs: Prentice Hall, 1967.
Catanese, Anthony James and Alan Walter Steiss, *Systemic Planning: Theory and Application*, Lexington: Heath-Lexington Books, 1970.
Cavallo, R. E., *The Role of Systems Methodology in Social Science Research*, The Hague: Martinus Nijhoff, 1979.
Cavallo, R. E., (editor) *Recent Developments in Systems Methodology for Social Research*, The Hague: Martinus Nijhoff, 1979.
Chadwick, G., *A Systems View of Planning: Towards a Theory of the Urban and Regional Planning Process*, New York: Pergamon, 1972.
Chartrand, R., *Systems Technology Applied to Social and Community Problems*, Hayden, 1970.
Churchman, C. West, *The Design of Inquiring Systems*, New York: Basic, 1972.
Churchman, C. West, *The Systems Approach*, New York: Dell, 1969.
Churchman, C. West, *The Systems Approach and Its Enemies*, New York: Basic, 1979.
Cooper, W. W., C. Eastman, Johnson, and Kortanec, *Systems Approach to Urban Planning: Mixed, Conditional, Adaptive and Other Alternatives*, CMU, Institute of Physical Planning, Res. Report #6, Pittsburgh, 1970.
DeGreene, Kenyon B., *Sociotechnical Systems: Factors in Analysis, Design and Management*, Englewood Cliffs: Prentice Hall, 1973.
DeGreene, Kenyon B., *Systems Psychology*, New York: McGraw-Hill, 1970.
Demereth and Peterson, *System Change & Conflict*, New York: Free Press, 1967.
Deutsch, K. W., et al. (editors) *Problems of World Modeling: Political and Social Implications*, Ballinger, 1977.
Deutsch, K. W., *The Nerves of Government*, second edition, New York: Free Press, 1966.
Dimitrove, *The Systems View of Planning*, New York: Oxford Polytechnic, 1972.
Emery, F. E., (editor) *Systems Thinking*, New York: Penguin, 1970.
Emshoff, James R., *Analysis of Behavioral Systems*, New York: MacMillan, 1971.
Ericson, R., (editor) *Improving the Human Condition: Quality and Stability in Social Systems*, Basel: Birkhouser Verlag, 1979.
Exton, William, *The Age of Systems; the Human Dilemma*, American Mgt. Association, 1972.
Faurre, Pierre and Depeyrot, Michel, *Elements of System Theory* Amsterdam: North Holland, 1977.
Forrester, J. W., *Principles of Systems*, Wright-Allen, 1968.
Fuller, Buckminster, *Synergetics*, New York: MacMillan, 1974.
Hall, Darl Meredith, *The Management of Human Systems*, Cleveland: Association for Systems Management, 1971.
Hoos, Ida, R., *Systems Analysis in Public Policy*, Chicago: University of Chicago Press, 1972.
Huse, E. and J. Bowditch, *Behavior in Organizations: A Systems Approach to Managing*, second edition, Reading: Addison-Wesley, 1977.
Jantsch, E., and C. H. Waddington, *Evolution and Consciousness: Human Systems in Transition*, Reading: Addison-Wesley, 1976.
Johnson, Richard Arird, F. E. Kast and J. E. Rosenzweig, *The Theory and Management of Systems*, New York: McGraw-Hill, 1963.
Karnapp and Rosenberg, *Systems Dynamics—A Unified Approach*, New York: Wiley Interscience, 1975.
Kast, F., and J. Rosenzweig, *Organization and Management: Systems and Contingency Approach*, third edition, New York: McGraw-Hill, 1979.
Katz and Kahn, *The Social Psychology of Organizations*, second edition, New York: Wiley & Sons, 1978.
Kelleher, G. J., (editor) *Challenge to Systems Analysis, Public Policy and Social Change*, New York: Wiley, 1970.
Kelly, William F., *Management Through Systems and Procedures; The Total Systems Concept*, New York: Wiley, 1969.
Kircher, Paul W. and R. N. Mason, *Introduction to Enterprise: A Systems Approach*, Los Angeles: Melville Publishing Co., 1975.
Klir, George J., *Trends in General Systems Theory*, New York: Wiley Interscience, 1972.
Klir, George J., *Applied General Systems Research: Recent Developments and Trends*, Plenum Press, 1977.
Kotter, *Organizational Dynamics: Diagnosis and Intervention*, Reading: Addison-Wesley, 1978.

Kramer and DeSmit, *Systems Thinking*, Boston: Kluner, 1977.
Laszlo, E., *Introduction to Systems Philosophy: Toward a New Paradigm of Contemporary Thought*, New York: Harper and Row, 1972.
Laszlo, E., (editor) *The Relevance of General Systems Theory*, New York: Braziller, 1972.
Laszlo, E., *The Systems View of the World: The Natural Philosophy of the New Developments in the Sciences*, New York: Braziller, 1972.
Laszlo, E., (editor) *The World System: Models, Norms, Applications*, New York: Braziller, 1973.
Laszlo, E., *A Strategy for the Future, the Systems Approach to World Order*, New York: Braziller, 1974.
Lilienfeld, R., *The Rise of Systems Theory: Ideological Analysis*, New York: Wiley, 1975.
Marx and Hillix, *Systems and Theories in Psychology*, third edition, New York: McGraw-Hill, 1979.
Matthies, Leslie H., *The Management System: Systems are for People*, New York: Wiley, 1976.
Merton, *Social Theory and Social Structure*, New York: Free Press, 1949.
Mesarovic, M. D., and Y. Takahara, *General Systems Theory: Mathematical Foundations*, New York: Academic Press, 1975.
Mesarovic, M., (editor) *Views on General Systems Theory: Proceedings*, second edition, Systems Symposium, Case Institute, 1963, Huntington: Krieger, 1974 (c1964).
Mesarovic, M., and A. Reisman, (editors) *Systems Approach and the City*, Amsterdam: North Holland, 1972.
Miles, R., (editor) *Systems Concepts: Lectures on Contemporary Approaches to Systems*, New York: Wiley, 1973.
Miller, J., *Living Systems*, New York: McGraw-Hill, 1978.
Milsum, John H., *Positive Feedback: A General Systems Approach to Positive/Negative Feedback and Mutual Causality*, New York: Pergamon Press, 1968.
Ruben, B. D. and Kim, (editors) *General Systems Theory and Human Communication*, Hayden, 1975.
Rubin, M. D. (editor) *Man in Systems*, New York: Gordon and Breach, 1971.
Saaty, T. L., *The Analytic Hierarchy Process*, New York: McGraw-Hill International, 1980.
Seiler, J., *Systems Analysis in Organizational Behavior*, Homewood, Dorsey Press, 1967.
Sutherland, J. W., *Administrative Decision Making: Extending the Bounds of Rationality*, Van Nostrand Reinhold, 1977.
Sutherland, J. W., *Societal Systems: Methodology, Modeling, and Management*, Amsterdam, North-Holland, 1978.
Sutherland, J. W., *A General Systems Philosophy for the Social and Behavioral Sciences*, New York: Braziller, 1973.
Teune, H. and Z. Milinar, *The Developmental Logic of Social Systems*, Beverly Hills, Sage, 1978.
Van Gigch, J. P., *Applied General Systems Theory*, New York: Harper Row, 1974.
Werck, K., *The Social Psychology of Organizing*, Reading: Addison-Wesley, 1969.
Weinberg, Gerald M., *An Introduction to General Systems Thinking*, New York: Wiley, 1975.
Weiss, P., *Hierarchally Organized System in Theory and Practice*, Hofner, 1971.
Weltman, *System Theory in International Relations*, Lexington: Lexington Books, 1973.
Wright, Chester and Michael D. Tate, *Economics and Systems Analysis: Introduction for Public Managers*, Reading: Addison-Wesley, 1973.
Young, Stanley, *Management: a Systems Analysis*, Glenview: Scott, Foresman, 1966.
Zadeh, L. A., et al. (editors) *Fuzzy Sets and Their Applications to Cognitive and Decision Processes*, New York: Academic Press, 1975.
Zadeh, L. A., and Polak, *Systems Theory*, New York: McGraw-Hill, 1969.

Journals

General Systems: Yearbook of the Society for General Systems Research (since 1956).
Behavioral Science (initially published by the Mental Health Research Institute of the University of Michigan, became a journal of SGSR with vol. 18, 1973, edited by J. G. Miller).
Cybernetica (Belgium): *Kybernetes; Kybernetik; Kybernetika.*
International Journal of General Systems.
IEEE Transactions on Systems, Man, and Cybernetics; Proceedings of the Nth Annual Symposium of the American Society for Cybernetics.
Information and Control; Information Sciences; Journal of Cybernetics.

CHAPTER 2

Systems

1. The Rationale for Systems Thinking

The planning and management sciences, including economics, policy analysis, business and public administration, have historically patterned their methods and procedures of analysis after the natural sciences, such as physics and chemistry, by embracing logical positivism and reductionist logic as the most rational approaches to scientific inquiry. Logical positivism is a set of philosophical propositions which suggest that there is an "objective" reality existing independently of, or not colored by, our personal perspectives or subjective interpretations of the world. For example, a positivist would maintain that a problem confronting our society, such as energy supply is perceived in the same, or at least highly similar ways by any number of different people and that solutions to these problems emerge from a consensus on the causes of the problem, its effect on other problems and from the "facts" as they present themselves. In the last chapter, however, we found that facts are relative and multidimensional in that they can say many things to different people. Usually people disagree in their perceptions of these problems and in the importance they assign to one dimension over another. Still each group would tend to emphasize the approach to deal with these problems that is more compatible with its philosophy and methodology. An economist, for example, might point to cost-benefit ratio and argue for a particular course of action on the basis that the numbers "speak for themselves." There are those whose strength of approach derives from challenging any specialized analytical approach, its interpretation of numbers, and how data are gathered and assumptions made.

Analytic deduction or reductionist logic maintains that the explanation of a whole is best obtained from the explanation of its parts. The reductionist will address a complex problem by breaking down or decomposing it to its component elements and then dealing with each. A consequence of reductionism, is the development of specialized disciplines, each with its particular scope of inquiry and sphere of influence. Plurality in approach is often a result of lack of communication across disciplinary domains. For the most part, scientists have not communicated across their disciplinary boundaries (MacRae, 1976). They do not understand each other's technical languages, and are unable to deal with systems problems in unified way; Kenneth

Boulding (1968, p. 4) writes:

"... physicists talk only to physicists, economists to economists—worse still, nuclear physicists talk only to nuclear physicists and econometricians to econometricians. One wonders if science will not grind to a stop in an assemblage of walled-in hermits, each mumbling to himself words in a private language that only he can understand... The spread of specialized deafness means that someone who ought to know something that someone else knows isn't able to find out for lack of generalized ears."

It is likely that reductionism in the social and behavioral sciences is largely a result of attempts to emulate the specialized methods and techniques of the physical sciences. Reductionism has provided a conceptual framework together with tools and procedures to identify and study the important factors that enter into the definition of a problem. But these methods do not work well when there are many factors or if the factors are interdependent or intangible. The tendency is to use a technique which treats these factors in the same way. For example, people have often used linear programming (sometimes in economic forecasting) to find best solutions to problems involving not tens or hundreds but thousands of variables all assumed to be linear and additive in the simplest way. This is not necessarily bad, except that it can encourage people to think they now have the answers to their problems. But the problems remain.

The inductive or expansionist view of science which generalizes on particular observations is based on the philosophical view that our perceptions of the world and our modes of analysis and synthesis are relative to the individuals involved in the inquiry because they make the particular observations. The various scientific disciplines are necessary but not sufficient bases from which we formulate theories about experience and knowledge. This is again because the practitioners of these disciplines have approached problems by methods more suited to their taste, training and world view. What is needed is a unified approach to combine the inductive or "expansionist" view of science with the deductive view to obtain a systemic view.

2. Causal Explanation—How Reductionism Works

According to Democritus, "By necessity are foreordained all things that were and are to come." To him all things connect together in a monolithic causal logic.

Assumptions of causality abound in most of our thinking. This is a result of a long range tradition of teaching and research. While social scientists have long avoided explicit causal inferences, even the physical sciences are now questioning the validity of the causal way of explanation. Causality has been partitioned according to the type of cause perceived to govern different outcomes. The following table lists these causes, their interpretations, illustrates them and describes their present status.

14   Analytical Planning

Causal working	Interpretation	Example	Present status
Formal cause	Idea realized in a formal process	The origin of the idea of a painting eludes causal explanation	No longer considered valid
Material cause	Substance undergoing change	The paint and canvas both necessary but not sufficient	No longer considered valid
Efficient cause	The external compulsion, the motive force	The effort of the painter- a creative act	Still of scientific concern
Final cause	The goal to be reached	The purpose it serves, its beauty	Now called purpose

All generality is obtained by some kind of inductive reasoning. We make observations on a few (no matter how large) instances of a phenomenon and postulate that the observation holds for all instances of the phenomenon. We say that all men are mortal but we only know that all men that we have known are mortal. Thus there can be no absolute certainty in generalized inferences. However, the alternatives for the validity of deductive reasoning about the real world has also come under intense questioning in our time.

In science, clear and definite causes are rejected and events are taken as partial causes. The significant observables, called the past state of a physical system, together with the laws of nature imply the future state. In physics differential equations are used to describe a system whose solution contains arbitrary constants whose values are determined by initial conditions such as present position and velocity computed by taking the ratio of the difference between present and past position and time. In the macro world past and present determine the future. On the micro scale according to Heisenberg's principle, it is not possible to determine the position of an electron because the process of observation alters that position. Hence it is not possible to determine the present with sufficient accuracy to predict the future. Instead a probabilistic notion of a state of a system is introduced to deal with prediction; traditional deterministic notion of causality has been abandoned at that level of thinking. In addition the probabilistic concept is considered more basic all around than the deterministic one because it is possible to rationalize the latter in terms of the former by showing that all measurement is subject to error and that what we use in actual Newtonian type of prediction are values taken from measurements done several times adopting that value with the greatest frequency of occurrence. In physics, causality can be interpreted probabilistically. Still, there are those who think that someday we may even give up this interpretation.

We have spoken of the present determining the future. How about the future determining the present? This idea has no supporters in physics. However, in the life and behavioral science some advocate that a future goal in which people believe can influence their present actions towards that goal.

The upshot of the criticisms levelled at the inductive and deductive modes of thinking is that individually they are inadequate and are not up to the task of dealing with complexity.

A hope resides in a synthesis of the two before resorting to looser methods of thinking such as spiritual inspiration, gestalt types of thinking or creative adhocracy.

3. Systems Theory Past and Present

The notion of a system, defined as "complexes of interacting parts," was first articulated by the biologist Ludwig von Bertalanffy. His ideas were presented orally in a series of lectures in the 1930s and, following a liberalization of the intellectual climate, in many other publications after WWII (see Bertalanffy, 1968, 1972).

Bertalanffy formulated a theory of *open systems*, which describes a process of exchange between living organism and its surrounding environment. As distinguished from closed systems, which generally attain a state of equilibrium characterized by maximum entropy, or chaos, and minimal use of free energy, open systems achieve a steady state through the continuous flow of component materials between the organism and its environment. Use of free energy by the organism produces negative entropy and allows for growth and stability. We shall discuss these ideas in greater detail later.

The theory of open systems was first applied in the life sciences, such as organismic biology and physiology, and later in psychology, sociology, anthropology, economics and organization theory.

While the explicit articulation of these concepts is attributed to Bertalanffy, scientists in other fields were simultaneously cultivating similar notions. A gathering of these scientists in 1954 led to the formation of the Society for General Systems Research. The primary purpose of this Society was to investigate isomorphisms, or similarities in concepts, laws, and models in various fields, and to assist in the transfer of these concepts from one field to another.

In an assessment of trends in general systems theory, von Bertalanffy (1975; 157–169) underlines three main aspects of the field. The first, identified as *Systems Science*, explores in an empirical manner the applications of systems concepts in the physical, behavioral and social sciences. Emphasis is on the scientific exploration of wholes and wholeness in contrast with the elementalistic/reductionistic approach which previously dominated much of scientific thought and modes of inquiry. In Systems Science attempts are made to evaluate levels of complexity and patterns of interactions and interrelationships among components of the system under analysis. Systems Science makes extensive use of mathematical models as well as cybernetics and network theory to identify similarities or isomorphisms in different kinds of systems.

The second aspect of systems theory, *Systems Technology* focuses on

16   Analytical Planning

problems arising in industry and society that may be addressed through applications of systems theory. In such fields as systems analysis, management science, operations research, computer science, and industrial engineering the concepts of systems theory are translated into operational terms in searching for practical solutions to concrete problems.

Lastly, *Systems Philosophy* refers to a reorientation of thoughts and worldviews which leads to the introduction of a "system" as a new and potentially fruitful scientific paradigm. Systems philosophy seeks to conceptualize the interdependence and interconnections of theories formulated within diverse fields of inquiry. It is an attempt to integrate traditional scientific fields within a philosophical framework of general systems concepts.

Systems philosophy provides heuristic hypotheses for the formulation of more specific scientific theories. It exemplifies the worldview used by systems scientists or systems technologists in formulating problems and asking relevant questions concerning perceived states of affairs.

Laszlo (1975) offers four central ideas in systems philosophy useful in formulating a coherent concept of a system:

— *Ordered Wholeness*: Ordered wholeness refers to the characteristics of the system rather than those of individual components. Since wholeness results from the dynamic interaction of component elements they become something *other* than the simple sum of their parts and their behavior cannot be predicted on the basis of the observed behavior of the parts in isolation.

— *Self-stabilization*: A self-stabilizing system achieves a dynamic balance between its internal, fixed constraints and the external, environmental forces which tend to disturb its stable configuration. When systems adjust the flow of disturbances from the environment, they are behaving in a self-stabilizing manner.

— *Self-organization*: The self-organizing system presents a more striking and more sophisticated example of adapting to the environment than the self-stabilizing system. A self-organizing system is capable of reorganizing its internal constraints rather than simply adjusting the flow of disturbances from the environment; self-organization results in new steady states which are more resistant to disturbances than previous states. Self-stabilizing systems *survive* in environments in which the disturbances are within the range of corrective action; self-organizing systems *evolve* into more sophisticated and more resilient systems.

— *Hierarchization*: A hierarchy results when systems which function as wholes on one level function as parts on a higher level, thus becoming subsystems of the higher level system.

Developments in a variety of disciplines mark a progression in scientific thought from considering individual elements to considering wholes and interdependencies. Examples of these attempts to make complexity manageable are: *Cybernetics* is the science of communication and control which deals with information-processing systems such as nerve networks in animals, servomechanisms for automatic control of machinery and electronic computers. One objective is to find features common to all such systems. Cybernetics overlaps with other fields, including neurophysiology, computer science, information theory and sociology and shares with general systems theory an interest in wholes and interdependence as opposed to reductionist analysis of information-processing functions of individual elements (Wiener, 1948).

Another approach to complex problems developed in World War II is Operations Research. It has its sets of theoretical models that may differ from the actual system under study but useful in obtaining solutions because they limit the problem within specified parameters. Probability theory has been utilized extensively in Operations Research to construct quantitative models employed to approximate the reality of the situation (Churchman *et al*, 1957).

Finally, we have a new approach to complexity through artificial intelligence exhibited in computers, now programmed by experts but eventually expected to learn on their own.

4. The Conceptual Value of Systems Theory

An individual just exposed to systems theory may believe that it can become the unifying science. But on deeper examination of its methods and applications that individual may find that the existing materials of systems theory do not represent a panacea for the manifold problems facing our world. Is the systems approach then a passing fancy or does it have a potential?

Despite the philosophical appeal of looking at a problem from many points of view, the solution of any problem will finally follow a certain plan with a defined line of thinking. As a result it is difficult to argue against reductionism without offering a better alternative. Pragmatic systems research synthesizes reductionism and expansionism by first conceptualizing problems in terms of their systemic characteristics and then identifying those components that have the greatest influence in the system. In other words, the systems approach must draw on our innate abilities to decompose complex phenomena into component elements while simultaneously conceptualizing and identifying relations of varying intensity among the elements of the system. Still systems theory has so far been criticized for its lack of a viable methodology.

Despite its shortcomings, systems theory has provided a conceptual foundation on which to construct a new methodology which allows us to describe a system and its problems in terms of an interconnected hierarchy. It also offers a means to set a priority order and measure the intensity of interaction of the components of the hierarchy describing the structure of a system. This methodology considers the human element of complex social and organizational problems and accommodates multiple and conflicting goals and objectives held by people whose interests are affected by the performance of the system.

References

Ackoff, Russell (1974) *Redesigning the Future*, New York: John Wiley.
Bertalanffy, Ludwig von (1968) *General Systems Theory*, New York: Braziller.
Bertalanffy, Ludwig von (1975) *Perspectives on General Systems Theory*, New York: Braziller.
Bertalanffy, Ludwig von (1972) The History and Status of General Systems Theory, in George Klir (ed.) *Trends in General Systems Theory*, New York: Wiley Interscience.
Blauberg, I., V. N. Sardovsky and E. G. Yudin (1977) *Systems Theory: Philosophical and Methodological Problems*, Moscow: Progress Press.
Boulding, Kenneth (1968) General Systems Theory: The Skeleton of Science, in Walter Buckley (ed.) *Modern Systems Research for the Behavioral Scientist*, Chicago: Aldine.
Churchman, C. W., R. L. Ackoff and E. L. Arnoff (1957) *Introduction to Operations Research*, New York: John Wiley.
Ellul, Jaques (1964) *The Technological Society*, New York: Alfred Knopf.
Kuhn, Thomas (1970) *The Structure of Scientific Revolution* (2nd ed.) Chicago: University of Chicago Press.
Lazlo, Ervin (1975) Basic Constructs of Systems Philosophy, in Brent Ruben and John Kim (eds.) *General Systems Theory and Human Communication*, Rochelle Park, N. Y.: Hayden.
MacRae, Duncan (1976) *The Social Function of Social Science*, New Haven: Yale University Press.
Saaty, Thomas L. (1980) *The Analytic Hierarchy Process*, New York: McGraw-Hill.
Wiener, Norbert (1948) *Cybernetics*, Cambridge: Technology Press.
Wilson, Edward O. (1975) *Sociobiology: The New Synthesis*, Cambridge: Harvard Press.

Suggested Readings

Bertalanffy, Ludwig von, *General Systems Theory*, New York: George Braziller, 1968.
   In this book von Bertalanffy, one of the founders of general systems theory, presents papers written over a period of 30 years. Included in this volume is the author's concept of open systems (Chapter 5) first introduced in 1941 and later modified to become an integral component of general systems theory. The book is particularly useful for highlighting basic concepts and illustrating applications of general systems theory in various realms of scientific inquiry. It is also useful for examining the intellectual development of systems thinking.

Bertalanffy, Ludwig von, The History and Status of General Systems Theory, in Trends in General Systems Theory, George Klir (editor) New York: Wiley Interscience, 1972.
   This article is one of the most concise statements of the rationale for and history of general systems theory. The article places the development of general systems theory in the proper historical context noting that simultaneous developments in other fields of inquiry including cybernetics, information theory, and economics contributed to the theoretical framework of systems theory and vice versa. Fundamental distinctions between systems science, systems technology, and systems philosophy are also presented.

Boulding, Kenneth, General Systems Theory: The Skeleton of Science, in *Modern Systems Research for the Behavioral Scientist*, Walter Buckley (editor) Chicago: Aldine Publishing Co., 1968.
   This article presents a concise yet thorough overview of general systems theory. Boulding portrays general systems theory not as a body of "knowledge" in the tradition of positivism but rather as a point of view, a way of conceptualizing complex problems, and as a stimulus for developing interdisciplinary methodologies, methods and techniques for practical problem solving. Boulding presents a hierarchy of systems which displays increasing levels of complexity. This hierarchy of complexity illustrates the present gaps in and weaknesses of traditional empirical knowledge and suggests how general systems theory has contributed to conceptual insights regarding systems at the highest level of complexity.

CHAPTER 3

The Analytic Hierarchy Process

1. Introduction

The Analytic Hierarchy Process is a systematic procedure for representing the elements of any problem, hierarchically. It organizes the basic rationality by breaking down a problem into its smaller and smaller constituent parts and then guides decision makers through a series of pairwise comparison judgments (which are documented and can be re-examined) to express the relative strength or intensity of impact of the elements in the hierarchy. These judgments are then translated to numbers. The AHP includes procedures and principles used to synthesize the many judgments to derive priorities among criteria and subsequently for alternative solutions. It is useful to note that the numbers thus obtained are ratio scale estimates and correspond to so-called hard numbers.

Problem solving is a process of setting priorities in steps. One step decides on the most important elements of a problem, another on how best to repair, replace, test and evaluate the elements, another on how to implement the solution and measure performance. The entire process is subject to revision and re-examination until one is satisfied that he has covered all the important features needed to represent and solve the problem. This process could be carried out in a sequence of hierarchies; i.e., by using the output of one hierarchy as the focus of concern of the next hierarchy. The AHP systematizes this process of problem solving.

Finally, if we were to assume that the unspoken feelings and experiences of people are the fundamental grounds on which an individual draws to articulate his creativity, then the judgments and their intensity can be used to express inner feelings and inclinations. They also enlarge the framework of the discourse itself by expanding the clusters and elements laid out in the hierarchy to deal with a particular problem.

This approach to systems design and problem solving draws upon the innate capacity of humans to think logically *and* creatively, to identify events *and* establish relations among them. In this respect we note that people have two communicable attributes. One is their ability to impart and observe things, therefore communicate what they observe. The other is their ability to discriminate by establishing relations and their intensity among what is observed and then synthesize these relations into a total understanding. These

20 *Analytical Planning*

are the principle of *identity and decomposition*, the principle of *discrimination and comparative judgment* and the principle of *synthesis*.

In this chapter we give a brief exposition and illustrate the use of the AHP. We also deal with questions of the consistency of a hierarchy and of dependence among its elements. Detailed exposition of the AHP is found in Saaty (1980). Saaty and Vargas (1982) illustrate applications of the AHP in various real-life systems.

2. The Principle of Identity and Decomposition

We have used the first of the two principles identified above to structure problems in a hierarchic or network fashion. The principle of identity and decomposition calls for structuring problems hierarchically which is the first step one must complete when using the AHP. In its most elementary form, a hierarchy is structured from the top (objectives from a managerial standpoint), through intermediate levels (criteria on which subsequent levels depend) to the lowest level (which is usually a list of alternatives).

There are several kinds of hierarchies. The simplest are *dominance* hierarchies, which descend like an inverted tree with the boss at the top, followed by successive levels of bossing. *Holarchies* are essentially dominance hierarchies with feedback. *Chinese box* (or modular) hierarchies grow in size from the simplest elements or components (the inner boxes) to the larger and larger aggregates (the outer boxes). In biology, neogenetic hierarchies are of interest because of their new top levels that emerge successively through evolution. We shall concentrate our attention on dominance hierarchies, although the theory described below has been generalized to the other hierarchical forms.

A hierarchy is said to be complete when every element of a given level functions as a criterion for *all* the elements of the level below (see Exhibit 3-1). Otherwise, it is incomplete. There is no problem with the weighting process in the case of an incomplete hierarchy, as one uses the priorities of the appropriate element with respect to which the evaluation is made. That is, the hierarchy can be divided into subhierarchies sharing only a common topmost element.

The hierarchic portrayal of a problem is best illustrated by a simple example which we will use throughout most of this chapter to explain the AHP. More complicated examples, introduced later, will illustrate a range of applications to which the AHP is appropriate.

A family of average income decided to buy a house and identified eight criteria which they thought they had to look for in a house. These criteria fall into three categories: economic, geographic and physical. Although one may have begun by examining the relative importance of these clusters, the family felt they wanted to prioritize the relative importance of all the factors without working with clusters. The problem was to decide which of three candidate houses to choose. The first step is the _decomposition_ or structuring of the problem as a hierarchy. In the first (or top) level is the overall goal of "Satisfaction with the House." In the second level are the eight factors or criteria which contribute to the goal, and in the third (or bottom) level are the three candidate houses which are to be evaluated in terms of the criteria in the second level. The definitions of the criteria and the pictorial representation of the hierarchy follow.

The criteria important to the individual family were:

(1) *Size of house*: Storage space; size of rooms; number of rooms; total area of house.
(2) *Location to bus lines*: Convenient, close bus service.
(3) *Neighborhood*: Little traffic, secure, nice view, low taxes, good condition of neighborhood.
(4) *Age of house*: Self-explanatory.
(5) *Yard space*: Includes front, back and side, and space from neighbors.
(6) *Modern facilities*: Dishwashers, garbage disposals, air conditioning, alarm system, and other such items possessed by a house.
(7) *General condition:* Repairs needed; walls, carpet, drapes, cleanliness; wiring; roof; plumbing.
(8) *Financing available*: Assumable mortgage, seller financing available, or bank financing.

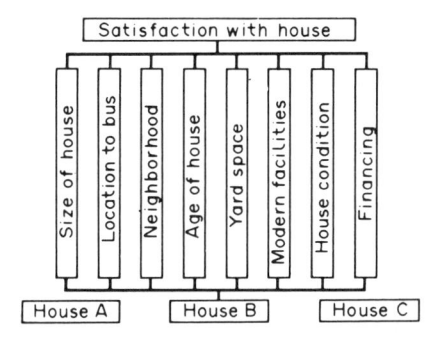

EXHIBIT 3-1. *Decomposition of the Problem Into a Hierarchy*

This downward decomposition format can easily be used on a wide range of problems. In addition, a slight modification to incorporate feedback loops will cover an even wider range.

The law of hierarchic continuity requires that the elements of the bottom level of the hierarchy be comparable in a pairwise fashion according to elements in the next level and so on up to the focus of the hierarchy.

For example, one must be able to provide meaningful answers to questions such as: "With respect to neighborhood, what is the desirability of House A relative to House B or to House C?" or "With respect to satisfaction with the house, what is the importance of size relative to location to bus line?" and so on. Whenever in doubt as to what levels to introduce in the hierarchy, the law of hierarchic continuity provides the linkage. The object is to derive priorities on the elements in the last level that reflect as best as possible their relative impact on the focus of the hierarchy.

It is important to note that the AHP demands that the problem be structured *by the participants* in the decision making process; in this simple example, the family members would devise the hierarchy in accordance with their perceived needs and their understanding of the constraints (i.e., limited funds) and opportunities (i.e., available houses) of the situation. This step requires dialogue and debate to ensure that the criteria and alternatives reflect the range of preferences and perceptions of those involved. It is not essential that *all* participants in the planning process agree on *every* component of the problem. For example, in this illustration, the criterion of yard space might have been included in the overall portrayal of the problem because only one of the family members thought it should be. Participants in the process will later have the opportunity to express the strength of their preference for criteria and alternatives and therefore, the arguments they present to justify those preferences will "sink or swim" at that time. In other words, one need not feel constrained in the initial hierarchic portrayal of the problem. It is crucial, however, that the planners agree on the uppermost level of the hierarchy—the objective or focus—since this will shape all of their subsequent judgments. Identifying this objective may require a great deal of prior research and negotiation. For example, in this case the family first decided that a fundamental change in the system was required (buying another house instead of modifying the old one) which may have involved an assessment of family needs, potential for family growth, and a forecast of changing neighborhood characteristics such as increased commercialization which might reduce the value of the present house.

3. The Principle of Discrimination and Comparative Judgments

Once a hierarchic or network representation of the problem has been achieved, how does one go about establishing priorities among criteria and evaluating each of the alternatives on the criteria perceived to be most important?

A. Pairwise Comparisons

In the AHP, elements of a problem are compared in pairs with respect to their relative impact ("weight" or "intensity") on a property they share in common. We reduce the pairwise comparisons to a matrix form—a square form in which an array of numbers is arranged as in the following example:

$$\begin{pmatrix} 3 & 2 & 1 & 0 \\ 4 & 1 & 0 & 2 \\ 3 & 1 & 4 & 7 \\ 2 & 6 & 1 & 9 \end{pmatrix}$$

The brackets that enclose this four-by-four matrix are used to identify such a group of numbers in its standard form.

When we compare a set of elements of a problem with each other a square matrix is produced that resembles the following:

$$\begin{pmatrix} a_{11} & a_{12} & a_{13} & \cdots & a_{1n} \\ a_{21} & a_{22} & a_{23} & \cdots & a_{2n} \\ a_{31} & a_{32} & a_{33} & \cdots & a_{3n} \\ \vdots & \vdots & \vdots & & \vdots \\ a_{n1} & a_{n2} & a_{n3} & \cdots & a_{nn} \end{pmatrix}$$

We observe that this matrix has reciprocal properties; that is:

$$a_{ji} = \frac{1}{a_{ij}}$$

where the subscripts i and j refer to the row and column, respectively, where any entry is located.

Later we will illustrate why reciprocals are important.

Now let $A_1, A_2, A_3, \ldots, A_n$ be any set of n elements and $w_1, w_2, w_3, \ldots, w_n$ their corresponding weights or intensities. Using the AHP, we want to compare the corresponding weights or intensities of each element with the weights or intensities of every other element in the set with respect to a property or goal that they have in common. The comparison of weights can be represented as follows:

	A_1	A_2	A_3	$\ldots$	A_n
A_1	$\dfrac{w_1}{w_1}$	$\dfrac{w_1}{w_2}$	$\dfrac{w_1}{w_3}$	$\ldots$	$\dfrac{w_1}{w_n}$
A_2	$\dfrac{w_2}{w_1}$	$\dfrac{w_2}{w_2}$	$\dfrac{w_2}{w_3}$	$\ldots$	$\dfrac{w_2}{w_n}$
A_3	$\dfrac{w_3}{w_1}$	$\dfrac{w_3}{w_2}$	$\dfrac{w_3}{w_3}$	$\ldots$	$\dfrac{w_3}{w_n}$
$\vdots$	$\vdots$	$\vdots$	$\vdots$		$\vdots$
A_n	$\dfrac{w_n}{w_1}$	$\dfrac{w_n}{w_2}$	$\dfrac{w_n}{w_2}$	$\ldots$	$\dfrac{w_n}{w_n}$

The first row is a "vector" of this matrix (row #1). Its entries are called components.

The second column is one column of this matrix (column #2). It is also known as a "vector" of the matrix.

24   Analytical Planning

One should note also that a matrix may consist of only one row or one column, in which case it is called a vector.

The square matrix obviously has an equal number of rows and columns, but it has other useful properties, such as eigenvectors and eigenvalues. These will be developed further in our attempts to "solve" this square reciprocal matrix. The reason for this computation is that it gives us a way to determine quantitatively the relative importance of factors or issues in a problem situation. The factors with the highest values are the ones that we should concentrate on in solving a problem or developing a plan of action.

It is important to see that if $w_1, w_2, w_3, \ldots, w_n$ are not known in advance, then we perform pairwise comparisons on the elements by using subjective judgments estimated numerically from a scale of numbers (which we describe later) and then solve the problem to find the ws.

When problems are structured hierarchically a matrix is arranged to compare the relative importance of criteria in the second level with respect to the overall objective or focus of the first level. Similar matrices must be constructed for pairwise comparisons of each alternative in the third level with respect to the criteria of the second level. The matrix is set up by providing the objective (or criterion) of comparison somewhere above and listing the elements to be compared on the left and on top. In the example of buying a new house nine such matrices would be required, one for the second level of the hierarchy and eight for the third level. The matrices are illustrated in Exhibits 3-2 and 3-3.

Note that the cells of these matrices have not been filled in; they are reserved

EXHIBIT 3-2. *Buying a House: Pairwise Comparison Matrix for Level 1*

Overall satisfaction with house	Size	Location to bus	Neighbor- hood	Age	Yard space	Modern facilities	General condition	Financing
Size								
Location to bus								
Neighbor- hood								
Age								
Yard space								
Modern facilities								
General condition								
Financing								

EXHIBIT 3-3. *Buying a House: Pairwise Comparison Matrices for Level 3*

Size	A	B	C	Location to bus	A	B	C
A				A			
B				B			
C				C			

Neighborhood	A	B	C	Age	A	B	C
A				A			
B				B			
C				C			

Yard space	A	B	C	Modern facilities	A	B	C
A				A			
B				B			
C				C			

General condition	A	B	C	Financing	A	B	C
A				A			
B				B			
C				C			

for assessments or judgments of the relative importance of the items being compared with respect to the objective or criterion identified at the top. If a scale of comparison exists (i.e., if there are measurable data available) they can be used to make the comparison; otherwise the cells are filled in with the subjective, yet informed judgments of the individual or group solving the problem. Later we will give the scale for entering such judgments.

B. The Need for a Scale of Comparison

For the present we note that often a scale underlying a problem exists and the judgments in that case are expressed as ratios from the scale. For example, if one is comparing the relative weights of stones and one has a stone A of weight W_A and a stone B of weight W_B the ratio W_A/W_B is entered in the matrix for the relative weight of stone A over stone B. The reciprocal, or W_B/W_A, is entered for the relative weight of stone B over stone A.

In the matrix, one begins with an element on the left and asks how much more important it is than an element listed on the top. When compared with itself the ratio is one. When compared with another element, either it is more important than that element, then an integer value, from the scale given later, is used or its reciprocal in the opposite case. In either case the reciprocal ratio is entered in the transpose position of the matrix. Thus we are always dealing

26 *Analytical Planning*

with positive reciprocal matrices and need only elicit $\frac{n(n-1)}{2}$ judgments where n is the total number of elements being compared. We do not assume that people are perfectly consistent and except for reciprocals in the transpose position do not force judgments for consistency. It is possible to construct a judgment matrix from fewer than $\frac{n(n-1)}{2}$ judgments taken from different people along what is known as spanning trees.

The reader may suspect (correctly) that comparing the relative weights of stones is far different than comparing the relative importance of criteria such as neighborhood or general condition of a house which the family in our example has identified as considerations in the problem they are confronting. In some comparisons we use units of measurements such as the dollar, the pound, the mile, or the second. But what do we do with social, political or emotional factors, the relative importance of which cannot be compared in physical measurements?

Suppose we had no scale with which to compare the relative weights of our stones. We would probably hold the two stones in our hands, one in the left and the other in the right, and attempt to "feel" their relative weights. Or we might pick them up sequentially with the same hand to avoid bias when one hand is stronger than the other. On the basis of such "experiments," we *would not* be able to state that stone A is precisely 3.5 pounds heavier than stone B but we *would* be able to say that stone A is "slightly heavier," "much heavier," and so on. Similarly, when comparing the relative importance of intangible or unquantifiable factors such as the neighborhood or general condition of a house, we need not despair simply because we have no physical or objective units of measurement. We would legitimately state that the neighborhood is slightly more important than the general condition, much more important, etc. depending on our tastes and preferences. Thus, the distinction between comparing physical objects and intangible feelings is not as clear-cut as it might at first appear.

C. *The Recommended Scale of Relative Importance*

We are now in a position to introduce the scale which we recommend for making subjective pairwise comparisons; it is illustrated in Exhibit 3-4. This scale has been validated for effectiveness, not only in many applications by a number of people, but also through theoretical comparison with a large number of other scales. We will demonstrate its effectiveness in the next section after we have learned how to use it and how to interpret the quantitative results it produces.

For the present, it will not hurt to repeat the steps in the AHP we have discussed thus far. First, a problem confronting people or an organization is portrayed in a hierarchic fashion. Next, elements in the second level of the hierarchy are arranged in a matrix in order to elicit judgments from people

The Analytic Hierarchy Process   27

who have the problem about the relative importance of the elements with respect to the overall goal.

EXHIBIT 3-4. *Scale of Relative Importance*

Intensity of relative importance	Definition	Explanation
1	Equal importance	Two activities contribute equally to the objective.
3	Moderate importance of one over another.	Experience and judgment slightly favor one activity over another.
5	Essential or strong importance.	Experience and judgment strongly favor one activity over another.
7	Demonstrated importance.	An activity is strongly favored and its dominance is demonstrated in practice.
9	Extreme importance.	The evidence favoring one activity over another is of the highest possible order of affirmation.
2, 4, 6, 8,	Intermediate values between the two adjacent judgments.	When compromise is needed.
Reciprocals of above non-zero numbers.	If an activity has one of the above numbers (e.g. 3) compared with a second activity, then the second activity has the reciprocal value (i.e., 1/3) when compared to the first.	

Additional matrices are constructed for each successive level of the hierarchy. The questions to ask, in the home buying example, when comparing two criteria in the second level are of the following kind: of the two criteria being compared, which is considered more important by the family buying the house and how much more important is it with respect to the family's concept of "satisfaction with a house" which is the overall goal? Similarly, in the third level, one would ask: of the alternative houses being compared, which is considered more desirable by the family and how much more desirable is it, with respect to a particular criterion (e.g., neighborhood) in the second level and on which the comparison is being made? For emphasis we again note that the convention is to compare the relative importance of elements on the left of the matrix with those on the top. Thus, if the element on the left is more important than the element on the top, then a positive integer (from 1 to 9) will be inserted in the cell; if it is less important the reciprocal value of the integer will be entered. The relative importance of any element compared with itself is 1; therefore the diagonal of the matrix (upper left to lower right cells) only contains 1's. Finally, reciprocal values are entered for reverse comparisons, that is if element A is perceived to be "slightly more important" (3 on the scale) relative to element B, then element B is assumed to be "slightly less important" (1/3 on the scale) relative to element A.

28   Analytical Planning

D. What Questions to Ask in Making Comparisons

In making the pairwise comparisons the following kinds of questions have been noted to occur.

In comparing A with B

— which is more important or has a greater impact?
— which is more likely to happen?
— which is more preferred?

In the wide diversity of applications made so far all the questions asked appeared to fall in one of these three categories. In comparing criteria one often asks which criterion is more important? In comparing alternatives with respect to a criterion one asks which alternative is more desired? In comparing scenarios which results from a criterion one asks which scenario is more likely to result from that criterion?

E. An Illustration of Subjective Judgments Using the Scale

Let us return to the family faced with the problem of purchasing a house and examine the matrix illustrated in Exhibit 3-5 which represents the second level of the hierarchy. Note that the cells of the matrix have now been filled in with the family's subjective judgments using the 1 to 9 scale and based on their preferences and perception of the constraints or opportunities of the situation. For example, when asked "With respect to overall satisfaction with a house, what is the importance of size relative to location to bus lines?" The family members agreed that size was strongly more important and therefore they entered the integer 5 in the corresponding cell; its reciprocal, or 1/5 was automatically entered for the reverse comparison. We have circled both of these judgments in Exhibit 3-5 to clarify the point.

When several people participate, judgments are often debated and people are requested to justify their judgments with reasons or data to which they may have access. In these cases the debate focuses on the assumptions which underlie judgments rather than the judgments themselves. Sometimes the group accepts the geometric mean of their combined judgments corresponding to a synthesis of the reciprocal judgments. If there is strong disagreement, the different opinions can each be taken and used to obtain answers. Those which subsequently display the highest consistency within the group are the ones usually retained.

The AHP incorporates equally both tangible factors which requires having hard measurements and intangible factors which requires judgments. Eventually one finds that so-called hard numbers have no meaning in themselves apart from their utilitarian interpretations.

The interdependence of criteria, such as house condition and age have to be considered carefully since there may be some perceived overlap. Judging the

EXHIBIT 3-5. *Buying a House: Pairwise Comparison Matrix for Level 2*

Overall satisfaction with house	Size	Location to bus	Neighborhood	Age	Yard space	Modern facilities	General condition	Financing
Size	1	5	3	7	6	6	1/3	1/4
Location to bus	1/5	1	1/3	5	3	3	1/5	1/7
Neighborhood	1/3	3	1	6	3	4	6	1/5
Age	1/7	1/5	1/6	1	1/3	1/4	1/7	1/8
Yard space	1/6	1/3	1/3	3	1	1/2	1/5	1/6
Modern facilities	1/6	1/3	1/4	4	2	1	1/5	1/6
General condition	3	5	1/6	7	5	5	1	1/2
Financing	4	7	5	8	6	6	2	1

relative importance of such things as condition and age, therefore, must be done as independently as possible avoiding overlaps.

We move now to the pairwise comparisons of the elements in the bottom level illustrated in Exhibit 3-6. The elements to be compared pairwise are the houses with respect to how much more desirable or better one is than the other in satisfying each criterion in the second level. There are eight 3 × 3 matrices of judgments since there are eight criteria in the second level, and three houses to be pairwise compared for each criterion. Again the matrices contain the judgments of the family. In order to understand the judgments, a brief description of the houses is given below.

House A—This house is the largest of them all. It is located in a good neighborhood with little traffic and low taxes. Its yard space is comparably larger than houses B and C. However, the general condition is not very good and it needs cleaning and painting. Also, the financing is unsatisfactory because it would have to be financed through a bank at a high rate of interest.

House B—This house is a little smaller than House A and is not close to a bus route. The neighborhood gives one the feeling of insecurity because of traffic conditions. The yard space is fairly small and the house lacks the basic modern facilities. On the other hand, the general condition is very good. Also an assumable mortgage is obtainable which means the financing is good with a rather low interest rate.

30 Analytical Planning

EXHIBIT 3-6. Buying a House: Pairwise Comparison Matrices for Level 3

Size	A	B	C	Location to bus	A	B	C
A	1	6	8	A	1	7	1/5
B	1/6	1	4	B	1/7	1	1/8
C	1/8	1/4	1	C	5	8	1

Neighborhood	A	B	C	Age	A	B	C
A	1	8	6	A	1	1	1
B	1/8	1	1/4	B	1	1	1
C	1/6	4	1	C	1	1	1

Yard space	A	B	C	Modern facilities	A	B	C
A	1	5	4	A	1	8	6
B	1/5	1	1/3	B	1/8	1	1/5
C	1/4	3	1	C	1/6	5	1

General condition	A	B	C	Financing	A	B	C
A	1	1/2	1/2	A	1	1/7	1/5
B	2	1	1	B	7	1	3
C	2	1	1	C	5	1/3	1

House C—House C is very small and has few modern facilities. The neighborhood has high taxes, but is in good condition and seems secure. The yard space is bigger than that of House B, but is not comparable to House A's spacious surroundings. The general condition of the house is good and it has a pretty carpet and drapes. Its financing is much better than A but not as good as B.

4. Synthesis of Priorities

At this point in our example, the family has constructed a hierarchy, arranged matrices, and offered subjective judgments in a pairwise fashion. But what do all of these numbers mean, and how can they help to guide the family in the choice that must be made? This section describes how hierarchic decomposition and the scale of relative importance are combined to yield meaningful approaches to multi-criteria planning problems.

A. Synthesis: Local Priorities

From the set of pairwise comparison matrices we generate a set of *local priorities* which express the relative impact of the set of elements on an element

The Analytic Hierarchy Process   31

in the level immediately above. We find the relative strength, value, worth, desirability, or probability of each of the items being compared by "solving" the matrices, each of which has reciprocal properties.

To do this we need to compute a set of eigenvectors for each matrix and then normalize to unity the result to obtain the vectors of priorities.

Computing eigenvectors is not difficult but can be time consuming. Fortunately, there are some easy ways to obtain a good approximation of the priorities. One of the best ways, is the geometric mean. This is done by multiplying the elements in each row and taking their nth root where n is the number of elements. Then normalize to unity the column of numbers thus obtained by dividing each entry by the sum of all entries. Alternatively, normalize the elements in each column of the matrix and then average each row. With the solution it is hoped that we can determine not only the priority rank of each item but also the magnitude of its priority. More simply stated, given ten desserts to choose from, we should be able not only to rank them in the order in which we favor them, but also to decide on the relative intensity of our desire for each one of them.

For a listing of other ways to approximate priorities see Thomas L. Saaty, *The Analytic Hierarchy Process*, New York: McGraw-Hill, 1980.

In using any approximation method, there is the danger of changing rank order and thus making a less desirable choice. The eigenvector approach makes use of the information provided in the matrix whatever the inconsistency may be and derives priorities based on that information without conducting arithmetic improvements on the data. The idea here is for the individual or group to decide whether they want to change their judgement. It is not up to the sophisticated mathematician to "improve" on what individuals may not want to change.

	A_1	A_2	A_3	A_4	
A_1	$\dfrac{w_1}{w_1}$	$\dfrac{w_1}{w_2}$	$\dfrac{w_1}{w_3}$	$\dfrac{w_1}{w_4}$	← If $\dfrac{w_1}{w_1} \times \dfrac{w_1}{w_2} \times \dfrac{w_1}{w_3} \times \dfrac{w_1}{w_4}$ are multiplied out and then the 4th root taken, an estimate of the first component of the principal eigenvector has been developed from this row.
A_2	$\dfrac{w_2}{w_1}$	$\dfrac{w_2}{w_2}$	$\dfrac{w_2}{w_3}$	$\dfrac{w_2}{w_4}$	
A_3	$\dfrac{w_3}{w_1}$	$\dfrac{w_3}{w_2}$	$\dfrac{w_3}{w_3}$	$\dfrac{w_3}{w_4}$	← If $\dfrac{w_2}{w_1} \times \dfrac{w_2}{w_2} \times \dfrac{w_2}{w_3} \times \dfrac{w_2}{w_4}$ are multiplied out and the 4th root taken an estimate of the second component of the principal eigenvector has been developed from this row, and so on.
A_4	$\dfrac{w_4}{w_1}$	$\dfrac{w_4}{w_2}$	$\dfrac{w_4}{w_3}$	$\dfrac{w_4}{w_4}$	

32   Analytical Planning

So the eigenvector component row $1 = \sqrt[4]{\dfrac{w_1}{w_1} \times \dfrac{w_1}{w_2} \times \dfrac{w_1}{w_3} \times \dfrac{w_1}{w_4}}$

eigenvector component row $2 = \sqrt[4]{\dfrac{w_2}{w_1} \times \dfrac{w_2}{w_2} \times \dfrac{w_2}{w_3} \times \dfrac{w_2}{w_4}}$

Once the n eigenvector components have been developed for all the rows, it becomes necessary to normalize them to do further computation.

	The matrix $A_1 \quad A_2 \quad A_3 \quad A_4$	Compute estimates of the eigenvector components from the rows		Normalize the result to get the estimate of vector of priorities
A_1	$\dfrac{w_1}{w_1} \ \dfrac{w_1}{w_2} \ \dfrac{w_1}{w_3} \ \dfrac{w_1}{w_4}$	$\sqrt[4]{\dfrac{w_1}{w_1} \times \dfrac{w_1}{w_2} \times \dfrac{w_1}{w_3} \times \dfrac{w_1}{w_4}} = a$	Now + add the	$\dfrac{a}{\text{Total}} = x_1$
A_2	$\dfrac{w_2}{w_1} \ \dfrac{w_2}{w_2} \ \dfrac{w_2}{w_3} \ \dfrac{w_2}{w_4}$	$\sqrt[4]{\dfrac{w_2}{w_1} \times \dfrac{w_2}{w_2} \times \dfrac{w_2}{w_3} \times \dfrac{w_2}{w_4}} = b$	column and + normalize	$\dfrac{b}{\text{Total}} = x_2$
A_3	$\dfrac{w_3}{w_1} \ \dfrac{w_3}{w_2} \ \dfrac{w_3}{w_3} \ \dfrac{w_3}{w_4}$	$\sqrt[4]{\dfrac{w_3}{w_1} \times \dfrac{w_3}{w_2} \times \dfrac{w_3}{w_3} \times \dfrac{w_3}{w_4}} = c$	+	$\dfrac{c}{\text{Total}} = x_3$
A_4	$\dfrac{w_4}{w_1} \ \dfrac{w_4}{w_2} \ \dfrac{w_4}{w_3} \ \dfrac{w_4}{w_4}$	$\sqrt[4]{\dfrac{w_4}{w_1} \times \dfrac{w_4}{w_2} \times \dfrac{w_4}{w_3} \times \dfrac{w_4}{w_4}} = d$	Total	$\dfrac{d}{\text{Total}} = x_4$

Multiplication of the matrix by the vector of priorities is achieved as follows: We multiply the first element of a row by the first element of the column of xs; the second element in the row, by the second in the column of xs; and so on. Then we add to obtain one number, Y, for that row as follows:

$$\begin{bmatrix} \dfrac{w_1}{w_1} & \dfrac{w_1}{w_2} & \dfrac{w_1}{w_3} & \dfrac{w_1}{w_4} \\ \dfrac{w_2}{w_1} & \dfrac{w_2}{w_2} & \dfrac{w_2}{w_3} & \dfrac{w_2}{w_4} \\ \dfrac{w_3}{w_1} & \dfrac{w_3}{w_2} & \dfrac{w_3}{w_3} & \dfrac{w_3}{w_4} \\ \dfrac{w_4}{w_1} & \dfrac{w_4}{w_2} & \dfrac{w_4}{w_3} & \dfrac{w_4}{w_4} \end{bmatrix} \begin{matrix} x_1 \\ x_2 \\ x_3 \\ x_4 \end{matrix} = \begin{matrix} \dfrac{w_1}{w_1}x_1 + \dfrac{w_1}{w_2}x_2 + \dfrac{w_1}{w_3}x_3 + \dfrac{w_1}{w_4}x_4 = Y_1 \\ \dfrac{w_2}{w_1}x_1 + \dfrac{w_2}{w_2}x_2 + \dfrac{w_2}{w_3}x_3 + \dfrac{w_2}{w_4}x_4 = Y_2 \\ \dfrac{w_3}{w_1}x_1 + \dfrac{w_3}{w_2}x_2 + \dfrac{w_3}{w_3}x_3 + \dfrac{w_3}{w_4}x_4 = Y_3 \\ \dfrac{w_4}{w_1}x_1 + \dfrac{w_4}{w_2}x_2 + \dfrac{w_4}{w_3}x_3 + \dfrac{w_4}{w_4}x_4 = Y_4 \end{matrix}$$

When the matrix has this form, it turns out that actually x_1, x_2, x_3 and x_4 are nothing but w_1, w_2, w_3 and w_4, respectively, which is what we are after; namely, from the ratio of the w's we want to determine each w. It is important to note that in the judgment matrix we don't have ratios like w_i/w_j but only numbers or reciprocals of numbers from the scale. That matrix is generally inconsistent. Algebraically the consistent problem involves solving $Aw = nw$, $A = (w_i/w_j)$ and the general one with reciprocal judgments involves solving $A'w' = \lambda_{\max} w'$, $A' = (a_{ij})$ where $\lambda_{\max}$ is the largest eigenvalue of the judgment matrix A.

B. Consistency of Local Priorities

An intrinsic useful by-product of the theory is an index of consistency which provides information on how serious are violations of numerical (cardinal, $a_{ij}a_{jk} = a_{ik}$) and transitive (ordinal) consistency. The result could be to seek additional information and reexamine the data used in constructing the scale in order to improve consistency. A structurally generated index is not available in other procedures for the construction of ratio scales. As already mentioned, the method also utilizes, for reasons suggested by consistency requirements, reciprocal entries ($a_{ji} = 1/a_{ij}$) in pairwise comparison matrices instead of the traditional $a_{ji} = -a_{ij}$ used for construction of interval scales.

All measurements, including those which make use of instruments, are subject to experimental error and to error in the measurement instrument itself. A serious effect of error is that it can and often does lead to inconsistent conclusions. A simple example of the consequence of error in weighing objects is to find that A is heavier than B, and B is heavier than C but C is heavier than A. This can happen particularly when the weights of A, B, and C are close, and the instrument is not fine enough to distinguish between them. Lack of consistency may be serious for some problems but not for others. For example, if the objects are two chemicals to be mixed together in exact proportion to make a drug, inconsistency may mean that proportionately more of one chemical is used than the other possibly leading to harmful results in using the drug.

But perfect consistency in measurement even with the finest instruments is difficult to attain in practice and what we need is a way of evaluating how bad it is for a particular problem.

With a pairwise comparison matrix, we have measures to assess the extent of the deviation from consistency. When such deviations exceed the limits specified, we say there is a need for the provider of the judgments in the matrix to re-examine his or her inputs into the matrix.

The consistency index for each matrix and for the entire hierarchy can be approximated by hand calculations. First add each column of the judgment matrix and then multiply the sum of the first column by the value of the first component of the normalized priority vector, the sum of the second column by that of the second component and so on. Then add the resulting numbers.

34 Analytical Planning

This yields a value denoted by λ_{max}. For the consistency index we have C.I. $= \frac{\lambda_{max} - n}{n - 1}$ where n is the number of elements being compared. For a reciprocal matrix, $\lambda_{max} \geq n$ always.

We now compare this value for what it would be if our numerical judgments were taken at random from the scale 1/9, 1/8, 1/7, ..., 1, 2, ..., 9 (using a reciprocal matrix). Below are the average consistencies for different order random matrices.

Size of matrix	1	2	3	4	5	6	7	8	9	10
Random consistency	0	0	.58	.90	1.12	1.24	1.32	1.41	1.45	1.49

If we divide C.I. by the random consistency number for the same size matrix we obtain the consistency ratio C.R. The value of C.R. should be around 10% or less to be acceptable. In some cases 20% may be tolerated but never more. If the C.R. is not within this range, the participants should study the problem and revise their judgments.

The Principle of Synthesis

The principle of synthesis is now applied. Priorities are synthesized from the second level down by multiplying local priorities by the priority of their corresponding criterion in the level above and adding them for each element in a level according to the criteria it affects. (The second level elements are each multiplied by unity, the weight of the single top level goal.) This gives the composite or global priority of that element which is then used to weight the local priorities of elements in the level below compared by it as criterion and so on to the bottom level.

An Illustration of Decomposition, Comparative Judgment and Synthesis

Let us return to the home buying family in order to illustrate these ideas with a concrete problem. Exhibit 3-7 presents once again the pairwise comparison matrix for the second level of the family's hierarchy which, as the reader will recall, contained the eight criteria perceived to have an impact on overall satisfaction with a house. This time the priority vector has been calculated as well as the eigenvalue λ_{max}, the consistency index, and the consistency ratio. Note that the consistency ratio is somewhat higher than we would like yet the family decided not to revise the judgments since they were not interested in rigorously consistent results. With relatively large matrices (i.e. 7 to 9 elements)

EXHIBIT 3-7. *Buying a House: Pairwise Comparison Matrix for Level 2, Solution and Consistency*

Overall satisfaction with house	Size	Location	Neighbor-hood	Age	Yard space	Modern facilities	General condition	Financing	Priority vector
Size	1	5	3	7	6	6	1/3	1/4	.173
Location	1/5	1	1/3	5	3	3	1/5	1/7	.054
Neighborhood	1/3	3	1	6	3	4	6	1/5	.188
Age	1/7	1/5	1/6	1	1/3	1/4	1/7	1/8	.018
Yard space	1/6	1/3	1/3	3	1	1/2	1/5	1/6	.031
Modern facilities	1/6	1/3	1/4	4	2	1	1/5	1/6	.036
General condition	3	5	1/6	7	5	5	1	1/2	.167
Financing	4	7	5	8	6	6	2	1	.333
								λ_{max} =	9.669
								C.I. =	.238
								C.R. =	.169

36 Analytical Planning

it is often difficult to achieve a high level of consistency. However, the level of consistency should correspond to the risk associated with inconsistent results. If, for example we were comparing the effects of drugs we would want a very high level of consistency.

Note also that the entries in the priority vector do not correspond exactly with those that one would obtain using the approximation method (normalized geometric means) described above. This is because the priorities in this example were generated from a computer program which calculated the actual (versus approximated) eigenvector components. (For a description of computer programs for the AHP see Saaty, 1982). One of the most successful and easy ways to structure and solve a problem with the AHP is to use the software package called Expert Choice by Decision Support Software, McLean, Virginia.

How does one now interpret the priorities thus obtained? Clearly the availability of adequate financing is perceived by the family to be the most important criterion in their choice of homes. In fact it is nearly twice as important as size (.333 versus .173) and far more important than age which has the lowest priority of .018. Indeed, one might choose to include only 3 or 4 of the most important criteria—say financing, neighborhood size, and general condition—when performing subsequent calculations since they will exert the most influence on the ultimate choice of a house. In order to do this one would simply add the priorities of the most important criteria, and divide each by the resulting total to obtain a new normalized vector of priorities for a smaller and more manageable set of criteria. In this illustration, however, we will retain each of the criteria in order to allow the AHP to run its course uninhibited.

Exhibit 3-8 reintroduces the pairwise comparison for the third level of the hierarchy which is concerned with comparing the relative desirability of houses A, B, and C with respect to the criteria of the second level. We observe that house B performed best on the criterion of financing, and that house A was perceived to be best with respect to size and location. Before going on the reader may wish to guess which house had the highest global priority ranking, given what we have witnessed in terms of the family's expressed preferences for the criteria and the performance of the three houses on those criteria.

The next step is to apply the principle of synthesis. In order to establish the composite or global priorities of the houses we lay out the local priorities of the houses with respect to each criterion in a matrix and multiply each column of vectors by the priority of the corresponding criterion and add across each row which results in the composite or global priority vector of the houses. For example, with House A we have: $(.754 \times .173) + (.233 \times .054) + \ldots + (.072 \times .333) = .396$. House A which was the least desirable with respect to financing (the highest priority criterion) contrary to expectation was the winner. It was the house that was bought. There were no reservations by the family in making the choice.

In retrospect the outcome was not surprising when we consider the fact that

The Analytic Hierarchy Process 37

EXHIBIT 3-8. *Buying a House: Pairwise Comparison Matrices for Level 3 Solutions and Consistency*

Size of house	A	B	C	Priority vector		Yard space	A	B	C	Priority vector
A	1	6	8	.754		A	1	5	4	.674
B	1/6	1	4	.181		B	1/5	1	1/3	.101
C	1/8	1/4	1	.065		C	1/4	3	1	.226

$\lambda_{max} = 3.136$ C.I. = .068 C.R. = .117
$\lambda_{max} = 3.086$ C.I. = .043 C.R. = .074

Location to bus	A	B	C	Priority vector		Modern facilities	A	B	C	Priority vector
A	1	7	1/5	.233		A	1	8	6	.747
B	1/7	1	1/8	.055		B	1/8	1	1/5	.060
C	5	8	1	.713		C	1/6	5	1	.193

$\lambda_{max} = 3.247$ C.I. = .124 C.R. = .213
$\lambda_{max} = 3.197$ C.I. = .099 C.R. = .170

Neighborhood	A	B	C	Priority vector		General condition	A	B	C	Priority vector
A	1	8	6	.745		A	1	1/2	1/2	.200
B	1/8	1	1/4	.065		B	2	1	1	.400
C	1/6	4	1	.181		C	2	1	1	.400

$\lambda_{max} = 3.130$ C.I. = .068 C.R. = .117
$\lambda_{max} = 3.000$ C.I. = .000 C.R. = .000

Age of house	A	B	C	Priority vector		Financing	A	B	C	Priority vector
A	1	1	1	.333		A	1	1/7	1/5	.072
B	1	1	1	.333		B	7	1	3	.650
C	1	1	1	.333		C	5	1/3	1	.278

$\lambda_{max} = 3.000$ C.I. = .000 C.R. = .000
$\lambda_{max} = 3.065$ C.I. = .032 C.R. = .056

	1 (.173)	2 (.054)	3 (.188)	4 (.018)	5 (.031)	6 (.036)	7 (.167)	8 (.333)	Composite or global priorities
A	.754	.233	.754	.333	.674	.747	.200	.072	.396
B	.181	.055	.065	.333	.101	.060	.400	.650	.341
C	.065	.713	.181	.333	.226	.193	.400	.278	.263

house A out-performed the others on 4 of the 7 criteria in which there were no tie scores. The example also illustrates that one should take care before deciding to exclude certain criteria following the first set of calculations.

5. A Summary of Steps in the AHP

It will be useful to reiterate the steps followed in the AHP. Particular steps may be followed more in some situations than in others.

1. Define the problem and determine what you want to know.
2. Structure the hierarchy from the top (the objectives from a managerial viewpoint) through the intermediate levels (criteria on which subsequent levels depend) to the lowest level (which usually is a list of the alternatives).
3. Construct a set of pairwise comparison matrices for each of the lower levels-one matrix for each element in the level immediately above. An element in the higher level is said to be a governing element for those in the lower level since it contributes to it or affects it. In a complete simple hierarchy, every element in the lower level affects every element in the upper level. The elements in the lower level are then compared to each other based on their effect on the governing element above. This yields a square matrix of judgments. The pairwise comparisons are done in terms of which element dominates the other. These judgments are then expressed as integers (see previous Exhibit 3-4 for judgment values.) If element A dominates element B, then the whole number (integer) is entered in row A, column B and the reciprocal (fraction) is entered in row B, column A. Of course, if element B dominates element A then the reverse occurs. The whole number is then placed in the B, A position with the reciprocal automatically being assigned to the A, B position. If A and B are judged to be equal, a one is assigned to both positions.
4. There are $n(n-1)/2$ judgments required to develop each matrix in step 3 (remember, reciprocals are automatically assigned in each pairwise comparison).
5. Having made all the pairwise comparisons and entered the data, the consistency is determined using the eigenvalue. The consistency index is tested then using the departure of λ_{max} from n compared with corresponding average values for random entries yielding the consistency ratio C.R.
6. Steps 3, 4 and 5 are performed for all levels and clusters in the hierarchy.
7. Hierarchical synthesis is now used to weight the eigenvectors by the weights of the criteria and the sum is taken over all weighted eigenvector entries corresponding to those in the next lower level of the hierarchy.
8. The consistency of the entire hierarchy is found by multiplying each consistency index by the priority of the corresponding criterion and adding them together. The result is then divided by the same type of expression using the random consistency index corresponding to the dimensions of each matrix weighted by the priorities as before. Note first the consistency ratio (C.R.) should be about 10% or less to be acceptable. If not, the quality of the

judgments should be improved, perhaps by revising the manner in which questions are asked in making the pairwise comparisons. If this should fail to improve consistency then it is likely that the problem should be more accurately structured; that is, grouping similar elements under more meaningful criteria. A return to step 2 would be required, although only the problematic parts of the hierarchy may need revision. (The reader can calculate the consistency of the hierarchy of the house buying example and show its value to be .081 which is acceptable.)

We note that in making the estimates, and to keep the comparisons relevant, an individual has to keep in mind all the elements being compared. It is not difficult to see that in order to develop valid numerical comparisons one should not compare more than 7 ± 2 elements. In that case a small error in each relative value does not alter that value significantly. If this is so, then how can we measure across wide classes of objects? The answer is, by hierarchical decomposition. The elements are grouped ordinally (as a first estimate) into comparability classes of about seven elements each. The element with the highest weight in the class of lighter-weight elements is also included in the next heavier class and serves as a pivot to uniformize the scale between the two classes. The procedure is repeated from one class to an adjacent one until all the elements are appropriately scaled.

In certain problems with a large number of alternatives, we do not always need to make pairwise comparisons among them. Instead we introduce subcriteria that are refinements of the criteria (e.g., high, medium, low) and prioritize the importance of these with respect to the criteria. We then take each alternative and examine which subcriterion describes it best and take the priority of that subcriterion. We add all these priorities for that alternative. Finally we normalize the values of the alternatives to obtain their overall priority.

6. Hierarchies as Representations of Complexity

The crucial advantage of the approach presented over most existing methods of assessing (project) alternatives is its contribution to analyzing the structure of a problem and articulating and debating judgments. Designing a hierarchy forces the planner or decision maker to penetrate the problem. Since the outcome of a decision process depends heavily on this initial step, one might want some ideas regarding how to design such—usually nonunique—hierarchies.

The reader may be concerned that he does not know how to formulate a hierarchy or at least he can only do the simplest kind as in the foregoing example. In this and in later chapters there will be other examples and he can begin by looking at them. However, in the next few paragraphs we hope to stimulate his thinking about how to structure a complex hierarchy.

Complexity as we know is characterized by a large number of interactions

40 Analytical Planning

among many subjective and objective factors of different type and degree of importance and of several parties with different objectives and conflicting interests all of which combine to influence the likelihood or impossibility of choosing an alternative outcome that is agreeable to all with a certain amount of compromise.

To deal with the mess associated with complexity we need an organized framework to represent the parties, their objectives, the criteria and policies governed by these objectives, the alternative outcomes and the resources to allocate to these alternatives.

The overall goal or focus of the problem such as choosing a best car, designing a best system, allocating a resource according to importance, is usually the top level of a hierarchy called the goal or focus. In planning, this level may consist of horizons (several intervals of time such as 3 or 5 years). The focus is then followed by a level of the most important criteria such as the cost, style, comfort and size of a car or in planning, profitability, investment, competition and so on. Each criterion may subdivide into subcriteria. These are then followed by a level of alternatives of which there can be a very large number.

As we shall see in certain hierarchies a level of actors may be included below the levels of the general criteria (sometimes this level of criteria may be totally absent) to determine which actor has the greatest impact on the outcome. This is then followed by a level of actor objectives for each actor, followed by a level of actor policies under the objectives of each actor and this is followed by a level of alternative outcomes.

In general the decomposition of a problem (or focus) into a hierarchy follows the train of thought of an individual. How do we know that we have selected the right focus or goal, the right criteria and have included the appropriate actors and so on? Can we follow a method which helps us to identify problems correctly, select objectives to solve them, and further structure the hierarchy? Here are some general guidelines.

Aids in Structuring a Hierarchy

1. Do a simple problem such as the House Buying example.
2. Look at many examples (see references).
3. Define the overall objective—what problem are you trying to solve? The objective should reflect assumptions regarding the cause of the problem within the system not just its manifestations (e.g., low employee morale as a cause of low productivity.) Low productivity is not the problem; it is its manifestation.
4. Identify assumptions (explicit and implicit) that are reflected in your definition of the problem (See Chapter 5.) Are these assumptions viable? If not, formulate new objectives.

5. Determine biases or preconceived notions that might affect your definition of the problem.
6. Identify who will be affected by your definition of the problem.
7. Find out how they define the problem. Can you give them an opportunity to participate in constructing the hierarchy? (see Chapter 5).
8. Determine if there are other definitions of the problem more viable than your own (Repeat steps 4–8 for all alternative definitions.)
9. Examine your problem as part of several problems in any overall goal.
10. Force a framework and refine it to fit the problem.
11. Brainstorm the problem's every conceivable facet. Then organize all the criteria listed as a hierarchy by grouping the factors in comparable classes appropriately aligned-positive or negative direction.
12. Make certain that you can answer questions about the importance of the elements in a level with respect to the elements in the upper level.
13. Formulate written questions you are going to answer for each level.

There are two general types of dominance hierarchies encountered in practice. These are studied in further detail in Chapter 6. We give them in outline form to encourage the reader to pursue his own structures with greater confidence.

How to Structure Dominance Hierarchies

The two generic types of dominance hierarchies are:

1. The forward process hierarchy:
   Project the present state of a problem into the *likely* or logical future (or consequence)
2. The backward process hierarchy:
   Determines control policies to help attain the *desired* future (or consequence)
   Both types of hierarchies are used in the planning process. Planning is an iterative process combining the forward and backward processes to produce convergence of the likely towards the desired.

The Forward Process Hierarchy

The levels of the hierarchy as they occur in descending order in the most general form. (In practice particular hierarchies are much more abbreviated) are:

(a) Macro environmental constraints
(b) Social and political constraints
(c) Forces

42   *Analytical Planning*

(d) Objectives
(e) Actors
(f) Actor objectives
(g) Actor policies
(h) Contrast scenarios
(i) Composite scenario. Details of this scenario are given by means of state variables, and an index is constructed to evaluate the composite impact of given control policies.

The Backward Process Hierarchy

The levels of this type of hierarchy are as follows:

(a) Anticipatory scenarios
(b) Problems and opportunities
(c) Actors and coalitions
(d) Actor objectives
(e) Actor policies
(f) Particular control policies to influence the outcome

As in the forward process hierarchy, some of the levels may be eliminated for some particular problems.

Note that the structure of a hierarchy may be altered to account for anomalies of choice. Here is a situation which presents itself in choice problems. An apple is preferred to an orange. More apples are then introduced. Should an apple continue to be preferred or does the presence of many apples now make an orange more preferred? On the one hand, the apples may be even more attractive than the orange—"the more the better." On the other hand, adding more apples can change the preference—"when there is a lot of it around, you never want it very much." The question is how can a theoretical approach be developed so that it can lead to both outcomes according to which one is desired? It is obvious that consciousness about a problem is in the mind of the user. A mathematical approach cannot by itself make such a distinction automatically. We need to represent our hidden expectations in the form of criteria in the hierarchy.

There are two other ideas to mention in this respect. The first is that a higher priority criterion in a hierarchy may have several alternatives to be judged under it while a lower priority criterion may have a few. It is desired to increase the priority of the elements in the larger set because if there are many of them they may each receive a smaller composite priority than each of the few elements under the low priority criterion. Sometimes it is the other rarer elements that need to receive a higher priority. In the first case one can multiply the priority of each criterion by the relative number of elements under it and normalize the weights of the criteria. In the second case a complementary set of weights can be used. A more general approach would be the one described above to introduce an additional criterion in the hierarchy called "importance of number of descendants." The prioritization is carried out under this criterion, which in turn has also been compared with the other criteria.

A third illustration of the need to augment the structure according to expectation is that of three secretaries who apply for a job: one excellent at English but poor at typing, the second is balanced but not excellent at either and the third is excellent at typing and poor at English. The way to surface the balanced secretary is to add to the criteria: English and typing, a third one: balance. In this manner the balanced secretary could receive the overriding priority.

To cover such situations which at first may appear paradoxical and whose variety can be infinite whether analyzed through an analytic hierarchy or by other means, we must usually modify the structure to satisfy these expectations.

Group Participation in Structuring Hierarchies

To understand how people participate in structuring a hierarchy, they are given a twenty-five minute lecture on how a problem is decomposed into levels of a hierarchy from the overall goal down to a level of alternatives with each level containing comparable clusters. They are shown the scale and how it is used verbally and then converted to numbers. They are encouraged not to use numbers but only judgments. They are shown one or two examples how pairwise comparisons are made, what the eigenvector priorities are, the inconsistencies, possible revision and the composite weights. Problems with benefits and costs are also illustrated combining the two in a single ratio scale. Following the presentation they begin to structure a simple problem with a three level hierarchy. As they see more complex examples they increase the complexity of their own structures.

At times before we had many examples people brainstormed their problem listing all the ideas they thought were relevant and then grouped these ideas into clusters of similar things. Then they arranged them in precedence levels to establish relations between what is more important, what is less important and what is still less important. It is in this fashion that our early examples of hierarchies were begun and out of which two distinct classes of hierarchies emerged. The forward hierarchy to project what is likely and the backward to determine what is desired and how to attain it. By combining the two we developed a planning or control hierarchy.

Thus we have tended to take the approach that we already have a hierarchic structure which has been defined formally in Saaty (1980), in each of whose levels there are clusters that are of nearly similar size or importance. But this need not be the case. We could start as in brainstorming by clustering everything and attempting to compare relative sizes (or importances) of clusters with respect to other clusters by taking the goal and comparing the levels according to relative importance each time making sure that adjacent

44 Analytical Planning

levels differ by no more than one order of magnitude. This is a complex operation which can be carried out along lines already described through the use of common elements. For our purpose it may be useful to first distinguish between noncomparable entities and then between comparable ones. We need primitives for this purpose.

7. Some Justification for the 1–9 Scale

The scale we recommend for use has been successfully tested and compared with other scales. The judgments elicited from people are taken qualitatively, and corresponding scale values are assigned to them. In general, we do not expect the judgments to be consistent.

Our choice of scale hinges on the following requirements:

1. The scale should make it possible to represent people's differences in feelings when they make comparisons. It should represent as much as possible all distinct shades of feeling that people have.

2. If we denote the scale values by $x_1, x_2, \ldots, x_p$, then let $x_{i+1} - x_i = 1$, $i = 1, \ldots, p-1$.

Since we require that the subject must be aware of all gradations at the same time, and we agree with the fact that for better consistency and accuracy an individual should not simultaneously compare more than seven objects (plus or minus one), we are led to choose a $p = 7 + 2$. Using a unit difference between successive scale values is all that we allow; by using the fact that $x_1 = 1$ for the identity comparison, it follows that the scale values will range from one to nine.

In using the scale, the reader should recall that we assume that the individual providing the judgment has knowledge about the relative intensities possessed by the elements being compared and that the numerical ratios he forms are nearest-integer approximations whose highest ratio corresponds to nine.

Presumably one would like to have a scale extend as far out as possible. But on second thought we discover that to give an idea of how large measurement can get, scales must be finite. We also note that one does not measure widely disparate objects by the same yardstick. Short distances on a piece of paper are measured in centimeters, longer distances in a neighborhood in meters, and still larger ones in kilometers and even in light years. To make comparisons of the sizes of atoms with those of stars, people, in a natural fashion, insert between these extremes objects that gradually grow larger and larger. This transition enables one to discriminate among the orders of magnitude of measurement. To make such distinction possible, the objects put in each group are within the range of the scale, and the largest object in one group is used as the smallest one in the next larger group. Its scale values in the two groups enable one to continue the measurement from one group to the next, and so on.

In practice, one way or another, the numerical judgments will have to be approximations, but how good the approximations are is the question at which this approach is aimed.

The Analytic Hierarchy Process

There is no satisfactory statistical theory that would assist us in deciding how well judgmental data correspond to reality. We have occasionally used the root mean square deviation (RMS) and the median absolute deviation about the median (MAD). These indicators are probably more useful when making interscale or inter-personal comparisons in judgments than as absolute measures of the goodness of fit. We have not found the Chi-square test useful. It is clear that this is an area of research worth pursuing.

Considerable effort has been concentrated on comparing the scale 1 to 9 with 28 other scales suggested to us by a number of people. Space limitation prevents us from showing that this scale and small perturbations of it are better than practically all others. We used five different problems for which the real answers were later determined. The reader should consult Saaty (1980) for this purpose.

Relative Weights of Objects

The following matrix Exhibit 3-9 gives pairwise comparisons of five objects indicated according to their relative weights:

EXHIBIT 3-9. *Relative Weights of Objects*

Weight	Radio	Typewriter	Large attache case	Projector	Small attache case
Radio	1	1/5	1/3	1/4	4
Typewriter	5	1	2	2	8
Large attache case	3	1/2	1	1/2	4
Projector	4	1/2	2	1	7
Small attache case	1/4	1/8	1/4	1/7	1

The largest eigenvalue $\lambda_{max} = 5.16$, with consistency index .04. The random value is 1.22. Estimates of the resulting eigenvector and vector of actual relative weights are obtained, as indicated earlier, by mutliplying the elements in each row, taking their fifth root, and then normalizing, which is only an approximation when we do not have perfect consistency; that is, $\frac{\lambda_{max} - n}{n - 1} > 0$.

Eigenvector	Actual relative weights
.09	.10
.40	.39
.18	.20
.29	.27
.04	.04

46 *Analytical Planning*

The root mean square deviation is given by .0158, less than 2% error indicating a good estimate. It is worth noting that comparing objects to estimate their weight by lifting them up with the hand is something people do rarely in their life. Thus, one would expect wider scatter in the results than, for example, in an optics experiment using the eyes to compare the relative brightness of objects from a light source to something the eye is trained to do nearly all the time. Greater precision is expected from the eye because of its experience.

8. Group Judgments and Variable Judgments

When a group participates in making a decision the question is how do we use these judgments in the process.

After debate and concensus, it is possible to combine the different judgments to satisfy the reciprocal property. Thus whatever rule we use to combine the judgments and take the reciprocal of the outcome, it should coincide with what we get by combining the reciprocals of those judgments. It turns out that there is one way to do this and that is to multiply the judgments and take the kth root if k people are participating. This is the geometric mean.

Next we ask, What happens to a decision when judgments whether of a single individual or a group change over time? If the decision has already been taken, it may be revised and reimplemented, if desired, incurring some costs. On the other hand, the AHP can be used as a learning tool in which case judgments can change. In that case either the last judgment is used, if it is thought to be the best one, or all p.evious judgments are synthesized by taking their geometric mean or some judgments are emphasized more by ensuring that they are represented more often before taking the geometric mean. It is also possible by using the AHP program, Expert Choice, on the personal computer, to carry out sensitivity analysis of judgments on outcomes.

In this manner change in judgment can be dealt with as part of the complexity being studied. Note that the AHP, like other analytic procedures, can be abused by forcing the data (judgments) to comply with the preconceived notions and biases of the analyst. Thus, one must be able to defend the weights assigned to the judgments.

9. Measuring Performance

Performance is measured in terms of the system's goals and objectives. As elementary as this principle is, it is often not reflected in standard methods of program evaluation. This is because programs are often undertaken without a clear and explicit statement of their goals and purposes. For example, government policies are formed through intense debate and compromise among legislators and, therefore, the stated goals may be an imperfect mixture of multiple and competing goals. The AHP facilitates performance measure-

The Analytic Hierarchy Process 47

ment by explicating goals and objectives, making them subject to monitoring and evaluation following implementation. Moreover, the AHP can be used as a performance measurement instrument by incorporating into the hierarchy assessment criteria with which to compare the actual performance of a system with its desired performance. This has been done to measure the deviation of buildings from architectural specifications, to assess the performance of aircraft designs against desired standards, and to assess alternative technologies for developing countries (Saaty and Erdener, 1979; Ramanujam and Saaty, 1981).

10. Additional Applications of the AHP

A. Selecting a Job

A student who had just received his Ph.D was interviewed for three jobs (A, B, and C). He decided to use the AHP to evaluate the jobs. The hierarchy of this example is complete (Exhibit 3-10). His criteria for selecting the jobs and their pairwise comparison matrix are given in Exhibit 3-11 together with the eigenvector (normalized) associated with the maximum eigenvalue. In this matrix, pairs of criteria are compared with respect to their relative contribution to the student's overall satisfaction with a job. The question asked was, which of a given pair of criteria is seen as contributing more to overall satisfaction with a job and what is the intensity or strength of the difference? For example, the value of 5 in row three, column four, indicates that benefits are strongly more important than colleague associations.

The eigenvectors (one for each criterion) just obtained are each weighted by

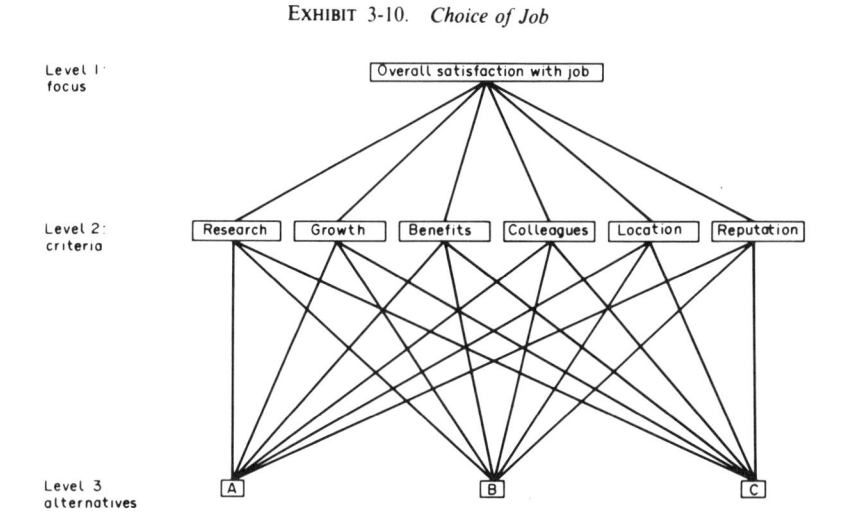

EXHIBIT 3-10. *Choice of Job*

48   *Analytical Planning*

EXHIBIT 3-11. *Pairwise Comparison Matrices for Choosing a Job*

Overall satisfaction with job	Research	Growth	Benefits	Colleagues	Location	Reputation	Eigenvector
Research	1	1	1	4	1	1/2	.16
Growth	1	1	2	4	1	1/2	.19
Benefits	1	1/2	1	5	3	1/2	.19
Colleagues	1/4	1/4	1/5	1	1/3	1/3	.05
Location	1	1	1/3	3	1	1	.12
Reputation	2	2	2	3	1	1	.30

The consistency index of this matrix is .07.

Research	A	B	C		Growth	A	B	C		Benefits	A	B	C
A	1	1/4	1/2		A	1	1/4	1/5		A	1	3	1/3
B	4	1	3		B	4	1	1/2		B	1/3	1	1
C	2	1/3	1		C	5	2	1		C	3	1	1

Colleagues	A	B	C		Location	A	B	C		Reputation	A	B	C
A	1	1/3	5		A	1	1	7		A	1	7	9
B	3	1	7		B	1	1	7		B	1/7	1	5
C	1/5	1/7	1		C	1/7	1/7	1		C	1/9	1/5	1

the eigenvector component of the associated criterion and the results summed and normalized. We obtain:

$$.16 \begin{pmatrix} 14 \\ .63 \\ 24 \end{pmatrix} + .19 \begin{pmatrix} .10 \\ .33 \\ .57 \end{pmatrix} + \cdots + .30 \begin{pmatrix} .77 \\ .17 \\ .05 \end{pmatrix} = \begin{pmatrix} .40 \\ .34 \\ .26 \end{pmatrix} \begin{matrix} A \\ B \\ C \end{matrix}$$

B. The Snail Darter and the Dam (*McConney and Verchota*)

In this example we elaborate on the environment of a complex, unstructured problem. The relevant factors were structured hierarchically (Exhibit 3-12) and the AHP was applied to determine which of the possible solutions was the most feasible.

The Tellico Dam, proposed by the Tennessee Valley Authority and approved by Congress in October 1966, has not yet been completed. The delay has been caused by a series of public demonstrations and legal battles. The $120 million project, which includes a dam on the Little Tennessee River, was intended to encourage economic and industrial development in the area. Early opponents of the project argued that the river's scenic, recreational, historical,

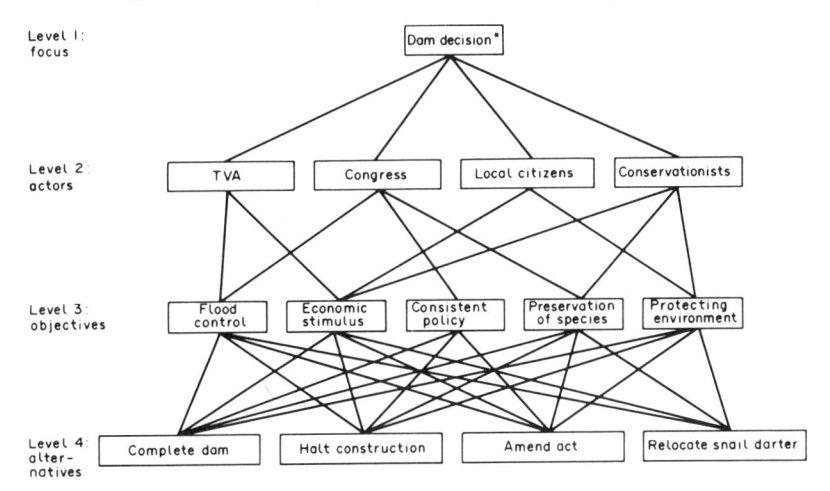

EXHIBIT 3-12. *The Tellico Dam Problem: Hierarchic Representation*

Level 1: focus — Dam decision*

Level 2: actors — TVA | Congress | Local citizens | Conservationists

Level 3: objectives — Flood control | Economic stimulus | Consistent policy | Preservation of species | Protecting environment

Level 4: alternatives — Complete dam | Halt construction | Amend act | Relocate snail darter

and archaeological attributes would be lost if the dam were completed and allowed to fill with water. Construction on the project was temporarily halted in 1971 and again in 1973 when opponents forced the Tennessee Valley Authority to comply with the regulations of the National Environmental Protection Agency. In 1973 the snail darter (a tiny, three-inch long member of the perch family) was discovered in the Little Tennessee River; it was declared to be an endangered species and the Little Tennessee River was declared a critical habitat. Consequently, construction of the Tellico Dam was halted in January 1977. This decision was based on the court's interpretation of the language of the Endangered Species Act, which provides absolute protection for endangered species and critical habitat. The Tennessee Valley Authority believed that the Endangered Species Act does not apply to this project since it was under construction before the Act was passed. In 1978 the Supreme Court upheld the earlier decisions: there could be no more work done on the dam. The situation has changed since then.

We may first identify the actors in this dispute; several groups are involved. The Tennessee Valley Authority (TVA) designed the Tellico Dam and received Congressional support amounting to nearly $120 million. Congress passed the Endangered Species Act and also made an appropriation after the snail darter had been declared an endangered species. Local citizens have wanted the economic development. Since its inception, however, conservationists have opposed the dam, saying that it would involve the loss of a natural, archaeological and historic amenity.

The objectives of the actors may be identified as follows:

TVA: (a) the provision of flood control, power, recreation and (b) the provision of local economic stimulus.

50 Analytical Planning

Congress: (a) the provision of flood control, power, recreation; (b) consistency in policy (to construct dam, protect species); and (c) the preservation of the endangered species.

Local citizens: (a) the provision of a local economic stimulus and (b) the preservation of a natural, scenic, historic and archaeological amenity.

Conservationists: (a) the preservation of endangered species; (b) the provision of a local economic stimulus; and (c) the preservation of a natural, scenic, historic, and archaeological amenity.

Possible solutions to the problem include:

(a) The completion of dam construction as planned.
(b) The halting of dam construction permanently.
(c) The amendment of the Endangered Species Act to include such phrases as "to the extent possible" and to allocate power to Congress or to a federal agency to exempt certain projects on which all major decisions have been made.
(d) The provision of a new habitat for the snail darter (and consequent declassification of the Little Tennessee River as its critical habitat).

A hierarchy (Exhibit 3-12) of three levels—actors, objectives and outcomes—was established; weights were assigned to the elements, and the final weighting of outcomes was found. The weights were as follows:

Completion of dam	.27
Permanent halt to construction	.10
Amendment of Endangered Species Act	.29
Relocation of snail darter	.35

Thus the process revealed the most likely outcome to be the relocation of the snail darter.

The hierarchy of this example is incomplete. It is illustrated in Exhibit 3-12. This exercise was carried out in the 1970s and a decision has been made to construct the Dam. If our information is adequate it was thought that the snail darter is not, after all, endangered by the dam.

C. Use of the AHP with Objective Data

Now we give an example of a comparison in linear utility. Let us show how the AHP may used to solve an ordinary decision problem. A person would like to buy a car that will cost him the minimum when totalled over the initial cost, maintenance costs over 3 years and driving gasoline costs over 3 years in the city (30,000 miles for 3 years) and in the country (20,000 miles for 3 years) at a cost of $1.50 per gallon. He must choose from 3 cars with the following data.

The Analytic Hierarchy Process 51

Cost	Maintenance per year	Gallons per mile in city	Gallons per mile in country
A $ 6,000	$600	$\frac{1}{10}$	$\frac{1}{20}$
B $ 8,000	$400	$\frac{1}{20}$	$\frac{1}{40}$
C $10,000	$200	$\frac{1}{40}$	$\frac{1}{60}$

Cost A = $6000 + 3 \times 600 + 30{,}000 \times 1.5 \times \frac{1}{10} + 20{,}000 \times 1.5 \times \frac{1}{20} = \$13{,}800$

Cost B = $8000 + 3 \times 400 + 30{,}000 \times 1.5 \times \frac{1}{20} + 20{,}000 \times 1.5 \times \frac{1}{40} = \$12{,}200$

Cost C = $10{,}000 + 3 \times 200 + 30{,}000 \times 1.5 \times \frac{1}{40} + 20{,}000 \times 1.5 \times \frac{1}{60} = \$12{,}225$

Car B would cost the minimum amount.
Now let us see how we could have arrived at this result hierarchically. Our hierarchy takes the following form:

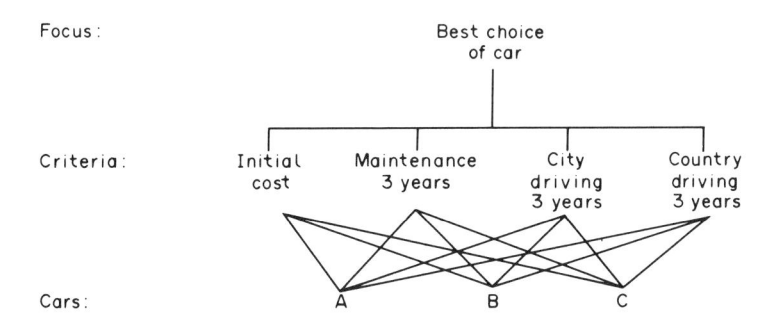

Focus: Best choice of car

Criteria: Initial cost | Maintenance 3 years | City driving 3 years | Country driving 3 years

Cars: A   B   C

Let us write the last three expressions for the costs (by normalizing over each factor) as follows:

Car A = $24000\left(\dfrac{6}{24}\right) + 3 \times 1200\left(\dfrac{6}{12}\right) + \dfrac{45000 \times 7}{40}\left(\dfrac{4}{7}\right) + \dfrac{30000 \times 5.5}{60}\left(\dfrac{30}{55}\right)$

Car B = $24000\left(\dfrac{8}{24}\right) + 3 \times 1200\left(\dfrac{4}{12}\right) + \dfrac{45000 \times 7}{40}\left(\dfrac{2}{7}\right) + \dfrac{30000 \times 5.5}{60}\left(\dfrac{15}{55}\right)$

Car C = $24000\left(\dfrac{10}{24}\right) + 3 \times 1200\left(\dfrac{2}{12}\right) + \dfrac{45000 \times 7}{40}\left(\dfrac{1}{7}\right) + \dfrac{30000 \times 5.5}{60}\left(\dfrac{10}{55}\right)$

The common weights for the cost of the car is 24000 (their total cost) that of maintenance is 3600 (the total over the 3 years). The weight of driving in the city is 7875 which is the total for the 3 cars over 3 years. Similarly for driving in the country the weight is 2750.

The matrix of pairwise comparisons of the criteria would involve the ratios of the weights just discussed whose principal eigenvector is simply these

52 Analytical Planning

weights given in normalized form, i.e., .6279, .0942, .2060, .0719. If we did not have this precise knowledge we could approximate the ratios of the weights using our 1 to 9 scale as follows:

$$\begin{vmatrix} 1 & 7 & 3 & 9 \\ 1/7 & 1 & 1/2 & 1 \\ 1/3 & 2 & 1 & 3 \\ 1/9 & 1 & 1/3 & 1 \end{vmatrix}$$

whose principal eigenvector is given by .6326, .0886, .2035, .0756 which is not very different from the exact value above.

The question to ask here can take the following form: overall which criterion is more important in buying, maintaining and operating the car? or: on the average, which criterion is more important in buying, maintaining, and operating the car? For comparisons of the three cars with respect to each of the four criteria we can use the ratios of the quantities in parenthesis in our expression for the costs which are simply the relative values. For example, when car A is compared with car B relative to cost we would write $\frac{6}{24} \div \frac{8}{24} = \frac{6}{8}$ and so on. The four eigenvectors are the three values normalized in each case. Finally the costs obtained by the hierarchic synthesis lead to the same answer and the choice of car B.

One advantage of this approach is that it is dimensionless so that the problem of having weights related to units does not arise. An alternative method would be to weight the actual attributes in their chosen units. In that case the weights should indeed reflect the units used in the measurement as well as the relative costs. The process used above corresponds to scaling the criteria according to the money involved and not to an intrinsic difference among them.

D. Generalization of the Approach to Network Systems

Sometimes it is not possible for planners to construct a *hierarchic representation* of a problem but a *network representation* is deemed to be more appropriate. There is an approach for handling these types of problems which is based on the same basic principles as the AHP. To adequately describe it here, however, would take us far afield. The interested reader should consult Saaty (1980) where the procedure is described in detail.

11. Comments on Dependence

The Analytic Hierarchy Process provides a simple and direct means for measuring interdependence in a system. The basic idea is that wherever there is interdependence, each of the activities (or criteria) becomes an objective and all the activities (or criteria) are compared according to their contributions to that activity (or criteria). This generates a set of dependence priorities indicating the relative dependence of each activity on all the activities. These priorities are then weighted by the independence priority of each related activity obtained from the hierarchy and the results summed over each row, thus obtaining the interdependence weights. By way of validation we find that this approach is compatible with, for example, what econometricians do in calculating input-output matrices.

To illustrate the method we take a manageable and self-contained example of the well being of an average American family. Three criteria are identified which affect this well-being. They are: "Security" (financial and psychological), "Love" and "Participation." The members of the family are "Mother," "Father," and "Children." A group of about nine people, six in their middle twenties, two older and one younger participated. They thought that the criteria could be regarded as independent. However, the members of the family depended on each other in making their contributions. Although the participants had no difficulty in relating all the elements according to dependence, it may be that in some problems not every element contributes to the others. In that case no judgments are provided for it and when finally it is listed with the others, it is assigned zero priority for that part of the dependence. The hierarchy has the following structure:

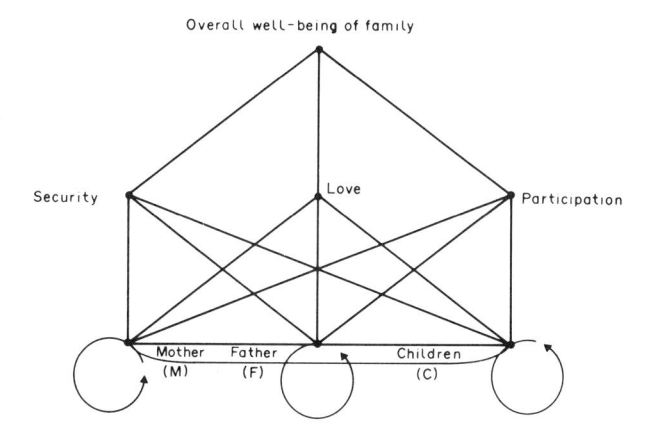

EXHIBIT 3-13. *Family Interdependence Priorities*

The pairwise comparison matrices are as follows: Which criterion contributes more strongly to the well-being of the family and how much more?

Well-being	Security	Love	Participation	Priorities
Security	1	3	7	.67
Love	1/3	1	3	.24
Participation	1/7	1/3	1	.09
			C.R. =	.006

54   Analytical Planning

Which member contributes more strongly to each criterion and how much more?

Security	Mother	Father	Children	Priorities
Mother	1	1/3	7	.30
Father	3	1	7	.63
Children	1/7	1/7	1	.06
			C.R. =	.12

Love	Mother	Father	Children	Priorities
Mother	1	2	7	.58
Father	1/2	1	6	.35
Children	1/7	1/6	1	.07
			C.R. =	.03

Participation	Mother	Father	Children	Priorities
Mother	1	4	5	.67
Father	1/4	1	3	.23
Children	1/5	1/3	1	.10
			C.R. =	.07

The independence weights with respect to each criterion are obtained by hierarchic composition. (Note that rounding errors may lead to slight deviations in the answers on the right.)

$$\begin{array}{c} \text{Security} \quad \text{Love} \quad \text{Participation} \\ (.67) \quad\quad (.24) \quad\quad (.09) \end{array}$$

$$\begin{array}{c} M \\ F \\ C \end{array} \begin{pmatrix} .30 & .58 & .67 \\ .63 & .35 & .23 \\ .06 & .07 & .10 \end{pmatrix} =$$

Composite weights of family member with respect to each criterion

$$\begin{pmatrix} .20 & .14 & .06 \\ .42 & .08 & .02 \\ .04 & .02 & .01 \end{pmatrix}$$

The independence weights are obtained by adding the entries in each row. We have:

$$\begin{bmatrix} M & .40 \\ F & .53 \\ C & .17 \end{bmatrix}$$

Next, we determine the dependence among the members of the family with respect to each criterion. How strongly do the members of the family contribute to each member with respect to the criterion indicated?

$M_{Security}$	Mother	Father	Children	Priority
Mother	1	1/5	6	.23
Father	5	1	7	.71
Children	1/6	1/7	1	.06
			C.R. =	.21

$F_{Security}$	Mother	Father	Children	Priority
Mother	1	5	7	.71
Father	1/5	1	6	.23
Children	1/7	1/4	1	.83
			C.R. =	.03

$C_{Security}$	Mother	Father	Children	Priority
Mother	1	3	7	.66
Father	1/3	1	4	.26
Children	1/7	1/4	1	.08
			C.R. =	.03

M_{Love}	Mother	Father	Children	Priority
Mother	1	1/5	1	.16
Father	5	1	3	.66
Children	1	1/3	1	.19
			C.R. =	.03

F_{Love}	Mother	Father	Children	Priority
Mother	1	5	3	.63
Father	1/5	1	1/5	.09
Children	1/3	5	1	.30
			C.R. =	.12

C_{Love}	Mother	Father	Children	Priority
Mother	1	1	1	.33
Father	1	1	1	.33
Children	1	1	1	.33
			C.R. =	.00

$M_{Participation}$	Mother	Father	Children	Priority
Mother	1	1/4	3	.22
Father	4	1	6	.69
Children	1/3	1/6	1	.09
			C.R. =	.05

$F_{Participation}$	Mother	Father	Children	Priority
Mother	1	4	6	.69
Father	1/4	1	3	.22
Children	1/6	1/3	1	.09
			C.R. =	.04

56   *Analytical Planning*

C Participation	Mother	Father	Children	Priority
Mother	1	1	5	.46
Father	1	1	5	.46
Children	1/5	1/5	1	.09
			C.R. =	.00

To obtain the final interdependence priorities, we multiply each column of dependence priorities by the composite weight of its respective factor and then add across to obtain the interdependence weight. Thus we have:

	M S (.20)	F S (.42)	C S (.04)	M L (.14)	F L (.08)	C L (.02)	M P (.06)	F P (.02)	C P (.01)		
M	.23	.71	.66	.16	.62	.33	.22	.69	.46	=	.48
F	.71	.23	.26	.66	.09	.33	.69	.32	.46		.41
C	.06	.06	.08	.19	.30	.33	.09	.09	.09		.11

By considering dependence in this example the priorities change somewhat from what we had used for independence changing the priorities of the mother and father. We have:

With independence	With interdependence
M ⎛ .40 ⎞ F ⎜ .53 ⎟ C ⎝ .07 ⎠	M ⎛ .48 ⎞ F ⎜ .41 ⎟ C ⎝ .11 ⎠

Our summary statement about dependence is as follows: In any cluster of the hierarchy whenever there is dependence among the elements of the cluster, that dependence must be measured in itself and separately from the usual independence evaluation. Dependence is measured for each criterion with respect to which it holds and the results synthesized over the criteria.

Ami Arbel of Tel-Aviv University has applied the AHP to aircraft design. The process involved repeated tradeoffs and interdependence assessment of design goals and design alternatives that lead to particular configurations. The design goals included such conflicting items as lateral stability, longitudinal stability, supersonic drag, roll rate and spin recover. The design approaches included wing positioning, control surface area, control travel and strake. The configuration selected included a combination of these design approaches, and one had to choose that one which best met the design goals.

12. Comparison With Other Methods

For a long time people have been concerned with the measurement of both physical and psychological events. The physical is concerned with things outside the person doing the measuring. It is objective. The psychological is concerned with how we perceive and interpret internally. What we experience and how we feel. It is subjective. Scientists have used a diversity of mathematical approaches to structure the problems they encounter and to perform measurement within this structure. Many have worked on measurement and on judgment solicitation. The AHP falls into this broad category of mathematical and behavioral science interests. In the AHP dominance matrices play a central role. Special effort has been made to characterize them.

Shepard (1972) has noted a more extensive research on proximity, profile and conjoint measurement than on measurement associated with dominance matrices.

The AHP uses pairwise comparisons in its dominance matrices. Thurstone's model (1927) of comparative judgment also uses pairwise comparison of the objects, but only to the extent that one is more preferred to or greater than another but does not get into how strongly greater. He then recovers information over the stimuli by imposing assumptions of normality on the judgmental process. Under additional assumptions on the parameters, he recovers various "metric" information on the stimuli. A number of restrictions are associated with Thurstone's approach. For example, Guilford (1928) recommends limiting the range of probabilities that one stimulus is judged to be more than another.

Torgerson (1958) has systematized and extended Thurstone's method for scaling; in particular, concentrating on the case in which covariance terms are constant, correlation terms equal, and distributions homoscedastic, i.e., they have equal variances.

Luce and Suppes (1964) and Suppes and Zinnes (1963) have proposed what Coombs (1964) calls the Bradley–Terry–Luce (BTL) model using the logistic curve which is a log transform of the probability distribution. Although this is different from assuming normality, in practice it is difficult to distinguish between the BTL model and the case in Thurstone's work where he assumes normal distributions and equal variances. The BTL model is more rigorously grounded in a theory of choice behavior. Coombs discusses the essential distinction between the two models.

We can contrast the assumptions used in the AHP with those used in the psychometric tradition above. We do not begin with the supposition that ratio judgments are independent probabilistic processes. Instead, we investigate the consequence of changes in the judgments through perturbations on the entire set of judgments. This type of approach leads to the criterion of consistency. Thus, obtaining solutions in our method is not a statistical procedure.

Briefly, many psychometric methods perform aggregation of judgments in the course of solving for a scale. We assume that if there is aggregation of judgments, it occurs prior to the ratio estimate between two stimuli. Therefore, our solution procedure is not concerned with assumptions of distributions of judgments. However, if we want to compare any solution with the criterion of consistency, we appeal to statistical reasoning and perturbations over the entire matrix of judgments.

Our use of metric information in the matrix of subjects' judgments generates strong parallels with principal component analysis, except that the data give dominance rather than similarity or covariance information. In principal component analysis λ_{max} is emphasized, but one also solves for all the λs. However, the results must be interpreted differently (Hotelling, 1973).

In our analysis the nature of the stimuli and the task presented to subjects are also similar to "psychophysical" scaling, as typified by Stevens and Galanter (1964) and recently used widely in many attempts to construct composite measures of political variables including "national power." Stevens' technique imposes consistency by asking the subjects to compare simultaneously each stimulus with all others, producing only one row of our matrix. This means that the hypothesis of unidimensionality cannot be tested directly. If Stevens' method is used, one should take care that the judgments over stimuli are known to be consistent or nearly so. In addition, there is no way of relating one scale to another as we do in the AHP.

Krantz (1972) has axiomatized alternative processes relating stimuli to judgments and has derived existence theorems for ratio scales. Comparable axiomatization has not been extended to hierarchies of ratio scales.

Some people have approached problems of scaling as if the cognitive space of stimuli were inherently multidimensional, but we choose instead to decompose this multidimensional structure hierarchically in order to establish a quantitative as well as qualitative relation among dimensions. The individual dimensions in multidimensional scaling solutions functionally resemble individual eigenvectors on any one level of our hierarchy.

The formal problem of constructing a scale as the normalized eigenvector w in the equation $Aw = \lambda w$, for λ a maximum, is similar to extracting the first principal component. When subjects are asked to fill the cells of only one row or one column and the other cells are computed from these (to insure "perfect consistency") the first eigenvalue, n, represents 100% of the variance in the matrix. If, however, "perfect consistency" applies to the data except that a normally distributed random component is added to each cell of the matrix, then one's theory of data would lead to principal factor analysis, and a "single-factor" solution would result. Thus, the imposition of perfect consistency by the experimenter produces an uninteresting result of exact scalability, which was assured by the experimental design of single comparisons. In fact, one can see that if the subjects fill only one row or column of the matrix and if the subjects' task is to generate ratios between pairs of stimuli, then the procedure is formally equivalent to having the subjects locate each stimulus along a continuum with a natural zero at one end: this is the "direct-intensity" technique of psychophysical scaling.

We have often used the logarithmic least squares approach as a quick way to estimate the eigenvector by normalizing the geometric mean of the columns. In a recent work with L. Vargas we have been studying the eigenvalue approach with the least squares and logarithmic least squares methods. With inconsistency, only the eigenvalue method is used.

Tucker (1958) presents a method for the "determination of parameters of a functional relation by factor analysis." He states, however, that "the rotation of axes problem remains unsolved . . .," that is, the factor analysis determines the parameters only within a linear transformation. Cliff (1975) suggests methods for the determination of such transformations where *a priori* theoretical analysis or observable quantities provide a criterion toward which to rotate the arbitrary factor solution.

The hierarchical composition is an inductive generalization of the following idea. We are given weights of elements in one level. We generate a matrix of column eigenvectors of the elements in the level immediately below this level with respect to each element in this level. Then we use the vector of (weights of) elements in this level to weight the corresponding column eigenvectors. Multiplying the matrix of eigenvectors with the column vector of weights gives the composite vector of weights of the lower-level elements.

Because the matrix of eigenvectors is not an orthogonal transformation, in general the result cannot be interpreted as a rotation. In fact, we are multiplying a vector in the unit n-simplex by a stochastic matrix. The result is another vector in the unit simplex. Algebraists have often pointed to a distinction between problems whose algebra has a structural geometric interpretation and those in which algebra serves as a convenient method for doing calculations. Statistical methods have a convenient geometric interpretation. Perturbation methods frequently may not.

In the works of Hammond and Summers (1965) concern is expressed regarding the performance of subjects in situations involving both linear and nonlinear relations among stimuli before concluding that the process of inductive inference is primarily linear. In our model, subjects' responses to linear and nonlinear cues seem to be adequately captured by the pairwise scaling method described here, by using the hierarchical decomposition approach in order to aggregate elements which fall into comparability classes according to the possible range of the scale used for the comparison.

Note that our solution of the information integration problem discussed by Anderson (1974) is approached through an eigenvalue formulation which has a linear structure. However, the scale defined by the eigenvector itself is a highly nonlinear function of the data. The process by means of which the eigenvector is generated involves complex addition, multiplication, and averaging. To perceive this complexity one may examine the eigenvector as a limiting solution of the normalized row sums of powers of the matrix.

Anderson (1974) also makes a strong point that validation of a response scale ought to satisfy a criterion imposed by the algebraic judgment model. Such a criterion in our case turns out to be consistency.

Multicriterion decision analysis offers a number of alternative approaches.

These have been recently reviewed by B. Roy and P. Vincke (1981). They include Multiattribute Utility Theory (MAU) which has been compared with the AHP on several occasions. From a theoretical standpoint MAU seeks to generate utilities on an interval scale whereas priorities in the AHP belong to a ratio scale. From a practical standpoint the AHP elicits judgments directly and uses them to synthesize priorities. MAU first derives a utility function by asking questions and then uses it to complete the analysis of a particular decision problem. Two other general approaches to multicriterion decision making are outranking methods and interactive methods. These often involve well defined decision rules in the form of indicators or objective functions sometimes leading to a linear program which is maximized or minimized as the case may be. There is no such optimization in the AHP unless of course one is allocating resources to maximize overall benefits. Finally, differing from most of these procedures the AHP allows for inconsistency as an integral part of the theory. Recognizing that people's ideas are in continuous change and growth, one should not insist on 100% consistency because that could change immediately after the problem is solved. Still one cannot make reliable decisions without an acceptable level of consistency. These concepts are dealt with through the formalization of the AHP.

13. Conclusion

The AHP has already been successfully applied in a variety of fields. These include: a plan to allocate energy to industries; designing a transport system for the Sudan; planning the future of a corporation and measuring the impact of environmental factors on its development; design of future scenarios for higher education in the United States; the candidacy and election processes; setting priorities for the top scientific institute in a developing country; the faculty promotion and tenure problem, and oil price predictions.

It should now be clear that designing an analytic hierarchy—like the structuring of a problem by any other method necessitates a substantial knowledge of the system in question. A strong aspect of the AHP is that the knowledge of individuals who supply judgments for the pairwise comparisons usually also plays a prominent role in specifying the hierarchy.

We have found that the use of the AHP has stimulated an increase in knowledge about specific planning problems, even in people who have a good deal of prior knowledge of and experience in a given situation. Moreover, we have found that even more light is shed on a problem and additional knowledge is gleaned when AHP is used in an iterative fashion, that is when the process is repeated in order to refine judgments, to allow for the introduction of new information, or simply to experiment with the effects of different assumptions. Dialogue, structured debate, and continuous interaction of participants in the process seem to be contributing forces in this learning process.

In the examples provided in this chapter, iteration would be a desirable component of the AHP. In Chapter 6 we illustrate applications of the AHP to planning and demonstrate its potential value in problems where one is attempting to produce convergence between the likely and desired futures. When the AHP is applied to planning problems, iteration is not only desirable but essential.

The approach to measurement with the Analytic Hierarchy Process tolerates a certain degree of inconsistency. Because of that, it is possible for a group to make a decision, whose degree of inconsistency for each of them is tolerable. In that case they will not feel that their preferences have been strongly violated. Thus the AHP obviates the need for an impossibility theorem like that of Kenneth Arrow's.

For readers interested in classical decision theory and notions of optimality, in particular Pareto Optimality, we note that the AHP can be used to determine the Pareto optimal state of a system; that is, the point at which some of the actors or players can be made better off without hurting someone else. Conversely, criteria representing surrogates for Pareto Optimality such as equity or fairness can be included in the hierarchic structure.

In summary we note that the Analytic Hierarchy Process is based on axioms of: pairwise comparisons, a valid scale to translate judgments to numbers in making these comparisons and the reciprocal relation, homogeneous clustering of hierarchic levels, hierarchic composition by weighting and adding and finally an axiom of expectations to be satisfied by introducing or deleting criteria from the hierarchy in order to address expectations based on criteria not already in the structure. A number of theorems have been developed from these axioms which make the AHP a mathematically viable approach for deriving ratio scales in solving complex problems.

References

Anderson, N. H. (1974) Information Integration Theory: A Brief Survey, In D. H. Krantz, R. C. Atkinson, R. D. Luce, and P. Suppes, Eds. *Contemporary Developments in Mathematical Psychology*, 2, San Francisco: Freeman.
Cliff, N. (1975) Complete Orders from Incomplete Data: Interactive Ordering and Tailored Testing, *Psychol. Bull.*, **82**, 2.
Coombs, G. H. (1964) *A Theory of Data*, New York/London/Sydney: Wiley.
Guilford, J. P. (1928) The Method of Paired Comparisons as a Psychometric Method, *Psychol. Rev.*, **35**, pp. 494–506.
Hammond, K. R. and D. A. Dummers (1965) Cognitive Dependence on Linear and Nonlinear Cues, *Psychol. Rev.*, **72**, 3, pp. 215–224.
Hotelling, H. (1933) Analysis of a Complex of Statistical Variables into Principal Components, *J. Educ. Psychol.*, **24**, pp. 498–520.
Krantz, D. H. (1972) A Theory of Magnitude Estimation and Cross Modality Matchings, *J. Math. Psychol.* **9**, pp. 168–199.
Luce, R. D. and P. Suppes (1964) Preference, Utility and Subjective Probability, in *Handbook of Mathematical Psychology*, III.
McConney, Mary and J. Verchota (1978) The Snail Darter Problem, unpublished paper: University of Pennsylvania.

Roy, B and P. Vincke (1981) Multicriterion analysis: Survey and Directions, *European J. Operat. Res.*, **8,** pp. 207-218.
Saaty, Thomas L. (1977) A Scaling Method for Priorities in Hierarchical Structures, *Journal of Mathematical Psychology.* **15,** 3, pp. 234-281.
Saaty, Thomas L. (1980) *The Analytic Hierarchy Process,* New York: McGraw-Hill.
Saaty, Thomas L. and Luis G. Vargas (1982) *The Logic of Priorities,* Boston: Kluwer-Nijhoff.
Saaty, Thomas L. (1982) *Decision Making for Leaders,* Belmont, CA: Wadsworth.
Saaty, Thomas L. (1982) Priority Setting in Complex Problems, *Proceedings of the Second World Conference on Mathematics at the Service of Man* Las Palmas, Canary Islands.
Shepard, R. N. (1972) A Taxonomy of Some Principal Types of Data and of Multidimensional Methods for their Analysis, in R. N. Shepard, A. K. Romney and S. B. Nerlove, Eds. *Multidimensional Scaling: Theory and Applications in the Behavioral Sciences,* 1, New York: Seminar Press, pp. 21-47.
Stevens, S. and E. Galanter (1964) Ratio Scales and Category Scales for a Dozen Perceptual Continua, *J. Experiment Psychol.*, **54,** pp. 377-411.
Suppes, P and J. L. Zinnes (1963) Basic Measurement Theory, in R. D. Luce, R. R. Bush, E. Galanter, Eds. *Handbook of Mathematical Psychology,* 1.
Thurston, L. L. (1927) A Law of Comparative Judgment, *Psychol. Rev.*, **34,** pp. 273-286.
Torgerson, W. S. (1958) *Theory and Methods of Scaling,* New York: Wiley.
Tucker, L. R. (1958) Determination of Parameters of a Functional Relation by Factor Analysis, *Psychometrika*, **23,** 1.

Suggested Readings

Saaty, Thomas, L., A Scaling Method for Priorities in Hierarchical Structures, *Journal of Mathematical Psychology*, **15,** No. 3, pp. 234-281.
This article provides a more detailed theoretical justification for the 1-9 scale.

Saaty, Thomas L., *Decision Making for Leaders,* Belmont; CA: Lifetime Learning Publications, Wadsworth, 1981.
This book provides additional applications of AHP with particular emphasis on non-technical explanations of cost-benefit, resource allocation, conflict resolution and so on. It is accompanied by a technical supplement containing computer programs for the AHP in Fortran, APL, Basic and even programs for hand calculators.

Saaty, Thomas L. and Luis G. Vargas (1982) *A New Logic for Priorities,* Boston: Klewer-Nijhoff 1982.

CHAPTER 4

Systems Characteristics and The Analytic Hierarchy Process

1. Introduction

This chapter has a dual purpose. The first is to identify properties of systems. The second is to relate some of these properties to the Analytic Hierarchy Process demonstrating that it is a systems method for dealing with systems problems. Our intention is to show that the AHP with its extensions to systems with feedback, captures the major properties embodied in systems theory and is its hand maiden. Perhaps the greatest value of this chapter is to highlight characteristics of systems that are important in hierarchic or network representation to obtain the most faithful and realistic interpretation and solution of problems. In other words we need to delve deeper into systems to discover what needs to be considered in our methodology. Examples are: the overall objectives of the system, its environment, the stability of the environment, its turbulence, people, their cooperation and conflict and so on.

We find it convenient and aesthetically satisfying to think of systems in terms of four major attributes. These are: purpose, function, flow and structure. To design a system one proceeds from the most general purpose to the particular functions of the parts, the flows necessary to perform the functions and the structure which constrains and directs the flows. This framework also makes it possible to differentiate and categorize a variety of systems.

We note that the whole universe may be regarded as one gigantic system. From a practical standpoint we do not deal with the entire universe every time we have a problem. Thus a particular system is a subsystem of the universe which in the broadest sense may be called its environment.

2. Purpose

Ackoff and Emery (1972) have drawn a distinction between *purposive* and *purposeful* systems. *Purposive* systems behave as programmed robots. They are tools used to fulfill needs perceived by their designers. Refrigerators serve the purpose of keeping food fresh; homes serve the purpose of protection from the environment; automobiles and airplanes serve the purpose of transportation. _Purposeful_ systems are inventive; examples are people and animals, universities and hospitals. Their purposes are determined by their ability to perceive needs to pursue alternative actions to satisfy those needs. They are also dynamic: their purposes and their style of selecting them change over time.

Both kinds of systems are open in that they exchange material or energy with their environment (see later); yet the inventive variety is distinguished by its ability to consider responses to environmental constraints. Systems which serve a purpose merely *react* to the environment with programmed outputs.

Preferred outcomes might be classified in terms of the amount of time required to bring them about. _Objectives_ are preferred outcomes attainable within a specified and relatively short period of time; *goals* are attainable in longer periods of time and require the prior satisfaction of one or more objectives; _ideals_ are states of a system never attained but merely approached with satisfaction of some objectives. Just as goals are clusters of objectives, ideals are clusters of goals.

It is worth mentioning that purpose itself need not be deterministically fixed. It can develop over time and is not necessarily unique. An interesting interpretation of this idea has been explored by the French microbiologist Jacques Monod in his book *Chance and Necessity* (1971). His thesis is that life is all a combinatorial accident based on chemistry and physics.

Purpose is a behavioral concept that is subjective and hard to define. Many people whose thinking is based on principles drawn from the natural sciences and engineering prefer to confine the definition of purpose to structure and flow and their interactions. Matter and motion are treated as intrinsic purposes. However, in social systems, human behavior is a powerful force that we do not understand adequately but that nonetheless appears to shape our approach to reality. It is difficult for us to understand systems, particularly those involving people, without reference to a human purpose. There is a kind of uncertainty principle in our attempt to define a system by looking at things we identify as systems. We are often led to modify our definitions as we become more and more specific. When one attempts to define a human as a system, causal explanations of the ultimate purpose of why people are designed the way they are fail to explain what their ultimate purpose is and how this design really contributes to that purpose. In the end one is led to circular arguments between the human design and the human purpose.

Human Purpose

Man is distinguished from other systems by an ability to perceive and differentiate among alternative courses of action and above all to design and control his own actions by a conscious effort. He establishes priorities and makes a choice on the basis of preference, necessity, caprice or whatever other forces impel him.

Our daily lives are dominated by a series of routine choices: when to get up in the morning, what to wear, what to eat, and the like; they are also dominated by a series of not so routine choices: where to go to school and what to study; whom to marry; when to retire; and sometimes even when to die. These choices, when followed by actions, give rise to new situations or states of existence. The cycle continues as new alternatives arise because of previous choices.

Groups of people form organizations and make choices to satisfy common purposes: what to produce and what to charge for it; what taxes to levy and what streets to pave; what weapons to build and how to fight a battle. In all decisions, the choices made today shape the alternatives of tomorrow.

While the notions of choice and purpose may be taken for granted, they are crucial to understand a particular system. We study systems to identify points of intervention where functions, flows, or structure can be modified to satisfy purpose. We also examine the purposes themselves to see if they are feasible or desirable in light of the existing circumstances.

The purpose of a system designed by people is, on the first level, given to it by the designer. Later the users of the system adapt it to their own purposes. An "ultimate" objective or purpose may or may not be perceived, even by the designer, as in the case of the use of nuclear energy. In this sense, a system should always be considered in the context of its users rather than of its designers—since they imbue it with purpose.

When designers and users basic purposes and viewpoints differ, their descriptions of a system may also differ, particularly when it relates to political and social impacts. This difference could give rise to conflict if actions are needed by one group, but they are being blocked by another group. A system can be regarded to have more than one purpose depending on the perspective of the observer. For example, recent research (Dunn, 1982) has demonstrated that some people regard the criminal justice system as primarily a punitive system because it imposes sanctions on violations of the law, while others see it as a means to focus on crime *prevention* by acting before violations occur. Still others perceive the criminal justice system as a vehicle for delivering many types of social services and assistance to citizens. Clearly, differing perceptions of the purpose of a system can lead to vastly different assessments or measures of the system's performance. Investigators in the field of evaluation research, who attempt to assess the performance of various types of systems, are discovering that many standard evaluation techniques fail to account for multiple and conflicting perceptions of the purpose of a system (Patton, 1978). It is, therefore, impossible to evaluate a system's performance in the absence of a synthesis of conflicting viewpoints.

The individual himself may not view the system the same way at all times. His view of it may depend on how it interacts with other systems he also uses. For example, a biologist may sometimes view a virus as a plant, sometimes as an animal—depending upon how it behaves in its environment.

An existing system may be thought of by various people (or even by the same individual) to have different purposes. For example, a car engine may be regarded by an aborigine as a source of heat for cooking while it is regarded by a member of a technological society as a means to transmit energy to rotate wheels. Conversely a given purpose may be satisfied by a number of different systems. For example, one can be transported by car, air or horse.

Because purpose is essential to the definition and evaluation of a system and because it is relative to the point of view of the people involved as a part of the system, we must include in our definition the variety of perspectives and possible differences among them, which can lead to conflict. Thus with every system there is a potential for conflict over what its purposes may be and what functions it performs.

We refer to the different perspectives of a system as the potential *conflict environment*. A basic problem in systems theory and particularly in social systems is how to obtain agreement on what the purpose is as a first step to the resolution of conflicts.

Organizations as systems cannot be studied in isolation from their participants. When people are components of systems, their behavior either facilitates or inhibits the fulfillment of purpose. The human element of purposeful systems makes them less predictable and less manageable than mechanical systems.

It follows that for social systems to achieve their purposes, people must cooperate with an implicit objective of making the system function better. We need to believe that our contribution to the system is important. It is also better to feel stimulated and creative at the tasks we perform. The quality of our working environment, the intellectual stimulation of our work, and our personal investment in the output of a product all contribute to our commitment to the purposes of the system. To create a cooperative atmosphere in a system, a manager must display strong leadership and have an ability to motivate people without manipulating them. Resolving conflicts in a way that keeps the "losers" committed to the organization is a task that requires specialized competence in negotiation strategies, arbitration, or organization development.

Purpose and the Environment

The purposes of a system are linked to the environment in which the system is embedded. We normally consider the environment of a system to be those factors external to the system that influence its behavior. Therefore, we need to study the environment to understand the compatibility of the purposes of the system with the functioning of the environment. A system may appear to be imperfect as far as its perceived objectives are concerned, yet it may be in harmony with the environment. A person who is lame, for example, may still be able to function well. Lack of appreciation of this connection between the

Systems Characteristics and the Analytic Hierarchy Process

individual and the environment can cause us to design systems that are in conflict with their environment. A system with an apparently clear and desirable purpose that is badly related to the environment would nevertheless be poorly designed. In our time, we have seen beautiful apartment complexes decay quickly because they were not well suited for either their users or the people who lived near them, or their environment.

A system may be related to the environment through the following criteria:

(1) *Purpose*— Is the purpose of the system compatible with the environment as we know it? If not, one should modify the purpose, abandon or discard the system, or reshape and adjust the environment.

(2) *Design*— Design involves the assembly of components so that they interact in harmony both among themselves and with the environment to achieve the purpose. The purpose is often modified to conform with what it is possible to realize and the cycle repeats.

(3) *Evaluation*— Is the system itself actually compatible with the environment? Does it accomplish its purposes efficiently? Does the system in operation suggest additional objectives to us that can be achieved with slight modifications?

A problem which occurs in a given system can be regarded either as improper functioning in the system itself or as a flaw in its interactions with the environment. The interface of the system with the environment is separate from either the system or the environment. Solving one problem can lead to disturbing other factors in the system or in its interface with the environment. Furthermore, solving a problem can disturb a system, even after a considerable lapse of time. For example, achieving the racial integration of schools through mandatory busing produced very noticeable impacts on the public school system more than a decade later. Declining enrollments in public schools has contributed to a cycle of decline in the quality of public education. Moreover, critics claim that mandatory busing may, in fact, intensify racial segration since minorities cannot afford the private school alternative.

Constraints on the Realization of Purpose

Despite the best efforts of highly trained analysts and problem solvers, social systems rarely realize their purposes. Here are some notable barriers to the fulfillment of these purposes.

A. *Internal Constraints*

1. *Perceptions*: Our separate views of the world shape our perceptions of the environment and may enhance or hinder our ability to identify and

distinguish among alternative needs and purposes and the means to achieve them.

2. *Unique Problems*: Often needs, when they are noticed, are ill-structured and there is no predetermined set of ordered procedures to satisfy them. Each need, or collection of needs, must be dealt with anew.
3. *Conflict and Power*: Perceived needs produce conflict in a system when decision makers cannot agree on the definition of the problem or else they disagree on the purpose itself, and that leads to fuzzy goals or objectives. Often, after compromising, one finds that the resulting system no longer has its original purpose to which there may have been considerable commitment of energy and principle and may even be simultaneously pursuing multiple and conflicting purposes.
4. *Inertia*: Major human decisions sometimes are attributable to uncontrolled sociological forces rather than to individuals. Individuals ossify and bureaucracies take on lives of their own in the process becoming less sensitive and adaptive.

B. *Environmental Constraints*

1. *Dynamics and Planning*: This constraint mainly has to do with our frustration to predict and plan the future. A large number of factors which influence decisions, their interdependence, and continuous change preclude the identification of an "optimal" solution, if indeed there is one. It is not clear what one can achieve in such a "mess."
2. *Turbulence*: Complex networks of inter-system relationships, combined with the dynamics of the environment, may create "turbulence" that inhibits the ability of any single system to survive and grow on the basis of its own adaptive capabilities (Emery and Trist, 1965).
3. *Delayed Feedback*: Feedback on the performance of a system or on the appropriateness of its purposes may not take place immediately. Since many events may occur in the intervening period, when feedback finally arrives, the results of feedback can be misinterpreted or overlooked and are seen to be of little use in adjusting the behavior of the system. Nevertheless, what is needed is a way to accommodate feedback enabling adjustments in the system.

These constraints on purposeful choice must be added to the list of more obvious ones, such as limited technical, financial, or human resources. We are coming to the realization that optimization is an ideal—something never attained in practice. Despite the availability of exotic techniques for optimization, it is not necessarily best in an overall systemic sense to always attempt optimization instead of simply satisficing (Simon, 1956). In real life, complexity and quick changes in factors and constraints leave little time for the kind of precision that may be aesthetically satisfying, like finding the optimum, but is of no practical consequence. The fact that factors, may change or have delayed impact makes it clear why it is often not as critical for us to optimize as it is to be satisfied at some reasonable level. Nature seems to have opted for the latter and only occasionally do we have the opportunity to indulge in the former in a deliberate and conscious way.

Values and Purpose

The traditional argument that science offers only factual rather than ethical or valuative statements is nowadays considered not very useful in systems thinking—particularly in discussions of purposeful systems. Purposeful systems are *not* value free, but value laden. They are selective systems that choose from available alternatives on the basis of normative statements such as "should" and "ought." They seek preferred outcomes with significant ethical and valuative implications. Even apparently objective statements of fact that are supported by hard data may turn out to be based on normative statements that could be challenged.

Truly value-free research would be devoid of content, for it would not touch our lives in meaningful ways (Rein, 1976). The presence of values does not mean we have to give up the quest for objectivity. Rather, normative statements of ethics and values, can be surfaced for open debate and actually contribute to rational objectivity. They can be treated like statements of fact. It is clear that there is a place for discussions of ethics and values in the conduct of systems research and for methodologies designed to deal with these issues.

3. Functions

Functions are transformations of purpose into action. These actions can then be called events which realize purpose. It is useful to think of the function of a component as an aggregate of its states in space and time. For example, the function of a wheel is the collection of all its positions as it rotates; when the wheel is not turning, we believe that it is not performing its proper function.

Functions may build upon one another in a sequential fashion, as in an assembly line. At each station, tasks are performed that add a new feature or dimension to the product. The process continues until the product emerges in its final form. In this example one might take a broader perspective by interpreting the entire assembly line as a single functional component of the larger system in which it is embedded, a manufacturing plant. Other functions such as product design, testing, marketing, and research and development are performed in relative isolation; yet they complement each other in the realization of purpose of the entire operation.

Interaction between the functions of two or more components often has an unanticipated, or emergent, quality that is not found in any single component.

For example, it is difficult to understand the purpose of an isolated automobile part; but its purpose becomes clear when we see the part interact with other components as the car is operated.

The same function may be performed in several different ways. Systems can be classified by the freedom or latitude displayed in the performance of functions. In mechanical or robotic systems, functional transformations are programmed into the system by the designer. The purpose of the functions is to maintain the system in a steady state of operation. The set of functional transformations performed by any mechanical system is finite, and the system has no choice in deciding how they should be performed.

In biological systems functional transformations are determined by the genetic code; yet they are also modified by changes in the conditions of the environment. A biological system may not choose its purpose or objective, but it may have a choice of functions to achieve the programmed objective. For instance, organs in the human body secrete a wide variety of antibodies to combat viruses. If one antibody fails, the organ may send another type to accomplish the objective. Thus biological functions can change in the face of different environmental influences.

Man as a purposeful system has the ability to perform the same function in different ways. Naturally, the number of ways of performing a function is limited by the purposes it is intended to serve. However, human systems generally have a choice from among several strategic or tactical functions in most of their pursuits.

4. Flows

All functions are carried out by *flows* of energy, materials, people, or information. A system may have several simultaneous flows. The following types of flows have been identified:

(a) Flow as transport and storage of matter;
(b) Flow as transduction and radiation of energy;
(c) Flow as transformation of information;
(d) Flow as conversion from one state to another;
(e) Flow as energy cost of triggering energy release.

In a concrete sense flow is movement of material and energy. A structure is essentially a set of constraints on the flows in space and in time. It channels them along designated routes and subjects them to various transformations with time lag, sometimes allowing for regulation and feedback. The structure itself may change in time and may be subject to transformation by the flow, as is the case with wearout due to continuous flow. The structure (which is a system within the system) may also change due to growth, evolution, or decay; thus structure, in turn, affects the efficiency of the flow.

Flows essential to stabilize or to keep the primary structure together (such as the flow of blood to the tissue) are called *sustaining flows*. Other flows that are the result of structural performance may be *waste* flows or *product* flows.

Fluid movement provides a simple example of how flow through pipes is constrained by the primary structure. Some of the more complex flows such as diffusion, radiation, or communication are also operated on by the structures through which they pass, albeit in more subtle ways than fluid flows. For example, the flow of communication in hierarchical organizations may be rigidly confined to certain "channels" whose boundaries are not defined in discrete physical terms but whose influence is, nevertheless, very real. The tradition of the organization, norms of behavior, unwritten rules of efficiency, and simple common sense dictate "who talks to whom". In this way, the organizational structure imposes constraints on the flow of communication and facilitates the efficient operation of the system.

Several levels of flow exist in any structure. For example there are flows in and out of red blood cells, which are themselves part of blood flow. There are flows at the level of the organic molecules that build these cells. There are flows among the atoms that in turn are part of the organic molecules. The human body contains many flows that interact with one another. None of these flows may appear meaningful by itself to the human mind. Together, however, the flows maintain life.

The reasons why transformation and change, realized through flow, are so basic to understanding is that consciousness by definition requires change from identity to diversity so that it can recognize things. To be conscious is to introspect and internalize the observation of change. The idea of transformation is associated with combining things in special ways to produce new entities (that is, the law of composition). To change is to seek variety. Change is the most basic attribute of all existence. For a system to function, it must seek change from instant to instant even if the process is repeated.

Flows, like the structures that constrain them, do not remain static over time. As the structural composition of a system changes, the character of the flow changes as well. Many management innovations such as Zero-Based Budgeting require structural reorganization that dramatically alters intraorganizational flows of communication and resources. Flows can also change without preceding or lagging behind changes in structure. For example, plants and certain animals enter dormant periods during which the structural and functional arrangement of components remain the same, yet the flows of food and energy sources are altered; that is, the metabolic process slows down.

Physical flows require a driving force to propel material or energy through the structure. A pump or gravity pushes fluid through pipes, and transmitters send radio and television signals through the air. There is a correspondence between the power of the driving force and the rate and direction or distance of flow.

In social systems we find that we cannot precisely isolate cause/effect relationships between driving forces and flows. Social forces such as prevailing economic conditions in a certain region may partially determine flows of people into and out of that area; but it is not possible to measure precisely the relationship between forces and flows.

5. Structures

Like many words, *structure* is used to refer to a wide variety of concrete objects and abstract ideas, yet it is generally possible to understand its meaning from the context in which it is used. We can usually form some preliminary conclusions when a neighbor tells us that his new home is structurally defective. The foundation may have been poured badly or the walls may be warped. Similarly when someone tells us that his life is structured, we can immediately surmise that he is referring to a high degree of routinization of tasks and sequencing of daily activities.

In the vocabulary of systems theory, structure has specific conceptual meaning. First, we must distinguish between the notions of *form*, *aggregate* and *structure*.

Form is the external overall appearance of an object without regard to its substance but with due regard to the organization of its parts. Thus two objects such as a ball of string and a ball of wax may have a different content but the same form. A form is a geometric concept that refers to an assemblage of things or ideas.

An *aggregate* is the conjunction or collection of particulars into a whole mass or sum without regard to form or order, like things in a hiker's backpack.

A *structure* is a set of parts or forms that relate together in a specific order (holism) to perform a function. The structure has the capacity to endure over a period of time through cohesive adjustment to maintain the parts and their relation in nearly the same order by responding to the pressures of the environment.

Structures are linkages of substructures or components, and these in turn are linkages of elements. All linkages are designed to allow some kind of flow. The structural composition and arrangement of a plant is such that water, nutrients, and solar energy pass through its structure, thereby sustaining life. Any structural damage may impede the plant's function, leading to structural decay. Piaget (1970) notes that the structure of a system is preserved and enriched by its functional transformations; at the same time the structure facilitates these transformations. This relationship is characterized by circularity and mutual dependence.

In organizations and in the broader social structure, there are cohesive forces that maintain the form of the structure. *Externally generated forces* are those whose origins are in the social structure itself. They include norms of behavior, mores, codes of ethics, and so on. They pattern our individual behavior and form linkages between ourselves and other like-minded persons or groups. *Internally generated forces* are those unique to the individual. They include personal needs such as physical sustenance, recreation, companionship, self-fulfillment, and the like These are the needs that prompt each of us to form some linkages with those around us; these needs are very strong and unique to the personality.

Characterizing the arrangement and linkages between elements in social structures or organizations presents many problems, since each element is itself a purposeful system. As individuals and groups we have at least a limited amount of control over our placement within the social structure and we also determine, in part, the extent to which we interact with other components. As systems, we act in self-determined ways, making the notion of a social structure more elusive than that of a mechanical or biological structure. Structure in the social realm refers to an abstraction—something that can be perceived and whose boundaries may be conceptualized; yet it cannot be dissected in the manner of mechanical or biological structures.

For practical purposes we must simplify the representation of structure in order to identify its elements and their interconnections. One of the simplest models for such a representation is a *network*. The network concept may be used to describe the actual "structural" connections of the elements of the system, as in transportation, or it may be an abstract "functional" representation of interactions between the components, as in a hierarchical representation of the various levels of regulation and control of an organization. Social network analysis has recently become a popular tool for studying the spread or diffusion of ideas in society. For example, several researchers have employed network analysis to explain and predict the diffusion of innovations among state and local government officials (Rossi and Gilmartin, 1981, Kearns, 1984). In this context, it is illustrative to note that flow of information within social networks is sustained and directed by the diffusion "infrastructure" (Roessner, 1979) characterized by formal linkages between producers, suppliers, and potential users of innovations.

Organizational structures change with the purposes of their designers, managers, and components. They change as new needs are perceived, new functions identified, and new flows designed to serve functions. They also change through growth and evolution as they respond to perturbations from the environment, assuming new structural arrangements that make them less vulnerable to damage in the future. The enactment of the myriad social welfare laws following the Great Depression and of civil rights legislation followed the racial disturbances of the 1960s are examples of structural evolution. Often, restructuring is a temporary "tactical" response to conditions in the environment that gives the system time to formulate a holistic or "strategic" response. For example, the contingency theory of organizational development states that firms are more likely to decentralize their internal structural arrangements in response to rapidly changing environmental conditions, such as intense competition, introduction of new products, changing economic conditions, and the like. Conversely, under relatively static environmental conditions the organization is more likely to assume a centralized and rigidly ordered hierarchical arrangement. Restructuring is always brought about to facilitate new flows that perform functions in pursuit of new goals and objectives (Lawrence and Lorsch, 1969). Thus organizations generally are thought to be self-organizing systems.

6. Characterization of Open Systems

Traditionally people have considered three basic categories of systems: (1) *transition* systems, which change from state to state with or without purpose; (2) *adaptive control* systems, which can be made to change from the current state to another desired state by appropriate feedback and information; and (3) *learning* systems, which can change from state to state by changing the purposes of the system (a process that requires imagination, adaptability, and originality).

A basic method for characterizing systems in terms of flow is to identify them as open or closed. A system is open when it exchanges matter, energy or information with its environment, importing and exporting building-up and breaking-down its material components.

By definition the only known perfectly closed system is the universe. Everything is in it, its boundary is empty, and nothing crosses the boundary. If nothing crosses the boundary, the system is *closed*. A closed system has no interaction with the environment.

The concept of a closed system is only intellectually interesting. To assist understanding we can use approximations of closed systems such as a Robinson Crusoe's economic system or the little greenhouse jar. Of course, such a system is not closed with respect to the intake of solar energy, for example, but it is closed with respect to transfer of goods and services.

An open system is a system that interacts with its environment. It is relatively easy to accept this definition of an open system, despite the fact that our understanding or knowledge of what defines the boundary of the system and what crosses this boundary is often fuzzy and cannot be readily specified. The environment places constraints on what crosses the boundary. Every open system is included in some closed system (the universe?). If a system S were to include a closed system C, C would be impossible to study through the purposes of S and would have no effect on anything in S. Thus there is no reason to consider the inclusion of C in S. Therefore, we state: (1) Closed systems are not subsystems of any system; (2) equivalently, *all subsystems are open*.

A closed system in equilibrium does not need energy for its preservation, nor can energy be obtained from it. For example, a closed reservoir contains a large amount of (potential) energy; but it cannot drive a motor. The same is true of a chemical system in equilibrium. It is not in a state of chemical rest; rather, reactions are continually going on, regulated by the law of mass action

Systems Characteristics and the Analytic Hierarchy Process

so that ions appear at the same rate as they disappear. Nevertheless, no work can be derived from this chemical equilibrium nor is work required by it or derived from it. The algebraic sum of work obtained from or used by elementary reactions equals zero. In order to perform work, it is essential that a system be not in a state of equilibrium but tend to it.

A basic difference between open and closed systems is that the latter must eventually attain a time-independent state of chemical and thermodynamic equilibrium, whereas open systems may, under prescribed conditions, attain a time-independent state, called a *steady state*. The same steady state can be reached from different initial conditions. In this state the composition of the system remains constant in spite of continuous exchange of elements, with the environment. Systems theorists have identified several properties of open systems that may be useful in designing social systems. These are listed and briefly defined below.

Properties of Open Systems

An open system has one or more of the following properties which involve variations on a system's purpose, function, flow or structure. Some of the properties may be incompatible, so the same system may not have all of them.

1. *Wholeness*. Let the system be determined by a set of variables. It is said to behave as a whole if changes in one variable cause changes in all other variables (this can happen in space, in time or in both). It may be that the changes do not occur instantly. This is a *holistic* system. An example of a holistic system is one defined by the set of linear differential equations:

$$\dot{x}_i = \sum_{j=1}^{n} a_{ij} x_j \quad i = 1, \ldots, n \text{ and } a_{ij} \neq 0 \text{ for all } i \text{ and } j.$$

This equation means that the rate of change in a particular coordinate may be expressed as a linear combination of all other coordinates. In this case change is interpreted to be with respect to time and only affected by space changes. Perhaps the best example to illustrate wholeness is that of the human body in which the parts depend on each other for their proper functioning. Organizations, particularly manufacturing firms, also behave as wholes since the success of each phase of the production process is contingent upon the success of previous and succeeding phases.

2. *Summativity*. In some systems each variable can be considered as independent of the others. The variation of the total system is the (physical) sum of the variations of its individual elements. As an illustration we take the system represented by $\dot{x}_i = a_i x_i$, $i = 1, \ldots n$. The whole is the sum of its parts; e.g.,

$$\sum_{j=1}^{n} \dot{x}_j = \sum_{j=1}^{n} a_j x_j$$

76   *Analytical Planning*

There are few good examples of this because whenever we apply information to order a set of scattered parts, the whole would have a new order which transcends the sum of the parts. Perhaps even a pile of stones is more than its individual stones, if it was put there for some purpose.

Clumps of matter may be regarded as collections of their individual parts despite some cohesion among these parts. It is clear that the more imagination one has the wider the purpose one would identify with anything and the greater the relations among the parts one would infer. Thus summativity is a property not often attributed to social systems such as organizations.

3. *Differentiation.* Open systems move in the direction of differentiation and elaboration, e.g., specialization of tissue. As an example of structural differentiation, we take the system represented by the two equations $\dot{x} = x + e^{-t}y$, $\dot{y} = e^{-t}x + y$, which is summative only as $t \to \infty$.

It is clear that in most systems, different parts perform different functions and the parts cannot be interchanged in the performance of those functions. In fact, often the parts are designed to specialize in function. Similarly, biological systems develop from a small homogeneous entity that is only potentially purposeful into a larger, heterogeneous, and purposeful system through growth which produces multiplicity and differentiation.

4. *Mechanization.* (a) Progressive segregation: When the interdependence of some of the elements decreases with time. (See 3 above.)

(b) As a result of (a) there is an increasing tendency for changes in the elements to be determined only by the elements themselves. Progressive segregation leads to a loss of regulability. Prior to segregation the system is a unitary whole, where control can be selectively applied to one or a few variables to most strongly affect the rest.

Families sometimes illustrate progressive growth followed by segregation. As the children mature they become independent, forgetting their origins and prior dependence. They take control of their own destiny, initiating new purposes and even creating new systems in the form of families, organizations, and the like.

5. *Centralization.* In time, one part becomes more and more dominant. Changes in this part cause changes in other parts but not conversely. As an example we take $x_1 = a_{11}x_1$, $x_2 = a_{21}x_1 + a_{22}x_2, \ldots, x_n = a_{n1}x_1 + \ldots + a_{nn}x_n$. Here x_1 is most dominant and x_n least. An example where only one element controls is $x_i = a_{i1}x_1 + a_{ii}x_i$, $i = 1, \ldots, n$. The system illustrated under wholeness may be called interaction of which this is a special case.

As organizations grow and experience segregation of their parts, centralization may be necessary to achieve at least a minimal acceptable level of coordination among these parts. Also, some types of organizations are inherently more centralized than others. Government bureaucracies, for example, tend to be more centralized than private corporations.

6. *Transformation of energy.* (a) Importing energy into the system is called an input.

(b) The transformation of the input energy within the system is called a throughput (which can often be described by an algorithm or a set of rules that define the transformation of the input step by step)..

(c) The flow of energy out of the system in the form of products and waste is called an output.

An illustration of an input-throughput-output system is given by $x = f(x, u, t)$, $y = g(x, u, t)$ where u is the input or control, x is the state or throughput and y is the output. Note that $u(t)$, $x(t)$ and $y(t)$ may be stochastic functions of t.

Biological systems provide the best examples of this concept as they take in nutrients, transform them into energy, and discard waste products. Mechanical and architectural systems also transform energy.

7. *Information input, negative feedback, and the coding process.* (a) Besides energy, information is also an input to a system.

(b) The simplest feedback information in a system is negative feedback, which enables a system to correct deviations from its course (e.g., a thermostat). Errors are corrected after they occur. When a system's negative feedback discontinues, its steady state vanishes and at the same time its boundary disappears and the system consisting of the controller and the device controlled is temporarily suspended. In positive feedback, a system instructs itself to behave in a prescribed manner in the future.

(c) Coding is a selective mechanism by which possible inputs are accepted and utilized or are rejected. It is a filter.

The human body is not only equipped with specialized sensors to deal with environmental stimuli and enhance its survival, but these sensors in turn filter the essential information to avoid overload. Businesses also develop a capacity to sense changes in their competitive environment and filter relevant information by using market analysts, planners and public relations experts.

8. *Negative entropy.* By the second law of thermodynamics, as a closed system moves to equilibrium, it tends toward maximal entropy or disorganization corresponding to minimum information. Open systems can reverse this trend toward maximum entropy by the importation of free energy from outside the system and thus maintain their organization.

9. *Growth in time.* Two examples of functional growth are exponential growth $\dot{x} = ax$ and logistic growth $\dot{x} = (a-x)x$. For growth in structure we have $\dot{x} = a(t)x$, $a(t) = \alpha t$.

10. *Equilibrium, stability, steady state, and dynamic homeostasis.* (a) The importation of energy to arrest entropy operates to maintain some constancy in energy exchange so that open systems that survive are characterized by a steady state which is not a true equilibrium but a kind of dynamic equilibrium (catabolic and anabolic processes preserve a steady state).

(b) Dynamic homeostasis involves the maintenance of a biological state by establishing a constant physical environment, which reduces the variability and disturbing effects of external stimuli. Thus the organism does not simply restore the prior equilibrium, but a new more complex and more comprehensive equilibrium is established. For example, to establish the habit of eating before becoming intensely hungry is a more complex equilibrium than simply responding to hunger. The result is a better preservation of the character of the system. An illustration is given by the predator-prey model $\dot{x} = ax - bxy$, $\dot{y} = cy + dxy$, $a, b, c, d \geqslant 0$.

11. *Cycles of events.* Stability is also characterized by cycles. Most systems, whether natural or man-made, perform their function through short or long range repetitions, interspersing different functions in this process. Mechanical systems are particularly restricted and cycle in the performance of their function. That is how they maintain stability.

Different cycling systems can themselves participate in a larger cycle where, for example waste products are used as fertilizers to hasten the growth of food which in turn initiates the cycle.

12. *The strange attractor.* Physicists who study chaos have recently identified a new property of systems. They introduced the notion of an attractor. All system motion is drawn towards some kind of attractor. If one puts water in a pan and shakes it up, after a while it stops swirling and comes to rest. This kind of equilibrium is the simplest attractor, mathematically called a fixed point. The periodic movement of a pendulum remains in a fixed cycle forever. It is known as a limit cycle of which there are many kinds. They are all predictable and form a second kind of attractor. A third variety is called the strange attractor. Many physical systems have been discovered to have pockets of disturbance built into them and can never be predicted accurately. The weather is an example, the final destination of a ball in a spinning roulette wheel is another. A waterfall is observed to be cascading regularly over jagged rocks when suddenly a jet of cold water is splashed at the observer. In an experiment a spigot has been observed to drip water droplets irregularly (though the spacing of the drops ought to be regular and predictable). This occurs despite the fact that the faucet is fixed, the water flow is constant and nothing perturbs the system. The pattern never repeats itself. Thus the new theory says that there are systems that are apparently unpredictable and not simply due to lack of knowledge that is usually modelled probabilistically.

13. *Finality of ultimate purpose.* (a) Static teleology or fitness, means that a system responds in the same way no matter what the external stimulus is. It may be perfectly appropriate for some stimuli, but totally inadequate for others. For example, the animal response of changing color for protection is the same whether the stimulus is external or internal. It can be simply described as a change from one predictable state to another.

(b) Dynamic teleology, means directiveness of processes.

(i) Behavior is directed toward a final state as if the present behavior is dependent on the final state (Purposeful system). From $\dot{x} = ax$, $x(t_0) = x_0$ we have $x_0 = x(t)e^{-a(t-t_0)}$ for the final state.

(ii) Directiveness based upon structure, means that the structural arrangement predetermines the process so that a certain result is achieved.

(iii) Equifinality or goal directiveness means that the system can reach the same final state from different initial conditions and by a variety of paths. This is a form of stability with respect to initial and boundary conditions (e.g., a sea urchin can develop from a normal ovum, half an ovum or from the fusion product of two ova.)

(iv) True Finality or Purposiveness means that the actual behavior is guided and influenced by the foresight of the goal. The original Aristotelian concept is illustrated by (iv), while the philosophy of Vitalism is an attempt to explain (ii) and (iii).

If a steady state is reached in an open system, it is independent of the initial conditions and determined only by the system parameters; that is by the rates of reaction and transport; it is called an equifinal state. In many organismic processes, such as physiochemical systems, the same final state can be reached equifinally from different initial conditions and after disturbances of the processes.

A steady state exhibits regulatory characteristics that are interesting to explore, particularly when the state is equifinal. Equilibrium in closed systems and stationary "equilibrium" in open systems show a certain similarity, since the system as a whole and the arrangements of its functioning parts remain constant.

According to the second principle of thermodynamics, the general trend of physical processes is toward increasing entropy; that is, toward states of increasing randomness and decreasing order. Living systems maintain themselves in a state of high order and low randomness. They may even evolve to higher order. This process is regarded by some scientists as accidental and possible in the myriad combinations of matter and flows; but then they say that nonetheless, the second law of thermodynamics eventually will make it come to naught. We have argued that our present interpretation of the world is closely tied to our limited senses, their type and depth of acuity and therefore there may be deeper forces operating behind sensual reality that keep the order of living beings evolving ever higher. This is also in part the philosophy of Teilhard de Chardin.

7. Prerequisites for an Effective Systems Methodology

A methodology for structuring and solving systems problems should itself be systemic, that is, it should display most of the attributes which have been used to characterize systems.

At a minimum the approach should guide decision makers toward a *holistic* approach to the definition and resolution of problems, accounting for the reciprocal interaction of elements in a system but still recognizing that some elements may exert effects independently (i.e., summativity) of others.

The methodology should be capable of handling problems of design and control when systems become progressively more differentiated and mechanized; that is when the interdependence of the system's components becomes less pronounced. Highly differentiated and mechanized systems may be thought of as aggregates of structures or as unrelated components which combine their individual functions through flow processes that give rise to an overall purpose for the system. The problem is that the relations among the elements may not be immediately apparent or measurable with standard instruments or research methods. Rather, they are combined in ways that may be understandable by only examining the system as a whole and sometimes by studying the effect of eliminating some of the parts. Sometimes intangible judgments based on extensive experience with the system are the only way to synthesize scattered but accurate observations which transcend the effect of the parts on the system.

Next, an effective approach to systems problems must be capable of isolating dominant elements in the system while placing them in the context of the system as a whole. *Centralization* in systems calls for the use of pragmatic reductionism to complement the idealism of holistic thinking. Reductionism attempts to understand a system by decomposing and looking at the details of its parts. Holism is the reverse. It attempts to understand a system by looking at its functions as they relate to its environment. Attempts to control or modify systems are often constrained by financial, material, and human resources. Thus, limited resources should first be devoted to the control of dominant elements. Fine tuning of the system through the modification of less influential elements can follow if time and resources permit. The identification of dominant elements must be preceded by a characterization of the system as a whole. Only through the exhaustive pairwise comparison of all elements can the relative influence of individual elements be determined. Thus, a methodology that is adequate for handling centralization in systems, must achieve a delicate balance between holism and reductionism.

Relevant information about the system must be combined using the creativity of decision makers as *input* specifying a desired purpose and structure for the system, identifying its component parts, and listing alternative intervention strategies. Next, throughput procedures should guide designers in establishing priorities among the system's elements. Also, the methodology should be output oriented, to facilitate comparison among alternative solutions and assist designers to arrive at a best solution and to implement it.

Finally, a systems methodology should incorporate a *feedback* mechanism in order to address issues related to the analysis of negative entropy, growth in time, and stability. Like an open system, the methodology should use information from the environment to test the viability of steps taken to control a system or modify its purposes. When decision makers do not have the time to wait for this information, the methodology should be capable of simulating environmental responses.

The AHP discussed in the previous chapter incorporates this wide variety of open system attributes and therefore should be a promising and powerful tool in the study of systems. Few other methodologies capture systemic qualities as completely.

A methodology with various systemic attributes is of little intrinsic value unless it is useful in solving problems of design and control. This is the topic of the following section.

8. The Object of Systems Study: Design and Control

The study of the design and control of systems revolves around a central idea: The system must be reliable enough to attain certain objectives; that is, it should be stable. We study systems to learn to design, control, and modify their behavior toward achieving their goals. For most natural systems it is difficult to identify an overriding purpose. Thus we assume that survival is the purpose. For example, man is a system and he works to keep himself alive.

While functioning toward its purpose, any system may be subject to perturbations not accounted for in its design. Also, the original set of constraints in the design of a system may not account for all difficulties that occur over time. Hence, the constraints and goals are periodically recalculated to take this possibility into consideration. Feedback information is needed to bring the system back to the desired behavior.

Clearly the analysis of the stability of systems is a major concern of systems theory. Because a system consists of several components, stability analysis must include them all. It is useful to study the stability of structure and flow separately so far as they fulfill purpose. It is also useful to study the stability of a system's goals so far as they are subject to revision, change, and conflicts. Finally, the stability of a system depends on other systems with which it interacts, and the totality of these systems is taken into consideration. Frequently the environment so affects a system that no internal changes can stabilize that system; in that case one must study the stability of the interaction of the two.

The analysis of stability is usually formulated in terms of *perturbations* of the *states* of a system. Perturbations are regarded as continuous phenomena. However, systems have been known to exhibit discontinuous behavior in the form of *catastrophy,* which is unaccounted-for discontinuity or sudden instability in structure and flow.

For a sensible understanding of a system one considers the following:

1. Admit the fuzziness of meaning or conflicting perceptions of the purpose(s) of a system and study a system as an ongoing process of interaction with the environment.
2. Define the purpose(s) of the system based on the input of its designers(s) and its user(s).

3. Describe the system and its environment.
4. Describe the system's elements and their relationships.
5. Identify the system's flows and functions and describe how they change.
6. Identify problems utilizing the experience of the users.
7. Study conditions that produce equilibrium to satisfy the purpose.
8. Develop means to produce stability of equilibrium with respect to perturbations in the elements and relations within the system as well as between the system and its environment.
9. Identify ways to introduce controls to produce stability (or instability) over time.

So far systems theory has offered no succint method of logical analysis that can avoid the pitfalls of reductionism. But by pointing to the influence of the environment, it has enriched our capability to understand complexity.

Various methods for dealing with systems and complexity have been used, ranging from wishful thinking to logical analysis and synthesis. Engineers study systems in terms of input-throughput and output as in an electrical network of wires, resistors, capacitors, and the like. They have also formulated the study of adaptive control systems along similar lines. Operations researchers look at systems as networks with the idea of maximizing or minimizing flows through them. Computer scientists use Boolean algebra to study relations and operations in electronic computers. Econometricians and applied mathematicians, as well as operations researchers, look at systems as a set of equations that describe their structural constraints and flow relations, often maximizing or minimizing a utility function, called an objective function, subject to these constraints. Probabilists, including queuing theorists, look at systems in terms of states and transitions among these states. Some physicists look at systems statistically in terms of particles and their collisions by applying ideas from mechanics and thermodynamics. The notion of entropy has formed the basis of information theory. Potential theorists and topologists have used the field concept. Modern behaviorists look at a system in terms of its purposes and its interactions with the environment.

It is clear that the physical scientists are more structure oriented, without giving undue attention to the hierarchy of purpose. They seem to be desirous of getting something done fast; with natural objects one has a wide tolerance for experimentation and access to many precise methods of measurement. Not so in fields that involve human beings directly, where human welfare, judgment and preferences are part of the system. One needs to ask many questions before plunging into complex social, political, and economic systems.

What should one do then if there is a problem? One should invite the people involved to participate in the process of designing the system and also in assessing its performance. The problem is often how to define and modify the purpose; how to design a system that meets the desired purpose and adapts to it; and how to take into consideration environmental impacts on the system. This is primarily a problem of redesign rather than of "problem-solving."

What we frequently fail to do well is to investigate the impact of implementing the solution of a problem within a system on the functioning of other parts of the system. Sometimes it may be advantageous to leave the problem unsolved. A relevant question to ask is whether modification of the old system is still useful to meet the objectives. As a chemical engineer once said of chemical plants (and it could be said of systems in general), "If it 'ain't' broke, don't fix it." Probably this philosophy had evolved from painful experience with the consequences of attempts to improve some operations with tinkering.

Occasionally, if the problem is serious, it may be better to re-examine the system as it is and to design a new one in light of changes in the objectives, environment, and behavior of the old system. Changes in technology, for example, make it preferable to revive an aging industry by redesigning it rather than by duplicating obsolete techniques. The resources available often determine whether one should repair the old system, replace it with a new replica, or create a completely new design.

The study of the design and control of systems focuses on two fundamental problems, which we consider briefly below and develop in later chapters.

The First Fundamental Problem of Systems Theory (Design). Given goals and objectives how do we design a system which achieves these goals and objectives? Given constraints on possible design we must modify the goals and objectives and continue until the two are matched in a compatible way. The solution of this problem is undertaken in the theory of planning. Bioengineering is an ambitious attempt of our time to generate and direct life forms iteratively in the hope of getting something useful in the end.

The Second Fundamental Problem of Systems Theory (Control). Given the *purpose* of a system, how do we control and modify its *structure* and flows to produce overall (dynamic) stability?

An example of a system that we wish to control to stabilize is society with its interacting economic, social, and political activities. An unambitious example that we can deal with very well is stabilizing the flows of a car or airplane so it can move us from point A to point B without serious difficulties despite impurities in gasoline, road bumps, or air turbulence, the presence of other vehicles, and so on. In fact, we can construct excellent systems that fulfill the purposes we devise. Knowledge of man-made systems may be useful (though possibly misleading) in the study of natural systems. We need to keep in mind here that although all systems are assumed to have structure and flows, man-made systems are endowed with a causal purpose by their designer, but those of nature evolve along with their purpose whose explanation we have not yet fully fathomed.

To understand the stability of systems, we need to develop (a) criteria for

84   *Analytical Planning*

evaluating the fulfillment of purpose and (b) methods for control that would maintain stability. Two fundamental properties used for testing the effectiveness of a set of goals use their *consistency* and their *priority*. After verifying that the goals are consistent, the causal process is unfolded through a sequence of prioritizations leading to a description of the state of the system and to methods of effective control.

In sum, the different stages in systems design and control are to (1) define the problem, (2) identify the purposes of the system, (3) identify the variables and their interactions, (4) identify the functions of the system, (5) identify the environment, (6) generate alternative flows, (7) prioritize the alternative flows, (8) compute resources needed for implementing each alternative, (9) determine the availability of resources, (10) choose a best alternative, subject to constraints, (11) implement that alternative, and (12) evaluate the effectiveness of the alternatives and revise the plan.

9. On Designing Adaptive Systems

It is clear that human beings are adaptive systems subject to both physical and mental change. These entail change in purpose or in the intensity of purpose. As people get older their physical drives and appetites may weaken but their intellectual drives may become broader and stronger. It is also true that the systems people designed in the past, may no longer meet their present needs. To diminish the rapid obsolescence of new systems, we need to incorporate a modicum of flexibility in their design so that we can modify them to meet our changing needs. The greater the sensitivity of these systems, the greater one would expect their responsiveness to be. This means that the system can continue to achieve stability under dynamic conditions of changing purpose. But such responsiveness can be very costly. In the end we learn to make compromises between stability and adaptiveness and instability and nonadaptiveness. Large investment in special purpose systems that we may outgrow in the long run could have more adverse effects on our lives in the form of massive unemployment than would smaller scale investments in a large number of broadly spread complimentary activities that cover our wide needs. This means that we should not become too deeply entrenched in massive production without gradually steering in and out of them with due consideration of turbulence. Today we cannot do this very well. In a better integrated world economy we might. Dispersed small systems can be modified in small steps without disastrous consequences to the lives of many people. In planning, one needs to eventually consider applying trade-offs between the performance of a large, well consolidated simple purpose hierarchic system and a much larger multipurpose collection or network of small systems with diffuse and fuzzy interconnections. From a theoretical point of view, only recently, we have learned to analyze the impacts and priorities of the subsystems of a network system. However, there is a close line between hierarchies and networks. Hierarchies are networks of a special kind. First we need to understand hierarchic systems well. Despite its apparent drawbacks, due to its simpler form, the hierarchic design is far more prevalent in the configuration of organizations than the network design. Moreover, hierarchies present an intuitively appearing framework to structure problems efficiently.

Hierarchies also reflect our current state of intellectual evolution. We have hardly begun to understand hierarchic structures when the world has thrust upon us the complexity of network structures. The basic theory for dealing with a network as a generalization of a hierarchy is found in the book by Saaty, The Analytic Hierarchy Process, Chapter 8.

In our applications to planning we have used both hierarchies and networks as appropriate. The forward-backward process of planning is essentially a feedback process between two hierarchies.

References

Ackoff, Russell (1973) Science in the Systems Age: Beyond Industrial Engineering, Operations Research and Management Science, *Operations Research Journal*, **21**, 3 pp.
Ackoff, Russell and Fred Emery (1968) *On Purposeful Systems*, Chicago: Aldine.
Allison, Graham (1971) *The Essence of Decision: Explaining the Cuban Missile Crisis*, Boston: Little Brown.
Bertalanffy, Ludwig von (1968) *General Systems Theory*, New York: Braziller.
Bertalanffy, Ludwig von (1950) The Theory of Open Systems In Physics and Biology, *Science*, 3, pp. 23–29.
Bryant, Stephens and Joseph Kearns (1982) Worker's Brains as Well as Their Bodies: Quality Circles in a Federal Facility, *Public Administration Review*, **42**, 2, pp. 144–150.
Churchman, C. W. (1968) *The Systems Approach*, New York: Delacorte.
Churchman, C. W. (1979) *The Systems Approach and Its Enemies*, New York: Basic Books.
Dunn, William N. (1980) Reforms as Arguments, paper presented at the International Conference on the Political Realization of Social Science Knowledge and Research Vienna, Austria June 19–20.
Dunn, William N. (1982) Measuring Police Performance, On-going research Pittsburgh: University of Pittsburgh Center for Study of Knowledge Utilization.
Emery, Fred and Eric Trist (1965) The Causal Texture of Organizational Environments, *Human Relations*, **18**, pp. 21–31.
Helmer, Olaf and Nicholas Rescher (1959) On the Epistemology of the Inexact Sciences, *Management Science*, **6**, pp. 25–52.
Holzner, Burkhart and John Marx (1978) *Knowledge Application: The Knowledge System in Society*, Boston: Allyn and Bacon.
Katz, D. and R. L. Kahn (1969) Common Characteristics of Open Systems, In Fred Emery (ed) *Systems Thinking*, New York: Penguin.
Kearns, K. P. (1984) Sociocognitive Networks and Local Government Innovation, Ph.D. Thesis. University of Pittsburgh, 1984.
Lawrence, Paul and Jay Lorsch (1969) *Organization and Environment*, Homewood IL: Richard D. Irwin Inc.
Mesarovic, M. D., D. Macko and Y. Takahara (1970) *Theory of Hierarchical, Multi-level Systems*, New York: Academic Press.
Mintzberg, Henry, D. Raisinghani and Andre Theorit (1976) The Structure of "Unstructural" Decision Processes *Administrative Science Quarterly*, **21**, pp. 247–275.
Monod, Jaques (1971) *Chance and Necessity*, New York: Random House.
Patton, Michael Quinn (1978) *Utilization Focused Evaluation*, Beverly Hills: Sage.
Piaget, Jean (1970) *Structuralism*, New York: Harper.

86   Analytical Planning

Rein, Martin (1977) *Social Science and Public Policy*, New York: Penguin.
Rosener, J. David (1979) Federal Technology Policy: Innovation and Problem Solving in State and Local Government, *Policy Analysis*, pp. 181–200.
Rossi, Robert and Kevin Gilmartin (1981) Information Exchange Among Public Agencies in Three California Counties, *Knowledge: Creation, Diffusion, Utilization*, **2**, 3, pp. 413–436.
Simon, Herbert A. (1956) Rational Choice and the Structure of the Environment, *Psychological Review*, **63**, pp. 129–158.
Sommerhoff, G. (1969) The Abstract Characteristics of Livings Systems, in Fred Emery (ed) *Systems Thinking*, New York: Penguin.
Sutherland, J. W. (1978) *Societal Systems: Methodology, Modelling and Management*, New York: North Holland.
Thom, R. (1972) *Stabilite Structurelle et Morphogemese*, New York: Benjamin.

Suggested Readings

Definition of a System

Monod, Jaques, *Chance and Necessity*, New York: Harper, 1971.
   This book presents an extremely abstract and complex view of living systems and how their evolution and functioning might be studied. The author concludes that human systems and their evolution cannot be studied in isolation of the laws of chance.

Sommerhoff, G. The Abstract Characteristics of Living Systems, in *Systems Thinking*, F. E. Emery (editor) New York: Penguin Books, 1969.
   The most distinctive characteristic of living systems is the goal directedness of their activities. According to Sommerhoff, goal directedness is an abstract concept that does not easily lend itself to analysis. The teleological organization of living systems requires modes of analysis that exist at a higher level of abstraction than those used to study geometrical order. Three criteria for goal directed behavior are set forth and an attempt is made to model this behavior in the language of abstract mathematics and theoretical physics. It should be noted that Sommerhoff is not concerned with predicting the behavior of goal directed systems but rather with conceptual clarification of the philosophical and methodological confusions which inhibit the rigorous analysis of living systems.

Problem Solving and System Design

Saaty, T. L., *The Analytic Hierarchy Process*, New York: McGraw-Hill, 1980.
   In this book the author introduces a new and powerful technique, the Analytic Hierarchy Process, which uses subjective judgment for structuring and solving multi-person, multi-criterion, and multi-time period problems. Structuring problems hierarchically allows for the identification of multiple actors and interests while resulting in prioritization of impacts and/or preferences through pairwise comparisons by judges. The Analytic Hierarchy Process allows for a margin of inconsistency (or intransitivity) of preferences and is equally suitable for scenario construction and policy selection. The technique draws upon the human ability to conceptualize problems as sets or systems of interdependent factors while simultaneously decomposing the problem in terms of those factors which are perceived to have the highest priorities.

PART II
Strategic Planning

What happens in the world is the result of many things interacting among themselves and with other things. With increasing complexity and without intervention we cannot be certain that those interactions would fulfill particular objectives. But the fulfillment of our objectives and those of others are important forces that give us satisfaction. Therefore, to improve the chances that what happens complements our objectives we need some control over events and over the relations among them. People plan so they can fulfill their objectives. At times people have succeeded in shaping the world to satisfy their objectives. At others they found, too late, that environmental forces or the objectives of other people negated their actions. In the three chapters of this second part of the book we examine philosophies of planning, present a new perspective and give a methodology for doing planning.

It is worth noting that our experience with problem solving indicates that reality is continuous, diffuse, and many layered more like very thick oils of different density continuously stirred in one bowl. To describe this dynamically mixed material, requires continued sampling from the different parts. Sometimes the sample may be taken from key areas of oil concentrations in which case we learn much and sometimes it is taken from a periferal region with thin oil in which case we don't know much about the mixture. Our hope is that with continued sampling in many areas, our knowledge of how to deal with this complexity would improve and we would also learn to be more successful in drawing samples and analyzing this complexity.

If one is to plan for a group of people or for a society, who are the people to be considered and how should the scope of the problem be defined to satisfy the conflicting interests of the many individuals involved? How should one invite participation and solicit ideas and judgments for the plan?

Planning itself is a system. It has a purpose (to achieve desired ends), functions (to study environments and situations, structure, select alternatives and evaluate performance), flows (of information among planners and users) and structure (a format within which the planner aligns the likely with the desired outcome using learning and feedback in the form of judgments and data to reevaluate the outcome). In order to address how purposes are identified, and how functions, flows, and structures are designed, we discuss types of rationality.

CHAPTER 5
Current Theories of Planning

1. Introduction: To Plan or Not to Plan?

While some people prefer to make no plans at all, leaving their fate in the hands of divine providence, luck or destiny, most of us believe that it is better to plan than not to plan. Advertising reinforces this belief; we are exhorted to plan for the education of our children, for personal illness or accidents, for retirement and so on. Advertisements attempt to sell us a pre-packaged plan, such as an investment portfolio, rather than encouraging us to actively engage in planning—portrayed in this chapter as a thinking and social process. They promote a sort of half-baked consumer oriented approach to planning.

Planning can best be envisioned as a continuous, and sometimes irregular, cycle of thought and action that can help us to design more durable and effective systems. It is not a discrete activity with a clear beginning and end. Systems thinking provides the philosophical outlook and methodological tools that help planners manage complexity rather than merely submit to it and hope that things will somehow work themselves out.

We do not advocate that planning should be applied in every area of human endeavor. There are convincing arguments in economics, for example, that the best way for things to arrange themselves is through the free market forces of supply and demand. Creativity and opportunity would be lost by interfering in a system that can find its equilibrium without too much control. However, there are many areas of human endeavor where we have no idea where to begin without a plan. Examples are the exploration of space, the design of cities, and the management of business enterprises. While there are situations where a *laissez faire* approach (allowing things to stabilize themselves) is called for, our concern in this chapter is with problems which call for intervention and planning.

There are three topics discussed in this chapter. They are:

1. *Ways of Thinking about Planning*: Planning has been studied from many perspectives. It has also been thought about in terms of general political, social, economic and cultural environments in which it takes place, the particular system in such environments to which planners direct their attention, and the level of detail needed to produce a plan. This is followed with a discussion of some characteristics of planning.

90   Analytical Planning

(2.) *A Definition of Planning*: Building on ways of thinking about the subject, a definition of planning is provided to capture the interrelations between the intellectual thought processes involved in planning and the policies and actions needed to bridge the gap between what is likely and what is desired.

(3.) *Philosophies of Planning*: Three philosophies of planning—formal, incremental, and systemic are compared according to how they are used (1) to structure problems, (2) to identify and evaluate alternatives and (3) to implement plans. Systemic planning is a synthesis of formal and incremental planning. Here are a few definitions that will be useful in what follows.

Goals: Desired ends or values one hopes to realize.

Alternatives: Available courses of action evaluated for their respective contributions to the attainment of goals.

Plans: Specified means for achieving goals requiring the simultaneous or sequential undertaking of several actions.

Policies: Authorized means of achieving goals arrived at through accepted decision making procedures. Among the latter might be voting, as in some governmental settings, or simply executive mandates as in many business settings. When a plan has been adopted it becomes a policy (see Jones, 1977: 4).

Outcomes: Potential states of a system derived from policies.

Rationality: A process of using reason to defend the selection of goals, the specification of alternative ways to achieve them, and formulation and implementation of plans.

The philosophical concepts discussed in this chapter are put to practical use in the two following chapters where we introduce a new method of systemic planning and illustrate its applications.

2. Ways of Thinking About Planning

Definitions of planning generally portray it as a future oriented decision making activity involving purpose and choice. To some, planning is a "process for determining appropriate future action through a sequence of choices" (Davidoff and Reiner, 1962: 103). To others, planning is "foresight in formulating and implementing programs and policies" (Hudson, 1979: 387). To still others, planning is a "process of preparing a set of decisions for action in the future, directed at achieving goals by preferrable means" (Dror, 1963: 48). There is a definition of planning which tells us much more about it; what it is and how it should be done. Before giving it we need to examine and sort out different planning concepts and theories.

A. How Should Planning Be Done? (*The Philosophies of Planning*)

—*Formal Planning*: Through this approach one narrows the scope of a problem in order to use quantitative models and optimization techniques.

—*Incremental Planning*: In this case one uses "common sense" and qualitative reasoning to make small modifications of existing policies. Here one relies on political bargaining, and compromise to reach a consensus (Lindblom, 1959).

—*Systemic Planning*: This is a broader approach in which one attempts to structure planning problems in terms of multiple intervening forces and the relations among them. Here one seeks convergence between idealized, optimal responses and feasible, incremental ones, relying on a mix of qualitative and quantitative methods.

B. What Steps Does Planning Follow? (Generic Planning Processes):

Whatever the philosophy, planning needs a general format to follow. This format consists of a set of activities or steps that remain relatively invariant across different planning philosophies. A generic planning process may take the following form:

—*Problem Structuring*: One must first define one or several objectives and the constraints imposed on achieving these objectives. The constraints may be political, economic, social, technological, environmental and so on. The problem should be formulated in such a way as to allow for some kind of intervention and control.

—*Identification and Evaluation of Alternative Responses*: The next step is to list possible solutions or resolutions and estimate costs and benefits—tangible and intangible—associated with alternative means of achieving a desired end. A selection is made from the list based on predetermined criteria.

—*Implementation*: Thirdly, one specifies a sequence of activities to realize the plan.

The final component of the planning process, not discussed here, is monitoring and evaluation which determines first whether plans have been properly implemented and, second, the extent to which they have produced the desired effects or outcomes. Evaluation frequently takes place months or even years after a plan has been implemented. It is an activity with its own set of theories and procedures (see for example, Guttentag and Struening, 1975; Campbell and Stanley, 1971). Frequently, the designers of a plan are not involved in its evaluation.

The sequence of activities identified above is an accurate portrayal of the planning process. However, it may not be followed exactly or with equal emphasis on the components by all planners in all settings. How to structure problems is the most important component of the process because it lays the foundation for all subsequent activities. Nearly as important are the methods used to identify several plans and to choose a good one.

People approach planning with different philosophical attitudes. Often the outcome is influenced by what attitude one takes.

C. Where is Planning Done? (*The Context of Planning*):

There is planning in government, in business, in universities, and in technology and even in personal life. Andreas Faludi (1973: vii) suggests that discussions of the different environmental settings of planning require consideration of the organizational, social, and political factors in each of these settings and their impact on ideas about how to do planning. For example, city planners, who examine urban needs such as transportation, housing, and recreation facilities devote significant attention to theories of urban development and growth, borrowing from the fields of sociology, economics, history, and political science (see also Bolan, 1969). Similarly, corporate planners draw upon the work of organization theorists in attempting to make their plans compatible with the administrative structure and interpersonal relations in specific organizational settings.

It should be clear that even with the best planning philosophy and the best tools to apply that philosophy, a plan may fail. Why? It may be because one does not understand the problem area and the forces behind it, the timing for intervention or whether it is possible at all, including past and present efforts in that area. Thus before one can hope to carry out a plan that as a minimum could be defended rationally, one must learn two things: (1) how to plan and (2) how are the history and philosophy of planning to be applied in a particular area, e.g., the economy, the city, technology, etc.

D. What Do We Plan For? (*The Object of Analysis*):

A fourth stream in the planning literature examines planning, whatever its philosophy and area of application, in relation to its object of analysis or, in other words, the specific phenomena to which planners direct their attention. Objects of analysis may be broadly classified as either *spatial* or *behavioral* phenomena. Spatial planning is primarily concerned with directing the evolution of physical systems. Land use planning in cities and location analysis in industry are two examples of spatial planning. It utilizes theories and methods of operations research, engineering, and architecture to determine, for example, **where to build** a factory so that it will have ready access to markets for the goods its produces or where shopping centers should be located given the economic development goals of a city.

Behavioral planning addresses social systems and attempts to determine the effects of proposed policies on the behavior of individuals or groups. It might be concerned, for example, with whether tax cuts will motivate people to put more of their money in banks, increasing funds available, contributing to lower interest rates, and ultimately stimulating economic growth. The design of advertising campaigns that encourage people to buy a certain product is another example of behavioral planning. It draws upon theories and concepts from fields such as social psychology, sociology, and economics.

E. How Much Do We Include In Planning? (*Level of Analysis*):

Planning may also be categorized according to whether it is broad or narrow in the scope of its analysis. For example, *comprehensive planning* in cities integrates into a single plan a broad range of socio-economic issues such as transportation patterns, land use, municipal revenues, social services, and intergovernmental relations. *Specialized planning* in the same context would limit the scope of its investigation to a single, narrowly defined issue, such as municipal revenues, while selectively considering environmental factors perceived to have direct or indirect impact on the primary issue.

The level of analysis may also be defined in *spatial* terms (national vs. local planning), *temporal* terms (long-range, strategic vs. short-term, tactical planning), or *behavioral* terms (group behavior vs. individual behavior). Thus, the level of analysis is sometimes a corollary of the object of analysis.

We may summarize the characteristics of planning as follows:

First, it is concerned with bringing about desired future states that are unlikely to occur without human intervention. Planning, therefore, addresses normative questions—what *ought* to be done—and as such it is a value-laden activity in which one must strive to include the values of those for whom planning is done.

Second, planning is concerned with the shaping of present as well as future events both by making better allocations of existing resources to fulfill short range (tactical) objectives and by looking into the future with certain beliefs or assumptions and directing present activity to meet long range (strategic) objectives. There is a trade-off or compromise between what appears best by looking only at the present and what appears best by simultaneously looking at the present and the future. The compromise is achieved by what is known as a discounting process since one is more certain about the present than the future.

Third, planning is a pragmatic activity concerned with selecting reasonable courses of action from among a set of alternatives. It must necessarily be constrained by what is humanly possible. Inadequate technology, incomplete information, and a limited ability to gather and process what information is available, present constraints or barriers that are difficult to overcome. Some people maintain that one must relax these rigid constraints by planning for "idealized" systems under the assumption that nearly everything is possible (see, for example, Ackoff, 1978). Freeing one's mind from the chains of reality can stimulate remarkable creativity. Moreover, planners are sometimes pleasantly surprised to discover that constraints originally believed to be unsurmountable are, in fact, negated by rapid developments in technology and science. In the end, however, the transformation of creative thought into pragmatic action requires tools that are either presently available or at least obtainable in the near future.

Fourth, planning involves rational choice. We have said that rationality deals with both reasoning from certain assumptions to conclusions and with the ability of the planner to defend or justify *both* assumptions and conclusions. In other words, a theory of rationality provides the primary epistemological support for the acquisition and use of knowledge in planning. It allows one to formulate a preliminary interpretation of a problem and select methods of analysis accordingly. Moreover, a theory of rationality is a prerequisite for communicating our ideas to others for feedback and possible modification. Departures from classic cause-effect rationality have been variously described as "subjective" or "nonrational." With the development of systems thinking, however, these departures have taken on special meaning: they are seen as alternative rationalities within a broader perspective of meaning and they are an entirely appropriate means of approaching a planning problem. Systems thinking acknowledges that what is meant by rational choice will vary across cultural, ideological, and disciplinary boundaries.

The following types of rational choice have been identified (Diesing, 1962):

Technical Rationality: Considers alternative courses of action on the basis of their potential to facilitate *effective* solutions to perceived problems; constraints such as cost or political feasibility of alternatives need not be considered.

Economic Rationality: Stresses need for *efficient* solutions to planning problems; cost per unit of benefit is the primary criterion for selection.

Legal Rationality: Assesses degree to which alternative plans conform to legally established rules of society. This has sometimes been extended to a point where people look to religion and heavenly justice to determine a choice.

Social Rationality: Compares plans according to their contribution to the maintenance or improvement of established social institutions.

Contextual Rationality: Considers the trade-offs or opportunity costs of attending to one set of problems to the relative exclusion of others.

Game Rationality: Focuses on behavior of self-interested individuals or groups who strive toward individual goals in relation to others who are perceived as competitors for "a piece of the pie;" examines the rationale for coalition building or development of mutual incentives (Rapaport, 1974).

Process Rationality: Considers the choice from among alternative planning processes rather than the choice of plans per se; concerned with the reasonableness of the process as opposed to the outcome (see Jones, 1977:6).

Common Sense Rationality: Owes no allegiance to techniques or standards of empirical inquiry; validity of plan rests on past experience, and casual empiricism. Views the world as essentially noncomplex (Geertz, 1975).

Meta-Rationality: Concerned with the choice of alternative rationalities—technical, economic, legal, and so on—according to which is (are) best in a particular context.

Planning invariably involves meta-rationality, which goes beyond any single model, because planning problems are generally multifaceted and intertwined. The rational mode that is best for examining one part of a planning problem is not necessarily a suitable way to examine the whole problem. For instance, planning a new highway system involves: factors of *technical* feasibility; *economic* factors relating costs and benefits to taxpayers; *legal* implications of obtaining rights of way through private land; *social* factors concerning the plan's impact on established neighborhoods; *contextual* factors concerning the trade-offs made by building a highway instead of directing resources elsewhere; *game* factors concerning competition among policy actors who have a vested interest in where the highway is constructed; *process* issues that will determine how much impact citizens and other stakeholder groups will have in the decision; and, finally, *common sense* standards for assessing alternative plans.

As we shall see in the next chapter, it is possible in a particular planning problem to trade off one kind of rationality for another and establish priorities among them as they are perceived to affect the outcome thus avoiding fragmentary solutions and explanations.

3. A Definition of Planning

With the characterization of planning provided above, we are in a position to define it as follows: *Planning is a thinking and social process of aligning what is deduced to be the likely outcome of a situation, given current actions, policies, and environmental forces, with what is perceived as a desirable outcome which requires new actions and policies.* Taking this definition a little at a time will reveal a deeper meaning.

To require that planning be a thinking process may seem strange. Is there something else besides thinking? Yes—blind adherence to a losing objective. A recent television program showed a method for trapping monkeys. The natives made a hole in a log and put bait inside. The monkey reached his hand in to get the bait, but when his fingers closed on it, he couldn't get his fist back through the hole. Determined to hang on to what he had, he was still hanging on when captured. All he needed to do to be free was let go. But to let go was to him incomprehensible—his priorities would not permit it. So he is destroyed by what he supposes is his highest priority objective.

Planning is a *thinking* process because it requires that one first make certain assumptions about current realities, future likelihoods, and available methods for eliciting and evaluating information about the two. One does this in order to draw what he believes to be valid conclusions which follow from the assumptions he makes and the methods or tools he uses to evaluate a problem. By reasoning from assumptions and following accepted rules or methodological guidelines, planners reach conclusions regarding actions necessary to attain a desired outcome and devise strategies for their implementation. As a *social* process planning takes place within a context of human interaction. The planning process and the plans themselves are shaped, defined, constrained, acted upon, or ignored, by forces in the socio-political environment. In other words, planning addresses the way decisions are made—who is involved and how they interact—as well as what decisions are made.

The thinking and social aspects of planning are mutually dependent. Our modes of reasoning from assumptions to conclusions are affected by the socio-political milieu in which they occur. Indeed, it may be that the theories and methods of science, in general, and planning, in particular, are as much reflections or rejections of historical social, political, or economic ideologies as they are products of pure intellectual energy (Laudan, 1977: 222). This is the view of historicism, a body of philosophical literature that stresses the impacts of historical settings on all thinkers. For example, during the 1960s Americans became increasingly concerned about the plight of poor people and minority groups. The Johnson administration launched the war on poverty with plans to increase the availability of low income housing and enhance equal employment opportunities. Out of this ideology regarding the expanded scope of government and its responsibility to its disadvantaged citizens flowed several distinct theories and methods of planning including "advocacy planning" and "radical planning" which sought to defend the interests of the weak against those of the powerful (Hudson, 1979).

On a more personal level, thinking and intellectual discourse in groups does not take place in a social vacuum. What one person says to another is not interpreted solely by the content of the words; rather, the words are assigned meaning and perhaps given greater or lesser credibility on the basis of who the speaker is, his role relationships with the listener, the power (intellectual or political) he wields and the context of the discussions. This is the view of the philosophy of relativism.

Edward Husserl, who developed a philosophical movement in the late 1800s known as phenomenology, believed that historicism and relativism provided inadequate explanations of how people interpreted the world around them as well as how they interpreted the knowledge claims or propositions made by scientists and others. In Husserl's view, knowledge claims are, in effect, phenomena or experiences which are "known in and by consciousness" including intuition, recollection, imagination and judgment. In other words, Husserl believed that informal knowledge plays an important role in shaping the cultural taxonomies (classification systems) and symbolic constructs that mediate between the planner and the problem imposed by the external environment. According to the modern day phenomenologist, Alfred Schutz:

> (Planners) have preselected and preinterpreted this world by a series of common sense constructs which determine their behavior, define the goal of their actions (and) the means available—which help them find their bearings in their natural and socio-cultural environment and to come to grips with it (Schutz, 1966: 5-6).

The acts of consciousness in any individual are, of course, difficult to bring to the surface and examine in an objective way. Phenomena are subjectively assigned meaning and they are perceived or interpreted in relation to other social and intellectual phenomena or experiences—past, present, and perhaps future—which an individual has also interpreted in a subjectively meaningful way. With regard to planning and other modes of knowledge production, the primary concern of phenomenology is the plan's relevance (or its lack) in terms of the subjective standards of assessment held by those involved in the planning process.

For example, by ignoring the unique evaluative criteria that decision makers bring to bear on a problem, the planner runs the risk of either producing knowledge that is perceived by decision makers to be irrelevant or, alternatively, adding to the time and expense of research by failing to take full advantage of the "knowledge" embodied in the consciousness of those around him. In either of these cases the prospects would not bode well for increasing the use of planning by decision-makers.

It is not difficult to see why these interconnections between the thinking and social aspects of the planning process, when combined with the inherent complexity and uncertainty displayed by the world, could make effective planning seem virtually impossible in the minds of some people (see Wildavsky, 1973). To others, they represent an opportunity for planners to extend the state of their art by developing new techniques and drawing upon these philosophical insights in their quest for creative means of guiding current actions toward future needs.

Let us continue with the dissection of our definition. Planning is a process of *alignment* because it is concerned with narrowing the *gap* between a likely (probable) future and a desired (optimal) future. This implies that planners are not likely to succeed in completely closing the gap between probable and optimal outcomes. Many of the constraints and opportunities to be encountered in the future are beyond the planner's control. Our limited ability to predict the future naturally constrains informed planning and control of the environment. Moreover, optimization may not always be a desirable, or a feasible objective. To optimize requires the planner to focus on one or several variables to the relative exclusion of others. This is the micro approach to planning.

An alternative is to simply "satisfice" (Simon, 1945) or "muddle through" (Lindblom, 1959) with plans that are just good enough to produce marginal (small) movement toward an objective given acknowledged constraints on our ability to gather and process information. It would appear that we need to strike a balance between optimization and satisficing with a method that allows us to simultaneously consider a wide range of environmental forces and alternative means of addressing them while focusing on the forces perceived to have the greatest impact and the alternatives believed to be most promising.

Thinking of planning as a process of alignment also provides a clue as to how planning should be done. It is an iteration or repetition of two distinct yet related processes. The first projects the *likely* future based on what seems reasonable given the current motivations of actors and the resources—technical, financial, intellectual—available to them. The second hypothesizes a *desired* and feasible future and the policies for its attainment. These policies are then added to the set of existing policies in a second projection to test the extent to which they facilitate or inhibit convergence toward the desired future. The process continues through enough iterations to conclude that the addition of new policies will not bring the likely and desired futures any closer together or, alternatively, that the slight amount of convergence produced by additional actions is not worth the cost of pursuing them.

The use of these two processes achieves a synthesis of the macro and the micro approaches to planning. The macro approach is concerned with identifying purposes, desired outcomes, and assessing the impact of forces in the environment while the micro approach seeks to modify details of a system's functions, flows, and structure to produce convergence of likely and desired futures.

4. Philosophies of Planning

Planning was characterized above as a process that includes a desired end state, available means to facilitate convergence of likely and desired futures, and rational criteria by which we measure convergence and judge its appropriateness to meet a perceived need. But how do we know what is good for us? Where do we come by such "normative" understanding? To understand planning as a thinking and social process requires that we look beyond its ontological character (the process as it is) to its philosophical and epistemological (how we know about it) foundations and assumptions.

Our approach will be to compare three philosophies of planning—formal, incremental, and systemic—in terms of the activities which comprise the generic planning process introduced earlier. Exhibit 5-1 provides an indication of how the planning process is affected by the assumptions and methods of these three prominent philosophies. We encourage the reader to examine carefully the exhibit because it serves as an outline for the detailed discussion which follows.

Formal Planning

The eighteenth-century political philosopher, Saint Simon, believed that his era would usher in a new approach to planning the public order. He envisioned planning as the domain, not of generals and politicians, but of scientists and engineers who possessed the specialized training to make objective rational choices in plotting the future direction of society.

Nearly two hundred years later, Robert Lane (1966) contended that the "domain of knowledge" in planning was expanding and "the domain of politics" was contracting. Lane's observations came at a time when the

Current Theories of Planning

EXHIBIT 5-1. *Comparison of Planning Philosophies*

<table>
<tr><th rowspan="2">Prominent planning philosophies</th><th colspan="3">Activities of a generic planning process</th></tr>
<tr><th>Problem structuring</th><th>Identification and evaluation of alternative responses</th><th>Implementation of chosen response</th></tr>
<tr><td>Formal planning</td><td>Assumes that problems can be accurately characterized by quantitative models and that there is consensus on the definition of a problem.</td><td>Alternatives limited to those whose costs and benefits may be objectively measured, preferably in terms of criteria common to all options. Selects optimal plan in terms of precise criteria.</td><td>Assumes that the implementation of a plan follows naturally from the logic of its formulation.</td></tr>
<tr><td>Incremental planning</td><td>Assumes lack of consensus on problem definition but offers no method for characterizing diversity.</td><td>Alternatives limited to those which represent marginal or small modifications of existing plans. Relies on bargaining and compromising to select plan that is "acceptable" versus "optimal". Criteria not explicit.</td><td>Relies on built-in flexibility that allows the users of a plan to adapt and modify it according to their needs and their interpretations of its intent.</td></tr>
<tr><td>Systemic planning</td><td>Assumes lack of consensus and proposes explicit methods of problem structuring that capture the range of possible perceptions.</td><td>Relaxes constraints on range of alternatives identified and uses mix of quantitative and qualitative methods to identify criteria, assign importance to criteria, and select that plan which is perceived to fulfill important criteria.</td><td>Assumes that implementation is affected by subjective assessments of adequacy and relevance in the minds of the users of the plans. Stresses modification of a plan to meet the needs of users.</td></tr>
</table>

planning sciences were inebriated with their new-found status in both the public and private sectors. For example, throughout the 1960s, rapid developments in computer technology (Forrester, 1969) were opening new frontiers of forecasting and modeling. Also, it was the "golden era" of operations research where planning specialists were orchestrating everything from the bombing of North Vietnam to the design of new methods of national budgeting.

Formal planning refers to a mode of planning whose assumptions and methods are consistent with the norms of classical science. This way of thinking ostensibly guarantees that plans will be determined by the "facts" as they present themselves and not by the subjective judgments or vested interests of the researcher/analyst. Simply stated, the formal planner seeks solutions to, not perspectives on a planning problem.

The Formal Approach to Problem Structuring

Problem structuring, the first set of activities in a generic planning process requires the planner to (1) define or categorize the problem as one which affects and is affected by one or more spheres of activity or environmental forces; (2) identify the variables or factors including people, policies, and other problems affecting or affected by the problem; and (3) assess the interrelations of variables—how they affect and are affected by each other.

The way one goes about structuring problems depends on his understanding of *complexity*. For example, a distinction has been drawn between two types of complexity (Weaver, 1948). Structured complexity may involve hundreds of variables but their interaction is easily handled by probability theory. One would feel fairly confident in predicting that out of 500 coin tosses, there would be roughly 250 heads and 250 tails even though there are many, many possible combinations. Insurance companies also use probability theory to predict how many clients will file claims and to determine what premium to charge for protection, given a client's chances of being in an accident. These are examples of structured complexity. Problems characterized by unstructured complexity, on the other hand, involve factors that interact in ways that do not lend themselves to analysis with conventional statistical methods. Predicting the behavior of people in response to policies is an example of unstructured complexity.

While most planning problems in government and private industry involve unstructured complexity, proponents of the formal approach define problems as though they were characterized by structured complexity. The problems are conceived as objective states which can be modeled in terms of deterministic or stochastic processes and treated independently of their valuative, subjective, or intangible components. In formal planning the most important step in structuring a problem is to identify the appropriate statistical method or modeling technique to characterize the problem at hand.

The Formal Approach to the Identification and Evaluation of Alternative Responses

The narrow way in which planning problems are defined or structured by the formal approach tends to limit the range of possible solutions which merge as candidates for subsequent evaluation. In other words, the way one structures a problem determines the method to solve it.

Consider once again the problem, discussed earlier, of planning a viable energy policy for the extended future. If the energy problem is seen as primarily an environmental one, then the range of alternative solutions will be limited to those that ostensibly address ecological concerns. If, on the other hand, it is viewed as a problem of national security, then alternative military or diplomatic solutions would receive the greatest attention. The key point is that formal planning limits the list of identified alternatives even further by confining them within a range that permits objective, quantitative comparisons. For example, in formal planning an environmental view of the energy problem would limit the list of alternative solutions to those whose ecological costs and benefits could be objectively and accurately measured; "ecological impact" would be operationally defined in measurable terms such as acreage of land consumed in the development of an energy source or pollutants produced by its consumption. The alternative plans or responses identified would be those that could be compared in these terms.

Evaluating alternative solutions in terms of their costs and benefits requires that rational choices and tradeoffs be made on the basis of agreed upon criteria. Even random choice is "rational" in the sense that it implies adherence to an assumption (i.e., each alternative is equally good or equally bad) which allows one to follow certain procedures (e.g., flipping a coin) for making selections. The formal approach to planning confines its conception of "rational choice" within relatively narrow boundaries.

In terms of the types of rational choice identified earlier, the formal planner most frequently adheres to the criteria of technical, economic, or legal rationality in selecting a preferred plan from a set of alternatives.

Comparing policy alternatives on the basis of these criteria is a fairly straightforward task. For example, economic methods can be used to justify that one alternative is more *cost efficient* than the others if, of course, one accepts the assumptions implicit in the method used. An alternative method is to pilot test plans, through small scale implementation or "experimentation" with selected target groups, which might demonstrate whether one plan is more *effective* than others in a technical sense. Again, however, interpreting the results of a pilot test can be difficult if there are many extraneous and intervening variables, some of which may be unmeasurable, that could provide different explanations.

There are quantitative methods which facilitate multi-criterion decision making yet the formal planner generally attempts to simplify the evaluation process by requiring that each alternative be considered on the basis of a limited set of criteria. Indeed, the scientific approach is most effective when one criterion (e.g., cost) applies to every alternative. To the formal planner, the inclusion of many diverse criteria such as political acceptability, social costs, and economic benefits—which may apply to some, but not every alternative—is like "comparing apples and oranges". He is likely to believe that it cannot be done in a scientifically acceptable manner.

The theories and methods of the formal approach are premised upon the epistemological foundations of logical positivism and they mimic those developed and refined in the natural and mathematical sciences (see for example, Nagel and Neef, 1979). Econometric forecasting models and simulation procedures (Greenberger, et al., 1976), probability theory and decision analysis (Baird, 1978), linear programming, cost-benefit analysis, and quasi-experimental pilot testing of policies are examples of methods used in this approach.

The Formal Approach to Implementation

After a plan is designed, formal planning assumes that its implementation—the third set of planning activities—will follow naturally or mechanically from the logic of its formulation. Just as problems are assumed to be objective states that exist independently of values and perceptions, the reasonableness of a proposed plan is assumed to speak for itself. In other words, the validity of the plan is assumed to rest *not* on the perceptions of potential users but rather on its conformity with criteria, such as its methodological rigor, established and maintained by the scientific community. These criteria do not acknowledge intuition, personal convictions, common sense, or practical experience. Therefore, they relieve the formal planner of the need to consult with those who will actively implement the plan or those who have a stake in the outcome.

In other words, the formal approach dismisses the possibility that administrators will tailor the goals and mechanics of the plan to fit the contextual requirements of the environment in which they are working. The formal approach stresses only that proposed plans be translated from the technical language of scientists to the pragmatic language of policy makers (see, for example, Sundquist, 1978; Glazer, 1981). Beyond that, the approach offers no means of resolving conflicts concerning the relevance and cogency of the plan itself.

Concluding Remarks on the Formal Approach

The formal philosophy has dominated modern planning and, indeed, has much to recommend it. Among its many strengths are its emphasis on clarity, its logical consistency, and the empirical validation of its tools. Proponents of this approach have expended a great deal of time and intellectual energy to devise and refine forecasting procedures and optimization models.

The weaknesses of the formal approach include a relative neglect of the human side of planning. Planning is regarded as separate from the purposeful character of social systems and the approach is silent on the fact that choices regarding desired futures are inherently value laden and frequently conflicting. Simply stated, the formal philosophy has no effective ways to make decisions that affect several individuals who have conflicting perceptions of the problem and different values they seek to satisfy. Even the theory of games, which deals with conflicts, has not been adequate to deal with this problem. Moreover, the formal philosophy assumes a mechanistic view of the future, where the outcomes are either known or at least calculable within statistical margins of error. Planning, however, takes place in a turbulent environment where decision outcomes are rarely known with certainty and where the consequences of a plan may be spread out over time, thus becoming irrelevant to the values that determined earlier choices. Some have suggested that the complexity and turbulence displayed by the environment dooms planners to a task analogous to that of Sisyphus who, in Greek mythology, was condemned to spend eternity rolling a huge stone up a hill, only to have it roll down again on reaching the top. However, turbulence paralyzes only planners whose view of the environment is based on simplicity, reductionism, or mechanistic reasoning.

Incremental Planning

The lack of perfect and complete knowledge and the limited intellectual capacities of planners to collect and process information have prompted some to call for a modification of the formal philosophy. Herbert Simon (1957) proposed the concept of *bounded rationality*—a process of selecting desired states and planning for their realization within the inherent limitations of human computational capability. Drawing largely on studies in cognitive psychology, he argued that human beings develop planning and decision-making procedures that are entirely "rational" given the constraints of the situation. Instead of optimizing desired values, as in the formal model, the constrained planner seeks merely to "satisfice" by identifying a course of action that is just "good enough" to produce a reasonable improvement in the present state of the system.

Simon was concerned, not with developing a theory of idealized choice behavior, but with describing *actual* choice behavior based on his observation of decision makers at work. There are those who believe that Simon's concept of bounded rationality is a more realistic portrayal of actual planning processes than the formal approach.

Charles Lindblom (1959) elaborated on Simon's work by suggesting that most planning takes place in groups and that the process is simplified by intentionally limiting the consideration of alternatives. Lindblom's theory of "incrementalism" states that in most planning situations the several decision makers involved consider only a limited set of policy alternatives. These alternatives represent incremental or marginal modifications of a base set of existing policies that are taken as "givens." Incrementalism suggests that conflicts over the values adopted by multiple actors and stakeholders are reduced through a process of "partisan mutual adjustment"—that is, through bargaining, compromising, and logrolling (each rolling the log just enough to maintain balance while dislodging his opponents). Lindblom's theory politicizes the formal philosophy of planning.

Problem Structuring in the Incremental Approach

Incremental planning subscribes to the post-positive assumption that there are many ways to structure or define a problem. While incremental planning acknowledges the presence of multiple definitions of a problem, it offers no formal method of capturing the range of possible perceptions. Rather, the problem definition which ultimately prevails is determined, in large part, by the relative power wielded by participants in the planning process. The perceptions and beliefs of those who are most powerful generally provide the foundation on which problems are structured and on which a tenuous "pseudo-consensus" is balanced. We call it "pseudo-consensus" because, in the presence of power differentials, people are rarely convinced (in a genuine sense) of others' points of view. Rather, they "submit" to a problem definition other than their own in the hope of establishing a *quid pro quo* relationship with their adversaries; that is they anticipate, and generally receive, future support from adversaries in return for their submission today.

The preoccupation of incrementalists with the incompleteness or unreliability of information and their scepticism regarding our intellectual capacity to process it produce problem definitions that intentionally limit the number of variables and simplify the relations among them. Thus, problem definitions in the incremental philosophy rarely consider the whole system and its interaction with its environment; rather, they focus on parts of the system and imply that resolutions require only slight modifications of the systems' functions, flows, or structure. A broad, macro-evaluation of the purposes of the system or an assessment of their compatibility with forces in the environment is rarely a topic of incremental planning.

The Incremental Approach to the Identification and Evaluation of Alternative Responses

Incrementalists maintain that, when identifying and evaluating alternative solutions, conflicts over the values and beliefs adhered to by multiple actors and stakeholders in the process are reduced through "partisan mutual adjustment" or, in other words, through bargaining, compromising, and power brokering. Several types of rationality, from the set identified earlier, may affect the processes and outcomes of partisan mutual adjustment. For example, *contextual rationality* may determine what trade-offs or sacrifices people are willing to make to appease others involved in the negotiation; *game rationality* might lay the foundation for coalition building which pits one group of interests against another in competition for limited resources; and, of course, *common sense rationality* may come into play when information is incomplete or unreliable which, as we have noted, is one of the primary assumptions of incrementalism.

The criteria used in incremental planning to select one plan over others are rarely expressed in objective and precisely measurable terms, as in the formal approach. Indeed, most of the literature and thinking on incrementalism displays a skeptical attitude regarding the appropriateness or reliability of quantitative methods in the selection of policy options (see Wildavsky, 1966). Therefore, the incremental approach generally repudiates precisely defined criteria in favor of intangible ones which more adequately reflect peoples' preferences, values, emotions, and fears. For example, congressmen may be concerned about the "political risks" associated with various taxing programs; or corporate executives might compare alternative marketing plans in terms of their respective contributions to the company's "image." Incrementalism claims that these criteria are difficult to define operationally in a rigorous way and, more importantly, in a way that all participants could agree upon; yet they are important criteria and should not be excluded from the planning process as they are in formal planning.

Thus, the incremental philosophy fosters an extreme level of heterogeneity (diversity) in planning by not requiring participants to agree on the meaning of the criteria used to compare alternative proposals. Instead, each participant may interpret the criteria differently and in ways that generally are not made explicit through reasoned discourse.

In incremental planning, the criteria themselves are not only intangible and submerged beneath imprecise rhetoric but the relative importance assigned to them by those involved in the planning process is not explicated; that is, incrementalism offers no formal methods of surfacing and synthesizing these subjective assessments of relative importance. The bargaining and compromising of the incremental approach focus solely on the alternative plans themselves, not on the criteria used to evaluate them.

The plan which is ultimately selected is that which, first, represents a marginal modification of existing practices and, second, addresses (at least superficially) the criteria perceived to be important by each of the many participants.

One can see that it is impossible to optimize the values of *each* participant in the process if there is no effort to place the criteria used to evaluate alternative plans in some order of priority; that is, if each actor or subgroup of actors clings to a unique set of values they wish to optimize. The result is a plan which is generally acceptable to all, but optimal to none. It follows that such plans are often extremely vague. Lending them greater specificity runs the risk of upsetting the delicate consensus achieved. It is fair to say that the product of incremental planning is not a specific plan but, rather, the broad parameters of a plan within which people holding different values and interests can agree to commit resources.

Consider, for example, the Supreme Court decision (Brown vs. Topeka Board of Education, 1954) requiring public school systems to take actions toward desegregation with "due speed." Some questions that might be posed are: What is "due speed"? Is there a specific time limit within which schools must be integrated? Is the time limit the same regardless of the size and complexity of the school system? These are questions that have not been answered precisely and which continue to plague implementation and enforcement efforts 30 years after the precedent-setting Supreme Court decision. There are many other examples of this sort of ambiguity in laws drafted by Congress. The incremental approach maintains that this imprecision is the only way to placate the many heterogeneous interests represented in the planning process. Moreover, equivocal plans help to ensure that no radical or dramatic actions will be taken to alter the basic character of the system; rather, policy changes are confined to incremental or marginal modifications of the status quo.

The Incremental Approach to Implementation

Incremental planning rarely specifies a rigidly defined strategy for implementation. Once the parameters of a plan have been drawn, its interpretation and designs for its implementation are frequently left to the judgments and perceptions of administrators whose daily activities are affected by it. Indeed, the built-in ambiguity of incremental planning allows users to adapt and modify plans according to personal interpretations of their intent (Pressman and Wildavsky, 1973).

When implementation procedures are specified in the incremental approach, they generally take the form of monitoring and enforcement. For example, there are several thousand regulatory agencies that are part of the American system of government. They have no authority to plan national policies; rather, they are charged with interpreting plans formulated by the executive, legislative and judicial branches of the government and with monitoring and enforcing their implementation. Even in monitoring and enforcement, however, the bargaining and compromising that were part of the earlier incremental planning process are carried over into implementation. The latitude in this type of bargaining depends, of course, on the nature of the policy. For example, there is no bargaining or compromising of drug safety standards between drug manufacturers and the Federal Drug Administration,

Current Theories of Planning

yet there is some bargaining between polluting industries and the Environmental Protection Agency on the enforcement of air quality standards.

In sum, the incremental approach to implementation is an offspring of its approach to the two previous sets of activities in the planning process—problem structuring and the identification and evaluation of alternative plans. All three sets of activities are characterized by political and intellectual conflict, bargaining and compromise to reach a pseudo consensus, and small movement toward desired objectives using existing policies as a point of departure.

Concluding Remarks on the Incremental Approach

Most of the literature on incrementalism does not claim that it is necessarily the *best* approach to policy planning and decision making; rather, it is portrayed as the *most prevalent* approach. We would not argue with this claim. Incrementalism is particularly prevalent in government planning and in large, multi-faceted private sector organizations. Moreover, the incremental approach to planning is not one which abounds with methods and techniques of analysis, nor does it boast of elaborate and carefully designed procedures for structuring human interaction, solving problems or resolving conflicts. Indeed, incrementalism is unapologetically *ad hoc* in its approach to planning problems; that is, it takes its form and identity from the particular setting in which it is embedded and there are no two settings in which incrementalism will display the same mode of information acquisition, exchange, and analysis.

Incrementalism has many strengths. It addresses the naivete of formal planning by acknowledging the human and political aspects of planning. It also admits that few things in life are known with certainty and that problems are not static but dynamic and, therefore, not likely to remain "solved" for long. Finally, it gives credence to human judgment, intuition, and knowledge derived from practical experience when objective data are incomplete or unreliable and when no adequate scientific theories exist to explain problems and design solutions.

Incrementalism also displays some important shortcomings. Among them is the inordinate credence given to partisan mutual adjustment which, in effect, guarantees that the interests of the most powerful or most highly organized groups prevail. The absence of specific methods for structuring debate and dialogue, or for surfacing the underlying criteria used to assess planning options renders incrementalism impotent in resolving fundamental conflicts. In the end, partisan mutual adjustment is little more than political arm twisting.

Moreover, the simplifications of the incremental model have a disturbing habit of becoming *over*-simplifications, especially if there is no effort to reexamine existing policies to test their reasonableness in light of rapidly changing environmental conditions. There is little consolation in the fact that planners are formulating only marginal adjustments to existing policies that are detrimental to or incongruous with the interest of the system. The incremental escalation of U. S. involvement in Vietnam illustrates a major problem in this form of planning (Frohock, 1979:55). Finally, incrementalism does not account for "fundamental decisions", which offer no base policy on which to formulate incremental adjustments (Etzioni, 1967). It has been observed that many of the pressing problems confronting government and industry are those which have never been encountered in the same form before and for which no pre-determined set of planning procedures exist (Mintzberg, et al, 1976). For example, the term "stagflation" was coined by economists in the late 1970s to refer to the presence of several economic phenomena — high unemployment and high rates of inflation — that had never occurred simultaneously before. Incrementalism is helpless when faced with an entirely new problem.

In sum incrementalism is the antithesis of formal planning. It appears, however, that in its zealous critique of formal planning, incrementalism has forsaken quantitative methods without bridging the gap with adequate qualitative procedures for addressing the complexity inherent in contemporary problems. In a Hegelian fashion, if we take formal planning as the thesis and incremental planning as its antithesis, then it appears that a *synthesis* of these two philosophies of planning is called for. The systems approach represents that synthesis.

Systemic Planning

We have noted that the assumptions of formal planning constrain the planner within boundaries that are unrealistically narrow. We may long for a hypothetical world where problems are well structured and where "solutions" emerge naturally through the comparison of cost/benefit ratios. Unfortunately, life is not that simple. Ours is a world in which finding the correct answers necessarily depends on asking the right questions. This statement cannot be dismissed as merely a clever play on words. Considering our rather dismal experience in predicting and adapting to events in the environment, we are apparently having a great deal of difficulty in asking the right questions. The systemic approach to planning has as its primary goal improving our ability to define and structure planning problems so that the right questions will be asked.

Incremental planning, in contrast with the formal philosophy, has allowed itself to be overwhelmed by complexity and has, in effect, admitted defeat in its unequivocal rejection of quantitative methods and in its explicit assumption that the best one can do is take small, tentative steps toward desired objectives by sequentially reacting to problems and opportunities as they arise.

Whereas the formal planning stresses *prediction* and the incremental planning stresses *reaction*, the systemic planning seeks to promote effective *interaction* with the environment while acknowledging the uncertainties associated with turbulence (Ackoff, 1974).

In systemic planning problems are not "solved" but rather resolved and continually redefined through a process of learning. Planning, therefore, is not a discrete activity but rather an ongoing process. The approach assumes that the future is uncertain and cannot be predicted from present conditions or past regularities. Emphasis is placed on creating alternative futures through action today rather than merely adapting to what the future will bring.

Finally, systemic planning is based on the explicit assumption that data or information about a problem cannot be conceived in isolation of the context of ideas that give them meaning. All data, in other words, are theory based. To understand the context of ideas in which planning takes place requires that we broaden our approach to include the subjective interpretations of meaning held by actors in the policy system, while not abandoning the precision and power of objective measurement and analysis of hard data.

The Systems Approach to Problem Structuring

The systemic planner is actively involved in the selection of desired end states and acknowledges this involvement as a normative, value-laden activity. The selection of goals and objectives is not conceived as an *a priori* "given" accomplished through the political system but rather as part and parcel of the planning process itself.

Problem definition and structuring is the single most important activity for the systemic planner. It was noted earlier that the manner in which a problem is defined or conceptualized determines to a large extent the search for and selection of alternative solutions. In systemic planning problems are not objectively determined only by the "facts" as they present themselves. Rather, this philosophy assumes that the same "facts" may be interpreted in radically different ways, depending on the world views and vested interests of participants in the planning process. For example, the problem of inadequate and poorly maintained housing units in central city areas may be defined in different ways by different people. To some it is a social-cultural problem resulting from a lack of interest by poor inner city residents to maintain standards of aesthetics and sanitation. To others it is a problem of infrastructure resulting from the paucity of job opportunities in the central city and inadequate transportation facilities to places where jobs are available. To some it is a problem of greed resulting from inadequate incentives for landlords to maintain and improve inner city dwellings. Finally, it may be a problem of education, of politics, of discrimination, or simply of "history." Note that even if there is general agreement on the definition of a problem, people may disagree on its scope, its severity, or its interrelatedness with other problems.

With this in mind, the systemic planner approaches problems with several assumptions (Dunn, 1981: 99). First, problems are *interdependent* and must be approached *holistically*. Second, problems are inherently *artificial* since they do not exist apart from the subjective interpretations of those who define them. In other words, problems do not exist in and of themselves but are the direct products of choice when individuals make judgments about altering a perceived state of affairs. Finally, problems are *dynamic* since there can be as many solutions as there are definitions of these problems. Moreover, problems and their solutions do not remain fixed but are in a constant state of flux.

Thus the systemic planner approaches every problem as if it were potentially ill-structured — one in which there are many decision makers, where alternatives and preferences are multiple and conflicting, and where the probability that a given alternative will produce a given end is either unknown or uncertain. The basic character of an ill-structured problem does not emerge from a table of facts and figures as suggested by the analytic philosophy nor from submitting to the preferences of a few top-level decision makers, as implicitly advocated by incrementalism. Defining and structuring problems under these circumstances requires insight, creativity and structured interaction among participants in order to surface and bring to the fore their values, assumptions, and interpretations of whatever data are available. In the process of structuring problems, the primary concern is not to avoid the wrong solution but to avoid asking the wrong questions and subsequently attempting to solve the wrong problem.

How does the systemic paradigm ensure that the "right" questions will be asked and the "right" problem addressed? Clearly, there is no simple formula that guarantees the planner with a correct definition of every problem. If there were a book entitled *How to Ask the Right Questions*, it would certainly occupy a place of honor in every planner's office. We are not writing such a book. However, we propose concepts that a planner can employ to avoid formulating a precise answer to the wrong problem when an approximate answer to the right problem would be far more useful.

The systemic planner should adopt an interpersonal mode of inquiry that is collaborative, dialogue-based, and educational. The fundamentally normative choices involved in the problem definition stage demand deliberate attention to and participation from those who affect and are affected by the problem situation. Therefore, planners should be actively involved in raising the consciousness of stakeholders by eliciting their judgments, and assumptions, and helping them to articulate their definitions of the problem and its relation to other problems. In this respect the systemic planner is acutely aware of the complex and highly subjective dimension of human choice and purposeful behavior. There is not only acknowledgment of but appreciation for alternative rationalities and alternative forms of knowledge including intuition, informed judgment, and common sense as well as scientific knowledge.

Systemic planning has produced several formal methods useful in structuring problems. We shall see in the next chapter that the Analytic Hierarchy Process provides a method for structuring problems hierarchically and graphically (visually) representing the relationships between desired objectives, global (general) and local (specific) factors impinging on those objectives, criteria for selection of alternatives, and finally the alternative plans themselves. The hierarchical representation is not devised arbitrarily but rather in collaboration with those affecting and affected by the ultimate outcome.

The Systems Approach to the Identification and Evaluation of Alternative Responses

In systemic planning the identification and evaluation of alternative responses takes place under far different assumptions than either formal or incremental planning. The most readily identifiable differences are that systemic planning relaxes assumptions that require strict adherence to quantitative expression of criteria and suspends *a priori* judgments as to how many and what types of alternative plans may be considered. Let us briefly examine these differences.

It is useful to keep in mind that the manner in which problems are structured which is the first set of activities in the planning process, affects the identification of alternative responses and the evaluation of their efficacy in addressing perceived needs.

First, by not structuring problems solely in terms of quantitative models or symbolic cause-effect relations, the systemic planner is free to consider alternative responses whose costs and benefits can only be assessed in qualitative terms. Second, by progressively expanding the boundaries of a problem to incorporate a complete representation of people's perceptions systemic planning admits the possibility of considering system-wide responses (including alterations of the system's purposes and modification of the environment in which it is embedded) in addition to small, marginal changes of its functions, flows and structure. In these two respects the systems approach to planning differs from the other two approaches.

When evaluating alternative means for achieving goals the systemic planners adheres to meta-rationality which, as the reader will recall, is concerned with choosing the most appropriate mix of criteria from other types of rationality such as economic, technical, social and so on. Systemic planning does not demand that all criteria apply to the consideration of all optimal plans. It does demand, however, that the criteria be made explicit and that people agree on their operational definitions regardless of whether or not they agree on the inherent value of one criterion relative to others. Thus, the systemic planner believes that it is indeed possible to compare "apples and oranges," in contradiction to the formal approach. Moreover, he is not satisfied with the ambiguity and confusion that result when the meaning of the criteria themselves and the relative importance people assign to them remain submerged or merely implicit as in the incremental approach.

Rationale for the Study of Values

Earlier we stated that systemic planners incorporate values and judgments into their mode of inquiry in order to represent fairly stakeholder interests and perspectives in a system of planning problems. The unique subject matter of the social sciences, the pluralistic character of planning problems, and the prescriptive dimensions of planning suggest that planners would be wise *not* to pattern their techniques after those employed by their counterparts in the natural sciences. A broader, postpositive theory of knowledge is required to address conflicts in purposeful human behavior and group planning and decision making. There are also other reasons for including values and human judgment in planning, which we discuss briefly below.

Complexity creates problems because we do not know the internal dynamics of whatever system we live in nor do we understand its relation to the environment in sufficient detail to formulate a reliable causal explanation. If we did, problems of planning could be reduced to simple linear relations, for which theories and techniques of social engineering would be entirely appropriate. The problems discussed in the first chapter illustrate the poverty of our causal theories when applied to really complex phenomena. We noted that current methods are not very useful in the absence of clear and fairly reliable causal understanding.

This, of course, begs the question: "What should we do when there are no good theories from which to deduce a rich description of the problem?" Or, more simply, how can we offer suggestions for problem resolution when we have little or nothing to go on? The answer provided by the techniques discussed below is that we should turn to *pre-causal* understanding found in human values and subjective judgments about the scope of the problem and the pattern of interrelationships among its variables. In other words, we must turn to deductive axiological (valuative) reasoning when faced with a system of planning problems for which no causal theories seem appropriate.

Our use of "deductive" in this sense diverges from the traditional usage of the term. Deductive reasoning usually refers to the process of formulating conclusions about specific observations on the basis of general theories or accepted truths. Theories in biology allow doctors to *deduce* a diagnosis in a specific case. Similarly, written laws and legal precedents allow judges to *deduce* an interpretation of the law in specific circumstances. In the absence of a clearly defined and accepted theory (or in the presence of multiple and conflicting theories), we believe that deductive reasoning may proceed from reflection on past experiences that shape our values and subjective judgments. To prevent deductive axiological reasoning from degenerating into little more than glorified guesswork, we place some constraints on judgments by requiring that they be supported by reasons or, in Toulmin's words, by warrants and backings. In this manner, judgments and values become informed by a body of factual knowledge and by previous relevant experience. Deductive reasoning is thus expanded and enhanced by its synthesis with inductive logic in the planning process.

Our reliance on human judgment in these instances is not merely a "last resort" or desperate search for something that will work. Instead, we are tapping a vast reserve of knowledge—a new frontier of human understanding—that has previously been unexplored. Reliance on axiological deduction is an approach that displays a high degree of optimism and faith in man's ability to conceptualize complex problems and to make valid judgments free from the rigid constraints of positive proof.

Dialectics and the Growth of knowledge

Another reason for incorporating values and judgments in resolving planning problems is a corollary of the first. We believe that in a problematic situation involving multiple perspectives, each perspective (theory) should be subjected to rigorous testing and scrupulous examination by those involved in the planning process. It may not be practical or even feasible to conduct empirical tests with carefully designed experiments in order to validate an expressed judgment. Indeed, we have said that the results of such experiments are themselves subject to personal interpretation. Rather, the testing of judgments should come from *within* the group of actors and stakeholders by surfacing and challenging hidden assumptions on which the plausibility of a knowledge claim rests. This demands interaction among actors and stakeholders. It demands the generation of internal *dialectics* or conflicts that will challenge an expressed judgment by pitting it against rival theories. The proponent of a particular judgment or theory must prove himself (and his theory) worthy of the challenge or yield to the opposition.

The rationale for this approach is that people not only have different feelings about the same situation, but these feelings change or can be changed by discussion, by new evidence, and by interaction with other experienced people. Sometimes, the outcome of a dialectical exchange is the rejection of *both* claims, and a synthesized perspective is formulated on the basis of assumptions common to both. In these cases the synthesis may yield new and creative insights not found in *either* of the judgments taken separately. In other cases the outcome is a compromise of many viewpoints involving substantial change in individual attitudes. Some people believe that a dialectical approach to inquiry is the only way to break the chains of inherent conservatism in science.

Note that this concept of knowledge generation and growth does not view

114   Analytical Planning

conflict as an obstacle to be avoided. Instead, conflict offers an opportunity to learn from the richness and diversity of information found in the group. Techniques that force consensus by mechanistically resorting to voting or before considering information that arises in the course of debate and argument do not take advantage of all knowledge held by participants.

Measuring Priorities

In most policy settings, planners, decision makers, and stakeholders generally agree that a "balance" or mix of values is desirable. For example, in debates on affirmative action programs, most people would agree that economic opportunities for minority groups should somehow be balanced against explicit provisions for non-discrimination against white males. Participants in the debate, however, are likely to disagree on the *relative* importance of these conflicting values or on the precise way to obtain a "mixture" of them. Some would say that minority groups should be compensated for past discriminatory practices with the imposition of a strict quota system of hiring. Others would contend that quota systems violate the principles of equality that affirmative action programs are designed to enforce. These people would say that if the overall principle of equality is pursued, equal treatment of minorities will follow naturally. Notice that the two groups agree on the ultimate value being pursued—equal treatment in hiring policies—yet they disagree on the mixture of values contained in each policy outcome.

We have learned to construct group priorities in planning problems with many potential mixtures of values. With the assistance of interactive techniques that acknowledge the importance of different values, we are able to identify and measure individual and collective priorities for combinations of potential policy outcomes. The concept of personal and group priorities have their roots in decision theory.

With these introductory remarks in mind, it is useful to review the several reasons for including values and judgments in the systemic paradigm. Values should be included in rational discourse to grant a fair representation of stakeholder interests, to explore untapped sources of knowledge in responding to complex problems, to enhance the body of knowledge by maximizing conflict in a structured and controlled manner, and to formulate richer conceptions of individual and collective priorities, for alternative policy outcomes.

The systems approach has produced several methods that allow one to include objective and subjective criteria and explicate the relative importance assigned to them by those involved in the planning process. We list some of these methods below and suggest that the reader consult the bibliographic references provided for a detailed description of how to use them, or for comparing their assumptions with those of the Analytic Hierarchy Process.

Systemic Methods of Planning

The Delphi Method

The delphi method, invented by Olaf Helmer (1967) and (e. g., Linstone and Turoff, 1975; Pill, 1971; Overbury, 1969), is a technique for eliciting expert judgments about phenomena that are not conducive to objective measurement or evaluation in the classical sense. Most frequently, the delphi method is used as a forecasting technique. For example, a delphi panel might be convened to examine the future of the American steel industry. This method represents a systematic approach for including multidisciplinary perspectives on planning problems. Delphi panels typically are composed of people who represent a wide range of professional modes of inquiry. Each perspective ostensibly contributes to a clearer understanding of the policy problem. Thus, if the delphi technique were used to assess the need for an expanded or modified public assistance program, it would be useful to obtain several perspectives on the problems of poverty including those of social workers, social psychologists, economists, doctors, politicians and of course, needy people.

Conventional delphi processes are characterized by anonymity and controlled feedback. The anonymity of panel members is preserved by physical separation and by the use of carefully constructed questionnaires or other communication procedures such as on-line computer communication. Thus the members of a conventional delphi panel do not debate their responses to questions posed by the planners. The purpose of maintaining anonymity and physical separation is to avoid several potential pitfalls of group decision making. The most frequently mentioned pitfall of group interaction is the "Ash Effect" — a phenomenon of group behavior that tends to encourage the domination of the group by one or more persons who are especially charismatic or who exert an extremely powerful influence due to their position within the organizational hierarchy.

Through controlled feedback the aggregate group response to a question presented on the delphi questionnaire is communicated to each panel member. The purpose of the feedback is to allow respondents to see how their judgments compared with those of others on the panel without being influenced of knowing who provided individual responses. The feedback is controlled because participants are offered only limited information on the responses of their colleagues. That is, they are shown the *average* or mean response of other panel members. This process eliminates the "noise" of extreme or "far-fetched" forecasts by removing outliers from the aggregate response. Controlled feedback following two or more rounds of questioning provides a foundation for group learning and an opportunity for panel members to modify their judgments in light of the responses of others.

After the controlled feedback, the delphi participants usually are convened as a group and allowed, for the first time, to communicate face to face. It is believed that after several rounds or iterations involving successive modification of individual forecasts, participants will converge to the point where they can reach consensus on the final forecast with minimum conflict and discussion.

The delphi process represents one of the first formalized methods for systematically obtaining and aggregating group judgments. In the early 1960s it stood apart as a unique and creative method of analyzing problems for which no good theory existed and for which there was insufficient data for the formulation of a new theory. However, experience with the technique has revealed several philosophical and practical problems. The designers of the method wished to maximize divergence by including a multi-disciplinary dimension. Yet, by including anonymity and controlled feedback and statistical group response, the designers unwittingly incorporated an element of "artificial consensus." Artificial consensus is imposed by precluding the opportunity for panel members to debate the merits and assumptions of their judgments and ultimately resorting to the summative measures of central tendency as the final product of the process. Thus, what appears on the surface to be an interdisciplinary approach to forecasting and planning may, in fact, degenerate into an arbitrary consensus that fails to capture the diversity of knowledge, values, and beliefs held by all participants. Moreover, the traditional delphi method may simply represent a disguised form of reductionist logic. Problems are merely decomposed into their respective disciplinary components, with each expert *further* reducing the problem in line with all of the assumptions and techniques that are unique to his disciplinary perspective.

In our view, although understandable, the most disturbing problem of traditional delphi methods is the anonymity and physical separation of the panel members. This arrangement tends to exclude information and new insights that could be generated and tested in the course of reasoned debate and argument. Traditional delphi processes are conspicuously incomplete because they fail to incorporate elements of dynamic interaction among participants on the panel. Instead, alternative appraisals of the problem are formulated individually and secretly, with only limited information provided after each of several rounds.

Finally, delphi processes may be extremely cumbersome. From the standpoint of simple logistics, the construction of delphi questionnaires is the most problematic component of the process. Following each round of a delphi process, new questionnaires must be devised on the basis of information obtained from the respondents in the previous round. Each new set of questionnaires is tested for reliability and validity. This process places significant demands on the time and resources of both the delphi panel members and the group moderators. Moreover, the questionnaire format does not allow respondents the freedom to "improvise" by providing information not requested by the questionnaire. Thus, to a large extent, the conclusions reached by a delphi panel are shaped or predetermined by the questions that are asked. As we noted earlier, the answers we find depend on the questions we ask.

Some of the shortcomings of traditional delphi methods have been addressed by a modified version called *policy delphi* which seeks to maximize conflict by eliciting the judgments of informed *advocates* instead of the judgments of impartial experts. Thus an attempt is made to include the interests and values of stakeholders or those who will be affected by the outcome of a plan. The problem of artificial consensus is addressed by a modified version of controlled feedback in which measures of group response accentuate conflict or polarization instead of central tendency. Moreover, in policy delphi participants have the opportunity to exchange ideas through limited interaction and debate.

Policy delphi improves upon the procedural weaknesses of traditional delphi processes, yet it remains a rather awkward and time consuming activity. Respondents remain isolated and "selectively" anonymous through the initial rounds of the process. Therefore, policy delphi does not satisfactorily address the problems associated with anonymous responses. Moreover, the practical problems of questionnaire construction and validation remain, as well as the philosophical problems of questionnaire responses.

The delphi process has met with only limited success, and its popularity relative to other more sophisticated methods seems to be waning. In some reported cases the forecasts obtained from a delphi process have been well off the mark (Overbury, 1969). Moreover, some people believe that the ultimate *purpose* of the process should be refined. Critics have suggested that delphi methods should not seek to determine what *will* happen in the future but rather what ought to happen. This suggestion reflects the belief that what happens tomorrow depends largely on what we do today.

In the Analytic Hierarchy Process we have addressed the weaknesses of the delphi technique while simultaneously drawing upon its strengths to improve decision making and planning under uncertainty. The AHP diverges from delphi by encouraging group interaction and debate. In this way, new and important knowledge emerges as the group explores the assumptions underlying individual judgments. Yet when judgments diverge, even after extensive debate and compromise, the AHP does not impose an artificial consensus by removing outliers from the calculation. Rather, extreme judgments are allowed to stand in testimony to the heterogenity of the group but within the requirements of tolerable inconsistency. In fact, we believe that diverging judgments point to the most crucial aspects of planning problems and to remove them is to create a "nonproblem" by camouflaging disagreement and conflict.

The AHP can also learn from the design of the delphi method. For example, the use of delphi-like questionnaires sent to many widely scattered stakeholders could be used to help structure hierarchies that would be the focus of an AHP workshop later. Also, we have used questionnaires to elicit judgments from many participants instead of relatively small face-to-face workshops. This strategy, of course, suffers from many shortcomings already described, yet it has the advantage of including different stakeholders whose judgments would otherwise not be solicited. The AHP can either synthesize individual judgments or synthesize solutions rising from individual judgments by weighting the individuals themselves according to the relevance of their knowledge.

Strategic Assumption Surfacing and Testing

Ian Mitroff and others (Mitroff and Sagasti, 1973; Mitroff and Emshoff, 1979) have suggested that the planning process would be improved if proposed solutions were challenged on the basis of their underlying assumptions:

> ... if the goal of planning is to test and to develop our theories/policies with the aid of data, then the existence of a single theory/policy can actually hinder further growth of the particular theory/policy under scrutiny. If only a single theory is operative, there is real danger of circularity and incentuousness — that the data uncovered by the theory can promote the appearance of compatibility between theory and data when such is not the case ... If theories/policies are to be tested by data ... they should be tested against the data uncovered by rival theories ... (Mitroff and Emshoff, 1979, p. 2).

A methodology called Strategic Assumption Surfacing and Testing (SAST) addresses the issue raised above. The SAST method is based on the belief that disagreements in planning debates generally hinge on conflicting *assumptions* about the parameters of the problem and the goals and objectives of actors in the planning process. When planners can agree on a common set of assumptions, they are more likely to reach consensus on a plan of action designed to address the perceived need. The SAST method follows a relatively simple sequence.

First, actors in the planning process are assisted in surfacing the underlying assumptions embedded in their respective strategies for resolving a problem. This stage proceeds backwards from a proposed plan of action, through supporting data, to the implicit assumptions that, in concert with the data, provide the logical deductive sequence of the proposed strategy. Formulating a complete listing of assumptions, including overall objectives of the organization and individual objectives held by policy actors, yields a fairly explicit articulation of the problem to which the plan is addressed. Mitroff has found it useful to use "stakeholder analysis" when surfacing assumptions. This interactive technique encourages decision makers to identify a set of people affecting or affected by a proposed plan. Decision makers are asked to examine the plan in light of what is assumed about the stakeholders, such as their rights, their desires, and their power to influence the decision.

The second step of the SAST method presents a "dialectic" in the form of counterassumptions that oppose those on which the initial strategy is based. Plausible counterassumptions are examined to see if they can serve as the basis for an entirely *new* formulation of the problem or an entirely new strategy. The

Current Theories of Planning 119

dialectic phase generates conflict in the hope that new options will emerge that are at least as plausible as the initial policy or the initial formulation of the problem.

The third stage uses negotiation to merge or integrate the assumptions of maximally different strategies into an acceptable pool that planners and decision makers acknowledge as the synthesized basis for a refined formulation of the problem. In applied settings, Mitroff has found that actors in the planning process will often agree on assumptions even when they disagree at the level of strategy. In the search for a common pool, participants are asked to rank their assumptions according to their relative importance to the proposed plan and according to their relative certainty or reliability which produces a grid chart like that illustrated below.

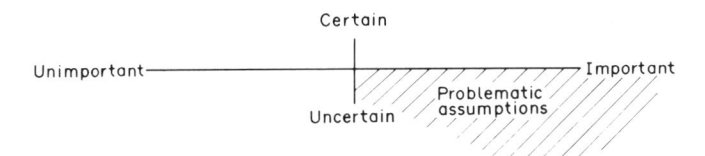

```
                    Certain
                       |
     Unimportant ——————+——————————————— Important
                       |   Problematic
                    Uncertain  assumptions
```

This simple grid allows actors to "see" those assumptions that are most important to their favored plan *and* those about which they are least confident or least certain, i.e., those in the lower right-hand quadrant. The integration stage of SAST focuses on these assumptions, since they are the ones on which the actors should agree if they are to proceed with the plan.

The fourth and final stage of SAST deduces a composite strategy or plan from the set of agreed-upon assumptions. It is assumed that at this point in the process there is sufficient agreement on the formulation of the problem to generate specific criteria for judging assumptions.

Strategic Assumption Surfacing and Testing has been employed to resolve planning problems in both the private and the public sectors. It is clear that the methodology is well suited to the analysis of ill-structured planning problems in which multiple strategies for resolution rest on sharply conflicting assumptions. It is equally obvious that the success or failure of SAST depends in large part on the skill and creativity of the facilitator or moderator of the exchange. This technique requires a moderator who is highly skilled in interpersonal dialogue and well versed in the theory of group dynamics. Imagination, resourcefulness, and courage are required to elicit assumptions that are "sensitive" or potentially destructive to the internal cohesion of the group. There are no guarantees that the dialogue will progress beyond the superficial noncontroversial and nonthreatening analysis of trivial assumptions. It is therefore doubtful that organizations could conduct SAST without the assistance of a trained and highly perceptive moderator. These caveats seem to make SAST relatively inaccessible to smaller and less affluent organizations.

120   Analytical Planning

The AHP and SAST can be used together in a complimentary way. It seems that assumption surfacing and testing would be most valuable in structuring a problem hierarchically, which is the most important phase of the AHP. For ill-structured problems with no prior experience, the establishment of the hierarchy's overall objective (the first level) may not be immediately apparent, and yet this single component of the hierarchy conditions the entire structure of the problem. The SAST could be used to define the first and successive levels of the hierarchy to ensure that judgments and priorities reflect the underlying assumptions of participants in the planning process, not just those of the workshop moderated.

Grouping of homogeneous elements into clusters and arranging clusters into levels that differ by no more than one order of magnitude at a time, are structural requirements of the AHP which facilitate the process of transmitting the large to the small in a way which clarifies the link between various assumptions.

The Symmetrical Linkage System

Kenneth Hammond and others (Hammond and Alderman, 1978; Hammond and Mumpower, 1979) have observed that the values and interests of citizen stakeholders are not *systematically* considered in the formation of public policy:

> Although social policies concerning public activities are assumed to be the product of social values and scientific facts, the means by which this product is achieved have not received close examination . . . That examination is required, however, because there is no established rational mechanism by which facts are brought to bear on social values. (Hammond and Mumpower, 1979, p. 246).

The integration of scientific facts and human values in the formation of public policy relies on the judgment of planners and decision makers who are supposedly acting in the interest of citizen stakeholders. In Hammond's view, the inherent flaws of human judgment may be partially controlled by improving the way information is collected and organized. He suggests that a systematic method of data collection and analysis that incorporates the judgments of citizens as well as those of experts is needed to avoid elitism and to increase the probability that the plan will be acceptable to those who will be affected by its outcome. The method should identify important social values, establish their relative importance, and determine the relevance of scientific facts to these values.

The Symmetrical Linkage System (SLS) is a method for integrating social values of citizens and scientific knowledge of experts in a systematic manner. This technique elicits value judgments from citizen stakeholders concerning preferred outcomes or purposes to be served by proposed policies. These values are aggregated and plugged into a mathematical model that includes policy-relevant information generated by experts. In the SLS social values are described in quantitative models that depict the relation between factors involved in a planning problem and stakeholder judgments concerning the relative importance or desirability of those factors.

In the first stage of the SLS, important factors that contribute to the choice from among alternative policy options are identified and organized. For example, in the choice from among alternative sources of energy for a municipal power plant, the relevant factors contributing to the decision might include:

1. The cost of construction
2. The future availability of fuel
3. The safety of operation
4. The long-range environmental impact of each alternative plant.

The second stage of the SLS develops quantitative models that describe stakeholder judgments about the relative social desirability of each policy option with respect to the factors identified in the first stage. Citizens are *not* asked to make judgments about scientific facts but rather to make normative judgments about a preferred mix of values contained in the chosen policy option. In our simple example a citizen may value a power plant that:

1. Is inexpensive to construct,
2. Uses fuel that is in plentiful supply,
3. Poses no threat to human life,
4. Discharges no contaminates into the air or water.

Obviously, this perfect energy source does not exist, and so the model must also describe the tradeoffs that the citizen is willing to make among the four factors.

In the third stage of the SLS, experts are called in to make scientific judgments regarding each dimension of the planning problem. The experts have no knowledge of the relative importance attributed to the factors by citizen stakeholders. They are asked merely to assess the policy alternatives on the basis of technical criteria. At this stage the experts may employ a host of traditional policy analytic tools such as cost/benefit analysis in order to rank the policy alternatives on each dimension identified in the first stage.

The final step of this technique aggregates the judgments of citizens and scientists and combines them in a relatively simple formula that reveals the preferred policy in terms of both social values and scientific facts.

The SLS represents an attempt to establish priorities among alternative policy options with respect to both technical feasibility and congruence with expressed social values. Unfortunately, the method is applicable only to planning problems for which a discrete set of policy alternatives has been defined. Thus the SLS seems to be of limited value in planning situations where there is strong disagreement on the definition of the policy problem and thus disagreement about the range of possible solutions.

122   *Analytical Planning*

Finally, the SLS displays many of the same shortcomings as in the delphi process discussed earlier. Specifically, the aggregation of judgments may create the illusion of consensus when in fact such is not the case. Thus the technique fails to take advantage of potential benefits to be derived from interaction and debate among participants.

The unique strength of the SLS is its attempt to incorporate the actual judgments of citizens rather than substituting those with the judgments of planners. Yet how many citizens must be sampled before we are confident that we have actually captured their values? Moreover, we must remember that planners are also citizens! In many applications of the AHP to problems involving social welfare we have incorporated the judgments of citizens.

Multiattribute Utility Theory (MAU)

This approach attempts to characterize planning options in terms of their objective and subjective attributes or characteristics and assigns numerical subjective utilities (which the theory assumes people innately have) to these attributes. This technique suffers from lack of a framework for structuring problems.

Conceived by Howard Raiffa and modified by others, (Raiffa, 1969; Keeney, 1972; Gardiner and Edwards, 1975), MAU is a method for reducing conflict by aggregating human judgments regarding the utility or value attached to alternative policy outcomes with multiple attributes. The theory of MAU measurement addresses issues pertaining to the relevance of policy attributes to the choice at hand, the measurement of values ascribed to those attributes by actors and stakeholders, the aggregation of values used to establish priorities from among a set of attributes, and the choice of a policy that contains the prioritized attributes.

The strength of MAU analysis is that it may be used to:

1. Predict the outcomes and impacts of policy alternatives.
2. Select a policy on the basis of a normative appraisal of its perceived attributes.
3. Evaluate the implemented policy by measuring the degree to which the desired attributes were actually displayed.

There are several versions of MAU measurement, which vary in their reliance on formal mathematical theory. We will not present a survey of these alternative approaches to MAU measurement but will focus instead on a relatively nontechnical approach that conveys the spirit of the technique. The Simple Multiattribute–Rating Technique (SMART) developed by Ward Edwards (1971) consists of the following sequence of steps:

1. Identify the actors and stakeholders whose utilities are to be considered in the choice from among alternative policies. If organizations or groups of citizen stakeholders have an interest in the policy outcome, then

representatives from these groups must be identified and encouraged to cooperate.
2. Identify the specific issue(s) around which there is disagreement. The issue must be placed in a specific context and the purpose for which the evaluation is being made must be explicated, since human values are generally contextually dependent.
3. Specify the range of outcomes associated with alternative courses of action; reliance on human judgment or deductive, inductive, or purely judgmental analysis is acceptable at this stage of the process when nothing is known with certainty. Moreover, outcomes have a "ripple effect" when they produce opportunities for future actions, future outcomes, and so on.
4. Identify the dimensions of value that are salient to the alternative policies being evaluated. Dimensions of value relate to the relevant attributes that make policy outcomes desirable or valuable. Each policy outcome contains different *types* of costs and benefits. They may be financial, aesthetic, ethical and so on.
5. Rank the attributes of each outcome in terms of their relative importance. Rankings are performed separately by the various actors and stakeholders involved in the planning process. Naturally the rankings will differ; yet every attempt is made to ensure that the participants are acting on the basis of common information. For instance, if the construction of our hypothetical convention center stimulates the local economy, this outcome may be valued for a number of different reasons: it may provide money for the improvement of transportation facilities; it may create opportunities for jobs; it may be used to enhance public assistance benefits or to improve the quality of locally supported schools, and so on. These attributes should be ranked by each participant according to their relative importance.
6. Rate the dimensions that have been ranked according to their importance. The least important dimension or attribute is arbitrarily assigned a rating of ten (10). The next least important attribute is then rated by asking how much more important (if at all) it is than the least important. This procedure is continued until the most important attribute in the list has been compared with all the others. It is important to note that each value assigned reflects a ratio of importance of that attribute relative to all others. For example, if one attribute has a value of thirty while another has a value of sixty, it means that the attribute rated sixty is twice as important as the attribute rated thirty, even though the two attributes may not have been directly compared when the ratings were assigned. Thus participants may want to constantly revise their ratings as they proceed up the list of attributes.
7. Sum the importance weights for each attribute, divide each attribute by the sum, and multiply by one hundred. This step standardizes the attributes that have been rated differently by different stakeholders.

8. Calculate the probability that each outcome is likely to result in the attainment of each attribute. Probabilities are estimated on a 0–100 scale, where zero is the minimum plausible value and one hundred is the maximum plausible value. Note that calculations of these probabilities may be objective, subjective, or a combination of both. Available data may be brought to bear on the calculations in order to make them as precise as possible. However, in the absence of past frequency distributions or other empirical data, subjective judgments will be elicited.
9. Calculate the utility for each outcome by using the equation:

$$U_i = \sum_j w_j u_{ij}$$

where U_i = the aggregate utility of the ith outcome;
w_j = the normalized value of the jth attribute;
u_{ij} = the probability of the ith outcome on the jth attribute

Thus w_{ij} is the output of step 7
and u_{ij} is the output of step 8.

10. Identify the outcome with the greatest value U_i and proceed to the selection of a specific policy designed to attain the desired outcome.

Other versions of the technique rely on more rigorous mathematical formulations designed to reflect the complexity of the situation facing planners and decision makers.

Unfortunately, the literature on MAU theory is silent on the value of this technique in structuring or defining problems *prior* to the elicitation of utility preferences. The implicit assumption seems to be that a discrete set of policy alternatives exists and, therefore, that there is consensus on the definition of the problem. Moreover, in the rating of attributes associated with alternative outcomes (see step 6), the technique requires both that intangible criteria can be assigned absolute values somehow, avoiding those which cannot and assumes a level of consistency that may be unrealistic. In other words, MAU analysis requires that preferences for various attributes be perfectly transitive. We have said that in group decision processes the rules of transitivity often break down and preferences may be circular: apples may be preferred to oranges and oranges may be preferred to bananas, yet *sometimes* bananas may be preferred to apples.

The Systems Approach to Implementation

Developing methods of planning which reflect the systems perspective requires a creative synthesis of deductive and inductive logic. In other words, a systemic planner may draw upon generally accepted theories when they seem appropriate to the problem at hand, but he must also acknowledge the validity of knowledge derived from experience when no good theories suggest themselves.

The task of the systemic planner is not complete when the plan is formulated and presented. This philosophy acknowledges the many difficulties in transferring knowledge to decision makers and guiding the plan through the phases of implementation. The systemic planner draws heavily on the work of scholars in an emerging discipline known generally as "knowledge utilization." Research in this field is dedicated to discovering why knowledge generated by planners and other social scientists is rarely used in the resolution of real world problems. A prominent theory is that planners and decision makers belong to two separate and largely isolated "communities." (Caplan, 1979). Each of these communities promotes norms, values, and reward structures that are frequently incongruent with those of other communities. For example, the planner who is also involved in academic research is "rewarded", (through publications and subsequent tenure appointments) for research that contributes to established theories or develops new theories in his particular discipline. In the mind of the decision maker, however, this research may be highly esoteric and largely useless in real world settings. Thus the determination of what constitutes valid, relevant, and useful knowledge depends on our frames of reference and the sociocultural environment in which we work.

With these thoughts in mind, the systemic planner attempts to encourage a process of constant learning not only for his clients but for himself by eliciting continuous feedback from decision makers and administrators and by modifying his plan for greater usability. The systemic planner knows that social learning or "paradigm shifts" are difficult to stimulate; yet the process need not be incremental nor inherently conservative. Often social learning takes place through a gestalt leap or a dramatic shift from one level of consciousness to another. This "event" is not likely to occur through traditional approaches to planning based on reductionism, incrementalism, and logical positivism. It is most likely to occur through a broader approach that draws from sources of knowledge heretofore ignored or excluded from the planning process.

Concluding Remarks on the Systems Approach

We began our discussion of systemic planning by claiming that formal planning is unrealistically narrow and that incremental planning is bereft of explicit methods of data collection and analysis. We have portrayed systemic planning as the next logical step in the *thesis-antithesis-synthesis* cycle. With such a synthesis we have broadened the scope of our inquiry and devised new methods for incorporating alternative modes of reasoning and problem solving.

We must realize, however, that a synthesis of alternative planning philosophies carries with it costs as well as benefits. For example, we may feel ill at ease without the high level precision provided by formal planning. Quite often, people feel more secure and confident when choices become "self-evident" from the comparison of quantitative costs and benefits. Even if we suspect that the precision of formal planning is an illusion or oversimplification, we may be reluctant to abandon its methods of comparing costs and benefits which, in effect, relieve us of the responsibility for our actions by portraying the "optimal" choice in clearly defined quantitative terms.

Alternatively, we may find it difficult to expand our horizons beyond those portrayed by incremental planning. Its rationale seems to come simply and naturally which, perhaps explains its predominance in many planning settings. It may be that planners are bargainers and compromisers by nature and that this mode of planning is more palatable than wrestling with complexity; it is easier to satisfice than it is to optimize, and it is less threatening to take small incremental steps toward an objective than it is to challenge and, perhaps, reformulate the assumptions which underlie the fundamental purposes of the system in its environment.

Despite these methodological and psychological costs, systemic planning addresses many of the inadequacies of the formal and incremental philosophies. We may be continually frustrated in our attempts to predict the future. However, a deeper understanding of the *present*, achieved by incorporating sources of knowledge previously ignored, offers the potential of helping us to shape and construct the future rather than merely adapt to it.

5. Conclusion

Our discussion of alternative rationalities and different philosophies of planning is rooted in a debate that has been raging in the social sciences for centuries. The debate concerns the distinction between "facts" and "values" and the role of values in the conduct of scientific inquiry.

We have dwelt on this topic because it is central to any discussion of the epistemology of planning. One's views on the fact-value dichotomy will necessarily shape one's approach to acquiring knowledge and using it in the planning process. The discussion is also pertinent to the ontology of planning. If planning is concerned with normative questions of what *ought* to be done, is it worthy of being labeled "science"? In other words, if the normative aims of planning lack objective scientific virtues, are they not relegated to the realm of "soft" ethics and not worthy of rational discourse?

Many problems are associated with logical positivism. There is reason to doubt that planning, decision making, or even inquiry in the "hard" sciences, such as physics, can be truly "value free" or objective. The mere selection of a problem for investigation and the subsequent "structuring" of that problem reflect values, preferences, and professional training. Moreover, we have seen that the same data can be used to support radically different perceptions of a planning problem. These conflicting perceptions are often the result of the different world views we bring to bear on a problem situation. Finally, the introduction of values into rational discourse can be justified with the provision of *reasons* for holding one value or another. When treated in this manner, values become analogous to facts that are relevant to the planning process and that can be debated rationally. The verification of any knowledge claim as "fact" is essentially a sociocultural process. The distinction between facts and values is not only a fiction but, more importantly, it can constrain planners within a narrow world view that verges on autocracy and stymies attempts to address systems of problems that are inherently pluralistic and conflictual.

Thus, a methodology for effectively dealing with ill-structured problems should first incorporate the informed judgments, assumptions, and intuition of experienced decision makers. Second, the methodology should allow for discussion of *conflicting* assumptions and judgments among multiple decision makers and stakeholders. Finally, the methodology should account for dynamic interaction among the elements of a planning problem, proceeding logically from objectives through performance criteria to alternative solutions or mixes of solutions.

Methods of formal, incremental, and systemic planning have both strengths and weaknesses. On balance, however, systemic planning is most relevant to our complex problems. To date, the major problem with systemic planning has been the operationalization of its concepts within a practical, problem-solving framework.

The AHP is a planning methodology which incorporates the best of formal, incremental, and systemic paradigms. In the following chapter, we examine applications of the AHP to strategic planning.

References

Ackoff, Russell (1974) Redesigning the Future: *A Systems Approach to Societal Problems*, New York: John Wiley.
Ackoff, Russell (1978) *The Art of Problem Solving*, New York: John Wiley.
Adelson, Marvin, Alkin, Marvin, Corey, Charles and Olaf Helmer, (1967) Planning Education for the Future, *American Behavioral Scientist*, **10**, No. 7, pp. 1–30.
Arrow, Kenneth (1951) Alternative Approaches to the Theory of Choice in Risk Taking Situations, *Econometrica*, **19**, pp. 404–437.
Baird, Bruce (1978) *Introduction to Decision Analysis*, North Scituate: Duxbury Press.
Bolan, Richard S. (1969) Community Decision Behavior: The Culture of Planning, *Journal of American Institute of Planners*, **35**, 5, pp. 301–310.
Campbell, Donald T. and Julian Stanley (1971) *Experimental and Quasi-Experimental Design*, Chicago: Rand-McNally.
Caplan, Nathan (1979) The Two Communities Theory and Knowledge Utilization, *American Behavioral Scientist*, **22**, 3, pp. 459–470.
Churchman, C. West (1971) *The Design of Inquiring Systems*, New York: Basic Books.
Dalkey, N. C. (1969) The Delphi Method: An Experimental Study of Group Opinion, Rand RM-5888-PR.

Davidoff, Paul and Thomas H. Reiner (1962) A Choice Theory of Planning, *Journal of the American Institute of Planners*, **28**, 2, pp. 103-115.
Diesing, Paul (1962) *Reason in Society*, Urbana: University of Illinois Press.
Dror, Yehezkel (1963) The Planning Process: A Facet Design, *International Review of Administrative Sciences*, **29**, 1, pp. 46-58.
Dunn, William N. (1981) *Public Policy Analysis*, Englewood Cliffs: Prentice-Hall.
Edwards, Ward (1971) Social Utilities, *The Engineering Economist*, Summer Symposium Series, **6**.
Enzer, Selwyn (1970) Delphi and Cross Impact Techniques: An Effective Combination for Systematic Futures Analysis, Institute for the Future, WP-8.
Etzioni, Amitai (1967) Mixed Scanning: A Third Approach to Decision Making, *Public Administration Review*, **27**, (December) pp. 385-392.
Farquhar, Peter, (1980) Advances in Multiattribute Utility Theory, *Theory and Decision*, **12**, pp. 381-394.
Faludi, Andreas (ed) (1973) *A Reader in Planning Theory*, New York: Pergamon Press.
Forrester, Jay (1969) *Urban Dynamics*, Cambridge: MIT Press.
Frohock, Fred (1979) *Public Policy: Scope and Logic*, Englewood Cliffs: Prentice-Hall.
Gardiner, Peter and Ward Edwards (1975) Public Value: Multi-Attribute Utility Measurement for Social Decision Making, in *Human Judgment and Decision Processes* Steven Schwartz and Martin Kaplan (eds) New York: Academic Press.
Geertz, Clifford (1975) Common Sense as a Cultural System, *Antioch Review*, **33**, 1, pp. 5-27.
Glaser, Edward (1981) Knowledge Transfer Strategies, paper presented at Conference on Knowledge Use, Pittsburgh, PA (March 18-20).
Gordon, T. J. and H. Hayward (1968) Initial Experiments with the Cross Impact Matrix Method of Forecasting, *Futures*, **1**, 2, p. 101.
Greenburger, Martin, Crenson, Mathew and Brian Crissey (1976) *Models in the Policy Process*, New York: Russell Sage.
Guttentag, Marcia and Elmer Struening (eds) (1975) *Handbook of Evaluation Research*, Beverly Hills: Sage.
Hammond, Kenneth and Leonard Alderman (1978) Science, Values and Human Judgment, in *Judgment and Decision in Public Policy Formation* Kenneth Hammond (ed) Boulder: Westview.
Hammond, Kenneth and Jeryl Mumpower (1979) Formation of Social Policy: Risks and Safeguards, *Knowledge: Creation, Diffusion, Utilization*, **1**, No. 2, pp. 245-258.
Helmer, Olaf (1969) *Analysis of the Future: The Delphi Method*, Santa Monica: Rand Corporation.
Helmer, Olaf and Nicholas Rescher (1959) On the Epistemology of the Inexact Sciences, *Management Science*, **6**, pp. 25-52.
Hudson, Barclay (1979) Comparison of Current Planning Theories, *Journal of the American Planning Association*, **45** (October) pp. 387-398.
Jones, Charles O. (1977) *An Introduction to the Study of Public Policy* (2nd edition), North Scituate: Duxbury Press.
Keeney, R. L. (1972) Utility Functions for Multi-Attribute Consequences, *Management Science*, **18**, pp. 276-287.
Lane, Robert (1966) The Decline of Politics and Ideology in a Knowledgeable Society, *American Journal of Sociology*, **31**, pp. 657-658.
Laudan, Larry (1977) *Progress and its Problems*, Berkeley: University of California Press.
Lindblom, Charles E. (1959) The Science of Muddling Through, *Public Administration Review*, **19**, 2, pp. 79-89.
Linstone, Harold and Murray Turoff (eds) (1975) *The Delphi Method*, New York: Addison-Wesley.
Mintzberg, Henry, Raisenghani, Duru, and Andre Theoret (1976) The Structure of "Unstructured" Decision Process, *Administrative Science Quarterly*, **21**, pp. 246-275.
Mitroff, Ian and Francisco Sagasti (1973) Epistemology as General Systems Theory, *Philosophy of the Social Sciences*, **3**, pp. 117-134.
Mitroff, Ian and James Emshoff (1979) On Strategic Assumptions Making: A Dialectical Approach to Policy Planning, *Academy of Management Review*, **4**.

Mumpower, Jeryl, Viers, Val and Kenneth Hammond (1979) Scientific Information, Social Values and Policy Formation, *IEEE Transactions on Systems, Man and Cybernetics*, Vol. SMC-9, No. 9, pp. 464–478.

Nagel, Stuart and Marion Neef (1979) *Policy Analysis in Social Science Research*, Beverly Hills: Sage.

Pill, Juri (1971) The Delphi Method: Substance, Context, a Critique and Annotated Bibliography, *Socio-economic Planning Science* 5, pp. 57–71.

Pressman, Jeffrey and Aaron Wildavsky (1973) *Implementation* Berkeley: University of California Press.

Raiffa, Howard (1969) Preferences for Multiattribute Alternatives Memorandum RM-5968-DOT/RC Santa Monica: Rand Corporation.

Rapaport, Anatol (1974) *Fights, Games and Debates* Ann Arbor: University of Michigan Press.

Rescher, Nicholas (1977) *Dialectics: A Controversy Oriented Approach to the Theory of Knowledge, Albany*: State University of New York Press.

Schutz, Alfred (1966) *Collected Papers Volume 2*, New York: McMillan.

Simon, Herbert A. (1957) *Administrative Behavior*, New York: McMillan.

Sundquist, James (1978) Research Brokerage: The Weak Link, in *Knowledge and Policy: The Uncertain Connection* Lawrence Lynn (ed) Washington: National Academy of Science.

Sztompka, Piotr (1979) *Sociological Dilemmas: Toward a Dialectical Paradigm*, New York: Academic Press.

Turoff, Murray, (1970) The Design of a Policy Delphi, *Technological Forecasting and Social Change*, 2, No. 2, pp. 149–171.

Weaver, Warren (1948) Science and Complexity, *American Scientist*, 36, pp. 536–544.

Wildavsky, Aaron (1966) The Political Economy of Efficiency, Cost-Benefit Analysis and Program Budgeting, *Public Administration Review*, 26, pp. 292–310.

Wildavsky, Aaron (1973) If Planning is Everything, Maybe It's Nothing, *Policy Science*, 4, pp. 127–153.

Suggested Readings

Types of Rationality

Ackoff, Russell (1978) *The Art of Problem Solving*, New York: John Wiley.
In this book the author suggests that effective problem solving often requires that we relax rigid constraining assumptions and free our imagination for the purpose at hand—the design of idealized systems. We are trained to think in terms of constraints which often inhibit creativity and innovation in planning. For instance, the solution to riddles and puzzles is generally obvious when we step outside the narrow world view which determines the way we structure problems and the methods we use to solve them. The book is supplemented with case studies of creative problem solving.

Campbell, Donald (1969) Reforms as Experiments, *Journal of the American Psychological Association*, 24, No. 4 pp. 409–429.
This article focuses on evaluation research or retrospective planning which is used to measure the degree to which plans have achieved the goals and objectives set from them. However, the article should be read from the point of view of prospective analysis since it presents an epistomology that is relevant to formulating plans as well as evaluating their outcomes. The author's experimental approach to policy evaluation is based upon his "threats to experimental validity" which are formalized counter-explanations or alternative hypotheses for assessing the effects of plans that have been implemented. In other words, Campbell has formulated a set of formalized challenges to the simple cause-effect assumptions that have dominated evaluation research in the past. The outcomes or effects of plans may, in fact, be due to many different factors. The plan itself may be only incidental to the outcomes that are observed. This article is highly recommended as a source for checking the rigor of planning

methodologies as well as suggesting alternative explanations for phenomena which, on the surface, appear to be crystal clear.

Dewey, John (1970) *How We Think*, Boston: D.C. Heath and Company.
This book naturally is dated by modern standards yet it is still useful as a guide to understanding the basis of hypothetical deductive modes of inquiry. Comprehensive rationality and value-free scientism are assumed to be the most defensible modes of inquiry in both the natural and social sciences.

Etzioni, Amitai (1967) Mixed Scanning: A Third Approach to Decision Making, *Public Administration Review*, **27**, pp. 385–392.
Etzioni issues a critique of both comprehensive rationality and incrementalism. Mixed scanning is portrayed as an alternative to the comprehensive and incremental approaches to planning. In the mixed scanning approach an attempt is made to conceptualize problems within a broader context while focusing on the high priority components. This approach is not formalized by the author but rather remains at the level of theory.

Geertz, Clifford, (1975) Common Sense as a Cultural System, *Antioch Review*, **33**, pp. 5–27.
A stimulating analysis of a generally ignored source of knowledge—common sense—in the context of its social and cultural determinants. Using case studies drawn from the field of anthropology, the author argues that common sense rationality is, in effect, a self-contained cultural system. Planners and policy makers should learn to recognize the subtle dynamics of common sense rationality and acknowledge its value as a viable mode of reasoning if they are to interact effectively in the real world of decision making.

Rescher, Nicholas (1977) *Dialectics: A Controversy-Oriented Approach to the Theory Knowledge*, Albany: Suny Press.
The author suggests that dialectics is a mechanism of rational validation within the socially conditioned interactions of the scientific community. Within the dialectical model of inquiry, the social and valuative aspects of the scientific enterprise are highlighted. The innovative scientist is viewed as an "advocate" of a certain thesis which opponents challenge in an adversarial manner. This notion of dialectical inquiry runs counter to the positivist philosophy of science since the status of a knowledge claim cannot be assessed outside the course of controversy from which it emerged.

Why Study Values?

Churchman, C. West, *The Design of Inquiring Systems*, New York: Basic, 1971.
In this book Churchman presents a contemporary interpretation of Leibnitz, Lock, Kant, Hagel and Singer with a view toward how philosophical traditions have shaped modern day systems of inquiry. The author illustrates the ontological and epistemological premises of these philosophers through examples of contemporary information systems. The philosophy of science has direct and immediate relevance for planners and other social scientists who are interested in developing methods and techniques of social inquiry.

Helmer, Olaf and Nicholas Rescher, The Epistemology of the Inexact Sciences, *Management Science*, Vol. 6 (1959) pp. 25–52.
This article suggests that the attainment of scientific status of a particular mode of inquiry is not determined by the "exactness" of methods used by inquirers but rather by the objectivity or, more appropriately, intersubjectivity of results or "ideas" which emanate from the methods used. The authors suggest that there is no fundamental epistemological difference

between the natural sciences and the social sciences. The role of expert judgment is discussed and the authors illustrate that judgment is not incompatible with scientific objectivity.

Feyerabend, Paul, *Against Method*, London: Verso, 1975.
This controversial essay portrays science as a chauvinistic social system which effectively resists alternatives to the status quo. Traditional definitions of "rationality" and rigid standards of what constitute acceptable modes of inquiry stifle creativity and subsequently inhibit the growth of knowledge. To counter the inherently conservative character of science, the author outlines an "anarchistic" epistemology based on counter-intuitive reasoning. Feyerabend argues that existing theories are best tested by formulating an incompatible alternative. The dialectic approach may refute or sustain existing theories but in either case knowledge grows.

Rein, Martin, *Social Science and Public Policy*, New York: Penguin, 1976.
Rein suggests that the central questions in policy planning do not involve issues of fact but rather issues of interpretation. In the author's view, it is futile to study how values enter into the policy process. A more fruitful area of inquiry is the boundary shared by factual and valuative premises. Policy analysis should be approached from a "value critical" perspective in which goals and values become the object of critical review. Problem structuring is as important as problem solving since the ideologies which organize our perceptions also shape the questions we ask and the solutions we reach. These concepts are discussed at the philosophical level and as they pertain to real life problems.

Rescher, Nicholas, Dialectics: *A Controversy-Oriented Approach to the Theory of Knowledge*, Albany: Suny Press, 1977.
The author suggests that dialectics is a mechanism of rational validation within the socially conditioned interactions of the scientific community. Within the dialectical model of inquiry, the social and valuative aspects of the scientific enterprise are highlighted. The innovative scientist is viewed as an "advocate" of a certain thesis which opponents challenge in an adversarial manner. This notion of dialectical inquiry runs counter to the positivist philosophy of science since the status of a knowledge claim cannot be assessed outside of the course of controversy from which it emerged.

Methods of Planning

Hammond, Kenneth and Leonard Alderman, Science, Values and Human Judgment, in Kenneth Hammond (editor) *Judgment and Decision in Public Policy Formation*, Boulder: Westview, 1978.
The authors suggest that a key element in integrating scientific facts and social values is human judgment. A framework is presented for integrating the value judgments of policy actors and stakeholders with the scientific judgments of experts in arriving at a choice from among alternative policy options.

Huber, George, Methods for Quantifying Subjective Probabilities and Multiattribute Utilities, *Decision Science*, Vol. 5 (1974) pp. 430–459.
This article is a non-technical discussion of methods for eliciting expert judgments of probabilities regarding the likely outcomes of alternative plans. The article also discusses methods of aggregating the utilities for multiple attributes displayed by each of several potential outcomes. This paper is an excellent introduction to the field of subjective judgment and should be used as a springboard into more recent and more technical discussions.

Mitroff, Ian and James Emshoff, On Strategic Assumption Making: A Dialectical Approach to Policy and Planning, *Academy of Management Review*, Vol. 4, No. 1, (1979) pp. 1–12.
This article introduces a methodology for dealing with ill-structured problems. It is suggested that policy debates are rarely resolved when attention is focused on alternative policies

themselves. Rather, such debates are most appropriate handled at the level of the assumptions which underlie preferences for one or another policy. When these assumptions are surfaced for critical review there is a greater change that policy makers will come to agreement on a set of assumptions that will serve as the basis for an acceptable policy which may or may not be one of the original set.

CHAPTER 6
Strategic Planning

1. Introduction

For the long range planner the important question is not what should we do tomorrow, but what should we do today to prepare for an uncertain future. Some factors of the future, however, need to be converged with various time spans into a decision in the present. As defined by Peter Drucker, decision making is, in essence, an attempt to synthesize into the present a great number of divergent time spans.

It is desirable to stay open to change and invention to attain better and more fulfilling futures. On the other hand, to cope with the future we need to design plans that will survive and be effective. How do we reconcile the two objectives—to ensure the survival of adaptive plans and also to admit change in the environment for variety, excitement, and progress in the future? This is the dilemma: no sooner do we have a plan to work with than the changes it brings about call for a new plan. Because of this contradiction some people have concluded that planning is useless. The rebuttal to this is that as long as things are changing it is better for us, if we want to control them to our advantage to be planning and replanning than to be simply reacting.

Strategic, adaptive planning is a process of learning and growth. Above all it is an ongoing event kept in the foreground to be seen, studied, used as a guide, and revised as change is noted in the environment. Strategic planning is the process of projecting the likely or logical future—the composite scenario—and of idealizing desired futures. It is the process of knowing how to attain these futures, using this knowledge to steer the logical future toward a more desired one, and then repeating the operation. The backward process of idealization inspires creative thinking. It affords people an opportunity to expand their awareness of what states of the system they would like to see take place, and with what priorities. Using the backward process, planners identify both opportunities and obstacles and eventually select effective policies to facilitate reaching the desired future.

The purpose of this chapter is to demonstrate how the systems approach of the Analytic Hierarchy Process can be used to plan for likely and desired futures. After a brief discussion of the planning process in general, we explore in some detail the forward-backward process. To illustrate the application of the AHP to planning problems, we offer several examples of actual situations in which the AHP was used. We conclude with some practical suggestions for implementing this systems approach to planning.

2. The Planning Process

In the simplest way all plans have three things in common—a starting point, a goal (or ending point), and a means of connecting the two. Furthermore, one ambition of the planning process is to combine the components at the least cost to achieve the greatest output—that is, to maximize efficiency.

The first component of any plan is its starting point. People's starting points are usually where they stand at the present time: they command certain resources that enable them to reach some other point; they make certain assumptions about influences beyond their control when designing a plan; they are locked by certain constraints of nature and environment that provide boundaries for the plan. Although usually taken for granted, one needs to make explicit account of all resources and constraints to facilitate maximizing planning efficiency. This would also require careful revision of the time to implement a plan because the starting point can be different than it was during the study. A much better assessment of the effect of the starting point is made when all available resources and all critical constraints are included explicitly.

The second component is the goal. Given that the other two components are conceived and executed properly, this component becomes merely a target. Goals may not be clearly defined, however, or they could be set at a point impossible to reach. The goal should not be envisioned without good knowledge of the forces and influences that affect and shape it. It must be well designed, reasonably accomplished, reevaluated, and changed as required by the circumstances.

The last component of a plan is the means. This component is the plan itself, since it describes the method by which one travels from the starting point to the goal. The other two components require mostly theoretical consideration; in contrast, this component is more concrete. It must include factors that affect the goal, the internal and external forces that affect these factors, the objectives of the operation, the conscientious sequence of steps to be followed, and the likely decision points required for control in the process. The factors could be environmental, economic, cultural, social, political, and technological. Further, they may or may not be controllable to some degree by the decision-maker. The factors should also account for any and all available information that needs to be considered.

3. The Forward-Backward Planning Process

Many planning processes move only in one direction. That is, they follow a time-sequenced order of events beginning at the present time $t = 0$ and terminating at some future point $t = T$. The first sequence, called the forward process, considers the factors and assumptions of the present state, which in turn generate some logical outcome. The second sequence, the backward process, begins with a desired outcome at time T and then works backward to identify and evaluate the factors and intermediate outcomes required to achieve that desired outcome. Both processes are theoretically sound and practical.

In the forward process, one considers the relevant present factors, influences, and objectives that lead to sensible conclusions or scenarios. The factors/influences/objectives may be economic, political, environmental, technological, cultural, and/or social in nature. The backward process begins with the desired scenarios then examines the policies and factors that might achieve those scenarios. Iteration of the two processes narrows or "converges" the gap between the desired and the logical scenarios.

The forward planning process provides an assessment of the state of the likely outcome. The backward planning process provides a means for controlling and steering the forward process towards a desired state.

Scenarios

The key to these processes is the scenario. A scenario is a hypothesized outcome that is conceived and specified by making certain assumptions about current and future trends. The assumptions must be reasonable and should include constraints of nature, time, people, and technology. One must guard against uninhibited imagination.

There are two types of scenarios—exploratory and anticipatory. The former proceeds from the present to the future, whereas the latter takes an inverse path by starting with a future point and works backward toward the present to discover what influences and actions are required to fulfill the desired goal. Each of the scenarios can be reiterated as needed.

The *exploratory* scenario examines the logical sequence of events generated by the components of the system under study. It is used often as a technique to fire the imagination, stimulate discussion, and attract the attention of people involved in the planning process. Its significance does not lie in answering questions. Its importance may be to force attention on factors formerly unconsidered.

There are two kinds of *anticipatory* scenario: normative and contrast. The *normative* scenario determines at the start a given set of objectives to be achieved and then defines a path for their realization. In this case, objectives may be idealized to find if the path truly exists. The *contrast* scenario, on the other hand, is characterized by both a desired and feasible future. Its main asset is to sharply emphasize claims on which assumptions of feasibility rest. The combination of normative and contrast scenarios forms a *composite* scenario, which in turn retains the properties of the specific scenario. This scenario allows for a synthesis of a wider range of considerations.

136   *Analytical Planning*

4. Rationale for the Forward-Backward Planning Process

One may question whether either the forward or the backward process is the most effective method of planning. Depending on the circumstances, one might be totally acceptable while the other is impractical. More importantly, each one alone may be inadequate to generate a good plan. Combining the two into a single forward-backward process can effectively overcome the problem. In this manner we conscientiously attempt to unite desired goals with logical goals, thereby providing a framework for the convergence of the two outcomes.

Perhaps the best reason for using the forward-backward planning process is classical planning theory itself. The theory states that there are essentially two planning goals. One is a *logical* or reachable goal that assumes the assumptions and factors affecting the outcome will remain substantially unchanged from the present state of affairs. Marginal changes in strategy and inputs will affect output only slightly or not at all. The other planning goal is a *desired* one whose attainment requires a great deal of change in inputs—both internal and external. These changes must not only be implemented, but they must survive against the entrenched policies of the system. Inertia is a powerful force. Good intuitions for making a change in course must be backed up with persistence.

5. Combining the Forward and Backward Processes

To integrate "forward" and "backward" hierarchical planning one projects the likely future from present actions, adopts a desired future, designs new policies, adjoins them to the set of existing policies, projects a new future, and compares the two futures—the projected and the desired—for their main attributes. The desired future is modified to see what policy modification is again needed to make it become the projected future, and the process is continued (see Exhibit 6-1).

EXHIBIT 6-1. *A Schematic Representation of the Basic Planning Orientation*

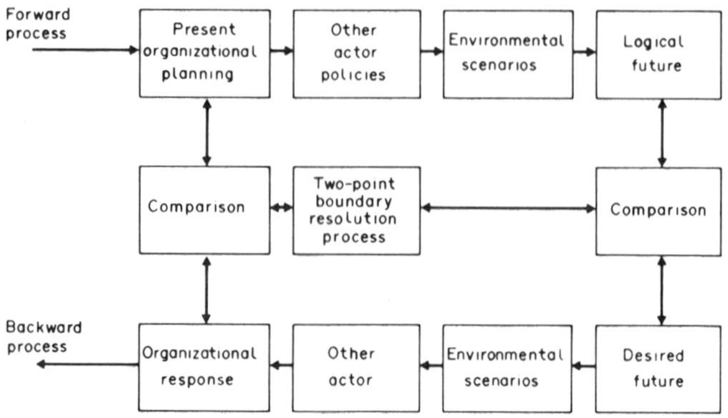

```
Forward
process  → [Present          ] → [Other    ] → [Environmental] → [Logical ]
           [organizational   ]   [actor    ]   [scenarios    ]   [future  ]
           [planning         ]   [policies ]
                ↕                                                    ↕
           [Comparison] ← [Two-point boundary resolution process] → [Comparison]
                ↕                                                    ↕
Backward
process  ← [Organizational] ← [Other] ← [Environmental] ← [Desired]
           [response      ]   [actor]   [scenarios    ]   [future ]
```

Strategic Planning 137

Formulation of a planning process for an organization as boundary problem enables us to explicitly structure the decision framework. Using decision theory notions, we identify three basic variables: (1) *planning policies* available to the organization, (2) *outcomes* the organization may realize in the future, and (3) *efficiencies* that show the probabilistic relationship between planning policies and outcomes.

These three variables are common to all decision processes, but the relationship among them is different for all projected planning processes and the desired planning processes. For the projected process the policies are *defined*, the efficiencies are estimated, and the probable outcomes are *deduced*. For the desired process the outcomes are *valued*, the efficiencies are *influenced*, and the policies are *developed*. This difference is due fundamentally to the way the problem is organized in each case. The organizing principle in both processes is *hierarchical*, but the dominance relationships are reversed. Our purpose is to show that the use of hierarchies as an organizing principle for the two-point boundary planning problem enables rich solutions to be developed because directions of dominance are made explicit.

The Forward Process

The hierarchy of the forward or projected process may be characterized in the following sequence:

```
[ Planning policies ] → [ Efficiencies ] → [ Outcomes ]
```

This process can be divided further by segmenting the efficiencies level into its two basic components: events caused by the purposeful behavior of other actors, and events caused by non-purposeful behavior (for example, by the weather). Purposeful behavior is itself a hierarchy, diagrammatically composed of the following elements:

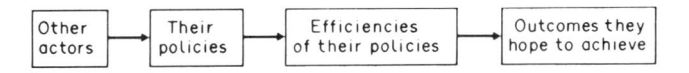

```
[ Other actors ] → [ Their policies ] → [ Efficiencies of their policies ] → [ Outcomes they hope to achieve ]
```

Some people have used the term transactional environment to describe other actors whose behavior directly affects organizational efficiencies. Such actors include suppliers, investors, customers, and the like. This analysis can, in turn, be expanded by adding another level to analyze the elements that contribute in the efficiency of the behavior of members of the transaction environment. Purposeful behavior of such actors has an indirect effect on the original organization; some use the term contextual environment to describe such effects. Exhibit 6-2 presents a diagram of the hierarchy of the projected process when transactional environment effects are explicitly included.

138 Analytical Planning

EXHIBIT 6-2. *Efficiencies*

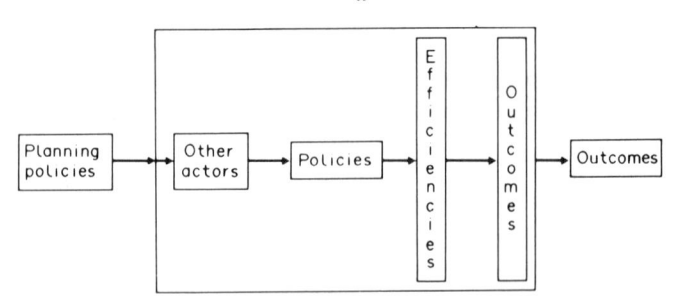

```
Planning  →  Other   →  Policies  →  Efficiencies  →  Outcomes  →  Outcomes
policies     actors
```

Note that the natural branching of the hierarchy for the projected process generates a large number of possible outcomes from a small number of initial policies. There are times when the elements (state variables) of the different outcomes are compatible and can thus be combined into a single composite outcome. From the pure outcomes of generating energy from nuclear power, fossil fuels, and solar energy one may use a strategy to combine all three outcomes. However, the outcomes may have incompatibilities that cannot be combined. For example, different plant site location outcomes cannot be combined to locate the plant in parts in each of them. Only one of the sites must be chosen.

The Backward Process

The hierarchy of the backward or desired process may be characterized in the following sequence:

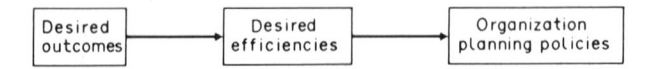

```
Desired    →  Desired       →  Organization
outcomes      efficiencies     planning policies
```

The desired process begins where the projected process ends. The organization first examines the range of projected outcomes and determines the set of outcomes for which it desires to increase the likelihood of achievement and also the set of outcomes for which it is desired to minimize the likelihood of achievement. Then it works back to the efficiencies to identify the changes that are critical to the achievement of this goal. These changes must occur through planning policies adopted by the organization to influence the action of key actors in the transactional environment. Such policies, called *counter-policies*, are developed to make other policies more effective. These counter-policies can achieve their purposes by (1) *instructing* the actors to change their choice directly, (2) *motivating* them to change the values of the outcomes, or (3) *inducing* them to change their behavior by affecting the efficiencies of their choices. Inducement can, of course, take place by direct action of the organization if it has the power to affect efficiencies, or by instructing or motivating members of the contextual environment, who are part of the actors' transactional environment.

The hierarchy for the desired process may be represented as in Exhibit 6-3.

Note that the two hierarchy processes produce opposite effects. The projected process starts with a small number of planning policies and produces a large number of possible outcomes. The desired process starts with a small number of outcomes and produces a large number of policy options. Hence an interesting and highly relevant two-point boundary problem is raised: how do we reconcile into one integrated solution the large number of options that are created when each problem is defined separately? As we shall see in the examples that follow: the vehicle to accomplish this is the prioritization principle of the Analytic Hierarchy Process used by iteration of the forward and backward planning processes.

EXHIBIT 6-3 *Desired Efficiency*

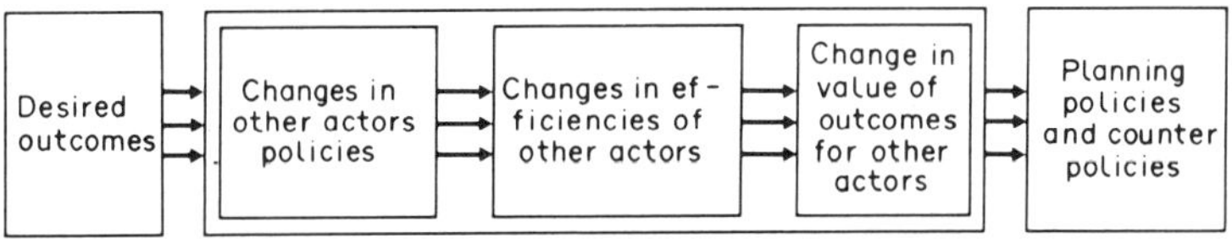

Desired outcomes → Changes in other actors policies → Changes in efficiencies of other actors → Change in value of outcomes for other actors → Planning policies and counter policies

6. Summary of Forward-Backward Analysis

The mechanics of carrying out the forward-backward process of planning can be summarized as follows.

Establish the forward process hierarchy by identifying the overall purpose of the planning exercise. It is the single element or focus of the hierarchy which occupies the top level. The second level should include the various forces, economic, political, social, which affect the outcome. The third level consists of the actors who manipulate these forces (sometimes it is possible to put the actors in the second level without any mention of the forces). In the fourth level one includes the objectives of each actor. The fifth level of the hierarchy is often optional and should include the policies that each actor pursues to fulfill his objectives. The sixth level is important. It involves the possible scenarios or outcomes that each actor is struggling to bring about as a result of pursuing his objectives (and applying his policies). The final level of the hierarchy is the composite outcome that is a result of all these different scenarios. After all, there is only one possible state of the world and it is a mixture of different people's attempts to shape it in a way which serves their interests. The composite scenario is also known as the logical outcome.

Because of the many and often conflicting interests that coalesce in this scenario, the result may be a dilution or weakening of what any of the actors wishes to see as an outcome. As a result one or several of the actors may work

140 *Analytical Planning*

to change some of their policies to bring about a new outcome that is closer to what they want to get.

This calls for the backward process. In this process each actor identifies for his second level one or several desired scenarios he wishes to see take place and sets priorities for them as to how well he wishes to see them affect his overall desired future. The third level consists of problems and opportunities that prevent the attainment of the scenarios. The fourth level includes actors (whether mentioned in the forward process or not) who can influence solution of the problems. The fifth level includes these actor's objectives. The sixth level may or may not include their policies. The seventh level includes one particular actor's policies (or change in objectives) which if pursued can affect the attainment of the desired futures.

After prioritization of these policies (or objectives) in the backward process, only the most important ones are used in a second forward process. They are included with the previous forward policies of just those actors desiring change. Prioritization of the second forward process is revised only from the level of objectives or if there is a level of policies then from that level downward. Then one compares the priorities of the composite likely outcome of the second forward process with the priorities of the *desired* futures of the first backward process to see if the logical future is driven closer to the desired future. If not, a second iteration of the backward process is carried out by changing the priorities of the desired futures and/or examining new policies. Again the important ones are substituted in a third forward process and scenario priorities are calculated and compared with those of the second backward process. The procedure is repeated until one has fairly exhausted the possibilities in search of ways to improve the logical or likely outcome.

State Variables

There is an alternative way to use the weights assigned to the outcomes. A scenario describes a state of a system. In that state the system has a particular structure and flows. To characterize these meaningfully one uses a set of variables called state variables which specify the structure and flows of the system in that state. Thus a set of state variables may be defined and used to describe an outcome of a planning process. These variables may range over the different aspects of an outcome: political, economic, social, legal. Each of the basic scenarios may be described in terms of the change in each of these variables from the status quo. The intensity of variations is indicated by a difference scale which ranges from -8 to 8. The interpretation of that scale is given in Exhibit 6-4.

7. Forward Planning Example: Future of Higher Education in the United States (1985–2000)

This illustration is based on an experiment conducted by twenty-eight college level teachers, mostly from the mathematical sciences, under the

Strategic Planning 141

EXHIBIT 6-4. *Scale For Difference Comparisons*

Difference in Values	Definition
0	no change in value
2(−2)	slight increase (decrease) in value
4(−4)	important increase (decrease) in value
6(−6)	remarkable increase (decrease) in value
8(−8)	maximum increase (decrease) in value
1, 3, 5, 7	intermediate values between the two
−1, −3, −5, −7	adjacent judgements

leadership of T. L. Saaty at an NSF Chautauqua type course in Operations Research and Systems Approach in February, 1976. The problem was to construct seven weighted scenarios and a composite scenario which would describe the future of higher education in the United States during the period 1985 through 2000.

Exhibit 6-5 presents the hierarchical structure of the factors, actors, and their motivating objectives which the group saw as a chain of influences that would affect the form that higher education will take between 1985 and 2000. No strict definitions of the various terms will be given, although during the development (which took approximately nine hours) comments were made on some of the intended meanings.

Seven scenarios are offered.

1. (PROJ)   1985-Projection of the present status quo (slight perturbation of present)
2. (VOTEC) Vocational-Technical Oriented (skill orientation)
3. (ALL)   Education for All (subsidized education)
4. (ELITE) Elitism (for those with money or exceptional talent)
5. (APUB)   All Public (government owned)
6. (TECH)   Technology Based (little use of classroom—use of media, computers)
7. (PT)   Part-Time Teaching—no research orientation

The characteristics which were considered and which were calibrated to give profiles of the various scenarios are given in Exhibit 6-6. The calibration numbers are integers between −8 and +8. These measurements were arrived at by consensus.

Zero (0) represents things as they now are (in the group's opinion). Positive integers represent the various degrees of "increasingness" or "more than now." Negative integers represent various degrees of "decreasingness" or "less than now." For example under Institution—Governance Structure we see 8 for Scenario 6. This means that the group thought that there would be a very large measure of administrative control (relative to the state of things as present) in a technology based higher education system in 1985 and after. On the other hand, if Scenario 3 (Education for All) were to prevail, then the value

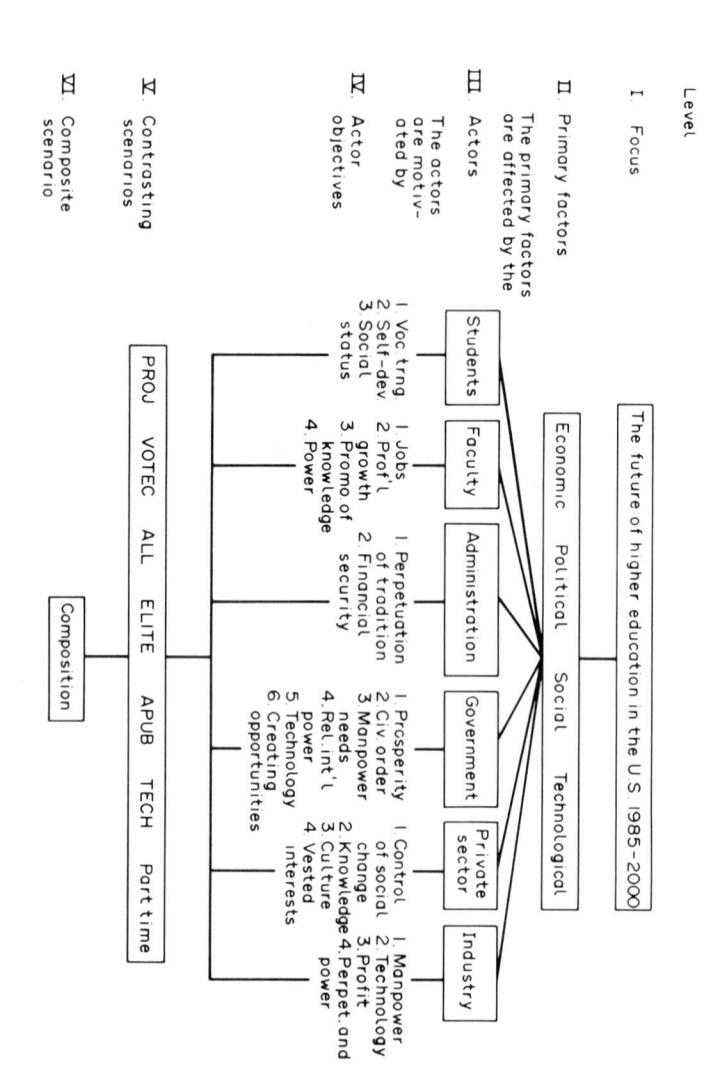

142   *Analytical Planning*

EXHIBIT 6-5 *A Hierarchy of Influences on Higher Education*

Level		
I	Focus	The future of higher education in the U.S. 1985–2000
II	Primary factors The primary factors are affected by the	Economic, Political, Social, Technological
III	Actors The actors are motivated by	Students, Faculty, Administration, Government, Private sector, Industry
IV	Actor objectives	Students: 1 Voc trng, 2 Self-dev, 3 Social status Faculty: 1 Jobs, 2 Prof'l growth, 3 Promo of knowledge, 4 Power Administration: 1 Perpetuation of tradition, 2 Financial security Government: 1 Prosperity, 2 Civ. order, 3 Manpower needs, 4 Rel. int'l power, 5 Technology, 6 Creating opportunities Private sector: 1 Control of social change, 2 Knowledge, 3 Culture, 4 Vested interests Industry: 1 Manpower, 2 Technology, 3 Profit, 4 Perpet. and power
V	Contrasting scenarios	PROJ, VOTEC, ALL, ELITE, APUB, TECH, Part time
VI	Composite scenario	Composition

Strategic Planning 143

EXHIBIT 6-6. *Seven Scenarios and the Calibration of their State Variables.* Scale: −8 +8

Scenario Weight Characteristics	.099 1 PROJ	.260 2 VOTEC	.203 3 ALL	.165 4 ELITE	.126 5 APUB	.067 6 TECH	.079 7 PT	COMP
STUDENTS								
1. Number	−3	+3	+6	−5	−2	+3	−3	.59
2. Type (I. Q.)	−2	−3	−5	+5	−2	−3	−2	−1.78
3. Function*	+2	−2	0	+2	0	−3	+3	.04
4. Jobs	+2	+6	−5	+6	+2	−3	+1	1.94
FACULTY								
1. Number	−3	+3	+6	−5	−2	−8	−6	− .39
2. Type (Ph.D.)	+2	0	−3	+3	+2	+3	−5	.14
3. Function (role on campus)	−3	−5	−3	+2	−3	−8	−8	−3.42
4. Job Security	−3	+2	+3	−5	−2	−6	−6	−1.19
5. Acad. Freedom	0	−3	0	+3	−2	−6	−8	−1.57
INSTITUTION								
1. Number	−2	+3	+3	−5	−2	−6	−2	− .45
2. Type (acad/non-acad)	−2	−6	−5	+5	−2	−5	−5	−2.93
3. Governance**	+3	+6	+4	−3	+3	+8	+8	3.31
4. Efficiency***	+3	+5	−3	+6	−2	−2	0	1.59
5. Accessibility	0	+3	+8	−5	+3	+6	+2	2.52
6. Culture-Entertain.	0	−3	+5	+5	+2	−5	−2	.82
7. Avail $ and other resources	−2	+3	+3	−3	0	−2	−5	.17
EDUCATION								
1. Curriculum (life-long learning)	+2	−3	+3	+5	+2	0	−2	.95
2. Length of Study	0	−5	+3	0	+2	+3	0	− .24
3. Value of a Degree	−2	0	−3	+6	−2	−3	−3	−.51
4. Cost per Student	+5	+5	+5	+6	+3	−2	−2	3.89
5. Research by Faculty	+2	−2	−2	+5	+2	−5	−6	−.46

144 *Analytical Planning*

of a degree (Education—Value of a Degree) would diminish considerably (−3) compared to how it is valued today. The row "Scenario Weight" and the column "Composite Weight" were empty at the beginning of this work. Filling them in is the object of this study.

The matrices listed below the Roman numerals refer to levels as indicated in Exhibit 6-5. Thus, for example, in the matrix I-1 the group believed that the Economy would have strong dominance over Technology *vis-à-vis* their impact on higher education in the United States in 1985. Thus a 5 is recorded in row 1 column 4.

There is only one matrix of pairwise dominance measures at the II-level since each pair is compared relative to its impact on higher education.

I-1 Which factor has the greatest impact on *Higher Education*?

Higher education	ECON	POL	SOC	TECH	EV
ECON	1	4	3	5	.549
POL	1/4	1	1/3	1	.106
SOC	1/3	3	1	2	.236
TECH	1/5	1	1/2	1	.109
					$\lambda_{max} = 4.06$

From this matrix we see, for instance, that the group considered the economic factor somewhat dominant (4) over the political factor in its impact on higher education.

Now each pair of items (actors) at level III is compared as to greater impact on the factors in level II. There are four dominance or importance matrices as shown.

II-1 Which actor has more impact on the economy?

ECON	S	F	A	G	P	I	EV
STU	1	3	1/2	1/8	1/5	1/8	.04
FAC	1/3	1	1/5	1/8	1/6	1/8	.02
ADM	2	5	1	1/7	1/3	1/5	.06
GOV	8	8	7	1	5	4	.47
PRI	5	6	3	1/5	1	1/5	.12
IND	8	8	5	1/4	5	1	.28
							$\lambda_{max} = 6.67$

Strategic Planning

II-2 Which actor has more impact in politics?

POL	S	F	A	G	P	I	EV
STU	1	1	3	1/7	1/5	1/7	.044
FAC	1	1	5	1/7	1/5	1/7	.044
ADM	1/3	1/3	1	1/7	1/5	1/7	.027
GOV	7	7	7	1	7	5	.500
PRI	5	5	5	1/7	1	1/6	.116
IND	7	7	7	1/5	6	1	.270
							$\lambda_{max} = 6.93$

II-3 Which actor has more impact on social issues?

SOC	S	F	A	G	P	I	EV
STU	1	3	3	1/5	1	1/5	.102
FAC	1/3	1	4	1/5	1/3	1/4	.067
ADM	1/3	1/4	1	1/5	1/5	1/5	.037
GOV	5	5	5	1	4	3	.411
PRI	1	3	5	1/4	1	1/3	.121
IND	5	4	5	1/3	3	1	.262
							$\lambda_{max} = 6.59$

II-4 Which actor has more impact on technology?

TECH	S	F	A	G	P	I	EV
STU	1	1/7	1/3	1/8	1/8	1/9	.022
FAC	7	1	7	1/4	1/3	1/5	.105
ADM	3	1/7	1	1/7	1/7	1/8	.034
GOV	8	4	7	1	2	1/3	.231
PRI	8	3	7	1/2	1	1/5	.165
IND	9	5	8	3	5	1	.443
							$\lambda_{max} = 6.67$

The objectives of each of the six actors are compared pairwise for each of the actors resulting in an eigenvector which essentially orders and weights the objectives.

III-1 Which objective is more important to the student?

STUDENT	VT	SD	SS	EV
Voc. Trng.	1	4	7	.687
Self-Devel.	1/4	1	5	.243
Soc. Status	1/7	1/5	1	.069
				$\lambda_{max} = 3.12$

III-2 Which objective is more important to the faculty?

FACULTY	J	PG	PK	P	EV
Jobs	1	5	4	6	.596
Prof. Growth	1/5	1	1	3	.151
Promo. Knowl.	1/4	1	1	5	.190
Power	1/4	1/3	1/5	1	.060

$\lambda_{max} = 4.17$

III-3 Which objective is more important to the administration?

ADMIN	P	FS	EV
Perpetuation (Tradition)	1	1/3	.250
Financial Security	3	1	.750

$\lambda_{max} = 2.00$

III-4 Which objective is more important to the government?

GOV	P	CO	M	RIP	T	OPP	EV
Prosperity	1	1/5	3	3	5	6	.203
Civ. Order	5	1	5	7	8	8	.516
Manpower	1/3	1/5	1	1/2	3	5	.092
Rel. Int'l Power	1/3	1/7	2	1	3	5	.110
Technology	1/5	1/8	1/3	1/3	1	4	.051
Create Oppor.	1/6	1/8	1/5	1/5	1/4	1	.027

$\lambda_{max} = 6.56$

III-5 Which objective is more important to private individual donors?

PRI	CSC	K	C	VI	EV
Con. Soc. Ch.	1	3	3	1/5	.220
Knowledge	1/3	1	3	1/3	.139
Culture	1/3	1/3	1	1/6	.065
Vest. Int.	5	3	6	1	.576

$\lambda_{max} = 4.31$

Strategic Planning

III-6 Which objective is more important to industry?

IND	M	T	P	P&P	E V
Manpower	1	1/4	1/9	1/7	.040
Technology	4	1	1/7	1/7	.084
Profit	9	7	1	1/3	.331
Perpetuation and Power	7	7	3	1	.546

$$\lambda_{max} = 4.40$$

The next step was to find the importance of the actors relative to their impact on the factors which affect higher education. This is done by multiplying the matrix of eigenvectors of the actors with respect to each factor in level III on the right by the eigenvector obtained for level II.

$$\begin{matrix} & \text{ECON} & \text{POL} & \text{SOC} & \text{TECH} \end{matrix}$$

$$\begin{bmatrix} S \\ F \\ A \\ G \\ P \\ I \end{bmatrix} \begin{bmatrix} .04 & .04 & .10 & .02 \\ .02 & .04 & .07 & .10 \\ .06 & .03 & .04 & .03 \\ .47 & .49 & .41 & .23 \\ .12 & .12 & .16 & .16 \\ .28 & .29 & .26 & .44 \end{bmatrix} \times \begin{bmatrix} .55 \\ .11 \\ .24 \\ .11 \end{bmatrix} \begin{matrix} \text{EC} \\ \text{POL} \\ \text{SOC} \\ \text{TE} \end{matrix} = \begin{bmatrix} .05 \\ .04 \\ .05 \\ \underline{.44} \\ .13 \\ \underline{.29} \end{bmatrix} \begin{matrix} S \\ F \\ A \\ G \\ P \\ I \end{matrix}$$

Since Government and Industry account for 73% (= .44 + .29) of the impact on the four primary factors which affect higher education, it was decided to use only these two actors to obtain the weights for the scenarios. Should one decide to use more actors, the computations follow the same procedure shown below, but the amount of work is increased.

Now we want to find the important objectives of the two actors; government and industry. To do this, we multiply the eigenvector for objectives by the respective actor weight which was just calculated.

For Government

$$.44 \begin{bmatrix} .20 \\ .52 \\ .09 \\ .11 \\ .05 \\ .03 \end{bmatrix} = \begin{bmatrix} .09 \\ .23 \\ .02 \\ .05 \\ .02 \\ .01 \end{bmatrix} \begin{matrix} \textit{Prosperity} \\ \textit{Civ. Order} \\ \textit{Manpower} \\ \textit{R I P} \\ \textit{Technology} \\ \textit{Create Oppor.} \end{matrix}$$

For Industry

$$.29 \begin{bmatrix} .04 \\ .08 \\ .33 \\ .55 \end{bmatrix} = \begin{bmatrix} .01 \\ .02 \\ .10 \\ .16 \end{bmatrix} \begin{matrix} \textit{Manpower} \\ \textit{Technology} \\ \textit{Profit} \\ \textit{Perpet \& Power} \end{matrix}$$

148   *Analytical Planning*

From this we see that the most influential objectives are *prosperity* and *civil order* for Government and *profit* and *perpetuation and power* for Industry. Using these four objectives and normalizing their weights we get the weight vector.

$$\begin{bmatrix} .16 \\ .40 \\ .17 \\ .27 \end{bmatrix} \begin{array}{l} \text{Prosperity} \\ \text{Civ. Order} \\ \text{Profit} \\ \text{Perpet \& Power} \end{array}$$

This vector will be used to get our scenario weights.

The final step necessary to get our scenario weights is to construct the dominance matrices for the seven scenarios with respect to each of the objectives (four in our case).

IV-1 Which scenario has more impact on the prosperity of the United States?

PROSP	PROJ	VT	EA	E	AP	TB	PT	EV
PROJ	1	1/5	1/5	5	1	5	5	.129
VOC TECH	5	1	3	7	1	5	5	.329
ED ALL	5	3	1	7	5	5	5	.275
ELITE	1/5	1/7	1/7	1	1/5	3	1	.041
ALL PUB	1	1	1/5	5	1	3	5	.149
TECH BASED	1/5	1/5	1/5	1/3	1/3	1	1/3	.032
PART-TIME	1/5	1/5	1/5	1	1/5	3	1	.045
								$\lambda_{max} = 7.96$

IV-2 Which scenario has more impact on the civil order of the United States?

CIV ORD	PROJ	VT	EA	E	AP	TB	PT	EV
PROJ	1	1/3	1/5	5	1	3	3	.125
VOC TECH	3	1	1/3	5	1	3	3	.180
ED ALL	5	3	1	5	3	5	5	.369
ELITE	1/5	1/5	1/5	1	1/5	1/3	1/2	.033
ALL PUB	1	1	1/3	5	1	5	5	.177
TECH BASED	1/3	1/3	1/5	3	1/5	1	1/3	.050
PART-TIME	1/3	1/3	1/5	2	1/5	3	1	.065
								$\lambda_{max} = 7.60$

Strategic Planning 149

IV-3 Which scenario has more impact on profitability?

PROFIT	PROJ	VT	ALL	ELITE	APUB	TECH	PT	EV
PROJ	1	1/5	4	1/5	3	1/3	1/3	.057
VOC TECH	5	1	7	1	3	5	5	.309
ED ALL	1/4	1/7	1	1/8	1/3	1/3	1/3	.028
ELITE	5	1	8	1	6	5	5	.331
ALL PUB	1/3	1/3	3	1/6	1	1/4	1/3	.048
TECH	3	1/5	3	1/5	4	1	3	.129
PART-TIME	3	1/5	3	1/5	3	1/3	1	.089

$\lambda_{max} = 7.79$

IV-4 Which scenario has more impact on perpetuating industrial methods and power?

P&P	PROJ	VT	ALL	ELITE	APUB	TECH	PT	EV
PROJ	1	1/7	7	1/5	1	1/3	1/4	.062
VOC TECH	7	1	5	1	5	3	5	.306
ED ALL	1/7	1/5	1	1/8	1/5	1/3	1/4	.026
ELITE	5	1	8	1	6	5	5	.330
ALL PUB	1	1/5	5	1/6	1	3	1/2	.085
TECH	3	1/3	3	1/5	1/3	1	1/2	.075
PART-TIME	4	1/5	4	1/5	2	2	1	.115

$\lambda_{max} = 7.94$

To obtain the scenario weights, we multiply the matrix of eigenvectors just obtained by the weight vector for the four most influential factors (prosperity, civil order, profit and perpetuation and power). This product yields the scenario weights. Exhibit 6-6 has these weights placed over the scenario names.

$$\begin{matrix} \text{PROS} & \text{CORD} & \text{PROF} & \text{P\&P} \end{matrix}$$
$$\begin{bmatrix} .129 & .125 & .067 & .062 \\ .329 & .180 & .309 & .306 \\ .275 & .369 & .028 & .026 \\ .041 & .033 & .331 & .330 \\ .149 & .177 & .048 & .085 \\ .032 & .050 & .128 & .075 \\ .045 & .065 & .089 & .115 \end{bmatrix} \begin{bmatrix} .16 \\ .40 \\ .17 \\ .27 \end{bmatrix} = \begin{bmatrix} .099 \\ .260 \\ .203 \\ .165 \\ .126 \\ .067 \\ .079 \end{bmatrix}$$

We note that the second scenario has the greatest weight (.260). This can be interpreted as the scenario most heavily favored by the group. A description of this scenario could be:

150 *Analytical Planning*

"Higher education in the United States in 1985 and beyond will be vocational-technical oriented. There will be more students who will be less bright (as measured by I.Q.) and who will be a little less active in influencing the institution, but they will have no problem in getting jobs upon graduation."

"There will be more faculty of about the same intellectual level as today, but they will have considerably less to say about the governing of the university. Their job security will be a little better than it is now, but there will be less academic freedom. As for the institutions, there will be more of them, but with much less academic orientation. The administration will control things to a much greater degree and the efficiency (less student attrition) will be considerably higher. The schools will be more accessible but their cultural and entertainment roles will decrease somewhat. The availability of dollar and other resources will be greater than at present."

"Finally, the type of curriculum will be more vocationally (skill) oriented with less of the learning experience which benefits one for a lifetime. The length of time it takes to complete a degree program will be considerably less and the value of a degree will not be any more or less than at present. The per student cost will rise quite a bit. There will be a little less research going on."

We now obtain the composite scenario: a single scenario obtained by finding composite scale measurement for each of the characteristics. The composite scale measurement for a characteristic is obtained by forming the sum of the products of scenario weight by the corresponding characteristic measurement, for example, for the number of students we have:

$(-3)(.099) + (2)(.260) + (6)(.203) + (-5)(.165) + (-2)(.126) + (3)(.067) + (-3)(.079) = .59.$

This measurement is found in Exhibit 6-6 in the last column on the right. Similarly for the other characteristics. An interpretation of the composite scenario might be:

"Higher Education in the United States in 1985 and beyond will witness not much, if any, increase in total enrollment. The student will exhibit slightly lower performance levels as measured by the type of standardized tests we have today. Students will play about the same role as they do today in setting university educational policy. Their chances for jobs upon graduation will be a little better than at present."

"The faculty characteristics will be about the same as today regarding numbers, Ph.D. holders. However, faculty will play considerably less of a role in campus affairs while possessing somewhat less academic freedom and job security."

"The number of institutions of higher education will not change much, if at all. They will be definitely less academically oriented with the administration exhibiting more control. There will be some increase in efficiency (less student attrition). Accessibility will be greater but their cultural and entertainment roles will be about the same as in 1976. There will be practically no increase in dollar resources."

"The Life-long learning qualities of the curriculum will not undergo much change, nor will the length of study, or the value of a degree. Costs will continue to increase significantly. The amount of faculty research will be about the same."

It was suggested that different results might be obtained had we not had Level II. Then we would need the eigenvector for the 6 × 6 dominance matrix for the actors. The dominance matrix was constructed yielding:

HIGHER EDUC	S	F	A	G	P	I	E V
STU	1	3	3	1/6	1	1/5	.09
FAC	1/3	1	1/3	1/6	1/3	1/5	.04
ADM	1/3	3	1	1/6	1/3	1/5	.05
GOV	6	6	6	1	5	3	.44
PRI	1	3	3	1/5	1	1/5	.09
IND	5	5	5	1/3	5	1	.28
						$\lambda_{max} = 6.50$	

When this vector is compared with the actors' weights obtained previously, we see close agreement.

It was further suggested that another primary factor, Ideology, be added at Level II. A new dominance matrix was formed for Level II (same as original with an added row and column). It follows:

HIGHER EDUC	ECON	POL	SOC	TECH	IDEO	E V
ECON	1	4	3	5	6	.50
POL	1/4	1	1/3	1	1	.29
SOC	1/3	3	1	2	3	.22
TECH	1/5	1	1	1	1	.10
IDEO	1/6	1	1	1	1	.09
					$\lambda_{max} = 5.05$	

Comparing this eigenvector with the original one for II we again see close agreement.

8. Backward Planning Example with Program Selection and Allocation of Resources for Commercial Power Generation Engineering

There is a component used in commercial power generation facilities that is technologically complex, has experienced problems in field operation, and is still in production. Research is performed to understand the field operations, prepare current units to go on line, and to devise improvements to be used in future construction. Strategic planning is required for program choice (the equivalent of policy choice in behavioral problems) for a five year time span to decide how to do this research.

A backward planning process takes the desired outcome and pyramids down to the programs and subprograms required to obtain the desired outcome. A backward planning hierarchy should be prepared after a forward planning process is complete. The results of the forward planning sketched in Exhibit 6-7 can and should impact the backward planning. The forward

152 *Analytical Planning*

EXHIBIT 6-7. *Forward Process Hierarchy*

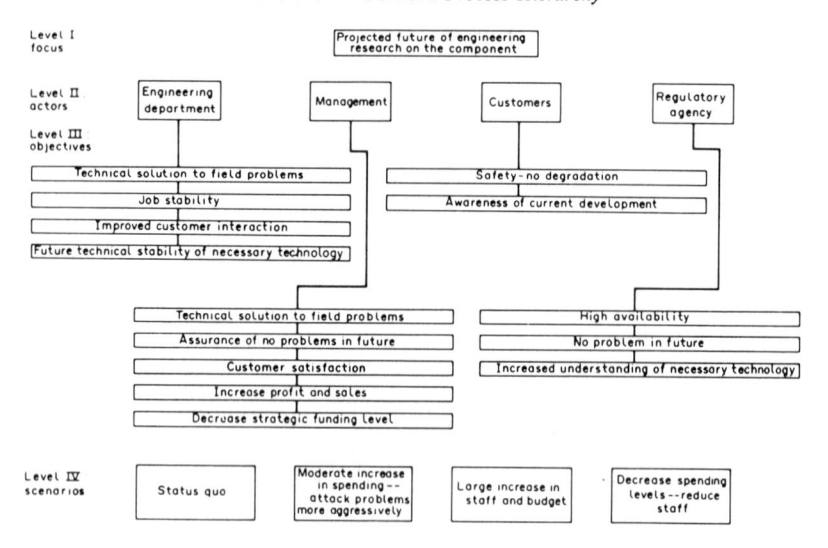

Level I focus	Projected future of engineering research on the component
Level II actors	Engineering department — Management — Customers — Regulatory agency
Level III objectives	Technical solution to field problems; Job stability; Improved customer interaction; Future technical stability of necessary technology; Safety-no degradation; Awareness of current development; Technical solution to field problems; Assurance of no problems in future; Customer satisfaction; Increase profit and sales; Decrease strategic funding level; High availability; No problem in future; Increased understanding of necessary technology
Level IV scenarios	Status quo; Moderate increase in spending — attack problems more aggressively; Large increase in staff and budget; Decrease spending levels — reduce staff

process was used to identify the contrast scenarios that are likely futures of engineering research on the component.

The backward process hierarchy is shown in Exhibit 6-8. Its focus is the desired future of engineering research on the component. The study was done to see what needed doing in order to improve the component. The desired scenario became "moderate increase in spending-attack problems more aggressively."

This scenario was adopted for the analysis because it provided the resources to deal with the various technical problems that could occur with the component. It is one of the four contrast scenarios of the forward process and was judged to be the most likely one.

EXHIBIT 6-8. *Backward Process Hierarchy*

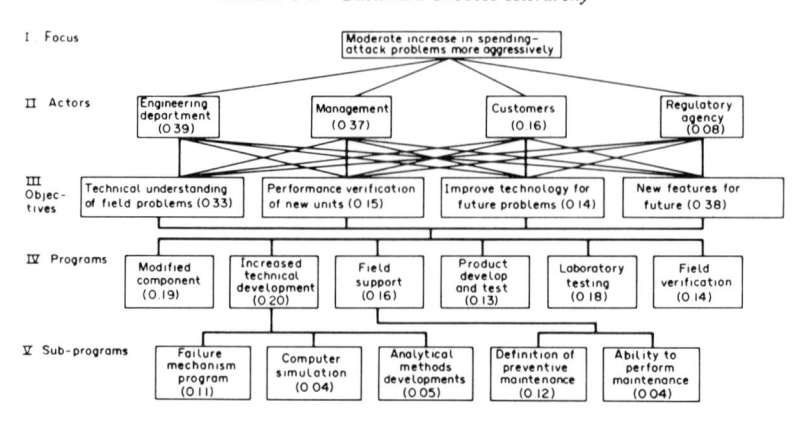

I Focus	Moderate increase in spending — attack problems more aggressively
II Actors	Engineering department (0.39); Management (0.37); Customers (0.16); Regulatory agency (0.08)
III Objectives	Technical understanding of field problems (0.33); Performance verification of new units (0.15); Improve technology for future problems (0.14); New features for future (0.38)
IV Programs	Modified component (0.19); Increased technical development (0.20); Field support (0.16); Product develop and test (0.13); Laboratory testing (0.18); Field verification (0.14)
V Sub-programs	Failure mechanism program (0.11); Computer simulation (0.04); Analytical methods developments (0.05); Definition of preventive maintenance (0.12); Ability to perform maintenance (0.04)

Level II of the backward process includes the four actors who had an impact on bringing about the desired scenario. Level III includes the objectives of the organization manufacturing the component and how important they are to each of the key actors. Level IV includes the possible programs to be pursued to bring about the desired future. Further details of this level are itemized in level V as subprograms. They are the divisible elements of the second and third programs. The first and last three programs are not divisible. The prioritization process elicited judgments in response to the question: Which of two elements being compared contributes more strongly to a higher level element in the hierarchy and how strongly? The priority of each element is listed in the exhibit. It indicates the relative benefit of that element.

Next a benefit-cost analysis was carried out using the benefit priorities for the programs identified in the backward hierarchy and relative costs estimated in dollars for each of the six programs. Both benefits and costs are shown in Exhibit 6-9. The benefit to cost ratios were formed and indicate that the third program is the most desired followed by the fourth and then the second programs. Also marginal analysis was carried out by listing the costs in increasing order and then simply bringing their corresponding benefits above them.

| Benefits | .13 | .16 | .20 | .14 | .18 | .19 |
| Costs | .06 | .07 | .11 | .17 | .29 | .30 |

EXHIBIT 6-9. *Benefit-Cost Comparison*

Program	Cost Normalized Dollars	Benefit	Ratio (Benefit-Cost)
Modified component	.30	.19	0.63
Increased technical development	.11	.20	1.82
Field support	.07	.16	2.29
Product develop and test	.06	.13	2.17
Laboratory testing	.29	.18	0.62
Field verification	.17	.14	0.82

Then we take the first elements and form its benefit to cost ratio and follow it by comparative differences between benefits divided by corresponding differences in costs. However, if any ratio has a negative value the program

154 Analytical Planning

producing that ratio is eliminated and the ratio of the differences is formed using the next program and so on. We have $\frac{.13}{.06} = 2.17$, $\frac{.16 - .13}{.07 - .06} = 3$, $\frac{.20 - .16}{.11 - .07} = 1$, $\frac{.14 - .20}{.17 - .11}$ which is a negative number therefore omit, $\frac{.18 - .20}{.30 - .11}$ which is also negative and omitted. Thus the most desired program is field support, the third one on the list, followed by the fourth and then the second programs.

9. Forward-Backward Planning for a Consumer Products Manufacturer*

Company X is a leading manufacturer of home products such as laundry detergents, dishwashing liquids, window cleaners, and the like. The position of Company X in the home products industry is volatile due to current economic conditions. For example, studies conducted by X's marketing department indicate that consumers are becoming more price conscious and less brand-loyal. Consequently, generic products and other inexpensive brands have increased their market share (per cent of total sales in the home products industry) at the expense of nationally known brands such as those produced by Company X.

The position of X in the industry is tenuous not only because of economic conditions and intensified competition but also because of X's historic dominance of the market. During the 1960s and 1970s, Company X held a majority share of the total industry market—nearly three times the percentage of its closest competition. Assured of its popularity with consumers, X was able to demand and receive many concessions from retailers. For example, X was able to withhold matching advertising resources from those retailers who did not adhere to rigidly defined promotional requirements including prominent and attractive store displays, local TV and newspaper advertisements, and restricting the shelf space available to competitors. Consequently, Company X gained a reputation among retailers as a "corporate bully" which freely used its consumer popularity as a weapon to ensure that the "rules of the game" served its interests. Relations between Company X and retailers steadily deteriorated and recently a group of large retailers filed a suit with the Federal Trade Commission alleging unfair trade practices and demanding compensation for X's past actions.

Decreased brand-loyalty has given retailers more ammunition to potentially reduce the control that X has in the industry. For example, retailers will often

---

*We acknowledge with thanks a first draft of this example developed by Regina Ceisler, Frank Domieson and Michelle Keane.

Strategic Planning 155

have the freedom to make additional price reductions on sale items or set shelf prices lower on some competitor's products than on others. Since customers are not as brand-loyal as they once were, they will buy the less expensive items. Such actions have been used by retailers in retaliation against a perceived abuse of power on X's part.

In summary, X is challenged with a changing environment and must make decisions to survive successfully in this new environment. Specifically, Company X has determined that it must first strive to improve its relations with retailers before it can hope to compete effectively with generic and other less expensive brands. Our purpose is to show how X might do this through the forward-backward planning process.

We note that improving relations with retailers is only one component of a larger plan that X is designing to regain its former prominence. For example, X has also decided to update the packaging of some of its older products to portray a new and more attractive image. Also, it is important to note that promotional strategies are the principal tools that might be used by X to improve its relations with retailers. Promotional strategies include specific arrangements between manufacturers and retailers concerning occasional product discounts, special offers (e.g., two for the price of one), local (versus national) advertising, store displays and so on. Company X has decided to design new promotional strategies which are congruent with its own interests and those of retailers.

A. First Forward Planning Process: Projecting Promotional Techniques in the Home Products Industry

In the first forward planning process, which is the descriptive arm of the Analytic Hierarchy Process, the planners constructed the hierarchy (Exhibit 6–10) after scanning the environment in which Company X is embedded. Recall that the purpose of the forward process is to project a logical future given certain assumptions about current trends such as the objectives being pursued by prominent actors who play a role in the home products industry.

In this example, Company X is attempting to project industry-wide promotional strategies for the next 10 years. The influence of X on these strategies, while potentially substantial, will be moderated by the influence of retailers and competitors in the home products industry. One might think that consumers should also be included among the prominent actors. Remember, however, that the problem is to improve X's relations with *retailers*. The perceived needs of consumers are subsumed within the objectives of retailers.

The hierarchy has the following levels:

Level 1: Focus of the Problem. The focus of this problem is to predict the future of promotional techniques in the home products industry.

Level 2: Actors. In this level the planners determined what actors exert influence on the industry-wide promotional techniques. Moreover, the planners weighed the relative influence of these actors. Therefore, the relevant question at this level was "with respect to the future of promotional techniques, what is the relative influence of Retailers, Company X, and Competitors?" These actors are described below.

Level 3: Actor's Objectives. In this level, for example, the planners asked "With respect to Retailers, what is the importance of weakening X, relative to decreasing promotional requirements?" and so on for each pair of objectives for each of the actors identified in the second level.

Level 4: Actor's Policies. In Level 4 the planners identified policies employed by actors in pursuit of their respective objectives. They asked themselves "With respect to weakening X, what is the relative importance of allocating shelf space between X's products and those of its competitors?" and so on for each objective identified in the third level.

Level 5: Exploratory Scenarios. In this level the planners identified three scenarios (discussed below) which best described the range of alternative futures.

Level 6: Composite Scenario. The planners realized that the most likely scenario will be some mixture of the three scenarios identified in the fifth level. The composite scenario will be described later.

From prioritizations for level 2, the planners were able to determine the normalized weight for each actor adjusted for power. In the interest of simplicity, the pairwise comparison matrices are not presented here.

However, a brief description of the actors will help to explain the priorities derived from the level 2 pairwise comparisons.

Retailers: Owners and operators of stores in which X's products (and those of its competitors) are displayed and sold. While retailers have some impact on which promotional strategies will be used, they are not as influential as manufacturers represented by X and its competitors.

Company X: Despite the fact that X has lost some of its former prominence, it is still the leading manufacturer in the home products industry. In fact, its influence over the future of industry-wide promotional strategies is judged to be greater than the influence of its competitors combined.

Competitors: The influence of competitors is substantial and seems to be increasing steadily. However, in the opinion of the planners, competitors still do not wield the power of Company X.

Next, the planners determined the priorities for the actors' objectives and for policies currently being used to fulfill those objectives. Note that the objectives of Company X and those of its competitors are very similar. Also, X and its competitors are utilizing similar policies in pursuit of those objectives. In other words, manufacturers in the home products industry are in a "zero sum" situation where greater fulfillment of X's objectives will have an adverse effect on competitors and vise versa.

Finally, the planners determined the priorities of the scenarios given the actors, objectives, and policies involved. These priorities indicate the relative likelihood of the three scenarios. A brief description of the scenarios follows:

(I) *Maintain Status Quo*—Billback system with strict adherence to promotional requirements. In a billback system the retailer pays the manufacturer a wholesale price for items and there are no incentives (i.e., reduced wholesale price) for retailer cooperation with promotional plans. Retailers must bill manufacturers for promotional costs incurred.

(II) *Off-Invoice with Flexibility*—Off-invoice system with performance flexibility and no retaliatory action (i.e., withholding cooperative advertising dollars) by manufacturers if retailers do not strictly adhere to promotional requirements. In an off-invoice system manufacturers will adjust the wholesale price as an incentive for retailer cooperation with or initiation of promotional plans.

(III) *Off-Invoice without Flexibility*—Off-invoice system without performance flexibility. If a supermarket uses only handbills and window banners for advertising specials and not newspaper as required by the manufacturers, they will not receive co-operative advertising dollars.

As illustrated in Exhibit 6-10, an off-invoice system with flexibility appears to be the most likely exploratory scenario for future promotional strategies in the home products industry, given the objectives of the retailers, Company X, and Competitors. However, as we have often pointed out, the composite scenario may involve a mix of the three scenarios because no single type of approach would work to satisfy everyone.

With relative weights assigned to the three scenarios, we are in a position to formulate a composite scenario. The composite scenario is represented by four state variables: sales revenue, volume of goods shipped, promotional dollars saved, and cash flow. A brief explanation of state variable cash flow is necessary. The present system allows X to invest the promotional dollars until retailers bill X for their performance. Under an Off-invoice system, retailers will receive the promotion allowances immediately and thus X cannot invest the money.

We will first place the state variables in the priority order according to their importance to company X (Exhibit 6-11). The importance index thus achieved will be used later when assessing the degree of convergence between the likely future and the desired future—convergence achieved through the addition of policies identified in the backward process which we discuss later.

Next, state variables are used to provide a profile of the various scenarios. The calibration numbers are integers between -8 and 8. As noted earlier, zero represents things as they are now in the planners' opinion. Positive integers represent various degrees of "increasingness" or "more than now." Negative integers represents varying degrees of "decreasingness" or "less than now." For example, in Exhibit 6-12 under Cash Flow we see -6 for scenario 2, off-invoice with flexibility. This reflects the fact that X will have significantly less cash on hand since retailers will receive cooperative promotional dollars immediately rather than upon receipt of a bill for retailer expenses. (If a state

158   *Analytical Planning*

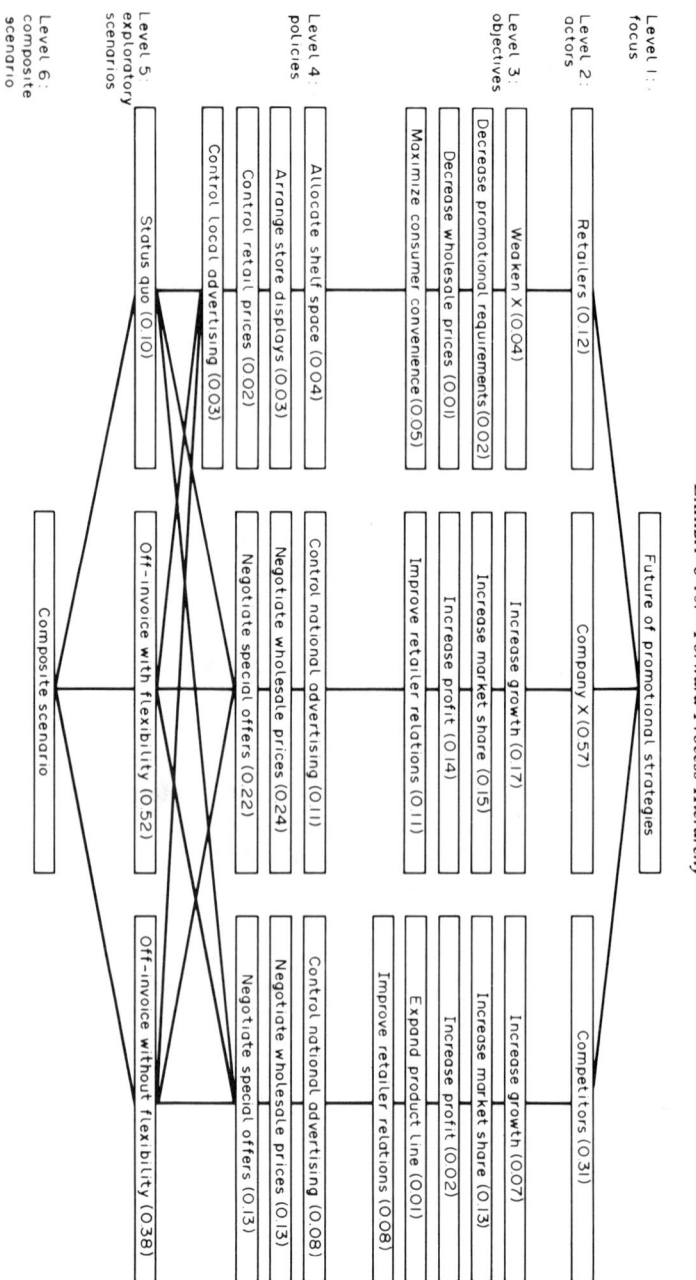

EXHIBIT 6-10. *Forward Process Hierarchy*

Level 1: focus		Future of promotional strategies	
Level 2: actors	Retailers (0.12)	Company X (0.57)	Competitors (0.31)
Level 3: objectives	Weaken X (0.04) Decrease promotional requirements (0.02) Decrease wholesale prices (0.01) Maximize consumer convenience (0.05)	Increase growth (0.17) Increase market share (0.15) Increase profit (0.14) Improve retailer relations (0.11)	Increase growth (0.07) Increase market share (0.13) Increase profit (0.02) Expand product line (0.01) Improve retailer relations (0.08)
Level 4: policies	Allocate shelf space (0.04) Arrange store displays (0.03) Control retail prices (0.02) Control local advertising (0.03)	Control national advertising (0.11) Negotiate wholesale prices (0.24) Negotiate special offers (0.22)	Control national advertising (0.08) Negotiate wholesale prices (0.13) Negotiate special offers (0.13)
Level 5: exploratory scenarios	Status quo (0.10)	Off-invoice with flexibility (0.52)	Off-invoice without flexibility (0.38)
Level 6: composite scenario		Composite scenario	

Exhibit 6-11.

State variables	Sales revenue	Volume shipped	Promotional savings	Cash flow	Vector weights
Sales revenue	1	1/3	4	6	.289
Volume shipped	3	1	5	7	.554
Promotional savings	1/4	1/5	1	3	.106
Cash flow	1/6	1/7	1/3	1	.051
				λ_{max}	= 4.173
				C.I.	= .058
				C.R.	= .064

Exhibit 6-12. *Calibration of State Variables With Respect to Scenarios*
(First Forward Process)

	(.10) Status quo	(.52) Off-invoice with flexibility	(.38) Off-invoice without flexibility	First forward process
Sales	2	7	5	5.74
Volume shipped	2	6	4	4.84
Promotional dollars saved	−2	4	5	3.78
Cash flow	2	−6	−5	−4.82
Composite				4.49

variable is a cost rather than a benefit variable, its increase would be negative and decrease positive so the total would still indicate net gain).

The next step is to obtain the composite scenario: As illustrated earlier, the composite scale measurement for a state variable is obtained by forming the sum of the products of scenario weights (given above the scenario name in Exhibit 6-12) by the corresponding state variable measurement. For example, for sales revenue we have: $(2)(.10) + (7)(.52) + (5)(.38) = 5.74$. The interpretation of this number is the same ("more than now"/"less than now") as for the calibration of the state variables themselves. Thus, it appears that sales revenues will increase rather dramatically given the likely promotional techniques of the future.

An interpretation of this scenario would be: "Promotional programs in the future will result in significant increases in sales revenues and a moderate increase in the volume of goods shipped. Promotional dollars saved will increase and there will be a rather substantial adverse effect on X's cash flows."

160 *Analytical Planning*

The composite scale measurement is obtained by forming the sum of the products of state variable weights (Exhibit 6-11) by the state variable measurement obtained above (Exhibit 6-12). Thus we have: $(.289)(5.74) + (.554)(4.84) + (.106)(3.78) + (.051)(-4.82) = 4.49$. This composite scale measurement (4.49) is not a "weight" or "priority ranking"; rather, it is used merely as a global measure or benchmark against which we will measure the degree of convergence between the likely and desired futures produced by the addition of policies identified in the backward process.

B. Backward Planning Process: Desired Future of X and its Retailer Relations

The backward process is the normative arm of the AHP and is critically important because it identifies policies which could produce convergence of the likely and desired futures of the company. In addition to identifying the best policies to pursue, the backward process enumerates various problems that could occur by implementing alternative promotional programs. The backward process has the following levels (Exhibit 6-13): Level 1—The Focus of the Desired Future; Level 2—Desired Scenarios of that Future; Level 3—Problems and Opportunities Facing the Future; Level 4—Actors Who Control Those Problems and Opportunities; Level 5—Objectives (or Policies) of a Particular Actor (in this case Company X) Wishing to Influence the Other Actors. On completing the priorities of this process, one selects the highest priority policies and adjoins them to those of the relevant actor in a second forward process to test their effect on the logical future. Prioritization in this case is done from that point downward.

EXHIBIT 6-13. *Backward Process Hierarchy*

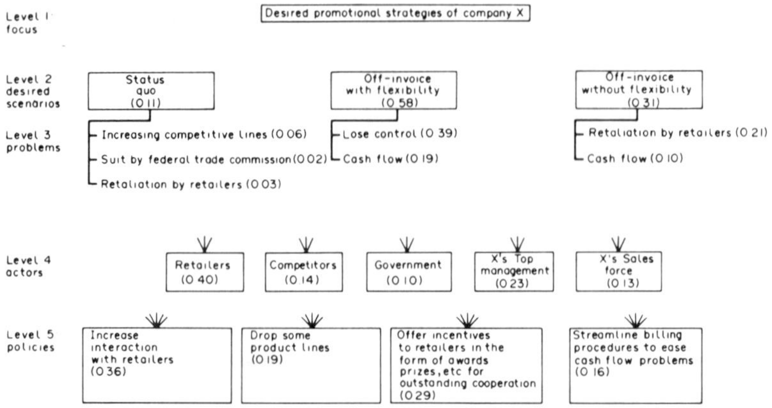

Level 1 focus: Desired promotional strategies of company X

Level 2 desired scenarios:
- Status quo (0.11)
- Off-invoice with flexibility (0.58)
- Off-invoice without flexibility (0.31)

Level 3 problems:
- Increasing competitive lines (0.06)
- Suit by federal trade commission (0.02)
- Retaliation by retailers (0.03)
- Lose control (0.39)
- Cash flow (0.19)
- Retaliation by retailers (0.21)
- Cash flow (0.10)

Level 4 actors:
- Retailers (0.40)
- Competitors (0.14)
- Government (0.10)
- X's Top management (0.23)
- X's Sales force (0.13)

Level 5 policies:
- Increase interaction with retailers (0.36)
- Drop some product lines (0.19)
- Offer incentives to retailers in the form of awards prizes, etc for outstanding cooperation (0.29)
- Streamline billing procedures to ease cash flow problems (0.16)

Strategic Planning 161

In the backward process, the planners for Company X identified Off-Invoice With Flexibility as the desired scenario which is the same exploratory scenario they projected to be the most likely future in the first forward process. Given that the likely and desired futures of promotional techniques coincide, in the planners' judgments, there is a high probability that the policies identified in the backward process will produce *some* convergence of the likely and desired futures. The primary concern of the planners is *how much* convergence will be produced with the addition of these policies. To measure this the planners must return to the forward process for a second iteration, this time taking into consideration the policies identified in the backward process.

C. Second Forward Process: Measuring Convergence

The planners selected the three policies with the highest relative weights in the backward process and introduced them into a second forward process to assess the amount of convergence they produce. A brief description of the three high priority policies is provided below.

Increase Interaction With Retailers: At present only X's sales force interacts directly with retailers. As a result, one of the major complaints of retailers is that X's top management is "distant" or "aloof" and, thus, not readily accessible. Not only are retailers frustrated in their efforts to register complaints with Company X, they also are discouraged from offering suggestions or innovative ideas that might help X enhance its position in the market. Therefore, X is considering the establishment of approximately eight regional offices from which top management officials will periodically "call" on retailers. Since management officials have more power than X's sales force, retailers' suggestions and complaints will have a greater impact on X's operating procedures. The regional officer will also be used to inform retailers of new products, special offers and the like. Finally, the regional officer will coordinate local advertising campaigns and will administer cooperative promotional arrangements with retailers thereby enhancing X's ability to monitor and control such arrangements as well as easing cash flow problems through decentralized billing procedures.

Offer Incentives to Retailers: Company X believes that retailers will respond to certain incentives *other* than merely relaxing promotional requirements. Therefore, X is considering a policy whereby special awards (e.g., "Retailer of the Year") and even prizes (e.g., a trip to Hawaii) will be offered to retailers in recognition of outstanding performance during a given promotional campaign.

Drop Some Product Lines: During the past several decades the product line of Company X has steadily expanded in response to consumer needs and new technological developments. Some of X's products actually compete with each other. For example, X produces two types of fabric softener—a liquid for

162   *Analytical Planning*

use in washers and a solid for use in dryers. Promotional campaigns for one of these fabric softeners have an adverse affect on the sales of the other. Consequently, X's net gain is zero. Therefore, X is considering the elimination of some of its older, less profitable product lines and concentrating its promotional efforts on its newer, more competitive products.

The second forward hierarchy is illustrated in Exhibit 6-14. The fourth level now includes the three high priority policies the weights of which have been determined with respect to their relative contribution to the objectives of Company X of the third level. Note that the three new policies relate only to the objectives of X, not those of retailers or competitors. The fifth level contains the exploratory scenarios which now have new weights given the addition of the policies in the fourth level. The relevant question in the fifth level would be posed as follows: "Given increased interaction with retailers, what is the relative likelihood of each of the three scenarios?"

Note that the addition of the policies increases the likelihood of the scenario—off-invoice with flexibility—from .52 in the first forward process to .66 in the second forward process.

While this convergence would appear to validate the effectiveness of the three new promotional policies, unless it is established that it is the only scenario to follow, the *true* convergence cannot be assessed accurately until a new composite scenario is constructed. A brief explanation is called for to illustrate why the composite scenario is a better basis for assessing convergence between the likely and desired futures produced by the addition of new promotional policies. The scenario characterized by off-invoice programs with performance flexibility is by far the most likely (and desired) future in the judgment of the planners. However, this does not preclude the possibility that all or parts of the other scenarios will come about. Specifically, there is a 34% chance (.07 + .27) that the two remaining scenarios will manifest themselves in the promotional programs of the future. Accounting for this possibility, through the composite scenario, allows for a more accurate (and perhaps more conservative) assessment of convergence of the two futures.

The composite scale measurements for the state variables, introduced earlier, are presented in Exhibit 6-15.

The algorithm used to derive these measurements in the same as that used to construct the first composite scenario (see Exhibit 6-12) except that we have substituted the new scenario weights above the scenario names to reflect the outcome of the second forward process. Thus for sales revenue we have: $(2)(.07) + 7(.66) + 5(.27) = 6.11$.

Comparing these new scenario weights with those obtained earlier (first forward process) demonstrates the value of formulating a new composite scenario instead of merely measuring the increased likelihood of the desired scenario.

Strategic Planning 163

EXHIBIT 6-14. *Second Forward Process Hierarchy*

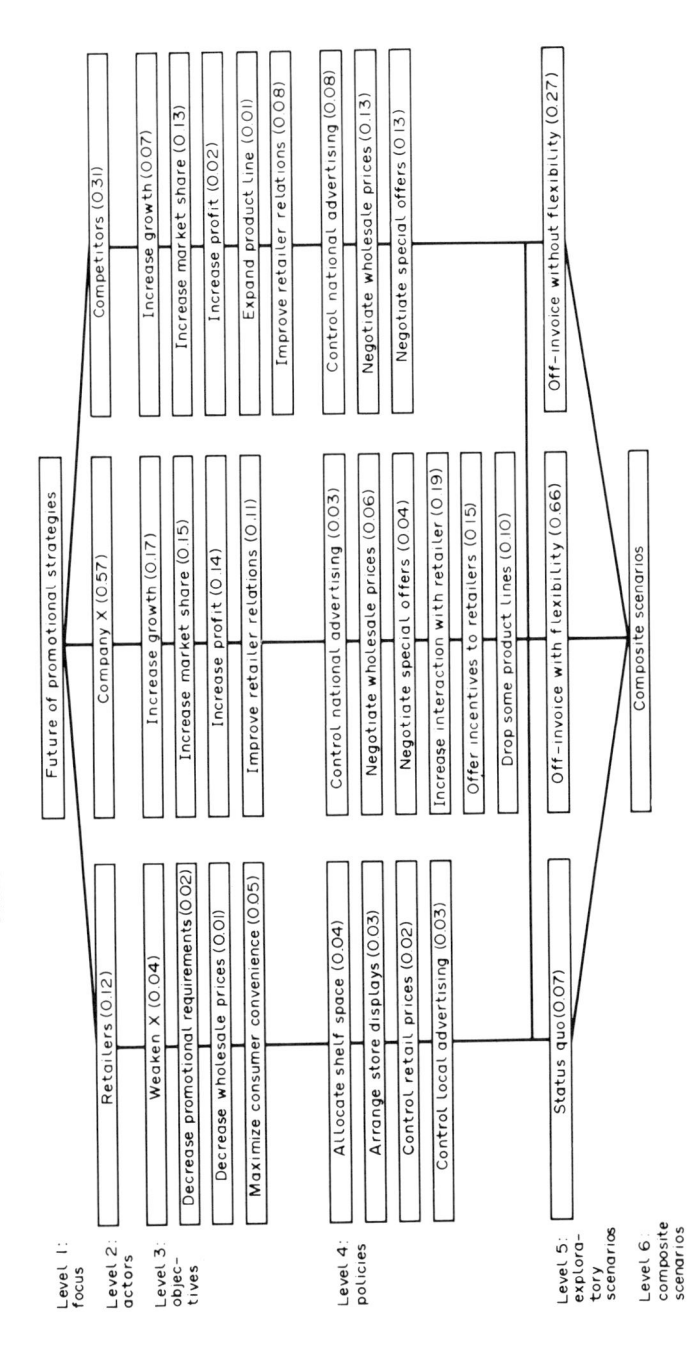

Level 1: focus
- Future of promotional strategies

Level 2: actors
- Retailers (0.12)
- Company X (0.57)
- Competitors (0.31)

Level 3: objectives
- Weaken X (0.04)
- Decrease promotional requirements (0.02)
- Decrease wholesale prices (0.01)
- Maximize consumer convenience (0.05)
- Increase growth (0.17)
- Increase market share (0.15)
- Increase profit (0.14)
- Improve retailer relations (0.11)
- Increase growth (0.07)
- Increase market share (0.13)
- Increase profit (0.02)
- Expand product line (0.01)
- Improve retailer relations (0.08)

Level 4: policies
- Allocate shelf space (0.04)
- Arrange store displays (0.03)
- Control retail prices (0.02)
- Control local advertising (0.03)
- Control national advertising (0.03)
- Negotiate wholesale prices (0.06)
- Negotiate special offers (0.04)
- Increase interaction with retailer (0.19)
- Offer incentives to retailers (0.15)
- Drop some product lines (0.10)
- Control national advertising (0.08)
- Negotiate wholesale prices (0.13)
- Negotiate special offers (0.13)

Level 5: exploratory scenarios
- Status quo (0.07)
- Off-invoice with flexibility (0.66)
- Off-invoice without flexibility (0.27)

Level 6: composite scenarios
- Composite scenarios

164 Analytical Planning

EXHIBIT 6-15. *Calibration of State Variables With Respect to Scenarios.*
(Second Forward Process)

	(.07) Status quo	(.66) Off-invoice with flexibility	(.27) Off-invoice without flexibility	Second forward process
Sales volume	2	7	5	6.11
Volume shipped	2	6	4	5.18
Promotional dollars saved	−2	4	5	3.85
Cash flow	2	−6	−5	−5.17
Composite				4.78

	First forward process	Second forward process
Sales revenue	5.74	6.11
Volume shipped	4.84	5.18
Promotional dollars saved	3.78	3.85
Cash flow	−4.82	−5.17
Composite	4.49	4.78

Note, for example, that sales revenues and the volume of products shipped will increase marginally. There will be a slight decrease in the promotional dollars saved and a slight reduction in the amount of cash X has on hand to invest given the increased likelihood of an industry-wide off-invoice promotional program. Thus, not all aspects of the composite scenario are favorable illustrating the trade-off that must inevitably be made in all planning problems. The saying "You can't have your cake and eat it too" has an element of truth in this example.

The composite scale measurement used to assess convergence is obtained as before by taking the sum of the products of the state variable weights by the state variable measurements. Thus we have: $(.289)(6.11) + (.554)(5.18) + (.106)(3.85) + (.051)(-5.17) = 4.78$.

The policies identified in the backward process improve the composite outcome in the second forward process. The composite score is improved by 6.5% from 4.49 to 4.78, i.e., $\frac{4.78 - 4.49}{4.49} = .065$.

Before pursuing these policies one must determine whether their costs justify the marginal increase in global benefits. If not the planners will have to proceed to a second backward process and reexamine their assumptions, formulating new judgments, or adding new policies that would address the weaknesses of those identified in the first backward process.

In this example the planners concluded that the costs of implementing the new policies were less than the global benefits they could be expected to produce. Therefore, they designed an implementation strategy which was presented to and approved by X's board of directors.

The next example illustrates a problem that required a second iteration of the forward-backward process.

10. Risk and Uncertainty

In many planning problems different time horizons need to be considered to cover elements of risk and uncertainty. The systems behavior is assessed in terms of various criteria applied to each time period. For example the time periods may be 1985–1990, 1990–2000, 2000–2010 and the criteria are industrial boom (high, medium, low) nuclear energy breakthrough and political stability in the Middle East.

Since a decision made now should have the future factored into it with appropriate discounting applied by the particular decision maker, the criteria are prioritized for each time period and conversely. To synthesize the weights of the criteria we must prioritize the time periods in terms of the criteria themselves. The priorities are obtained by taking a supermatrix with block matrices. One block (in the 1, 2 position) has its columns for the priorities of the criteria in terms of each time horizon and the second block (in the 3 position) has for its columns the priorities of the time periods in terms of each criterion (see below).

The priorities are obtained from any column in the limiting power of the supermatrix which is column stochastic (i.e., each of its columns adds to unity). See Saaty, 1980 for detail.

Applications have been made of this approach whereby one does the evaluation of priorities for the entire hierarchy three times, once for each time period. An easy way to do this is to use three entries for each pairwise comparison but do the appropriate calculation for each and then use the weights for the time periods obtained from the supermatrix to carry out the synthesis over time. Each of the criteria would use its three priorities with respect to the three time horizons. In other words only the priorities of the time periods are used from the supermatrix. In this manner one can deal with problems of risk and uncertainty. The pairwise comparisons dealing with this cycling process are as follows:

Which criterion is more likely during the time period indicated and how much more likely is it?

166   *Analytical Planning*

1985–1990	Industrial boom	Nuclear energy breakthrough	Mid-East stability
Industrial boom	1		
Nuclear energy breakthrough		1	
Mid-East stability			1

1990–2000	Industrial boom	Nuclear energy breakthrough	Mid-East stability
Industrial boom	1		
Nuclear energy breakthrough		1	
Mid-East stability			1

2000–2010	Industrial boom	Nuclear energy breakthrough	Mid-East stability
Industrial boom	1		
Nuclear energy breakthrough		1	
Mid-East stability			1

This leads to three priority vectors which when arranged as columns give rise to a matrix B_{12} giving the impacts of the criteria on time. Similarly we have: During which time period is the indicated criterion most likely and how strongly?

Industrial boom	1985–1990	1990–2000	2000–2010
1985–1990			
1990–2000			
2000–2010			

Nuclear energy breakthrough	1985–1990	1990–2000	2000–2010
1985–1990			
1990–2000			
2000–2010			

Mid-East stability	1985–1990	1990–2000	2000–2010
1985–1990			
1990–2000			
2000–2025			

This leads to three priority vectors which when arranged as columns give rise to a matrix B_{21} giving the impact of the time periods on the criteria. The supermatrix has the following form.

$$S = \begin{array}{c} \text{Criteria} \\ \\ \\ \text{Time} \\ \\ \end{array} \begin{array}{c} (1) \\ (2) \\ (3) \\ (1') \\ (2') \\ (3') \end{array} \begin{pmatrix} \begin{array}{c} \text{Criteria} \\ (1)\ (2)\ (3) \end{array} & \begin{array}{c} \text{Time} \\ (1')\ (2')\ (3') \end{array} \\ 0 & B_{12} \\ B_{21} & 0 \end{pmatrix}$$

We are also interested in the continued interaction between these two levels in the form of a cycle.

$$\text{TIME} \circlearrowleft \text{CRITERIA}$$

Thus we compute $\lim_{k \to \infty} S^k$ from which we obtain the limiting priorities of the time period. The powers of S indicate the impact of repeated cycling of interaction. It is known that the limiting matrix has identical columns and hence the priorities can be obtained from any column. The rest of the story as we said requires that we proceed as if we have three hierarchies, one for each time period, using the same criteria under each. Each time period has the priority just obtained from the supermatrix. The first one from the fourth entry of the supermatrix, the second from the fifth and the third from the sixth since in the supermatrix the components of the time vector follow those of the criteria components. Note that the hierarchy used in the energy example above could be augmented by putting the time periods as the first level, the criteria as the second and the rest of it as given here beginning with actors. One would have to prioritize for each time period the importance of the actors with respect to each criterion.

The synthesis of the exercise is to discount the final three outcomes using the weights of the time periods thus obtaining an overall weight for each scenario through the year 2010.

11. The Future of Synthetic Transportation Fuels

The OPEC oil embargo of 1973–74 focused America's attention on the need to develop viable energy alternatives to foreign crude oil. Efforts were initiated to develop a synfuels industry with particular attention to transportation fuels.

With the passage of the Energy Security Act of 1980 and the creation of the Synthetic Fuels Corporation (SFC), the federal government displayed an interest in cooperating with the private sector in the development of synthetic fuels. The government, however, has not followed up on its early initiatives and has yet to develop an explicit synfuels policy. In fact, recent government actions, including its announced intent to dismantle the Department of Energy, suggest that it intends to divorce itself from the synfuels industry leaving the private sector to develop its own initiatives.

Unfortunately, synfuels technology is not well developed. Enormous capital investments are required to construct even prototype demonstration plants and there is no promise that synthetic fuels will be economically competitive in the market place. Consequently, the private sector has been unwilling to take the substantial risks required for the development of a viable synfuels industry.

Also, there is a considerable controversy regarding environmental and social consequences associated with the development of synfuels technology. Much of America's vast coal and shale reserves are located in the relatively sparsely settled West. In fact, some of the richest reserves are located in national parks and other protected areas, thereby setting the stage for a heated national debate on the trade-offs between ecological protection and energy independence. Thus, even on the tenuous assumption that the mass production of synthetic fuel is economically feasible, there is a thicket of regulations and environmental concerns that may impede progress in the synfuels industry.

Finally, the policies of the Oil and Petroleum Exporting Countries (OPEC) have an impact on the future of the synfuels industry. OPEC is interested in ensuring that the western industrialized nations (particularly the U. S. and Western Europe) remain dependent on Middle Eastern oil. A viable synfuels industry would enhance competition thus forcing OPEC to lower its prices in order to survive in the marketplace. OPEC may use its pricing policies to discourage investment in synfuels research and development. For example, it might temporarily stabilize oil prices in order to defuse the occasional clamoring for viable energy alternatives. OPEC might then gradually increase its prices in order to continue to reap enormous profits. In this manner, the synfuels industry would become little more than a puppet with OPEC pulling the strings.

It is evident from the discussion above that the future of the synfuels industry in the United States with respect to transportation fuels is uncertain due to (1) the conflicting signals which the industry is receiving from the federal government; (2) the high cost of developing the synfuels industry, (3) the environmental concerns associated with the development of synthetic fuels, and, (4) the pricing policies of OPEC.

Where does the industry appear to be going and where should it go if the environment becomes more favorable? This problem is approached from the standpoint of an emergy company who, in the first forward process, is attempting to envision what type of environment the synfuels industry will

Strategic Planning 169

have to adapt to in the next 10 years. By "environment" we are referring to the general political, economic, technological and social milieu, within which the synfuels industry will develop or, perhaps, stagnate and die.

The First Forward Process

Exhibit 6-16 illustrates the hierarchy for the first forward process. The focus or objective is to portray the likely environment facing the synfuels industry in the U.S. in the next 10 years. Note that for purposes of this example the synfuels industry pertains to transportation fuels, not fuels for industrial use, home heating, and the like.

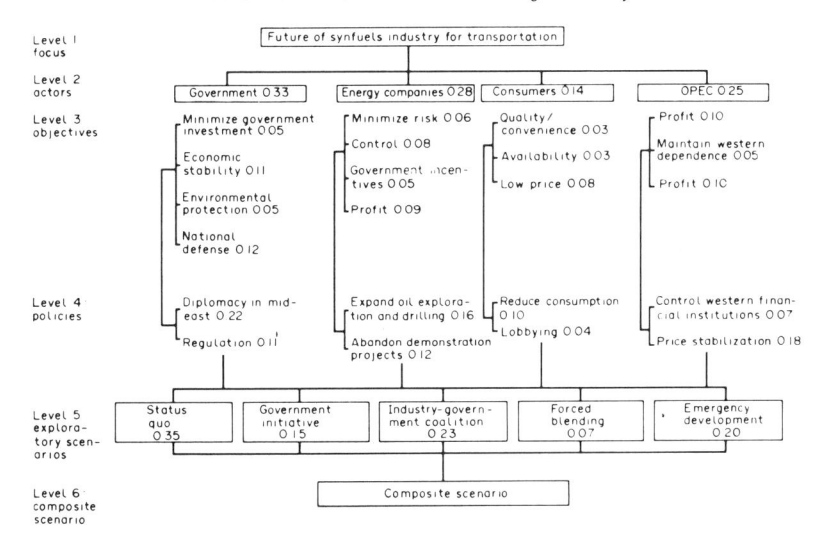

EXHIBIT 6-16. *First Forward Planning Hierarchy*

Level 1 focus	Future of synfuels industry for transportation
Level 2 actors	Government 0.33 | Energy companies 0.28 | Consumers 0.14 | OPEC 0.25
Level 3 objectives	Minimize government investment 0.05; Economic stability 0.11; Environmental protection 0.05; National defense 0.12 | Minimize risk 0.06; Control 0.08; Government incentives 0.05; Profit 0.09 | Quality/convenience 0.03; Availability 0.03; Low price 0.08 | Profit 0.10; Maintain western dependence 0.05; Profit 0.10
Level 4 policies	Diplomacy in mideast 0.22; Regulation 0.11 | Expand oil exploration and drilling 0.16; Abandon demonstration projects 0.12 | Reduce consumption 0.10; Lobbying 0.04 | Control western financial institutions 0.07; Price stabilization 0.18
Level 5 exploratory scenarios	Status quo 0.35 | Government initiative 0.15 | Industry-government coalition 0.23 | Forced blending 0.07 | Emergency development 0.20
Level 6 composite scenario	Composite scenario

The main actors affecting the future of the synfuels industry are: (1) government; (2) energy companies; (3) consumers, and (4) OPEC. Each actor has certain objectives and is pursuing certain policies in order to fulfill those objectives. Finally, the hierarchy contains five exploratory scenarios which will comprise the composite scenario. The exploratory scenarios are briefly described below.

Status Quo: This scenario is characterized by continued government disinvestment in synfuels accompanied by reluctance on the part of the private sector to take the necessary risks to enhance the economic viability of the synfuels industry. The scenario assumes that OPEC oil prices will remain relatively stable thereby diminishing the attractiveness of alternative energy sources. Also there will be little or no change in the regulatory and environmental concerns which currently pose barriers to synfuel development.

170 *Analytical Planning*

Government Initiative: This scenario assumes that the federal government will act preemptively to minimize the capability of OPEC to once again bring the Western nations to their knees with an oil embargo. The scenario forecasts increased government involvement in and subsidization of synfuels research and development. Relatedly, the government will breathe new life into the synthetic Fuels Corporation, giving it the political mandate and financial resources necessary to design the research agenda and to develop a coherent national policy on synthetic fuels. The synfuels industry would be closely monitored and regulated in the same way that utility companies are controlled by government today. Finally, the scenario assumes that environmental concerns will be diminished by a combination of new technologies that will minimize adverse environmental effects and by the diminishing power of environmental interest groups.

Industry-Government Coalition: This scenario is similar to "Government Initiative" in that the federal government will take a renewed interest in synfuels research and will provide financial and technical support for those research efforts. The major difference is that the energy companies will control the research agenda and will maintain private ownership of demonstration plants, patents, and the like. Moreover, the industry will not be strictly monitored or controlled by government; rather, the free market system will prevail; therefore supply and demand patterns, not government regulations, will determine both the quantities of synfuels produced and the market price for those fuels.

Forced Blending: Some countries, such as Brazil, have implemented a policy of forced blending. In this scenario refiners are required to blend conventional fuels with prescribed percentages of synthetic fuels; the prescribed percentage increases over time. The policy would be analogous to the government forcing industry to conform to air quality standards by a particular date. The burden of developing the appropriate technology falls, of course, on the energy and transportation companies alone with the government providing little or no assistance.

Emergency Development: This scenario portrays a repetition of the 1973-74 oil embargo. Increased military and political tensions in the Middle East combined with continuous U.S. support of Israel will prompt retaliatory action by OPEC. The U.S. will react with an emergency research and development program. A "crisis atmosphere" will prevail and, therefore, the research and development agenda will not be systematically planned or coordinated. Most social and environmental concerns will be ignored as the country makes a concerted effort to establish energy independence. Also, energy companies will be encouraged (or coerced), through government appeals to their patriotism, to temporarily abandon the profit motive as the driving force behind their research and development activities.

Exhibit 6-17 illustrates the prioritization of the state variables. Note that the state variables and their associated priorities reflect the interests of the energy

EXHIBIT 6-17. *Priorities of State Variables*

State variables	Priority
Control	.32
Government incentives	.16
Free market	.28
Research funds	.15
Citizen support	.09

company since the planning exercise is being conducted from its perspective. Exhibit 6-18 illustrates the calibration of the state variables with respect to the exploratory scenarios. The first forward process produced a composite measurement of $(-.31)$.

EXHIBIT 6-18. *State Variable Calibration*

	Status quo (.35)	Government initiative (.15)	Coalition (.23)	Forced blend (.70)	Emergency Development (.20)	First forward process
Control	0	−5	+4	−7	−7	−1.72
Government incentives	−3	+2	+5	+2	+5	1.54
Free market	0	−7	+3	−2	−4	−1.30
Research funds	−3	+5	+4	0	+6	1.82
Citizen support	0	+2	−2	+1	+5	91
Composite						−.31

The First Backward Process

The first backward process hierarchy is illustrated in Exhibit 6-19. Note that, while "Status Quo" is projected to be the most likely scenario, "Industry-Government Coalition" is the desired scenario from the point of view of the energy companies. The fifth level of this hierarchy contains policies that are being considered by the energy companies. A brief explanation of those policies follows.

Industrial Consortium: The consortium would serve as an industry-wise advisory body which would present a unified voice to the federal government on matters pertaining to synfuels research and development. The consortium would be a strictly voluntary organization with no formal policy making authority; it would, therefore, not violate laws pertaining to restraint of trade. It would serve as an informal forum for industry-government planning. It is

172 *Analytical Planning*

EXHIBIT 6-19. *First Backward Planning Hierarchy*

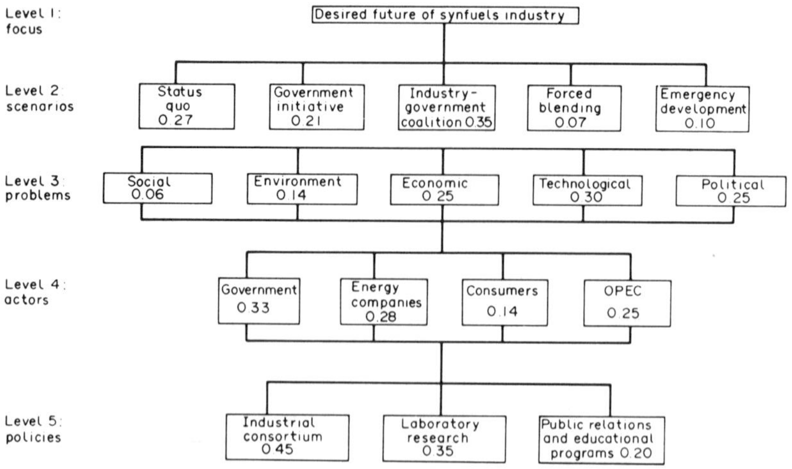

Level 1: focus — Desired future of synfuels industry

Level 2: scenarios
- Status quo 0.27
- Government initiative 0.21
- Industry-government coalition 0.35
- Forced blending 0.07
- Emergency development 0.10

Level 3: problems
- Social 0.06
- Environment 0.14
- Economic 0.25
- Technological 0.30
- Political 0.25

Level 4: actors
- Government 0.33
- Energy companies 0.28
- Consumers 0.14
- OPEC 0.25

Level 5: policies
- Industrial consortium 0.45
- Laboratory research 0.35
- Public relations and educational programs 0.20

believed that such a forum would streamline patterns of communication between government and industry.

Laboratory Research and Development: Even small scale field demonstration, e.g., coal gasification plants, have proved to be extremely costly and thus far have offered little promise of short term or long term pay-offs. Some industry representatives believe that synfuels researchers should "go back to the drawing board" so to speak through intensified laboratory research which is relatively inexpensive compared with field demonstration projects. Only when such research produces highly promising results would the industry approach the federal government for direct financial assistance or indirect incentives to proceed with the construction of demonstration plants.

Public Relations and Educational Campaigns: It is suspected that the relatively stable oil prices combined with the disappointing performance of demonstration projects has produced widespread complacency and apathy toward synfuels research. A national media campaign would stress America's growing reliance on foreign oil, highlighting the politically volatile situation in the Mid-East and calling for long range planning to avoid a repetition of the 1973–74 embargo. In general, such a campaign would attempt to sway public opinion toward synfuels research.

Remark: At this point it should be noted that pairwise comparison of the scenarios, with respect to the desired future (as was done in Exhibit 6-19), is based on implicit assumptions of the scenarios without looking at the state variable values. Imprecision in judgment can be a result of lack of a more detailed understanding of the state variables whose values define each scenario.

If we use the state variable priorities given in Exhibit 6-17 and the state

Strategic Planning

variable calibrations given in Exhibit 6-18, a composite for each scenario in Exhibit 6-18 can be obtained by multiplying the values of the state variables by their priorities. For example for the "status quo" we obtain

$$(0)(0.32) + (-3)(0.16) + (0)(0.28) + (-3)(0.15) + (0)(0.09) = -0.93$$

Doing this for the remaining four scenarios yields values of -2.31, 3.34, -2.39, and -1.21, respectively.

Here "coalition" with the only positive value (3.34) is the most favored future outcome, and "forced blend" is the least favorable one. The desired priorities of the exploratory scenarios for the backward planning hierarchy in Exhibit 6-19 can then be adjusted relying in part on the magnitudes of these individual composites.

The Second Forward Process

The two high priority policies, Industrial Consortium and Laboratory Research, were introduced into the second forward process hierarchy as policies of the energy companies. The prioritization proceeded from the level of policies downward.

The relative likelihood of "Industry-Government Coalition" (the desired scenario) occurring improved somewhat from .23 to .29 as illustrated in Exhibit 6-20. The "true" convergence, as determined by the composite measurement improved by nearly 100% from $-.31$ to $-.003$. Remember that a move toward zero in this case is a positive move. Exhibit 6-21 illustrates the

EXHIBIT 6-20. *Second Forward Process: Relative Likelihood of Exploratory Scenarios*

Scenarios	Relative likelihood
Status quo	.32
Government initiative	.13
Coalition	.29
Forced blending	.05
Emergency development	.21

EXHIBIT 6-21. *State Variable Calibrations for First and Second Forward Processes*

State variables	First forward	Second forward
Control	-1.72	-1.31
Government incentives	1.54	1.90
Free market	-1.30	$-.98$
Research funds	1.82	2.11
Citizen support	.91	.78
Composite	$-.31$	$-.003$

Analytical Planning

state variable calibrations and the composite measurement for the first and second forward processes.

The Second Backward Process

Even though significant convergence was achieved, the future prospects for the synfuels industry do not appear very bright. It was determined, therefore, that another iteration of the forward-backward process was required. In the second backward process the planners decided to add a policy that would have a short term impact on shaping the future of the synfuels industry. "Industrial Consortium" and "Laboratory Research" would require time to produce meaningful results; the planners believed that the efficacy of these two policies might be enhanced if they were complemented with some policies that had positive impacts in the short term as well as long term. A second backward process hierarchy was constructed which was identical to that illustrated in Exhibit 6-19 (the first backward process) with one exception—a new policy ("Gasohol") was added and the weights of the three previous policies were adjusted to reflect the new alternative. A brief explanation of the new policy follows:

Gasohol: Alcohol may be produced from excess foodstuffs through fermentation and blended with gasoline to produce a fuel ("gasohol") suitable for use in conventional engines. At present, conventional engines can operate efficiently on fuel with up to a nine to one gas to alcohol ratio, above which there is a need to modify conventional engines. Also, large quantities of grain are required to produce relatively small quantities of alcohol. Despite these drawbacks the technology for producing gasohol is currently being used, with high consumer satisfaction, especially in the Mid-West States. Also, there are relatively few technological, social or environmental patterns associated with increasing its usage. While the long term prospects for gasohol may not be as promising as those for synfuels derived from shale, coal and other natural resources, it offers significant short-term potential. Specifically, if the energy companies can increase the short-term demand for gasohol, through price reductions, advertising campaigns, and the like, they may be more successful in gaining government and public support for long-term research and development efforts related to other synfuel technologies.

The Third Forward Process

In the third forward process hierarchy all four policies from the second backward process were included as policies of the energy companies. With the addition of short term as well as long-term policies, the perceived likelihood of "Industry-Government Coalition" (the desired scenario) increased again from .29 in the second forward process to .34 in the third forward process as illustrated in Exhibit 6-22.

EXHIBIT 6-22. *Third Forward Process: Relative Likelihood of Exploratory Scenarios*

Scenarios	Relative likelihood
Status quo	.31
Government initiative	.13
Coalition	.34
Forced blending	.01
Emergency development	.21

Exhibit 6-23 illustrates the composite measurements for the first, second, and third forward hierarchies. Note that the convergence between the likely and desired futures improved rather significantly (186%) between the first and third iterations. On the basis of this convergence, the planners recommended that the company pursue all four policies with emphasis corresponding to the priorities. A description of the scenario that will result from the implementation of these four policies follows.

EXHIBIT 6-23. *State Variable Calibrations For First, Second, and Third Forward Processes*

State variable	First forward	Second forward	Third forward
Control	−1.72	−1.31	−.83
Government incentives	1.54	1.90	2.10
Free market	−1.30	−.98	−.75
Research funds	1.82	2.11	2.34
Citizen support	.91	.78	.64
Composite	−.34	−.003	.269

It appears inevitable that the energy companies will lose a small amount of control over the synfuels industry by attempting to foster an industry-government coalition. Relatively, the free market forces of supply and demand will not be allowed to seek their true equilibrium point due to anticipated government intervention in the synfuels industry. On the positive side, however, government incentives to engage in synfuels research will be enhanced. Available research funds will increase slightly and public support for synfuels research will also increase slightly.

12. Conclusion

We have seen how to actualize our intuitive understanding of planning by successive iterations of the forward-backward process. The purpose is to decide on what is likely to happen, what we want, what we must control or bring about, and how effective this control is likely to be in directing the likely future towards the desired future. This approach not only unfolds our understanding but provides logical dynamics to test for promising alternatives. This kind of understanding must precede action. Before we proceed to alter the world we live in, with the hope that we can change it for the better, we need a means to test the soundness of our approach.

The complexity of the environment is increasing so rapidly that the impetus to plan and replan to keep up with change must always be present. As any plan is used to make a change, it must soon after be revised to incorporate the full impact of the change it has brought about. There are several reasons why no plan can be so fully dynamic that all aspects of change can be anticipated in it. One is that we always plan for a part of our world, and occurrences elsewhere tend to overtake the system being planned for; hence the plan must be periodically revised. Another is that not all impacts can be anticipated, particularly those of a synergistic nature, which give rise to completely new entities that cannot be fully characterized in advance. This is true both of concrete physical constructions and of relations among people or among ideas. The close association of a few ideas could lead to the emergence of a new idea that is radically different from its constituent parts. The plan must now be rethought to take into consideration the new developments and their impacts.

Revising a plan may involve the addition or deletion of factors or preferably it can be restructured *ab initio* to incorporate subtleties that have come to light which cannot be easily accommodated in the older framework.

We propose that in the process of implementing the composite scenario the plan should be revised periodically in periods ranging from 3 to 5 years: 3 years to allow the effects of actions to have sufficient time to become noticeable; 5 years to prevent the system from becoming too resistant to change. The ideas in the plan should be constantly reviewed and changed or interpreted on a daily basis as a means of tactical revision. But the structure and recommendations of the strategic plan, once adopted, should not be questioned every day.

The systems approach requires that a plan be approached as an organic whole, not in pieces. Thus major revisions must encompass the entire plan and not simply relate to some parts, leaving out others. This necessitates that not only the components of the plan but their interactions be studied and synthesized, that applications in one part be thought of in terms of their effect on the organization with regard to its structure and its function. Planning is more effective when practiced as an integrated whole.

References

Emshoff, James and Thomas Saaty (1982) Applications of the Analytic Hierarchy Process to Long Range Planning Processes, *European Journal of Operations Research*, 10, 131–143.

Saaty, Thomas L. and Paul C. Rogers (1976) Higher Education in the United States (1985–2000): Scenario Construction Using a Hierarchical Framework with Eigenvector Weighting, *Socio-Economic Planning Sciences*, **10**, pp. 251–263.

We are grateful to Dr. Thomas E. Esselman, Regina Ceisler, Frank Domieson, Michelle Keane, Jeffrey J. Cher and Richard Gaffney for their contributions to this chapter.

Suggested Readings

Bates, Donald and David Eldredge (1980) *Strategy and Policy: Analysis, Formulation and Implementation*, Dubuque: Brown.

Brown, George E. (1981) The Uses of History in Policy Analysis and Strategic Planning, *Technological Forecasting and Social Change*, **20**: 365–368.

Bryant, Coralic and Louise White (1975) The Calculus of Competing Goals: Planning, Participation and Social Change, *Growth and Change*, **6**: 38–43.

Davidoff, Paul (1965) Advocacy and Pluralism in Planning, *Journal of the American Institute of Planners*, **31**: 331–338.

Davidoff, Paul and Thomas Reiner (1962) A Choice of Theory of Planning, *Journal of the American Institute of Planners*, **28**: 331–338.

Emshoff, James, Ian Mitroff and Ralph Kilmann (1978) The Role of Ideolization in Long Range Planning: An Essay on the Logical and Social Emotional Aspects of Planning, *Technological Forecasting and Social Change*, **11**: 335–348.

Epstein, I. and T. Tripodi (1977) *Research Techniques for Program Planning*, Monitoring and Evaluation, New York: Columbia University Press.

Goehlert, Robert (1983) *Policy Studies on Planning: A Selected Bibliography*, Monticello: Vance.

King, William and David Cleland (1978) *Strategic Planning and Policy*, New York: Von Nostrand Reinhold.

Mackett, R. L. (1976) Hierarchical Planning Relationships, Consistency, and Indicators in the Planning Process, *Socio-Economic Planning Sciences*, **10**: 1144–1155.

Mandell, Marvin, *et al.* (1982) Making Planning More Responsive to Its Users: The Concept of Meta-Planning. *Environment and Planning*, 14.

Mason, Richard O. and Ian Mitroff (1981) *Challenging Strategic Planning Assumptions*, New York: John Wiley.

McAllister, D. W. *et al.* (1979) Contingency Model for the Selection of Decision Strategies, *Organizational Behavior and Human Performance*, **24**: 228–244.

Moskow, Michael H. (1978) *Strategic Planning in Business and Government*, New York: Committee for Economic Development.

Nagler, T. H. (1979) Organizing for Strategic Planning, *Managerial Planning*, **28**: 3–9.

Norman, O. Gene (1980) *Business Policy and Business Strategy: A Selected Bibliography*, Monteicello: Vance.

Rittel, Horst and Melvin Webber (1973) Dilemmas in a General Theory of Planning, *Policy Sciences*, **4**: 155–169.

Steiner, George A. (1979) Strategic Planning, *What Every Manager Must Know*, New York: Free Press.

Wildavsky, Aaron (1973) If Planning is Everything, Maybe It's Nothing, *Policy Sciences*, **4**: 127–153.

CHAPTER 7

Benefit-Cost Analysis and Resource Allocation

1. Introduction

In this chapter, we illustrate the highly relevant applicability of the Analytic Hierarchy Process to project evaluation and resource allocation. Benefit-cost analysis supplies the underlying principles to guide resource allocation while the AHP is used to structure the allocation problem and measure the factors consequential to the decision.

In order to measure the relative importance of the components and benefits and costs, we can resort to sampling public opinion, employ expert judgment and compare with the consequences of past projects of this kind.

Resources, in a general sense, are the means we have at our disposal to bring about a change in the state of a system or to direct it toward a desired end. We use intellectual resources to achieve high marks in school; we use natural resources (oil, gas, etc.) to drive machines; and we use other kinds of natural resources (flour, sugar, etc.) in combination with intellectual resources to bake a cake. In planning, resources are often monetary and they are almost always finite, or even scarce; that is, they do not exist in unlimited quantities and, therefore, cannot be devoted to the achievement of all of one's objectives. As a result, resources are usually allocated in different amounts to different projects or proposals according to the perceived worthiness of the alternatives. There are actually three different types of resource allocation problems: (1) selection of one project to be undertaken with the total resources available; (2) selection of a mix of projects to which available resources will be allocated in equal or unequal portions; and (3) allocation of resources to existing projects according to their remaining (marginal) potential.

By applying the AHP to structure benefit-cost problems, we achieve two extensions of traditional methods: (a) we can quantify intangible, non-economic factors which have so far not been effectively integrated in decision making, and (b) make explicit and informed tradeoffs among multiple selection criteria, including multiple performance objectives and output activities. To achieve these extensions, one first constructs complementary hierarchies of benefits and costs. Benefit-to-cost ratios which we call "preference ratios" are computed and projected into the future in order to identify projects that may be desirable to implement at a later date. In this way, the analysis can be given an explicit temporal dimension, permitting one to apply different discounts to the future.

Where intangible factors are essential to problem characterization, the lack of a common "currency" for effecting comparisons and tradeoffs forces the analyst to seek combinatorial solutions. This type of problem, which traditionally deals with the disposition of fixed "inventories" of resources (Marglin, 1967) is more central to the field of allocation than has been widely recognized. Traditional analysis has followed Marglin in taking the goal of benefit-cost analysis and of economic choice generally to be the maximization of utility subject to whatever constraints the economic and political environment imposes. The AHP offers a procedure to integrate fully the economic and political environment as objectives or criteria to evaluate an allocation scheme.

Later we also explore combinatorial formulations of assigning input resources to activities by identifying several types of problems in which sets of heterogeneous inputs must be optimally assigned to sets of indirectly commensurable activities or outputs. Traditionally, these give rise to "knapsack" and "double knapsack" problems. Solutions to these problems have so far been obtained by exhaustive enumeration and while we do not offer algorithms for their solution the applicability of the AHP as a modeling framework will be demonstrated.

2. Benefit-Cost Analysis: Traditional and AHP Approaches

How do planners determine worthiness? They might, for instance, attempt to assess the benefits of alternative plans and choose the one from which the maximum benefit would be derived. But more resources (i.e., dollars) will generally buy more benefits and, as we have noted, resources are usually limited. Therefore, the benefit criterion alone is not a very meaningful basis for comparison. Alternatively, planners could attack the problem from the opposite direction by assessing the respective costs of alternatives, and select the plan which would minimize the required investment. This is not a valid way to compare projects either, because minimizing costs might lead to a "do nothing" approach or, more realistically, doing so little that no significant movement is made toward the desired end.

It appears that a more meaningful approach is to consider benefits and costs simultaneously. This approach, known as benefit-cost analysis, seeks to compare the "units" of benefits per "unit" of resource (e.g., dollar) that would have to be expended on each alternative plan.

Benefit-cost analysis has a long history and was first used on a large scale by the federal government in its assessment of various water resource projects (dams, flood control, etc.) in the late 1930s. Some elaborate techniques of benefit-cost analysis have been developed (e.g., converting future costs and

180   *Analytical Planning*

benefits to present value) and sometimes the components of the techniques are modified depending whether it is applied to public or private sector problems. Fundamentally, however, the method calls for an assessment of total costs and total benefits of each of several alternatives. The benefit-cost ratio, total benefits divided by total costs, is then calculated to determine how many benefit units are purchased with each unit of cost. The alternative with the highest benefit-cost ratio is then selected, assuming, of course, that its total costs are within the feasibility range established by the planners given their limited resources.

Exhibit 7-1 presents the estimated costs and benefits of highway construction projects. Project A offers by far the greatest benefits but it is also rather expensive. Project C is the least expensive, yet, understandably, offers fewer benefits. The benefit-cost ratio of Project D is the highest and therefore would probably be selected in this case, although another in-depth comparison with Project B might be justified since its ratio is rather close to that of Project D.

Exhibit 7-1. *Cost-Benefit Analysis*

Project	Costs (in millions of dollars)	Benefits	Benefit-Cost ratio B/C	Rank
A	300	600	2.0	3
B	150	350	2.33	2
C	100	175	1.75	4
D	200	500	2.50	1

In light of our earlier discussions, the reader might surmise that there are many problems of measurement in benefit-cost analysis. The benefit-cost ratio is, in fact, not the clear-cut objective measure of performance that it appears to be. For instance, how does one first go about identifying benefits and costs and, second, assigning a dollar value to those that are intangible? These are subjective and valuative judgments that are beneath the facade of objectivity which the benefit-cost ratio portrays. Even when all factors can be compared in terms of identical units of measurements there is a *risk* factor in predicting certain outcomes (e.g., Project D will produce 500 benefit units) that does not seem to be adequately accounted for in benefit-cost analysis as it is traditionally practiced. Moreover, the technique is further complicated by the need to account for both direct (primary) and indirect (secondary) costs and benefits. Finally, we know from systems theory that benefits and costs may be categorized under many labels—social, economic political, managerial—and that the interdependence of these categories should be accounted for in the assessment of alternatives.

The AHP stresses the need to structure benefit-cost problems hierarchically and to compare alternatives and their attributes in a pairwise fashion in terms of the strength of their respective contribution to the fulfillment of objectives.

Benefit-Cost Analysis and Resource Allocation 181

The costs of alternatives should also be portrayed as a hierarchy or network in order to capture their dynamic interactions and relative impacts on the problem. Moreover, the AHP acknowledges that two or more alternatives together may accrue a greater benefit to cost ratio than a single one.

In addressing these issues the AHP calls for the construction of two hierarchies, one for costs and one for benefits with the same alternatives in the bottom level. Thus one obtains a benefits priority vector and a costs priority vector. The benefit-cost ratio for each alternative is then calculated on the basis of these two priority vectors obtained in the first step rather than on arbitrary conversions to "units" of benefit and cost as in the traditional approach. Marginal analysis can be carried out using the benefits and the costs derived in this way.

Consider the case of a manufacturer that has decided to establish a production facility is another country in order to gain access to foreign markets and decrease production costs by taking advantage of lower foreign wage rates. The potential costs of such an expansion include such factors as loss of managerial control, the predominance of unskilled labor, and the risk of changing political and economic conditions in the host country. Assume, further, that the manufacturer has done some preliminary analysis and has narrowed the choice to four countries: Great Britain, Egypt, Yugoslavia, and Italy.

The benefit and cost hierarchies are illustrated in Exhibits 7-2 and 7-3 respectively. We have not included the matrices since the reader is now familiar with how to conduct pairwise comparisons and calculate local and global priorities. Please note that the factors included in the hierarchies are not intended to be exhaustive; they are merely suggestive of the type of consideration one might want to include in such an analysis. Note that the criteria for benefits and the criteria for costs need not be simply opposites of each other but could be totally different.

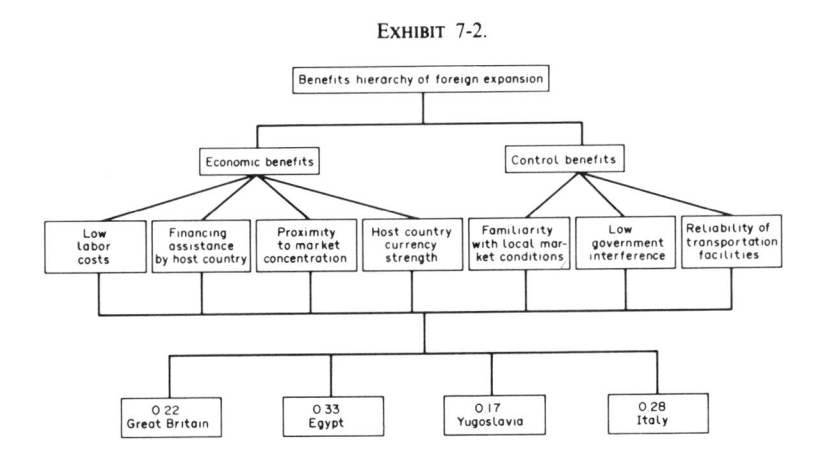

EXHIBIT 7-2.

182 *Analytical Planning*

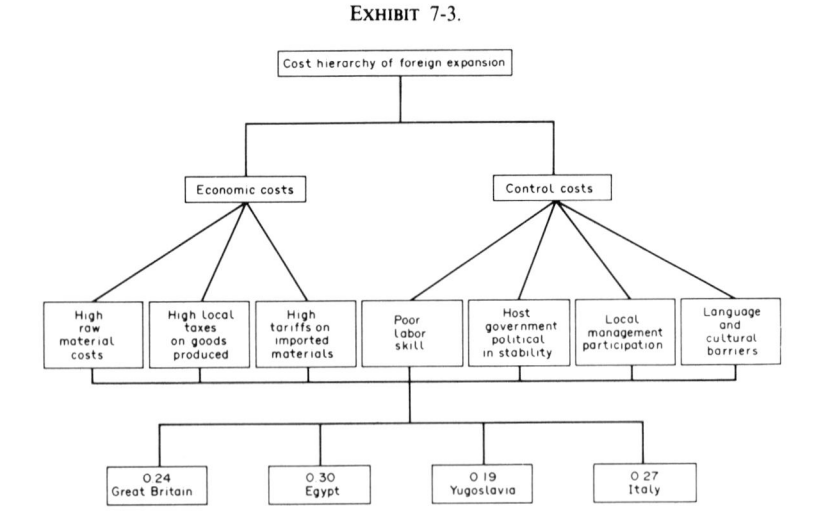

EXHIBIT 7-3.

```
                    Cost hierarchy of foreign expansion
                           /              \
                  Economic costs      Control costs
```

- High raw material costs
- High local taxes on goods produced
- High tariffs on imported materials
- Poor labor skill
- Host government political instability
- Local management participation
- Language and cultural barriers

| 0.24 Great Britain | 0.30 Egypt | 0.19 Yugoslavia | 0.27 Italy |

We will assume that the benefit and cost priorities for the four countries emerged as follows:

	Great Britain	Egypt	Yugoslavia	Italy
Benefits	.22	.33	.17	.28
Costs	.24	.30	.19	.27

Calculation of the benefit-cost ratio yields the following results which favor location of the new production plant in Egypt with Italy close behind.

Great Britain	Egypt	Yugoslavia	Italy
$\frac{.22}{.24} = .92$	$\frac{.33}{.30} = 1.1$	$\frac{.17}{.19} = .89$	$\frac{.28}{.27} = 1.03$

When making the pairwise comparisons in the cost hierarchy, one must remember that a high rank for an alternative reflects the relatively high "costs" associated with it. In this example, one would ask: Which of the two countries being compared is likely to have a generally lower level of labor skill and how much lower is it? We mention this because in the hierarchies we have discussed so far, a high rank for an alternative has represented a high level of desirability relative to the elements with which it is compared. The rankings reflect just the opposite in a hierarchy of costs.

The AHP approach to benefit-cost analysis does not attempt to impose standard units of measurement (e.g., dollars) on costs or benefits that are not amenable to such conversions. Moreover, the AHP is a convenient and conceptually useful way to explicate both direct and indirect factors by portraying the benefit and cost problems hierarchically and accounting for the relationships of many elements simultaneously. It is also important to remember that the hierarchies are constructed and subsequently the judgments made by the participants in the planning process.

Another Example: Decision to Build a Bridge

A governmental agency which has jurisdiction over the building of bridges and tunnels in a certain area must decide whether to build or not to build a tunnel and/or a bridge across a river presently served by a privately owned ferry. The factors which affect both the benefits and the costs of crossing a river are given in the two hierarchies shown in Exhibits 7-4 and 7-5. These factors fall into three categories: economic, social, and environmental. A decision will be made by comparing benefits and costs.

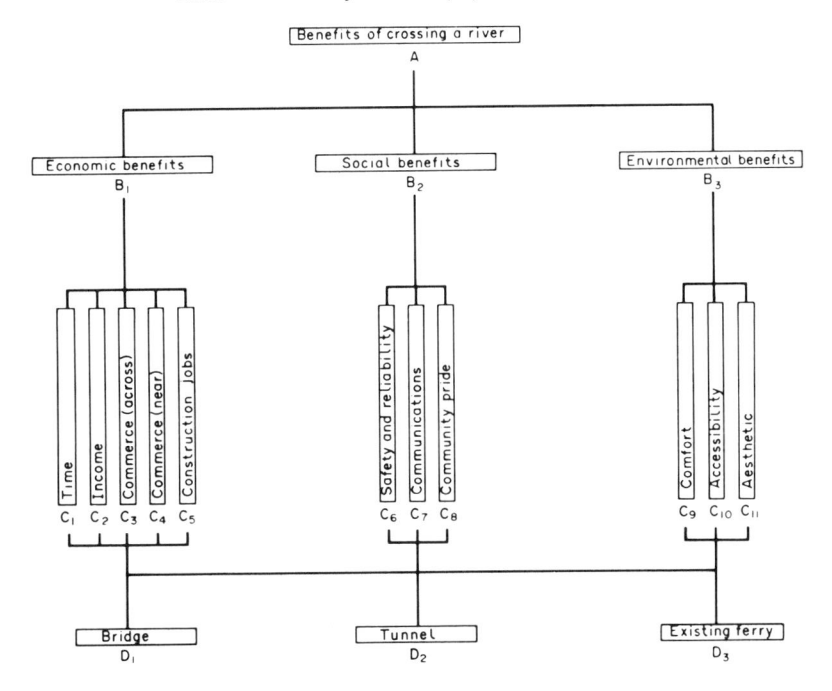

EXHIBIT 7-4. *Benefit Hierarchy of Illustrative Problem*

Benefits

The economic factors affecting the choice consist of the benefit derived for the time saved by using a new bridge or tunnel rather than using the existing

184   *Analytical Planning*

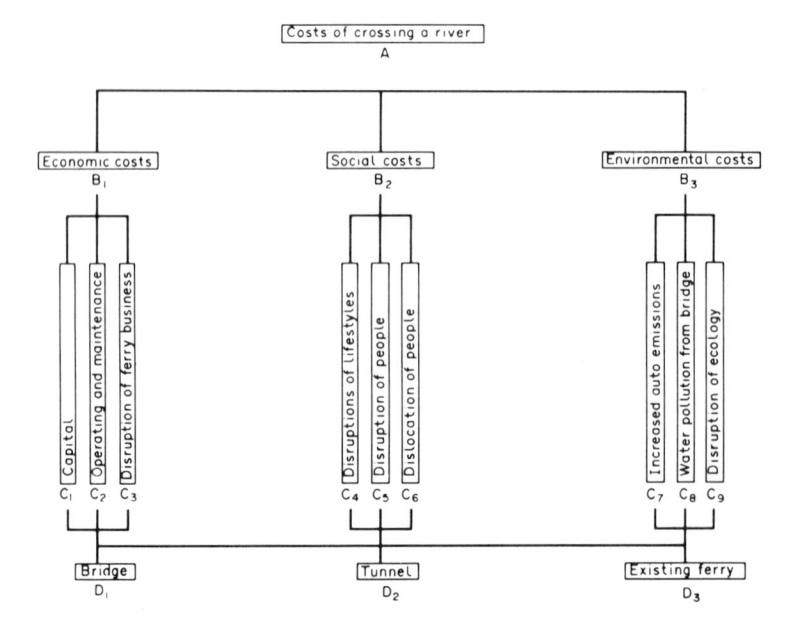

EXHIBIT 7-5. *Cost Hierarchy of Illustrative Problem*

```
                    ┌─────────────────────────┐
                    │ Costs of crossing a river│
                    │            A            │
                    └─────────────────────────┘
           ┌────────────────┼────────────────┐
    ┌──────────────┐  ┌──────────────┐  ┌─────────────────┐
    │Economic costs│  │ Social costs │  │Environmental costs│
    │      B₁      │  │     B₂       │  │       B₃         │
    └──────────────┘  └──────────────┘  └─────────────────┘
```

B_1 Economic costs	B_2 Social costs	B_3 Environmental costs
C_1 Capital	C_4 Disruptions of lifestyles	C_7 Increased auto emissions
C_2 Operating and maintenance	C_5 Disruption of people	C_8 Water pollution from bridge
C_3 Disruption of ferry business	C_6 Dislocation of people	C_9 Disruption of ecology

Bridge	Tunnel	Existing ferry
D_1	D_2	D_3

ferry. The increased traffic into the area could bring in toll revenue which, in turn, increases the general income of the local government. The traffic will also aid the commerce both in the area and those nearby (such as gas stations and restaurants). Another economic benefit comes from the construction jobs created. If economic factors are the only ones which need to be considered, most of these factors could be calculated quantitatively. The associated cost could also be computed quantitatively and a benefit-cost ratio could be immediately calculated and used to make the decision. But we have to consider social and environmental factors which do not directly translate into dollars.

The social benefits of the project represent the benefits which society-at-large will derive from the presence of a bridge or a tunnel. For example, a bridge or a tunnel can provide greater safety and reliability than a ferry. The bridge or tunnel can also contribute to a greater number of trips across to visit relatives, friends, museums, etc. Finally, either alternative can generate community pride not present to the same degree in using the ferry.

Environmental factors are viewed in terms of their contribution to individual personal benefits. They differ from benefits to society in that society often considers benefits to an abstract collection which does not represent the interest of any particular individual. In our example, the environmental factors of interest to the individual are the comfort derived in using the bridge, tunnel or ferry; the ease of accessibility in using one over the others; and the aesthetics affecting the choice of alternative for crossing the river.

Costs

As with benefits, the costs of crossing a river also involve economic, social, and environmental factors. Exhibit 7-5 shows three economic costs that are relevant to the decision problem: the capital costs of the alternatives, the operating and maintenance costs associated with the three projects, and the economic consequence of not having a ferry boat business.

The social costs again represent costs to society at large. The degree to which lifestyles will be disrupted when using any of the alternatives to cross the river may be important. The congestion of traffic differs between the various modes of crossings and thus is deemed a relevant cost. The third type of social cost is the effect on society of the dislocation of people from their homes according to the alternate chosen. Environmental costs differ from benefits in that they represent possible harm done to the ecosystem by the alternatives. For example, the three modes of crossing the river may vary as to the amount of auto emissions generated in the area. Additionally, pollution of the water and the general disruption of the ecology contribute to environmental costs.

Results

In the calculation of both benefits and costs, economic factors outweighed the other factors. The benefits derived from the commerce across the bridge, the added safety and reliability, and the quick accessibility of crossing the river all received high priorities. As for costs, the capital required, the dislocation of people from their homes and the amount of auto emissions all received high priorities.

The composite benefits and costs are as follows:

	Bridge	Tunnel	Ferry
Benefits (b_i)	.57	.36	.07
Costs (c_i)	.36	.58	.05

We stated earlier, one criterion used in benefit-cost analysis is to choose the project with the largest benefit-to-cost ratio (b_i/c_i). In this example we have:

Bridge	Tunnel	Ferry
$\dfrac{b_1}{c_1} = 1.58$	$\dfrac{b_2}{c_2} = .62$	$\dfrac{b_3}{c_3} = 1.28$

which favors the construction of a bridge across the river. Note that this has taken into consideration the capital requirements.

186 *Analytical Planning*

A common mistake often made in employing benefit-cost analysis is to rank the alternatives by the first benefit-cost ratio. To determine which of the three alternatives is best, it is necessary to compare the alternatives with each other. Thus, the appropriate decision rule is: *The best alternative is the one with the highest total cost priority which has a benefit-cost ratio greater than a prespecified standard when compared with all lower cost-priority alternatives.*

The rationale for this is that whenever we are comparing two or more alternatives, we are not concerned with the absolute magnitudes of their respective benefits and costs. Rather we are concerned with their relative magnitudes; that is, we compare incremental benefits with incremental costs. Thus, in general, a shift from a present state A to an allegedly "better" state B is justifiable only when the additional costs of moving from state A to state B are justified by the benefits from the shift.

For the above example we order the costs $.05 < .36 < .58$ and form the ratio of successive positive difference in benefits and costs obtaining $\frac{.07}{.05}$ and $\frac{.50}{.31}$. Again marginal analysis favors the construction of the bridge.

3. Resource Allocation*

At this point, we have discussed the derivation of priorities and benefit-cost ratios from benefit-cost hierarchies. Once these measurements have been obtained, we can turn our attention to more complex resource allocation problems. Specifically, we shall be interested in combinatorial optimization problems where, in its simplest terms, the task becomes one of determining that combination of projects which maximizes "total benefits" subject to constraints on costs. This section must be more technical than the previous sections in order to explore the richness of the theory and practice of resource allocation. Some knowledge of linear programming would be helpful (see Gass, 1975).

In the discussion that follows, the following notation will be adopted:

N = number of resources or inputs to be allocated to the projects or activities.

M = number of alternative projects or activities under consideration.

b_j = composite priority of the jth project in the hierarchy of anticipated benefits.

c_j = composite weight of the jth project in the hierarchy of anticipated costs, i.e., the relative rates of which bundles of inputs can be traded off among projects in the long term.

---

* The authors gratefully acknowledge the contribution of James P. Bennet to a paper entitled *A New Perspective on Benefits and Costs: The Analytic Hierarchy Process*, coauthored with the first author in 1979.

such that

$$\sum_{j=1}^{M} b_j = \sum_{j=1}^{M} c_j = 1$$

$$0 \leqslant b_j, c_j \leqslant 1 \text{ for all } j$$

To implement any jth project, one must allocate to it a minimum amount of the ith resource, denoted by r_{ij} such that $r_{ij} \geqslant 0$. The resource requirements of all projects give rise to the matrix

$$R = \|r_{ij}\| \text{ of size } N \times M$$

which has at least one non-zero element in each row and column; that is, each point required at least one resource and each resource is required in at least one project.

It has already been indicated that allocation problems generally force us to allocate resources over this matrix of requirements under three kinds of criteria:

1. Do *as much* as possible.
2. Do something *as cheaply* as possible.
3. Get a *benefit-cost ratio as high* as possible.

Before explicating these three groups of allocation objectives, let us specify some additional properties of the resources. We define the matrix

$$A = \|a_{ij}\| \text{ of size } N \times M$$

to be the *actual* (rather than the minimum) distribution of the ith resource to the jth project. Assuming that the resources are not infinitely divisible, we let n_i be the number of indivisible units of each ith resource.

The nature of resource indivisibility may take many forms, of which we can point out two. First, they may be functionally indivisible—such as the unit of the firm. Second, they may be indivisible only for convenience of measurement within a particular problem—such as the unit of " # 1 million." We denote by n_{ij} the number of units of the ith resource allocated to the jth project with

$$\sum_{j=1}^{M} n_{ij} < n_i, i = 1, \ldots, N$$

For a sufficiently homogeneous set of projects, we can measure the relative effectiveness v_{ij} of several resources i when used to perform a particular project j. One might, for instance, employ a plumber, a carpenter or even a dentist to fix a leaky faucet. Presumably, the latter two would perform less effectively. By choosing the most efficient resource as the base of comparison, we have $v_{ik} < 1$, for all resources i, substituted for resources k with $v_{ij} = 1$. For problems in which some substitution is possible we may obtain the a_{ij} amount of i equivalent resources assigned to project j by first converting n_{ik} units of

188   *Analytical Planning*

resource i into resource k at efficiency v_{ik}; that is,

$$a_k = \sum_{i=1}^{N} n_{ik} v_{ik}$$

We have converted an amount a_i of the ith resource. From this we would allocate an amount $a_{ij} \left(\text{with} \sum_{j=1}^{M} a_{ij} \leq a_i \right)$ to the jth project. When conversion is impossible, $v_{ik} = 0$ and allocation can be made simply in terms of "natural units of the resource," i.e., $a_{ij} = n_{ij}$.

The cases to be discussed below are chosen on the basis of three criteria:

1. They reflect real-world problems of allocation.
2. Their solution involves comparison among discrete combinations of resources.
3. They offer opportunities for the use of prioritized measures of benefits, costs, or both.

The cases have been classified according to the character of the objectives function. Then in each case, we discuss those variations in the constraints that seem to be prevalent in practical problem solving.

Case I. *Do as Much as Possible with Limited Resources*

As an illustrative problem, consider a firm with several product lines. Each product line can be accorded a priority (b_j) from a hierarchical analysis of factors such as its anticipated profitability, strategic significance for maintaining a market share, cash flow requirements and diversity of markets. We initially assume that the production economics are such that a fixed number of units of each product line must be produced in a batch. This batch may correspond to a one day's output as in the case of partially automated clothing manufacture. Here, pattern cutting is performed by programmable equipment; while reprogramming and resupply of materials is accomplished in the evenings when the rest of the plant is idle. To produce fewer units than possible in a full working day creates an expensive suboptimality, so that only one-day-long runs are most probably considered by management.

Several resources $(i = 1, \ldots, N)$ are required for each potential batch of clothing $(j = 1, \ldots, M)$. Resources include not only cloth but also labor, supervision and specialized tools. If the firm fails to allocate enough resources to each batch undertaken (i.e., $a_{ij} \leq r_{ij}$), then we assume that the entire batch is spoiled and cannot be sold. (Below we shall relax this restriction.) Thus, the allocation problem is to choose those batches of product lines yielding maximal total priority subject to constraints imposed by the available resources.

Each project is "worth" nothing unless it is implemented entirely, in which case the project is "worth" its priority of benefit. We wish to maximize the total benefit of projects by a judicious allocation of n_i, $i = 1, 2, \ldots, N$. Our problem is then to select x_j that maximizes

$$\sum_{j=1}^{M} b_j x_j \tag{1}$$

Subject to

$$\sum_{j=1}^{M} b_j = 1 \tag{2}$$

$$\sum_{j=1}^{M} a_{ij} \leqslant n_i, \; i = 1, \ldots, N \tag{3}$$

$$x_{ij} = 1 \text{ if } (a_{ij} - r_{ij}) \geqslant 0, \; x_{ij} = 0 \text{ otherwise} \tag{4}$$

$$x_j = 1 \text{ if } \sum_{i=1}^{N} x_{ij} = N, \; x_j = 0 \text{ otherwise} \tag{5}$$

Note that this is not a standard linear program but a combinatorial allocation problem of the knapsack type. Condition 4 states that project j can be performed only if the requirement for every input to the project is met or exceeded by the amount of resources allocated to the project.

However, it is unrealistic, as in the basic model above, to assume that a shortfall in the allocation of any resource makes the whole batch worthless. A more reasonable assumption is that each minor shortfall reduces the worth (or benefits) of the batch which leads us to a variation of the foregoing mode.

Variation 1. The first variation of the model arose in energy planning for contingencies. Consider an economy which faces a small cutback in all types of energy resources (e.g., coal, oil, gas and nuclear) for industrial uses. Let us assume for simplicity that the pre-cutback distribution of energy inputs is optimal for the productive efficiency of the economy.

It is not unreasonable to assume, at the margin, that a reduction in any type of energy input produces a reduction in the efficiency of the industry's operations (denoted by e_{ij}). In the simplest case, the reductions may be proportionate and identical for all inputs and industries. Larger cutbacks require examination through input/output interdependence among industries as well as input-and industry-specific measurement of the decrease in efficiency (Saaty and Mariano, 1979).

We take the "worth" of each industry before the cutbacks as its priority derived from a general hierarchy that assesses the industry's importance of the broader economy. The task of a public agency charged with administering the cutbacks in the various forms of energy is to maximize the total priority of the industrial activity after the cutbacks have been made. Thus, it must allocate the reductions of each type of energy to the industries such that the remaining total industrial "worth" is as large as possible. This assumes that

190   *Analytical Planning*

each project may be "worth" something even if it is not fully implemented, with this "worth" lying somewhere between the projects priority (fully implemented) and zero (not implemented at all). The nature of this model variation requires defining a measure of inadequacy of the allocation and relate it to the priority of the project. Let e_{ij} be a measure of inadequacy of allocation of the ith resource to the jth project. Then e_{ij} is some function of the difference between what is required and what is allocated, i.e.,

$$e_{ij} = f(r_{ij} - a_{ij}),$$

such that

if $a_{ij} \geq r_{ij}$ then $e_{ij} = 1$, and

if $r_{ij} > 0$ (i.e., if at least some of the ith resource must be allocated)

and $a_{ij} = 0$, then $e_{ij} = 0$

A simple way to define f, plausible for small shortfalls, is as follows:

$$e_{ij}^* = \frac{a_{ij}}{r_{ij}} \text{ for those } r_{ij} > 0,$$

Variation 2. Still greater generality is obtained if, instead of taking resources and their uses to be fixed (such as would occur with a pre-existing inventory of material inputs) we assume that substitutions can be made among them. In the major planning endeavor discussed below, a 10-year time frame and nationwide perspective suggested that determining the substitutability and convertibility of potential inputs should be a major focus of the research.

A comprehensive transport plan to 1985 for the Sudan was recently constructed around a set of scenarios which represented alternative developmental paths for that country (Saaty, 1977). From the scenarios were drawn a set of transport projects. Hierarchical analysis of the impact of these projects upon a composite national scenario yielded priorities as measures of overall benefit. Additionally, project costs and scheduling, the availability of specific resources, and substitutions among resources were examined under the alternative developmental paths. In this illustration, we ignore complicating factors of project interdependence and scheduling which can, nevertheless, be handled by the imposition of additional project alternatives and additional cost constraints, respectively.

Again, we wish to maximize the total benefit of projects that can be completed. In this variation, however, conversion among resources can be undertaken over the lifetime of the plan. For example, certain classes of Sudanese labor can be hired to work on transport projects directly, or can be encouraged to emigrate and remit a portion of their hard currency earnings.

It may be possible for the pre-existing resource endowment to convert units of resource i for use in the transport system. In that case, we make allocations for a_{ij} as follows:

$$(a_{ij} - r_{ij}) \geq 0, \text{ subject to } \sum_{j=1}^{M} a_{ij} < n_i \quad i = 1, \ldots, N$$

for the case in which a project must be totally completed to be of any benefit. (In a transportation plan, many projects are typically preliminary to others and the former requires full implementation to be of any value.)

Note two features of this problem. First, a budgetary limitation is implicit in the vector $N = n_1, \ldots, n_N$ representing a pre-existing factor endowment. In the decade covered by the plan, growth and change in this resource base can be expected. Because the effective budget is dynamic, its projection is part of the planning process.

Second, there are two "stages" of allocation required to maximize total benefit. Each trial combination of projects creates a demand for selecting a scheme for converting resources. The conversion coefficients can be interpreted as an input/output matrix, and this stage of the allocation can therefore be performed by linear programming methods.

Case II. *Do Something as Cheaply as Possible*

Suppose, in these times of university contraction, that an entrepreneurial chairman of an academic department receives a large number of "requests for proposals" to do sponsored research. The chairman prioritizes these by hierarchical analysis of factors such as the amount of overhead yielded, the potential for scholarly achievement which they accord, and the amount of graduate employment which they generate. Recognizing the success of a proposal is problematic and that he lacks sufficient resources to respond to all the requests, the chairman sets as a target the submission of proposals with a given total benefit, i.e., a given aggregate priority. His target perhaps responds to hints by his dean about the level of research activity required to safeguard departmental size and autonomy.

The chairman's principal resource is his faculty. To each he assigns values reflecting the scholar's effectiveness at each of the activities that comprise proposal writing: literature summaries, budgeting, contacting colleagues in funding agencies, and the like.

On the minus side, the diversion of faculty from their normal duties engenders costs which may also be prioritized. Generally, the cost will differ among the N faculty members. If we denote by c_i the cost per hour of the ith scholar, and by n_{ij} the number of hours that scholars devote to proposal j, then the objective is to

Minimize $$\sum_{i=1}^{N} \sum_{j=1}^{M} c_i n_{ij} x_j,$$

192 Analytical Planning

Subject to $\sum_{j=1}^{M} b_j x_j \geq L$, L a minimum level of performance (6)

$$\sum_{j=1}^{M} b_j = 1 \tag{7}$$

$$\sum_{j=1}^{M} a_{kj} \leq a_k = \sum_{i=1}^{N} n_{ik} v_{ik} \tag{8}$$

For $j, k = 1, \ldots, M$,

$$x_{ij} = 1 \text{ if } (r_{ij} - a_{ij}) > 0, \tag{9}$$

$x_{ij} = 0$ otherwise;

$$x_i = 1 \text{ if } \sum_{j=1}^{M} x_{ij} = M$$

$x_i = 0$ otherwise

Variation. In the preceding example, proposals are an all-or nothing product. But there are many instances in which partial project performance is meaningful. Consider a political machine consisting of several professional party workers capable of performing a variety of services, such as getting snow removed, arranging school transfers, cutting red-tape, and so on. We assume that the machine has a well-defined territory so that each party worker takes the constituency as a whole as the object of service. Each worker's unique characteristics enable him to perform the gamut of services with varying degrees of effectiveness. The machine cannot completely provide all the services at the level demanded by its constituents. Indeed, it only needs to satisfy some minimal level of demand in order to gain re-election. The constituents reward even partial performance of each service with a degree of support. We assume that the machine has prioritized the services on the basis of their contribution to future electoral victory.

In analyzing earlier cutbacks in energy usage (Case I), we hypothesized that marginal reductions in each input debilitated the system's performance in a manner proportionate to the magnitude of that reduction. If this interpretation of partial project performance is retained, the machine may manage to get re-elected by doing many jobs poorly or partially. The political machine, we posit, wishes simply to minimize the total costs to party workers of performing services while ensuring re-election. In other words it,

Minimizes $\sum_{j=1}^{M} \sum_{i=1}^{N} c_i n_{ij} f_j$

Where $f_j = \prod_{i=1}^{N} e_{ij}$ given below,

Subject to
$$\sum_{i=1}^{N} c_i = 1$$

$$\sum_{j=1}^{M} b_j f_j \geq 1/2$$

$$\sum_{j=1}^{M} n_{ij} \leq n_i.$$

Define
$$e_{ij}^* = \frac{r_{ij} - \sum_{i=1}^{N} n_{ik} v_{ik}}{r_{ij}} \text{ for } a_{ij} > 0$$

if $e_{ij}^* > 0$ or if $r_{ij} = 0$, then $e_{ij} = 1$; otherwise $e_{ij} = 0$

Minimizing the objective function may still impose unacceptable costs on the party workers. In this case, the machine contracts an additional "budgetary" constraint on the objective function itself, which may not be satisfied. Consequently, the machine collapses because the party workers cease to support it.

Case III. Make the Benefit-to-Cost Ratio of a Package of Projects as Large as Possible

Taking both benefits and costs as priorities, we can form the benefit-to-cost ratio for any project j by dividing benefit priority (b_j) by cost weight (c_j). If we decompose the cost measure into units of partially substitutable resources, we have
$$\frac{b_j}{\sum_{i=1}^{N} c_i n_{ij}}$$
where c_i is the "cost" priority of one unit of resource i.

To make this quantity as large as possible, we add projects until constraints are exceeded. Specifically, the object is to

Maximize
$$\sum_{j=1}^{M} \frac{b_j f_j}{\sum_{i=1}^{N} c_i n_{ij}}$$

Where the sum is taken over those projects on which some resources are spent, i.e., for which $n_{ij} > 0$. The constraints are

$$\sum_{j=1}^{M} b_j = 1$$

$$\sum_{i=1}^{M} n_{ij} \leq n_i$$

and f_j is computed as above.

194 Analytical Planning

As an illustrative example, consider a public agency. With a fixed budget, it seeks to choose projects to maximize its cumulative benefit-to-cost ratio. The agency will attempt to expend all of its resources, fully aware that the B/C ratio of the "last" project chosen may be small. Indeed, if both benefits and costs are expressed as priorities, then the B/C ratio lacks the usual interpretation that unity is a "break-even" point. Because we have formed both benefit and cost priorities from hierarchical analysis over possibly heterogeneous components expressed in different units, it is entirely appropriate that B/C analysis should abandon its concern with the "break-even" concept and focus upon maximizing the aggregate ratio of a package of projects. To the extent that projects $j = 1, \ldots, N$ are a fairly exhaustive set of alternatives, the objective function above seeks allocation by maximization of the aggregate opportunity B/C ratios.

Variation 1. A variety of extensions of this benefit-cost analysis model can be developed. First, the ratio b_j/c_j can be rewritten in a form analogous to Marglin's formula which discounts future benefits and costs and allows investment and returns to extend asynchronously over several periods. A more sophisticated extension can be made to permit one to propose "cash flow" constraints or their analogue in priorities. We might seek to:
Maximize

$$\sum_{t=1}^{T} \sum_{j=1}^{M} \frac{b_{it} x_{jt}}{\sum_{i=1}^{N} c_i n_{ijt}}$$

where the indexing by t merely decomposes costs and benefits over time. An additional constraint for all $t = 1, \ldots, T$, which is a requirement for "cash flow" would then be:

$$\sum_{j=1}^{M} \frac{b_{jt} x_{jt}}{\sum_{i=1}^{N} c_i n_{ijt}} \geq F$$

where F itself may be a function of time.

Variation 2. A second dimension for extension is to make temporal interdependencies among projects explicit in their priorities. The simplest such scheme considers only pairs of projects and asks how their benefits and costs vary depending upon which is implemented first. For example, let $B = [b_{hj}]$ and $C = [c_{hj}]$ be $M \times M$ matrices for which project h precedes project j. Let $x_{hj} = 1$ if h precedes j (and $x_{hj} = 0$ otherwise) and if all the relevant conditions above are satisfied, then one might adopt the objective to:
Maximize

$$\sum_{h=1}^{M} \sum_{j=1}^{M} \frac{b_{hj} x_{hj}}{\sum_{i=1}^{N} c_i n_{ij}}$$

subject to the appropriate constraints.

More detailed temporal interdependencies are perhaps revealed through PERT or CPM, but these lie beyond the scope of this discussion.

To illustrate the models outlined earlier, consider a hypothetical problem confronting an air force officer who must select missions with a given unit of weapons systems. The example is constructed to capture some of the variations discussed above.

We initially assume that each of the missions has been prioritized by the senior staff and that the officer is evaluated on his ability to obtain the greatest benefit with forces available to him. The missions and their benefit priorities are:

	Ground support	Air defense	Transport	Reconnaissance
Priority:	.30	.40	.15	.15

The inventory of weapons systems available is as follows:

	Fighter bomber	Interceptor	Transport	Gunship	Attack helicopter
Number:	8	6	4	2	6

The matrix of resource requirements for each mission is as follows:

Regional units	Fighter bomber	Interceptor	Transport	Gunship	Attack helicopter
Ground support	7	0	0	1	4
Air defense	4	6	0	0	2
Transport	0	0	3	0	5
Reconnaissance	1	1	0	0	0

If the officer performs the highest priority mission, air defense, he is left with the following resources:

	Fighter bomber	Interceptor	Transport	Gunship	Attack helicopter
Remaining:	4	0	4	2	4

and achieves a benefit of 0.40. He can perform no other mission with the remaining resources. However, if he chooses to perform ground support plus

196 Analytical Planning

reconnaissance, he achieves a total benefit of .45 with some remaining resources.

	Fighter bomber	Interceptor	Transport	Gunship	Attack helicopter
Remaining:	4	0	4	1	2

By performing reconnaissance plus transport, a third possible option, he achieves a benefit of only .30. The choice of ground support and reconnaissance is thus seen to be the best solution available to the officer.

It is highly plausible that substitutions among weapons systems will enable the officer to perform missions in various ways. Let us assume that the officer has available the following estimates of the effectiveness of each weapon system in performing each mission. (Note that physical conversion of resources is not involved here.)

	Fighter bomber	Interceptor	Transport	Gunship	Attack helicopter
Fighter bomber	1	1/4	0	1/2	1/2
Interceptor	1/3	1	0	0	0
Transport	0	0	1	1/3	1/4
Gunship	0	0	1/5	1	1/2
Attack helicopter	0	0	0	1/3	1

For instance, cell (1, 2) gives the rate of substitution as requiring 4 fighter-bombers to do the work for which one interceptor is designed.

Again, we examine the choices available to the officer seeking to maximize mission benefits.

	Number of Units Remaining					
Missions	Fighter-bomber	Interceptor	Transport	Gunship	Attack helicopter	Cumulative benefits
A. Start with Ground Support	1	6	4	1	2	.30
Add Reconnaissance	0	5	4	1	2	.45
Use Gunships as Attack Helicopters	0	5	0	1	3	.45
Use Transports as Attack Helicopters	0	5	0	0	$3\frac{1}{2}$	.45

B. Start with						
Air Defense	4	0	4	2	4	.40
Use Gunships as Attack Helicopters	4	0	4	0	5	.40
Add *Transport*	4	0	1	0	0	.55

Examination of options shows that judicious substitution among weapon systems now make the choice of "air defense plus transport" superior to "ground support plus reconnaissance." The situation is obviously more complex if the officer receives some benefit from partial missions performed, a topic beyond this example.

Now suppose that the cost of mission performance is prioritized as follows:

Ground support	Air defense	Transport	Reconnaissance
0.35	0.35	0.24	0.06

Because we already know the performance possibilities, we can readily compute the benefit-cost ratios for each alternative as follows:

1. Air Defense and Transport

$$(0.40 + 0.15)/(0.35 + 0.24) = 0.55/0.59 = 0.93$$

2. Ground Support and Reconnaissance

$$(0.30 + 0.15)/(0.35 + 0.06) = 0.45/0.41 = 1.10$$

3. Reconnaissance and Transport

$$(0.15 + 0.15)/(0.24 + 0.06) = 0.30/0.30 = 1.00$$

These first benefit-cost ratios compare the desirability of each alternative with respect to the "do nothing" reference situation. Since the ratios are greater than some prespecified standard (say 0.8) any of the three alternatives is justified rather than doing nothing.

In our example, the "ground support plus reconnaissance" alternative has the highest preference ratio. However, the first preference ratio does not show whether the additional costs required for higher-cost alternatives are justified. As is done in Exhibit 7-6 we must compute an incremental preference ratio for every higher-cost alternative in comparison with every lower-cost alternative.

From Exhibit 7-6, "ground support plus reconnaissance" and "air defense plus transport" are clearly justified by comparison with the lowest cost "reconnaissance plus transport" alternative. However, the "air defense plus transport" is not justified in comparison with "ground support plus reconnaissance." From the foregoing, it can be seen that "ground support plus reconnaissance" is the preferable alternative.

198 Analytical Planning

EXHIBIT 7-6. *Incremental Benefit-Cost Ratios*

Alternatives	Benefit index	Cost index	Benefit-cost ratios of testing column alternatives compared to lower-cost alternatives in rows	
			Ground support plus reconnaissance	Air defense plus transport
Reconnaissance plus transport	0.30	0.30	0.15/0.11 = 1.36 > 0.8	0.25/0.29 = 0.86 > 0.8
Ground support plus reconnaissance	0.45	0.41		0.10/0.18 = 0.56 > 0.8 (Not justifiable)
Air defense plus transport	0.55	0.59		
Benefit index			0.45	0.55
Cost index			0.41	0.59

Before concluding, two points are in order. That the preferable alternative "ground support plus reconnaissance" also has the highest benefit-cost ratio is coincidental. Had we specified a lower standard (say 0.50), "air defense plus transport" would have been the preferred alternative. Secondly, this procedure assumes the absence of restrictions on capital financing which is not necessarily realistic. In the presence of capital rationing, we modify the decision rule by adding that the preferred alternative (using the decision rule) should be within capital restrictions; otherwise, we choose the next lower-cost alternative which meets the decision rule.

4. Conclusion

Normative economic theory, which provides the conceptual foundation for conflict-cost analysis and resource allocation, has been criticized for its restrictive assumptions and inapplicability to systematic problems particularly as they occur in the public sector (e.g., Zechauser and Schaefer, 1968). Specifically, *traditional* methods of benefit-cost analysis and resource allocation are incapable of adequately addressing three sets of problems frequently encountered by planners:

(1) *The Multiattribute Problem*: The costs and benefits of alternative policies or projects generally are characterized by many attributes, the relative importance of which cannot be sufficiently explored in two dimensional indifference maps, transformation curves, or other restrictive models derived from normative economic decision theory, systematic pairwise comparisons of the relative importance of attributes—in terms of benefits and costs—are made possible only with the construction of an N-dimensional analytic framework which does not attempt to force-fit decision criteria within the narrow confines of theoretical models.

(2) *The Qualitative Problem*: The costs and benefits of alternative projects cannot always be converted to a common metric such as dollars, gallons, or pounds. It is not possible, for instance, to devise "units" of urban renewal and "units" of national defense such that trade-offs can be made between the two and resources allocated accordingly. Thus, values placed on alternative outcomes must be based on subjective informed judgment and priorities should reflect knowledge derived from objective data as well as experience.

(3) *The Problem of Group Decision Making*: The emphasis of normative economic theory on personal utility functions and optimizing behavior fails to account for the likelihood that in any given planning context there are likely to be *multiple* decision makers each of whom may be pursuing unique and, perhaps conflicting objectives. Bargaining, compromise, and other political strategies often produce decisions that are acceptable to each actor yet optimal to none.

Traditional methods of benefit-cost analysis and resource allocation provide no explicit technique for eliciting and synthesizing the preferences of multiple decision makers.

The AHP addresses these three sets of problems without sacrificing the logical appeal and methodological rigor of normative economic theory. As such the AHP has successfully bridged the intellectual and philosophical gap which here-to-fore has stymied meaningful dialogue between economists and statisticians who have designed elegant normative decision models and organization theorists and political scientists who have constructed realistic descriptive models of actual decision making processes. Moreover, this dialogue will be enriched by the presence of a fully developed methodology which can be applied and studied in many planning contexts.

References

Gass, S. I. (1975) *Linear Programming*, 4th Edition, McGraw-Hill, New York.
Marglin, Stephen A. (1967) *Public Investment Criteria: Benefit-Cost Analysis for Planned Economic Growth*, MIT Press: Cambridge, MA.
Saaty, Thomas L. (1980) *The Analytic Hierarchy Process: Planning, Priority Setting, Resource Allocation*, McGraw-Hill: New York.
Saaty, Thomas L. (1977) The Sudan Transport Study, *Interfaces*, **8**, No. 1, pp. 37–57.
Saaty, Thomas L. and Mariano (January 1979) Rationing Energy to Industries: Priorities and Input-Output Dependence, *Energy Systems and Policy*, **8**, pp. 85–111.
Saaty, Thomas L. and Luis G. Vargas (1979) A Note on Estimating Technological Coefficients by Hierarchical Measurement, *Socio-Economic Planning Science*, **13**, pp. 333–336.
Shepard, R. N. (1962) The Analysis of Proximities: Multidimensional Scaling with an Unknown Distance Function, *Psychometrika*, **27**.
Wind, Yoram and Thomas L. Saaty (July 1980) Marketing Applications of the Analytic Hierarchy Process, *Management Science*, **26**, pp. 641–658.

Suggested Readings

Arrow, Kenneth and Leonid Hurwicz (1977) *Studies in Resource Allocation*, Processes, New York: Cambridge Press.

After a brief general introduction, this book turns to a theoretical treatment of selected and highly specialized topics in resource allocation. Multiple objective programming is treated in detail.

Mishan, Edward J. (1976) *Cost-Benefit Analysis* (2nd edition) New York, Praeger.
This book provides a sound basis on which to expand one's exploration of cost-benefit analysis. After a brief treatment of simplified applications, the author examines economic principles and assumptions of the technique and proceeds through progressively more sophisticated applications.

Sugden, Robert and Alan Williams (1978) *The Principles of Practical Cost-Benefit Analysis*, Oxford: Oxford University.
This book limits its treatment of economic principles to those that are directly relevant to cost-benefit analysis. Moreover explicit discussions of cost-benefit analysis are presented only after a lengthy review of issues in project appraisal.

Thompson, Mark S (1980) *Benefit-Cost Analysis for Program Evaluation*, Beverly Hills: Sage.
This book is a straight forward and relatively non-technical exploration of benefit-cost analysis. Several useful discussions include those on interpreting benefit-cost calculations and use of subjectivity.

Other Books on Benefit-Cost Analysis and Resource Allocation

Anderson, Lee G. (1977) *Benefit-Cost Analysis: A Practical Guide*, Lexington: Lexington Books.

Dantzig, George (1963) *Linear Programming and Extensions*, Princeton: Princeton University Press.

Gramlich, Edward M. (1981) *Benefit-Cost Analysis of Government Programs*, Englewood Cliffs: Prentice Hall.

Marglin, Stephen A. (1967) *Public Investment Criteria: Benefit-Cost Analysis for Planned Economic Growth*, Cambridge: MIT Press.

Mishan, Edward J. (1982) *Cost-Benefit Analysis: An Informal Introduction*, Boston: G. Allen and Unwin.

Oxenfeldt, Alfred R. (1979) *Cost-Benefit Analysis for Executive Decision Making: The Danger of Plain Common Sense*, New York: AMACON.

Vance, May (1982) *Cost-Benefit Analysis: A Book List*, Monticello: Vance Bibliographies.

Author Index

Ackoff, R. 9, 18, 63, 85, 93, 109, 128, 129–130
Allison, G. 85
Anderson, L. 200
Anderson, N. H. 59, 61
Arbel, A. vii, 56
Arrow, K. 199
Ashby, W. 9

Baird, B. 102, 128
Baker, F. 9
Bates, D. 177
Beckett, J. A. 9
Beer, S. 5, 9
Beishon, J. 9
Berlinski, D. 9
Berrien, F. 9
Bertalanffy, L. 8, 9, 15, 18, 85
Blauberg, I. 8, 18
Braners, W. K. 9
Boguslow, R. 9
Bolan, R. 92, 128
Bonathy, B. 9
Bossel, S. 9
Boulding, K. 8, 13, 18
Bowditch 10
Brown, G. 177
Bryant, C. 177
Bryant, S. 85
Buckley, W. 9

Campbell, D. 91, 128, 130
Caplan, N. 124, 128
Catanese, A. 10
Cavallo, R. E. 10
Ceisler, R. 154
Chadwick, G. 10
Chardin, T. 79
Chartrand, R. 10
Chen, J. 177
Churchman, C. W. 8, 10, 17, 18, 85, 130
Cliff, N. 59, 61
Coombs, G. H. 57, 61
Cooper, W. W. 10

Dalkey, N. C. 128
Dantzig, G. 200

Davidoff, P. 90, 128, 177
DeGreen, K. 10
Democritus 13
Depeyrot, M. 10
Deutch, K. 10
Dewey, J. 130
Diesing, P. 94, 128
Domieson, F. 154
Dror, Y. 90, 128
Dunn, W. N. 65, 85, 110, 128

Eastman, C. 10
Edwards, W. 122, 128
Ellul, J. 8, 18
Emery, F. E. 10, 63, 68, 85
Emshoff, J. 8, 10, 118, 129, 176, 177
Enzer, S. 128
Epstein 177
Ericson, R. 10
Esselman, T. 177
Etzioni, A. 108, 128, 130
Exton, W. 10

Faludi, A. 92, 128
Farquar, P. 128
Faurre, P. 10
Feyerabend, P. 131
Forrester, J. W. 10, 100, 128
Frohock, F. 108, 128
Fuller, B. 10

Gaffney, R. 177
Gallanter, E. 58, 62
Gardiner, P. 122, 128
Gass, S. 199
Geertz, C. 94, 128, 130
Gilmartin, K. 73, 86
Glazer, E. 102, 128
Goehlert, R. 177
Gordon, T. 128
Greenberger, M. 102, 128
Guilford, J. D. 57, 62
Guttentag, M. 91, 128

Hall, D. 10
Hammond, K. R. 59, 61, 120, 128, 130

Author Index

Helmer, O. 85, 115, 128, 131
Holzner, B. 85
Hoos, I. 10
Hotelling, H. 58, 61
Huber, G. 131
Hudson, B. 90, 96, 129
Huse, E. 10
Husserl, E. 96

Jantsch, E. 10
Johnson, N. 10
Johnson, R. 10
Jones, C. 90, 94, 129

Kast, F. E. 10
Keeney, R. L. 122, 129
Keane, M. 154
Kearns, J. 85
Kearns, K. P. 73, 85
Kelleher, G. J. 10
Kelly, W. F. 10
King, W. 177
Kircher, P. 10
Klir, G. 10
Krantz, D. H. 58, 61
Kuhn, T. 7, 8, 18

Lane, R. 98, 128
Laudan, L. 96, 128
Lawrence, P. 74, 85
Lazlo, E. 11, 16, 18
LeShan, L. 7, 8
Lilienfeld, R. 11
Lindblom, C. 97, 103, 128
Linstone, H. 115, 129
Lorsch, J. 74, 85
Luce, R. D. 57, 61

MacRae, D. 12, 18
Margenan, H. 7, 8
Marglin, S. 179, 199
Mandell, M. 177
Marx, J. 85
Mason, R. 10, 177
Matthies, L. 11
McAllister, D. 177
McConney, M. 48, 61
Mesarovic, M. P. 11, 85
Merton, C. 11
Miles, R. 11
Milinar, Z. 11
Milsum, J. H. 11
Mintzberg, H. 85, 108, 129
Mishan, E. 200

Mitroff, I. 8, 9, 118, 129, 132
Monod, J. 64, 85
Moskow, M. 177
Muller, N. 9
Mumpower, J. 129

Nagel, S. 102, 129
Nagler, T. 177
Neef, M. 102, 129
Norman, O. 177

Oxenfeldt, A. 200
Odum, H. 8

Patton, M. 65, 85
Peters, G. 9
Piaget, J. 72, 85
Pill, J. 115, 129
Pressman, J. 106, 129

Raiffa, H. 122, 129
Raisinghani, D. 85
Rapaport, A. 99, 129
Rein, M. 69, 86, 131
Reiner, T. 90, 128
Reiman, A. 11
Resoher, N. 85, 128, 130
Rittel, H. 177
Roessner, J. D. 73, 86
Rogers, P. 177
Rosenzweig, J. E. 10
Rossi, R. 73, 86
Roy, B. 62
Ruben, B. D. 11

Saaty, T. 8, 11, 18, 20, 31, 36, 43, 47, 86, 176, 177, 189, 190, 199
Sagasti, F. 9
Sardovsky, N. 8, 18
Schutz, A. 96, 129
Seiler, F. 11
Shannon, C. 8
Shepard, R. N. 62, 199
Simon, H. 4, 8, 68, 86, 97, 103, 128
Sommerhoff, G. 86
Stanley, J. 91, 128
Steiner, G. 177
Steiss, A. 10
Stevens, S. 58, 62
Struening, E. 91, 128
Sugden, R. 200
Summers, D. A. 59, 61
Sundquist, J. 102, 129

Suppes, P. 57, 61
Sutherland, T. W. 11, 86
Sztompka, P. 129

Takahara, Y. 11
Tate, M. 11
Teune, H. 11
Theorit, A. 85
Thom, R. 86
Thompson, M. 200
Thurstone, L. L. 57, 62
Torgerson, W. S. 58, 62
Trist, E. L. 68, 85
Tucker, L. R. 59, 62
Turoff, M. 115, 129

Vance, M. 200
Vargas, L. 20, 59

Van Gigch, J. P. 11
Verchota, J. 48, 61

Watson, J. 8
Weaver, W. 4, 8, 100, 129
Weinberg, G. 11
Wein, P. 11
Werck, K. 11
Wiener, N. 8, 17, 18
Wildavsky, H. 97, 105, 106, 129, 177
Wilson, E. O. 8, 18
Wind, Y. 199
Wright, C. 11

Young, S. 11
Yudin, G. 8, 18

Zadeh, L. A. 11

Subject Index

Actors 142, 155
Adaptive systems 84
AHP steps 38
Alternatives 90
Analytic Hierarchy Process 19, 133
Anticipatory scenario 135
Arms race 6
Artificial intelligence 17
Assumptions 118
Attractor 78

Backward planning, power generation 151
Backward process 42, 138
Benefit-cost 178
Brand-loyalty 154

Causal explanation 13
Causality, physics 14
Cause
  efficient 14
  final 14
  formal 14
  material 14
Centralization 76, 80
Chaos 78
Choice, optimal 126
Coding 77
Common sense rationality 94, 105
Comparative judgment 22
Competitors 156
Complexity 3, 4, 17, 39, 100
Composite scenario 135, 156
Conflict 8, 68
Conflicting goals 5
Congress 49
Conservationists 50
Consistency 33
Consortium 171
Constraints 67
Consumer product company 154
Contextual rationality 94, 105
Contrast scenario 135
Control 81
Convergence 98, 161
Cost efficient 101
Cost-benefit 12
Criteria, intangible 105

Cultivation 6
Cybernetics 17
Cycles of events 78

Dam, Tellico 48
Decision making 22
Decomposition 21
  principle 20
Delphi method 115
Dependence 52
Design 67, 81, 84
Desired future 160
Deterministic 14
Diagnosis 112
Dialectics 113
Difference scale 141
Differentiation 4, 76
Directiveness 79
Discrimination 22
Dynamic homeostasis 77
Dynamic teleology 78

Econometric forecasting 102
Economy 6
Effective plan 101
Efficiencies 137
Efficient cause 14
Energy importation 76
Entropy 77
Environment 66
Environmental constraints 68
Equifinality 79
Equilibrium 75, 77
Evaluation 67
Expansionist 13
Expert Choice 36
Explanation, causal 13
Exploratory scenario 135, 156

Facts 12
Faculty 142
Feedback 63, 80, 115
  delayed 68
Final cause 14
Finality 78
Flows 70

Subject Index

Food production 5
Forecasting, econometric 102
Formal cause 14
Formal planning 90, 98
  higher education 140
Forward process 41, 137
Forward-backward 154
  planning 134
  synfuels 167
Functions 69
Fundamental problems 83
Future 167
  desired 98
  likely 97
Fuzziness 81

Game rationality 94, 105
Gap 97
Gasohol 174
Generic planning 91
Goal directedness 86
Goal, influence 14
Goals 64, 90
  conflicting 5
Government 142
Group decision making 199
Group judgments 46
Group participation 43
Groups 114
Growth in time 77

Hierarchies
  and complexity 39
  dominance 41
Hierarchization 16
Hierarchy
  aids to structure 40
  analytic 19
  backward 42
  crossing a river 183
  foreign expansion 181
  forward 41
  higher generation 142
  power generation 152
  promotional strategies 158
  synfuels 169
Higher education
  forward 140
  hierarchy 142
  planning 140
Holistic 79, 110
Homeostasis 77
House buying 20
Human purpose 64

Ideals 64
Identification 91
Identity, principle 20
Ill-structured problem 9
Implementation 91, 106, 124
Incremental planning 91, 103
Inductive 13
Industry 142
Information 77
Input 77
Intangible 6
  criteria 105
Intensity 4
Interaction 4
Interdependence 4
Isomorphism 15

Job selection 47
Judgments, group 46

Knowledge 7
  growth of 113

Laissez faire 89
Legal rationality 94
Local priorities 30
Logical positivism 12
Logistics curve 57

Management Science 7
Material cause 14
MAU method 122
Mechanization 76
Meta-rationality 94
Multiattribute problem 198
Multiattribute utility 60
Multiattribute Utility Theory 122
Multicriterion decision analysis 59

Negative entropy 77
Negative feedback 77
Network systems 52
Newtonian physics 7
Normative scenario 135

Objective data 50
Objective reality 12
Objectives 64
  tactical 93
Open system 14
  characterization 74
  properties 75

Subject Index 207

Operations Research 7, 17
Optimal choice 126
Optimal, pareto 61
Optimization 68, 97
Organization structure 73
Organization, self 16
Outcomes 90, 137

Pairwise comparison 22
Pareto Optimal 61
Participant 105
Participants 22
People 87
Perceptions 67
Performance, measurement 46
Physics 14
Plan, effective 101
Planners 96
Planning definition 95
Planning process 134
Planning theories 89
Planning
  as a system 87
  as alignment 97
  definition 90
  formal 90, 98
  forward-backward 134, 154
  generic 91
  higher education 140
  incremental 91, 103
  philosophies 90, 98
  power generation 151
  rational choice 93
  strategic 87
  systematic 108
  systemic 91
Plans 90
Policies 90
Policy analysis 12
Power 68
Power generation 151
Principal component analysis 58
Principle of synthesis 34
Priorities 114
Priority 167
Probabilistic 14
Problem solving 8
  group 12
Problem structuring 91, 104, 109
Problem, ill-structured 9
Problematique 5
Process rationality 94
Process
  backward 138
  forward 137
Promotional strategies 158
Promotional techniques 155

Purpose 63, 67, 69, 78, 117
  human 64
Purposeful systems 63
Purposive systems 63

Question to ask 28
Questions 144

Rationality 87, 90
  common sense 105
  contextual 105
  game 105
  types 94
Reality 87
Reciprocal matrix 34
Reciprocal property 23
Reductionism 13
Reductionist logic 12
Relative weights 45
Resource allocation 178, 186
Resources, limited 188
Retailer relations 160
Retailers 156
Risk 165

SAST method 118
Satisficing 68, 97
Scale 27
Scale comparison 25
Scale justification 44
Scenario
  composite 135, 156
  exploratory 156
Scenarios
  contrast 135
  examples 141
  exploratory 135, 156
  normative 135
Scientific revolutions 7
Self-organization 16
Self-stabilization 16
SLS method 120
Snail darter 48
Social rationality 94
Stability 77
Stabilization 16
State variables 140
Status quo 171
Steady state, 75, 77
Steps of AHP 38
Strange attractor 78
Strategic assumptions 118
Strategic planning 87, 133
Structure, hierarchies 40
Structures 72
Students 142

Subject Index

Subjective 6, 7
Subjective judgment 28
Subsystems 74
Summativity 75
Symmetrical Linkage System 120
Synthesis 30
Synthetic fuels 167
System
  flow 70
  function 69
  implementation 124
  open 15
  planning 87
  purpose 63
  structure 72
  Symmetrical Linkage 120
Systemic planning 91, 108
Systems 12, 15, 63, 74, 81
Systems approach 8
Systems characteristics 63
Systems philosophy 16
Systems sciences 15
Systems study, object 81
Systems technology 15
Systems theory 17
Systems theory and record first fundamental problems 83
Systems
  adaptive 84
  design 84

problem structuring 109
purposeful 63
purposive 63
Synthesis 34

Technical rationality 94
Teleology 78
Tellico Dam 48
Tennessee Valley Authority 48
Third World 5
Time horizons 166
Transformation 76
Turbulence 68

Ultimate purpose 78
Ultimate truth 7
Uncertainty 165
Unique problems 68
Unstructured problems 100

Value free 69
Values 69
  study of 112
Vitalism 79

Wholeness 16, 75

Ratio scale, 17
Rationing, 10, 182, 184
Reciprocal, 24; matrix, 18
Reference projection, 56
Regulations, government, 255
Reliability, 88
Requirement process, 167
Requirements, 166
Resource: allocation, 9, 98; optimization, 177; relations, 173
Revolution, 123
Risk, 83, 247, 252; of obsolescence, 70
Rockwell International, 257
Royal Dutch Shell, 149

Saudi Arabia, 49
Scale, 21, 23
Scaling, 138
Scenario, composite, 59
Scenarios, 231; environmental, 229; priorities of, 58; of Sudan, 55
Second-order convergence, 70
Sensitivity analysis, 177
Shell Oil, 148
Shortfall, 91
Socal Oil, 148
Social factors, 254
Software, 95
Solar energy, 79
South Africa, 118, 134
Soviet influence, 197
Soviet Union, 122
Space limitations, 172
Spanning trees, 276
Stability: economic, 150; of hierarchy, 272
State variables, 106, 130, 131
Status quo, 138, 229
Stocks, 251
Storage, 94
Storage capacity, 84
Strategies, 290; investment, 63; management, 64
Subobjectives, 241, 244

Sudan, 45, 281; scenarios of, 55; map of, 46
Supermatrix method, 266

Tappan, 257
Technological: choice, 66; coefficients, 279; factors, 254
Technology, 77
Technology: choice, 73; transfer, 68
Texaco, 148
Time periods, 241
Time-dependent judgments, 261
Tradeoffs, 3
Training, 76
Transitivity, 18
Transmission, 88
Transport: plan process, 52; study, 4
Transportation, 77, 84
Tree, spanning, 276

Uganda, 50
Uncertainty, 83, 90, 247
United States, 122, 139, 153
U.S.: economy, 27; health system,
Utilization, 172

Vacation site, 34
Validity, 19
Value: constant and current, 148, 156, 292; expected, 155, 156
Variables, 106, 130
Vector, 18
Volatility, 229

Western powers, 121
White minority, 122
Win-draw-lose, 214
World Bank, 45, 65
World Energy Conference, 140

XYZ Research Institute, 83
XYZRI hierarchy, 87

Zaire, 50
Zimbabwe, 119

INDEX 301

Nile, 48
Normative planning, 104
Nuclear energy, 79, 94
Objective function, 166
Objectives, 12, 127; corporate, 229
Oil, 139
Oil: actors, 142; discovery rate, 200; embargo, 152; exporting countries, 144; market, 141, 151; price factors, 198; prices, 195; prices computation, 202; production capacity, 200; supply hierarchy, 158
OPEC, 139, 149, 195
OPEC behavior, 199
Optimization, 166
Options: diplomatic, 135; electric, 136; military, 135
OR people, 110
Ordered set, 30
Ordinal, 18
Organizing principle, 103
Outcomes, 105
Outline of AHP, 265

Pairwise comparisons, 17, 20
Parametric analysis, 224
Pareto optimal point, 153
Participants, 4
Participation, 102
Payoff, 290
Payoffs, 148
Peakload, 95
Peakload problems, 84
Performance, 101
Perron-Frobenius, 18
Persian Gulf, 197, 202
Plan, 47, 83; National Health Insurance, 179; problem areas, 48; transport, 52
Planning, 5, 99, 101; continuous, 102; corporate, 102; descriptive, 103; desired, 104; efficiencies, 105; integrated, 102; normative, 104; outcomes, 105; practice, 102; principles, 7; projected, 103; purpose of, 47

Planning: horizon, 89; policies, 104, 106; scheme, 105
Policies, 106; critical, 161; desired, 157; essential, 161; necessary, 161; significant, 161
Policy, Bantustan, 122
Political: climate, 85; cluster, 197; factors, 200, 254
Portfolio, 11; corporate, 240; and hierarchical model, 253; investment, 247; product, 228; selection, 227
Possible future, 8
Power, relative, 209
Powers, Western, 121
Prediction, 10, 215; of oil prices, 195; chess, 207
Preference, transitive, 21
Price increases, estimation of, 201
Prices of oil, 195
Pricing policies, 84
Prioritization, 51, 184
Priority, 4, 5, 14, 95, 182; absolute, 266; calculation of, 38; composite, 168; estimation of, 38; function of, 31; impact of, 266; range of, 261; ratio of, 241; of regions, 60; of scenarios, 58; sectoral, 71; setting of, 16
Problems, types of, 16
Processes: causal, 15; purposive action, 15
Product portfolio, 228
Production capacity of oil, 200
Products, new, 233
Profit maximization, 152
Profitability, 251
Programming model, 176
Projected future hierarchy, 112

Questionnaire, 276
Questions, types of, 22

R&D, 77
R&D: hierarchy, 86; planning, 83; policies, 108

Funding, 92; R&D, 88
Future, desired, 58
Future technology transfer, 69

Game, 215; nonzero sum, 161; two-person, 290
Game theory, 116
Geometric mean, 24
Goals, prioritization of, 248
Great Britain, 9
Great powers, 199
Group: interactions, 111; judgments, 115
Group of "77," 66
Gulf Oil, 148

Health, 75
Health care, 165; problem areas in, 179
Hierarchical: analysis, 207; composition, 33; decomposition, 109
Hierarchy: Bunge's definition of, 31; chess factors, 213; complete, 32; consistency, 36, 266; continuous, 270; corporate benefits, 242; corporate costs, 243; cost/benefit, 81; definition of, 31; desired future, 113; energy demand, 187; health resources, 170; Koopmans's definition of, 31; levels of, 31; marketing benefits, 237; marketing portfolio, 230, 232; medical objectives, 169; new-products, 235; oil price factors, 198; oil supply, 158; and portfolio model, 253; projected future, 112; purpose of, 4; Saaty's definition of, 31; South African conflict, 120; stability, 272; technology choice, 73; vacation site, 35
Hospital: requirements, 165; service data, 171; utilization data, 174
Human Rights, 137

I. D. Industries, 257
Impact priorities, 266

Implementation, 64
Inconsistency, 20
Independence, 27
Industry, 76
Input-output, 182
Input-output: analysis, 279; tables, 287, 288
Insurance, 229
Integer programming, 176
Integrated planning, 102
Intensity, 22
Interdependence, 153, 172
Intrinsic factors, 251
Investment: portfolio, 227, 247; strategies, 63
Investor, 12; objectives of, 251

Judgment, 24, 115

Karpov-Korchnoi Match, 215, 220
Kenya, 50
Kuwait Fund, 47

Leontief, W., 280
Less developed countries, 66
Light water reactor, 98
Linear programming, 188
Loop, 241
Loss functions, 85

Management strategies, 64
Managerial assessment, 103
Market share, 229, 233
Marketing benefits hierarchy, 237
Marketing mix, 236
Matrix powers, 270
Measurement, ratio scale, 17
Middle East oil, 197
Miller, G., 22
Mining, 75
Mobil Oil, 148
Morbidity, 167
Mortality, 167

NAFA Foundation, 269
Nash equilibrium, 148
Network structures, 266

INDEX

Clustering, 38, 241, 282, 283
Clustering schemes, 245
Coal, 94
Colonial Penn, 229
Communications, 76
Company future, 112
Competition, 207
Complete hierarchy, 32
Complexity, 3
Components, range of, 274
Composite scenario, 59
Computer algorithm, 270
Conflict, 118; Arab-Israeli, 197; South African, 118
Consistency, 19, 266; cardinal, 21; hierarchy, 36; index, 25; ratio, 25
Constant value, 148, 281, 292
Constraint matrix, 172
Consumption, 183
Continuous: hierarchy, 270; planning, 102
Control, 102
Coordination, 110
Core value, 274
Corporate: benefits hierarchy, 242; objectives, 229, 240; planning, 102; portfolio selection, 240
Corporations, 227
Cost(s)/benefit(s) hierarchy, 81; for corporation, 243; criteria for, 243
Counter policies, 107
Courses of action, 229
Criteria, 74, 185, 252; costs, 243; extrinsic, 252; intrinsic, 258; performance, 101
Current value, 148, 292
Customer, 230
Cutback, 183, 189

Data General, 257
Decision theory, 14
Decomposition, 39
Demand constraints, 172
Dependence, 27, 128
Descriptive planning, 103

Desired: future, 58, 139; future hierarchy, 113; planning, 104
Diplomatic options, 135
Discount rate, 85
Discounting, 97
Distance, estimate of, 25
Distribution, 77
Dominance, 21

Econometric models, 54
Economic, 26; activities, 53; clusters, 207; factors, 196, 254; options, 136
Economists, 110
Economy, 282
Education, 76
Efficiency, 105, 107
Egypt, 49
Eigenvalues, 18
Eigenvector, 267
Eigenvector range, 274
Electric power, 86
Electricity, 84; rationing of, 189
Energy, 182; demand hierarchy of, 187; nuclear, 79; solar, 79; sources of, 200; users of, 185. *See also* World Energy Conference
Environment: contextual, 106; transactional, 106
Environmental effects, 88
Ethnic group, 119
Expected value of strategies, 155
Extrinsic factors, 251
Exxon, 86

Factors: extrinsic, 252; intrinsic, 258; oil price, 198; technical and behavioral, 212
Feedback, 101, 208
Financial institutions, 201
Fischer-Spassky match, 216
Forward process: first, 123; priority, 126; second, 128; third, 129
Forward-backward process, 101, 103, 114
Fredholm integral equation, 272

INDEX

Absolute Measurement, 290
Actors, 68, 106; influence of, 70; oil, 142, 143
Adaptability, 70; ease of, 78
Adaptation capability, 103
ADAR, 281
Agriculture, 74, 284
Algorithm, 276
Allocation, 9, 85, 247
Analytic Hierarchy Process, 3, 4, 13, 15, 16, 40, 103, 116, 195, 227, 261, 281; extensions of, 264; network structures, 266; outline of, 265
Apartheid, 122
Applications, other, 275
Arab-Israeli conflict, 197
Aramco, 148
Aswan Dam, 50

Backward process, 65, 107, 155; first, 125; second, 128
Balanced regional growth, 57
Bantustan policy, 122
Behavior, 212
Benefit(s)/cost(s) hierarchy, 81, 91; for corporation, 242; criteria for, 242
Black majority, 121
British Petroleum, 148
Budget constraints, 172
Business: interests, 122; segments, 242; units, 243

Cardinal consistency, 18, 21
Cause-effect, 15
Chess, 208
Chess factors, 212
CIA, 140

The priorities for the intensities for DEPNBLTY in the main model are (0.479, 0.275, 0.157, 0.060, 0.029). They are "adjusted", by multiplying each by 1/0.479, where 0.479 is the highest priority among the intensities, for Outstanding, to (1.000, 0.574, 0.328, 0.125, 0.060). The priority for the DEPNBLTY criterion itself is 0.0746. The first employee, F. Hyat, is rated Outstanding, and receives a score of 0.0746 x 1.000 for DEPNBLTY, and so on for the remaining criteria. Had Hyat been rated V. Good under DEPNBLTY, the score would have been 0.0746 x 0.275. The verbal ratings are shown in Table 2, with corresponding scores shown in Table 3.

An "ideal" alternative, one that receives a top rating under every criterion, gets the highest possible overall score of 1.000 (since the sum of the global priorities of the lowest level criteria equals 1.000). Note that there is an "ideal" candidate, T. Peters, in row 3, who gets a perfect composite score of 1.000.

ALTERNATIVES	DEPNBLTY .0746	EDUCAT'N .2004	EXPER'NC .0482	QUALITY .3604	ATTITUDE .0816	LEADERSP .2348	TOTAL
1 HYAT, F	0.0746	0.0868	0.0482	0.3604	0.0816	0.2348	0.886
2 ADAMS, V	0.0746	0.0356	0.0207	0.3604	0.0293	0.2348	0.755
3 PETERS, T	0.0746	0.2004	0.0482	0.3604	0.0816	0.2348	1.000
4 BECKER, L	0.0746	0.0868	0.0482	0.1154	0.0816	0.2348	0.641
5 TOBIAS, K	0.0746	0.0868	0.0081	0.1154	0.0816	0.2348	0.601
6 O'SHEA, K	0.0746	0.0178	0.0482	0.1154	0.0816	0.2348	0.572
7 KESSELMAN, S	0.0245	0.0356	0.0034	0.3604	0.0816	0.2348	0.740
8 KELLY, S	0.0245	0.0356	0.0081	0.3604	0.0293	0.2348	0.693
9 WILLIAMS, E	0.0746	0.0868	0.0034	0.1154	0.0293	0.2348	0.544
10 WASHINGTON, S	0.0428	0.0868	0.0081	0.1154	0.0816	0.2348	0.570
11 JOSEPH, M	0.0094	0.0178	0.0081	0.3604	0.0125	0.2348	0.643
12 GOLDEN, B	0.0428	0.0356	0.0482	0.1154	0.0125	0.2348	0.489
13 BELL, W	0.0245	0.0868	0.0482	0.1154	0.0125	0.2348	0.522
14 ROGERS, M	0.0428	0.0356	0.0081	0.1154	0.0293	0.2348	0.466
15 EVANS, S	0.0245	0.2004	0.0081	0.1154	0.0125	0.2348	0.596
16 ZIMMERMAN, A	0.0428	0.0868	0.0081	0.1154	0.0125	0.2348	0.500
17 FRANK, P	0.0245	0.2004	0.0207	0.0599	0.0125	0.2348	0.553
18 WOODHEAD, A	0.0428	0.0178	0.0034	0.1154	0.0293	0.2348	0.443
19 LARSON, B	0.0245	0.0868	0.0482	0.0599	0.0125	0.2348	0.467
20 MILTON, D	0.0428	0.0356	0.0482	0.0599	0.0293	0.2348	0.451

From Expert Choice Software ratings utility

Table 2. Ratings Table Showing Numerical Scores.

The composite score for an employee is independent of the other employees that happen to be in the group being rated, though if an employee is up against a group of superior performers their scores will be higher and they will consequently rank higher. But the employee is rated against standards, and not against other employees directly.

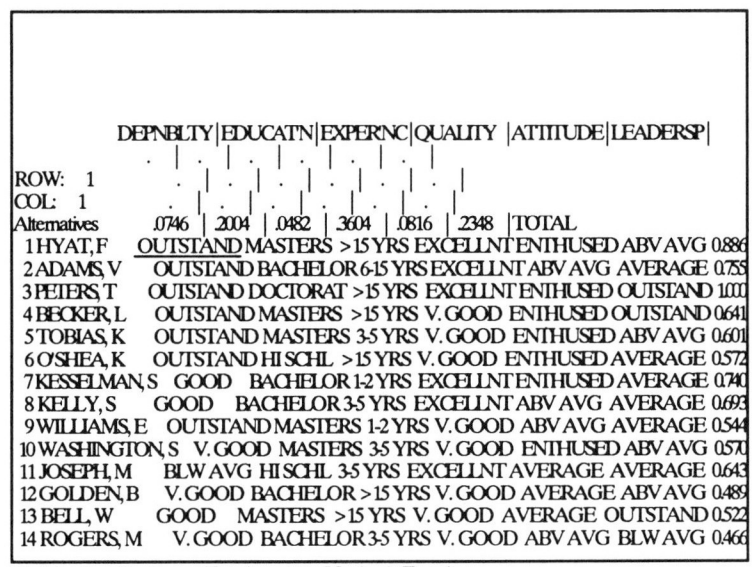

```
                DEPNBLTY|EDUCATN|EXPERNC|QUALITY |ATTITUDE|LEADERSP|
                    .  |   .   |   .   |   .    |    .   |    .   |
ROW:  1             .  |   .   |   .   |   .    |    .   |    .   |
COL:  1             .  |   .   |   .   |   .    |    .   |    .   |
Alternatives      .0746| .2004 | .0482 | .3604  |  .0816 |  .2348 |TOTAL
 1 HYAT, F        OUTSTAND MASTERS  >15 YRS EXCELLNT ENTHUSED ABV AVG  0.886
 2 ADAMS, V       OUTSTAND BACHELOR 6-15 YRS EXCELLNT ABV AVG AVERAGE  0.755
 3 PETERS, T      OUTSTAND DOCTORAT >15 YRS EXCELLNT ENTHUSED OUTSTAND 1.000
 4 BECKER, L      OUTSTAND MASTERS  >15 YRS V. GOOD ENTHUSED OUTSTAND  0.641
 5 TOBIAS, K      OUTSTAND MASTERS  3-5 YRS V. GOOD ENTHUSED ABV AVG   0.601
 6 O'SHEA, K      OUTSTAND HI SCHL  >15 YRS V. GOOD ENTHUSED AVERAGE   0.572
 7 KESSELMAN, S   GOOD     BACHELOR 1-2 YRS EXCELLNT ENTHUSED AVERAGE  0.740
 8 KELLY, S       GOOD     BACHELOR 3-5 YRS EXCELLNT ABV AVG AVERAGE   0.693
 9 WILLIAMS, E    OUTSTAND MASTERS  1-2 YRS V. GOOD ABV AVG AVERAGE    0.544
10 WASHINGTON, S  V. GOOD  MASTERS  3-5 YRS V. GOOD ENTHUSED ABV AVG   0.570
11 JOSEPH, M      BLW AVG  HI SCHL  3-5 YRS EXCELLNT AVERAGE AVERAGE   0.643
12 GOLDEN, B      V. GOOD  BACHELOR >15 YRS V. GOOD AVERAGE ABV AVG    0.489
13 BELL, W        GOOD     MASTERS  >15 YRS V. GOOD AVERAGE OUTSTAND   0.522
14 ROGERS, M      V. GOOD  BACHELOR 3-5 YRS V. GOOD ABV AVG BLW AVG    0.466
```

Table 1. Ratings Table with Verbal Entries.

The employees are now entered into a ratings table, shown in Table 1, and rated under each criterion by selecting the appropriate intensity for it. Verbal intensities are shown in Table 1 and the corresponding scores are shown in Table 2. The scores thus obtained are added across all the criteria to get a composite score. And now a word about how the scores are obtained. If an alternative gets the top rating for a criterion, it receives the entire global or weighted priority of that criterion for its score under that criterion. If it gets a lower rating it receives a proportionate amount of the priority. This is in accordance with the theory of the Analytic Hierarchy Process which says that priorities are ratio scale numbers. The ratio of the priorities for any two intensities gives their relative importance. The highest rating is assigned all the priority of the criterion, lower ratings get their proportionate share.

For example, suppose there were a criterion with three categories of intensities: Excellent (.60), Average (.30) and Poor (.10). An Excellent rating for an alternative would receive the entire priority of the criterion (.60/.60 or 1 times the priority of the criterion), an Average rating would receive .30/.60 or 1/2 times the priority of the criterion, and a Poor rating would receive .10/.60 or 1/6 times the priority of the criterion. Multiplying the priority of each rating in the set by 1/.60 to adjust them to the correct proportion of the "ideal". Multiply the priorities of (.60,.30,.10) by 1/.60 to get the adjusted values of (1.000,.5000,.1667). The score of an alternative for the criterion is the product of its adjusted rating and the priority of that criterion.

EMPLOYEE EVALUATION

The goal in this example is to evaluate employees using absolute measurement and compare the employees individually against established standards. The criteria are DEPNBLTY, EDUCAT'N, EXPERNCE, QUALITY, ATTITUDE and LEADERSHP. The rating intensities for DEPNBLTY are Outstanding, Above average, Average, Below average, and Unsatisfactory, for EDUCAT'N the rating intensities are Doctorate, Masters, Bachelor, High School, and so on for the other criteria. The main part of the model is shown in Figure 1.

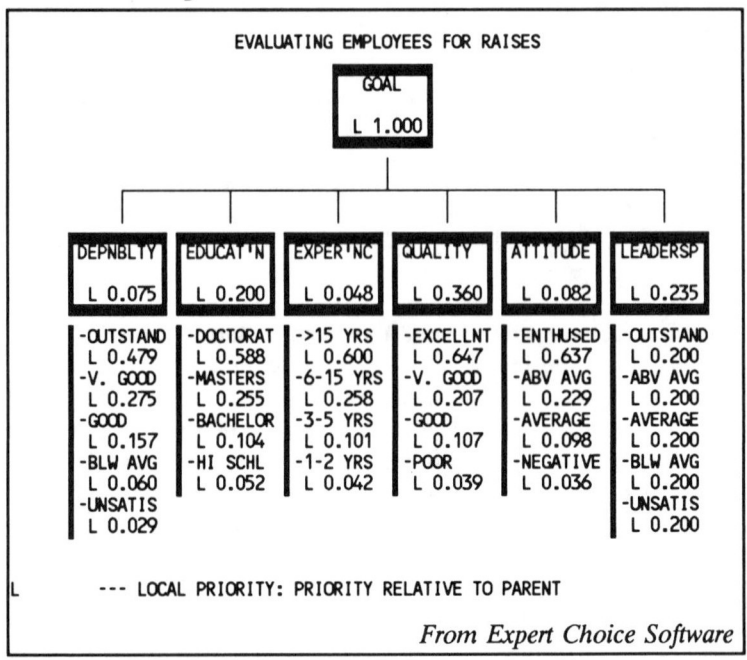

```
EVALUATING EMPLOYEES FOR RAISES
                GOAL
              L 1.000
```

DEPNBLTY	EDUCAT'N	EXPER'NC	QUALITY	ATTITUDE	LEADERSP
L 0.075	L 0.200	L 0.048	L 0.360	L 0.082	L 0.235
-OUTSTAND L 0.479	-DOCTORAT L 0.588	->15 YRS L 0.600	-EXCELLNT L 0.647	-ENTHUSED L 0.637	-OUTSTAND L 0.200
-V. GOOD L 0.275	-MASTERS L 0.255	-6-15 YRS L 0.258	-V. GOOD L 0.207	-ABV AVG L 0.229	-ABV AVG L 0.200
-GOOD L 0.157	-BACHELOR L 0.104	-3-5 YRS L 0.101	-GOOD L 0.107	-AVERAGE L 0.098	-AVERAGE L 0.200
-BLW AVG L 0.060	-HI SCHL L 0.052	-1-2 YRS L 0.042	-POOR L 0.039	-NEGATIVE L 0.036	-BLW AVG L 0.200
-UNSATIS L 0.029					-UNSATIS L 0.200

L --- LOCAL PRIORITY: PRIORITY RELATIVE TO PARENT

From Expert Choice Software

Figure 1. Employee Evaluation Hierarchy with Criteria Intensities.

The priorities are derived through the usual pairwise comparison process, including those for the rating intensities. For example, when comparing the intensities for DEPNBLTY one would be answering such questions as "How much more preferred is an 'Outstandingly dependable employee' than an 'Above average dependable employee'?" "How much more preferred is an 'Outstandingly dependable employee' than an 'Average dependable employee'?" Or, for EDUCAT'N, "How much preferred is an 'Employee with a college Bachelor's degree' to an "Employee with a high school degree'?"

USING RANGES FOR INTENSITIES

Often people are more comfortable making judgments if the intensities are expressed as ranges. To use ranges name the nodes representing the intensities appropriately. For example, to evaluate employees for "Years of Experience" use four nodes: 1-2 YRS, 3-5 YRS, 6-15 YRS, > 15 YRS (more than than 15 years). Categories such as this are easier to conceptualize and compare. Notice that the ranges do not have to be equal in span. The important thing is to convey the information about the individual being rated and to use ranges that are logical to the evaluator. Years of experience convey something about how useful the employee is to the company and an experienced evaluator knows, just about, what experience of 1-2 YRS, or 6-15 YRS means. It would perhaps make no sense to the evaluator to distinguish between 9 years and 10 years of experience. But the same evaluator might be very comfortable with ranges for the categories; these ranges might equally well have names such as Novice, Some experience, Solid experience, and Senior person. To establish the priorities one needs to answer such questions as: How strongly preferred is 3-5 years of experience over 1-2 years of experience? And 6-15 years of experience over 1-2 years of experience? These are meaningful questions and can be answered by an expert experienced at evaluating the criterion in question.

NONLINEAR RANGES

The priorities for the intensities are custom made for the situation at hand and cannot be derived independently from the problem to which they relate. Notice that priorities do not have to increase or decrease uniformly; the only requirement is that they increase understanding of the problem. Priorities for the intensities might go from small to large and back to small. Consider the following example. Suppose the problem were to evaluate temperature for comfort. The intensities are expressed as temperature ranges in Fahrenheit: below 32 degrees, 33-55 degrees, 56-90 degrees, 91-110 degrees and 110-140 degrees. Priorities might end up something like this, respectively: .06, .26, .53, .11, and .03, with temperatures at both extremes getting low priorities. Conversely, if the problem were to establish priorities for temperature ranges for *preventing* bacteriological growth, the reverse would occur. Temperature ranges above boiling or below freezing would get the highest values, and temperatures in the intermediate ranges would get the lowest values.

then allow rank to take its natural course. Forcing rank preservation can lead to wrong results in problems where rank should naturally be allowed to reverse if it must. For new or one-of-a-kind situations in which there is no history of decision making, and no standards have been developed through experience, the relative approach, involving pairwise comparisons throughout, is best.

Absolute measurement requires prior information on the intensities of the criteria. These intensities are set independently of the current crop of alternatives. Any alternative coming along is then rated on these intensities. Contrast this with the relative measurement approach of comparing particular alternatives in pairs with respect to each criterion. Thus absolute measurement is prioristic, relative measurement is oriented to the present and what one has in hand. The former depends on past experience for information from which the standards are derived. The latter needs no standards and simply compares currently available alternatives in relative terms.

An added benefit of absolute measurement is that it can handle hundreds of alternatives more efficiently than the relative measurement method which is to cluster them hierarchically in groups until the groups are small enough to compare the elements in pairs. Many decision problems of an evaluative nature tend to have large numbers of alternatives and *are* well-understood problems with established guidelines and procedures. The rating approach is appropriate for such problems as: evaluating personnel, admitting students, prioritizing road repair projects, and evaluating research projects. However, one should not force the use of the rating approach in the absence of prior experience merely because there are a large number of alternatives to be ranked.

In a rating model there are rating sets or intensities such as A,B,C,D and F in the school grading system, or Excellent, Average, Poor in a general evaluation system, or whatever subranges of a continuous range from which one exclusively and exhaustively is able to make distinctions. The alternatives are then rated on these ranges of intensity for each criterion. Priorities are established throughout the model in the usual way by making paired comparisons. Thus the intensities themselves are pairwise compared according to preference or dominance for each criterion. The number of intensities and their kind may differ from one criterion to another. They will serve as our yardsticks for absolute measurement once priorities have been established for them. The alternatives themselves do not appear in the main model, but are entered into a rating table where they are "rated" by selecting the appropriate intensity for each on each lowest level criterion. A score is computed for each alternative by adding up its intensity scores for all the criteria.

may have been preferred to item B, but when item C is added to the group, item B is now preferred to item A, as in Forman's example above.

Marketing professionals make an interesting use of this phenomenon. A phantom item is introduced, which is not actually available for purchase, solely to sway the consumer's perception of the items that are available. One of the available items, which otherwise would be ranked low, now gets ranked high because of the phantom. Consider the real estate salesman. He takes a couple to see an inexpensive house which they dislike, and an expensive house which they like, but think costs too much. Price is their most important criterion, so they end up preferring the inexpensive house overall. The salesman now takes them to see a model of houses to be built in the future that will be much more expensive, but will have only a few more features than the house they liked, but had decided not to buy on grounds of price. The salesman knows this house is not a true candidate, as it is far too expensive: it is a phantom. The couple goes back and buys the more expensive house after all, reversing their preferences after mentally adding in the "phantom" house and doing relative comparisons.

ABSOLUTE MEASUREMENT AND RATINGS

Criteria need to be always compared in pairs. The alternatives are sometimes compared and at other times rated one by one. Let us see when, how and why.

Absolute measurement is measurement against a standard. It is a very different concept from relative measurement. When a yardstick is used to measure a room, one is performing absolute measurement using the yardstick as a standard. Those measurements are not changed by measuring other items later with the same yardstick. The measurements are independent. Absolute measurement in a multicriteria environment is an extension of this idea. For each criterion or subcriterion we develop a kind of yardstick that we then apply independently to any alternative that comes along.

In absolute measurement, rank adjustment, or reversal, cannot take place. Once an alternative has a score, that score does not change. If alternative A has a higher score than alternative B, A will always rank higher than B, no matter how many alternatives are rated later, nor how many are slipped into place between A and B, having gotten intermediate scores.

In any decision one must first decide whether one has enough experience and knowledge to set norms as a result of which one wants to preserve rank. If not, one still needs enough knowledge to make paired comparisons, but must

The following example of desirable rank adjustment is due to Ernest Forman.

"Consider the evaluation and ranking of employees in a small firm with half a dozen or so employees. Suppose that Susan is as good as or slightly better than John with respect to all attributes except one; John is the only employee who is proficient in the use of personal computers and in understanding what needs to be done with both the hardware and software in order to meet the firm's clients' needs. Suppose a multicriteria evaluation is performed and that the results indicate that John is the most valuable to the firm, with Susan a close second.

Subsequently, a new employee is hired, who is very knowledgeable about the use of PC's, but not quite as knowledgeable as John. John is also superior to the new employee in all other criteria as well. Since John dominates the new employee, the new alternative is "irrelevant" and, according to some decision theory practitioners, "should not" affect the ranking of the pre-existing employees. Is this necessarily reasonable? Since John's *relative* value to the firm has certainly been diminished, "should" John still be more valuable to the firm than Susan?

To see that a prohibition of rank adjustment in this evaluation is not reasonable, suppose more and more (similar) "irrelevant" alternatives are hired. Surely there would come a point where the value of John's ability with PC's would be diluted to the point where Susan would be considered to be the most valuable employee."

In relative measurement, rank adjustment or reversal never happens under a single criterion, but only happens in multicriteria ranking. Susan will never be ranked higher than John in computer skills, no matter how many other employees are later hired and evaluated for their computer skills. But she can be ranked higher on overall value to the company, a multicriteria assessment, later when other employees are added.

Stated generally, if item A is preferred to item B on a single criterion and item C is then added to the comparison set, it can never happen if the judgments are consistent that then one would assess item B to be preferred to item A because item C is now in the picture. With overall composite priorities in multicriteria settings with relative measurement, however, item A

APPENDIX B:
Absolute Measurement - Rating Alternatives One at a Time

ABSOLUTE VERSUS RELATIVE MEASUREMENT

Here we talk about another method for ranking alternatives known as absolute measurement. We have seen examples of relative measurement where the priorities of the criteria and subcriteria are computed using relative measurement, comparing them in pairs, as are the priorities of the alternatives. Now we look at another way to rank the alternatives, although the criteria must continue to be ranked using relative measurement. To gain a better understanding of it, we shall first point out what effect comparing alternatives relatively in pairs has on their rankings. We then transit to a discussion and an illustration of absolute measurement.

In relative measurement, the alternatives under consideration affect each other's rank, scales that are derived are tailored to the particular problem at hand with its criteria and its alternatives. Anything one does to change the structure of the problem, by adding new criteria, or new alternatives, or dropping some out, can change everything. The goal, the criteria, the alternatives, their characteristics and their number are the *structural* features of the model. The model is a package and comprises the universe of the decision. Everything is relative and it is a closed world - what one takes, another gives.

For example, in comparing cars where engine power is a criterion, if one car in the group has a powerful engine and the rest have smaller variable power engines, the car with the powerful engine is going to get most of the priority in the comparison under engine power. If engine power has a high priority, the cars with small engines are going to suffer in engine power, and consequently in overall priority. But if the powerful car is removed, it can no longer take up most of the priority under engine power and the rest of the cars in the group split the newly available priority among themselves. If their engine power is about the same, it may be that it is no longer such an important factor to distinguish among the cars, and some other criterion such as style, or cost, on which the cars differ substantially, will become the one that determines their overall ranking. The overall priority of the cars, and their rankings in the new situation, may be entirely different than they were before. We call this rank adjustment, sometimes referred to as rank reversal, and it may take place under relative measurement whenever members of the comparison group (or the criteria themselves) are changed. Rank adjustment here is entirely normal and desirable.

———. 1941. *Structure of the American Economy, 1919-1929*. New York: Oxford University Press.
Levine, H.S. 1962. "Input-Output Analysis and Soviet Planning." *American Economic Review* 52:127-37.
Lombardini, S. 1970. "A Model for Regional Planning Applied to the Piedmont Region." In A.P. Carter and A. Brody, eds., *Applications of Input-Output Analysis*. New York: North-Holland.
Ministry of Finance and Economics. 1962. *The Ten-Year Plan of Economic and Social Development, 1961/62-1970/71*. Khartoum.
Nelson, H.D.; M. Dobert; G.C. McDonald; J. McLaughlin; B.J. Marvin; and P.C. Moeller. 1973. *Area Handbook for the Democratic Republic of Sudan*. Washington, D.C.: GPO.
Newman, P.C. 1952. *The Development of Economic Thought*. Englewood Cliffs, N.J.: Prentice-Hall.
Phillips, A. 1955. "The Tableau Economique as a Simple Leontief Model." *Quarterly Journal of Economics* 69:135-44.
Spiegel, H.W. 1952. *The Development of Economic Thought*. New York: Wiley.
United Nations. 1958. *Structure and Growth of Selected African Economies*. New York: United Nations Publication.
Wonnacott, R.J. 1961. *American-Canadian Dependence: An Interindustry Analysis of Production and Prices*. Amsterdam: North-Holland.
Yan, C. 1968. *Introduction to Input-Output Economics*. New York: Holt, Rinehart & Winston.

Table A.3. Actual Input-Output Coefficients Obtained in the Sudan Transport Study

	AGR	P.U.	M&M	T&D	CONS	SERV
AGR	.00737	0	.21953	.00042	.06721	0
P.U.	.00024	0	.01159	.00618	0	.00283
M&M	.00393	0	0	.00857	.04216	.00322
T&D	.06993	.14536	.12574	0	.09879	.00641
CONS	0	0	0	0	0	.05402
SERV	0	.01030	.02549	.02422	.00520	.00021

Comparison with table A.3, constructed by the Wharton Econometric Forecasting Associates, which itself involved considerable approximation, shows that most differences between the elements of the two tables are small.

REFERENCES

ADAR. 1975. *The Sudan Transport Study*, vols. 1-5. The Democratic Republic of the Sudan in Association with the Kuwait Fund for Arab Economic Development. The ADAR Corporation.

Bank of Sudan. 1963. *Economic and Financial Bulletin.* Economics Department of the Bank of Sudan.

Carter, H.O., and D. Irery. 1970. "Linkage of California-Arizona Input-Output Models to Analyze Water Transfer Patterns." In A.P. Carter and A. Brody, eds., *Readings of the Fourth International Conference of Input-Output Techniques.* New York: North-Holland.

Collins, R.O., and R L. Tignor. 1967. *Egypt and Sudan.* Englewood Cliffs, N.J.: Prentice-Hall.

Gherity, J.A. 1965. *Economic Thought: A Historical Anthology.* New York: Random House.

Government of Sudan. 1962. *Ten Year Plan of Economic and Social Development.*

Gusten, R. 1966. *Problems of Economic Growth and Planning: The Sudan Example.* New York: Springer-Verlag.

Hirsch, W.Z. 1959. "Interindustry Relations of a Metropolitan Area." *Review of Economics and Statistics* 41:360-69.

IIFT. 1967. *Export Market on Sudan.* New Delhi: Indian Institute of Foreign Trade.

Leontief, W. 1936. "Quantitative Input-Output Relations in the Economic System of the United States." *Review of Economics and Statistics* 18:105-25.

ESTIMATION OF INPUT-OUTPUT TECHNOLOGICAL COEFFICIENTS

Contribution from Services	P.U.	M&M	T&D	Cluster	Weights
P.U.	1	1/2	1/2	3	0.1930
M&M	2	1	1	5	0.3680
T&D	3	1	1	5	0.3680
Cluster	1/3	1/5	1/5	1	0.0704

The weights of construction and services are obtained by multiplying 0.0704, the weight of the cluster, by 0.9 and 0.1, respectively. The contribution of services to the other sectors is given by:

Sectors	AGR	P.U.	M&M	T&D	CONS	SERV
Relative contribution of services	.0000	.1930	.3680	.3680	.0634	.0070

The eigenvector of weights obtained in the second step is used to form the *rows* of a matrix, with zeros in positions where no interaction was indicated in the matrix of interactions. They represent the distribution of the output produced by a sector to the sectors related to it. We now use the first entry of the first eigenvector we obtained for the relative importance of the sectors to weight each element of the first row of this matrix, the second entry to weight each element of the second row, and so on. This yields the estimate of the input-output matrix given in table A.2.

Table A.2. Estimates of Input-Output Coefficients

	AGR	P.U.	M&M	T&D	CONS	SERV
AGR	.0079	0	.2331	.0008	.0699	0
P.U.	.0009	0	.0130	.0075	0	.0033
M&M	.0041	0	0	.0089	.0379	.0037
T&D	.0691	.1694	.1281	0	.1115	.0153
CONS	0	0	0	0	0	.0546
SERV	0	.0117	.0224	.0224	.0039	.0004

Gov't of Sudan (1962), Gusten (1966, p. 15), I.I.F.T. (1967), Ministry of Finance and Economics (1962), and United Nations (1958, p. 148):

Contribution from T&D	AGR	P.U.	M&M	CONS	SERV	Weights
AGR	1	1/3	1/2	1/2	7	0.1400
P.U.	3	1	1	2	9	0.3434
M&M	2	1	1	1	7	0.2596
CONS	2	1/2	1	1	7	0.2260
SERV	1/7	1/9	1/7	1/7	1	0.0310

The construction sector allocates outputs only to services. Thus the priority associated with services is 1.

For the contribution of the services sector we have a cluster consisting of:

$$\text{Cluster} \begin{cases} \text{Construction} \\ \text{Services,} \end{cases}$$

for which we get (with information from Nelson et al., 1973, p. 294):

Contribution from Services	CONS	SERV	Weights
CONS	1	9	0.9
SERV	1/9	1	0.1

Construction receives most of what is allocated to the cluster (Nelson et al., 1973, pp. 210-19).

With information from ADAR (1975), Collins and Tignor (1967), Gov't of Sudan (1962), Gusten (1966), and Nelson et al. (1973, pp. 190-92), we compare the remaining sectors, together with the cluster, and get:

Sectors	AGR	P.U.	M&M	T&D	CONS	SERV
Relative contribution from agriculture	.0225	.0000	.7500	.0025	.2250	.0000

Similarly, we have the following matrices and eigenvectors for the contributions of the other five sectors. Our estimates for the contribution of public utilities are based on information from Gusten (1966, p. 17), I.I.F.T. (1967, p. 293), Ministry of Finance and Economics (1962), and United Nations (1958):

Contribution from P.U.	AGR	M&M	T&D	SERV	Weights
AGR	1	1/9	1/7	1/5	0.0410
M&M	9	1	2	5	0.5242
T&D	7	1/2	1	3	0.3030
SERV	5	1/5	1/3	1	0.1318

Our estimates of the contribution of manufacturing and mining are based on information from Ministry of Finance and Economics (1962, p. 291):

Contribution from M&M	AGR	T&D	CONS	SERV	Weights
AGR	1	1/2	1/9	1	0.0758
T&D	2	1	1/5	3	0.1628
CONS	9	5	1	9	0.6941
SERV	1	1/3	1/9	1	0.0681

For the estimation of the contribution from transportation and distribution, we use information from ADAR (1975, vol. 1), Collins and Tignor (1967),

are preoccupations of the government. The activities within the subcluster are compared among themselves:

Contribution from Agriculture	AGR	T&D	Weights
AGR	1	9	0.9
T&D	1/9	1	0.1

Agriculture receives by far the greater input in the form of earnings, seeds, and related materials than does the transportation sector because the outputs of the agricultural sector that are not exported or allocated to manufacturing and mining are used to grow new crops and to satisfy domestic consumption. It is natural to assume that private earnings of the agricultural sector are allocated to construction. If the subcluster is compared with construction, we have:

Contribution from Agriculture	Subcluster	CONS	Weights
Subcluster	1	1/3	0.3333
CONS	3	1	0.6667

Hence construction is weakly superior to the subcluster because the government invests more in agriculture and transportation than in any other sector. What agriculture produces serves two objectives: (1) to satisfy internal needs and (2) to provide benefits for the people in agriculture. Since the industrial sector is the most rewarding sector for investing private earnings, and since it is not a significant part of the total GDP (3 percent), the only nongovernment-controlled sector remaining in which agriculture can allocate its outputs is the construction sector.

Composing the weights obtained for the cluster and subcluster, we obtain the priority weights for the sectors related to agriculture:

Sectors	AGR	P.U.	M&M	T&D	CONS	SERV
Total index of relative importance	.3108	.0248	.0546	.4934	.0546	.0608

The next step is to compare the sectors according to the contribution they receive from each of the six sectors.

Using information from Bank of Sudan (1963), I.I.F.T. (1967), Nelson et al. (1973, p. 255), and United Nations (1958), we aggregate all but manufacturing and mining into a cluster:

$$\text{Cluster} \begin{cases} \text{Agriculture} \\ \text{Transportation and distribution} \\ \text{Construction} \end{cases}$$

and compare the two according to the contribution they receive from agriculture. We have:

Contribution from Agriculture	Cluster	M&M	Weights
Cluster	1	1/3	0.3333
M&M	3	1	0.6667

Manufacturing and mining is considered weakly superior to the cluster receiving inputs from the agricultural sector. The reason for this is that the main crop is cotton, which is allocated to manufacturing and exports.

Within the cluster, a subcluster consisting of agriculture and transportation and distribution is formed:

$$\text{Subcluster} \begin{cases} \text{Agriculture} \\ \text{Transportation and distribution} \end{cases}$$

The reason why these two sectors belong together is that the government itself makes most of the investment in agriculture and transportation. Thus the agricultural sector does not allocate much to itself and to transportation since they

From three studies (Gov't of Sudan, 1962; Gusten, 1966; I.I.F.T., 1967), it was determined that agriculture and transportation and distribution were comparable, but that the remaining sectors had to be clustered to be in a class comparable to these two. Thus we have:

$$\text{Cluster} \begin{cases} \text{Public utilities} \\ \text{Manufacturing and mining} \\ \text{Construction} \\ \text{Services} \end{cases}$$

We also have the matrix of pairwise comparisons and principal eigenvector of weights shown in table A.2 (see p. 287).

Contribution to Economy	AGR	T&D	Cluster	Weights
AGR	1	1/2	2	0.311
T&D	2	1	2	0.493
Cluster	1/2	1/2	1	0.195

All sectors in the cluster fall in the same comparability class; their pairwise comparison matrix according to their contribution to the economy (from information in I.I.F.T., 1967; Nelson et al., 1973, p. 293), together with their corresponding eigenvector of weights, is given by:

Contribution to Economy	P.U.	M&M	CONS	SERV	Weights
P.U.	1	1/2	1/2	1/3	0.127
M&M	2	1	1	1	0.280
CONS	2	1	1	1	0.280
SERV	3	1	1	1	0.312

The eigenvector above is then multiplied by the weight of the cluster, which is 0.195 from the previous eigenvector. Finally, we concatenate the weights of the six sectors and obtain for the index of relative importance of the sectors in the economy of the Sudan:

ESTIMATION OF INPUT-OUTPUT COEFFICIENTS

Application of the AHP to generate input-output coefficients proceeds in two steps. The first utilizes judgments to determine the relative impact of the different sectors on the economy. This is essentially an "a priori" or constant value of the sectors. The second step involves analysis of the interdependence among the sectors. We take each sector and determine the relative strength of utilization of its output by the remaining sectors. The second step is a calculation of the current value of a sector in terms of its influence on the remaining sectors. Finally we compose the results of the two steps to obtain the input-output matrix.

A portion of the Sudan transport study involved the construction of econometric models with an input-output table by our colleague L.R. Klein at the Wharton Economic Forecasting Associates. This particular input-output table was developed on the basis of information from surrounding countries and not directly from Sudanese data. Thus it is an indirect estimate. We used our procedure to obtain an input coefficients table based on qualitative information on the economic sectors of the Sudan. Since the number of sectors is small, it serves as a good, short illustration of the method. Similar applications have been made with respect to Pakistan and Iran.

The approach we followed was to have one of us (L. Vargas), who had no knowledge about the Sudan, examine the literature regarding interaction among the sectors of the economy in the Sudan. We then used the AHP to construct the input-output matrix.

The sectors of the economy of the Sudan were identified by using the ADAR's *Sudan Transport Study* (1975), and their interactions were noted (see table A.1).

Table A.1. Pairwise Comparisons of Economic Sectors

	1 AGR	2 P.U.	3 M&M	4 T&D	5 CONS	6 SERV
Agriculture	X		X	X	X	
Public utilities	X		X	X		X
Manufacturing & mining	X			X	X	X
Transportation & distribution	X	X	X		X	X
Construction						X
Services		X	X	X	X	X

developed a modified "macroeconomic" version of the tableau, which represented the entire economy of his day in the form of circular flows (Newman, 1952; Phillips, 1955; Gherity, 1965).

In 1874, L. Walras, in his "Eléments d'Economie Politique Pure," examined the simultaneous computation of all prices in an economy. His model consisted of a system of equations, one for each price. He was also interested in the general equilibrium of production. In his theory he made use of the coefficients of production, which were determined by the technology and measured the amount of each factor needed to produce one unit of each kind of finished product (Spiegel, 1952). The model developed by Walras considers interdependence among the producing sectors of the economy, together with the competing demand of each sector for the factors of production.

In 1936, W. Leontief developed a general theory of production based on the notion of economic interdependence (Leontief, 1936, 1941). Leontief's input-output analysis is an adaptation of the theory of general equilibrium to the study of the quantitative interdependence among related economic activities. It was first formulated to analyze and measure the connection between the producing and the consuming sectors within a national economy, but it has also been applied to the economies of a region (Lombardini, 1970), of several regions (Carter and Irery, 1970), of metropolitan areas (Hirsch, 1959), and of the entire world (Levine, 1962; Wonnacott, 1961).

In all applications, whether the system is small or large, the interdependence among its sectors is described by a set of linear equations; its structural characteristics are expressed by means of the numerical magnitude of the coefficients of these equations. If we denote by y_i the quantity of the product of sector i allocated to the final demand sector, and by x_i the total output of sector i, the system of equations that provides the general equilibrium point of the economy is:

$$x_i = \sum_{j=1}^{n} a_{ij} x_j + y_i, \ i=1, 2, \ldots, n.$$

Then the solution of the system of equations, in matricial form, is given by:

$$X = (I - A)^{-1} Y.$$

Thus, once the coefficients of the system of equations are known, it is easy to compute the inverse of the matrix $(I-A)$. Our method estimates the coefficients a_{ij} in a simpler manner than is currently done, and hence computing the equilibrium point of an economy is considerably simplified.

APPENDIX A:
Estimation of Input-Output Technological Coefficients

The study of the Sudanese economy at a macrolevel required the development of an econometric model based on an input-output approach. This was done by using traditional methods. In this appendix we present a new systems-oriented method for estimating the input-output coefficients of a given economy. A major advantage is that it generally does not require extensive detail to capture the significant relations among the sectors.

Often one's general understanding about an economy can be an adequate tool for doing this without the use of an enormous amount of statistical data. Also, the process does not require knowledge of valuation of outputs, secondary products, dummy industries, imports, inventory change, and gross inputs and outputs, which are usually needed and often prove to be problematic in input-output analysis (Yan, 1968).

BACKGROUND

Input-output models emerged through a process of historical development. In 1758, F. Quesnay published "Tableau Economique," in which he emphasized the importance of the interdependence among economic activities. Later he

This appendix was written by T.L. Saaty and L.G. Vargas (*Socioeconomic Planning Sciences* 13 [1979]:333-36).

CONCLUDING REMARKS ABOUT APPLICATIONS

We have shown how to set priorities in a variety of applications including transportation, technological choice, resource allocation under uncertainty, planning, conflict resolution, determination of requirements, energy rationing, prediction, and portfolio selection.

The book highlights major problem areas of application and possible extensions of the method. The examples make it amply clear that complex problems can be structured in a reasonable way and decisions made by using the logic of priorities developed here.

Useful observations stand out in the use of the method. It makes it possible to incorporate judgments and hard data by an individual or a group. The group can participate in defining its own problem and deciding on the most suitable hierarchic structure for its representation. The AHP allows one to deal with both tangible and intangible factors. The output of the process may be a set of priorities for ranking or a set of numbers expressed in the form of dollars, percentages, games won or lost, and the like.

The framework has great potential for application in areas of social and political disagreement and in planning systems compatible with the broad or specialized objectives of various groups and individuals. Work is under way for using the process to generate new criteria and options in the hierarchy; the attempt is to extend the boundaries of consciousness to include additional elements in order to diminish lurking uncertainties in decision making. In this manner one can hope to face with greater assurance, understanding, and control the forces that shape the future.

REFERENCES

Saaty, T.L. 1979. "Mathematical Modeling of Dynamic Decisions: Priorities and Hierarchies with Time Dependence." *Mathematics and Computers in Simulation* 21:352-58.

———. 1981. *Decision Making for Leaders.* Belmont, Calif.: Lifetime Learning.

———, and H. Ait-Kaci. 1978. "Continuous Hierarchies." University of Pennsylvania, Philadelphia.

Vargas, L.G. 1979. "Measurement and Optimal Resource Allocation in Social Systems." Ph.D. dissertation, University of Pennsylvania, Philadelphia.

———. 1981. "Random Reciprocal Matrices." Submitted to *Journal of Mathematical Modeling.*

edges and identify the corresponding pair of vertices that form its end points. For each pair we ask for a judgment expressing the intensity of dominance with respect to the criterion. The question is: does A dominate B or does B dominate A with respect to this criterion? Indicate how strongly next to the proper alternative below.

	Equal Importance	Weak	Strong	Demonstrated	Absolute
A over B or B over A	— —	— —	— —	— —	— —

This is done for the $(n-2)$ other pairs indicated by edges in the tree.

Random generation of spanning trees saves time and can help in avoiding conflicts. Also it allows one to elicit judgments from decisionmakers who feel that their collective judgment could be used without having to reach a consensus on each of the judgments. Thus, by generating random spanning trees, one for each decisionmaker, we can capture the diversity of opinions within a given group. Each group member will make $(n-1)$ comparisons, but for different pairs of activities or criteria. The resulting $(n-1)$ judgments are used to generate a consistent matrix of pairwise comparisons. All matrices are then combined into a single matrix by taking the geometric mean of the judgments corresponding to the same entry.

The next step is to take the $(n-1)$ judgments of each decisionmaker and place them in a matrix, rather than construct all entries of the matrix from them. If we do this for all participants, taking the geometric mean of judgments if several decisionmakers answer questions corresponding to the same pairwise comparison, the resulting matrix may have all its entries filled. If this is not the case, the blank entries must be filled by using the consistent matrix we constructed with the judgments of all participants.

This matrix is used to estimate the relative priorities of the alternatives and the consistency of the group for the criterion in question. The process is then repeated for each criterion in the hierarchy.

GROUP JUDGMENTS BY QUESTIONNAIRE

There have been times when participants in problem-solving sessions with the AHP have felt that the judgmental process taxed their minds and their patience. For this reason we have developed a procedure to elicit judgments by questionnaire.

In general, given n activities, one has to elicit $n(n-1)/2$ judgments to generate pairwise comparison matrices from which priorities can be generated. As n increases, the total number of judgments also increases. The process becomes tedious and time consuming when it is too large.

To cope with this problem, we have constructed an algorithm that requires only $(n-1)$ judgments to construct the matrix of pairwise comparisons. The algorithm consists of generating spanning trees on the set of alternatives (vertices) being compared with respect to a given criterion. The procedure is as follows:

0. Start at any vertex selected at random.
1. Call your present vertex v_p.
2. If there are any untraveled edges out of v_p, select one at random and proceed along it to an adjacent vertex; call it v_a.
   a. If you have visited v_a before, retreat to v_p, labeling that edge "nontree"; go to 1.
   b. If you have never visited v_a before, label this edge "tree"; go to 1.
3. If there are only "tree" and "nontree" edges incident with v_p, retreat along a "tree" edge, relabeling this edge "tree-deadend"; go to 1.
4. If there are only "tree-deadend" and "nontree" edges incident with v_p, you are finished.

This algorithm has been implemented on the computer as follows: First, after the activities or criteria have been numbered, $1, 2, \ldots, n$, we select two numbers a and b ($a \neq b$) at random from the set $(1, 2, \ldots, n)$. The first branch of the spanning tree is the edge joining the vertices a and b, (a,b). Next we label those two vertices 1 and 2 and select 1 or 2 at random. If we obtain, for example, 1, then we select a as the starting point of the next branch of the tree. In the next step we randomly generate a number c from the set $(1, 2, \ldots, n)$ such that $a \neq c$ and $b \neq c$. Our tree now consists of the branches (a,b) and (a,c). Again, we would label a, b, and c as 1, 2, and 3, respectively, and the procedure is iteratively applied. These steps are repeated until all vertices have been reached.

After the spanning tree has been constructed, we take each of the $(n-1)$

sibility of assumptions that might violate group expectations and on their acceptability.

The problem of the sensitivity of the eigenvector to changes in judgment and how to relate the answer to the judgmental data was solved earlier by Vargas (1979) in his Ph.D. dissertation.

APPLICATION OF THE AHP TO SOME PROBLEM AREAS

In *Decision Making for Leaders* (1981), T.L. Saaty has dealt with many situations in which the AHP has been used. For brevity we present only a partial list:

1. *Home or personal decisions:* Buying a car, choosing household appliances, selecting snow radial tires, selecting a home computer, choosing a career, getting a Ph.D., choosing the ideal investment, choosing a spouse, deciding on how many children to have, selecting a school, choosing a city in which to reside, purchasing a house;
2. *Social/psychological issues:* Judging parental influence on overall psychological well-being, predicting the number of children of an average family;
3. *Corporate context:* Purchasing of urethane equipment, purchasing of word-processing equipment, buying or leasing equipment, selecting a management position;
4. *Nonprofit agencies:* Assessing the benefits of crossing a river, developing programs for research and development of a research institute, deciding on the capacity of a harbor;
5. *Public policy issues:* Selection of beverage containers, evaluation of energy storage systems, higher education, resource allocation for juvenile correction, staggering industry hours for energy conservation, likelihood of technical innovation as related to forms of corporate control, analysis of the school busing conflict, conflicts of interest in health administration, planning for the steel industry, selection of regional projects, site selection of combustion turbines, resource allocation among research and development projects in a bank, product-market decisions, financial decision making, division performance evaluation, normative backward planning process;
6. *International context:* Economic strategy for an underdeveloped country, mineral extraction;
7. *Estimation/prediction:* Selection of musical groups, prediction of elections.

Table 14.5. Priorities of Activities

Activities	Limiting Impact Priorities
Replacement	
Predict car resale prices	.014
Determine vehicle requirements and specifications	.015
Determine replacement cycle of cars	.027
Maintenance	
Plan maintenance facilities	.042
Formulate preventive maintenance schedule	.064
Develop reliability and usage records of parts	.079
Inventory	
Develop optimum inventory policy	.079
Management information system	
Develop information base for:	
Maintenance types and hours	.098
Spare parts consumption	.094
Vehicle types and specifications	.122
Old car price movements	.057
Period budget	.062
Fuel consumption and allocation	.071
Personnel	
Communicate maintenance information	.043
Resource allocation	
Identify constraints and priorities	.059
Develop fiscal budget allocation schedule	.032
Develop fuel allocation schedule	.039

Vargas (1981) has investigated the converse problem: given a wide diversity of judgments that distribute stochastically around a core value, what is their effect on the eigenvector, and how acceptable is this variability as a guide for action?

If we have reasonable judgments and could surmise an outcome around which we can act, before acting we ask how the public feels about it. We take the distribution of potential judgments, compute a range of eigenvector components and look at the deviation from the core value, and answer questions on fea-

Table 14.4. Matrix W

	R_1	R_2	R_3	M_1	M_2	M_3	I	MIS_1	MIS_2	MIS_3	MIS_4	MIS_5	MIS_6	P	RA_1	RA_2	RA_3
R_1	0.089	0.011	0.033					0.019	0.014	0.011	0.069	0.012	0.012				0.073
R_2	0.011	0.089	0.067		0		0.019	0.027	0.042	0.009	0.012	0.012	0				0.364
R_3	0.011	0.011	0.011				0.057	0.054	0.042	0.017	0.071	0.071					0.364
M_1	0.037	0.032	0.032	0.178	0.022	0.022	0.073	0.021	0.063	0.063	0.015	0.063	0.063				0
M_2	0.037	0.032	0.032	0.022	0.178	0.022	0.110	0.021	0.063	0.063	0.073	0.063	0.063				0
M_3	0.148	0.159	0.159	0.022	0.022	0.178	0.015	0.148	0.063	0.063	0.110	0.063	0.063				
I		0		0.111	0.111	0.111	0.094	0.095	0.095	0.095	0.094	0.095	0.095	0			0.125
MIS_1	0.047	0.047	0.051	0.259	0.334	0.047	0.158	0.032	0.038	0.038	0.073	0.073	0.032	0.235	0.113	0.062	0.062
MIS_2	0.047	0.047	0.153	0.037	0.047	0.334	0.031	0.159	0.038	0.038	0.073	0.073	0.032	0.141	0.188	0.062	0.062
MIS_3	0.041	0.430	0.257	0.185	0.143	0.143	0.095	0.095	0.191	0.038	0.044	0.044	0.095	0.235	0.113	0.062	0.062
MIS_4	0.430	0.047	0.103	0.037	0.047	0.047	0.031	0.032	0.038	0.191	0.014	0.014	0.032	0.046	0.038	0.062	0.062
MIS_5	0.047	0.047	0.051	0.111	0.047	0.047	0.031	0.032	0.038	0.038	0.102	0.102	0.032	0.046	0.113	0.313	0.188
MIS_6	0.047	0.047	0.051	0.037	0.047	0.047	0.031	0.032	0.038	0.038	0.073	0.073	0.159	0.046	0.188	0.188	0.313
P		0			0		0.048	0.048	0.048	0.048	0.048	0.048	0.048	0.125	0.200			
RA_1							0.141	0.063	0.063	0.063	0.113	0.113	0.021		0.200	0.135	0.083
RA_2		0			0		0.024	0.063	0.063	0.063	0.057	0.057	0.063	0	0.025	0.019	0.028
RA_3							0.024	0.063	0.063	0.063	0.019	0.019	0.106		0.025	0.096	0.139

Table 14.3. Priorities of Subsystems

	R	M	I	MIS	P	RA
Replacement (R)	.111			.095		
Maintenance (M)	.222	.222		.190	.800	
Inventory (I)		.111	.125	.095		
MIS (MIS)	.666	.666	.750	.381		.750
Personnel (P)			.125	.048	.200	
Resource allocation (RA)				.190		.250

The basic eigenvalue problem $Aw = \lambda_{max} w$ that we solved to obtain priorities is transformed into the Fredholm integral equation of the second kind:

$$w(s) = \int_a^b \frac{1}{\lambda} J(s,y) w(y) \, dy,$$

where $J(s,y)$ is a function of the arguments s and y, which define points of the "effect" interval $[a,b]$. $J(s,y)$ plays a parallel role to that of a_{ij} in the discrete eigenvalue problem. Thus $J(s,y)$ satisfies the property $J(y,s) \cdot J(s,y) = 1$ for all $(s,y) \in [a,b]^2$. An example of a judgment function is $J(s,y) = \exp\{k(s-y)\}$, $s,y \in [a,b]$, for $0 < |k| \leq (\ln \alpha)/(b-a)$, α is the judgment scale. The solution to the integral equation is:

$$w(s) = k \, e^{ks}/(e^{kb} - e^{ka}).$$

The principle of hierarchic composition is also derived along similar lines. One may hope that when people or computers can deal with attributes of reality in a continuous fashion, then this sort of approach would be applicable.

THE STABILITY OF HIERARCHIES

The authors have also studied the stability of a hierarchy—that is, of the composite vector of the lowest-level alternatives—with respect to changes in the elements or, more generally, in the structure of the hierarchy; with respect to changes in the judgments at a fixed period; and with respect to changes in judgments over time.

One problem here is: given a certain range of variability of the components of the eigenvector, and given a certain value of the consistency, what is the range of values of the judgments on the scale $1/9, 1/8, \ldots, 1, \ldots, 8, 9$ that could give rise to this perturbed vector, and are these ranges feasible to arrive at in practice?

Table 14.2. Elements Impact Priorities

	R_1	R_2	R_3	M_1	M_2	M_3	I	MIS_1	MIS_2	MIS_3	MIS_4	MIS_5	MIS_6	P	RA_1	RA_2	RA_3
R_1	.900	.100	.300														
R_2	.100	.800	.600														
R_3	.100	.100	.100														
M_1	.167	.143	.143	.800	.100	.100		.200	.143	.111	.727	.125	.125	.091			
M_2	.167	.143	.143	.100	.800	.100		.200	.286	.444	.091	.125	.125	.455			
M_3	.667	.714	.714	.100	.100	.800		.600	.571	.444	.182	.950	.750	.455			
I				1.000	1.000	1.000	1.000	.385	.111	.333	.333	.077	.333				
MIS_1	.071	.071	.071	.389	.500	.071	.313	.583	.111	.333	.333	.385	.333		.150	.083	.083
MIS_2	.071	.071	.230	.056	.071	.500	.188	.077	.777	.333	.333	.583	.333		.250	.083	.083
MIS_3	.071	.645	.385	.278	.214	.214	.313	1.000	1.000	1.000	1.000	1.000	1.000				
MIS_4	.645	.071	.154	.056	.071	.071	.062	.417	.083	.100	.100	.192	.083		.150	.083	.083
MIS_5	.071	.071	.071	.167	.071	.071	.062	.083	.417	.100	.100	.192	.083		.250	.083	.083
MIS_6	.071	.071	.077	.056	.071	.071	.062	.250	.250	.500	.100	.115	.250		.150	.083	.083
								.083	.083	.100	.500	.038	.083		.050	.083	.083
								.083	.083	.100	.100	.269	.083		.150	.417	.250
								.083	.083	.100	.100	.192	.417		.250	.250	.417
P							1.000	1.000	1.000	1.000	1.000	1.000	1.000	1.000			
RA_1								.750	.333	.333	.333	.600	.111		.800	.538	.333
RA_2								.125	.333	.333	.333	.300	.333		.100	.077	.111
RA_3								.125	.333	.333	.333	.100	.555		.100	.385	.555

side of the table impacts the activity at the top of the table. Only some of the components interact.

Following the procedure previously outlined, we first develop the matrix of impacts of the elements of a component on the elements of another. We then tabulate the eigenvectors as shown in table 14.2. Next, we prioritize the components that impact a given component, repeating this for each component. We obtain the matrix given in table 14.3. Finally, we weight each block of the matrix of table 14.2 by the corresponding priority of table 14.3 to obtain table 14.4. This (column stochastic) matrix is then raised to powers to compute the priorities of the activities given in table 14.5. One must ensure that the column totals are precisely equal to unity; otherwise, raising the matrix to powers does not converge to a finite solution.

The outcome indicates that the development of an information base for vehicle types and specifications is the most important activity of the fleet manager, and so on.

The computer algorithm (in APL language) for raising the matrix to powers is as follows:

```
        ∇    R←NETWORK X
[1]          R ← X
[2]          L:R←R+.×R
[3]          R←R+.×R
[4]          R1←|R[;1]-R[;2]
[5]          R1←R1 [⍋R1]
[6]          →L×⌿R1[1↑⍴X]≤1.000000000E-10
[7]          Q←'PRIORITIES'
[8]          Q← 1 10 ⍴Q
[9]          Q1←((1↑⍴X),10)⍴(10 8 - R[;1])
[10]         Q←Q,[1]Q1
[11]         R←Q
        ∇
```

THE CONTINUOUS HIERARCHY

In an unpublished work by Ait-Kaci and Saaty (1978), the AHP was generalized to the case in which hierarchic decomposition can no longer be made into a discrete set of components but may consist of a continuous interval of components.

tem (*MIS*), personnel (*P*), and resource allocation (*RA*). The components have the following activities:

1. Replacement:
   a. Predict car resale prices,
   b. Determine vehicle requirements and specifications,
   c. Determine replacement cycle of cars.
2. Maintenance:
   a. Plan maintenance facilities,
   b. Formulate preventive maintenance schedule,
   c. Develop reliability and usage records of parts.
3. Inventory:
   Develop optimum inventory policy.
4. Management information system:
   a. Develop information base for maintenance types and hours,
   b. Develop information base for spare parts consumption,
   c. Develop information base for vehicle types and specifications,
   d. Develop information base for old car price movements,
   e. Develop information base for periodic budget,
   f. Develop information base for fuel consumption and allocation.
5. Personnel:
   Communicate maintenance information.
6. Resource allocation:
   a. Identify constraints and priorities,
   b. Develop fiscal budget allocation schedule,
   c. Develop fuel allocation schedule.

In order to put the right amount of effort into the right activity, we need their priorities. An *x* in table 14.1 indicates that the component on the left-hand

Table 14.1. Relationships among Subsystems

	R	*M*	*I*	*MIS*	*P*	*Resource Allocation*
Replacement	x			x		
Maintenance	x	x		x	x	
Inventory		x	x	x		
MIS	x	x	x	x		x
Personnel			x	x		x
Resource allocation				x		x

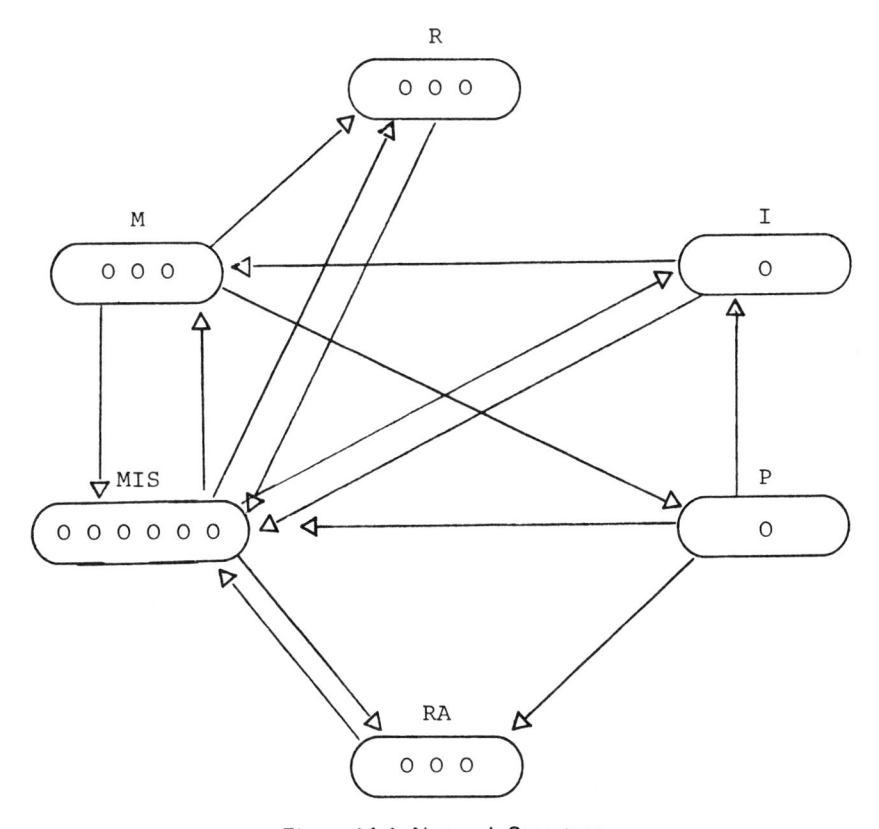

Figure 14.1. Network Structure

entries of the first matrix are then multiplied by these priorities. The resulting matrix, whose columns sum to unity, is the desired matrix W.

The limiting priorities are obtained by raising this matrix to infinite power. In practice the process of raising the matrix to powers is stopped when all columns of the matrix are nearly equal. The limiting priorities are given by any of these columns. The application of the AHP to the study of systems with feedback was developed by the first author in *The Analytic Hierarchy Process* (New York: McGraw-Hill, 1980), pp. 206-22.

We now present a brief example developed in our research for the NAFA Foundation. Those who buy cars for the use of corporate personnel usually deal with the following clusters of issues that define the components of the system: replacement (R), maintenance (M), inventory (I), management information sys-

SOME EXTENSIONS IN APPLICATION AND THEORY 267

1. Construct the following matrix:

$$
\begin{array}{c}
\begin{array}{ccc} C_1 & \cdots & C_N \\ c_{11}\,c_{12}\cdots c_{1n_1} & & c_{N1}\,c_{N2}\cdots c_{Nn_N} \end{array} \\[4pt]
\begin{array}{cc}
\begin{array}{cc}
& c_{11} \\
C_1 & c_{12} \\
& \vdots \\
& c_{N1} \\
\vdots & \\
& c_{N1} \\
C_N & c_{N2} \\
& \vdots \\
& c_{Nn_N}
\end{array}
&
\begin{bmatrix} W_{11} & \cdots & W_{1N} \\ \vdots & & \vdots \\ W_{N1} & \cdots & W_{NN} \end{bmatrix}
\end{array}
\end{array}
$$

where the (i,j) block is given by

$$W_{ij} = \begin{bmatrix} w_{i1}^{(j1)} & w_{i1}^{(j2)} & \cdots & w_{i1}^{(jn_j)} \\ w_{i2}^{(j1)} & w_{i2}^{(j2)} & \cdots & w_{i2}^{(jn_j)} \\ \vdots & \vdots & \vdots & \vdots \\ w_{in_i}^{(j1)} & w_{in_i}^{(j2)} & \cdots & w_{in_i}^{(jn_j)} \end{bmatrix},$$

each of whose columns is an eigenvector that represents the impact of all the elements in the ith component on each of the elements in the jth component. If the ith component does not impact on the jth component, then the block w_{ij} would consist of zeros.

2. Assess the importance of the contributions of the components as a whole to the system; that is, for a given component, identify all other components that have an impact on it and calculate their priorities. The

problem $Aw = \lambda_{max} w$ and test the consistency (see chapter 2, section on "Methods of Estimating the Vector of Priorities and Clustering Schemes").

6. Repeat steps 3, 4, and 5 for all levels and clusters in the hierarchy.
7. Now use hierarchical composition to weight the eigenvectors by the weights of the criteria and take the sum over all weighted eigenvector entries corresponding to each element to obtain the composite priority of the elements in a level. These are then used to weight the eigenvectors corresponding to those in the next lower level, and so on, resulting in a composite priority vector for the lowest level of the hierarchy.
8. Evaluate consistency for the entire hierarchy (see chapter 2, section on "The Consistency of a Hierarchy") by simply multiplying each consistency index by the priority of the corresponding criterion and adding overall such products. Divide the result by the same type of expression with the use of the random consistency index corresponding to the dimensions of each matrix weighted by the priorities as before. The ratio should be about 10 percent or less for acceptable overall consistency. Otherwise, the quality of the judgmental data should be improved.

A natural extension of hierarchic structures in decision making is a situation in which the levels of the hierarchy are no longer connected in the form of a descending chain, but each level may interact with several others at the same time. The network structure can have the form shown in figure 14.1. In this network, an arrow directed from one component to another indicates that the second component has an impact on the first component.

Here we are interested in two types of priorities: (a) *impact* priorities, which indicate the influence or impact of one element on any other element in the system, and (b) *absolute* priorities, or priorities of any element regardless of which elements they influence. Obviously the impacts of the elements may be of the first order, namely, interactions along single paths; of the second order, namely, interactions along paths of length 2; and so on. Usually one seeks the limiting priorities of the system as a whole; that is, by computing net effects along all paths. Thus we would be able to show where existing trends might lead if there was no change in preferences affecting the priorities and to steer the system toward a more desired outcome by modifying the priorities and noting their limiting trends (the supermatrix method).

The procedure used to obtain these two types of priorities consists of constructing a matrix whose entries are themselves matrices. To see how this is done, let us consider a system decomposed into N clusters or components C_1, $C_2, \ldots, C_N$. Let us denote the elements in component C_k by $c_{k1}, \ldots, c_{kn_k}$, where n_k is their number. The matrix W that measures the impacts of the components among themselves is constructed as follows:

SOME EXTENSIONS IN APPLICATION AND THEORY   265

RCA
R.J. Reynolds
Standard Oil of Ohio
System Simulation Ltd. (London)
Westinghouse Electric Corporation
The British Department of Health and Social Security
The Electric Power Research Institute
The Government of Mauritania
The Government of the Sudan
The Kuwait Fund for Arab Economic Development
The Leonard Davis Institute at the Wharton School
The NAFA Foundation
U.S. Air Force and U.S. Navy
U.S. Patent Office
Woods Gordon (Canada)

We felt it would be useful to group selected applications in separate categories to show the reader the flexibility of the method.

SUMMARY OUTLINE OF THE ANALYTIC HIERARCHY PROCESS AND EXTENSIONS

1. Define the problem and specify a desired solution.
2. Structure the hierarchy by starting with the most general objectives, followed by subobjectives, criteria, and perhaps alternatives as the bottom level; that is, start with the overall purposes and continue through relevant intermediate levels until a level is reached where control would alleviate, or maybe solve, the problem.
3. Construct a pairwise comparison matrix of the relative contribution or impact of each element on each governing objective or criterion in the adjacent upper level. In such a matrix the elements of a level are compared in pairs with respect to a criterion in the next higher level. In comparing the i,j elements, people prefer to give a judgment that indicates the dominance as an integer. Thus, if the dominance does not occur in the i,j position while comparing the ith element with the jth element, then it is given in the j,i position as a_{ji}, and its reciprocal is automatically assigned to a_{ij}.
4. Obtain all $[n(n-1)]/2$ judgments.
5. Having collected the pairwise comparison data and entered the reciprocals together with n unit entries down the main diagonal, solve the eigenvalue

14 SOME EXTENSIONS IN APPLICATIONS AND THEORY

In this final chapter we summarize the steps of the Analytic Hierarchy Process and discuss its extensions to other areas of prioritization and problem solving. We illustrate an extension dealing with structures more complex than hierarchies: systems with feedback.

The AHP has also been extended to include time-dependent judgments already described in the literature (see Saaty, 1979) and hierarchies with a finite number of levels, each with an infinite number of alternatives. The latter will be briefly described. Another idea we mention briefly is the stability of a hierarchy with respect to changes in structure, judgment, and time.

Our experience with the AHP has produced a great variety of applications. The following list includes some of the corporations and international bodies that have used the AHP to carry out planning and problem solving by the direct involvement mostly of the first author:

Alcoa
Cerveceria Cuauhtemac (Mexico)
Colonial Penn Insurance Co.
Cooperativa de Seguros de Vida (Puerto Rico)
Gulf Oil

quire setting up an implementation and tracking program aimed at monitoring the outcomes resulting from decisions based on AHP recommendations.

REFERENCES

Forester, J.N. 1961. *Industrial Dynamics.* Cambridge, Mass.: MIT Press.
Gass, S. 1975. *Linear Programming Methods and Applications,* 4th ed. New York: McGraw-Hill.
Green, P.E., and Y. Wind. 1975. "New Way to Measure Consumers' Judgment." *Harvard Business Review* 53 (July-August):107-17.
——, and V. Srinivasan. 1978. "Conjoint Analysis and Outlook." *Journal of Consumer Research* (September).
Johnson, C., and C. Jones. 1957. "How to Organize for New Products." *Harvard Business Review* 35 (May-June):49-62.
Resource Priorities, Inc. 1980. *Corporate Portfolio Selection.* (Work done by T.L. Saaty and L.G. Vargas.)
Saaty, T.L. 1980. *The Analytic Hierarchy Process: Planning, Priority Setting, Resource Allocation.* New York: McGraw-Hill.
——, and J.P. Bennett. 1978. "A New Perspective on Benefits and Costs—The Analytic Hierarchy Process." University of Pennsylvania, Philadelphia.
——, P.C. Rogers, and R. Pell. 1980. "Portfolio Selection through Hierarchies." *Journal of Portfolio Management,* Spring Issue (3):16-21.
Wind, Y. 1978. "Organizational Buying Center: A Research Agenda." In T.V. Bonoma and G. Zaltman, eds. *Organizational Buying Behavior.* Chicago: American Marketing Association.
——, and T.L. Saaty. 1980. "Marketing Applications of the Analytic Hierarchy Process." *Management Science* 26 (7):641-58.

as the selection of channels of distribution) and choice prediction (for example, concept or product testing) situations. In addition, it can also be applied to cases in which the buying or marketing decision involves a number of participants (Wind, 1978) with conflicting perceptions or objectives.

The extent to which the analytic hierarchy would offer a *better* (more reliable and valid) procedure than some of the other existing approaches to these decisions is an empirical question. Managers have had no difficulty in completing pairwise matrices. In fact, many of them find the task challenging, interesting, and of intrinsic value because it forces them to examine relationships often left unexamined.

Future research on the AHP and its marketing applications should explore the following areas:

1. Conceptually, whether a set of general hierarchical structures can be developed to provide management with a basis from which they can deviate (to reflect their idiosyncratic characteristics) in the structuring of the hierarchy. The attractiveness of having a general conceptual framework for the structuring of hierarchies should be weighted against the advantages of flexibility; that is, the ability of the AHP to process *any* structure.

2. The structuring, data collection, and analysis of hierarchies that take into consideration the real-world complexity of many allocation type of problems — that is, interdependence among elements within the same level and symmetrical relations with the environment (the environment affects the actions, but the actions in turn can affect the environment) — and the occasional need to deal with incomplete hierarchies.

3. Simplification of the data collection procedure. Although some shortcut designs have been utilized to reduce the number of pairwise judgments required for the analysis, a more systematic effort is required to explore the suitability of experimental designs of the fractional factorial type. The development of designs that require only a small number of judgments is essential if top management is to participate in and provide input into the process. This latter issue is especially critical, given the current magnitude of the data collection task and the reluctance of many top executives to spend much time on such a process.

4. Comparison of the AHP with other approaches. Given that there are a number of areas in which the AHP is only one of several possible approaches (conjoint analysis for determining the importance of the objectives, cross-impact analysis to assess interaction, and so on), studies should be undertaken to compare the results of the competing approaches, assess the conditions under which each is more appropriate, and explain the advantages, if any, of incorporating the AHP with other research procedures.

5. Assessing the validity of the AHP's recommendations. This would re-

PORTFOLIO SELECTION 261

maintain the same relative standing except when the investor's objectives are emphasized. A certain amount of stability is shown here.

Should we want to use these weights as a guideline for allocating funds among the stocks and should we use the criteria-weighting scheme (2:1:1) where the extrinsic criteria are deemed twice as important as each of the other two, we would invest about 40 percent in Data General, about 26 percent in Rockwell International, about 19 percent in Tappan, and about 15 percent in I.C. Industries.

COMMENTS

Although other procedures such as conjoint analysis can and have been used to assess the relative importance of management objectives (Green and Wind, 1975; Green and Srinivasan, 1978), conjoint analysis to date has not been used for the solution of problems such as the ones discussed in this chapter. For this class of allocation problems, the AHP seems to be more appropriate.

In some cases both AHP and conjoint analysis can be used. It is desirable to compare the results of the two approaches in areas that conceptually, at least, can be measured by either approach. The determination of the relative importance of corporate objectives is one such area.

The AHP has been applied to three marketing decisions—(a) determining the desired target product portfolio and allocation of resources among the components of the portfolio (at any level of specificity), (b) determining the desired directions for new-product development, and (c) generating and evaluating marketing mix strategies—as well as to the construction of corporate and investment portfolios.

The AHP, when applied to these types of decisions, offers specific guidelines for resource allocation among the firm's current and potential products, markets, and distribution outlets; among various new-product ideas; and among various marketing mix strategies under alternative environmental conditions and various objectives. The guidelines suggested by the AHP can be subjected to a number of sensitivity analyses aimed at establishing the critical *priority range* for each of the portfolio components. This approach can be undertaken at any level of the organization (corporate-SBU or product group) and at various degrees of specificity, including, for example, portfolios of specific brand positioning by specific market segments and distribution outlets. The procedure can also be extended to more complex cases such as the construction of nonlinear hierarchies (see next chapter), construction of time-dependent judgments, and the weighting of the judgments by the respondents' perceived expertise.

Conceptually, the AHP can be applied to any allocation of resources (such

Table 13.9. Weights of Firms for Investor's Objectives

Firm	Profit (.34)	Control (.28)	Security (.25)	Excitement (.13)
Rock. Int'l.	.27	.06	.04	.38
Tappan	.03	.04	.13	.03
Data Gen.	.63	.75	.29	.55
I.C. Ind.	.07	.15	.54	.04

When the four firms are compared pairwise relative to each of these objectives, we obtain the results in table 13.9.

The final list of weighted firms relative to the investor's objectives is:

Rockwell International	Tappan	Data General	I.C. Industries
.17	.05	.58	.20

To obtain the final prioritization of the firms (the portfolio), we weight each of the criteria (extrinsic, intrinsic, and objectives) and perform the multiplication and addition. In table 13.10 we show the final weights for three weighting schemes for the criteria. The scheme 2:1:1 means weights of 2/4, 1/4, 1/4, and so on.

We note that Data General and Rockwell International rank first and second, respectively, in all the weighting schemes. Also, I.C. Industries and Tappan

Table 13.10. Final Weights of Firms

Firm	Weights Relative to Ext. Criteria	Weights Relative to Int. Criteria	Inv. Obj.	1:1:1	1:1:2	2:1:1	1:2:2
Rockwell Int'l.	.29	.29	.17	.25	.23	.26	.26
Tappan	.29	.13	.05	.16	.13	.19	.15
Data General	.27	.47	.58	.44	.47	.40	.45
I.C. Industries	.15	.11	.20	.15	.17	.15	.14

Innovativeness	Management Quality	Research and Development Quality	Sales
.46	.21	.17	.16

The four firms in our extrinsic factors list are now compared pairwise relative to each of the intrinsic criteria. The results are summarized in table 13.8.

The final list of weighted firms relative to the intrinsic criteria (after multiplying and adding) is:

Rockwell International	Tappan	Data General	I.C. Industries
.29	.13	.47	.11

The investor's objectives with weights computed under an average risk class are:

Profit	Control	Security	Excitement
.34	.28	.25	.13

Table 13.8. Weights of Firms for Intrinsic Criteria

Firms	Innovativeness	Management Quality	Research and Development Quality	Sales[a]
Rock. Int'l.	.34	.32	.12	.25
Tappan	.27	.03	.04	.05
Data Gen.	.30	.55	.74	.52
I.C. Ind.	.09	.10	.10	.18

[a]Sales-to-assets ratios were used to compare the firms in order to remove size consideration.

Now we turn to the intrinsic factors and repeat the same process: construct a two-level hierarchy of factors and criteria; obtain weights for the factors; obtain weights for the criteria relative to the corresponding factor; then obtain an overall list of weighted criteria; and finally obtain a prioritized list of firms.

The intrinsic factors hierarchy consists of the following:

Primary Intrinsic Factors	*Criteria*
Profitability	Management quality, market share, earnings, innovativeness, diversity, payout ratio
Size	Sales, labor force, assets, market structure
Technological Control	Research and development, quality, age distribution of product, energy dependence, pollution effects
Business Philosophy	Social responsibility, participatory decision making

After comparing the four primary factors pairwise in each of the three levels of risk and taking the average of the resulting three weights, we obtain the weighted list of factors:

Profitability	*Size*	*Technological Control*	*Business Philosophy*
.51	.17	.26	.06

Thus, profitability and technological control exert about 76 percent of the total influence on a firm's behavior when we consider only the intrinsic factors. Business philosophy doesn't seem to have much impact.

After we derive the weights of the criteria for each of the factors and multiply these weights by the weight of the factors, we obtain a list of sixteen factors. Using the four whose total weight was about 60 percent of the total, we obtain an abbreviated list of weighted *intrinsic criteria:*

PORTFOLIO SELECTION

Table 13.7. Weights of Firms for Extrinsic Criteria

Firm	State of Tech (.33)	Emp. Cond. (.26)	Elas. of Dem. (.16)	Int. Rates (.10)	Fam. Dis. (.08)	Gov. Inv. in Tech. (.07)
Tappan	.07	.36	.03	.03	.45	.03
Ingersoll Rand	.10	.05	.07	.07	.02	.10
I.C. Ind.	.17	.14	.05	.05	.12	.18
Allied Chem.	.03	.03	.03	.02	.02	.03
Rockwell Int'l.	.21	.23	.12	.12	.21	.38
Data Gen.	.38	.02	.23	.23	.10	.20
Butler	.02	.06	.17	.17	.06	.02
Chemetron	.04	.11	.31	.30	.02	.06

A glance at table 13.7 shows that, in a technological environment, Data General, Rockwell, and I.C. Industries are heavily favored, as one might expect. Tappan and Rockwell are beneficiaries of good employment conditions reflecting their consumer markets—appliances for Tappan (80 percent of sales) and home and auto products for Rockwell International (35 percent of sales).

To get an overall prioritized list of firms, vis-à-vis the extrinsic factors, we multiply the weights of the firms for a given criterion by the weight of that criterion (shown in parentheses in table 13.7) and then total these new weights for each firm. This yields:

Tappan	Ing. Rand	I.C. Ind.	All. Chem.	Rock. Int'l.	Data Gen.	Butler	Chem.
.16	.07	.13	.03	.20	.21	.07	.13

For purposes of illustration, we will use only the four highest ones with their weights adjusted, as we did when shortening the list of criteria. The prioritized list of firms relative to the extrinsic criteria are:

Rock. Int'l.	Tappan	Data Gen.	I.C. Ind.
.29	.23	.30	.19

	State of Technology	Government Involvement
Technological	*.29*	.07

The weights in italics are the largest ones. We will shorten our list to include only these. In order to have the weights total one, we divide each weight by the total of all the weights in the shortened list. We now have our weighted list of *extrinsic criteria:*

State of Technology	Empl. Cond.	Elas. of Demand	Int. Rates	Family Disint.	Gov. Involve. in Tech.
.33	.26	.16	.10	.08	.07

The firms being considered (eight in this illustration) are now prioritized relative to each of the six extrinsic criteria. This process is the same pairwise comparison and weighting procedure we have been applying. For example, when comparing the firms pairwise relative to the state of technology, we would ask, "Which firm will respond more favorably to the technological environment of the future?" The matrix for this criterion is shown:

Tech	Tap	IR	IC	AC	RI	DG	B	Ch
Tappan	1	1/3	1/5	4	1/5	1/7	6	5
Ingersoll Rand	3	1	1/4	4	1/4	1/6	7	6
I.C. Ind.	5	4	1	5	1/2	1/4	6	5
Allied Chem.	1/4	1/4	1/5	1	1/16	1/7	4	3
Rockwell Int'l.	5	4	2	6	1	1/3	7	6
Data Gen.	7	6	4	7	3	1	9	7
Butler	1/6	1/7	1/6	1/4	1/7	1/9	1	1/3
Chemetron	1/5	1/6	1/5	3	1/6	1/7	3	1

Table 13.7 summarizes the weights each of the eight firms received for each criterion.

	Gov. Regulations	Int'l. Exposure	Employment Conditions
Political (.10):	.24	.06	.70

	Family Disintegration	Age Dist.	Educ. Achievement	Empl. Cond.
Sociological (.22):	.30	.11	.11	.48

	State of Technology	Government Involvement
Technological (.36):	.80	.20

To obtain the final weights for a criterion, we must multiply the criterion weights just found by the weight of the factor associated with that criterion:

	Empl. Cond.	Elas. of Demand	Elas. of Supply	Int'l. Econ.	Int. Rates
Economic	.05	.14	.02	.02	.09

	Gov. Regulations	Int'l. Exposure	Employment Conditions
Political	.02	.01	.07

	Family Disintegration	Age Dist.	Educational Achievement	Empl. Cond.
Sociological	.07	.02	.02	.11

These weights point out that, in a high-risk future, technological factors have the greatest impact on a firm's behavior. In a medium-risk environment, both economic and technological factors are the most influential, and in a low-risk environment social factors are the most important. Economic factors have appreciable impact on all three levels, whereas the impact of political factors is rather low.

We could carry through our analysis under each of the three risk levels, but for illustrative purposes we will use the average weight for each factor. A weighted average could be used if we wished to favor one type of future over the other. Averaging, we obtain the following weights:

Economic	*Political*	*Social*	*Technological*
.32	.10	.22	.36

Now we compare the criteria for each factor to determine their order of importance. In each pairwise comparison we ask, "Which criterion has more impact on the factor and by how much?" In the case of technology and its two criteria we have the following comparison matrix:

	S	G
State of technology	1	4
Government involvement in technology	1/4	1

which indicates the state of technology has more impact on technology in general than does the government's involvement in it. This matrix and three others yield the following sets of weights for the various criteria:

	Empl. Cond.	*Elas. of Demand*	*Elas. of Supply*	*Int'l. Econ.*	*Int. Rates*
Economic (.32):	.16	.45	.07	.05	.27

PORTFOLIO SELECTION

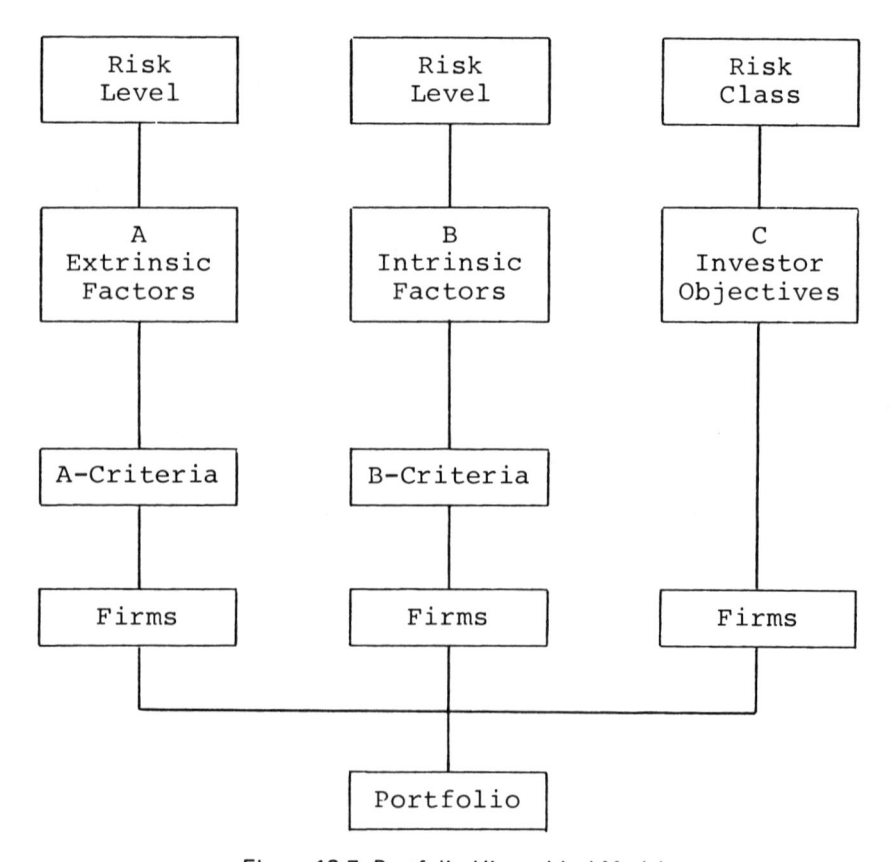

```
┌─────────┐        ┌─────────┐        ┌─────────┐
│  Risk   │        │  Risk   │        │  Risk   │
│  Level  │        │  Level  │        │  Class  │
└────┬────┘        └────┬────┘        └────┬────┘
     │                  │                  │
┌────┴────┐        ┌────┴────┐        ┌────┴────┐
│    A    │        │    B    │        │    C    │
│Extrinsic│        │Intrinsic│        │Investor │
│ Factors │        │ Factors │        │Objectives│
└────┬────┘        └────┬────┘        └────┬────┘
     │                  │                  │
┌────┴────┐        ┌────┴────┐             │
│A-Criteria│       │B-Criteria│            │
└────┬────┘        └────┬────┘             │
     │                  │                  │
┌────┴────┐        ┌────┴────┐        ┌────┴────┐
│  Firms  │        │  Firms  │        │  Firms  │
└────┬────┘        └────┬────┘        └────┬────┘
     │                  │                  │
     └──────────────────┼──────────────────┘
                   ┌────┴────┐
                   │Portfolio│
                   └─────────┘
```

Figure 13.7. Portfolio Hierarchical Model

believed that technology would have a generally strong influence on a firm's behavior compared to the other factors.

The weights for each of the factors for each risk level are computed and turn out to be:

Risk	Economic	Political	Social	Technological
High	.25	.12	.06	.57
Medium	.43	.11	.05	.41
Low	.30	.10	.54	.07

the uncertainty of the general business environment, the firm's behavior (high, medium, or low risk), and the risk class of the investor (high, medium, or low).

As our first step we look at the hierarchy of extrinsic factors. At the first level we have the primary extrinsic factors that affect a firm's behavior. At the second level we have the criteria that influence each of the primary factors.

Primary Extrinsic Factors	Criteria
Economic	Employment conditions, elasticity of demand, elasticity of supply, international economy, interest rates
Political	Government regulations, international exposure, employment conditions
Social	Family disintegration, age distribution, educational achievement, employment conditions
Technological	State of technology, government involvement

The extrinsic factors are compared pairwise for a high-risk environment, a medium-risk environment, and a low-risk environment. In each case the comparisons are based on the question, "Which factor has more impact on a firm's behavior and by how much?"

Firm	High Risk				Medium Risk				Low Risk			
	E	P	S	T	E	P	S	T	E	P	S	T
Economic	1	3	4	1/3	1	5	7	1	1	5	1/3	4
Political	1/3	1	3	1/5	1/5	1	3	1/5	1/5	1	1/5	2
Social	1/4	1/3	1	1/8	1/7	1/3	1	1/6	3	5	1	5
Technological	3	5	8	1	1	5	6	1	1/4	1/2	1/5	1

We can see that in a high-risk environment the group constructing the matrix

First we must answer the question, "How shall we compare the stocks?" The general answer is, "The stocks will be compared ultimately to criteria that exercise the most direct influence on the stocks." These criteria occupy the level of the hierarchy immediately above the stock level. But because these criteria are not all of equal importance, they in turn must be compared relative to factors that will enable us to gauge their importance. Going one step further, these factors must be weighted in terms of their effect on the overall market and business conditions.

Our task then is to make these comparisons truly reflect our information, judgments, or feelings. One of the strengths of our method is the ease with which feelings and informed judgments can be reflected and synthesized in the model. Masses of data need not be utilized directly.

The hierarchical model consists of three separate hierarchies: one based on extrinsic factors, one on intrinsic factors, and a third on the investor's objectives. The firms being considered are ranked (weighted) relative to the criteria in each hierarchy. The weights are then combined to provide an overall preference list of firms. Figure 13.7 gives an overall view of the model we will use.

We will now define the various factors and objectives we used that influence firms' portfolio selections (the particular details of the design that we have chosen are less important than the use of this design to illustrate the technique involved).

A. *Extrinsic Factors.* These are the outside factors or environmental characteristics that affect an industry's (or firm's) performance. The firm, in turn, has no direct influence on them. These factors are *economic, political, social,* and *technological.* By incorporating the analysis of the extrinsic variables, we can determine the sensitivity of a particular firm to changes in these factors.

B. *Intrinsic Factors.* These are the internal factors or operational characteristics of the firm. They may be considered as a measure of the way the firm is making its decisions or, in general, the degree to which the firm has the capacity to compete successfully. These factors are *profitability, size, technology,* and *philosophy.*

Each of the above factors is characterized in turn by criteria that describe that factor.

C. *Investor's Objectives.* These are the values of each investor that define his actions in the business world. We are aware of the great variety of objectives and combinations of objectives that a particular investor may have. To make the model simple, however, we consider four mutually exclusive types of objectives: *profitability, security, excitement,* and *control.*

Finally, since we are dealing with a model based on future conditions, we must consider *risk,* the uncertainty of future events. The model incorporates

Table 13.4. Composite Priorities of Corporate Objectives

	Objectives	Priorities
I	Market standing	0.12
II	Innovation	0.07
III	Ability to manage physical and financial resources	0.23
IV	Productivity and added value	0.08
V	Corporate commitment	0.39
VI	Worker performance and attitude	0.07
VII	Management development	0.03
VIII	Public responsibility	0.02

Table 13.5. Prioritization of Corporate Commitments Subobjectives

Corporate Commitments	1	2	3	4	5	6	7	8	Priorities
1. Earnings	1	2	2	3	7	5	9	1	0.26
2. % of sales (net income)	1/2	1	1	2	5	5	7	1	0.18
3. Operating profit	1/2	1	1	2	5	5	7	1	0.18
4. Sales growth	1/3	1/2	1/2	1	3	4	7	1/2	0.11
5. Debt ratio	1/7	1/5	1/5	1/3	1	1/2	2	1/3	0.04
6. Times interest coverage	1/5	1/5	1/5	1/4	2	1	4	1/3	0.05
7. Dividend payout ratio	1/9	1/7	1/7	1/7	1/2	1/4	1	1/6	0.02
8. Return on equity	1	1	1	2	3	3	6	1	0.17

Table 13.6. Prioritization of Clustering Schemes with Respect to Subobjectives

Operating Profits as a % of Sales	1	2	3	4	Priorities
1. Product life cycle	1	7	1/4	8	0.30
2. Investment turnover	1/7	1	1/8	2	0.07
3. Market share	4	8	1	7	0.59
4. Method of manufacturing	1/8	1/2	1/7	1	0.05

Table 13.3. Pairwise Comparisons of Corporate Objectives with Respect to Corporation's Higher Objectives

Growth, Sales, and Earnings	I	II	III	IV	V	VI	VII	VIII	Priorities
I	1	1/2	1/4	3	1/5	7	7	9	0.13
II	2	1	1/3	5	1/2	5	6	8	0.17
III	4	3	1	4	1/2	6	6	8	0.25
IV	1/3	1/5	1/4	1	1/4	4	3	7	0.07
V	5	2	2	4	1	7	9	9	0.31
VI	1/7	1/5	1/5	1/4	1/7	1	1	3	0.03
VII	1/7	1/6	1/6	1/3	1/9	1	1	3	0.03
VIII	1/9	1/8	1/8	1/7	1/9	1/3	1/3	1	0.02

C.R. = 0.08

Survival of Organization and Management	I	II	III	IV	V	VI	VII	VIII	Priorities
I	1	5	1/2	2	1/6	1	5	4	0.12
II	1/5	1	1/4	1/4	1/7	1/3	1/2	2	0.03
III	2	4	1	5	1/3	4	7	7	0.22
IV	1/2	4	1/5	1	1/6	1	1	3	0.07
V	6	7	3	6	1	7	8	9	0.42
VI	1	3	1/4	1	1/7	1	2	3	0.08
VII	1/5	2	1/7	1	1/8	1/2	1	2	0.04
VIII	1/4	1/2	1/7	1/3	1/9	1/3	1/2	1	0.03

C.R. = 0.05

Table 13.2. Prioritization of Goals

	Focus	SR	LR	Priorities
	Short Range	1	3	0.75
	Long Range	1/3	1	0.25

Short Range	Shareholder Improvement	Growth	Mgt. Perp.	Survival	Priorities
S/H Imp.	1	3	1/2	1/7	0.13
Growth	1/3	1	1/4	1/6	0.07
Mgt. Perp.	2	2	1	1	0.32
Survival	7	6	1	1	0.48

Long Range	Shareholder Improvement	Growth	Mgt. Perp.	Survival	Priorities	Composite Priorities
S/H Imp.	1	4	1/2	1/4	0.16	0.14
Growth	1/4	1	1/4	1/5	0.13	0.09
Mgt. Perp.	2	4	1	1	0.32	0.32
Survival	4	5	1	1	0.40	0.46

	Priorities
Growth, Sales, and Earnings	0.23
Survival of Organization and Management	0.78

PORTFOLIO SELECTION

Legend for Figures 13.5 and 13.6 (continued):

Elevator:
    Maintenance – Equipment
    Engineered Product
    Standard Product Low Rise
    Components and Parts
    Standard Product High Rise
    International
    Commercial Escalators
    Transit/Airport/Multibuilding
    Maintenance – Noncorporate Equipment

Architectural Systems:
    Office Systems Furniture
    Other – Flooring and Partition
    International

important to attaining the overall objective of the corporation? The final priorities of the horizons and the criteria are obtained using the supermatrix method illustrated in the next chapter. The remaining questions in the hierarchy proceed downward from the level of criteria. This is an important step for dealing with risk and uncertainty.

Benefits (and costs) are often observed to have greater value in the future than in the present. However, these values have a certain worth in the present that affects the decision being made. Thus the output of both the benefits and costs hierarchies are often discounted in terms of their utility in the present. This discounting decreases over the time horizon. Discounting (which is a weighting process) of both tangible and intangible factors is done in a similar fashion to discounting money (i.e., by estimating the worth of benefits and costs in present value).

This application is particularly useful for showing how a large set of activities can be clustered with respect to a set of clustering criteria. As shown in chapter 2, this procedure reduces the number of pairwise comparisons required, thereby increasing the consistency and efficiency of the overall process.

Finally, we show how the AHP can be used to select a set of stocks to construct an investment portfolio. This analysis can easily be extended to different types of investments, not only stocks, to diversify the portfolio and minimize the risk involved in the operation.

INVESTMENT PORTFOLIO SELECTION

Our ultimate objective is to rank a set of stocks. The ranking or preference numbers we obtain will serve as a guide for allocating our dollar resources to the stocks (see Saaty, Rogers, and Pell, 1980).

Legend for Figures 13.5 and 13.6 (continued):

BU_3: Power Generation
BU_4: Transformer
BU_5: Credit Corporation
BU_6: Met & LVIT
BU_7: T&D International
BU_8: Offshore Power Systems
BU_9: Power Systems Projects
BU_{10}: Uranium Resources
BU_{11}: Motors
BU_{12}: Broadcasting
BU_{13}: Proc. Equipment & Systems
BU_{14}: Ind. Services
BU_{15}: Distribution Products
BU_{16}: Industrial Control
BU_{17}: Control Equipment International
BU_{18}: Electronic Components
BU_{19}: Community Development
BU_{20}: Industrial Materials
BU_{21}: Lighting
BU_{22}: Lamp
BU_{23}: Defense
BU_{24}: Architectural Systems
BU_{25}: Elevator
BU_{26}: . . . . , BU_{37}

Some Business Segments

Business Unit	Business Segments
Industrial Services:	Aparatus Repair U.S.
	Engineering Service U.S.
	Other U.S. Services
	Overseas Service Businesses
Lighting:	Industrial Lighting Market – Interior
	Outdoor – Construction
	Outdoor – Utility
	Commercial Lighting Market
	HUB Electric
Lamp:	Incandescent – Grocery
	Incandescent – Electric Wholesale
	Incandescent – Mass Merchandiser
	Fluorescent – Consumer
	Fluorescent – Electric Wholesale
	Fluorescent – OEM
	High-Intensity Discharge
	Sealed Beam
	Photoflash

PORTFOLIO SELECTION 245

Legend for Figures 13.5 and 13.6 (continued):

    Receivable Ratios
    Debt/Equity Ratio
    Investment Turnover
D. Productivity and Value Added:
    Value Added per Employee
    5% Increase per Year
    Capital Expenditure
    Value Added (% Sales Billed)
    $ per Employee and Equipment
E. Corporate Commitment:
    Operating Profit (% Sales)
    IAT (% Sales)
    ROI
    Earnings Growth
    Sales Growth
    Absolute IACC
F. Worker Performance and Attitude:
    Corporate Representation
    Work Stoppages
    EEO
    Size of Plant
    Plant Age
    Turnover
G. Management Development
H. Public Responsibility

Clustering Schemes
CS_1: Type of Manufacturing and/or Service
CS_2: Driving Force
CS_3: Market End Use
CS_4: Distribution Channels
CS_5: Investment Intensity
CS_6: Cyclicality
CS_7: Inherent Cash Flow
CS_8: Sensitivity to Technological Changes
CS_9: Financial Performance
CS_{10}: Environmental Impact
CS_{11}: Labor Intensity
CS_{12}: Growth Rate/Potential
CS_{13}: Product Life Cycles
CS_{14}: Geographic Segmentation
CS_{15}: Internationalization
CS_{16}: Nuclear Sensitivity
CS_{17}: Financial Leverage
CS_{18}: Risk Classification (e.g., advantages of being a large corporation)
CS_{19}: Knowledge Sensitivity

Business Units
BU_1: Water Reactor
BU: Advanced Power Systems

Legend for Figure 13.6 (continued):

C_{17}: Intrinsic costs that give rise to benefits
C_{18}: Costs incurred to attain benefits (disbenefits)
C_{19}: Strategic costs
C_{20}: Operating costs
C_{21}: A weak position (the business segments) as major elements of a cost chain
C_{22}: Low value-added opportunities
C_{23}: Poor market position with low potential (or unjustified cost) for significant improvement
C_{24}: Small size with poor growth potential
C_{25}: Unmanageable cyclicality
C_{26}: Low or uncertain growth potential
C_{27}: Low return on the cost of capital (long-term return)
C_{28}: Decline in the productivity of the employees due to decrease in amount of time they spend doing their jobs
C_{29}: Loss of productivity due to strikes
C_{30}: Environment changes and the product may not be needed
C_{31}: Air pollution controls
C_{32}: Water pollution controls
C_{33}: Noise control
C_{34}: Reputation
C_{35}: Solid waste controls
C_{36}: Mandatory costs to maintain a license
C_{37}: Returns not commensurate with manageability of the risks

Legend for Figures 13.5 and 13.6:

Subobjectives
A. Market Standing
    Market Share
    Concentration Ratio
    Defensibility of Market Share
    Distribution Effectiveness
    Service
    Image
    Growth Rate
    Coverage
    Market Share Trends
    Product Synergy
    Size
B. Innovation:
    Number of Product "Firsts"
    Number of Patents
    Number of Engineers
    Engineering Expenditures
C. Ability to Manage Physical and Financial Resources:
    Age of Facilities
    Inventory/Sales Ratio

```
                                    FOCUS
                          SHORT RANGE  LONG RANGE
                            (.75)       (.25)
                    SHAREHOLDER  GROWTH  SURVIVAL  MANAGEMENT
                    IMPROVEMENT  (.09)   (.46)     PERPETUATION
                      (.14)                          (.32)
                        GROWTH, SALES        SURVIVAL OF THE ORGANIZATION
                         & EARNINGS               & MANAGEMENT
                           (.23)                      (.78)

MARKET     INNOVATION  ABILITY TO      PRODUCTIVITY &  CORPORATE    WORKER PERFORMANCE  MANAGEMENT   PUBLIC
STANDING   (.07)       MANAGE PHYS.&   VALUE ADDED     COMMITMENT   & ATTITUDE          DEVELOPMENT  RESPONSIBILITY
(.12)                  FIN. RESOURCES  (.08)           (.39)        (.07)               (.03)        (.02)
                       (.23)
  (A)       (B)          (C)             (D)            (E)           (F)                (G)          (H)
```

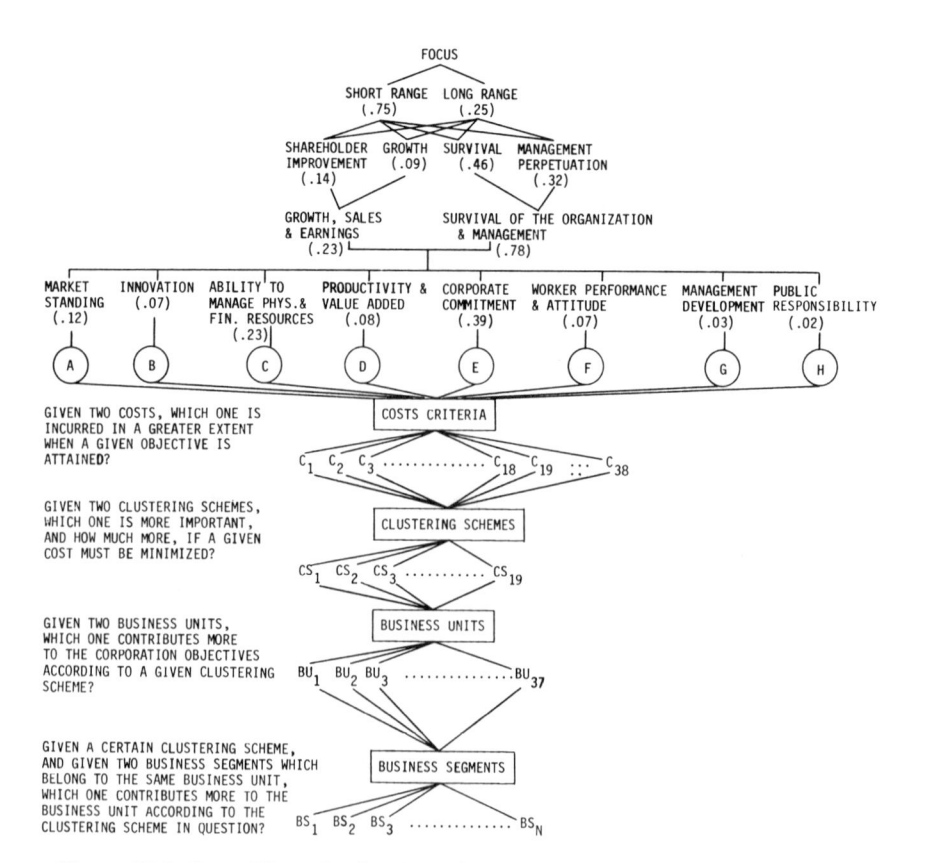

GIVEN TWO COSTS, WHICH ONE IS
INCURRED IN A GREATER EXTENT   COSTS CRITERIA
WHEN A GIVEN OBJECTIVE IS
ATTAINED? C_1 C_2 C_3 .... C_{18} C_{19} ::: C_{38}

GIVEN TWO CLUSTERING SCHEMES,
WHICH ONE IS MORE IMPORTANT,   CLUSTERING SCHEMES
AND HOW MUCH MORE, IF A GIVEN
COST MUST BE MINIMIZED?
                                         CS_1 CS_2 CS_3 .... CS_{19}

GIVEN TWO BUSINESS UNITS,
WHICH ONE CONTRIBUTES MORE   BUSINESS UNITS
TO THE CORPORATION OBJECTIVES
ACCORDING TO A GIVEN CLUSTERING BU_1 BU_2 BU_3 .... BU_{37}
SCHEME?

GIVEN A CERTAIN CLUSTERING SCHEME,
AND GIVEN TWO BUSINESS SEGMENTS WHICH   BUSINESS SEGMENTS
BELONG TO THE SAME BUSINESS UNIT,
WHICH ONE CONTRIBUTES MORE TO THE
BUSINESS UNIT ACCORDING TO THE
CLUSTERING SCHEME IN QUESTION? BS_1 BS_2 BS_3 .... BS_N

Figure 13.6. Costs Hierarchy for Assessing Business Segments of a Corporation

Legend for Figure 13.6:

Costs Criteria

C_1: A strong environmental impact similar to that of steel mills
C_2: Catastrophic events from one of the company's products
C_3: Costs of disseminating technological benefit
C_4: Investment in undeveloped technologies
C_5: Insufficient knowledge to start a business
C_6: A negative public image or cost (this characteristic is more important than having a positive public image)
C_7: Deceptive promotion
C_8: Return per unit of right effort to make the business successful or to fix a poor business
C_9: Unsafe, impure, and defective products
C_{10}: Occupational diseases
C_{11}: Industrial accidents
C_{12}: High negative market impact
C_{13}: Costs of sales promotions
C_{14}: Capital charge
C_{15}: Interest
C_{16}: Depreciation

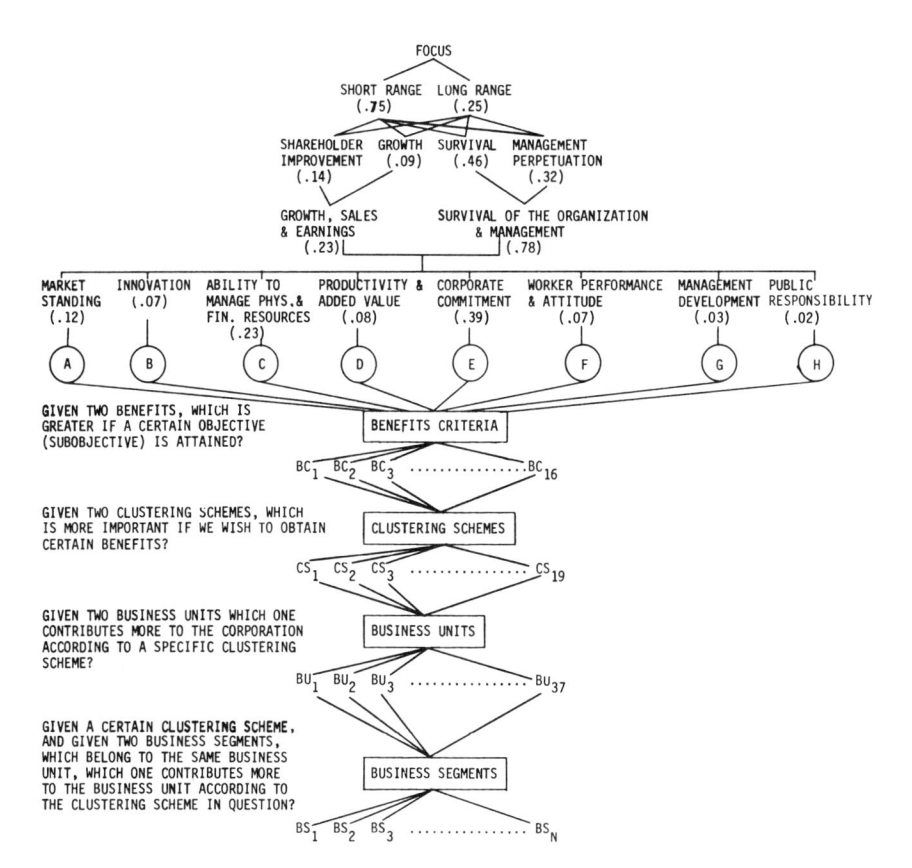

Figure 13.5. Benefits Hierarchy for Assessing Business Segments of a Corporation

Legend for Figure 13.5:

Benefits Criteria
BC_1: Competition
BC_2: Licensing technologies (royalties)
BC_3: Make or have the potential to make money
BC_4: Have an acceptable growth potential
BC_5: Have an acceptable investment turnover
BC_6: Are not sensitive/vulnerable to unmanageable controlling factors
BC_7: Have the potential (opportunity) to occupy a strong or dominant position in the market
BC_8: Size
BC_9: Good value-added opportunities
BC_{10}: Have a strong position as major elements of a cost chain
BC_{11}: Good product differentiation
BC_{12}: Image of a socially responsible corporation
BC_{13}: Business involving technologies that give a unique market position
BC_{14}: Investment in many technologies to identify the right one and avoid the wrong one
BC_{15}: Perpetuation of power
BC_{16}: Greater industrial efficiency

turn are grouped into two major objectives that drive the corporation's operations: (a) growth, sales, and earnings and (b) survival of the organization and management. The next level consists of a set of criteria or lower objectives in terms of which the benefits (costs) are prioritized. This level is inserted here to consider financial objectives, such as corporate commitment, that must be attained by all operations. They also provide a measure of the performance of business segments, to be classified as good or bad businesses. These criteria include market standing, innovation, ability to manage physical and financial resources, productivity and value added, corporate commitment, worker performance and attitude, management development, and public responsibility. Each of these lower objectives is decomposed into subobjectives (see figures 13.5 and 13.6). At this level, the hierarchy is incomplete; that is, each objective has a set of subobjectives that are not necessarily related to the subobjectives of the other objectives. The sixth level (level of benefits or costs) is the point of departure of the two hierarchies. Up to this level, all other levels coincide. In figures 13.5 and 13.6 we have included some of the benefits mentioned by the corporate executives and some others suggested by our review of the literature. This set of benefits (costs) is not exhaustive, in the sense that another corporation could have a totally different set of benefits (costs). The remaining levels are common to the two hierarchies. They consist of clustering schemes (level 7), business units (level 8), and business segments (level 9). The clustering schemes are used to classify business segments as indicated in the figures. Tables 13.2, 13.3, and 13.4 give the results of the prioritization sessions for the first four levels of the hierarchies.

For illustrative purposes we have prioritized some of the clustering schemes with respect to one of the subobjectives: operating profits as a percentage of sales. The priorities obtained must be discounted according to the priority of operating profits (table 13.5), which in turn is multiplied by the composite priority of corporate commitment. The results are given in table 13.6.

The same procedure is used to prioritize the clustering schemes with respect to costs. Once benefits and costs have been obtained, ratios of benefits to cost (priority ratios) are formed and the resources allocated accordingly. It is recommended that long-range benefit/cost analyses consider the individual periods of time (e.g., short, medium, and long-range) of the study in the second level. The following level should itemize the overall benefit criteria (or cost criteria for the cost hierarchy). The second- and third-level elements are prioritized in terms of each other. This creates a loop between the time periods and the criteria. Two types of questions are answered here: (1) given a time period, which criterion is the most desired, and (2) given a criterion, in which time period the criterion is most important. Using the priorities obtained from both questions, one then derives priorities for the horizons and for the criteria without having to answer such direct questions as, Which time horizon is more

of conditions: (a) various marketing mix strategies (for specified segments and positioning); (b) competitive, market, and government actions; and (c) overall environmental conditions. The separate cost hierarchy reflected management decision to base its selection on an explicit and detailed cost/benefit analysis. In other cases, the cost can be included as one of the objectives of the basic hierarchy.

Given, however, a separate cost hierarchy and resulting priorities, the selection of the "best" marketing mix was constructed by developing the cost/benefit ratio for each marketing mix option.

Actual experience with this approach is more limited than that with the application of the AHP to portfolio decisions or to the generation and evaluation of new products. Yet even the pilot study has suggested that this approach is viable for (1) generating more innovative marketing mix strategies, (2) evaluating the various strategies, and (3) reaching consensus among conflicting intents on the desired strategy.

CORPORATE PORTFOLIO SELECTION

Many corporations consist of several business segments. In some instances their number can exceed 100. Not all these business segments may be successful. There are four kinds of segments, identified by their degree of success: the "dogs" are the basic failures; the "problem children," as the name indicates, are segments whose success is uncertain; the "cash cows" bring money but require care and nurturing; and the "stars" are the total successes.

The problem is to decide which business segments to allocate more resources to, which ones to sell or close down, which ones to buy, and which ones to expand. The AHP provides an effective vehicle for doing this assessment in terms of cost and benefit hierarchies by using the ratio of the two as the indicator for allocating resources (Resources Priorities, Inc., 1980).

This approach was used to decide on the business segments of a large corporation. The benefit and cost hierarchies are shown in figures 13.5 and 13.6, respectively. These hierarchic structures join the objectives of the corporation, the benefits (costs) accrued from its business segments, and the business segments.

Since the objectives may change over time, we included a level (level 2) to deal with this issue. Thus the objectives of the corporation are prioritized with respect to short- and long-range plans. These two periods are used to discount the future and to observe which business segments would survive in the short- and in the long-range plans.

The third level of the hierarchies consists of four major objectives: shareholder improvement, growth, survival, and management perpetuation. They in

Adv. Obj.	Camp. 1	2	3	4
Cam. 1	1			
Cam. 2		1		
Cam. 3			1	
Cam. 4				1

Pro. Obj.	Pro. 1	2	3	4
Pro. 1	1			
Cam. 2		1		
Cam. 3			1	
Cam. 4				1

Price Obj.	Price 1	2	3	4
Price 1	1			
Cam. 2		1		
Cam. 3			1	
Cam. 4				1

Dist. Obj.	Dist. 1	2	3	4
Dist. 1	1			
Cam. 2		1		
Cam. 3			1	
Cam. 4				1

Alternative Formulation:

Prod. Pos. 1	Mktg. Mix 1	Mktg. Mix 2	Mktg. Mix 3	Mktg. Mix 4
Mktg. Mix 1	1			
Mktg. Mix 2		1		
Mktg. Mix 3			1	
Mktg. Mix 4				1

Prod. Pos. 2	Mktg. Mix 1	Mktg. Mix 2	Mktg. Mix 3	Mktg. Mix 4
Mktg. Mix 1	1			
Mktg. Mix 2		1		
Mktg. Mix 3			1	
Mktg. Mix 4				1

Prod. Pos. 3	Mktg. Mix 1	Mktg. Mix 2	Mktg. Mix 3	Mktg. Mix 4
Mktg. Mix 1	1			
Mktg. Mix 2		1		
Mktg. Mix 3			1	
Mktg. Mix 4				1

Table 13.1. Illustrative Pairwise Judgments

Opti-mistic	Profit	M/S	Growth		Status Quo	Profit	M/S	Growth		Pessi-mistic	Profit	M/S	Growth
Profit	1				Profit	1				Profit	1		
M/S		1			M/S		1			M/S		1	
Growth			1		Growth			1		Growth			1

Profits	Seg. A	B	C		M/S	Seg. A	B	C		Growth	Seg. A	B	C
Seg. A	1				Seg. A	1				Seg. A	1		
Seg. B		1			Seg. B		1			Seg. B		1	
Seg. C			1		Seg. C			1		Seg. C			1

Seg. A	Pos. 1	2	3		Seg. B	Pos. 1	2	3		Seg. C	Pos. 1	2	3
Pos. 1	1				Pos. 1	1				Pos. 1	1		
Pos. 2		1			Pos. 2		1			Pos. 2		1	
Pos. 3			1		Pos. 3			1		Pos. 3			1

Pos. 1	Adv.	Pro.	Price	Dist.		Pos. 2	Adv.	Pro.	Price	Dist.		Pos. 3	Adv.	Pro.	Price	Dist.
Adv.	1					Adv.	1					Adv.	1			
Pro.		1				Pro.		1				Pro.		1		
Price			1			Price			1			Price			1	
Dist.				1		Dist.				1		Dist.				1

PORTFOLIO SELECTION

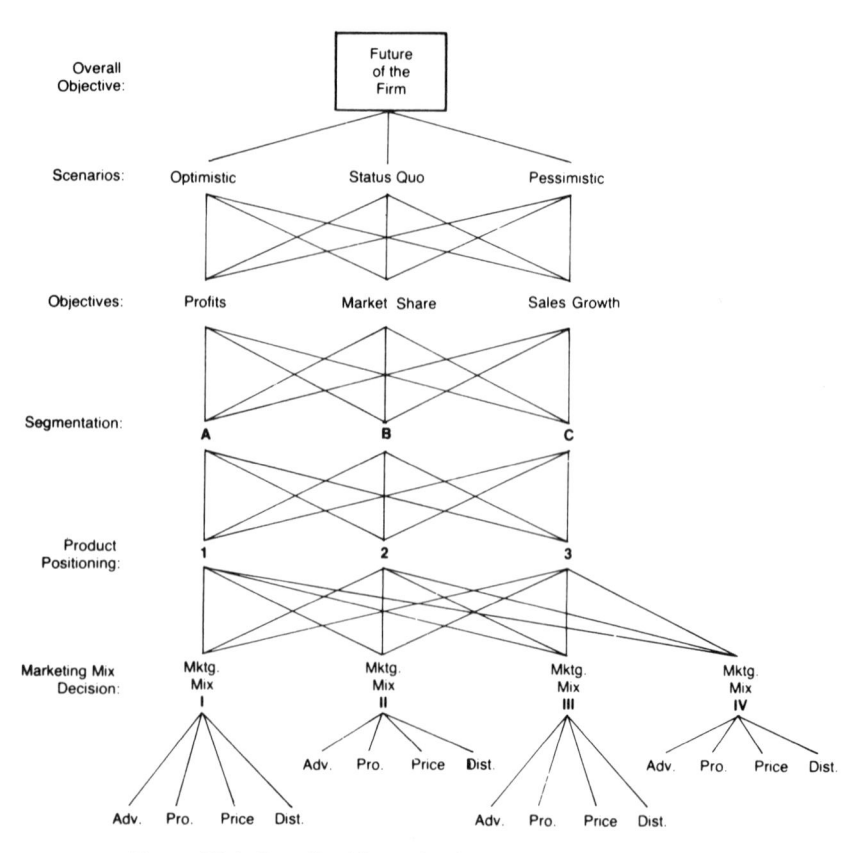

Figure 13.4. Benefits Hierarchy for Marketing Mix Decision

the formulation of the marketing mix decisions (the bottom level of the hierarchy) and therefore also examined a number of alternative formulations. The alternative selected used the same top five levels but changed the bottom level of the hierarchy from a set of *mixes* to *components*. The structure of the pairwise matrices used to generate the executive judgments are illustrated in table 13.1.

When completed, the reciprocal matrices of table 13.1 were analyzed to obtain priorities for each level of the hierarchy. This hierarchical structure, however, succeeded in capturing only the *benefit* side. To overcome this limitation, a second hierarchy—a cost hierarchy—was constructed. This hierarchy focused on three cost components: monetary costs, time costs, and management time costs. It also included the evaluation of the costs under three sets

d. Evaluation of the projects identified in step *a* with respect to the criteria for 1980 and 1985.
e. Selection of two sets of projects: first-tier projects with the highest priority on the 1980 "speed of entry" objective and second-tier projects with high priority on the 1985 ROI objective.
f. Evaluation and selection of the desired mix of 1980/1985 projects consistent with the allocation of resources suggested in figure 13.3 among projects with short-term payoffs (80 percent) and long-term payoffs (20 percent). This process resulted in the identification of ten first-tier projects aimed at achieving the short-term corporate objective in product areas *A, B, C, D,* and *E*. The projects involved three for products *A,* three for *B,* two for *C,* and one each for *D* and *E*. In addition, five second-tier projects were identified with expected long-term payoffs.

Management reaction to the results were favorable, and they started implementing the recommendation.

MARKETING MIX DETERMINATION

The design of a marketing program is conceptually not much different from any other resource allocation problem that requires:

Creativity in generating alternative (marketing mix) components and strategies;
Interactive and congruence assessment among the components (the congruence of prestige positioning with high price and prestigious distribution outlets, for example);
Evaluation of performance on multiple objectives (sales, share, attitude, and so on)—despite difficulties in such evaluation due to long-term effects (for example, carry-over advertising effects);
Multiple decisionmakers.

This complexity of the marketing mix decision suggests the advisability of formulating it with the use of the AHP.

Illustrative Application

Figure 13.4 illustrates the structure of a marketing mix hierarchy for a consumer service. The managers who constructed this hierarchy had some difficulty with

PORTFOLIO SELECTION   235

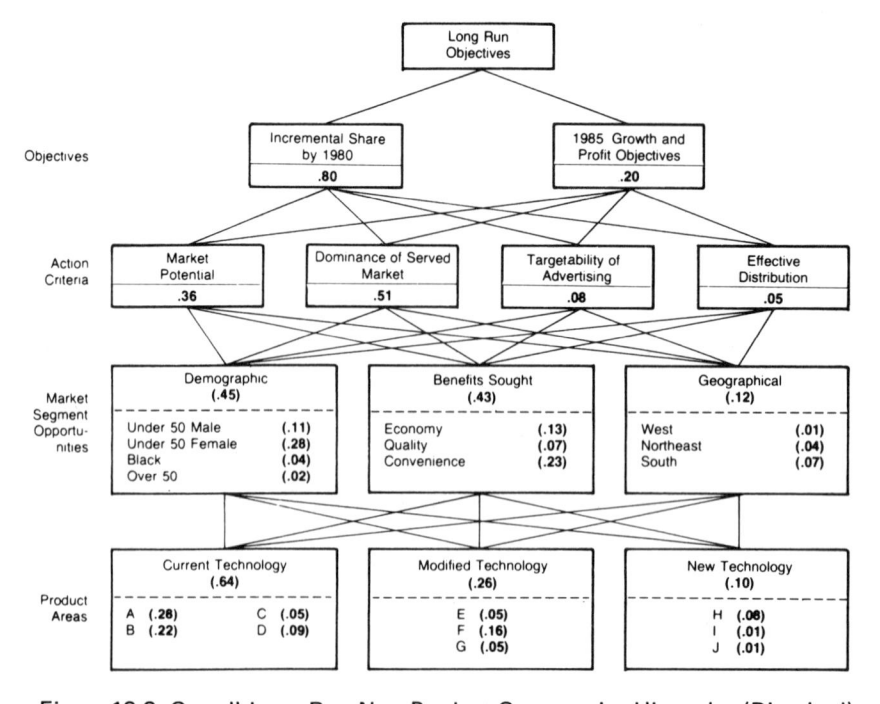

```
                            ┌─────────────────┐
                            │   Long Run      │
                            │   Objectives    │
                            └─────────────────┘
                              /              \
                    ┌──────────────────┐   ┌──────────────────┐
Objectives          │ Incremental Share│   │ 1985 Growth and  │
                    │     by 1980      │   │ Profit Objectives│
                    │       .80        │   │       .20        │
                    └──────────────────┘   └──────────────────┘
```

	Market Potential .36	Dominance of Served Market .51	Targetability of Advertising .08	Effective Distribution .05
Action Criteria				

	Demographic (.45)		Benefits Sought (.43)		Geographical (.12)	
Market Segment Opportunities	Under 50 Male	(.11)	Economy	(.13)	West	(.01)
	Under 50 Female	(.28)	Quality	(.07)	Northeast	(.04)
	Black	(.04)	Convenience	(.23)	South	(.07)
	Over 50	(.02)				

	Current Technology (.64)		Modified Technology (.26)		New Technology (.10)	
Product Areas	A (.28)	C (.05)	E (.05)		H (.08)	
	B (.22)	D (.09)	F (.16)		I (.01)	
			G (.05)		J (.01)	

Figure 13.3. Overall Long-Run New-Product Opportunity Hierarchy (Disguised)

2. Detailed evaluation of high-priority product areas and the establishment of the *desired project mix*. This phase involved six steps:
    a. Selection of the five top product areas—*A, B, F, D,* and *H*—for each area and identification of major project areas.
    b. Identification of criteria for evaluating new-product development projects. Four criteria were identified: speed of entry, required investment, long-run ROI, and likelihood of success.
    c. Evaluation of these criteria with respect to their importance for 1980 and 1985. This evaluation was conducted with the use of two AHP matrices and resulted in the following priorities:

	1980	*1985*	*Change*
Speed of entry	.47	.14	−.33
Investment	.05	.05	.00
Long-run ROI	.16	.45	+.29
Likelihood of success	.31	.36	−.05

context allows management to proceed concurrently with three other critical phases of new-product development efforts and to integrate them with the first phase of determining the direction for new-product development efforts. These three additional tasks are:

1. Generating new-product ideas. Managers participating in the AHP often possess a tremendous amount of knowledge about their product category and markets. It is desirable, therefore, to capture this cumulative knowledge and to utilize the AHP sessions also as "brainstorming" sessions aided by relevant background information—in the form of a synthesis of previous research—to generate additional new-product ideas.
2. Pulling together the new-product ideas that were generated from a variety of sources (for example, R&D, marketing research, and so on) and content analyzing them to group all similar ideas. This clustering of ideas is essential for any new-product development system because it collapses hundreds of ideas, many of which are closely related, into a manageable number of idea groups.
3. Initially evaluating the various ideas based on the degree to which they can help achieve the desired corporate objectives under a variety of scenarios.

Illustrative Application

A leading manufacturer of a frequently purchased product line who was concerned with the lack of innovativeness of the firm's new-product activities applied the AHP. Seven executives representing diverse groups within the firm (marketing, marketing research, new-product development, technical R&D) and an advertising agency spent two days in a concentrated effort, following the AHP framework, aimed at determining the directions the firm should take to achieve its long- and short-term objectives and at identifying specific new-product opportunities.

The overall hierarchy developed by the group, together with disguised results, is presented in figure 13.3. This hierarchy provided only the first phase in the overall process. The entire process involved two phases:

1. Identification of a basic hierarchy (figure 13.3) relating the 1980 new-product opportunities of the firm to action criteria, market segment opportunities, and specific product areas. An examination of the priorities of the action criteria with respect to the importance of achieving the firm's 1985 objectives suggested that the importance of these objectives is not likely to change in evaluating projects for 1980 or 1985.

ditions of status quo, and .1434 under pessimistic conditions). An examination of the results suggests that the relative importance of the various objectives varies considerably by the anticipated scenario. For example:

> Sales growth is twice as important under continuation of status quo as under the other two scenarios (0.92 versus .045 and .042).
> Market share is most important under an optimistic scenario (.093 versus .068 and .057).
> Profit level, volatility, and demand on resources are most important under a pessimistic scenario.

A sensitivity analysis was conducted with the use of alternative hierarchical formulations as well as under different assumptions concerning the likely occurrence of the various scenarios. These analyses resulted in a *range of priorities*. Given that this range suggested an allocation of resources significantly different from the firm's current resource allocation pattern, it led the president to reevaluate his firm's activities and assign task forces to those aspects of the portfolio that did not receive the attention and resources they deserved.

GENERATION AND EVALUATION OF NEW-PRODUCT CONCEPTS

New-product development efforts are often designed to minimize the constraints on R&D and marketing in generating new-product ideas. Although such freedom is often considered desirable, in many cases it has resulted in a focus on low-risk "me-too" products or, at the other extreme, on new products that may be innovative but do not capitalize on the firm's strengths. In both cases, the firm loses the benefits of potentially synergistic new-product entries. In these cases, it might be desirable to determine the boundaries of and direction for new-product development efforts.

Such explicit consideration could help to increase the likelihood that at least some new-product development efforts will be directed toward truly innovative new products. This latter consideration is critical, given the prevailing risk-avoidance tendency and the time pressures often imposed on many new-product development activities, both of which lead to the development of minor product modifications or the development of "me-too" products. Consider the large numbers of industries in which all new-product introductions center on slight variations in a limited number of dimensions.

The AHP can thus offer a useful approach for determining desired new-product development directions. Furthermore, utilization of the AHP in this

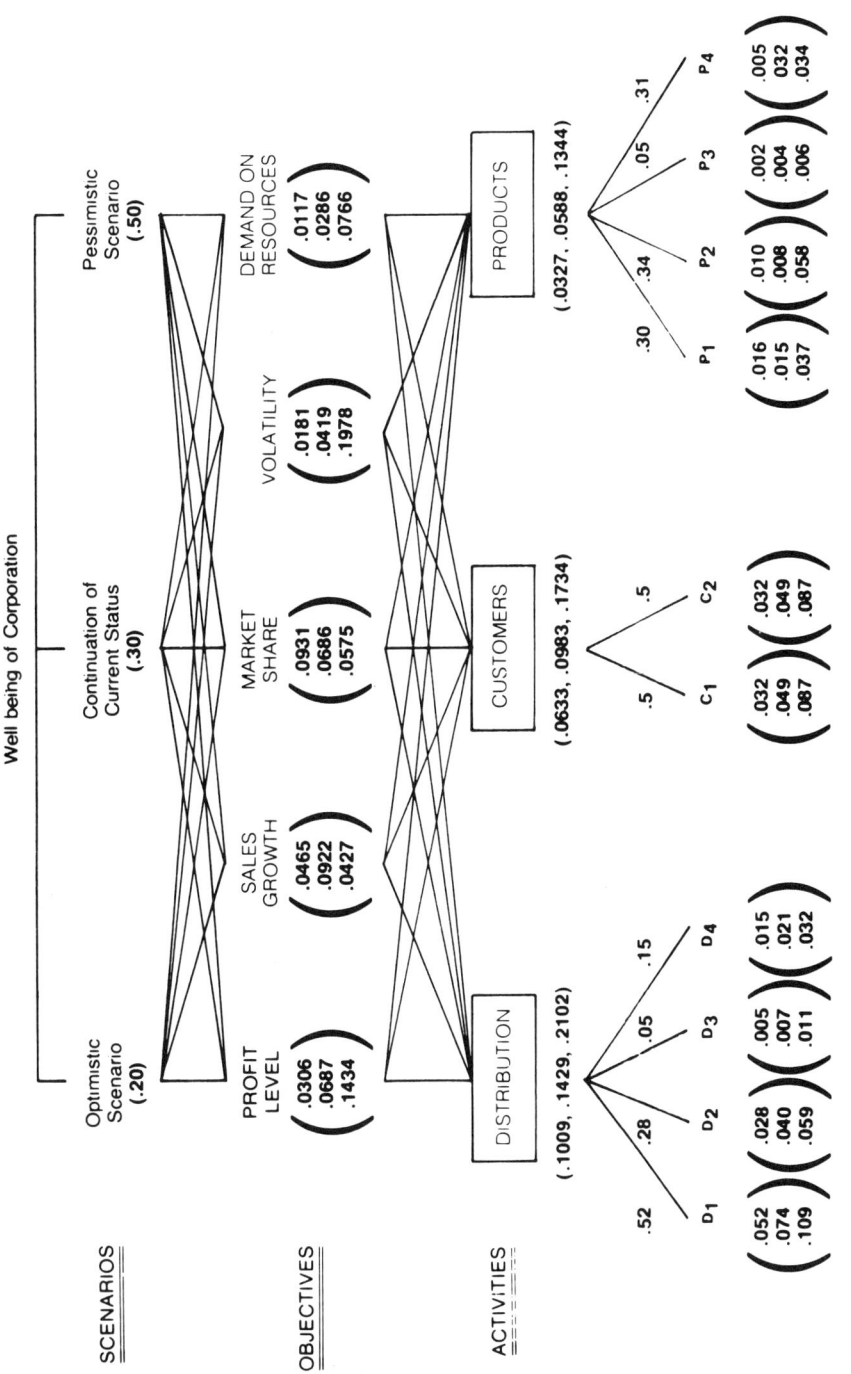

Figure 13.2. Hierarchy for Selecting Products/Customers/Distribution Portfolio

In this case, the president judged distribution to be of strong importance (5) over product in leading to the achievement of the firm's target profit level, but somewhat less important when compared to customers (4). In evaluating customers versus products, the president judged customers to be of weaker importance than products (3). Given the three judgments, the reciprocals were added and the president continued with the pairwise comparison tasks of other matrices. These tasks included the evaluation of:

Scenarios with respect to the overall objectives of the firm;
Objectives with respect to each scenario;
Classes of activities and subactivities with respect to each of the objectives;
Likely occurrence and impact of each component, given each of the other components at the same level of the hierarchy (that is, a cross-impact evaluation).

The results obtained from these data are given in figure 13.2. Examination of these results suggests explicit rules for allocating the firm's resources in developing products, markets, and distribution vehicles under three alternative scenarios. In the disguised example presented in figure 13.2, the president had a strong preference for the development of distribution outlets. In fact, the allocation of the developmental resources of the firm in this example should be .45 to the development of (current and new) distribution outlets, .35 to (current and new) market segments, and .22 to (current and new) products. This rule suggests allocating resources in proportion to the priorities. Other resource allocation rules, such as the ratio of priorities (benefits) to costs (see Saaty, 1980, p. 113; Saaty and Bennett, 1978), can also be used. The output as presented in figure 13.2 provides a significant amount of information such as:

Perceived likelihood of occurrence of the three scenarios:
Optimistic .2
Status quo .3
Pessimistic .5
Relative importance of the five objectives:
Profit level   .2427
Sales growth   .1814
Market share   .2192
Volatility   .2578
Demand on resources .1169

The overall weight of each objective reflects the importance of the objective under the three scenarios (for example, the overall importance of profit level is .2427, which is based on .0306 under optimistic scenarios, .0687 under con-

230　　　　　　　　　　　　　　　　　　　　　　　　　　CHAPTER 13

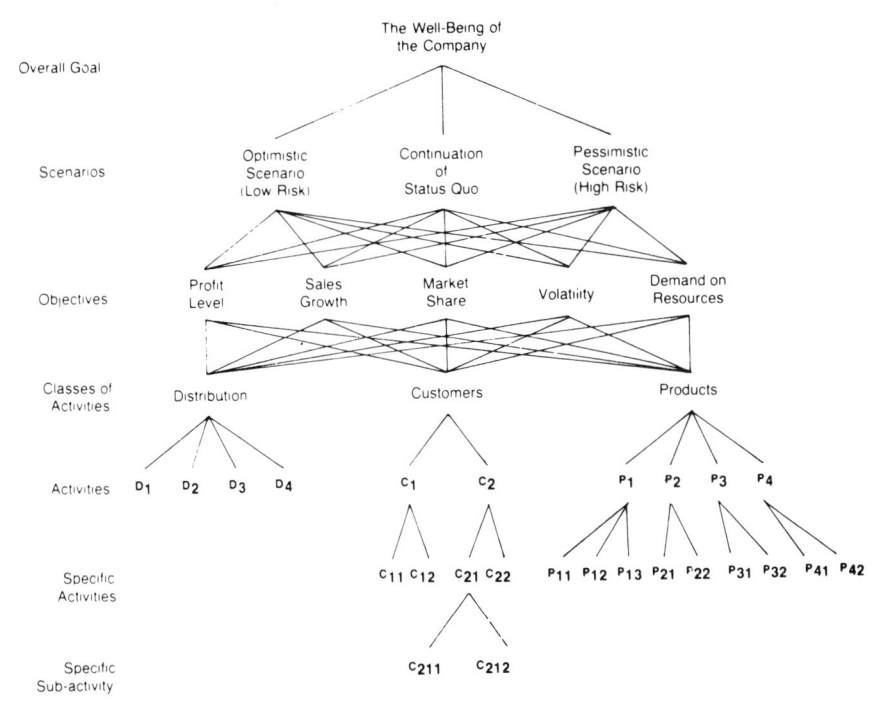

Figure 13.1. Hierarchy for Selecting Target Product/Market/Distribution Portfolio

Given the sensitive nature of information on the firm's plans for allocation of its resources among alternative courses of action, the actual options are disguised and are referred to by letters and numbers that do not correspond in any order to the items listed on the previous page.

Having selected the hierarchical structure outlined in figure 13.1, the president evaluated all pairwise comparisons with the use of the scale given in chapter 2. These evaluations resulted in reciprocal matrices of the components of each level with respect to the items in the level above. Consider, for example, the evaluation of the three major sets of activities with respect to the objectives. This involved five pairwise matrices such as the following:

Profit Level	Products	Customers	Distribution
Products	1	1/3	1/5
Customers	3	1	1/4
Distribution	5	4	1

folio models requires a different portfolio allocation model that is not subject to the limitations of the conventional resource allocation procedures and is not restricted to products (Wind and Saaty, 1980).

Illustrative Application

The Colonial Penn Insurance Company is a fast-growing company, specializing in developing and marketing auto and homeowner's policies to the over-50 market segment. Company management faces the key strategic question of determining the company's direction for future growth. Should the company continue to focus its efforts only on insurance products and, in particular, the over-50 market or should they diversify into other products and markets? Furthermore, given the firm's historical strength in the direct mail operation, should they focus their operation on products and markets that can be reached effectively by mail or should they consider developing new distribution vehicles such as telephone, stores, agents, and the like?

The AHP was used to help guide the selection of the desired target portfolio of products/markets and distribution outlets and to direct the allocation of resources among the portfolio's components. A hierarchy was developed jointly with the company president and is presented in a disguised form in figure 13.1. This hierarchy is based on three major levels:

1. *Environmental scenarios* – expressed as three summary scenarios reflecting:
   a. An optimistic environment (low risk and potentially high-return environmental conditions),
   b. Continuation of the status quo,
   c. A pessimistic scenario (high risk and potentially low-return environmental conditions).
2. *Corporate objectives* – criteria for the evaluation of the various courses of action. Five objectives were identified:
   a. Profit level,
   b. Sales growth,
   c. Market share,
   d. Volatility,
   e. Demand on resources.
3. *Courses of actions* – activities. These included the three sets of products, markets, and distribution outlets but went into considerably greater specificity of potential activities, including various new distribution outlets not currently used by the firm, new market segments, and specific new-product activities.

and in the case of international operations:

> Existing and new countries and their associated mode of entry (export, joint venture, and so on).

This focus on both the existing activities/markets and distribution outlets as well as the new directions of growth is a critical component of any strategic planning effort. It incorporates not only resource allocation under existing conditions but forces manager/planners to incorporate their assessment of likely future scenarios and their anticipated impact on the firm and its ability to achieve its objectives.

From a conceptual point of view, we should extend the product (corporate or investment) portfolio to the portfolio of activity/market/distribution options that explicitly recognizes that most companies can grow by introducing (by internal development or mergers and acquisition) new activities, entering new markets (domestic and foreign), and utilizing new methods of distribution, or any combination of the above.

This reformulated view of a firm's portfolio options is an extension of the more conventional product by market matrix proposed by many corporate strategists (see, for example, Johnson and Jones, 1957). It further suggests that the portfolio decision should not be limited only to products as in the case of product portfolio or to business segments as in the case of corporate portfolio.

PRODUCT PORTFOLIO SELECTION

Most product portfolio approaches such as the Boston Consulting Group share-growth matrix, the Shell International Sector profitability and competition matrix, and the other commonly used portfolio models of A.D. Little and McKenzie are helpful in portraying the current position of the firm's products on the selected dimensions. But they do not provide explicit rules for the selection of the target portfolio and are based on a small set of a priori selected dimensions that might not include the dimensions (criteria) critical to specific management situations such as risk, demand on resources, and so on.

In contrast, the desired portfolio approach would provide explicit guidelines for the allocation of resources among the components of the target portfolio and would base such an allocation on the relevant management criteria and their relative importance.

Accepting this basic departure from the more conventional product port-

13 RISK AND UNCERTAINTY IN PORTFOLIO SELECTION

The objective of the AHP, as established in chapter 2, is to provide priorities (weights) reflecting the importance of activities with respect to multiple criteria ordered in a hierarchical structure. These priorities can be used to allocate a resource such as money among the activities at the lower levels of the hierarchy (see chapter 5). As such, the approach is ideally suited to the allocation of a firm's resources among the activities in its (1) target production portfolio, (2) corporate portfolio—the activities are the business segments, and (3) investment portfolio.

Current approaches to resource allocation (see, for example, Forester, 1961; Gass, 1975) are rarely used by top management for the allocation of resources among the various products and businesses of the firm. The limitations of the current approaches to resource allocation at the corporate level are especially evident if one considers, not a simple allocation among the current activities, but rather an allocation that takes a more realistic posture and incorporates the following alternatives:

New activities and businesses;
Existing and potential new markets;
Existing and new modes of distribution;

The multiple authorships of this chapter are indicated in the text.

Karpman, B. 1937. "The Psychology of Chess." *Psychoanalytic Review* 24 (January):54-69.

Krogius, N. 1976. *Psychology of Chess*. New York: R.H.M. Press.

Reinfeld, F. 1952. *The Human Side of Chess*. New York: Pellegrini & Cudahy.

Roberts, R.; H.C. Schonberg; A. Horowitz; and S. Reshevsky. 1972. *Fischer-Spassky: The New York Times Report on the Chess Match of the Century*. New York: New York Times.

Table 12.9. Probabilities of Fischer-Spassky Match under Altered Expectations

	M_1	M_2	M_3	M_4	M_5
P_{AW}	.45	.50	.50	.50	.54
P_{AD}	.30	.24	.24	.23	.19
P_{AL}	.25	.26	.26	.27	.27
Expected number of games	21	21	21	21	20

Table 12.10. Probabilities of Karpov-Korchnoi Match under Altered Expectations

	M_1	M_2	M_3	M_4	M_5
P_{AW}	.35	.382	.3819	.3818	.41
P_{AD}	.30	.24	.29	.23	.19
P_{AL}	.34	.378	.3781	.3782	.40
Expected number of games	35	32	32	32	30

2. The players' expectations of winning, drawing, or losing. For this purpose pairwise comparisons can be used to assess their expectations in the particular match. The outcome is not very sensitive to small (justifiable) changes indicating differences in opinion on players' expectations.

The procedure described here can serve to illustrate a more analytic approach to prediction in competition that incorporates the effect of the behavioral as well as the technical abilities of players.

REFERENCES

Hearst, E.S. 1967. "Psychology across the Chess Board." *Psychology Today* 1 (June):29-37.

PARAMETRIC ANALYSIS

Let us now introduce some alterations in the players' expectation matrices. If we consider the following matrices:

M_1	W	D	L	a_i and b_i
W	1	3	7	0.63
D	1/3	1	7	0.30
L	1/7	1/7	1	0.06

M_2	W	D	L	a_i and b_i
W	1	5	9	0.71
D	1/5	1	9	0.24
L	1/9	1/9	1	0.05

M_3	W	D	L	a_i and b_i
W	1	5	7	0.70
D	1/5	1	7	0.24
L	1/7	1/7	1	0.06

M_4	W	D	L	a_i and b_i
W	1	5	5	0.68
D	1/5	1	5	0.23
L	1/5	1/5	1	0.08

M_5	W	D	L	a_i and b_i
W	1	7	9	0.76
D	1/7	1	7	0.19
L	1/9	1/7	1	0.05

then the probabilities of winning, drawing, and losing, and the expected number of games played for each matrix of expectations, are those given in tables 12.9 and 12.10.

Of the two contests, the Fischer-Spassky match yields more stable results because the total number of games was fixed in advance.

COMMENTS

The expected outcome of games won, drawn, and lost in chess seems to be determined by two types of factors:

1. The relative strength of the players derived from their technical and behavioral characteristics as assessed by expert judgment such as those of grandmasters.

HIERARCHICAL ANALYSIS OF BEHAVIOR IN COMPETITION   223

and substituting in equation (12.1) we have:

$$P_{AW} = 0.38 = P_{BL},$$
$$P_{AD} = 0.24 = P_{BD},$$
$$P_{AL} = 0.37 = P_{BW}.$$

From equation (12.4) we have:

$$6 = n_1 \, (.5064)(.38)$$

and

$$6 = n_2 \, (.4936)(.37),$$

which yield $n_1 \cong 31.18$ and $n_2 \cong 32.85$. Thus n should be between 31 and 33. The average of 31.18 and 32.85 is 32.02. We have:

$$n \cong 32,$$
$$N_W = 32 \times .38 \times .5064 = 6.2 > 6 \Rightarrow N_W \cong 6,$$
$$N_L = 32 \times .37 \times .4936 = 5.9 < 6 \Rightarrow N_L \cong 5.$$

Actually, Korchnoi won his fifth game in the thirty-first game of the match. The tie was broken by Karpov in the thirty-second game, who thus won by the required number of six games. These results were predicted in the midst of that match, witnessed, and signed.

If the technical and behavioral categories are not equally weighted, then the results of the analysis are those given in table 12.8.

Table 12.8. Composite Power Indexes, Unequally Weighted Categories

	[1 : 0]	[9 : 1]	Technical : Behavioral [8 : 2]	[7 : 3]	[6 : 4]	[5 : 5]
S_A	0.5298	0.5244	0.5191	0.5137	0.5084	0.5064
S_B	0.4703	0.4757	0.4810	0.4864	0.4917	0.4936
n	32	32	32	32	32	32

Table 12.7. Composite Power Indexes for Karpov and Korchnoi

	Karpov		Korchnoi	
Grandmasters	Technical	Behavioral	Technical	Behavioral
1	0.5428	0.6667	0.4572	0.3333
2	0.5417	0.5000	0.4583	0.5000
3	0.4417	0.3056	0.5583	0.6944
4	0.5167	0.4167	0.4833	0.5833
5	0.6854	0.5000	0.3146	0.5000
6	0.4375	0.3899	0.5625	0.6101
7	0.5688	0.6833	0.4313	0.3167
8	0.5000	0.5833	0.5000	0.4167
9	0.6000	0.2167	0.4000	0.7833
10	0.5313	0.5000	0.4687	0.5000
Average	0.5366	0.4762	0.4634	0.5238
Relative power	$S_A = 0.5064$		$S_B = 0.4936$	

ceding example, we obtain the final weights assigned to the players, shown in table 12.7.

The next step is to calculate P_{AW}, P_{AD}, P_{AL}, P_{BW}, P_{BD}, and P_{BL}. Since these players are nearly equal in power, their expectations would tend to be symmetrical and perhaps somewhat cautious. Their matrices would be the same. Winning is preferred strongly over drawing and absolutely over losing. We shall see in the next section that small alterations in their expectation matrices do not affect the outcome significantly. Actually, this is also true for small changes in the relative strength of the players.

Their matrices of expectations are:

Karpov	W	D	L	a_i	Korchnoi	W	D	L	b_i
W	1	5	9	0.71	W	1	5	9	0.71
D	1/5	1	9	0.24	D	1/5	1	9	0.24
L	1/9	1/9	1	0.05	L	1/9	1/9	1	0.05

Table 12.6. Grandmasters' Judgments on Karpov and Korchnoi

Grandmasters	Technical Criteria													Behavioral Criteria				
	C	EX	GH	IM	IN	GA	LRP	M	PR	Q	RY	S	T	E	G	GNWW	P	ST
1	1	1/4	1	1/4	1	—	1/3	3	3	—	4	—	4	1	—	5	5	1/4
2	—	1/4	3	1/3	4	—	—	1	1	—	5	—	1	1	1	—	1	—
3	—	1/4	1/3	1	1	—	—	1	1/3	—	5	—	1	1/3	1	—	1/5	—
4	—	1/3	1/3	1/4	5	—	—	4	5	—	4	5	1/5	1	1/3	—	1	—
5	—	1/3	3	1	4	—	—	3	4	—	5	—	4	1	1/3	—	3	—
6	—	1/4	1/3	1	3	—	—	1	1/3	—	4	—	1/3	1	1/5	—	1	—
7	—	1/3	1	1/4	3	1	—	4	3	5	4	—	1	3	1	—	4	—
8	—	—	1	—	1	—	—	1	1	—	—	—	—	1	1	—	3	—
9	—	1/5	3	1/4	4	—	—	3	1	—	5	—	4	1/3	1/3	—	1/3	—
10	—	1/5	3	1/4	5	—	—	1	4	—	5	—	1/5	1	4	—	1/4	—

Table 12.5. Games Played, Won, Drawn, and Lost by Fischer

	[1 : 1]	[1 : 2]	[2 : 1]	[3 : 1]	[1 : 3]	[1 : 0]	[0 : 1]
n	20	20	20	20	20	20	20
N_W	7	7	7	7	7	7	7
N_D	11	11	11	11	11	11	11
N_L	2	2	2	2	2	2	2

using $S_A = 0.6791$, $S_B = 0.3209$ for the (1 : 1) proportion in table 12.4, we have:

$$P_{AW} = 0.5321 = P_{BL},$$
$$P_{AD} = 0.2060 = P_{BD},$$
$$P_{AL} = 0.2618 = P_{BW}.$$

Substituting in equation (12.5) yields $n \cong 20$,

$$N_W \cong 7,$$
$$N_D \cong 11,$$
$$N_L \cong 2.$$

The actual results were: Fischer won 7 games, lost 3, and drew 11. A total of 21 games were played. One game was forfeited by Fischer due to absence, so 20 were in fact played.

Using the full range of proportions in table 12.4, we obtain the results shown in table 12.5 for the number of games played, won, drawn, and lost by Fischer.

The 1978 Karpov-Korchnoi Chess Match

From the questionnaire in table 12.1, we also have the judgments shown in table 12.6 for Karpov versus Korchnoi. For that match the total number of games played was open until one of the players succeeded in winning six games. Entries in table 12.6 represent how much more strongly Karpov is rated over Korchnoi. For example, the sixth grandmaster indicated that with respect to intuition Karpov is weakly superior to Korchnoi. However, with respect to good health Korchnoi is weakly superior to Karpov. Following the same steps as in the pre-

Table 12.4. Composite Power Indexes for Fischer and Spassky

	Technical : Behavioral						
	[1 : 1]	[1 : 2]	[2 : 1]	[3 : 1]	[1 : 3]	[1 : 0]	[0 : 1]
S_A	0.6791	0.6795	0.6786	0.6784	0.6797	0.6778	0.6803
S_B	0.3209	0.3205	0.3214	0.3216	0.3203	0.3222	0.3197

have here. This suggests that Fischer would follow a more daring strategy than Spassky. He would press very strongly for wins over draws. His matrix of expectations according to his resolve is:

Fischer	W	D	L
W	1	7	9
D	1/7	1	7
L	1/9	1/7	1

and his expectations toward winning, drawing, or losing are in the following proportion: $a_1 = 0.76, a_2 = 0.19$, and $a_3 = 0.05$, respectively.

Spassky, on the other hand, may need more caution and hence opts for draws more often; but he has the same feeling about losing as Fischer:

Spassky	W	D	L
W	1	5	9
D	1/5	1	9
L	1/9	1/9	1

Spassky's expectations toward winning, drawing, or losing are in the proportion $b_1 = 0.71, b_2 = 0.24$, and $b_3 = 0.05$, respectively. Applying equation (12.1) and

Table 12.3. Grandmasters' Judgments on Fischer and Spassky

Grandmasters	Technical Criteria												Behavioral Criteria			
	C	EX	GH	IM	IN	GA	LRP	M	PR	Q	RY	S	T	E	G	GNWW	P	ST
1	—	—	1	1	5	—	—	5	5	—	5	—	5	5	1	—	5	—
2	4	1/3	1	3	3	—	4	4	5	—	3	—	5	1	—	1	3	4
3	—	1/3	1	2	3	—	—	1	4	—	3	—	3	3	4	—	5	—
4	—	1	1	4	3	—	—	3	4	—	5	—	3	5	5	—	3	—
5	—	1	1/3	1/4	3	—	—	5	5	—	1	1/4	4	4	3	—	1/3	—
6	—	1	3	1	3	—	—	4	5	—	1	—	3	4	3	—	3	—
7	—	1	3	1	1	4	—	5	5	5	1	—	4	5	1	—	1/4	—
8	—	1	4	1	1	—	—	3	5	—	3	—	3	3	3	—	1	—
9	—	1/4	1	3	4	—	—	4	4	—	4	—	4	5	1	—	1/4	—
10	—	1/5	5	1	4	—	—	5	5	—	4	—	5	4	4	—	—	—

HIERARCHICAL ANALYSIS OF BEHAVIOR IN COMPETITION   217

from the one-to-nine scale. For the purpose of these matches, we assumed that the players, being grandmasters, would differ as much as "strongly" but not "very strongly" or more with respect to the characteristics considered.

Table 12.3 provides the judgments given by the grandmasters. An integer number in the table indicates how much more strongly Fischer was rated over Spassky with respect to the criterion indicated. Reciprocals represent how much more strongly Spassky was rated over Fischer. A dash indicates the lack of an evaluation from the corresponding grandmaster on the given criterion. Some of the criteria were mentioned only by a single respondent.

From this table the judgments are used as follows. Let us pick the judgment given by the third grandmaster, for example, when he compared Fischer with Spassky with respect to intuition. As a result, we have for that judgment a matrix of pairwise comparisons and its principal eigenvector:

Intuition	*Fischer*	*Spassky*	*Eigenvector*
Fischer	1	3	0.75
Spassky	1/3	1	0.25

The principal eigenvector, according to the Analytic Hierarchy Process, provides the relative standing of the players with respect to each other according to intuition. For each grandmaster we obtain the relative weight of the players with respect to each criterion. Averaging the relative priorities of the players for those criteria within the two categories, we obtain their relative technical and behavioral strengths.

Now we are faced with the problem of weighting the two categories according to importance to obtain a single overall index for both. It is clear that however they are weighted, the resulting weights of the actors will be between the two values indicated for each actor. It is very likely that a player's chess play could improve through exposure to a variety of behavioral situations so that he would no longer be greatly affected by behavioral factors. We note that a strong behavioral strategy that breaks the other person's ability to cope with the game would cause the opponent to quit (100 percent behavioral and 0 percent technical strategies are unacceptable as there would be no game) and may even induce the referee to nullify the game or the match. The composite power indexes S_A for Fischer and S_B for Spassky associated with the different weightings of the technical and behavioral categories are shown in table 12.4.

In the next step we compute the expectations of the players. It is reasonable to assume, for example, that both Fischer and Spassky, being experienced grandmasters, can generate something similar to the relative power indexes we

Substituting equation (12.4) into equation (12.2), we have for the number of games played:

$$n = \begin{cases} (N+1)/(1+S_A P_{AW} - S_B P_{BW}) & \text{if } N_D \text{ is odd} \\ (N+2)/(1+S_A P_{AW} - S_B P_{BW}) & \text{if } N_D \text{ is even.} \end{cases} \quad (12.5)$$

Case B: Variable Number of Match Games;
Decision by Number of Games

When the total number of games allotted to the match is not fixed but one of the players must win six games for the title, the total number of games played is obtained as follows: If N_A is the total number of games won by player A, then we have $N_A = n S_A P_{AW}$, which yields an estimate of n denoted by n_1. Similarly, we have for player B $N_B = n S_B P_{BW}$, which yields a second estimate of n denoted by n_2.

In general, one would expect n, the total number of games played, to fall between these two values. When the players are equally or nearly equally matched, n may be reasonably approximated by the average of these two values. In case one player is much stronger than his opponent, we argue that only the expression corresponding to the stronger player should be used. To see this, we add both expressions and solve for n, thus obtaining $n = (N_A + N_B)/(S_A P_{AW} + S_B P_{BW})$. If a_1, a_2, and a_3 are the expectations of player A with respect to winning, drawing, and losing games, respectively, and if b_1, b_2, and b_3 are the corresponding expectations of player B, where $0 \leq a_i, b_i \leq 1$, then P_{AW} and P_{BW} are given by $P_{AW} = a_1 S_A + b_3 S_B$ and $P_{BW} = a_3 S_A + b_1 S_B$. Since $S_A + S_B = 1$, S_B must tend to zero as $S_A \to 1$. Hence, n tends to N_A/a_1.

This may be interpreted as follows: If the relative power of one of the players is close to unity—that is, he is clearly the superior player—the result of the match is independent of the expectations of the weaker player. In that case a_1 would tend to unity, and n would be close to $N_A = 6$.

APPLICATIONS

The procedure developed above is now applied to the 1972 Fischer-Spassky match to illustrate how the theory works and to the 1978 Karpov-Korchnoi match for prediction purposes.

The 1972 Fischer-Spassky Match

The questionnaire in table 12.1 indicated what the grandmasters were asked to do. Their qualitative responses were then given corresponding numerical values

HIERARCHICAL ANALYSIS OF BEHAVIOR IN COMPETITION

where P_{ij} is the likelihood that outcome j will occur to a given player i, $i = A$ or B, and j = win, draw, or lose.

PREDICTING THE NUMBER OF GAMES PLAYED AND WON

Knowing the likelihoods of the outcomes for each player, we can then predict the number of games played, drawn, and won. Let us begin by describing relationships between the power index of the players and the number of games played in a chess championship match for two situations: the earlier situation in which a maximum of twenty-four games was allotted to the match, and the more recent one in which a match had to go on until one player won six games.

Case A: Fixed Maximum Number of Match Games N; Decision by Number of Points

Prior to the Karpov-Korchnoi match of 1978, the rule was to allocate a value of 1/2 point to a draw and a value of 1 to a win and to allow the play to go on for no more than a total of N games ($N = 24$). N is always even to equalize whites and blacks. Thus to be declared a winner, a player must accumulate a total of at least $(N/2 + 1/2)$ points.

If N_W is the number of games won by the winner, N_D the number of draws, and N_L the number of games won by the loser, then n the number of games played satisfies:

$$N_W + (1/2)N_D = \begin{cases} N/2 + 1/2, & \text{if } N_D \text{ is odd} \\ N/2 + 1, & \text{if } N_D \text{ is even} \end{cases} \quad (12.2)$$

$$N_W + N_D + N_L = n. \quad (12.3)$$

Since the number of games won by a player is determined by his power index and the result is weighted by his expectation of winning, our approach leads to the following definition of the number of games won, drawn, and lost by the winner:

$$\begin{aligned} N_W &= n\, S_A\, P_{AW}, \\ N_D &= n\, (1 - S_A\, P_{AW} - S_B\, P_{BW}), \\ N_L &= n - N_W - N_D. \end{aligned} \quad (12.4)$$

mates his opponent in one game, he quickly learns to change his expectation for the next game.

In chess, the possibility of a draw complicates the calculation of outcomes. The power index computed from technical and behavioral factors gives only the relative strength of the players and does not allow for draws. It divides each game into two parts: the relative number of games won and drawn by one player and the relative number won and drawn by the other. Since our prediction must also cover the number of drawn games, we assess the attitude or expectation of each player toward a win, a draw, or a loss by constructing pairwise comparison matrices of the three outcomes of a game:

Player i	Win	Draw	Lose	Expectation
Win	1			
Draw		1		$\begin{pmatrix} \\ \\ \end{pmatrix}$
Lose			1	
$i = A$ or B				

Let us denote the expectations of players A and B as follows:

Outcome	Expectations	
	A	B
Win	a_1	b_1
Draw	a_2	b_2
Lose	a_3	b_3

Now, given the relative strengths and the expectations of the players, the relative priorities of the outcomes are obtained by weighting the expectations of the players by their relative strengths and adding them. Thus we have:

Outcome	Likelihood of Occurrence
Win	$a_1 S_A + b_3 S_B = P_{AW} = P_{BL}$
Draw	$a_2 S_A + b_2 S_B = P_{AD} = P_{BD}$
Lose	$a_3 S_A + b_1 S_B = P_{AL} = P_{BW}$

(12.1)

```
                    ┌─────────┐
                    │  CHESS  │
                    └─────────┘
              ┌──────────┴──────────┐
        ┌───────────┐         ┌────────────┐
        │ TECHNICAL │         │ BEHAVIORAL │
        └───────────┘         └────────────┘
```

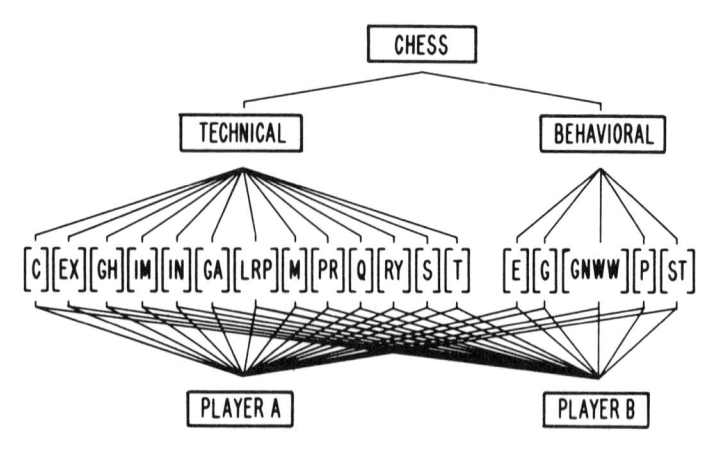

[C][EX][GH][IM][IN][GA][LRP][M][PR][Q][RY][S][T]   [E][G][GNWW][P][ST]

```
        ┌──────────┐              ┌──────────┐
        │ PLAYER A │              │ PLAYER B │
        └──────────┘              └──────────┘
```

Figure 12.1. Hierarchy of Factors Affecting a Chess Match

exploit his psychology to his own advantage. This requires skill in decoding one's own and the opponent's individualities.

The foregoing characterization of chess may be represented schematically for our purposes as in figure 12.1. (The key is provided in table 12.2.) The prioritization of the hierarchy given in the figure yields the relative strengths (power index) of the players with respect to the criteria of the second level. We have left open the relative importance of technical versus behavioral criteria and carried out our prediction under different assumptions of relative values. Thus we average over the weights of the players in each category. We note that there is no unanimity as to what the priorities of the criteria should be. Also, because of the large number of factors, we assume that they are equally important as a first estimate. However, we note that there is no significant change in the outcomes predicted if priorities are adequately assigned to the criteria.

DISPOSITION OF THE PLAYERS TOWARD THE GAME

Let us assume that the two players in a match are designated by A and B. Let S_A and S_B be their relative strengths. The next step is to assess the expectations of the players in the match.

A player will go for a win or a draw depending on who his opponent is. If he expects his opponent to be strong, his expectation for a win is not as high because he allows a possibility for a draw or even for a loss. This is not so if he plays a weak player, in which case he would go for a win without reservation and with absolutely greater commitment than for a draw or a loss. If he underesti-

Table 12.2. Technical and Behavioral Factors in Chess

T *Calculation (C)*: Ability to evaluate different alternatives or strategies in light of the prevailing situation.

B *Ego (E)*: Self-image with respect to general abilities and qualifications and desire to win.

T *Experience (EX)*: Composite of the versatility of opponents faced before, the strength of the tournaments previously participated in, and the length of time one has been exposed to a rich variety of chess players.

B *Gamesmanship (G)*: Ability to influence the opponent's game by destroying his concentration and self-confidence.

T *Good Health (GH)*: Physical and mental strength to withstand pressure and provide endurance.

B *Good Nerves and the Will to Win (GNWW)*: Attitude of steadfastness that ensures a healthy perspective when the going gets tough. Player keeps in mind that the situation involves two people and that if one holds out, the tides may go in one's favor.

T *Imagination (IM)*: Ability to perceive and improvise good tactics and strategies.

T *Intuition (IN)*: Ability to guess the opponent's intentions.

T *Game Aggressiveness (GA)*: Ability to exploit the opponent's weaknesses and mistakes to one's advantage, occasionally referred to as killer instinct.

T *Long-Range Planning (LRP)*: Ability to foresee the outcome of a certain move, set up desired situations that are more favorable, and work to alter the outcome.

T *Memory (M)*: Ability to remember previous games.

B *Personality (P)*: Manners and emotional strength – their effect on the opponent in playing the game and on the player in keeping his wits.

T *Preparation (PR)*: Study and review of previous games and ideas.

T *Quickness (Q)*: Ability to see rapidly and incisively the heart of a complex problem.

T *Relative Youth (RY)*: Vigor, aggressiveness, and daring to try new ideas and situations, a quality usually attributed to youth.

T *Seconds (S)*: Availability of other experts to help analyze strategies between games.

B *Stamina (ST)*: Physical and psychological ability to endure fatigue and pressure.

T *Technique (T)*: Ability to use and respond to different openings, improvise mid-game tactics, and steer the game to a familiar ground to one's advantage.

	Fischer over Spassky					Spassky over Fischer		
	(5) Strongly	*(4)* Moderately	*(3)* Weakly	*(1)* Same	*(3)* Weakly	*(4)* Moderately	*(5)* Strongly
Experience							
Good health							
Imagination							
Intuition							
Memory							
Preparation							
Relative youth							
Technique							
Ego							
Gamesmanship							
Personality							
Others[a]							

Note: This questionnaire is for comparing Karpov and Korchnoi, and Fischer and Spassky from what is known about them. We ask: Given two players (e.g., Karpov and Korchnoi), whom do you feel has the characteristic in question in a stronger fashion? For example, who has more experience by comparison, Karpov or Korchnoi? If you feel that, for example, Karpov has more experience than Korchnoi, check one of the three entries "weakly, moderately, or strongly" next to experience under "Karpov over Korchnoi." If you consider both players equal according to some of the characteristics, check the middle column—"same." Otherwise, check one of the three columns under "Korchnoi over Karpov." This process must be repeated for each characteristic so that in each row there is a single check mark.

[a] If you feel that additional characteristics should be considered, write them below and compare the players with respect to them.

Table 12.1. Questionnaire for Comparing Chess Players

	Karpov over Korchnoi			(1) Same	Korchnoi over Karpov		
	(5) Strongly	(4) Moderately	(3) Weakly		(3) Weakly	(4) Moderately	(5) Strongly
Experience	——	——	——	——	——	——	——
Good health	——	——	——	——	——	——	——
Imagination	——	——	——	——	——	——	——
Intuition	——	——	——	——	——	——	——
Memory	——	——	——	——	——	——	——
Preparation	——	——	——	——	——	——	——
Relative youth	——	——	——	——	——	——	——
Technique	——	——	——	——	——	——	——
Ego	——	——	——	——	——	——	——
Gamesmanship	——	——	——	——	——	——	——
Personality	——	——	——	——	——	——	——
Others[a]	——	——	——	——	——	——	——

useful for predicting how that person will fare against a champion challenger. In general, statistics cannot serve as a measure of performance under the special and highly demanding conditions of the match between two nearly equal contenders. Thus the assessment of the outcome of a match must be made in terms of the competition between the particular players. Occasionally such statistics between the same opponents can be decisive; for example, the Karpov-Korchnoi matches of 1974 and 1978 were decided by one game. The output must be evaluated both in terms of the power of each player and in terms of how strongly a player is assessed to press for a win or a draw. This appears to be a reasonable way to deal with the fine structure involved in predicting the actual numbers we seek.

RELATIVE POWER OF THE PLAYERS: THE INPUT

The questionnaire sent to the grandmasters (see table 12.1) and the literature we examined (Karpman, 1937; Krogius, 1976; Reinfeld, 1952) were concerned with individual technical characteristics and the psychology of chess players. These gave rise to the set of factors given in table 12.2, which was divided into a technical category (or expertise on the board) T and a behavioral category (or knowledge of how to deal with the opponent) B. These categories are indicated beside each factor. We admit that some factors may appear to belong to both categories, but refinements of the approach might eventually sort out such ambiguity either by focusing on redefining the factors or by a different process of aggregation, such as factor analysis.

It is clear that for players who are technically mismatched, behavioral factors have little effect. Even for well-matched players it is sometimes possible that one will tune out his opponent and continue to play a good game. But in certain situations, such as a long match, this may not be possible.

Behavioral factors may be applied to the game and to the environment. In the former, a player may introduce an innovative play in the midst of a conventional opening game. Alternatively he may apply possibly distracting, misleading, or irritating mannerisms in his approach to moving the pieces.

When the players are equally matched in their technical characteristics, behavior becomes important and may even be a decisive factor. Krogius (1976, p. 167) points out that almost 80 of the 100 masters and grandmasters he polled said that they took into account all the emotional nuances of their opponent's behavior. He also found that players who took into consideration the psychology of the opponent (for instance, inferring his state of mind by observing changes in his breathing and perspiration) later developed a counterbehavioral strategy to their own advantage. A player must also consider his own behavior to

necessarily mathematical, or artistic, or more intelligent. . . . You attack a person's psychological weaknesses. You put him under tremendous strain, push him to where he consumes his energy, where he gets exhausted . . . when he reaches a point of demoralization, a player can crash, go to pieces, lose.

In general, however, mathematical analyses of indoor games have been made purely in terms of the strategies of the players without due consideration to their behavior.

To be accurate, prediction must deal with the inputs of a system, the actual operation of that system, and the outputs. The problem is: given certain inputs, what is the likelihood that a certain output will result?

In chess, the raw input into the game is the experience and know-how of the players in manipulating or transforming the system (that is, the chess board and its psychological surrounding environment) to an output that in practice is a win, a draw, or a loss indicated by the resignation of one player — a checkmate rarely occurs among experts — or by an agreed-upon tie.

Thus our task is to assess the quality of the input by considering all "relevant" characteristics and deriving a relative index of the power of the players. We then use this power to assess the kind of output it would produce over a set of several encounters in a match. Our object is to predict the total number of games played and the number of games won by each player. We also analyze the sensitivity of the results to changes in the expectations of the participants.

A successful predictive model should be based on feedback, leading to revision and enrichment, from similar situations. An ongoing interaction between our initial representation of a situation and our practice of it is necessary until a degree of alignment is produced that makes the two correspond more closely. It is only then that prediction becomes realistic and accurate. Otherwise, we would be dealing with a random guessing game.

Of course, we do not pretend that we have included every relevant factor in chess or that our understanding of the players' abilities with regard to these factors is complete. What we present is a proposed approach that organizes our understanding of the game in a more effective way than we believe is otherwise available.

To do this for chess, we compute the input and, given certain common knowledge about the actual game and its rules, we predict the output (the outcome) for a particular set of players. The judgments we use were obtained by questionnaires sent to twenty-one chess grandmasters in the United States (ten responded). We feel that their understanding and experience are much more valuable than our own judgments or those gathered from books, magazines, newspapers, or lay acquaintances.

To compute the output, we note that the statistics of a player's past wins, losses, and draws against various opponents form a mixed bag and are not very

12 HIERARCHICAL ANALYSIS OF BEHAVIOR IN COMPETITION:
Prediction in Chess

Our purpose in this chapter is to explore, through an example, the roles of technical competence and of behavior in predicting the outcome of a competitive situation. Of course, factors arising from uncontrollable natural events (such as bad weather) and from human intervention (such as referee error) could have a marked effect on the outcome. In most competition, however, an effort is usually made to minimize the effect of natural causes to avoid unfair outside intervention.

We use competition in chess to develop our proposed systems approach, which we apply to the 1972 Fischer-Spassky match as well as to the 1978 Karpov-Korchnoi match (still in progress at the time of the study).

The importance of behavior in chess competition has been highlighted in the literature. For example, E.S. Hearst (1967, p. 37) points out that "psychological combat takes place almost every time a wooden piece is shifted from one square to another. Top flight chess is as much psychological battle as technical ability." And according to Roberts et al. (1972, p. 19):

> The essential quality of a high-level player is a kind of enjoyment of a very intense, physically and mentally exhausting struggle. Chess players are not

This chapter, by T.L. Saaty and L.G. Vargas, has been reprinted from *Behavioral Science*, Volume 25, No. 3, 1980, by permission of James Grier Miller, M.D., Ph.D., Editor.

COMMENTS

Our predictions show a 28.32 percent increase by 1985 and a 40.18 percent increase by 1990. Based on the price of Arabian light crude of $32 per barrel, we obtain $41.06 and $44.86 for 1985 and 1990, respectively, as the real price. These results are higher than those predicted by the Exxon Corporation (1980).

Based on the price of Arabian light crude in October 1979 or $18 per barrel, the Exxon study predicted that the real price would be $25 per barrel in 1985 and $28 in 1990. The Exxon study has indicated that its estimates are below those assumed by the U.S. Senate Finance Committee in its predictions.

Considering costs of energy resources other than oil of $35 to $50 per barrel of oil equivalent, our results are reasonable. According to our predictions, by 1985 the price of crude will be equal to the cost of its cheaper substitutes, and by 1990 it will still remain cheaper than most of its alternatives. Higher oil prices will also raise the production costs of alternative energy resources. Therefore, this level of oil prices will provide major oil exporters with long-term security of demand for their oil.

It may be useful to note that in the extreme situation of internal disorder or breakout of hostilities among the major oil producers of the Persian Gulf or between them and other industrial nations, oil supplies may be completely cut off with skyrocketing effect on the spot market of oil. In that case the price of a barrel could go over $100, at least temporarily, before 1990.

For a revised version contrasting assumptions and improved predictions see *Prediction, Projection, and Forecasting*, T. Saaty and L. Vargas, Kluwer Academic Publications, 1991.

REFERENCES

Exxon Corporation. 1980. *World Energy Outlook*. New York.

Table 11.3. Expected Increases in Oil Prices in 1985 and 1990

1985

Price Increases	H_1	M_1	L_1	H_3	S_1	S_2	P_2	M_4	H_5	M_5	(W_6) M	Likelihood Weights
E 80%	.066	.029	.033	.043	.101	.046	.066	.060	.513	.101	.046	.126
H 40%	.171	.081	.063	.086	.502	.102	.171	.153	.262	.503	.102	.238
S 20%	.527	.162	.129	.201	.251	.245	.528	.576	.129	.251	.245	.285
M 10%	.171	.416	.513	.469	.101	.504	.171	.153	.063	.101	.504	.253
L 5%	.066	.312	.262	.201	.044	.102	.066	.060	.033	.044	.102	.098
V —	—	—	—	—	—	—	—	—	—	—	—	—

1990

Price Increases	M_1	L_1	L_3	S_1	P_3	L_4	H_5	(W_5) M	Likelihood Weights
E 160%	.041	.037	.056	.041	.037	.033	.096	.044	.044
H 80%	.199	.078	.240	.199	.078	.121	.148	.163	.154
S 40%	.430	.191	.374	.430	.191	.251	.513	.297	.327
M 20%	.199	.425	.240	.199	.425	.445	.179	.424	.323
L 10%	.090	.191	.056	.090	.191	.118	.039	.044	.103
V 5%	.041	.078	.034	.041	.078	.033	.023	.029	.049

Table 11.2. Composite Weights of Subfactors Influencing Oil Prices in 1985 and 1990

Factors	Composite Weights		Selected Factors (Normalized)	
	1985	1990	1985	1990
H_1	.078	.012	.095	–
M_1	.044	.075	.054	.102
L_1	.066	.093	.081	.127
H_3	.045	.006	.055	–
M_3	.024	.014	–	–
L_3	.008	.073	–	.099
S_1	.167	.138	.204	.188
S_2	.068	.035	.083	–
S_3	.028	.015	–	–
P_2	.047	.030	.057	–
P_3	.026	.070	–	.095
H_4	.007	.014	–	–
M_4	.069	.052	.084	–
L_4	.030	.123	–	.167
H_5	.112	.051	.137	.069
M_5	.046	.013	.056	–
L_5	.019	.005	–	–
$V(W_5)$	–	.018	–	–
$M(W_5)$	–	.112	–	.152
$R(W_5)$	–	.045	–	–
$V(W_6)$	.008	–	–	–
$M(W_6)$	.077	–	.094	–
$R(W_6)$	.033	–	–	–

ing real prices based on 1980 dollar value: $32 \times 1.2832 = \$41.06$ in 1985; and $32 \times 1.4018 = \$44.86$ in 1990.

Assuming average annual inflation rates of 10 percent, 12 percent, and 15 percent in the United States, the price of a barrel of oil can be: $41.06 (1 + .10)^5 = \$66.13, \$72.36, \$82.59$, respectively, in 1985; and \$116.36, \$139.33, \$181.48, respectively, in 1990.

A referee of the paper from which this chapter has been excerpted indicated that the most recent forecast in his organization projected oil price increases of 4.35 percent and 2.01 percent per year for the periods 1980-1985 and 1985-1990, respectively. These yield $32(1.0435)^5 = \$39.59$ and $39.59(1.0201)^5 = \$43.73$ for the two periods.

Table 11.1. Relative Weights of Factors Influencing Oil Prices in 1985 and 1990

Factors	Weights		Selected Factors (Normalized)	
	1985	1990	1985	1990
W_1	.176	.169	.188	.181
W_2	.025	.023	–	–
W_3	.072	.087	.077	.093
W_4	.577	.515	.616	.550
W_5	.040	.165	–	.176
W_6	.111	.042	.119	–

some substitutes for oil. For 1985, great-power struggle is seen to have a relatively strong influence on escalating the price of oil as a result of the great powers (a) competing to get for themselves the quantity needed by paying more for it and (b) attempting to improve their political status in the world (as France and Japan are doing). In 1990 the influence of this factor declines but remains important owing to a tightening of the oil market as the supply shrinks relative to the demand. A subfactor that ranks third in influence in 1985 but is not as important in 1990 is the unfavorable disposition of OPEC to managing prices in a reasonable manner. By 1990 the influence of OPEC in the world energy market will decline because of the diminishing reserves of some members and the increased domestic needs of other members and as the views of OPEC members diverge in search of greater opportunities in the world. The development of alternative energy resources will be of significant importance by 1990 as the industrialized world will increase its efforts to secure its energy needs. Because of the long lead times required for the development of such resources, their impact on oil prices in 1985 will be negligible.

From table 11.2, the surviving subfactors for both 1985 and 1990 are used to prioritize the various percentage increases. Table 11.3 summarizes the results. According to this table, the expected increases for 1985 and 1990 are obtained by weighting the percentages by the values of their likelihood and adding. We have for 1985: $80 \times .126 + 40 \times .238 + 20 \times .285 + 10 \times .253 + 5 \times .098 = 28.32\%$; and for 1990: $160 \times .044 + 80 \times .154 + 40 \times .327 + 20 \times .323 + 10 \times .103 + 5 \times .049 = 40.18\%$. Considering the present price of Arabian light crude (market crude) of \$32 per barrel, these percentages amount to the follow-

4. For great-power struggle (P_4), which of the three levels of intensity is most likely for the period under consideration: high (H_4), medium (M_4), or low (L_4)?
5. For OPEC behavior (P_5), which of the three levels of intensity of unfavorable disposition is most likely for the period under consideration: high (H_5), medium (M_5), or low (L_5)?
6. Compute the composite weights for each subfactor and select subfactors with high relative weights.
7. Compute the relative likelihoods for each level of price increase for each selected subfactor.
8. Compute the composite weights of the levels of price increase. The result will be a set of numbers representing the likelihood of each price increase.
9. Compute the expected price increase by multiplying each price increase level by its corresponding likelihood.

Remark: Some of the judgments used here were initially provided by five experts from major oil companies and were later modified to enforce consistency and to cope with other factors not included in the first version of the model.

COMPUTATION OF OIL PRICES

The two columns of weights in table 11.1 indicate, as one would expect, that political factors have by far the dominant influence in both periods. The next most important factor in both periods is the increase in oil consumption, which we surmise will take place mainly in the developing countries, particularly in the oil-producing countries themselves. The third most important factor differs in the two periods. In 1985 it is the influence of international financial institutions, whereas in 1990 it is the development of energy resources other than oil. The fourth ranking factor, the oil discovery rate, is the same in both periods. In each period there are two factors with such negligible relative influence that they were eliminated and the remaining four values renormalized. They appear in the last two columns of table 11.1. The remainder of the analysis is based on these surviving factors for each period.

In table 11.2 we give the composite weights of the subfactors. Note that there is one subfactor that dominates in both periods: social strains (together with tension between individual states, such as Iraq and Iran, in 1985) within the countries of the Persian Gulf region. This is seen to contribute substantially to the instability of the region. The current concern of the Western world for the stability of this area validates this outcome. Oil consumption is the next most important concern in 1985 but ranks third in 1990, as nations will have

W_6: *International Financial Institutions.* Most of the excess oil revenues are circulated around the world by these institutions. If the funds are circulated properly, they will provide greater incentive to a special group of oil producers to increase oil supply beyond their domestic financial needs. The resulting pressure to raise the price of oil will not be as great as it would be if the surplus money is not invested in profitable ways, leading to depreciation in the value of the funds. It is often said that in such a situation, oil in the ground is more valuable than money in the bank.

ESTIMATION OF PRICE INCREASES

The following steps are required to estimate price increases when using the AHP:

1. Compute the relative weights of the factors $(W_1, \ldots, W_6)$ according to their effectiveness in increasing the price of oil (see the legend of figure 11.1 for their definition).
2. For each W_i, compute the relative likelihood of its corresponding subfactors. For example, for the period under consideration, we ask the following questions:
   a. Which of the two strategies of the oil-consuming countries is more likely: collective or unilateral?
   b. Which of the three levels of oil consumption increase is most likely: 4 percent, 2 percent, or 1 percent per year? And so on.
   c. Which of the three levels of excess production capacity is most likely: 10 percent, 5 percent, or 1 percent above production level?
   d. Which of the three rates of oil discovery is more likely: 20 billion barrels/year (BB/y), 10 BB/y, or 5 BB/y?
   e. Which of the five political factors would have the greatest influence in determining future oil prices: degree of instability in the Persian Gulf region (P_1), intensity of the Arab-Israeli conflict (P_2), increasing Soviet influence in the Middle East (P_3), great-power struggle (P_4), or OPEC behavior (P_5)?
   f. Which of the three levels of development in alternative energy resources is most likely: vigorous, moderate, or restrained?
   g. Which of the three levels of influence of international financial institutes is most likely: vigorous, moderate, or restrained?
3. For instability in the Persian Gulf region (P_1), compute the relative importance of its three subfactors; namely, social strains within countries (S_1), tension between individual states (S_2), and continuing disorder in Iran (S_3).

toward stable and reasonable oil prices. The actions of the Soviet Union could encourage radicalization, whose dangers are greatest for Saudi Arabia and Kuwait.

The Economic-Technological Cluster

W_1: *World Oil Consumption Increase.* In 1979 the United States, Japan, and Europe accounted for about 75 percent of the total world oil consumption. No substantial increase in demand is anticipated for these countries. But in the developing countries, particularly the oil-exporting ones, demand for oil is expected to increase significantly owing to industrialization and development. The oil consumption increase depends greatly on the strategies—whether cooperative or unilateral—of the oil-consuming nations.

W_2: *World Excess Production Capacity.* Today the world's excess production capacity is more than 10 million barrels per day (MBD), two-thirds of which is from the Middle East. At this level of excess capacity, only large oil producers can affect oil prices significantly by fluctuating their production levels. However, when the excess capacity declines substantially, say to 2 or 3 MBD, even small producers can cause a sudden jump in oil prices by cutting back their production (or large producers by cutting back on a small portion of their production).

W_3: *Oil Discovery Rate.* Before 1970, oil discovery rates were much higher than oil production rates. Therefore, the volume of the world's discovered reserves was increasing. But since the early 1970s, oil discovery has declined steadily while production rates have increased continuously. This downward trend for discovery rates is predicted to continue slowly until 1985 and rather sharply thereafter.

W_4: *Political Factors.* These factors have been discussed under the political cluster above.

W_5: *Development of Energy Sources Other than Oil.* A substantial amount of oil could be replaced by synthetic fuels from large coal, oil shale, and tar sand reserves and from biomass resources. But because of the long lead times (about six to ten years), large capital requirements, and environmental constraints, such fuels are not expected to make a significant contribution during the next decade. In the 1990s, however, synfuels will play an important role in the world energy market.

Legend for Figure 11.1:

W_1: World Oil Consumption Increase
W_2: World Excess Production Capacity
W_3: Oil Discovery Rate
W_4: Political Factors
W_5: Development of Energy Sources other than Oil
W_6: Influence of International Financial Institutions

H_i: High $i = 1, 2, 3, 4, 5$
M_i: Medium
L_i: Low
V: Vigorous
M: Moderate
R: Restrained

P_1: Degree of Instability in the Persian Gulf
P_2: Intensity of the Arab-Israeli Conflict
P_3: Increased Soviet Influence in the Middle East
P_4: Great-Power Struggle
P_5: OPEC Behavior (Intensity of Unfavorable Disposition)

S_1: Social Strains within Countries
S_2: Tension between Individual States
S_3: Continuing Disorder in Iran

Baluchistan was, among other things, to provide the Soviet Union with a secure oil and gas supply source in the future by gaining access to the Persian Gulf.

Increasing Soviet influence in the Middle East will enhance its position in the oil market vis-à-vis the West. And, if it is to their advantage, the Soviets would not hesitate to use oil as an economic weapon against the West, particularly the United States. This action will lead to higher oil payments for the Western countries.

P_4: *Great-Power Struggle.* This factor represents all major economic and military powers as they individually and collectively work to enhance their influence in the world and to secure their domestic economic needs. To do this, some have been known to pay higher prices, thus gradually encouraging their adoption by oil producers. Some of these nations are able to absorb higher prices through increased exportation.

P_5: *OPEC Behavior.* OPEC as a cartel managed well for its members in the 1970s. Increased radicalization in member nations would force prices upward. Moderate members have had a damping effect on price increase, but in the long run they will tend to be outnumbered and may gradually lose their influence. In the next decade, OPEC's behavior is likely to be increasingly unfavorable

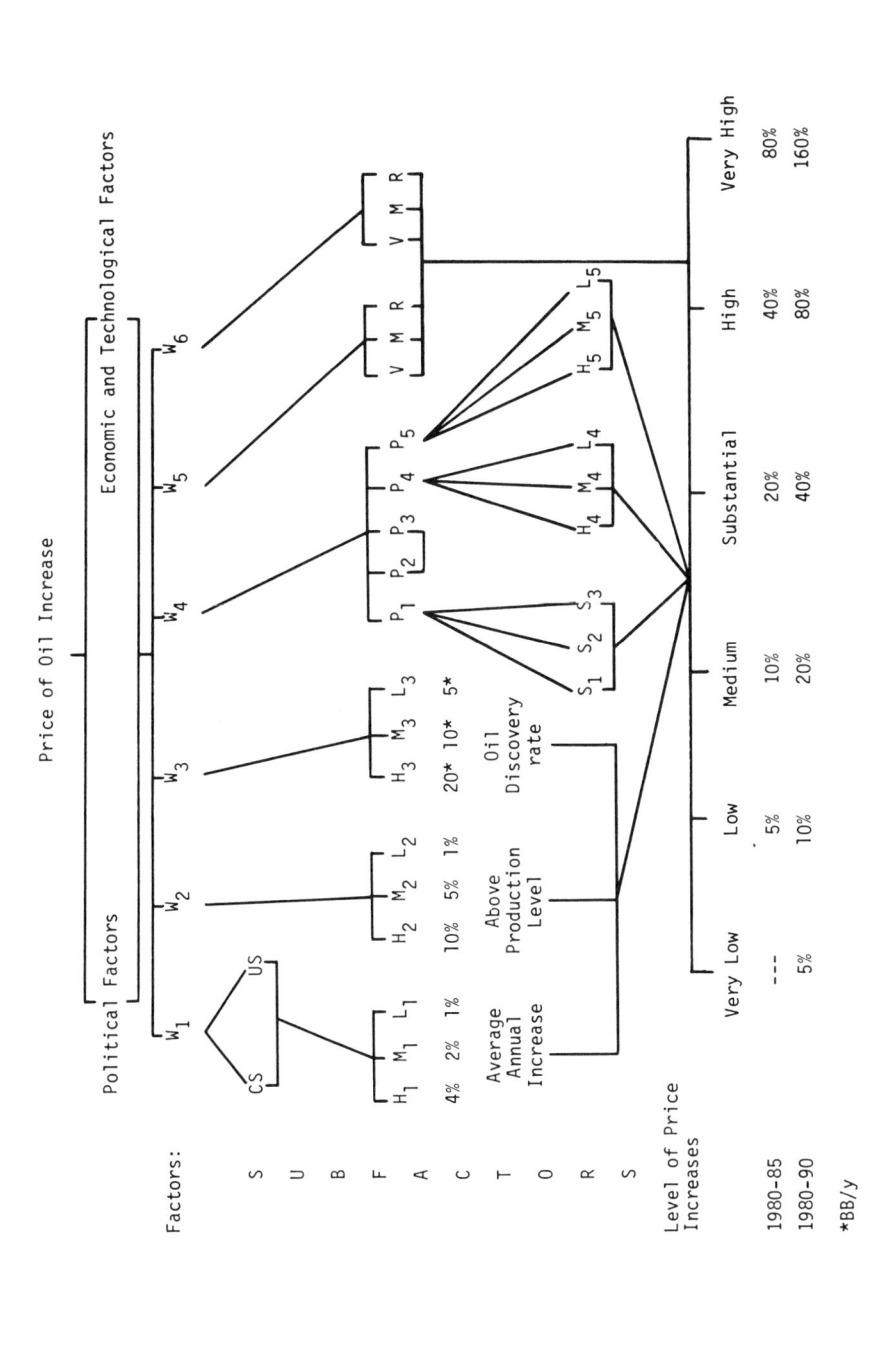

Figure 11.1. Hierarchy of Factors Affecting Future Oil Prices

FACTORS AFFECTING FUTURE WORLD OIL PRICES

The Political Cluster

Political factors play an extremely important role in the world oil market. The Arab oil embargo of 1973, the Iranian revolution, and the consequent disruptions in world oil supplies have demonstrated the significance of political factors in the supply, demand, and price of oil. Great political dangers still threaten the supply and therefore the price of oil. (Incidentally, the political cluster is denoted by the symbol W_4 in the analysis that follows and is called political factors.)

P_1: *Instability in the Persian Gulf Region.* The region that will continue to be of extreme importance in the future supply and price of oil is the Middle East, particularly the Persian Gulf states. The Persian Gulf is surrounded by a number of major oil-exporting countries such as Iran, Saudi Arabia, Iraq, Kuwait, Qatar, Bahrain, and the United Arab Emirates. These countries, excluding Bahrain (which is not a major oil exporter) are members of OPEC and altogether account for over 80 percent of its proved oil reserves, or nearly half of the world's total reserves. Over 30 percent of the world's oil supply comes from this region.

Stability of the Persian Gulf itself depends on several other factors, particularly the social strains due to rapid economic development, industrialization, unstable political systems, and religious movements. Also, tensions between the individual states, as we are now witnessing between Iran and Iraq, could lead to a regional war. Another factor to be considered is the possibility of continued disorder in Iran, which would not only keep Iranian oil output as low as it is today but may also increase instability in the region.

P_2: *Continuation of the Arab-Israeli Conflict.* The Arab oil embargo of 1973 demonstrated the impact of the Arab-Israeli conflict on the flow of oil to the industrialized world. Long delays in resolving the conflict will discourage the major Arab oil producers from cooperating in meeting the demands of the industrialized world. This will put more pressure on the world oil market; consequently, oil prices will rise drastically.

P_3: *Increasing Soviet Influence in the Middle East.* The Soviet bloc is currently a net exporter of oil. But because of expected decline in oil production in the Soviet Union, it is predicted to become a net importer of oil in the near future. Therefore, the Soviet Union will be competing with the Western countries for Middle East oil. Some political observers believe that the purpose of Soviet intervention in Afghanistan and assumed assistance to the rebels in

of oil in 1985 and 1990. For our purposes, we assume that eleven macrofactors will affect the price of oil over the two time horizons. They are grouped into two clusters: political and economic-technological.

The political factors include the following: the degree of instability of the Persian Gulf region, the intensity of the Arab-Israeli conflict, increased Soviet influence in the Middle East, great-power struggle, and OPEC behavior.

The economic-technological factors consist of world oil consumption increase, which depends on the strategies of the consuming countries, whether they are unilateral or collective, in the oil market; world excess production capacity; oil discovery rate; development of energy resources other than oil; and influence of international financial institutions.

All economic factors were further subdivided according to three levels of intensity: high (vigorous), medium (moderate), and low (restrained).

Only three of the five political factors were decomposed. The first, concerning Persian Gulf instability, was divided into social strains within countries, tension between individual states such as Iraq and Iran, and continuing disorder in Iran. The fourth and fifth political factors, concerning great-power struggle and OPEC behavior were divided into high, medium, and low according to the intensity of unfavorable disposition toward cooperation. We have selected and used a range of percentage increase in oil prices for the two periods.

Our object is to estimate the likelihood of the subfactors, which is derived in terms of the relative influence of the major factors for the two periods as we perceived this likelihood in 1980. We calculate the likelihood of percentage increase in terms of the subfactors as well as the major factors and their estimated numerical values by using a straightforward weighting process.

In a problem where a few factors clearly dominate the outcome, it is unnecessary to include every conceivable factor in the structure. The weighting process will eliminate factors that are perceived to have little or no effect. The process is repeated four times over a period of several months to ensure adequate representation, and the judgments are what we consider to be fairly reliable.

The judgments used here are our own, based on our experience and extensive research. However, there is nothing sacred about the specific interpretation we give to the problem. We consider this example to be illustrative of the power of the process.

For a shared understanding of a problem area, one would expect the results to be close to our estimates unless there is a wide controversy over some of the interpretations. This is indeed what we have found by comparing our results with those obtained by others who used elaborate techniques. It is crucial that the important factors be represented in the structure. Figure 11.1 represents the factors and their interconnections as they affect future oil prices.

11 OIL PRICES: *1985 and 1990*

Today oil is the world's major energy resource. It accounts for about 54 percent of the world's total energy consumption. Because of conservation and the development of alternative resources in industrialized countries, the share of oil in the world's total energy consumption is expected to decline. But the total volume of oil consumption will still rise, and it will remain the largest single source of energy for the next two decades.

Despite oil price hikes between 1974 and 1980, the real price of OPEC oil has not increased significantly when adjusted for inflation and depreciation of the dollar. Actually, devaluation of the dollar against the Japanese yen and the West German mark caused the real price of oil to decline in Japan and West Germany. However, because of depletion of the world's proven oil reserves, increasing demand, and possible political unrest in the major oil-producing countries, oil prices are expected to rise during the next decade.

A number of predictions of world oil prices have been made by major oil companies and government agencies during the recent past. Most are based on demand and supply. But in today's world, oil market economics and politics are interwoven, and political decisions increasingly influence the levels of oil production, consumption, and price.

In this chapter, by using the Analytic Hierarchy Process we predict the price

This chapter was written by T.L. Saaty and A. Gholamnezhad; also published in *Energy Systems and Policy* (1981, forthcoming).

V PREDICTION

sentation of the major groups of industries in the economy. On the other hand, it was sufficiently consolidated to keep computational time within reasonable bounds.

COMMENTS

Even if energy rationing does not become a reality, it is always useful to know the price level of energy resources in order to plan better for the future. A straightforward extrapolation of past trends in the prices of oil would not have predicted the price of oil after the 1973 embargo. Only an analysis of the situation involving political and social influences as well as economic ones could have envisioned a similar outcome.

In chapters 11 and 12 we present two approaches to predict (a) oil prices in 1985 and 1990 and (b) outcomes resulting from competitive situations such as the world chess championship. The common feature of the two approaches is that to predict an event we do not have to predict intermediate outcomes. For example, in the oil market, price hikes adopted by OPEC every time they meet could be considered an intermediate step necessary to reach a certain price level. In chess matches we predict the final outcome without due consideration of the outcome of each individual game.

REFERENCES

Mariano, R. 1975. "Allocation Models for Energy Planning" (T. L. Saaty, supervisor). Ph.D. dissertation, University of Pennsylvania, Philadelphia.
U.S. Bureau of Economic Analysis, U.S. Department of Commerce. 1963. *Survey of Current Business.* November.
———. 1972. *Survey of Current Business.* July.

RATIONING ENERGY TO INDUSTRIES

Table 10.1. Continued.

Energy Level R = 55000.00000		Energy Level R = 62000.00000		Energy Level R = 63000.00000		Energy Level R = 64000.00000	
Required Share	Allocated Share	Required Share	Allocated Share	Required Share	Allocated Share	Required Share	Allocated Share
0.06520	0.06520	0.05784	0.05784	0.05692	0.05692	0.05603	0.05603
0.00208	0.00000	0.00185	0.00000	0.00182	0.00000	0.00179	0.00000
0.04988	0.04988	0.04425	0.04425	0.04354	0.04354	0.04286	0.04286
0.01076	0.01076	0.00955	0.00955	0.00940	0.00940	0.00925	0.00925
0.01904	0.00000	0.01689	0.01689	0.01663	0.01663	0.01637	0.01637
0.00650	0.00000	0.00577	0.00000	0.00568	0.00000	0.00559	0.00000
0.07059	0.07059	0.06262	0.06262	0.06162	0.06162	0.06066	0.06066
0.01739	0.01739	0.01543	0.01543	0.01518	0.01518	0.01494	0.01494
0.27371	0.27371	0.24281	0.24281	0.23895	0.23895	0.23522	0.23522
0.05447	0.05447	0.04832	0.04832	0.04755	0.04755	0.04681	0.04681
0.02821	0.00000	0.02502	0.02502	0.02462	0.02462	0.02424	0.02424
0.00326	0.00000	0.00289	0.00000	0.00284	0.00000	0.00280	0.00000
0.05457	0.00000	0.04941	0.01935	0.04764	0.03494	0.04689	0.04689
0.29569	0.29569	0.26231	0.26231	0.25814	0.25814	0.25411	0.25411
0.03855	0.03855	0.03420	0.03420	0.03366	0.03366	0.03313	0.03313
0.05861	0.05861	0.05200	0.05200	0.05117	0.05117	0.05037	0.05037
0.05212	0.05212	0.04623	0.04623	0.04550	0.04550	0.04479	0.04479
0.06390	0.01303	0.05669	0.05669	0.05579	0.05579	0.05492	0.05492
0.00731	0.00000	0.00649	0.00649	0.00639	0.00639	0.00629	0.00629
0.00864	0.00000	0.00767	0.00000	0.00755	0.00000	0.00743	0.00000
0.00864	0.00000	0.00767	0.00755	0.00755	0.00000	0.00743	0.00312

2. A larger percentage of the shortage is distributed to the final demand sector in *all* the cases covered by the analysis.
3. Sectors with larger requirements for an energy resource in short supply are normally allocated a larger percentage of the shortage, whereas those with lower requirements are usually allocated smaller fractions of the shortfall.
4. For all cutback levels, the final demand levels of agriculture, new construction, transportation, communication, wholesale and retail trade, and finance and insurance are set at the maximum by the optimization procedure.

The aggregation of industries was sufficiently detailed to give a good repre-

Table 10.1. Allocation of Electricity to Industries for Short-Term Rationing

Industry	Priority Weight	Dependence Numbers	Required Energy	Energy Level $R = 32500.00000$		Energy Level $R = 48000.00000$	
				Required Share	Allocated Share	Required Share	Allocated Share
Food and kindred	0.10157	14376.47102	3585.16680	0.11034	0.11034	0.07471	0.07471
Tobacco	0.01159	181.39660	114.56599	0.00353	0.00000	0.00239	0.00000
Textile	0.03114	2839.46529	2743.19473	0.08441	0.00000	0.05715	0.00000
Apparel	0.05006	2841.17580	591.89919	0.01821	0.00000	0.01233	0.00000
Lumber and wood	0.02895	1768.74080	1047.41498	0.03223	0.00000	0.02182	0.00000
Furniture	0.02263	541.22518	357.60323	0.01100	0.00000	0.00745	0.00000
Paper	0.03790	3065.05919	3882.25951	0.11945	0.00000	0.08088	0.01948
Printing	0.05940	4893.87393	956.36315	0.02943	0.00000	0.01992	0.01992
Chemicals	0.07583	10293.97888	15053.95061	0.46320	0.38926	0.31362	0.31362
Petroleum and coal	0.06304	5800.38977	2995.88664	0.09218	0.00000	0.06241	0.06241
Rubber-plastics	0.03108	1549.66000	1551.29271	0.04773	0.00000	0.03232	0.00000
Leather	0.01461	272.73290	179.17935	0.00551	0.00000	0.00373	0.00000
Stone-clay-glass	0.03314	1474.06757	3001.27611	0.09235	0.00000	0.06253	0.00000
Primary metals	0.06551	10628.30554	16263.09798	0.50040	0.50040	0.33381	0.33381
Fabricated metals	0.06638	4893.52550	2120.33036	0.06524	0.00000	0.04417	0.04417
Mach. except elec.	0.08579	8713.45036	3223.80323	0.09919	0.00000	0.06716	0.06716
Electric machinery	0.08546	8791.32987	2866.56275	0.08820	0.00000	0.05972	0.05972
Transportation	0.04742	2591.74988	3514.70850	0.10814	0.00000	0.07322	0.00000
Instruments	0.03483	1478.17196	402.29716	0.01238	0.00000	0.00838	0.00000
Miscellaneous	0.01869	453.98767	475.45303	0.01463	0.00000	0.00991	0.00000
Ordnance	0.03500	1300.88456	475.45303	0.01463	0.00000	0.00991	0.00000

This was the first run of the example using highly aggregated industries and dealing with short-term energy shortages. It is clear that society would not tolerate a complete and permanent shutdown of some major industries when energy shortage is prolonged. This work has been carried to the next step of long-range rationing by R.S. Mariano (1975) in a Ph.D. dissertation. Mariano's study uses an eighty-five-sector breakdown of the U.S. economy, with the input-output relationships among the sectors used as constraints. Some of the major findings are as follows:

1. The distribution of the shortage is dependent on the "tightness" of the allowable drop in the level of final demand of each sector, as well as on the degree of assumed drop in electric energy output.

SHORT-TERM RATIONING OF ELECTRICITY TO INDUSTRIES

We now summarize the results for the real-life electricity rationing problem described earlier and indicate the cutback of electricity (partial or complete) for the activities. There are cases in which a complete cutoff of certain activities for a short time period is warranted to prevent the deterioration of the entire system.

Table 10.1 shows how much of the total available energy (in kilowatt-hours) will be allocated to each industry, assuming that the total requirement for energy by all industries exceeds the available supply for a specified time period, say an hour.

The first and second columns of the table list the industries and their priorities, respectively. The dependence numbers in the third column were obtained by multiplying each entry of the input-output matrix by the associated priority weights and summing by rows. The numbers shown in this column were obtained by multiplying the numbers obtained through the above operation. The projection of the total electric energy requirement during the specified time interval is 65,402.76 (in kilowatt-hours). The fourth column gives the breakdown of this total for each industry. In subsequent columns R denotes the total amount of electric energy (in kilowatt-hours) available. Each industry requires a fractional part of R to fulfill its requirements. These portions are listed in the column headed "Required Share." Since there is not enough energy to fulfill the total energy requirement of all industries, an optimization procedure is used to allocate a fractional part of R to each industry. These allotments are given in the column headed "Allocated Share." This procedure has been performed for different levels of R: 32,500; 48,000; 55,000; 62,000; 63,000; 64,000.

Some interesting results can be read from this table. The tobacco, furniture, leather, and miscellaneous (for example, jewelry, musical instruments and parts, pens) industries are never allocated a portion of the available energy at *all* cutback levels. Ordnance is allocated about 50 percent of what it requires only when the available energy R is equal to 64,000 and is allocated none at lower levels. Food and primary metals are given their full requirements at all levels. The chemical industry is given its full requirement at all levels except when the amount available is only half of what is required by all industries; then it is allocated about 85 percent of its requirement.

This research shows that rationing can be approached scientifically for the maximum benefit of society without excessive reliance on traditional economic supply and demand. We can include factors that are needed to make rationing a socially and economically fair process.

Suppose that the energy requirements R_i (measured in appropriate units) of the three users are as follows:

Activity (C_i)	Energy Requirements (R_i)
C_1	4,616
C_2	7,029
C_3	3,297
Total	14,942

Also assume that the total energy available has been cut back to a level of $R = 12,000$ units. We have the following linear programming problem:

Maximize
$$z = 0.39w_1 + 0.07w_2 + 0.08w_3,$$

whose coefficients are the corresponding elements of the vector, subject to:

$$0 \leqslant w_1 \leqslant 0.39$$
$$0 \leqslant w_2 \leqslant 0.59$$
$$0 \leqslant w_3 \leqslant 0.28,$$

in which the quantities on the right are respectively R_i/R, $i = 1, 2, 3$, where

$$\sum_{i=1}^{3} R_i > R \quad \text{and} \quad w_1 + w_2 + w_3 = 1.$$

The optimal allocation is given by:

$$w_1 = 0.39$$
$$w_2 = 0.34$$
$$w_3 = 0.28.$$

Thus only C_2 is not given its full requirement because of the priority assignment and interdependence relationships. In the case of a hospital, the priority assigned to it will far outweigh any contribution it might make to other activities because it deals with life and death situations. Hence its share of the allocation would remain high.

Note that here we have simplified the linear programming problem to make the procedure easier to grasp. There is a more sophisticated way of using the input-output table to generate constraints.

RATIONING ENERGY TO INDUSTRIES

Level 1: Focus — NATIONAL WELFARE

Level 2: Factors — Economic Strength, Environmental Quality, National Security

Level 3: Activities — C_1, C_2, C_3

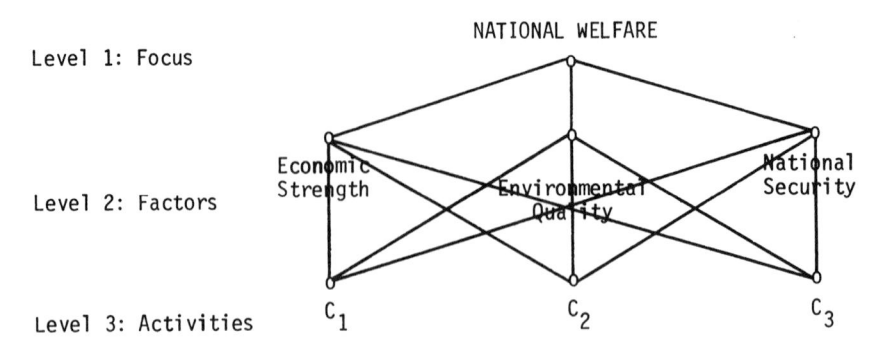

Figure 10.1. Energy Demand Allocation Hierarchy

The corresponding priorities are, respectively, the three columns of the following matrix:

$$\begin{pmatrix} 0.65 & 0.09 & 0.54 \\ 0.23 & 0.17 & 0.30 \\ 0.12 & 0.74 & 0.16 \end{pmatrix}$$

This matrix is multiplied by the vector $P(0)$, yielding the following composite priority vector of activities C_1, C_2, and C_3:

$$\alpha = \begin{pmatrix} \alpha_1 \\ \alpha_2 \\ \alpha_3 \end{pmatrix} = \begin{pmatrix} 0.55 \\ 0.24 \\ 0.21 \end{pmatrix}$$

The input-output or interdependence matrix is:

$$\begin{array}{c} \\ C_1 \\ C_2 \\ C_3 \end{array} \begin{pmatrix} C_1 & C_2 & C_3 \\ 1.09730 & 0.22680 & 0.19020 \\ 0.07990 & 1.06570 & 0.06010 \\ 0.03950 & 0.33210 & 1.20710 \end{pmatrix}$$

These data come from the U.S. Bureau of Economic Analysis, 1963, 1972.

When the coefficient in the (i, j) position of the above matrix is weighted by α_i and α_j and summed over each row, we obtain the following vector of dependence numbers:

$$\beta = \begin{pmatrix} 0.39 \\ 0.07 \\ 0.08 \end{pmatrix}$$

Let us now consider a small hypothetical example that illustrates, with less complexity than the actual example, how one performs a rationing problem.

AN EXAMPLE

The problem in the energy allocation is to find allocation weights for several large users of energy according to their overall contributions to different goals of society. Let us assume the following conditions:

1. There are three large users of energy in the United States: C_1, C_2, and C_3.
2. The goals against which these energy users will be evaluated are: contribution to economic growth, contribution to environmental quality, and contribution to national security.

On the basis of the overall objective of national welfare, shown in the hierarchy in figure 10.1, the matrix of paired comparisons of these three goals on the previously described scale from one to nine is:

	Econ.	Env.	Nat. Sec.
Econ.	1	5	3
Env.	1/5	1	3/5
Nat. Sec.	1/3	5/3	1

The priority (normalized eigenvector) of level 2 with respect to level 1 is given by:

$$P(0) = \begin{pmatrix} 0.65 \\ 0.13 \\ 0.22 \end{pmatrix}$$

The decisionmaker, after a thorough study, has made the following assessment of the relative importance of each user from the standpoint of the economy, environment, and national security. The matrices giving these judgments are, respectively:

Econ.
$$\begin{array}{c} \\ C_1 \\ C_2 \\ C_3 \end{array} \begin{pmatrix} C_1 & C_2 & C_3 \\ 1 & 3 & 5 \\ 1/3 & 1 & 2 \\ 1/5 & 1/2 & 1 \end{pmatrix}$$

Env.
$$\begin{pmatrix} C_1 & C_2 & C_3 \\ 1 & 1/2 & 1/7 \\ 2 & 1 & 1/5 \\ 7 & 5 & 1 \end{pmatrix}$$

Nat. Sec.
$$\begin{pmatrix} C_1 & C_2 & C_3 \\ 1 & 2 & 3 \\ 1/2 & 1 & 2 \\ 1/3 & 1/2 & 1 \end{pmatrix}$$

one business is more important to the nation than another. There is no argument, for example, that the food industries take precedence over the tobacco industry. The situation may not be as clear-cut with others.

Although the application made for this purpose is intended to show that this type of analysis leads to reasonable and sensible results, it is too lengthy to present in full detail. Thus after we identify the classes of industries and the criteria by which they are evaluated, a small example is briefly worked out. Then we simply present the allocation of electricity given to the various industries for different cutback levels and interpret the results.

CLASSIFICATION OF ENERGY USERS BY INDUSTRY

In this application, we confine our analysis to manufacturing industries and classify them according to the standard industrial classification system. The major groups in this system are (1) food and kindred products, (2) tobacco manufacturers, (3) textile mill products, (4) apparel and related products, (5) lumber and wood products, (6) furniture and fixtures, (7) paper and allied products, (8) printing and publishing, (9) chemicals and allied products, (10) petroleum and coal products, (11) rubber and plastics products, (12) leather and leather products, (13) stone, clay, and glass products, (14) primary metal industries, (15) fabricated metal products, (16) machinery, except electric, (17) electric machinery, (18) transportation equipment, (19) instruments and related products, (20) miscellaneous manufacturing, and (21) ordnance and accessories.

The optimal weights generated below for these classes of industries are applicable to peak-power demand considerations where shortage of power may occur in a short time duration. In this case the optimal scheduling of power and its allocation will be determined as a function of time.

CRITERIA USED TO EVALUATE ENERGY USERS

To evaluate energy users, we used the following objectives, which fall into two classes: class 1, characterized by two measurable indicators: contribution to economic growth (measured in dollars) and impact on the environment (measured in tons of pollutants); and class 2, characterized by three qualitative indicators: contribution to national security, contribution to health, and contribution to education. The measures for these indicators were derived by using judgments and the eigenvalue procedure. The results of the two classes were composed hierarchically to obtain an overall priority for each industrial group.

50 percent of the crude oil used in the United States is imported, and it would take time to readjust this dependence on outside suppliers of energy.

2. Discovery or development of new forms of energy such as coal gasification, geothermal energy, nuclear fission, nuclear fusion, and solar energy. Again, these forms are now in short supply and cannot be counted on to satisfy the increasing demand.

3. Rationing energy. Although rationing is not an attractive alternative, we have seen that in cases of severe weather in the Midwest, energy has to be diverted from schools and industries to accommodate homeowner needs. The pressure to ration energy may increase if supplies dry up or continuity in importing oil is seriously threatened. It is difficult to see how this could be allowed to happen—but it can happen, and over the next twenty years the alternative of rationing will have to be given serious consideration. Rationing will also have to be considered when the market mechanism fails to adjust quickly to prevent serious deterioration in the economy.

The problem is to allocate scarce energy resources according to priority; that is, on the basis of the combined contribution of an activity to the economic, social, political, technological, and environmental welfare of the society. The objective function will include these priorities, using as constraints an input-output type of interdependence among the activities. This will ensure equitable cutbacks in resource allocation when rationing becomes inevitable.

RATIONING ENERGY THROUGH PRIORITIZATION

The problem in the energy allocation is to find allocation weights for several large users of energy according to their overall contribution to different goals of society. Let us admit at the start that we do not foresee a major energy crisis in the short run that would necessitate drastic rationing measures. However, we believe that it is beneficial for us to see how activities that have mushroomed out of proportion to basic needs would fare through rationing.

It is widely known that energy consumption rises as the gross national product rises. However, the gross national product is a measure of economic activity, not of social progress. If energy rationing becomes necessary, consumers must be evaluated on the basis of the importance of their activities to general social and national welfare as well as to direct economic growth. It is with this goal in mind that we undertook this preliminary study of rationing. Its findings are interesting inasmuch as they serve as indicators for industries that are not critical. The study required appreciation of the contributions of these industries through a diversity of factors considered important. It is no heresy to say that

rationing, priority plays an important role, particularly in activities in which economic adjustment to the production of only certain types of goods requires a long time to stabilize and hence immediate, carefully weighed action is needed.

What is a rational basis for allocation to meet the demand for energy, given a limited supply? This is the problem we wish to address here.

It is clear that if the shortage is small, a correspondingly small cutback may be made in delivering electric energy to consumers, generally without adverse effects. Thus a percentage cut at low levels of scarcity should not entail major difficulties.

But suppose that the shortage is sufficiently large and prolonged enough over time that a corresponding amount of cutback would harm the consuming activity. For example, certain industries require a threshold amount of energy, below which they cannot operate. In this case either the industry would have to rearrange and perhaps reduce its production activity if possible, or it might have to shut down. Thus the problem is a matter of assignment of priority and interdependence. Priority considerations are needed to determine the precedence of the activities; and interdependence considerations are needed to ensure that higher-priority activities that receive some inputs from lower-priority activities are not penalized indirectly by the lack of adequate energy available to the lower-priority activities on which they depend. When the time period for rationing is short (such as during severe weather conditions), interdependence is not an effective constraint on the solution, and straight allocation according to priority is sufficient. In this chapter the short-term rationing problem is illustrated.

The general approach is to develop an objective function that reflects allocation in proportion to priorities. Hence its coefficients are priorities of the activities concerned, and its variables are the amounts of electricity (or whatever form of energy) to be allocated to the corresponding activities. For long-term rationing we would maximize this function subject to input-output constraints, indicating interdependence among the activities. For short-term rationing we would simply use the objective function. Let us first look at the problem of how to determine priorities.

In addition to improving efficiency, for the long range we need to consider several alternatives to prevent severe energy shortages. (In chapter 8 policies were identified to provide the best alternative ways of action in response to policies implemented by oil-exporting countries.) The alternatives include the following:

1. Reduction of U.S. consumption to the level of domestic energy production. It is doubtful that Americans can or would cooperate to pursue this alternative of equating consumption with domestic production. For example, over

10 RATIONING ENERGY TO INDUSTRIES: Priorities and Input-Output Dependence

A short time ago it was unthinkable and deemed an academic exercise to speak of rationing. People thought that there could be no crippling energy crisis because our energy czars and planners would presumably take our needs into their projections. Today the situation looks very different. Witness the lack of natural gas in the cold winter of 1976-77, which caused the shutdown of some schools and industries, and the coal strike of 1977-78. Lack of coal caused a shortage of electric power in the Midwest, and electric power companies planned to ask for an end to all outdoor lighting and evening sports events plus a cutback of retail business schedules. The companies were also prepared to slice industrial electric usage to between 50 percent and "maintenance level," forcing the shutdown of many factories.

In any case, we must face the needs of our homes, offices, industries, and massive transportation systems not simply by producing additional supplies of energy but also by rationing energy. Electricity is easier to ration because it is generated, transmitted, and distributed at central locations. It is not unreasonable to expect that cutbacks in energy and the use of other conservation schemes would also entail careful allocation of electricity to users. Some of the rationing decisions will be left to the consumer through pricing; others will be made on a government level and through inducement incentives. In a balanced approach to

This chapter was written by T.L. Saaty and R.S. Mariano; previously published in *Energy Systems and Policy* 3, No. 1 (1979):85-111.

Avnet, H.M. 1967. *Physician Service Patterns and Illness Rates.* New York: Group Health Dental Insurance, Inc.
Bergwall, D.F.; P.N. Reeves; and N.B. Woodside. 1974. *Introduction to Health Planning.* Washington, D.C.: Information Resources Press.
Berki, S.E. 1972. *Hospital Economics.* Lexington, Mass.: Lexington Books.
Berry, F.C., Jr. 1978. "Health Care: The Broken Contract." *Armed Forces Journal International.* February.
Carner, D.C. 1968. *Planning for Hospital Expansion and Remodeling.* Springfield, Ill.: Charles C Thomas.
Daly, S. 1978. "Inside the O.R." *Sunday Bulletin/Discoverer.* February 12.
DHEW. 1970. *Planning for Health Manpower.* Washington, D.C.: GPO.
Gainsborough, H., and J. Gainsborough. 1964. *Principles of Hospital Design.* London: Architectural Press.
Georgeopoulos, B.S. 1975. *Hospital Organization Research: Review and Source Book.* Philadelphia: Saunders.
Griffith, J.R. 1972. *Quantitative Techniques for Hospital Planning and Control.* Lexington, Mass.: Lexington Books.
Hospital of the University of Pennsylvania. 1977. *Vital Signs* 2(2).
Klarman, H.E., ed. 1970. *Empirical Studies in Health Economics.* Baltimore: Johns Hopkins University Press.
Magnuson, W.G., and E.A. Segal. 1974. *How Much for Health?* Washington, D.C.: R.B. Luce.
March, J.G., and H.A. Simon. 1958. *Organizations.* New York: Wiley.
Odynocki, B. 1979. "Planning the National Health Insurance Policy: An Application of the AHP in Health Policy Evaluation and Planning." Ph.D. dissertation, University of Pennsylvania, Philadelphia.
Public Law 79-725. 1946. Hospital Survey and Construction Act.
Public Law 91-296. 1964. Health and Medical Facilities and Construction Act.
Research and Policy Committee. 1973. *Building a National Health Care System.* Washington, D.C.: Committee for Economic Development.
Rose, C. 1978. "Can We Put a Price on Premature Babies?" Associated Press. February.
Sidel, V.W., and R. Sidel. 1977. *A Health State – An International Perspective on the Crisis in U.S. Medical Care.* New York: Pantheon.
Silver, G.A. 1976. *A Spy in the House of Medicine.* Rockville, Md.: Aspen Systems.
Silvers, J.B., and C.K. Prahalad. 1974. *Financial Management of Health Institutions.* New York: Halsted Press.
WHO. 1958. *Constitution, Annex I: The First Ten Years of the World Health Organization.* Geneva, Switzerland.

Table 9.5. Project Area Rankings

	Economic-to-Service Ratio		
	1 : 1	1 : 2	2 : 1
Reimbursement	.35	.36	.36
Quality outcome measures	.17	.14	.12[a]
Budget development process	.12	.12	.12[a]
Conflict in institutional planning	.11	.12	.12[a]
Governance	.11	.12	.12
Interorganization relations	.08	.09	.09
Service utility payoff	.08	.06	.06

[a]Before values were rounded off, the projects were ranked, by several thousandths of a point, in the following order: conflict in institutional planning, quality outcome measures, and budget development process.

The three plans are evaluated in terms of their contribution to what the author calls an "adequate" health care system. Adequacy is defined in terms of medical needs and medical services. Medical needs are expressed as functions of prevention, treatment, and rehabilitation, and medical services are defined as a function of availability, accessibility, quality, and financial efficiency.

Then he compares the three proposals within a forward and backward context to identify possible actor coalitions that would make one of the plans successful. The results of the forward process show that although Kennedy's plan fulfills better the needs of the American health care system, it violates the existing legal and political framework of health insurance and has no chances of passage. A coalition among the American Medical Association, the American Hospital Association, and the Health Insurance Association of America provided a strong ground versus organized labor and the Carter administration to make Senator Long's plan more likely to succeed than the other two. In this case, political influences seem to steer the system more strongly toward the final outcome, since the coalition has come into being because of common economic interests, the same ideology of "free enterprise," and the continuing threat of government regulation.

REFERENCES

American Hospital Association. 1973. *Distribution of Physicians in the U.S.* Chicago.
———. 1974. *Hospital Statistics, 1973.* Chicago.

could be defined in greater detail. Thus the value of rare but very complex medical procedures such as open heart surgery (which typically requires two anesthesiologists, a heart surgeon, three residents in surgery, one scrub nurse, an anesthetist, a circulating nurse, and three pump men [Rose, 1978]) or neonatal intensive care (which may cost more than $150,000 per baby [Silvers, 1974]) could be traded against equally critical but less resource-intensive common procedures such as an appendectomy or a delivery.

If requirements are to be evaluated in greater depth, demand and duration data on approximately 100 surgical procedures and numerous diagnostic and other medical procedures can be found in Gainsborough's *Principles of Hospital Design* (1964). Additionally this resource provides data that may be used to evaluate the underlying service distributions if a queuing approach is to be used as a part of the process for requirements determination.

We note that the applications of the AHP within the context of health care have not been restricted to the determination of requirements. The regional advisory committee of a well-known national health care management center met in two full-day sessions, in June and in August of 1978, to identify problem areas for research. They first structured a hierarchy of actors who would influence the research, but then decided to focus on one important actor embodied in the providers of health care in order to identify his influence. The final ranking of problem areas was as follows:

1. Institutional management and governance;
2. Financial management;
3. Service delivery;
4. Environmental control and regulation;
5. Consumer behavior/health education;
6. Manpower and industry structure.

The focus of the second meeting was on the first three ranked problem areas, within which projects were identified and classified. Seven projects with the highest priorities were then selected. The sensitivities of their priorities where economic and service-related objectives were weighted differently are given in table 9.5. These projects have been the center of study of the regional advisory committee.

A second area in health care to which the AHP has been applied is health policy evaluation and planning (Odynocki, 1979). Here the author evaluates three national health insurance proposals: the Health Care for All Americans plan by Senator Edward M. Kennedy, the National Health plan by former President Carter, and the Catastrophic Health Insurance plan (S.760) by Senator Russell B. Long.

Table 9.4. Resource Optimization and Sensitivity Analyses

Variable	Resource	[1,1]	[.9,1]	[.8,1]	[1,.9]	[1,.8]	[.8,.8]
X_1	Psychiatrists	5	5	5	0	0	0
X_2	Psych. rooms	30	30	30	0	0	0
X_3	Radiologists	11	0	0	11	11	1
X_4	Anesthesiologists	23	21	8	23	1	1
X_5	M.D.s	130	130	130	130	130	130
X_6	Anesthetists	32	32	18	32	1	1
X_7	Chem/bacteriologists	31	31	31	31	31	31
X_8	X-ray technicians	20	20	14	20	20	20
X_9	Patients' rooms	497	497	497	497	458	458
X_{10}	Labor rooms	5	5	4	1	0	0
X_{11}	Delivery rooms	3	3	2	1	0	0
X_{12}	Chem/bac. labs	12	12	12	12	12	12
X_{13}	X-ray labs	5	5	4	5	5	5
X_{14}	Pathologists	7	0	0	7	7	0
X_{15}	Therapists	6	0	0	6	6	3
X_{16}	Electrocardiologists	7	0	0	7	7	7
X_{17}	Therapy rooms	3	0	0	3	3	3
X_{18}	Life-saving equip.	30	30	30	30	30	30
X_{19}	Radiology labs	2	0	0	2	2	1
X_{20}	Elec. cardio labs	2	0	0	2	2	2
X_{21}	Nursery beds	36	36	36	11	0	0
X_{22}	Incubators	5	5	5	0	0	0
X_{23}	Surgeons	13	4	0	17	0	0
X_{24}	Recovery rooms	6	2	0	3	0	0
X_{25}	Operating rooms	3	1	0	3	0	0
X_{26}	Emergency rooms	28	28	28	28	28	28

in the elimination of services that are high-space consumers. Inflicting budget and space cuts simultaneously drives the hospital toward primarily providing emergency and intensive care services and deleting high-cost or space-consuming services like surgery and psychiatric care.

COMMENTS

In determining requirements for an actual hospital, the hierarchy of objectives and services displayed in figure 9.3 might be expanded to consider services at a more detailed level. In this manner the resources required to provide the service

where indirect = 375 $(X_2 + X_9 + X_{21} + X_{22})$. The twenty-six demand constraints (with constants equal to the expected yearly requirement for the resource) are:

$$X_1 \leq 5, X_2 \leq 30, X_3 \leq 11, X_4 \leq 23, X_5 \leq 130, X_6 \leq 32,$$
$$X_7 \leq 32, X_8 \leq 20, X_9 \leq 497, X_{10} \leq 5, X_{11} \leq 3, X_{12} \leq 12,$$
$$X_{13} \leq 5, X_{14} \leq 7, X_{15} \leq 6, X_{16} \leq 7, X_{17} \leq 3, X_{18} \leq 30,$$
$$X_{19} \leq 2, X_{20} \leq 2, X_{21} \leq 36, X_{22} \leq 5, X_{23} \leq 17, X_{24} \leq 6,$$
$$X_{25} \leq 3, X_{26} \leq 28.$$

Finally, the interdependencies (with related coefficients) include the following:

$$6X_1 \geq X_2, X_3 \leq 6X_{19}, X_3 \geq 3X_{19}, 3X_1 \leq X_2,$$
$$X_7 \leq 2.6 X_{12}, X_7 \geq 1.3 X_{12}, X_8 \leq 4 X_{13}, X_8 \geq 2 X_{13},$$
$$X_{10} \leq 2 X_{11}, X_{14} \leq 2.6 X_{12}, X_{15} \geq X_{17}, X_{15} \leq 2 X_{17},$$
$$X_{21} \leq 9 X_{10}, X_{22} \leq 3 X_{10}, X_{20} \leq .6 X_{16},$$
$$X_4 \geq 4.2 X_{11} + X_{23},$$
$$X_4 \geq 8.4 X_{11} + 2 X_{23},$$
$$X_6 \leq 4.2 X_{11} + .75 X_{23} + .02 X_{18},$$
$$X_6 \leq 8.4 X_{11} + 1.5 X_{23} + .04 X_{18},$$
$$2 X_{19} \leq X_{16} \leq 3.5 X_{20},$$
$$X_{25} \leq X_{24} \leq 2 X_{25},$$
$$4 X_{25} \leq X_{23} \leq 6 X_{25}.$$

RESOURCE OPTIMIZATION AND SENSITIVITY ANALYSIS

After the complete integer programming model is formulated, the final step of the analysis is to solve the program that determines the requirements. This is accomplished here by using the branch-and-bound method; the first column of table 9.4 provides the results of the optimization. The sensitivity of the optimum resource allocation to the following constraint changes is shown in columns 2 through 6:

1. Change budget to 90 percent of original level.
2. Change budget to 80 percent of original level.
3. Restore budget to original level and reduce available space to 90 percent of original level.
4. Reduce space to 80 percent of original level.
5. Reduce budget and space to 80 percent of their original levels.

As can be seen from the data of table 9.4, increased budgetary constraints reduce the most sophisticated and costly services, while space reductions result

of hospital organization and function as a system is critical to the development of accurate and meaningful interdependencies. The following discussion displays the complete model, both objective function and constraint matrix, developed for this example. It should be noted that a large amount of intermediate data analysis and manipulation have been excluded, as they add little to the insight derived from the application.

The integer programming model (with coefficients equal to the resource priorities) for hospital requirements determination is as follows:

Maximize $.0018 X_1 + .0282 X_2 + .0034 X_3 + .0056 X_4 + .0661 X_5$
$+ .0082 X_6 + .0123 X_7 + .0256 X_8 + .5540 X_9 + .0058 X_{10}$
$+ .0029 X_{11} + .0433 X_{12} + .0266 X_{13} + .0007 X_{14} + .0007 X_{15}$
$+ .0011 X_{16} + .0017 X_{17} + .1520 X_{18} + .0005 X_{19} + .0012 X_{20}$
$+ .0444 X_{21} + .0060 X_{22} + .0027 X_{23} + .0046 X_{24} + .0023 X_{25}$
$+ .0102 X_{26},$

subject to the following constraints:

1 budget constraint $\equiv \Sigma_{i=1}^{26} \pi_i x_i \leqslant$ budget - indirect, where π_i are resource costs;

26 demand constraints $\equiv x_i \leqslant \Sigma_{j=1}^{7} \rho_j v_j$, where $v_i = 1/$resource availability;

26 interdependencies $\equiv$ various descriptions;

1 space constraint $\equiv \Sigma_{i=1}^{26} S_i x_i \leqslant$ space - indirect, where S_i are resource space requirements.

The budget constraint (with coefficients equal to the resource cost per unit) is:

$\quad 40027 X_1 + \quad 1050 X_2 + \quad 49415 X_3 + \quad 51347 X_4 + \quad 49415 X_5$
$+ 15000 X_6 + \quad 11572 X_7 + \quad 11572 X_8 + \quad\quad 930 X_9 + \quad\quad 1700 X_{10}$
$+ \quad 1700 X_{11} + 100000 X_{12} + 367000 X_{13} + \quad 49415 X_{14} + \quad 49415 X_{15}$
$+ 11572 X_{16} + \quad 10000 X_{17} + 100000 X_{18} + 370000 X_{19} + 300000 X_{20}$
$+ \quad\quad 100 X_{21} + \quad\quad 100 X_{22} + \quad 58774 X_{23} + \quad\quad 1700 X_{24} + \quad\quad 2500 X_{25}$
$+ \quad\quad\quad 80 X_{26} \leqslant$ budget - indirect,

where indirect = $(.34)(10000)(X_1 + X_3 + X_4 + X_5 + X_7 + X_8 + X_{14} + X_{15} + X_{16} + X_{23}) + (11250)(X_2 + X_9 + X_{21} + X_{22})$.

The space constraint (with coefficients equal to per unit resource space requirement in square feet) is:

$\quad\quad 0 X_1 + 516 X_2 + \quad 0 X_3 + \quad\quad 0 X_4 + \quad\quad 0 X_5 + 0 X_6$
$+ \quad 0 X_7 + \quad\quad 0 X_8 + 476 X_9 + 506 X_{10} + 506 X_{11} +$
$+ \quad 0 X_{12} + \quad\quad 0 X_{13} + \quad 0 X_{14} + \quad\quad 0 X_{15} + \quad\quad 0 X_{16} + 0 X_{17}$
$+ \quad 0 X_{18} + \quad\quad 0 X_{19} + \quad 0 X_{20} + 236 X_{21} + 236 X_{22} + 0 X_{23}$
$+ 340 X_{24} + \quad\quad 0 X_{25} + \quad 0 X_{26} \leqslant$ space - indirect,

Table 9.3. Resource Priorities ($P_{i,j}$)

x_i	Resource	Surgery	Med. Care	Ped. Care	Mat. Care	Emer. Care	Int. Care	Psych. Care	Composite Priority
1	Psychiatrist							.06	.0018
2	Psych. rooms							.94	.0282
3	Radiologists	.0058	.0035		.0014	.0045	.0010		.0034
4	Anesthesiologists	.0290			.0411		.0042		.0056
5	M.D.s		.0500	.0600	.0411	.0900	.0336		.0661
6	Anesthetists	.0290		.0500	.0411		.0042		.0082
7	Chem/bacteriologists	.0290	.0060		.0041	.0135	.0163		.0123
8	X-ray technicians	.0043	.0030		.0014	.0405	.0004		.0256
9	Patient rooms	.7300	.9000		.7140	.4800	.5750		.5540
10	Labor rooms				.0822				.0058
11	Delivery rooms				.0411				.0029
12	Chem/bac. lab	.0290	.0125	.0500	.0411	.0585	.0168		.0433
13	X-ray lab	.0043	.0085		.0014	.0450	.0004		.0266
14	Pathologist	.0029	.0026				.0018		.0007
15	Therapists		.0012				.0084		.0007
16	Electrocardiologists	.0029	.0025				.0084		.0011
17	Therapy rooms	.0058	.0050				.0084		.0017
18	Life-saving equip.					.2400	.3160		.1520
19	Radiology lab	.0008	.0025				.0006		.0005
20	Elec. cardio lab	.0029	.0025				.0084		.0012
21	Nursing			.7400					.0444
22	Incubator			.1000					.0060
23	Surgeons	.0340							.0027
24	Recovery rooms	.058							.0046
25	Operating rooms	.029							.0023
26	Emergency rooms					.0135			.0102
	Basic Service Priority	.08	.15	.06	.07	.55	.06	.03	

Table 9.2. Hospital Utilization Data

	Service Category														
	Surgery		Med. Care		Ped. Care		Mat. Care		Emer. Care		Int. Care		Psych. Care	
Resource	λ	μ	λ	μ	λ	μ	λ	μ	λ	μ	λ	μ	λ	μ
Psychiatrist													500	3/4
Psych. rooms													500	21.5
Radiologists	2,520	1/4	7,800	1/12			313	1/12	1,006	1/12	240	1/12		
Anesthesiologists	4,235	1/4					3,130	1/4			350	1/4		
M.D.s			1,300	1/2	3,130	1/3	3,130	1/4	40,232	1/24	1,400	1/2		
Anesthetists	4,235	1/4					3,130	1/4			350	1/4		
Chem/bacteriologists	4,235	1/4	3,250	1/4	3,130	1/4	313	1/4	1,005	1/4				
X-ray technicians	2,118	1/12	6,500	1/12			313	1/12	10,058	1/12	100	1/12		
Patient rooms	4,235	6.5	13,000	9.4			3,130	4.5	1,006	9.4	1,400	9.4		
Labor rooms							3,130	1/2						
Delivery rooms							3,130	1/4						
Chem/bac. lab	4,235	1/4	3,250	1/4	3,130	1/4	3,130	1/4	4,023	1/4	1,400	1/4		
X-ray lab	2,118	1/12	6,500	1/12			313	1/12	10,053	1/12	100	1/12		
Pathologists	423	1/4	1,300	1/4							375	1/4		
Therapists			1,300	1/8							700	1/4		
Electrocardiologists	424	1/4	1,300	1/4										
Therapy rooms	423	1/2	1,300	1/2							700	1/4		
Life-saving equip.									503	9.0	1,900	4.7		
Radiology lab	423	1/12	1,300	1/4							140	1/12		
Elec. cardio lab	423	1/4	1,300	1/4							700	1/4		
Nursery					2,874	4.5								
Incubator					156	11.5								
Surgeons	4,235	1/3												
Recovery rooms	4,235	1/2												
Operating rooms	4,235	1/2												
Emergency rooms									40,232	1/4				

Note: λ = arrivals per year, μ = service duration in days.

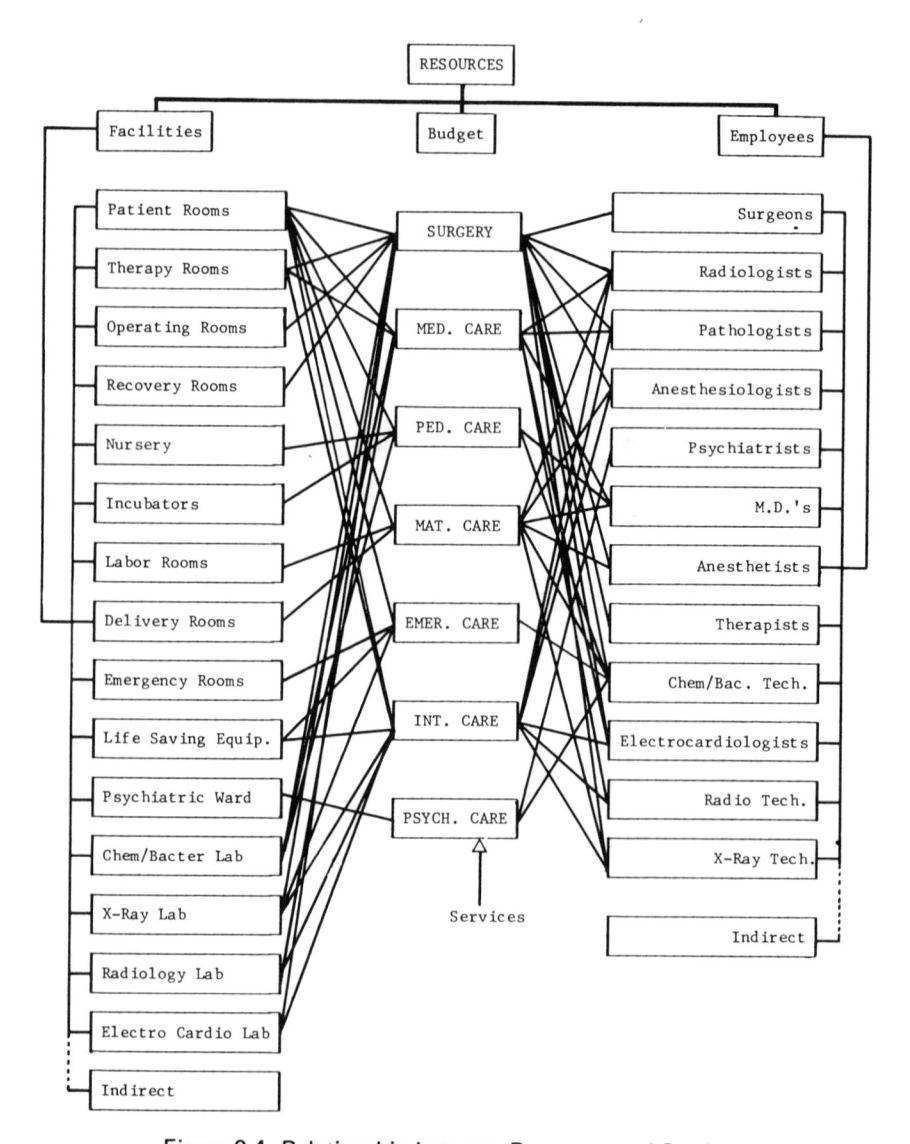

Figure 9.4. Relationship between Resources and Services

relevant services. Figure 9.4 displays the relationship of the various resources to the objectives (services).

Then we derive the priorities of each resource. A utilization analysis has been performed to identify the demand rate (λ) and service rate (μ) with respect to the seven service categories identified in figure 9.4. The demand data in terms of arrivals per year and the service rate data in terms of days of service required per arrival are displayed in table 9.2. From these data, resource utilizations have been calculated by using the following relationship:

$$\text{Utilization } (\rho) = \frac{\text{arrivals per year } (\lambda)}{\text{services per day } (\mu)} \cdot \frac{1}{365}.$$

$\rho_{i,j}$ = rate of utilization of the ith resource by the jth service.

Once $\rho_{i,j}$ have been calculated, the priorities ($P_{i,j}$) of the resources are obtained as follows:

$$P_{i,j} = \frac{\rho_{i,j}}{\sum\limits_{i} \rho_{i,j}} \quad \text{for } j = 1, 2, \ldots, 7.$$

The various $P_{i,j}$ values are displayed in table 9.3.

Finally, the objective function constants c_i (composite priorities) are determined through the following relationship:

$$c_i = \sum_{j} \pi_j P_{i,j} \quad \text{for } i = 1, 2, \ldots, 26.$$

The various composite priorities for each of the twenty-six variables with a direct influence on hospital service are also displayed in table 9.3.

RESOURCE CONSTRAINT MATRIX DEVELOPMENT

Four kinds of constraints are considered in the determination of hospital requirements:

Budget constraints;
Demand constraints;
Interdependencies;
Space limitations.

A great deal of preparatory data analysis is required for the development of demand, budgetary, and space constraints. Additionally a thorough understanding

Table 9.1. Summary of Hospital Service Data and Priorities

Service	Demand (per Year)	Demand Priority	Service Duration (Days)	Patient Days	Patient Days Priority	Unavailability Priority	Criticality Priority	Composite Priority (π_j)
Medical	13,000 [1]	.18	9.4 [1]	122,200	.55	.05	.04	.15
Surgery	4,235 [2, 4]	.06	6.9 [4]	29,211	.14	.23	.09	.08
Pediatrics	3,130 [1]	.04	4.0 [4, 5]	12,520	.06	.10	.14	.06
Maternity	3,130 [1]	.04	4.4 [4]	13,772	.07	.10	.23	.07
Emergency	44,996 [1, 4]	.65	.25 [a]	11,249	.05	.14	.23	.55
Intensive care	1,340 [1, 2]	.02	12.0 [4]	16,080	.08	.24	.23	.06
Psychiatric	500 [5]	.01	21.5 [3]	10,750	.05	.14	.05	.03

[a] Added on a per bed basis.

[1] Research and Policy Committee, 1973.
[2] March and Simon, 1958.
[3] American Hospital Association, 1974.
[4] Gainsborough, 1964.
[5] Daly, 1978.

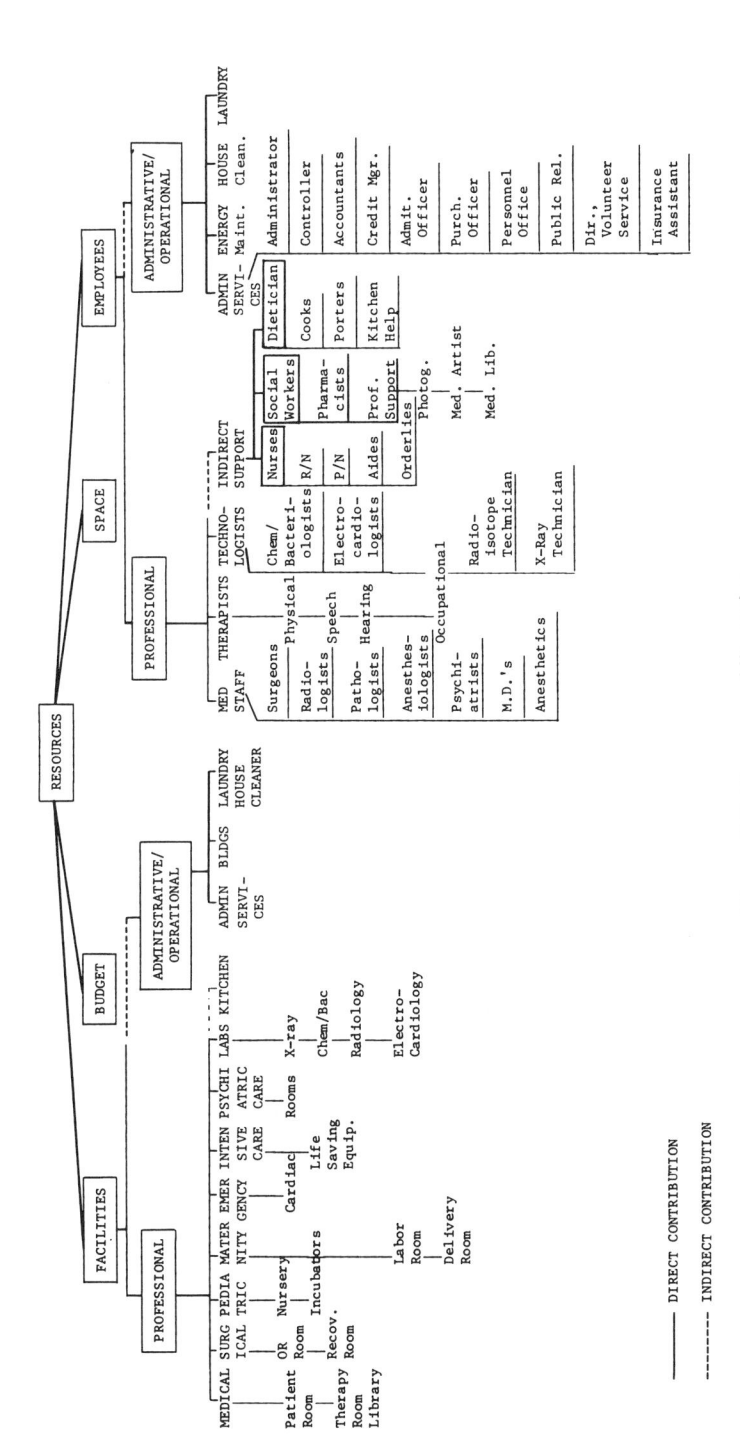

Figure 9.3. Resources Hierarchy

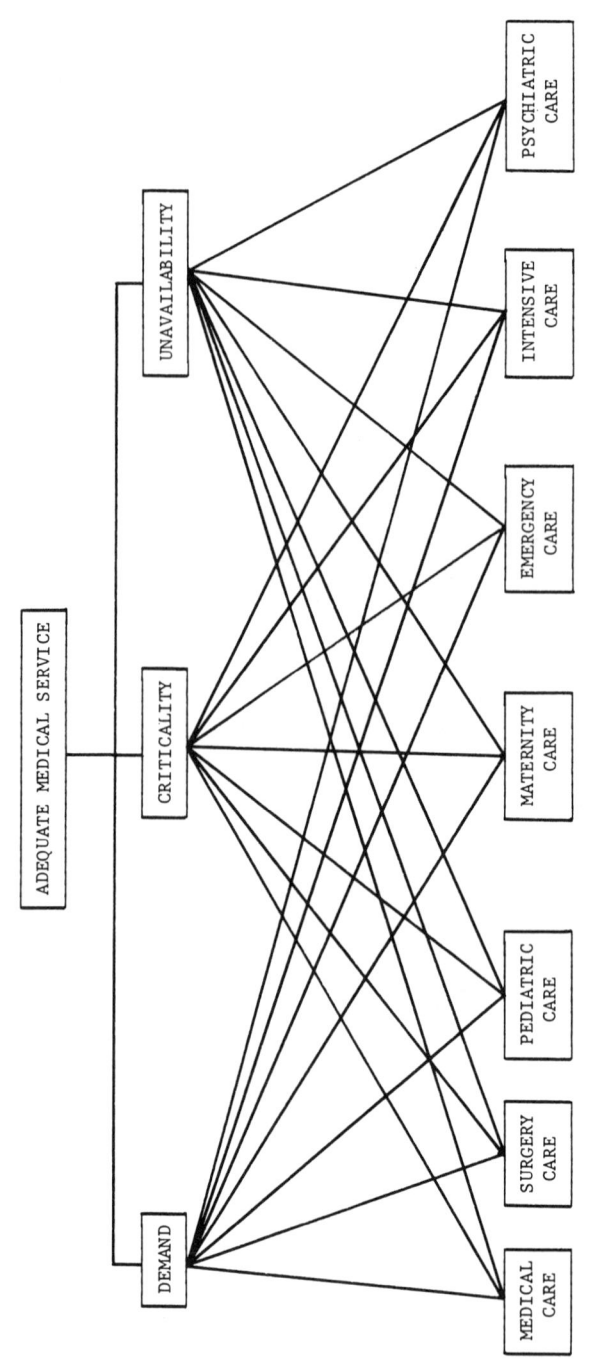

Figure 9.2. Objectives Hierarchy

Berki (1972) and Griffith (1972) have considered the possibility of using an objective function. The first author attempts to optimize the goals of the hospital decisionmakers rather than those of the community, whereas the second attempts to maximize profit.

The model for determining optimum hospital requirements proceeds in three steps. First, we construct the hierarchy of objectives by which we obtain the priorities of the subobjectives. Next, we construct the resource hierarchy, which we combine with the hierarchy of objectives to obtain the resource priorities. These priorities are used as coefficients in the objective function of the optimization problem. Finally, we determine the constraints and then solve the optimization problem. Figures 9.2 and 9.3 show the objectives and resources hierarchies, respectively.

Many different types of hospitals and forms of service are available. In determining requirements for a hospital, the first step is to identify community needs and the role of the hospital in serving these needs. Toward this end, the board of directors must decide on the scope of services the hospital will provide (American Hospital Association, 1974). In the analysis we consider the mental and physical health care aspects of a long-term, voluntary hospital. However, the application of the approach to any type of hospital would require minimal modification of the hierarchy and the basic decision-making parameters.

More than twenty medical specialties are currently in existence. In 1900, three of five health professionals were doctors. By 1960 only one of five health professionals was a doctor, and seven of every ten doctors were specialists. There are now over 200 health occupations (Klarman, 1970). In this analysis we consider only those specialties felt to be of major or unique value to a hospital and implicitly cover all others under the heading MDs. Again, explicit treatment of more specialties would present no conceptual problem; but demonstrating the methodology would make our analysis unnecessarily detailed. Furthermore, the majority of hospital types and medical specialties are covered by the categories explicitly treated in this example (American Hospital Association, 1973; Avnet, 1967). As such, the results of this analysis should be applicable for determining the majority of hospital requirements.

Proceeding toward the development of an objective function, table 9.1 summarizes the results of pairwise comparisons for elements of the first and second levels of the objectives hierarchy, along with other quantitative data used to derive the composite priorities (π_j) of the various kinds of medical service.

Now in order to derive the constants of the objective function, it is necessary to combine the various prioritized objectives (see table 9.1) with the various direct resources under evaluation (see figure 9.3). By doing this, we compute the composite priorities of each of the resources when considered across all

OPTIMUM DETERMINATION OF HOSPITAL REQUIREMENTS 167

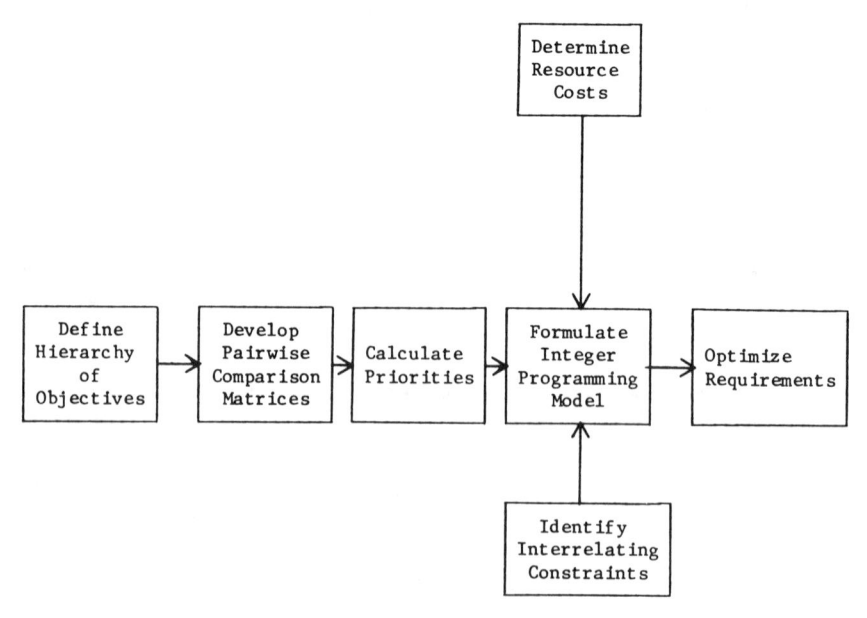

```
                                    ┌───────────┐
                                    │ Determine │
                                    │ Resource  │
                                    │  Costs    │
                                    └─────┬─────┘
                                          │
                                          ▼
┌─────────┐   ┌──────────┐   ┌─────────┐ ┌──────────┐   ┌──────────┐
│ Define  │   │ Develop  │   │         │ │Formulate │   │          │
│Hierarchy│──▶│ Pairwise │──▶│Calculate│▶│ Integer  │──▶│ Optimize │
│   of    │   │Comparison│   │Priorities│ │Programming│  │Requirements│
│Objectives│  │ Matrices │   │         │ │  Model   │   │          │
└─────────┘   └──────────┘   └─────────┘ └─────┬────┘   └──────────┘
                                               ▲
                                               │
                                        ┌──────┴──────┐
                                        │  Identify   │
                                        │Interrelating│
                                        │ Constraints │
                                        └─────────────┘
```

Figure 9.1. Process for Requirements Determination

Although methods of determining quality of hospital care have been suggested, none have established measures of quality in statistically meaningful samples (Klarman, 1970). We have elected to evaluate all medical services considered in our analysis in light of the demand for that medical service, the critical importance of receiving it when it is needed, and its unavailability from other sources.

Regardless of the measures used in the literature to determine health status, an underlying consideration pervading all decisions concerning the determination of health requirements is whether these requirements should be planned on the basis of demand or on the basis of need. Demand is consumer generated according to people's ability to afford the service. Need is that level of health care deemed essential according to professional consensus (Bergwall, 1974).

Three frequently used methods of determining requirements for health care are morbidity (illness rates), mortality (death rates), and utilization (hospital occupancy rates) analyses. The first two methods are based on need, and the third on demand (Bergwall, 1974). We have used the demand type of data within a hierarchical framework to determine the coefficients (reflecting community priorities) of the objective function and also the resource constraint equations.

mining requirements to meet community demand. We need a way to make tradeoffs among the various requirements by taking both the costs and the value of treatment into consideration. The intent of this chapter is to describe a process for defining the medical priorities of the community and subsequently determining hospital requirements in an optimum manner consistent with these priorities.

MODEL FOR HOSPITAL REQUIREMENTS DETERMINATION

Like any other complex system, a hospital must function within the bounds of numerous internal and environmental constraints. It must allocate its resources within these constraints in the most efficient manner consistent with its own (or the community's) objectives and priorities. It is this perception of the hospital as a purposeful system with its own basic objectives, subject to internal and external constraints, that gives rise to the formulation of the optimization procedure carried out in this chapter. It has the following form:

$$\text{Maximize } z = \sum_{j=1}^{M} c_j x_j \qquad x_j = 0, 1, 2, \ldots,$$

$$\text{subject to } \sum_{j=1}^{M} a_{ij} x_j \leq b_i, \qquad i = 1, \ldots, N.$$

The objective function z represents the social value of a hospital to the community it serves. The c_j's represent the importance of each unit of x_j, where the x_j's represent hospital resources such as doctors, nurses, beds, and X-ray machines. Finally, in the model some of the a_{ij} values represent the costs of the resources, while other constraints represent interrelationships among resources that must be considered, such as not adding doctors without adding hospital beds and not adding X-ray machines without adding X-ray technicians. The approach is outlined in figure 9.1.

HOSPITAL REQUIREMENTS PRIORITY DETERMINATION

For the purpose of this study, the primary objective of a hospital is the maintenance of community health through the provision of adequate medical service. Health is defined as a state of complete physical, mental, and social well-being and not merely the absence of disease or illness (Berki, 1972).

9 OPTIMUM DETERMINATION OF HOSPITAL REQUIREMENTS

The United States spends 8.6 percent of its total gross national product (the highest percentage in the world) on health care systems (Sidel and Sidel, 1977); yet it ranks nineteenth in the world in providing care necessary to decrease mortality and morbidity rates. Conversely there are countries such as Great Britain, whose expenditures are closer to 5 percent, that rank higher in the provision of quality medical care (Silver, 1976). Considerable medical expenditure in the United States goes into duplication of equipment and personnel in a single community and even within a single hospital.

Despite the current availability of elaborate equipment for both diagnosis and medical treatment, the quality of the health care system in the United States needs to be improved and the cost of health services reduced. Faulty allocation of hospital resources is an acknowledged cause of inadequacies in the U.S. health service system (Research and Policy Committee, 1973; Magnuson and Segal, 1974; DHEW, 1970). Numerous authors have discussed at great length the reasons for hospital inefficiency (Hospital of the University of Pennsylvania, 1977; Klarman, 1970; Carner, 1968; Georgeopoulos, 1973; Bergwall, 1974), governmental efforts to improve efficiency (Public Law 79-725, 1946; Public Law 91-296, 1964), and the lack of success of previous efforts (Berry, 1978).

One of the major areas to examine for conserving resources is that of deter-

This chapter is the work of J.J. Dougherty, III, and T.L. Saaty ("A Hierarchical Approach to Optimum Determination of Hospital Requirements," University of Pennsylvania, Philadelphia, 1977).

IV RESOURCE ALLOCATION

Table 8.9. Types of Desired Policy

Policy Type	P_i	Priority
Critical	P_{15}	.159
Essential	P_1	.069
	P_2	.079
	P_3	.075
	P_{22}	.073
	P_{24}	.058
	P_{26}	.087
Necessary	P_4	.042
	P_5	.041
	P_6	.038
	P_8	.026
	P_{20}	.030
	P_{23}	.028
	P_{25}	.022
	P_{27}	.023
Significant	Rest of Policies	Between .02 and .0004

a possible alternative would be the implementation of energy-rationing strategies. The problem then becomes one of resource allocation. This is the topic of the next two chapters. First we see how to assess the needs of a system (chapter 9); then resources are allocated accordingly (chapter 10).

REFERENCES

Gholamnezhad, A. 1981. "Critical Choices for OPEC Members and the United States." *Journal of Conflict Resolution* 25 (1):115-43.

Saaty, T.L. 1979. "U.S.-OPEC Energy Policy Application: Eigenvalues, Hierarchies, and the Payoff Matrix." *International Journal of Game Theory* 8:225-34.

P_3: Improving the existing policy constraints such as stiff environmental controls, siting and legal restrictions in order to encourage replacement of oil and natural gas in industry, and electric generation by coal and other abundant resources

P_4: Ensuring a favorable economic climate for energy investments

P_5: Intensifying research and development in the areas of new sources of energy, improving energy efficiency, and nuclear waste

P_6: Raising the domestic price of oil gradually

P_7: Encouraging public transportation by improving services

P_8: Encouraging home insulation through loans, tax credits, and other means

P_9: Mandatory efficiency standards for new automobiles, home appliances, and other energy-using machinery

P_{10}: Urban planning aimed at the development of communities combining residential, work, and recreational activities to a greater extent than at present

P_{11}: Intensifying research and development to improve the efficiency of energy-using equipment and to find alternative ways to reduce wasteful use of energy

P_{12}: Petroleum stockpiling

P_{13}: Preparation of an emergency scheme for petroleum rationing

P_{14}: Emergency oil sharing

All the Actors Concerned

P_{15}: A "just" political settlement of the Arab-Israeli conflict as soon as possible

Saudi Arabia

P_{16}: Expand education, training, and health care

P_{17}: Improve the infrastructure

P_{18}: Develop capital- and energy-intensive industries

P_{19}: Develop a regional common market

P_{20}: Make trilateral agreements with industrialized countries and the LDCs

P_{21}: Encourage immigration of skilled labor and highly educated people

OPEC Members

P_{22}: Invest in food production in LDCs along with industrialized countries in order to have guarantees for the investment

P_{23}: Invest in those industries in the oil-consuming countries for which products are needed by the investor

P_{24}: Invest "downstream" in the consumer countries

P_{25}: Invest in LDCs with rich nonoil minerals in order to have access to the raw materials needed for domestic industries as well as markets for their products

P_{26}: Invest in LDCs through international organizations

P_{27}: Invest in research and development in the field of petroleum in order to explore new and better ways for the utilization of this valuable resource and better ways of utilizing desert lands such as harnessing of solar energy for desalination, irrigation, and electricity generation

nonzero sum two-person game—that is, the Nash equilibrium solution—is "to increase the interdependence between OPEC members and the United States." This appears to be a rational strategy. However, as in all conflicts, the actual outcome may vary significantly from the one predicted. If this were the case,

CRITICAL CHOICES FOR OPEC MEMBERS AND THE U.S. 159

Legend for Figure 8.6:

U.S. Desired Strategies
S_1: Increase production of crude oil
S_2: Produce synthetic oil from coal
S_3: Produce oil from shale
S_4: Increase production of natural gas
S_5: Increase use of coal
S_6: Expand nuclear generating capacity
S_7: Increase hydroelectric generating capacity
S_8: Increase use of solar heating and cooling
S_9: Increase use of geothermal energy
S_{10}: Produce synthetic gas from coal
S_{11}: Increase efficiency in the use of energy
S_{12}: Discourage overconsumption of energy
S_{13}: Improve energy management

Constraints on Accelerating Development of Indigenous Resources
C_1: Availability of resources
C_2: Lead times for exploration, development, and utilization of resources
C_3: Technological bottlenecks
C_4: Environmental and safety regulations
C_5: Economic problems
C_6: Price controls and regulatory constraints other than environmental

Constraints on Energy Conservation
C_7: Economic
C_8: Technological
C_9: Lead times
C_{10}: Social

Constraints on Saudi Arabia's Industrialization
C_{11}: Small size of population
C_{12}: Shortages of skilled laborers and experienced managers
C_{13}: Inadequate infrastructure
C_{14}: Access to markets for its future industrial products
C_{15}: Access to Western technology and know-how
C_{16}: Shortages of known nonoil mineral resources
C_{17}: Social problems

Constraints on OPEC Members' Foreign Investment
C_{18}: Devaluation
C_{19}: Expropriation
C_{20}: Access to markets for products of industries in which OPEC members have investments

DESIRED POLICIES

United States
P_1: Providing incentives for new oil and natural gas discoveries by removing price controls and relaxing other regulatory constraints
P_2: Subsidizing those energy resources that could directly replace oil, such as synthetic oil from coal and oil shale

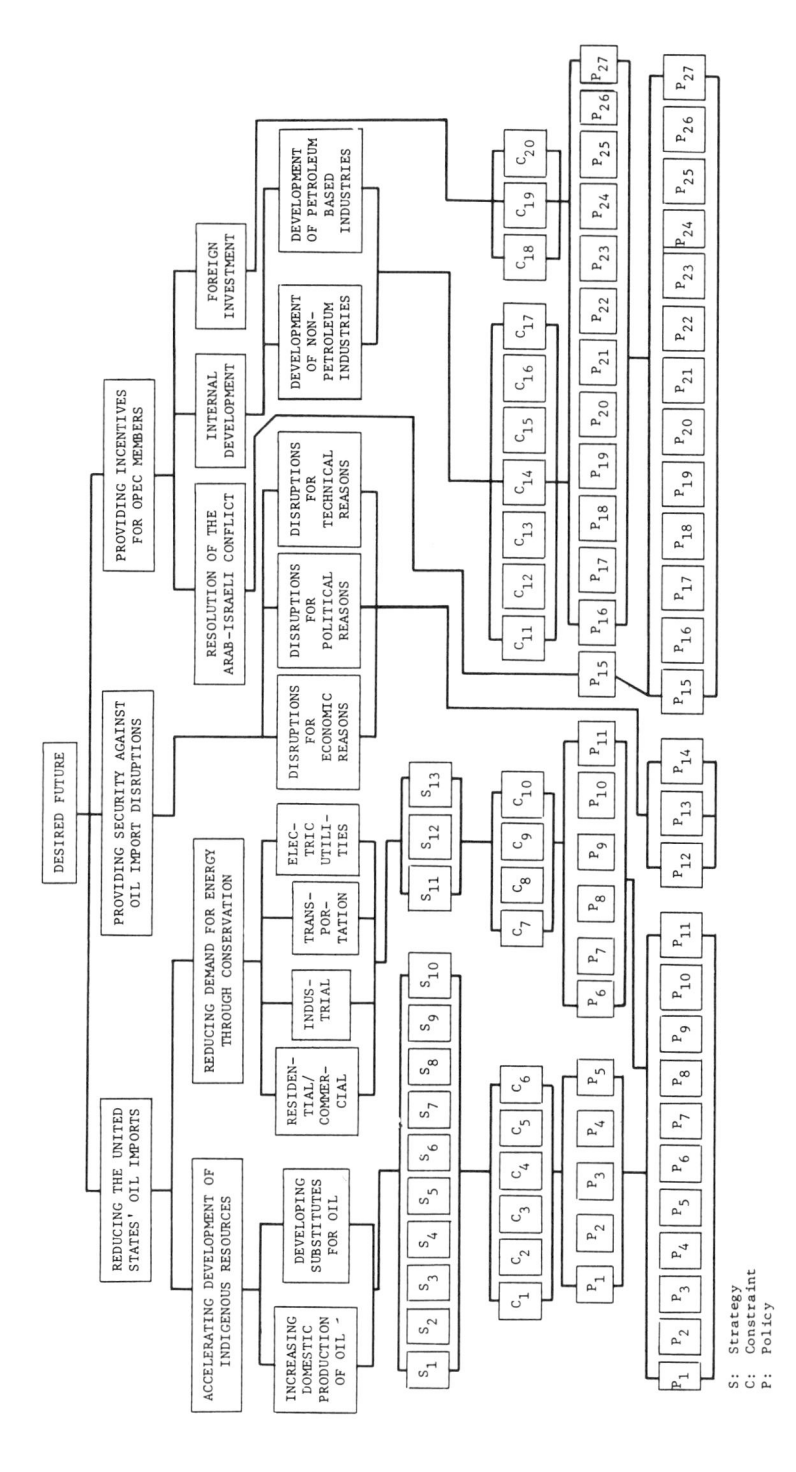

Figure 8.6. Hierarchy for Attaining Adequate Oil Supply at Reasonable Prices

S: Strategy
C: Constraint
P: Policy

Scenario I: Reducing U.S. demand for imported oil;
Scenario II: Enhancing the security of oil supplies;
Scenario III: Providing incentives for OPEC members to expand their oil production.

These scenarios and the desired strategies and policies are shown in figure 8.6. The prioritization of the desired policies is given in table 8.8. The policies are then divided into four categories according to their priority, as shown in table 8.9.

The most important policy, the critical one (see figure 8.6), concerns all actors. It calls for a "just" political settlement of the Arab-Israeli conflict as soon as possible. It is followed by P_{26}, which requires the investment of U.S. capital into LDCs through international organizations.

COMMENTS

This chapter has examined possible alternative strategies of the United States for attaining the desired future defined as: "Having sufficient oil supply in the international market at 'reasonable' and 'stable' prices." The solution of this

Table 8.8. Desired Policies

Policies	Composite Weights	Policies	Composite Weights
P_1	.069	P_{15}	.159
P_2	.079	P_{16}	.009
P_3	.075	P_{17}	.008
P_4	.042	P_{18}	.019
P_5	.041	P_{19}	.015
P_6	.038	P_{20}	.030
P_7	.020	P_{21}	.013
P_8	.026	P_{22}	.073
P_9	.011	P_{23}	.028
P_{10}	.013	P_{24}	.058
P_{11}	.013	P_{25}	.022
P_{12}	.0014	P_{26}	.087
P_{13}	.0011	P_{27}	.023
P_{14}	.0004		

Table 8.6. Constant, Current, and Expected Values of U.S. Strategies

Strategies	Constant Values	Current Values	Expected Values
U_1	.337	.323	.587
U_2	.067	.076	.027
U_3	.103	.096	.053
U_4	.043	.022	.005
U_5	.010	.001	.0001
U_6	.012	.003	.0002
U_7	.064	.078	.027
U_8	.010	.001	.0001
U_9	.166	.038	.034
U_{10}	.114	.347	.269
U_{11}	.043	.015	.004

Table 8.7. Constant, Current, and Expected Values of OPEC Strategies

Strategies	Constant Values	Current Values	Expected Values
O_1	.009	.146	.013
O_2	.085	.122	.100
O_3	.099	.012	.012
O_4	.241	.112	.260
O_5	.015	.036	.005
O_6	.097	.045	.042
O_7	.133	.082	.105
O_8	.035	.058	.019
O_9	.124	.077	.091
O_{10}	.140	.254	.342
O_{11}	.021	.054	.011

these problems, we must find the most feasible solutions and their urgency. To explore ways to implement the desired strategies derived in the previous section, we apply the backward planning process as discussed in chapter 6.

The desired future is defined as "adequate supply of oil at 'reasonable' prices." First, desired scenarios are identified:

has decreased more than six times while the U.S. payoff has increased slightly. The reason is that by cutting back production, OPEC members' oil revenues would be reduced significantly. If countries such as Iran, Iraq, and Indonesia participate in the production cutbacks, their reduced oil revenues would slow their economic development plans and lead to economic, social, and political problems. On the other hand, if countries with large oil reserves, such as Saudi Arabia, Kuwait, and the UAE, whose main source of income is oil, reduce their production drastically, the tightening of oil supplies and higher oil prices would accelerate the development of alternatives, which would lead to a loss of revenues to these countries in the future. In other words, the value of their oil in the ground would depreciate over time. Although the U.S. payoff is greater in the (U_1, O_2) equilibrium point, carrying out such a strategy requires large investments in non-OPEC oil-exporting countries in order to enable them to boost their production and exports to the United States (assuming they are willing to do so). Also, the necessity of increasing the use of nonoil resources such as coal and nuclear would lead to more environmental and social problems contrary to basic objectives of the United States ("better quality of life").

If OPEC does not cut back production, then the equilibrium point would be (U_1, O_4): "U.S. reducing its oil imports" and "OPEC linking the price of crude oil to an index of prices of goods that OPEC members need to import." Note that at (U_1, O_4) equilibrium point, OPEC would still have a lower payoff and the U.S. payoff would be reduced as well.

If the strategies (U_{10}, O_{10}) and (U_1, O_2) are eliminated, there would be no equilibrium solution, and the likelihood of conflicts of interest between OPEC members and the oil consumers, particularly the United States, would be great. This would bring losses to all the actors in the international oil market.

Another way to look at the conflict problem is to assume that each actor will try to maximize the "expected value" for its strategies. "Expected value" is defined here as the value of a strategy that takes into account both its constant and its current values. In doing so, we must sum the payoffs of each actor against each strategy of the opponent and normalize the results. This leads to prioritized strategies for each actor. With payoffs from table 8.5, the expected values of U.S. and OPEC strategies are those shown in tables 8.6 and 8.7.

THE BACKWARD PROCESS

To attain a desired future for oil supply, demand, and prices for the United States and OPEC, we would encounter "real-world" problems of mixed technological, economic, environmental, social, and political origins. To overcome

Table 8.5. U.S.–OPEC Payoff Matrix (U_i, O_j)

	O_1	O_2	O_3	O_4	O_5	O_6	O_7	O_8	O_9	O_{10}	O_{11}
U_1	6.6, 0	12, 1.2	14, 0	10, 1.1	5.6, .6	9.7, 0	13, 0	8.2, 0	19, .35	3.5, 3.5	17, .28
U_2	.22, .14	.25, 2.5	.26, .42	.25, .65	2.8, 0	.59, .76	.41, .25	.17, .4	.37, .38	0, 3.3	.34, 0
U_3	3, 0	2.6, 0	.78, .26	0, 2.9	.35, 0	.49, .46	.34, 1.3	.71, 0	1.2, .5	0, .6	1.2, .5
U_4	0, 0	.14, 1.1	0, .65	0, 9.3	0, 0	0, 2.3	.47, .44	.43, .34	0, .32	0, .27	0, 0
U_5	.02, .51	0, 2.3	0, 0	0, 0	0, 0	0, .39	0, 0	0, 0	0, 0	0, 1.8	0, 0
U_6	.05, .24	0, 1.1	0, 0	0, 0	0, 0	0, .54	0, 0	0, .15	0, 0	0, 7.1	0, 0
U_7	6, .05	.79, 2	1.1, 0	.52, .67	.45, 0	.31, 0	.75, 0	.99, .43	0, 5.7	0, 1.4	0, 0
U_8	.02, .51	0, 1.1	0, 0	0, 0	0, 0	0, .39	0, 0	0, .93	0, 0	0, 0	0, 0
U_9	2.6, 0	0, 0	0, 0	0, 6.3	0, 0	0, 0	0, 1.6	0, 0	0, 0	4.3, 7.9	0, .12
U_{10}	2.3, 0	2.7, 0	4.2, 0	6.9, 2.8	3.5, 0	7.6, 0	4.3, 0	6.1, 0	3.8, 3.2	9.2, 7.9	4.6, .12
U_{11}	0, 0	0, 0	0, 0	.31, 6.2	.31, 0	0, 0	0, 8.5	0, 0	0, 0	0, 0	0, .22

The payoff matrix of the U.S.-OPEC conflict is given in table 8.5. The (U_i, O_j) entry in the matrix represents the payoff to the United States if it adopts policy U_i and OPEC chooses policy O_j. Those payoffs are obtained by weighting each current value (the relative strength of the strategies of one actor against those of the opponent) by the constant value (the relative effectiveness of each strategy in satisfying the actors' objectives) of the corresponding strategy.

The next step is to find the Nash equilibrium solution of the nonzero sum U.S.-OPEC game. The Nash equilibrium solution is a pair of strategies (one for each player) such that no player is able to improve his payoff by changing his strategy choice while the other player holds his strategy fixed. In our case the solution is (U_{10}, O_{10}); that is, to increase the interdependence between the United States and OPEC members.

Increasing interdependence between the oil consumers and oil producers appears to be a rational strategy. By exercising restraint in price hikes and by investing in the economies of the oil-consuming countries, particularly the United States, OPEC members are encouraging this type of outcome. (U_{10}, O_{10}) places the United States in a good position against threats by OPEC members regarding production cutbacks and oil price hikes. It also boosts U.S. exports, thereby providing more jobs and improving the U.S. balance of payments. From the OPEC members' viewpoint, interdependence not only ensures an oil market but also provides OPEC countries with U.S. technology, capital, and management skills needed for development.

Looking at the equilibrium solution (U_{10}, O_{10}), we see that the payoff for the United States is higher than that for OPEC ($U_{10} = 9.2$, $O_{10} = 7.9$). This is because the oil producers, with their large oil revenues, should be able to buy capital, technology, and know-how almost anywhere. The United States, however, does not have a wide choice for its oil imports.

If other consumers were to follow a policy of interdependence, the difference between the two payoffs (of producers and consumers) would be drastically reduced. This is because each oil consumer would be tied to several oil producers, which would reduce the chances of OPEC members switching customers. (A pareto-optimal point has a payoff not worse coordinatewise than that of any other point).

If the "interdependence" strategies of the United States and OPEC (U_{10}, O_{10}) are removed, we would have several pareto-optimal points at (U_{11}, O_4), (U_1, O_4), (U_1, O_2), (U_1, O_1), and (U_1, O_9). Among these points, only (U_1, O_2) is an equilibrium solution, with the United States "reducing its dependence on OPEC by increasing its imports from non-OPEC sources, accelerating the development of indigenous resources, and reducing oil consumption through energy conservation"; and OPEC "cutting back production in order to prevent a glut in the oil market due to reduced demand for its oil and to keep the price of oil from falling." Note that in the (U_1, O_2) equilibrium, OPEC's payoff

U_6 = Impose embargoes of various kinds of goods and services to OPEC.
U_7 = Weaken or break up OPEC by a joint consumer action.
U_8 = Help Israel in its confrontations with the Arabs.
U_9 = Encourage and support a "just" political settlement of the Arab-Israeli conflict.
U_{10} = Increase interdependence with OPEC members.
U_{11} = Increase arms sales to OPEC members.

OPEC members' basic objectives, which are periodically stated by their government officials, are as follows:

1. Profit maximization.
2. Maintenance of sovereignty over natural resources, which may be defined as:
    a. Freedom of action in petroleum production and sales,
    b. Security against political and economic sanctions by the oil-consuming governments,
    c. Security against terrorist attacks,
    d. Access to markets.
3. Cohesion between members; for example, by balancing their political, social, legal, and commercial interests.
4. Raising their people's standard of living.
5. Developing diversified and productive economies.

OPEC members, either individually or collectively, may choose one or a mixture of the following strategies in the future:

O_1 = Impose an oil embargo.
O_2 = Cut back production.
O_3 = Base the price of oil on the nearest alternative energy source.
O_4 = Link crude oil prices to an index of prices of goods that OPEC members need to import.
O_5 = Reduce the price of oil drastically.
O_6 = Use SDRs (Saudi Dinars) or a basket of major currencies as the petroleum price indicator.
O_7 = Increase oil prices gradually.
O_8 = Impose sudden oil price hikes.
O_9 = Search for an alternative to OPEC.
O_{10} = Increase interdependence with the oil importers.
O_{11} = Do nothing.

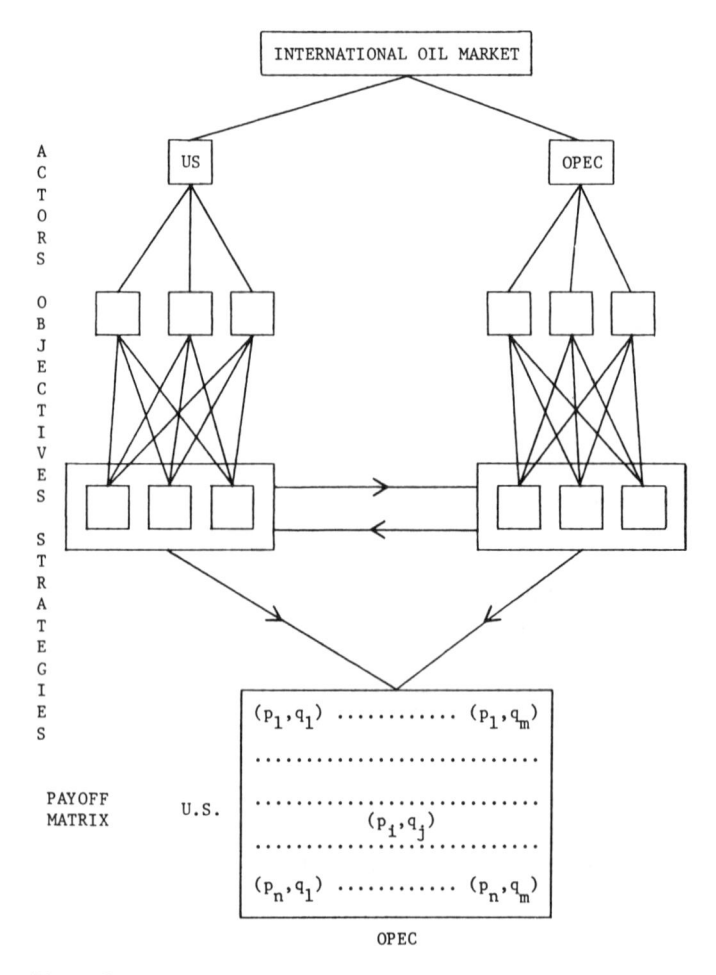

CRITICAL CHOICES FOR OPEC MEMBERS AND THE U.S. 151

Figure 8.5. Hierarchy for Reshaping the Future of the International Oil Market

U_2 = Limit petroleum imports by tariffs and quotas.
U_3 = Prepare an emergency scheme for dealing with sudden oil shortages, such as establishing strategic petroleum reserves, oil rationing programs, and emergency oil sharing.
U_4 = Devalue the dollar against other major currencies.
U_5 = Take military action against OPEC.

is therefore questionable whether OPEC members will continue to meet the increasing demands of consumers in the future.

Among OPEC members, Saudi Arabia, Kuwait, and the UAE will play the most important role in the future world oil market. These countries together hold more than 50 percent of OPEC proven oil reserves, about 45 percent of its current production capacity, and more than 60 percent of its excess capacity. They are therefore highly capable of expanding their oil production in the future. However, because of their small populations, large surplus oil revenues, and low "absorption capacities," they are not willing to expand their oil production beyond their needs. These three countries, particularly Saudi Arabia, will actually determine whether there will be shortages of oil supplies in the future world market.

In conclusion, among the actors of the international oil market, the United States and OPEC members—particularly Saudi Arabia, Kuwait, and the UAE—are the actors who could reshape the future of the world oil market. Hence the methodology is applied to the United States and OPEC. A hierarchical representation is given in figure 8.5.

The basic objectives of the United States that are continually mentioned by U.S. government officials and other responsible authorities are the following:

1. Economic stability and growth, defined as:
    a. Achieving a higher level of employment,
    b. Achieving a higher level of production of goods and services,
    c. Improving the U.S. balance of payments.
2. Maintenance of national security, defined as:
    a. Establishing an adequate supply of oil,
    b. Providing security against import disruptions,
    c. Reducing U.S. dependence on imported oil.
3. World peace. In achieving this objective, the United States would seek to:
    a. Maintain peace in the Persian Gulf area,
    b. Reach some solution to the Arab-Israeli conflict.
4. Higher quality of life, defined as:
    a. Protecting the basic American standard of living,
    b. Safeguarding the quality of the environment.

The United States may choose one or a mixture of the following strategies in the future:

U_1 = Reduce oil imports from OPEC by increasing imports from non-OPEC oil producers, accelerating the development of indigenous resources, and reducing oil consumption.

Among the non-U.S. majors, Royal Dutch Shell is expected to play a significant role because of its North Sea operations, particularly its role in refining and petrochemicals. BP's activities are concentrated in a few countries. All of these countries, except for the United Arab Emirates (UAE), do not have potential for production expansion. In the UAE, BP is just one of the seven majors with operations in that country. CFP, though small compared to other majors, is owned partly by the French government. Because of the "special relationship" between the French government and some of the important oil producers, it seems that CFP's role will become more significant in the future.

Observe from tables 8.1 and 8.2 that the United States and OPEC will continue to play the most important role in the future world oil market. The United States is the largest oil consumer and oil importer in the world. In 1978 its oil demand comprised about 30 percent of the world total, some 43 percent of which was imported. Besides its oil and gas reserves, which are rather large but declining, the United States has substantial amounts of other energy resources. Its known coal resources are the second largest in the world (after those of the USSR); even with a significant increase in production, they will be adequate to supply a significant portion of U.S. energy needs well beyond the twentieth century. Coal can also be converted to oil and gas to replace part of the imported oil in the future. The United States also has the largest known uranium resources.

In addition to conventional sources of energy, the United States has huge deposits of oil shale and tar sands. Oil shale deposits are estimated to be as high as 2 trillion barrels. Having the world's highest per capita energy consumption, the United States has more potential for energy conservation than any other industrialized country.

The United States is also the largest trade partner of the oil-exporting countries; it supplies them with goods and services and offers them outlets for their investments. In addition to a number of independents, the United States is the home country for five of the seven major oil companies. Its "special relationship" with several major oil producers, its diplomatic and military role in the security of oil supplies, its active role in the Arab-Israeli conflict, and especially its leadership in energy technologies place the United States in a leading position among the oil-importing countries.

OPEC members currently hold over 65 percent of the world's proven oil reserves and more than 33 percent of the world's proven gas reserves. In 1978 OPEC members accounted for nearly 50 percent of world oil production. Because of relatively insignificant domestic consumption, most of the oil produced by OPEC members is being exported. However, the decline in outputs of some major oil producers; the accumulation of oil revenues by some less populated, rich oil producers; and the possibility of change in leadership of some major oil-producing countries make future OPEC supplies uncertain. It

Table 8.4. Nonpetroleum Activities of Major Oil Companies

Factors Actors	Horizontal Integration .250	Development Assistance .750	Nonpetroleum Activities
Exxon	.403	.289	.317
Gulf	.151	.055	.079
Mobil	.145	.144	.144
Texaco	.113	.289	.245
Socal	.059	.144	.123
BP	.020	.020	.020
Shell	.091	.020	.038
CFP	.019	.038	.033

THE BASIC METHODOLOGY

The next steps in the process are as follows:

1. Construct a hierarchy of objectives and strategies for each actor.
2. Prioritize these objectives.
3. Compute "constant values" of each actor's strategies; for example, the relative effectiveness of each strategy in satisfying the actor's objectives.
4. Compute "current values" of the strategies; for example, the relative strengths of the strategies of one actor against those of the opponent.
5. Compute the payoffs to each actor by multiplying the current values of each strategy by its constant value. This results in a payoff matrix showing the payoffs to the actors for each pair of their strategies.
6. Search for a "Nash equilibrium solution."

This approach is an application and expansion of a new work on conflict analysis developed by T.L. Saaty (1979). The objective of the method is first to assign payoffs to the strategies of the actors by taking into consideration both their "constant" and their "current" values and then to determine the equilibrium solution(s).

Of the five U.S. majors, all except Gulf are partners of Arabian-American Oil Company (Aramco), which is the biggest oil-exporting company in the world and has access to about a quarter of the world's proven oil reserves. (The Saudi government owns 60 percent of Aramco's producing assets, and the four U.S. major oil companies own 40 percent—namely, Exxon, 12 percent; Mobil, 4 percent; Texaco, 12 percent; and Socal, 12 percent.)

Table 8.3. Petroleum-Related Activities of Major Oil Companies

Factors\Actors	Exploration and Capital Expenditures .485	Production .030	Transportation .090	Refining and Petrochemicals .228	Marketing .167	Petroleum-Related Activities (Composite Weights)
Exxon	.399	.395	.389	.376	.366	.387
Gulf	.034	.022	.058	.036	.029	.035
Mobil	.089	.050	.147	.062	.044	.079
Texaco	.195	.208	.076	.128	.164	.164
Socal	.115	.092	.047	.079	.084	.095
BP	.055	.092	.020	.038	.108	.058
Shell	.095	.122	.244	.264	.187	.163
CFP	.018	.019	.020	.018	.019	.018

Table 8.2. Future Role of Oil-Exporting Countries in International Oil Market

Clusters Countries	USSR .114	Newcomers .114	OP_1 .451	OP_2 .236	OP_3 .063	OP_4 .023	Future Role
USSR	.114						.038
China		.240					.037
Egypt		.150					.024
Mexico		.340					.055
Norway		.280					.043
Saudi Arabia			.487				.225
Kuwait			.269				.122
U.A.E.			.244				.109
Iran				.461			.109
Iraq				.311			.073
Libya				.228			.055
Algeria					.146		.012
Indonesia					.136		.012
Venezuela					.165		.014
Nigeria					.550		.049
Ecuador						.269	.006
Gabon						.448	.012
Qatar						.284	.006

```
                THE FUTURE ROLE IN THE WORLD
                        OIL MARKET
                   /                \
    PETROLEUM-RELATED          NON-PETROLEUM
       ACTIVITIES                ACTIVITIES
          .75                       .25
              |
  ┌──────┬──────┬──────┬──────┬──────┬──────┬──────┐
 Exxon  Gulf  Mobil Texaco Socal   BP   Shell   CFP
 .370   .046  .096  .184   .102  .049   .132   .022
```

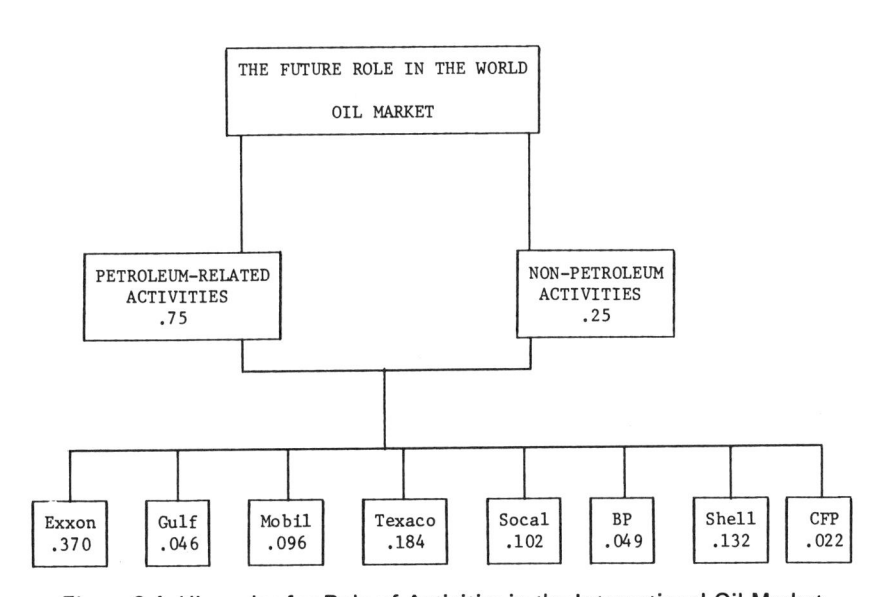

Figure 8.4. Hierarchy for Role of Activities in the International Oil Market

Table 8.1. Future Role of Oil-Importing Countries in International Oil Market

Clusters / Members	United States .562	Japan .257	Western Europe and Canada .112	Eastern Europe .026	LDCs .044	Future Role
United States	.562					.324
Japan		.257				.146
Canada			.053			.021
France			.343			.115
Italy			.195			.063
United Kingdom			.142			.042
West Germany			.267			.084
Bulgaria				.127		.010
Czechoslovakia				.216		.021
East Germany				.196		.021
Hungary				.230		.004
Poland				.026		.004
Romania				.039		.021
Yugoslavia				.165		.031
Low income					.308	.021
Middle income					.207	.021
High income					.205	.021
India					.281	.031

Figure 8.4 shows that two of the major American oil companies, Exxon and Texaco, will have a leading role among the majors in the future activities of the world oil market, followed by Shell, Socal, and Mobil, the latter two of which are also American companies. The other three companies, BP, Gulf, and CFP, will have lesser roles in the future markets. This is mainly because of their relatively limited participation in exploration and refining and petrochemical activities, two of the main activities that would lead to greater supplies in the future.

In 1975 over 70 percent of all oil-related investments in the world were undertaken by five American companies of the eight majors. In that year, they also reduced the price of oil.

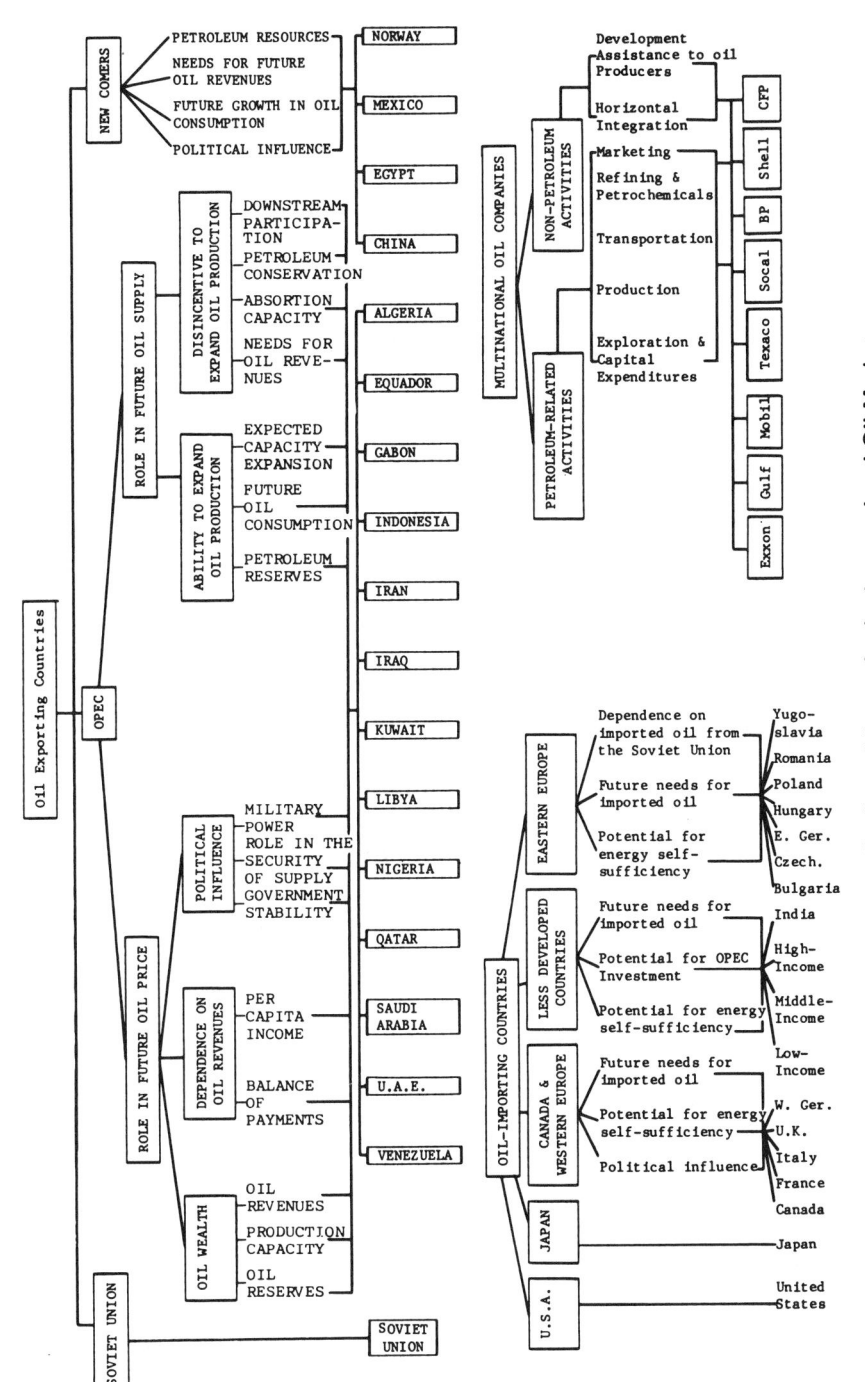

Figure 8.3. Detailed Outline of Actors in the International Oil Market

CRITICAL CHOICES FOR OPEC MEMBERS AND THE U.S.   143

```
                    ACTORS OF THE INTERNATIONAL
                            OIL MARKET
                    ┌──────────────┼──────────────┐
                OIL            OIL          MULTINATIONAL
            IMPORTING       EXPORTING           OIL
            COUNTRIES       COUNTRIES        COMPANIES
```

Oil Importing Countries: UNITED STATES, JAPAN, CANADA & W. EUROPE, EASTERN EUROPE, NON-OIL LDCs

Oil Exporting Countries: SOVIET UNION, OPEC, NEW COMERS

Multinational Oil Companies: EXXON, GULF, MOBIL, TEXACO, SOCAL, BP, SHELL, CFP

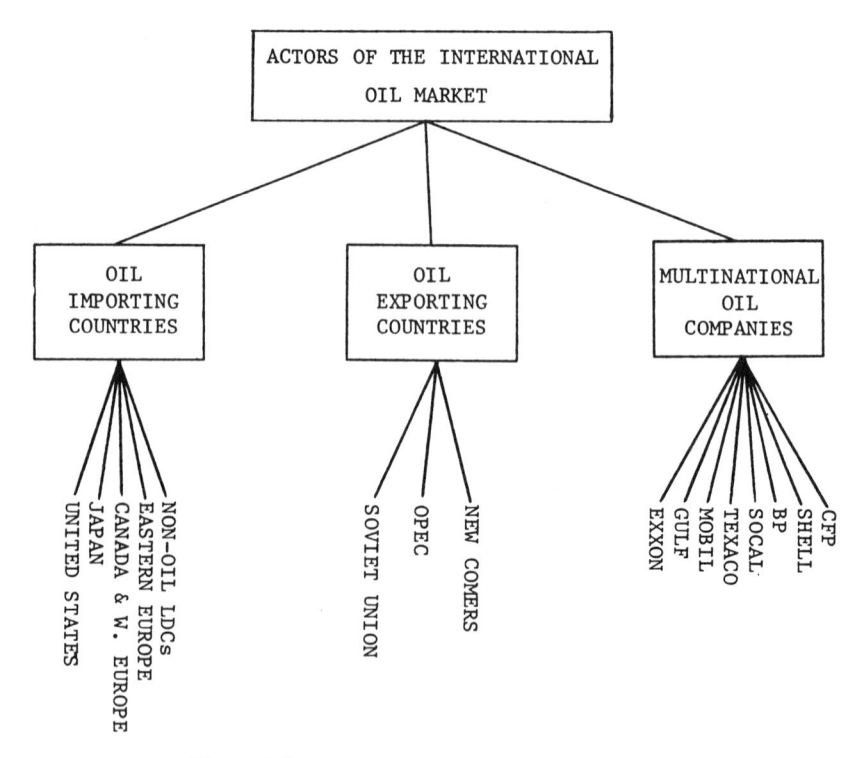

Figure 8.2. Actors in the International Oil Market

Tables 8.1 and 8.2 summarize the priorities of oil-importing and exporting countries with respect to their future role in the international oil market. To show how these weights are obtained, we have chosen the multinational oil companies because fewer constraints are involved in the prioritization process than in the case of the other two major sets of actors (see figure 8.3).

First, the constraints are prioritized with respect to their importance in the future role of the oil companies in the world oil market (see figure 8.4). Second, petroleum-related activities and nonpetroleum activities are prioritized within each cluster. Finally, the oil companies are assessed with respect to each activity, or constraint (see tables 8.3 and 8.4). The composite priorities of the multinational oil companies can be seen in figure 8.4.

national oil market. Their strategies are matched against one another; by using a game theoretical approach, the most desirable strategies are derived and analyzed for their effectiveness and stability.
3. To formulate policies in order to attain the desired future. Using previously derived information, we show how a desired goal can be attained by the United States and OPEC countries regarding oil supply and demand and price structure. The problems arising in the process are identified, and desired policies to solve these problems are formulated. Figure 8.1 outlines the analysis.

In general, a conflict hierarchy consists of the following levels (see chapter 6):

$$\text{Conflict} \to \text{constraints} \to \text{actors} \to \text{objectives} \to \text{policies} \to \text{outcomes} \to \text{composite or stable outcome}.$$

ACTORS IN THE INTERNATIONAL OIL MARKET

The three groups of actors in the world oil market of today are the oil-importing countries, the oil-exporting countries, and the multinational oil companies (Gholamnezhad, 1981). Figure 8.2 identifies the major actors in each group. A more detailed outline of the actors is given in figure 8.3.

For convenience, the many countries involved within each major set of actors have been clustered into subsets as follows:

Oil-Importing Countries (table 8.1):
  United States;
  Japan;
  Western Europe and Canada;
  Eastern Europe;
  LDCs.
Oil-Exporting Countries (table 8.2):
  USSR;
  Newcomers;
  OP_1;
  OP_2;
  OP_3;
  OP_4.

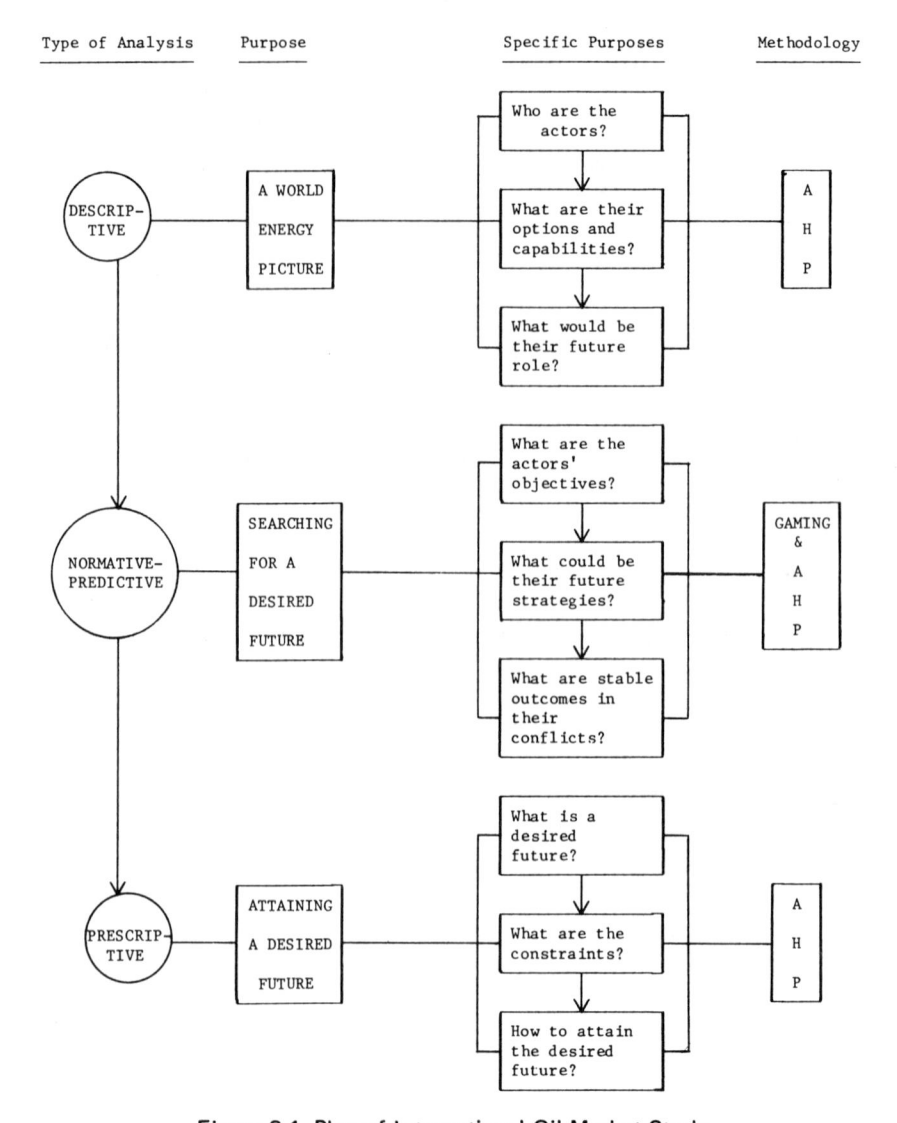

Type of Analysis	Purpose	Specific Purposes	Methodology
DESCRIPTIVE	A WORLD ENERGY PICTURE	Who are the actors? → What are their options and capabilities? → What would be their future role?	A H P
NORMATIVE-PREDICTIVE	SEARCHING FOR A DESIRED FUTURE	What are the actors' objectives? → What could be their future strategies? → What are stable outcomes in their conflicts?	GAMING & A H P
PRESCRIPTIVE	ATTAINING A DESIRED FUTURE	What is a desired future? → What are the constraints? → How to attain the desired future?	A H P

Figure 8.1. Plan of International Oil Market Study

An important quality in planning for the international oil market is to be realistic and open-minded; we should look at the possibilities of both desirable and undesirable outcomes. This vision gives us a sense of appreciation for a desired future and motivation to attain it. If we are too idealistic or too narrow in our vision, our actions could lead us to disaster. We have tried to be both realistic and fair in our efforts to analyze the factors most critical to world oil supplies: demand and prices. We search for a desired future that would provide adequate supplies of oil for the world, sufficient income for oil exporters, and a way of assisting the forgotten part of the world (the poor less developed countries; see chapter 4) in its struggle for survival.

The international oil market has become the playground for economists, political scientists, technologists, and even sociologists and theologians. Most of these "players" support only one particular group of actors in the international oil market (the oil-exporting countries, oil-importing countries, or the multinational oil companies). Only a few are concerned about the world community as a whole. Most of the players, who in most cases greatly influence their government's decision making, compete with each other to gain the most benefits for their individual group. Many times these competitions have resulted in confrontations among the actors of the oil market, particularly the oil producers and consumers.

A number of studies have been conducted on the future of world energy, especially on the availability of oil. Noteworthy among them are those by the Workshop on Alternative Energy Strategies (WAES), the Central Intelligence Agency (CIA), the Organization for Economic Cooperation and Development (OECD), and the World Energy Conference. Although based on different assumptions, they all conclude that unless appropriate actions are taken soon by oil producers and consumers, particularly OPEC members and the United States, oil shortages in the late 1980s are inevitable.

The preponderance of energy studies analyze only economic and technological factors affecting world energy supply, demand, and price structure. But it has become increasingly necessary also to include relevant political, social, and environmental factors. So far, the major problem encountered in the consideration of such diverse factors has been the lack of a framework to analyze their complex joint interactions and impacts.

This study of the international oil market has the following objectives:

1. To analyze the international oil market by identifying the major actors and analyzing their capabilities and projected future role in this market.
2. To search for a desired future for OPEC members and the United States. This is the central theme of the study. It will focus on U.S. and OPEC members' national objectives and possible future strategies in the inter-

8 CRITICAL CHOICES FOR OPEC MEMBERS AND THE UNITED STATES: *A Hierarchical Search for Their Desired Future*

The international oil market is the most complex trade market in the world. The actions taken by one major actor affect the whole world community. The market's influence not only is felt in the economic affairs of nations but also reaches out to the technical, social, environmental, and political domains, all continually interacting and affecting each other. Some actors who organize and operate this large market belong to the poorest nations; others are multinational corporations; and still others are superpowers whose potential confrontations in the world today include the security of oil sources and oil supplies. The ideologies and politics of the actors are diverse. With such a complex system one cannot possibly make accurate judgments or prescriptions without understanding the interrelationships among the actors and the factors that influence the system. Thus it seems crucial to do long-range planning by scrutinizing the capabilities and behavior of the actors, defining their objectives, investigating their possible future strategies, examining the impact of these strategies on each actor, searching for strategies that could lead to a desired future, and exploring ways that would make such a future attainable. Through this planning we can control the future; we can direct it toward a desired goal and prevent the emergence of disastrous outcomes. Planning would also provide us with the time needed for change and adaptation to a new environment as we proceed toward our desired goal.

This chapter is a summary of a Ph.D. dissertation by A. Gholamnezhad, University of Pennsylvania, Philadelphia.

been identified in terms of which the scenarios are represented in a more detailed manner (see also Blair, 1978). These variables are quantified by using a -5 to +5 scale. This scale is a useful tool to evaluate the impact of coalitions on the scenarios, not just by examining the scenario weights, but also by analyzing what aspect of a scenario in a conflict is influenced the most when different options are implemented.

Instead of difference numbers, we could use for each state variable pairwise comparisons of the scenarios including the status quo to determine the increase or decrease in the variable relative to the status quo. One can then compose the values as usual and compare this result with the corresponding value at the status quo to assess the increase or decrease in the contribution of the variable. Pairwise comparisons of the variables for either each scenario or once and for all yield weights for the composite answer that make it possible to compare across variables.

REFERENCES

Alexander, J.M., and T.L. Saaty. 1977a. "The Forward and Backward Processes of Conflict Analysis." *Behavioral Science* 22:87-98.

———. 1977b. "Stability Analysis of the Forward-Backward Processes: Northern Ireland Case Study." *Behavioral Science* 22:375-82.

Barrat, J. 1976. "Southern Africa: A South African View." *Foreign Affairs* 55 (1):147-68.

Blair, P.D. 1978. "Hierarchical Systems and Multiobjective Energy Planning: Applications to the Energy Park Concept." Ph.D. dissertation, University of Pennsylvania, Philadelphia.

Ferguson, C., and W.R. Cotter. 1978. "South Africa: What Is to Be Done?" *Foreign Affairs* 56 (2):253-74.

Nyerere, J.K. 1977. "America and Southern Africa." *Foreign Affairs* 55 (4): 671-84.

Woods, D. 1978. "South Africa's Face to the World." *Foreign Affairs* 56 (3): 521-28.

10. Enforce Decree No. 1 of the U.N. Council on Namibia calling on all states to seize any exports from Namibia that reach their shores and to hold them in trust for the Namibian people.
11. Reduce or terminate landing rights for South African Airways in the United States.
12. Prohibit the importation of South African goods into the United States on the grounds that they violate U.S. laws banning importation of goods produced by "slave" labor.
13. Use U.S. influence in the International Monetary Fund and in other ways to depress the world gold price.

With many of these options, a mere threat of undertaking that measure may be sufficient to influence the South African government. While we suggest that these options outline alternatives for action by the United States, the important point to be learned from the preceding discussion is that the AHP, when applied in the forward-backward fashion, is useful for describing the necessary components of conflict resolution and the general characteristics of actions that must be taken to reach a desirable outcome.

Finally, Julius Nyerere (1977) provides some useful thoughts concerning the situation in South Africa:

[Human rights] are denied by any law or practice which distinguishes the rights and duties of men and women according to their racial origin. . . . Domination of one racial group by another is inconsistent with human rights when the majority dominates the minority. It is not made more consistent when 83 percent of the South African population is denied elementary political, economic, and social justice by legislation and economic power used by and in the interests of the whites. . . . Despite everything which the South African state can and will do, instability is inherent in a situation where the majority of the people are excluded from benefits of a society that depends on their work. . . . Change can be delayed by an intensification of oppression and human suffering. But apartheid is doomed. The only question is whether the society subsides into chaos, or whether there is an orderly but speedy movement toward justice. . . . For nations have learned, and mankind has learned, that the hope for world peace and justice precludes indifference in the face of the organized racialism.

Also, Donald Woods (1978) appropriately writes: "During the time it took to read this article [about the same length as this chapter], five black babies in South Africa died of malnutrition in one of the richest countries of the world, with two-thirds of the world's gold, more than half the world's diamonds, more than three-quarters of the world's uranium, and the best agricultural land in all Africa. It is not only in detention that the victims of apartheid die."

A new approach has been brought up in this chapter: state variables have

4. Make certain that NATO does not collaborate with South African military personnel in any fashion and make it explicit that the Western security umbrella does not extend to protect South Africa from internal or external military pressure.

Options with Respect to Refugees and Nonmilitary Support of Liberation Movements and African States:
1. Support multilateral (via the Organization of African Unity or the United Nations) or bilateral programs of humanitarian assistance to the liberation movements, including the provision of educational and medical supplies.
2. Increase support to the front-line African states affected by their proximity to South Africa. These states include Angola, Botswana, Lesotho, Mozambique, Swaziland, and Zambia. These nations have been shouldering huge economic losses resulting from the liberation struggle in southern Africa and, unless there is a change of course in South Africa, are likely to suffer even more in the future. Botswana and Lesotho are particularly vulnerable to counterpressures by the South African government, and the international community should be making contingency plans now for supplying needed resources (including oil) to these countries in the event of South African cutoffs.

Economic Options:
1. Discourage foreign business expansion in South Africa and vote for the Swedish resolution in the United Nations that calls for no new international investment.
2. Advise U.S. businesses that if they decide to stay in South Africa, they do so at their own risk and that, in the event of difficulties with liberation movements, the U.S. government would not protect them.
3. Encourage U.S. firms in South Africa to establish fair employment practices including a new program to recognize and deal with black labor unions.
4. Amend Executive Order No. 10925 so that, with respect to U.S. businesses in South Africa, fair employment practices in their South African enterprises would be made a condition for their eligibility for U.S. government contracts.
5. Warn U.S. traders with South Africa that they should be seeking alternative suppliers since the security of supply, given the unsettled internal conditions, cannot be guaranteed.
6. Discourage the travel of U.S. tourists to South Africa—now totaling more than 50,000 a year.
7. Prohibit U.S. banks and other financial institutions from providing financing to the South African government or its parastatal corporations.
8. Deny foreign tax credits to U.S. firms operating in Namibia.
9. Embargo the transfer of new technology that might assist the South African government in enforcing repression.

as those listed below, which are a subset of a list compiled in 1979 by Ferguson and Cotter (1978). Within each category, the options are arranged from weaker to stronger measures.

Diplomatic Options:
1. Give continued presidential attention to detained black dissidents in South Africa (as has been done in the case of Russian dissidents).
2. Eliminate U.S. commercial, defense, and agricultural attachés to South Africa and end all U.S.-South Africa cooperative agency agreements such as those with the Treasury and the Defense Departments.
3. Institute an expanded educational and cultural exchange program with South African blacks, coloureds, Asians, and institutions and individuals working for meaningful change.
4. Appoint a black American ambassador.
5. Join the U.N. Council in Namibia, the Apartheid Committee, and other bodies of the United Nations engaged in increasing international pressures on South Africa.
6. Put U.S. visa policy toward South Africa on a reciprocal quid pro quo basis.
7. Make it clear that South Africa's internal situation itself—not merely the supply of arms to South Africa—constitutes a threat to peace under Chapter VII of the U.N. Charter. (The arms embargo is ambiguous on this point.)
8. Arrange for the president to meet with liberation movement leaders from South Africa and Namibia when they visit this country.
9. Cease condemnation of the efforts of blacks in South Africa to achieve their freedom by forceful means and in reaffirmation of the principles enunciated in the Declaration of Independence, acknowledge their right to use whatever means are necessary to achieve self-determination when moderate paths fail.
10. Downgrade our representation from ambassadorial to chargé level in South Africa and close our outlying consulates.

Military Options:
1. To the extent that it has already been significantly broadened, broaden further the definition of what constitutes "military" equipment.
2. Terminate the sale of weapons-grade uranium to South Africa and end all other nuclear collaboration.
3. Encourage our allies, particularly the Israelis, French, and Italians, to abide by the U.N. mandatory arms embargo and to give the broadest possible interpretation to such "gray areas" as the provision of spare parts, components, and repairs, light aircraft (including civilian aircraft), the training of South African military personnel (including correspondence courses and participation at conferences), and cooperation in research and development of military know-how (including the testing of military equipment).

may be prohibitive in very complex conflict situations. In our example, we see that the access and mobility of blacks are enhanced the most by the third composite outcome, decided as a U.S.-West coalition applying significant pressures to reduce the power index of the S.A.-white coalition by 60 percent.

COMMENTS

The internal conflict in South Africa remains a major issue not only for the parties directly affected but for the international community as well. As John Barrat (1976), an informed expert on South Africa, states: " . . . the situation developing in South Africa is such that it is in the interests of other governments, in the West at least, to make a positive contribution to the resolution of conflict and avoid the easy escape of offering simplistic solutions to African problems. Ultimately, the peaceful and constructive development of the region as a whole will depend on a resolution of the potential conflict situation within South Africa itself."

Several conclusions can be drawn from the ensuing analysis. It is readily apparent that the United States and the West must be concerned about their ability to continue foreign trade in commodities found in South Africa that are important to their productivity. The irony, though, is that by identifying themselves with the South African regime to hope naively for a "coming around" of the leaders of the apartheid government, the United States and the West are risking the realization of the very things they fear the most—growth of communist interference, radicalization of the opposition to apartheid to the extent of violent revolution, and politically irreparable damage to economic interests.

As Clyde Ferguson and William Cotter (1978) declare: "[There is] no sign that white South Africa is prepared to consider an effective sharing of political (and hence, economic) power. . . . Thus a violent and protracted collision seems inevitable unless a combination of internal pressures and resources in the international community can be used to enlarge the gambit of what is 'acceptable' to the minority ruling establishment." This outcome was clearly brought out by the forward-backward iterative process. It was shown that unless the United States and the West can effectively influence the white apartheid government through various pressures or sanctions, then a collision of the sort mentioned above seems likely.

Several policy options have been noted in government circles and in the literature as having promise for bringing about the desired outcome of a transition to a just power-sharing arrangement with minimum violence. From our previous discussion, it is clear that the limited pressures being applied by the United States and the West can no longer affect the outcome significantly. Therefore we suggest a serious reexamination of stronger policy measures such

Propensity for violence against blacks	0	-1	-2	0	5	-.30	-.38	-.64	-.57
Racism in Africa	0	-1	-5	1	-1	-.90	-.92	-1.66	-1.47
Interracial marriage	0	0	2	0	1	.37	.37	.68	.60
Access to basic services	0	2	5	0	-2	1.16	1.23	1.92	1.74
Malnutrition in black communities	0	-1	-4	0	3	-.72	-.79	-1.36	-1.21
Legal								
Right to due process for all	0	0	5	0	-1	.75	.80	1.56	1.36
Right to trial for all	0	0	5	0	-1	.75	.80	1.56	1.36
Political arrests	0	0	-5	0	-2	-.90	-.91	-1.68	-1.48
Brutality by police	0	1	-4	0	-5	-.66	-.62	-1.28	-1.11
Freedom of the press	0	0	5	0	3	.95	.95	1.72	1.52

Composite 1: first forward iteration.
Composite 2: second forward iteration.
Composite 3: third forward iteration with S.A.-white coalition's power equal to .10.
Composite 4: third forward iteration with S.A.-white coalition's power equal to .25.

Table 7.4. Continued.

Variables	Outcomes					Composites			
	1	2	3	4	5	1	2	3	4
Voting rights of blacks	1	0	5	0	5	1.43	1.40	2.05	1.89
Power of black leaders	0	0	5	-1	5	.87	.84	1.62	1.42
Citizenship of blacks	0	0	5	0	5	1.05	1.02	1.80	1.60
Procurement of Western military equipment	0	0	5	0	-3	.65	.72	1.48	1.28
Peaceful settlement of disputes in region	0	1	5	1	-5	.96	1.07	1.78	1.59
Procurement of communist military equipment	0	0	-5	0	5	-.55	-.64	-1.40	-1.20
Social									
Ability to organize in black communities	-3	1	5	0	5	.14	.14	1.25	.94
Social work practiced by blacks	0	1	5	0	5	1.28	1.26	2.00	1.81
Education for whites	0	0	0	0	-5	-.25	-.19	-.20	-.20
Education for blacks	0	0	3	0	-3	.33	.39	.84	.72
Propensity for violence against whites	2	0	-1	2	5	1.21	1.14	.74	.86

Table 7.4. State Variables

Variables	Outcomes					Composites			
	1	2	3	4	5	1	2	3	4
Economic									
Foreign trade	0	0	-2	1	-5	-.39	-.34	-.66	-.58
New internal investment	1	0	-1	0	-3	.07	.09	-.19	-.11
New foreign investment	0	0	-2	1	-5	-.39	-.34	-.66	-.58
Profitability of business	0	0	-5	0	-5	-1.05	-1.02	-1.80	-1.60
Black wage discrimination	0	-1	-4	0	-5	-1.12	-1.09	-1.68	-1.53
Black employment discrimination	0	-1	-4	0	-5	-1.12	-1.09	-1.68	-1.53
Black access to natural resources	1	1	5	0	5	1.66	1.63	2.25	2.1
Land ownership by blacks	2	1	5	0	5	2.04	2.01	2.5	2.39
White economic control	0	0	-3	0	-5	-.73	-.69	-1.16	-1.04
Natural resource development	0	0	1	0	-5	-.09	-.02	.12	.08
Rate of economic growth (SR)	1	1	-1	0	-5	.2	.25	-.07	.02
Political									
Problem of communist presence in South Africa	2	1	-4	1	5	.78	.69	-.20	.05
Power of white minority	0	0	-4	2	-5	-.53	-.48	-1.12	-.96
Access and mobility of blacks	0	1	5	0	5	1.28	1.26	2.00	1.81

continued

Table 7.3. Results of Varying Power of South African Government-White Coalition in Second Step of Third Forward Iteration

Outcomes	Power of South African-White Coalition			
	.632	.25	.10	0
Bantustan policy	.372	.29	.25	.23
Abolish petty apartheid	.217	.21	.20	.20
National conference	.17	.28	.32	.35
Three parliaments	.23	.18	.18	.18
Revolution	.039	.04	.04	.04

white coalition's influence weight. How much does the weight have to be reduced in order to cause a shift from the Bantustan policy outcome to the desired result, a national conference? Table 7.3 summarizes the outcome structure at various weights for the S.A.-white coalition. One can see that parity between the two outcomes is achieved when the influence weight equals .25, and the national conference emerges as dominant when the weight is reduced to .10. Thus pressures must be applied by other parties to the conflict to reduce the S.A.-white coalition's influence by 60 percent in order to change the outcome to a more desired result. This signals that continuation of the policy of rhetorical coaxing without strong international economic and political pressure will prove fruitless toward changing the outcome to the national conference.

STATE VARIABLES

A more detailed assessment of the effects of changes identified in the forward-backward process can be made by applying the outcome weights at each iteration to a set of state variables. These variables, which appear in table 7.4, describe particular aspects of the conflict that may be affected by each alternative outcome. The effect of each outcome on a variable is determined by applying an interval scale from −5 to +5 that indicates how a variable changes from the status quo under a particular outcome.

The normalized weights for the outcomes from each iteration in the forward-backward process are used to obtain a weighted average, or composite outcome. The values of these state variables describe the characteristics of a composite outcome at various iterations of the forward-backward process. Thus specific features of the conflict can be identified as major issues for peaceful resolution. Otherwise, effects must be inferred from generalized outcomes, a process that

Objectives:
1. Resist U.S.-West pressure .20;
2. Consolidate apartheid .40;
3. Suppress blacks .20;
4. Protect investments .13;
5. Gain support .04;
6. Curb communism .03.

Outcomes:
1. Bantustan policy .19;
2. Abolish petty apartheid .35;
3. National conference .08;
4. Three parliaments .35;
5. Revolution .03.

In addition, we assume the U.S.-West coalition recognizes that additional sanctions must be applied to reduce the influence of the S.A.-white coalition in order to change the dominant outcome to a desired result.

THIRD FORWARD PROCESS

There are two steps to this iteration. The first step investigates the effect of the S.A.-white coalition and their new objective structure on the outcome weights. The new influence weights and the resulting outcome weights appear as follows:

Parties:
1. S.A.-white coalition .632;
2. Black majority .031;
3. U.S.-West coalition .194;
4. Business interests .143.

Outcomes:
1. Bantustan policy .372;
2. Abolish petty apartheid .217;
3. National conference .170;
4. Three parliaments .230;
5. Revolution .039.

The Bantustan policy remains the dominant outcome, with slight changes in the weights of other outcomes.

The second step involves a systematic investigation of a reduction in the S.A.-

Outcomes:
1. Bantustan policy .10;
2. Abolish petty apartheid .15;
3. National conference .62;
4. Three parliaments .10;
5. Revolution .03.

SECOND FORWARD PROCESS

Using the changes in the structure of the hierarchy identified above, another iteration of the forward process is carried out. The new influence weights for the parties and the resulting outcome weights are as follows:

Parties:
1. South African government .367;
2. Black majority .031;
3. White minority .265;
4. U.S.-West .194;
5. Business interests .143.

Outcomes:
1. Bantustan policy .374;
2. Abolish petty apartheid .234;
3. National conference .167;
4. Three parliaments .187;
5. Revolution .038.

The outcome mix is virtually unchanged from the first forward process. Thus the conclusion is that a mere coalition of the United States and the West with support from the black majority is ineffective toward changing the dominant outcome to the more desired result (national conference).

SECOND BACKWARD PROCESS

The second iteration of the backward process looks at a coalition of the South African government and the white minority. Their objectives are consolidated and a new objective is added — resist pressure from the U.S.-West coalition. The result is:

Table 7.2. Continued.

Business Interests	
Protect investment	.69
Ensure economic stability	.26
Curb communism	.05
Soviet Union	
Support blacks	.11
Gain influence	.55
Minimize influence of West and China	.28
Disrupt economy and trade	.06
Outcomes	
Bantustan policy	.38
Abolish petty apartheid	.23
National conference	.16
Three parliaments	.18
Revolution	.05

allocated proportionately to each of the other parties by multiplying their weights by:

$$\frac{1}{(1 - \text{power of Soviets})} = \frac{1}{.98}.$$

Second, because the United States and the West have very similar objectives and prefer the same outcome, a coalition is formed between the two by adding their influence weights together and combining their objectives. Third, because the black majority cannot be highly selective as to where they acquire assistance, we add to the set of black objectives one of support to the U.S.-West coalition and delete the objective of opposition to big-power intrusion. The new priority vectors for the black majority appear as follows:

Objectives:
1. Majority rule   .55;
2. Economic equality   .23;
3. Human rights   .14;
4. Support to U.S.-West coalition   .08.

Table 7.2. Priority Vectors from the First Forward Process

Parties	
United States	.12
Black majority	.03
South African government	.36
White minority	.26
West	.07
Business interests	.14
Soviet Union	.02
Objectives	
United States	
Human rights	.26
Curb communism	.06
Peace in region	.03
Protect investments	.16
Minimize violence	.49
Black Majority	
Majority rule	.54
Economic equality	.16
Human rights	.25
Oppose big powers	.05
South African Government	
Appease whites	.36
Consolidate apartheid	.29
Suppress blacks	.17
Protect investment	.11
Gain sympathy	.04
Resist communism	.02
White Minority	
Maintain apartheid	.55
No outsiders	.13
Abolish petty apartheid	.03
Protect profits	.29
West	
Protect investment	.18
Ensure self-determination	.49
Curb communism	.03
Human rights	.25
Remain neutral	.05

to influence the conflict. Another example is the entry of 7 in the first row, second column, which reflects the judgment that the United States is demonstrably or very strongly better able to influence the outcome of the conflict than the black majority because of the variety of sanctions and resources at its disposal. This judgment was articulated in the discussions of Woods (1978), Ferguson and Cotter (1978), and Barrat (1976). It is this familiarization process of recognizing issues from research of the recent literature that has inspired the remainder of the judgments used to characterize the South African conflict in the rest of the chapter.

The priority vectors for each level of the hierarchy from the first forward process appear in table 7.2. These priority vectors are then weighted throughout the hierarchy to derive an overall weight for each of the outcomes. The result is as follows:

1. Bantustan policy: .38;
2. Abolish petty apartheid: .23;
3. National conference: .16;
4. Three parliaments: .18;
5. Revolution: .05.

Thus, in the first forward process, we see that the Bantustan policy emerges as the most likely outcome, given the influence of the parties, the importance of their respective objectives, and the contribution of each outcome to the fulfillment of those objectives.

FIRST BACKWARD PROCESS

An noted earlier, the purpose of the backward process is to identify a desired outcome and changes in the hierarchy that might lead to an emergence of that outcome as dominant through a subsequent iteration of the forward process. In the South African case, the desired outcome of a national conference was chosen because it is the most preferred from the perspective of the blacks, the United States, and the West. The most preferred outcome from the perspective of the South African government, the white minority, and business interests has already emerged as dominant — the Bantustan policy.

Three changes in the hierarchy are investigated in this first backward iteration. First, the Soviet Union is eliminated from the parties level because its weight is very low, reflecting the low level of influence the Soviets have within South Africa. Because the AHP requires that the components of the vector of priorities on a particular level sum to unity, the weight of the Soviet Union is

Table 7.1. Matrix of Pairwise Comparisons of the Influence of Parties over the Outcome

	United States	Black Majority	South African Government	White Minority	West	Business Interests	Soviet Union
United States	1	7	0.20	0.20	4	0.50	8
Black majority	0.14	1	0.125	0.125	0.14	0.14	5
South African government	5	8	1	2	6	4	9
White minority	5	8	0.50	1	6	2	9
West	0.25	7	0.167	0.167	1	0.33	8
Business interests	2	7	0.25	0.50	3	1	8
Soviet Union	0.125	0.20	0.11	0.11	0.125	0.125	1

Consistency index = .18.

chosen representatives of all groups would decide the power-sharing and transitional arrangements toward a more equitable governing structure in South Africa.

4. *Three parliaments:* This outcome involves a constitutional reorganization where three parliaments would be formed of coloreds, Indians, and whites (not blacks). A varying percentage of the representation would be formed, and an executive president would preside instead of a prime minister.

5. *Revolution:* This outcome is one of violent uprisings by the black community toward the goal of total overthrow of the apartheid regime, accompanied by heavy violence against whites.

FIRST FORWARD PROCESS

The judgments used throughout this discussion are those of the authors and reflect an understanding of the problem in South Africa derived from extensive research into recent developments in the area as described in the literature, some of which is cited in the reference section of this chapter. From a theoretical standpoint, it has been proven mathematically that moderate perturbations in the judgments can be made without affecting the overall priority vectors significantly. This is important because it allows one to account for what will inevitably be less than perfect judgments about a highly volatile political situation. Ideally, judgments would be elicited from parties to the conflict or from a group of experts. However, we believe that judgments about particular relationships and objectives of parties to the conflict derived from secondary sources (that is, publications) are reasonably reliable. (One should note, however, that the judgments used in this analysis were made during late 1978 and early 1979 and may be partially outdated.)

This discussion is presented to illustrate the issues and likely outcomes reflected in the conflict hierarchy. Each level of the hierarchy is evaluated with respect to elements of the next higher level. Thus, for example, the influence of the parties over the conflict is given in table 7.1. As an example of a numerical entry in the table, the pairwise comparison of the relative influence of the South African government and the West over the conflict in South Africa is reflected by an entry of 6 (between strong and demonstrated influence) in the third row, fifth column. This entry means experience has shown that the South African government has stronger and somewhat more demonstrated ability to influence the conflict than the West has. We determined the judgment from the discussions of Ferguson and Cotter (1978) and Nyerere (1977), where they allude to the inability of the West in the recent past to bring about a change in the apartheid policies of South Africa and the West's reluctance to apply significant sanctions

3. White minority:
    a. Maintain apartheid in the economic and political sense,
    b. Minimize outside intervention into internal matters,
    c. Abolish petty apartheid,
    d. Protect profitability of business interests.
4. United States:
    a. Maintain commitment to human rights,
    b. Curb communism,
    c. Secure peaceful settlements in region surrounding South Africa,
    d. Protect U.S. investments in and trade with South Africa,
    e. Ensure transition to just power sharing with a minimum of violence.
5. West:
    a. Protect investment and trade,
    b. Ensure black self-determination,
    c. Curb communism,
    d. Ensure human rights,
    e. Remain neutral in the conflict.
6. Business interests:
    a. Protect trade and internal investments,
    b. Ensure continuation of economic situation,
    c. Curb communism.
7. Soviet Union:
    a. Support revolutionary blacks and leaders,
    b. Gain political influence in South Africa,
    c. Minimize Western and Chinese influence,
    d. Disrupt economic trade and investment by West in South Africa.

The bottom level of the hierarchy is formed from possible future outcomes that may emerge in the conflict. These may be briefly described as follows:

1. *Bantustan policy:* This outcome would maintain the "homelands" where blacks are allowed to reside. The difference from the status quo is that this policy would allow ownership of land by blacks and citizenship in their respective homelands, or Bantustans. Also, independence would be granted for each homeland, except that work requirements and several other apartheid policies would still be enforced.

2. *Abolition of petty apartheid:* This outcome would provide for the reduction of discrimination in the social sphere against blacks. Blacks would be allowed access to basic services and facilities and social organizations.

3. *National conference:* The black majority are proponents of this outcome, which would provide for the convening of a national conference where freely

3. The white minority in South Africa;
4. The United States;
5. The West;
6. Business interests;
7. The Soviet Union.

The South African government, the white minority, and the black majority have obvious influence over or concern about the conflict. The United States has several reasons for maintaining influence in South Africa. A combination of factors, including the racial composition of the United States, a commitment to human rights, the interest of the Soviet Union in South Africa, and economic considerations of trade and investment, preclude U.S. indifference to the internal events of South Africa. For much the same reasons, the West (Britain, France, Portugal, and so on) has influence over the conflict. Commitment to human rights and protection of trade and investment are the key elements explaining their interest. In particular, Western Europe has a much larger economic stake in South Africa than does the United States. Business interests, both foreign and internal, are vitally concerned with the outcome of the conflict. Investments in vital and profitable resources such as gold, diamonds, chrome, iron ore, and uranium are the key elements of the business interests' concern. The Soviet Union has interest in the outcome because of its policy of projecting its influence and presence in critical global regions. This policy is further evidenced by its presence in other African conflicts (Angola and Zimbabwe in particular).

The next level of the hierarchy contains each party's objectives with respect to the South African situation. These objectives, listed here, are relatively self-explanatory:

1. South African government:
   a. Appease white electorate,
   b. Consolidate apartheid by commitment to racial separation and subordination,
   c. Suppress black revolutionary opposition,
   d. Protect economic interests,
   e. Gain worldwide sympathy through propaganda,
   f. Resist communist intrusion.
2. Black majority:
   a. Provide for majority rule and abolish apartheid,
   b. Ensure economic equality,
   c. Provide basic human rights for blacks,
   d. Oppose intrusion of big-power politics.

likely outcome and its desirability to the parties. In our example, the dominant outcome of a Bantustan policy (explained later) is favored by the South African government, the white minority, and business interests and is strongly opposed by the black majority, the United States, the West, and the Soviet Union. To induce a more desired outcome from the perspective of the black majority, the United States, and the West, the backward process identifies the necessary conditions, the revised objectives of the parties, and the amount of pressure needed to achieve the desired outcome (see Alexander and Saaty, 1977a, 1977b).

THE CONFLICT HIERARCHY

The top level of the hierarchy contains the parties to the conflict (see figure 7.1). They appear in this position because their ability to influence the outcome is the dominant consideration. The parties to the South African conflict are:

1. The South African government;
2. The black majority in South Africa;

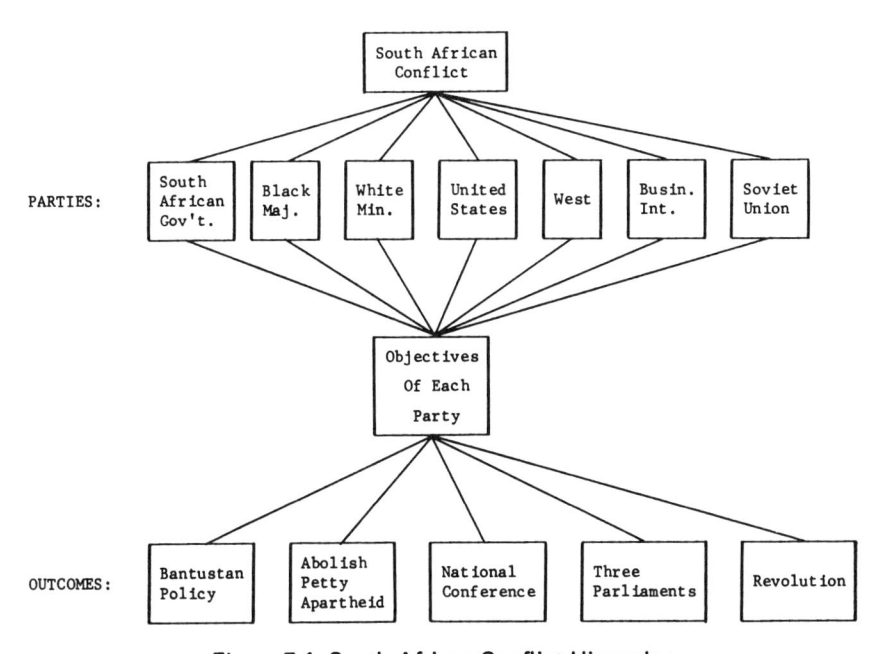

Figure 7.1. South African Conflict Hierarchy

Since the appearance of whites in southern Africa, internal political problems as well as human rights issues have existed. For over seventy-five years, blacks in South Africa have been struggling to organize opposition to legislated policies of the apartheid regime. These policies include citizenship and voting restrictions; mixed marriage restrictions; jobs reservation laws; separation-of-residence requirements; and assorted legal instruments designed to deprive blacks of basic rights of free assembly, political self-determination, and social justice. The main bulwark of the apartheid government has been the Group Areas Act, which established separate tribal living areas for each so-called ethnic group. This "independence strawman" is characterized by the fact that 12 to 13 percent of South Africa's territory belongs to its 18.7 million blacks, while 87 percent is reserved for its 4.3 million whites. Significantly, this 87 percent includes the gold and diamond mines as well as all the developed industrial and metropolitan areas and harbors.

Instability in the region also promises to fuel the potential for conflict in South Africa. The support provided to several revolutionary black movements by the Frontline states and the increasing boldness of black youths in South Africa add to internal instability. The recent emergence of an independent, black-ruled Zimbabwe has encouraged those who see a possibility for a similar transition in South Africa; but the influence of the Soviet Union as indicated by its presence in Angola and Mozambique as well as by its ties to the major political faction ZAPU (led by Nkomo) in Zimbabwe, combined with the desire of the West to circumvent further spread of this influence and presence, has sown the seeds of confrontation between the major powers and created a further potential for an unstable and violent outcome.

Our purpose here is to investigate the stability of potential outcomes of the conflict. In this process we explore the likelihood that a desired less violent outcome will emerge as a consequence of more stringent policies than the existing policy of rhetorical condemnation that could be applied and enforced by a coalition of the Western powers. It will be shown that this can be the only promising path to a just power sharing in South Africa with a minimum of violence.

We construct a hierarchy of the forward, or projected, path of the conflict interests of parties to the conflict, their objectives, and the potential political outcomes. The forward process identifies an outcome that is most likely to occur given the influence of the parties and their objectives. The backward process identifies a desired outcome and outlines necessary actions to achieve the desired result. This backward perturbation of the hierarchy is then applied in another iteration of the forward process to test the effect of the changes on the weights associated with the outcomes. The conflict can thus be investigated by successive iterations of the forward-backward process in order to either test stability of a particular outcome or identify actions or policies necessary to achieve a desired result. Thus, in the forward process, we examine the most

7 THE CONFLICT IN SOUTH AFRICA

The domestic strife in South Africa between ruling whites and subordinated blacks threatens to become a major conflict of violent dimensions in the African continent. This strife is primarily a consequence of racial policies promulgated by the white apartheid regime. Donald Woods (1978) describes apartheid in South Africa as "government of the blacks, by the whites, for the whites." Since the early 1970s, a new black movement has emerged to challenge the white regime, "taking as its leitmotif the raising of black consciousness" (Ferguson and Cotter, 1978). This has led to increasingly violent uprisings in black communities mainly by university students and urban blacks, inviting white police intervention and serious suppression of black organizations.

In recent years worldwide attention has been drawn to the rioting incidents at Soweto; to the death in detention of the new black movement's acknowledged leader, Steve Biko; and to "the arrest of Percy Qoboza, editor of the *World,* the largest black newspaper in South Africa; the banning of Donald Woods, editor of the 'white' *Daily Dispatch;* and the closure of the *World* itself" (Ferguson and Cotter, 1978). But apartheid has resulted in even greater denial of human rights than indicated by these incidents.

The resignation of Prime Minister John Vorster and the selection of Defense Minister P.W. Botha to replace him signal to the international community the uncertainty surrounding the potential outcome of apartheid policies in the area.

This chapter is by D.S. Tarbell and T.L. Saaty; previously published in *Journal of Peace Science* 4, No. 2 (1980):151-68.

Mace, M.L. 1965. "The President and Corporate Planning." *Harvard Business Review* 43 (January–February):49–62.

Saaty, T.L., and P.C. Rogers. 1976. "The Future of Higher Education in the United States." *Socioeconomic Planning Sciences* 10:251–54.

———, and J.P. Bennett. 1978. "Terrorism: Patterns for Negotiation. A Case Study Using Hierarchies and Holarchies." In *Terrorism: Threat, Reality and Response.* Stanford, Calif.: Hoover Institution Press.

Steiner, G.A., and H. Schollhammer. 1965. "Pitfalls in Multi-National Long Range Planning." *Long Range Planning* 8 (April):2–12.

Finally, and perhaps most significantly, the process has been put to general use inside the company since the original test. A number of staff groups are using the process to plan their own functional activities, engaging members of the department in a prioritized hierarchy for issues that are relevant to their area of control. Furthermore, strategies for interacting with external actors have been modified as a result of the prioritized hierarchy assessments. The vehicle has thus become a concise communication tool by which different groups can understand the bases of long-range planning decisions taken by other groups in the company. As use of the process spreads, coordination in planning becomes practically more meaningful and easier to implement.

This application did not use the forward and backward processes in an iterative fashion because the results from the first iteration revealed significant differences between projected and desired corporate management views. We have, however, deemed it necessary to show how these iterations from present to future are done.

COMMENTS

In this chapter we have described how the AHP can be applied to planning to identify projected and desired futures. The outcome of the backward process is a set of policies to attain the desired future. Thus, policy formulation is crucial in planning. It provides an opportunity to consider not only policies related to our desired future but also policies that may curtail the functioning of the system. The next two applications deal with policy formulation and how it is accomplished through the iterative application of the forward and backward processes. First, the process is applied to the conflict in South Africa (chapter 7). In the second application, the energy conflict between the United States and OPEC members is looked at in the context of a game (chapter 8) where the payoff matrix (a tool used in game theory to measure numerically the impact of the actions of a party on the counteractions of another party) is estimated with the use of the AHP (see Appendix B). The outcome in both applications is a set of policies that could steer the conflict toward an equilibrium.

REFERENCES

Emery, F.E., and E.L. Trist. 1972. *Towards a Social Ecology*. London: Plenum Press.

Lucado, W.E. 1974. "Corporate Planning—A Current Status Report." *Managerial Planning* 23 (November–December):27–34.

3. What do you think are the important long-range problems that the company will be addressing through its policies?

The following observations on these questions emerged from the process:

Question 1. Even though there was consensus about the factors in the hierarchy, different individuals had used different factors to describe the future of the company. Some issues, such as increased taxation, were mentioned by only a few participants individually but turned out to be very significant in the prioritized hierarchy analysis. Other factors, such as personnel productivity, were felt to be important by a number of individuals before the session, but did not come out that way in the collective process.

Question 2. Both the collective process and the preponderance of individual judgments had identified the government, investors, and suppliers as important actors. However, a large number of actors, such as consumers and union groups, considered important by many individuals prior to the process were determined actually to have low influence.

Question 3. Here we have the greatest difference between individual perceptions and those produced as a result of the process. Competition and investment risk, hardly considered significant by the management meeting, turned out to be dominant problems in the prioritization process. Conversely a number of problems proposed by individuals were not incorporated into the final prioritized design because no significant weights were assigned to them.

The fact that outcomes of the group judgments in the organized approach were very different from the unorganized individual judgments is testimony to the learning and possible change achieved in the process. Even more significantly, there was unanimous agreement that the picture of the company's future developed in the process was in fact an adequate representation of the combined beliefs of the group who participated. In addition, the outcome was obtained with no major conflict, as each individual had ample opportunity to explain his or her beliefs.

A second basis for assessing the usefulness of the test was the follow-up. The corporation completely revised its strategy for dealing with the government and proceeded to act on it with regard to policies affecting the company's future. Furthermore, individual members who were part of the planning staff took the result of this preliminary exercise and began to reassess the priorities of the model-building activities that had already been initiated by staff groups in the corporation. Substantial changes in those priorities were made as a result of the reassessment process.

maximization of investment return. The government desired political control, development, and revenue, in that order. Suppliers were assumed to seek profit return and were not particularly loyal to the customers who purchased their products; hence, risks of supply availability existed.

The major conclusions for the backward planning projection were as follows:

1. International expansion was seen as a much more desirable future than was domestic expansion.
2. The major problems relevant to achieving the desired future were: (a) competition in domestic and international markets, (b) the risk involved in investing in new products and markets, and (c) political and social problems. For the desired future, the supply of raw material and organizational development were judged to be less significant than other problems.
3. The most significant actors that would affect the outcome of the desired future were (in order of importance): the government, investors, competitors, and the company's management. It is significant that the government appeared to be the key actor in creating desired change. Also, the company's own management, which was the most influential actor in the forward process, is much less important here.
4. Counterpolicies by company management were discussed only briefly because of time limitations. However, the findings were that there is urgent need for (a) further knowledge, analysis, and understanding of the behavior of key external stakeholders; (b) a method for evaluating risk and returns on alternative new growth strategies; and (c) developing methods for exerting greater influence over external factors that have a major impact on future courses the company might desire to pursue.

ASSESSMENT OF FORWARD AND BACKWARD PROCESSES

The value of the process was assessed in three specific ways. The first was that the two-day intensive session using the prioritized hierarchy system provided a rich learning experience with nontrivial results for the participants. Each participant was asked to fill out a questionnaire individually before the process started. The questionnaire analyzed each member's beliefs about major factors in the company's planning strategy that would be reassessed after the process. The following questions were asked of the participants:

1. What do you believe the company will look like in 1985 in general terms?
2. What do you think are the major elements in the environment of the company that will have a significant role in shaping its future?

LEVEL I: DESIRED SCENARIOS

- Internalization .55
- Domestic Diversification .28
- Basic Business Boom .10
- Vertical Integration .07

LEVEL II: PROBLEMS

- Competition .25
- Investment Risk .27
- Political and Social Problems .18
- Raw Material Supply .12
- Organizational Development .08

LEVEL III: ACTORS

- Suppliers .05
- Government .25
- Consumers .10
- Investor .20
- Competitors .18
- Society .06
- Company Executives .16

LEVEL IV: POLICIES

- Political Control .20
- Low Risk Investment .24
- High Return .12
- Discourage Competition .15
- Increase Market Share .09
- Company Success .13
- Personal Success .07

Root: Desired Future of the Company

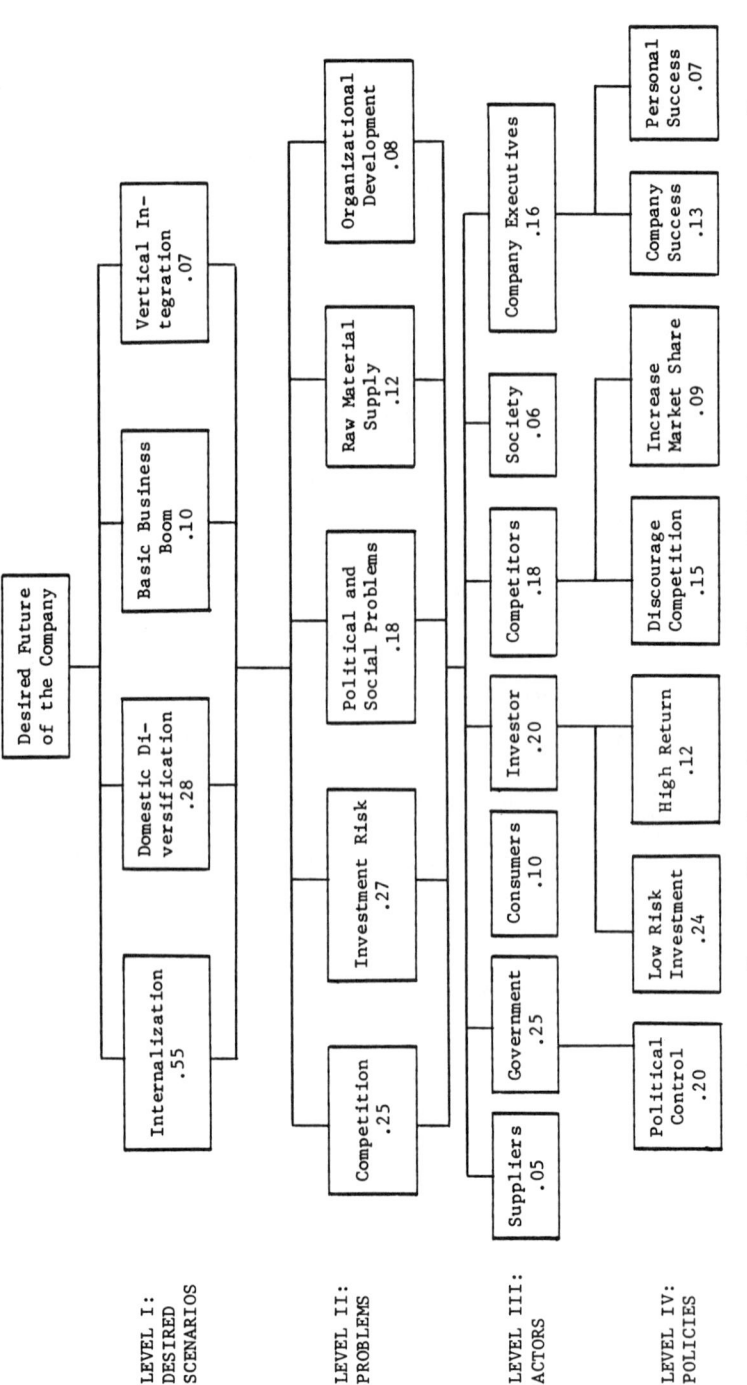

Figure 6.5. Backward Planning Process (Numbers Represent Elements' Weights of Importance at Analysis Level)

LEVEL I: ACTORS

| Distributors .06 | Company Executives .31 | Consumers .03 | Investors .23 | Competitors .05 | Government .14 | Employees .05 | Suppliers .13 | Society .01 |

Projected Future of the Company

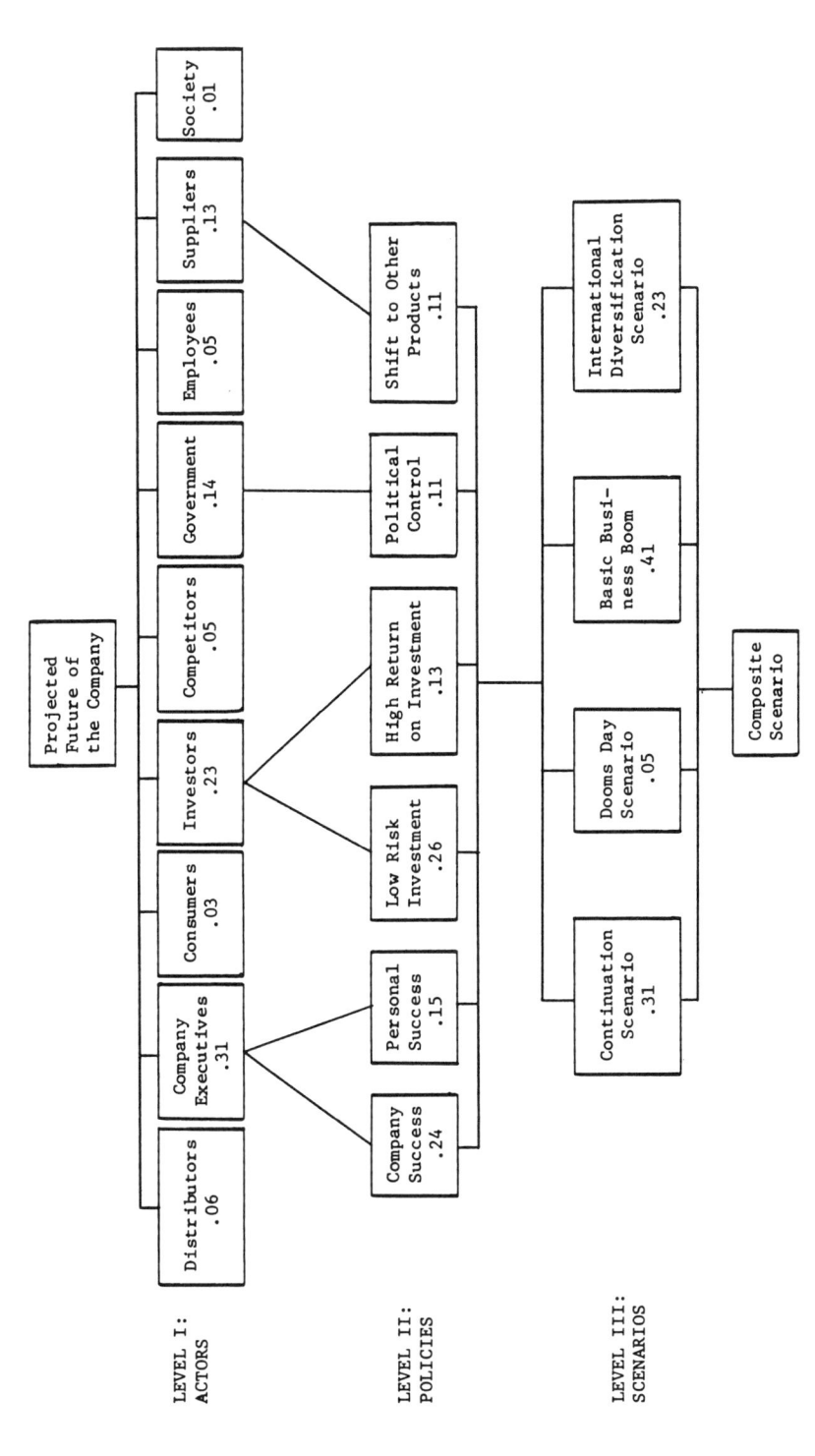

LEVEL II: POLICIES

| Company Success .24 | Personal Success .15 | Low Risk Investment .26 | High Return on Investment .13 | Political Control .11 | Shift to Other Products .11 |

LEVEL III: SCENARIOS

| Continuation Scenario .31 | Dooms Day Scenario .05 | Basic Business Boom .41 | International Diversification Scenario .23 |

Composite Scenario

Figure 6.4. Forward Planning Process (Numbers Represent Elements' Weights of Importance at Analysis Level)

progressed. However, the decisions were made entirely by the company representatives who participated.

The first step in the process was an explanation of the forward and backward planning processes, which were to become the basic orientation of the planning session. The stated and accepted objective of the session was for the group to make one complete iteration through both the forward and the backward processes, with one day allotted to each.

Next, the consultants proposed a basic hierarchical structure for the forward and backward planning processes. In the actual procedure of hierarchy assessment and prioritization, each level of a hierarchy was dealt with individually. At any particular level, a set of elements relevant to the planning process was presented to the company's management group and discussed for completeness and relevance. After the final list was agreed upon, the process of prioritization was conducted. After each level of the hierarchy was prioritized, the managers were provided with resulting priorities. With this information, decisions were made as to the relative importance of components at the next level of the hierarchy.

Summaries of the elements selected for each level of the hierarchy and weights assigned to each element are presented for the forward and backward planning processes in figures 6.4 and 6.5, respectively. The forward planning process results are straightforward and seem like natural conclusions. They are, however, considerably different from the backward process conclusions given later. The forward process conclusions can be summarized as follows:

1. The projected future suggests a successful concentration by the company on the development of the business area that has made it successful in the past. Some efforts for international diversification will take place; but this program will be driven more by the failure of domestic markets to develop rapidly than by the attractiveness of internationalization. The projected future indicates a distinct possibility that the domestic market will not provide an acceptable growth rate, primarily because of either supplier or government actions.

2. The actors most significant to the company's projected future are (in order of importance) the company's own vice presidents, the major financial investors in the company, the government, and raw material suppliers. Product consumers were not considered to be particularly significant in the projected future, implying that purchasing habits would not change unless there were new actions by the company itself.

3. The policy and objectives of the key company managers were oriented first toward company success and then toward personal success, implying that the development of existing functional areas had a high priority as long as that led to acceptable growth for the company as a whole. Financial investors were thought to be motivated primarily by risk minimization and secondarily by

The four functional areas were split up and nine new vice presidencies established. Each vice president had decentralized operating responsibility for his area. A corporate planning committee was formed, consisting of the president and each of the nine vice presidents. This committee was to focus on establishing corporate growth objectives and planning explicit strategies for achieving the objectives.

Although the reorganization helped promote corporate planning by removing some obstacles, the committee mechanism proved inadequate to ensure a coordinated corporate planning process for the company. The corporate planning committee initiated a series of reviews of the divisional plans. It was intended that this review process would familiarize all the vice presidents with the planning issues addressed by the other divisional areas. This review was to provide a perspective for the vice presidents to collectively define corporate level planning issues. It had precisely the opposite effect. The corporate planning committee began to spend more and more time on the details of each other's plans as they were reviewed. The committee began to manage the major decisions of each of the divisions and gave decreasing attention to their original corporate planning charter.

As this process was going on, the corporate planning staff, made up of economists and OR people, found themselves with little meaningful work to occupy their time. Therefore, they began to develop economic forecasting models that they believed would be of some benefit to the corporate planning process. However, the staff was operating with little or no managerial direction from the committee.

Thus the initial attempts at organizational change were unsuccessful. The company was no closer to having a corporate planning process than it had been with the previous structure; furthermore, day-to-day operating efficiency was substantially eroded by bureaucratic intervention of the corporate planning committee.

At this point a proposal was made to coordinate the corporate planning committee's activities and to integrate the effort of the corporate planning staff with these activities. The idea was to use the prioritized hierarchy procedure to accomplish this integration. The procedure was introduced to the committee and explained in more detail to the company president and to the planning vice president. A pilot test of the planning process was proposed and accepted by the committee.

A representative set of managers who were active participants in the corporate planning committee and corporate planning staff met in an intensive two-day planning session; the prioritized hierarchy methodology was used to see if it could produce agreement among the group on key corporate planning issues. The responsibility for running the actual session was given to outside consultants who coordinated the schedule of discussion and decision making as the meeting

Table 6.1. General Format for Hierarchical Decomposition

Generic for a System	Environmental Constraints and Forces	Perspectives (Actors)	Objectives of Actors	Policies	Outcomes	Resultant Outcome
Conflict	Constraints	Actors	Objectives	Policies	Outcomes	Compromise or Stable Outcome
Forward Planning	Present Organizational Policies	Other Actors	Objectives	Policies	Scenarios	Logical Future
Backward Planning	Organizational Response Policy	Other Actors	Other Actor Objectives	Other Actor Policies	Problems and Opportunities	Desired Future
Portfolio Selection	Criteria	Subcriteria	Objectives	Policies	Options	Best Option or Mix
Investment Choice	Risk Level	Major Forces	Criteria	Problem Areas	Specific Projects	
Prediction	Risk Level	Major Forces	Criteria	Problem Areas	Categories	

outcomes and may produce a large number of policy options. Hence we must reconcile the large number of options that are created when each problem is defined separately into one integrated solution. This is done by a "telescoping" process in which the lower priority policies are ignored; that is, elements that contribute only marginally to the overall results are eliminated from the analysis.

For example, we often begin the forward planning process by asking managers to list those policies of their organization that they feel will have a major impact on the company's future. Frequently they initially react by saying that there are none. But after some implicitly or explicitly stated thought about R&D policies, marketing policies, management development policies, financial policies, and so on, the list grows rapidly. After the list is refined to ensure that all policies are at the same level of generality, we go through the prioritization assessment. Very often this process shows that there is only a small core of policies essential for shaping the future. Following this, we proceed to the next level of the process; for example, identifying external actors who affect the core policies we just determined. We note that the managers by now have participated in the definition of the original list of policies and through the prioritization process have accepted the reduction of that list to its most influential policies. They now sense that there is no pressing need to list every actor they can imagine, but only the important ones. They know that they can go back and reintroduce factors left out if they so desire. Two major reasons why these simplifications are accepted seem to be that the managers (1) participated in making them and (2) accepted the fact that not everything itemized has a significant effect.

Table 6.1 gives the general format for hierarchical decomposition. Also included is the general decomposition of conflicts, portfolio selection, and investment choice, which will be discussed in later chapters.

APPLICATION: A CASE STUDY

To illustrate the foregoing theory, we present an application based on a real-life study done for a major corporation. The company produces and markets a number of consumer goods, with one major product dominating its sales and profits. For many years the company had been organized around four strong functional vice presidents: production, marketing, administration, and new business development. Each of these vice presidents had complete autonomy for his particular area, and there was little cooperative interaction among them.

The president wished to increase the corporate rate of growth. Realizing that the company's resources had to be coordinated to develop activities outside its traditional dependence on one dominant product, he reorganized the company.

The Backward Process

The hierarchy of the backward or desired process may be characterized as follows:

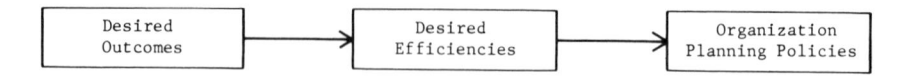

```
[Desired Outcomes] → [Desired Efficiencies] → [Organization Planning Policies]
```

The desired process begins where the projected process ends. The organization first examines the range of projected outcomes and determines the set of outcomes for which it desires to increase the likelihood of achievement and also the set of outcomes for which it desires to minimize the likelihood of achievement. Then it works back to the efficiencies to identify the changes that are critical to the achievement of the goals. These changes must occur through planning policies adopted by the organization to influence the actions of key actors in the transactional environment. Such policies, called *counterpolicies,* are developed to make other policies more effective. These counterpolicies can achieve their purposes by (1) *instructing* the actors to change their choice directly, (2) *motivating* them to change the values of the outcomes, or (3) *inducing* them to change their behavior by affecting the efficiencies of their choices. Inducement can, of course, take place by direct action of the organization, if it has the power to affect efficiencies, or by instructing or motivating members of the contextual environment, who are part of the actors' transactional environment.

The hierarchy for the desired process may be represented as in figure 6.3. Note that the two hierarchy processes produce opposite effects. The *projection* process starts with a small number of planning policies and may produce a large number of possible outcomes. The *desired* process starts with a small number of

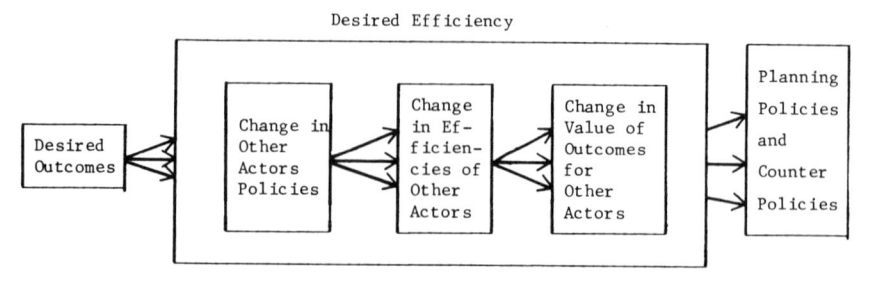

Figure 6.3. Hierarchy for Desired Process

This process can be divided further by segmenting the efficiencies level into its two basic components: events caused by the purposeful behavior of other actors, and events caused by nonpurposeful behavior (for example, the weather). Purposeful behavior is itself a hierarchy, diagramatically composed of:

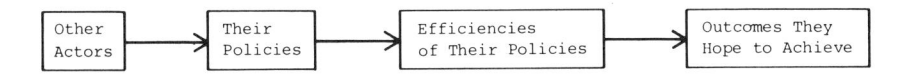

```
┌────────┐    ┌──────────┐    ┌──────────────┐    ┌──────────────┐
│ Other  │ →  │ Their    │ →  │ Efficiencies │ →  │ Outcomes They│
│ Actors │    │ Policies │    │of Their Policies│  │ Hope to Achieve│
└────────┘    └──────────┘    └──────────────┘    └──────────────┘
```

Emery and Trist (1972) use the term *transactional environment* to describe other actors whose behavior directly affects organizational efficiencies. Such actors include suppliers, investors, customers, and the like. This analysis can, in turn, be expanded by adding another level to analyze the elements that contribute to the efficiency of the behavior of members of the transactional environment. Purposeful behavior of such actors has an indirect effect on the original organization; Emery and Trist use the term *contextual environment* to describe such effects. Figure 6.2 presents a diagram of the hierarchy of the project process when transactional environmental effects are explicitly included.

Note that the natural branching of the hierarchy for the projection process may generate a large number of outcomes from a small number of initial policies. There are times when the elements (state variables) of the different outcomes are compatible and can thus be combined into a single composite outcome (see chapter 7). However, the outcomes may have incompatibilities that cannot be combined (see Saaty and Bennett, 1978). This is the case of mutually exclusive outcomes.

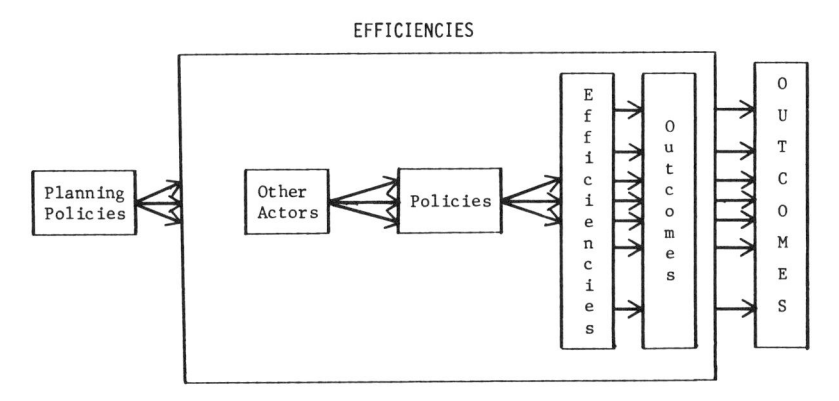

Figure 6.2. Hierarchy Including Transactional Environment

PLANNING: FORWARD AND BACKWARD PROCESSES 105

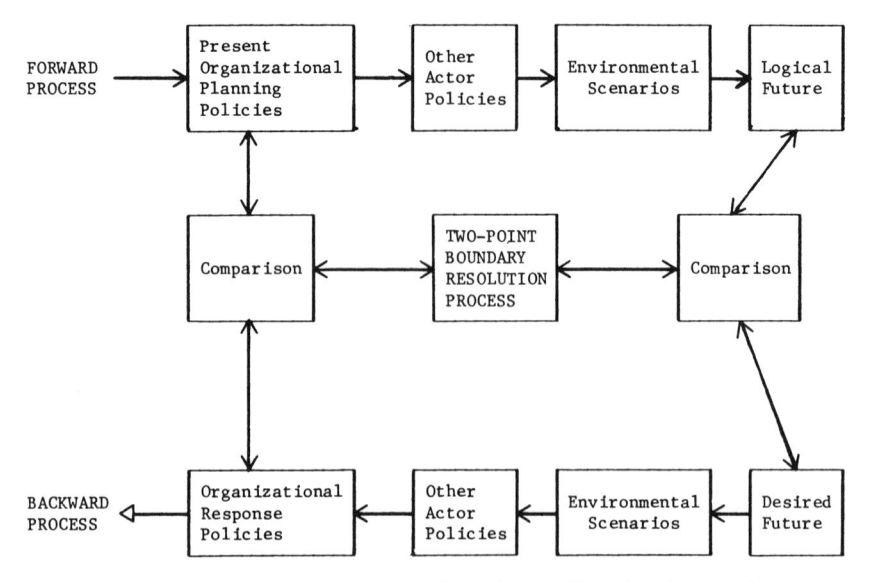

```
FORWARD       Present                Other                                  
PROCESS  -->  Organizational  -->    Actor    --> Environmental --> Logical
              Planning               Policies    Scenarios          Future
              Policies

                    ↕                                                 ↕
                                   TWO-POINT
              Comparison  <--      BOUNDARY    <--   Comparison
                                   RESOLUTION
                                   PROCESS
                    ↕                                                 ↕

BACKWARD      Organizational        Other                                   
PROCESS  <--  Response        <--   Actor    <-- Environmental <-- Desired
              Policies              Policies    Scenarios          Future
```

Figure 6.1. Schematic Representation of Basic Planning Orientation

future, and (3) *efficiencies* that show the probabilistic relationship between planning policies and outcomes.

These three variables are common to all decision processes, but the relationship among them is different for the projected and the desired planning processes. For the projected process the policies are *defined*, the efficiencies are *estimated*, and the probable outcomes are *deduced*. For the desired process the outcomes are *valued*, the efficiencies are *influenced*, and the policies are *developed*. This difference is due fundamentally to the way the problem is organized in each case. The organizing principle in both processes is hierarchical, but the dominance relationships are reversed.

The Forward Process

The hierarchy of the forward or projected process (Saaty and Rogers, 1976) can be characterized in the following sequence:

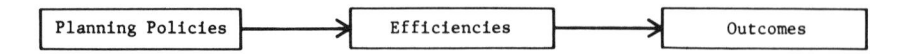

```
| Planning Policies | --> | Efficiencies | --> | Outcomes |
```

The aspect of planning that is concerned with working backward from a desired or idealized future and developing plans to bring such a future about is what we call the *desired planning process* or the *backward process*. It is a *normative* approach concerned with the question: Given a desired future, what *should* our policies be to attain that future? This again is a one-point boundary problem fixed at the future.

It is clear that the backward process is limited by constraints on the policy to be developed and by possible conflicts with existing policies. One is not at complete liberty to select policies to meet that future even if these policies are workable. This is due to the substantial constraints imposed by present habits, commitments, and policies. Conversely, projecting a likely future from present policies comes in conflict with the valued or desired future. When put together, the forward and backward processes demonstrate that we are not free to pursue planning from the present without understanding and evaluating where we want to go, nor to plan where we want to go without examining our present potentials and capabilities. If our existing policies fall short of what is needed to attain that future, then just as strongly, futures that result from present policies may fall short of the desired future we value. Making these two processes compatible is one of the major challenges facing planners. It is an evenhanded pragmatic process that is both an enrichment of the conservative tendencies of the forward process and a "pragmatization" of a fantasy-prone backward process. It seems then that the study of planning is not a simple benevolent art freely concerned with the improvement of living. Rather it makes a psychological contribution to the fulfillment of our values and desires for the future as strongly and intrinsically as it does to our satisfaction in the successes of our present actions.

The two-point boundary problem—present to future and future to present—is concerned with the following management process: given both the present set of policies and a desired future, modify the existing policies and design new compatible policies to attain that future. Then modify the desired future for greater compatibility with the effectiveness of the new policies. Iterate the process until an acceptable solution arises.

The starting point is to project the likely future from present actions, adopt a desired future, design new policies, adjoin them to the set of existing policies, project a new future, and compare the two futures for their main attributes: *the projected and the desired*. The desired future is modified to see what policy modification is again needed to become the projected future, and the process is continued. The process is diagrammed in figure 6.1.

Formulation of a planning process as a two-point boundary problem enables us to structure explicitly the decision framework to be formulated. Using decision theory notions, three basic variables are involved: (1) *planning policies* available to the organization, (2) *outcomes* the organization may realize in the

however, specialization in one of the areas is not sufficient to reflect the full domain of planning.

One major reason why systemic planning processes are difficult to start is that many relevant factors must be simultaneously coordinated. It is very easy either to skip some of them or to bog down in factors that are actually irrelevant to the process. Once the systemic planning process is started, adaptive learning procedures can be designed to ensure improvement in the quality of the planning functions. But without designing all the functions into the process at the start, success is about as likely as getting an automobile to run without a fuel pump; work to improve the other components will not correct for basic design deficiencies.

What then is needed to ensure that a planning process maintains its systemic properties? We believe that the process must be defined with four explicit characteristics. The first is a *basic orientation* to the process; that is, a succinct statement of the core problem to be addressed through the long-range planning process. Such a statement enables planning systems to begin with a relatively modest effort focused on the core, with later elaboration of the process evolving as the need arises. The second characteristic is an explicit *organizing principle* for the process that enables all relevant information about the variables affecting planning decisions to be systematically organized. Third, a *managerial assessment procedure* is required that incorporates attitudes and beliefs of decisionmakers and thus defines factors for further analysis in the system as well as factors to be eliminated. Finally, an *adaptation capability* must be incorporated to ensure that new facts or analyses developed by staff groups or managers can be reflected in the planning strategy assessment. The Analytic Hierarchy Process enables us to integrate these four characteristics into a long-range planning process.

FORWARD AND BACKWARD PROCESSES

Planning consists of two basic interacting phases. The first phase involves an assessment and optimum utilization of present capabilities. It is called the *projected planning process,* which is a one-point boundary problem whose boundary is fixed at the present state. It is what we also call the *forward process,* a primarily *descriptive* approach concerned with the following kind of question: Given the present actors and their policies, what *will* (is believed or is likely to) be the future resulting from their actions? Assessment of the impact of the present is usually made in terms of projection scenarios that span the future. The result is a composite scenario that is an integrated assessment of the individual projections.

pact is long term; hence the correctness of strategies is difficult to evaluate because of the lack of feedback.

3. *Controllability:* In short-term decisions, the factors that are under the organization's control can normally be separated from those that are not; over the long term there is less pure control over any single factor but more potential influence over many other factors.

The complexity of issues raised in strategic planning processes has led to the belief that to achieve a measure of success it is essential that there be *coordinated participation* of managers and staff throughout the organization. Furthermore, the planning must be a *continuous* process that is *integrated* with day-to-day tactical decisions. This implies that planning is a systemic property of the organization's management.

A complete picture also requires consideration of the *practice* of planning. Our experience with planning in a number of public and private sector organizations, both inside and outside the United States, suggests that the gap between planning theory and practice is rather large. Published studies of planning practices are consistent with these observations (see, for example, Lucado, 1974; Steiner and Schollhammer, 1975).

We believe the gap between the theory and practice of long-range planning in most organizations is related more to what is not done in the process than it is to the way activities that are part of the process are carried out. For example, one of the most commonly reported omissions in planning is managerial participation. Mace (1965) identified this in an early assessment of the role of the president in corporate planning:

> Probably the single most important problem in corporate planning derives from the belief of some chief operating executives that corporate planning is not a function with which they should be directly concerned. They regard planning as something to be delegated, which subordinates can do without responsible participation by chief executives. They think the end result of effective planning is the compilation of a "plans" book. Such volumes get distributed to key executives, who scan the contents briefly, file them away, breathe a sigh of relief, and observe "thank goodness that is done – now let's get to work." [p. 50]

When the implementation of a plan omits one or more of the essential components designed in the planning process, some of the richness of the plan is lost, thereby leading to a more specialized and perhaps less useful system. Typical consequences of such specialization are that planning becomes a process for specifying annual budgets, an activity for preparing scenarios of organization futures, a means of forecasting changes in the external environment, or a merger/acquisition function. Clearly all these activities are part of long-range planning;

6 PLANNING:
Forward and Backward Processes

Planning is an ongoing decision process whose purposes are: (1) to specify the ideals, objectives, and goals an organization desires to obtain in the future; (2) to define the programs that must be undertaken to achieve these ends; and (3) to procure the resources, create the organization, and control the results of planning implementation.

An implicit assumption underlying an organization's long-range planning process is that actions based only on what is best for present-day considerations (that is, tactical decisions) will not be sufficient for getting the organization to where it ought to be in the future. Were this assumption not so, the future could "take care of itself when we get there." However, the process by which an organization determines its strategic decisions is tremendously more complicated than it is for day-to-day tactical decisions. Among the complexities are the following:

1. *Performance criteria:* Long-range strategies must address a wider range and less quantifiable set of values in determining ends to be achieved than do short-range decisions.
2. *Feedback:* Long-range planning requires actions now, but the major im-

This chapter is the work of J.R. Emshoff and T.L. Saaty ("Prioritized Hierarchies for Long Range Planning," University of Pennsylvania, 1977).

III PLANNING

ASSURING CONTINUITY OF OPERATIONS

As an alternative to directly increasing the level of disaggregation in successive levels of the hierarchy, at some point in the unfolding of the allocation program the analyst may think it wise to ensure the projects supported will more or less continuously be coming on line. In other words, the failure to distribute resources in any program area over technologies at different stages of development may produce hiatuses in new capacity for some future years.

The purpose of level G' in table 5.3 – priorities of whose elements have been computed but, in this illustration, not integrated into the composed hierarchy – is to monitor and direct resources into a balanced pattern over R&D phases for any single program area. For instance, with reference to nuclear generation of electricity, the normalized eigenvectors show that the predominance of funds will go to design and research, with much less apportioned to demonstration and prototypes. Except for the light water reactor (LWR), little will be allocated to testing. There may be entirely valid grounds – given XYZRI's mission and limited funds – to specialize in one phase of R&D. For example, the unit cost of nuclear prototypes might exceed the entire organization budget! In such areas, XYZRI may require joint funding with the Department of Energy and other utilities and vendors. However appropriate the spending pattern, the elaboration of allocations into R&D phases enables one to examine at a glance the propriety and sufficiency of the time horizons used in various programs. (An entirely compatible method is to chart critical events, as is done in XYZRI's volumes on its R&D program through 1985.)

Table 5.3 shows that the major emphasis in power generation is at present largely given to design and research, whereas in transmission/distribution it is given to testing. These emphases may be appropriate, but they require justification in terms of the existing stocks, coordinate ventures made by other organizations and businesses in the phases of R&D, and technological opportunities. Such factors exceed the scope of the present study. One should note, however, that allocating to phases of R&D is a form of programming: the objective is to ensure capacity on line when required by attending to provision of sufficient resources at each point in a developmental sequence. Table 5.4 gives the composite priorities of the R&D hierarchy where level G' is considered.

COMMENTS

In this application resources are allocated to projects in research and development areas to ensure continuity of operations and to eliminate projects that do not provide the expected results. However, to allocate resources to projects whose outcomes may be uncertain, we must adopt a long-range view of the problem. In other words, we must do planning, the topic of the next chapter.

Table 5.4. Composition of the R&D Hierarchy

	1980	1990	2000	Discounted
LEVEL C				
Availability	.05	.06	.08	.05
Reliability	.08	.07	.06	.07
Efficiency	.09	.09	.10	.09
Profitability	.15	.15	.19	.15
Environmental safeguard	.64	.63	.58	.63
LEVEL D				
Generation	.47	.45	.47	.46
Transmission/distribution	.07	.07	.05	.07
Storage & conversion	.15	.14	.14	.14
Environment & health	.06	.05	.07	.06
Resource availability	.26	.28	.26	.27
Forecasting & analysis	.01	.01	.02	.01
LEVEL E				
Nuclear	.249	.251	.357	.259
Coal	.318	.321	.200	.302
Solar	.025	.025	.044	.025
Geothermal	.025	.025	.025	.025
AC	.047	.036	.025	.041
DC	.021	.034	.023	.027
Underground	.007	.008	.007	.008
"Distribution"	.003	.003	.002	.003
Rotating electrical machinery	.003	.003	.002	.003
Planning & control	.011	.012	.007	.011
Batteries	.099	.106	.090	.096
Thermo-mechanical	.052	.041	.041	.045
Fuel cell demo	.004	.025	.009	.013
Fuel cell advanced development	.026	.018	.032	.023
Chemical energy conversion	.016	.008	.015	.011
Physical effects	.005	.004	.006	.005
Ecological effects	.015	.013	.018	.015
Health effects	.060	.053	.071	.061
Demand & conservation	.009	.008	.005	.008
Supply	.003	.004	.005	.003
Systems synthesis	.001	.002	.016	.002

Table 5.3. An Alternative Level G' to the R&D Hierarchy: Allocating Funds over R&D Phases

	Design & Research	Demonstration & Prototype	Testing
NUCLEAR GENERATION			
LWR	.17	.08	.75
LWR variants	.76	.18	.06
LMFBR	.73	.19	.08
Fusion reactor	.82	.09	.09
COAL-FUELED GENERATION			
Pulverized coal-steam plants	.13	.08	.79
Fluidized bed combustion	.77	.16	.07
Gasification	.65	.29	.06
Liquefaction & clean solids	.65	.29	.06
SOLAR GENERATION			
Heating and cooling	.64	.27	.09
Conversion	.73	.19	.08
Technical assessment	1.00	.00	.00
TRANSMISSION/DISTRIBUTION			
AC	.05	.25	.69
DC	.05	.25	.69
Underground	.56	.31	.12
"Distribution"	.08	.15	.77
Rotating electrical machinery	.79	.13	.08
System planning & control	1.00	.00	.00
STORAGE			
Batteries	.72	.21	.08
Thermal-mechanical	.74	.19	.06
Fuel cells demo	.05	.66	.29
Fuel cells advanced development	.79	.13	.08
Chemical energy conversion	1.00	.00	.00
ENVIRONMENT & HEALTH			
Physical factors	1.00	.00	.00
Ecological effects	1.00	.00	.00
Health effects	1.00	.00	.00
FORECASTING & ANALYSIS			
Demand & conservation	—	—	—
Supply requirements	—	—	—
Systems synthesis	—	—	—

Note: The question asked for G' is: In terms of funding this year, relatively how important are the research phases of each technology?

disparity lies in the need for R&D in batteries. Our experts thought that peak-load problems toward the end of the century when solar heating begins to make a substantial contribution to total energy production necessitated radically increased attention to storage devices. Thermal-mechanical devices also got much more importance in the analysis of benefits.

The disparity of importances assigned to the division of environment and health is greater than apparent from the table. This arises because substantial portions of the benefit from resource availability should be assigned to XYZRI's category of environment and health. In general, although XYZRI does a very large amount of research on the environmental effects of power generation and transmission, it gives—our experts believed—inadequate attention to disposal of nuclear wastes. XYZRI finds itself in a difficult position: revision of pollution and safety standards forces large expenditures toward marginal improvements in environmental protection. However, this focus debilitates an effective program concerning nuclear wastes; public concern with wastes is much more the cause of lagging nuclear generating capacity than is accident. A full study of XYZRI's cost and benefit priorities should devote perhaps first-order attention to the quandary of environmental safeguards.

Forecasting and analysis includes much but not all of the "software" research. The table shows XYZRI as spending more than is justified by the benefit priorities. However, prorating the relevant "software" projects from the category of resource availability and reallocating program-specific analysis would erase most of the differences.

Allocating budget proportionally to priorities ignores the different unit costs of projects and technologies. For example, a single project in fusion generation may necessarily cost several orders of magnitude more than a project in studying emissions of coal combustion. Therefore, one cannot naively take the priorities of this analysis as the sole basis for allocating money. One can extend the hierarchy "downward" to include detailed implementation schedules, as is done in XYZRI's project planning to allocate money for each subtask of a project.

This study is obviously inadequate to assess definitively XYZRI's cost effectiveness. First, it fails to sufficiently detail the programs into projects. Second, it relies on a relatively narrow set of external experts. Third, it does not construct a full hierarchy of costs. Nevertheless, it does effectively demonstrate the directions in which further analysis can proceed and, most crucially, the power of the kinds of comparisons—of programmatic consistency and coherence and benefit/cost analyses—that are facilitated by the method of analytic hierarchies. We suggest that XYZRI's advisory committee participate in a two-day planning session to construct a more applicable hierarchy and to supply authoritative judgments. This program could establish a framework for systematic planning of resource allocations on an ongoing basis.

the second column were truly a priority, the second and third columns would be directly comparable for each technology.

We find that for all generation R&D, XYZRI budgets a slightly larger proportion than the benefit priority justifies. However, if we look at the last row of the table, we will find one cause for this apparent disparity. Our experts found it difficult to make judgments about the relative importance of program areas without inclusion of R&D on resource availability as an alternative for funding. This category does not appear in XYZRI's budget, although many of its activities are subsumed under nuclear and coal generation as well as forecasting and analysis. However, if the priority assigned to resource availability were plausibly prorated over the relevant XYZRI budget categories, one would discern a closer fit to the benefit priorities in generation.

Within the technologies for generation, there is a close correspondence between nuclear energy and coal, although coal receives relatively greater priority than money. This is, overall, a consequence of our experts' conservatism in power generation: they felt that coal-derived generation would remain a rewarding area for development well into the next century. Nor did they share the pessimism about the effectiveness of fluidized bed combustion prevalent within XYZRI. Our benefit priority assigns a low importance to solar power. Had political costs been considered, we might well have accorded roughly 5 percent of the priority to this area, as does XYZRI. As a unique institution in our society, XYZRI has a sometimes expensive responsibility not to ignore attractive technologies despite their apparent cost ineffectiveness for its own objectives. The possible extension of XYZRI's activities into electrical automotive systems is evidence of this unique status.

The major disparity between our benefit priorities and XYZRI spending occurs in transmission and distribution. Our experts simply did not accept a legitimate XYZRI mandate for extensive testing in this area. They felt perfection of existing technologies was more the responsibility of the most directly affected utilities, either alone or in combination, and that XYZRI should reserve its funds for efforts more in the nature of "public goods." A major exception arose in connection with direct current transmission. Here they thought that technologies developed abroad could in large measure be borrowed and adapted at relatively low cost.

We do not claim that the benefit priorities are somehow valid evaluative criteria: this study is deliberately a pilot effort. The order-of-magnitude disparities in importance assigned to the programs within the transmission/distribution area point out the wisdom of devoting more attention to this facet of XYZRI's operations.

Storage and conversion, on the other hand, received stronger importance from our benefit priorities than in XYZRI's budget. The major source of this

STORAGE & CONVERSION	13.6	8	14.0	19.2
Batteries	3.5	2	9.6	13.2
Thermal-mechanical	1.1	1	4.5	6.2
Fuel cell demo	5.2	3	1.3	1.8
Fuel cell advanced development	3.7	2	2.3	3.2
Chemical energy conversion	0.1	0	1.1	1.5
ENVIRONMENT & HEALTH	26.5	15	6.0	8.2
Physical factors	20.3	11	0.5	0.7
Ecological factors	2.9	2	1.5	2.1
Health effects	3.3	2	6.1	8.3
FORECASTING & ANALYSIS	9.0	5	1.0	1.4
Demand & conservation	2.1	1	0.8	1.1
Supply requirements	3.9	2	0.3	0.4
Systems synthesis	3.0	2	0.2	0.3
RESOURCE AVAILABILITY		27		

Note: Where necessary, some XYZRI expenditures have been reallocated from their actual division to the category most descriptive of the activities supported. Analysis and "software" pertinent to a single program is included within that program category. Analysis pertinent to systems integration is within FORECASTING & ANALYSIS.

Table 5.2. Proportionate XYZRI Funding, 1977, Compared with Priorities of Benefits

Program	I 10^6	II % XYZRI Budget	III Priority $\times 10^2$ from Figure 5.1	IV Priority Prorated over XYZRI Operations
GENERATION	97.0	54	46.0	69.7
Nuclear	50.7	28	26.0	35.6
Coal	39.7	22	30.0	41.1
Solar	4.4	5	2.5	3.4
Geothermal	2.2	2	2.5	3.4
TRANSMISSION/DISTRIBUTION	33.0	18	7.0	9.6
AC	7.5	4	4.1	5.6
DC	10.5	6	2.7	3.7
Underground	7.4	4	0.8	1.1
"Distribution"	5.2	3	0.3	0.4
Rotating electrical machinery	.6	0	0.3	0.4
System planning & control	1.8	1	1.1	1.5

In table 5.1 we illustrate how to incorporate the uncertainties discussed earlier in this chapter. The levels of table 5.1 are labeled as in figure 5.1 except that two additional levels—loss functions of supply and project commitment—have been inserted. As in figure 5.1, the rate at which XYZRI discounts the return on its R&D investment is retained as level A_1. Level A_2 presents a schedule for assessing the loss function of an excess or shortfall in the supply of electricity with regard to each of the sources of production of level B. The third source of uncertainty is treated by the lead time at which commitments are made to the development of a given technology, specified by the elements of level F, and the degree of reversibility of that commitment. We have lacked the information required to prioritize levels A_2 and A_3, as done for the rest of the hierarchy in the following section. Consequently, the resource allocations presented here are expressed as single numbers; elaboration of the levels of uncertainty would enable us to prescribe schedules or distributions of investments and to address more directly the degree of prudence.

BENEFIT/COST ANALYSIS OF PROGRAMS

We have completed the benefit hierarchy of figure 5.1. Its quantification goes far, we believe, to providing a powerful means with which to answer the second question concerning coherence and consistency of XYZRI's R&D program. The third question remains largely unanswered, although we have established the foundation to answer it as well. Yet to provide a satisfactory means of assessing cost effectiveness, we require an analytic hierarchy of costs—not merely dollar costs, but also political, social, and cultural costs; in short, a full realization of the notion of "opportunity costs" of choosing and supporting one technology at the expense of another. And support of one technology is ultimately and inevitably done at the expense of another.

We have not had the information necessary to construct a hierarchy of costs. Had we done so, we could divide the priorities assigned to programs in the benefit hierarchy by those assigned in the cost hierarchy and deduce a powerful and general basis for selecting among programs. Instead, we have had to rely on the proportion of 1977 funding XYZRI assigned to each program area to undertake a first cut at benefit/cost assessment. We first discuss the results of this comparison, which are presented in table 5.2. Subsequently, we enumerate a number of very important qualifications to this analysis.

Table 5.2 presents for each element of level D (in capital letters) and each of level E, respectively, the 1977 budgeted figure, the proportion of the XYZRI that figure represents, and the priority obtained. *If* the proportionate cost of

divided — eventually into individual research projects and even tasks. To continue decomposition requires engineering skills and familiarity with R&D in the electric power industry.

Before becoming involved in the quantitative aspects of the analysis, however, we should sum up our answer to the second question. XYZRI can evaluate the consistency and coherence of its R&D program by constructing an analytic hierarchy of its activities. The hierarchy would disclose the relations among programs *and* their justifications in terms of "virtues" or planning criteria *and* an explicit rate of discounting future returns on R&D. Such a hierarchy helps make clear to the expert what is omitted, what system boundaries have been drawn suboptimally narrow, and where principles and programs extraneous to XYZRI's basic mission are being used to justify expenditures.

XYZRI has already constructed such a hierarchy without, however, explicitly discounting returns on R&D investment. Yet in its scheduling of critical events within each program, the relative emphasis on near- versus far-term accomplishments is clearly shown. Furthermore, normative criteria are explicitly included in XYZRI's hierarchy as objectives. Although our analytic hierarchy in figure 5.1 differs from XYZRI's publication in minor respects, this is largely because we anticipate eliciting pairwise judgments and thus require elements as distinct as possible.

Table 5.1. Levels of Uncertainty in Revised Analytic Hierarchy with Levels Corresponding to Those in Figure 5.1

A_1	Discount	\% per year, or discretely, return in given year 1980, 1990, 2000						
B	Background scenario							
A_2	Loss functions of supply[a]		Excess				Shortfall	
		High	Medium	Low	Low	Medium	High	
C	Criteria							
D	Operational areas							
E	Programs							
F	Technologies							
A_3	Project commitment	Long/prespecified Long/revisable Short/yearly						
G	Projects							

[a]That is, loss functions as ratios of costs of missing optimum production level in integrated electric power system. A similar level for loss functions could be inserted between levels D and E to assess costs by operational area.

casting and analysis. We have broken down the industry's operations at this level as far as possible in conformance to XYZRI's usage. Thus storage and conversion are treated as a single element, as are environmental and health protection. Yet we have added—on expert advice—an additional category, resource availability. Here the physical accessibility of energy resources interacts with the cost of discovering and proving reserves and extraction. This is typically not an area of XYZRI's responsibility (except for preprocessing of nuclear fuels and the production of intermediate stages in coal derivatives). However, it was thought that resource availability might so centrally affect the success of any R&D program that it should be explicitly included. The reader must be cautioned that the pattern of resource allocation derived from expert evaluation of this hierarchy must consequently differ somewhat from XYZRI's pattern.

Each of the elements of this level—roughly corresponding to XYZRI's divisions except for the inclusion of "advanced" (liquefaction and clean solids) and coal-steam systems in the element of generation—may be further decomposed into program areas. To allocate R&D funds, one must know the priorities within the divisions; for example, nuclear versus solar, alternating current versus direct current or underground transmission. However, as one continues decomposition, putting together in a single element those activities that strongly affect one another either by applying the same technology or by addressing the same industry need, the probability increases that the elements will be neither clearly functionally distinguishable nor mutually exclusive. To supplement the hierarchy designed here, a full-scale review of XYZRI's programs should employ a surrogate for the technological input-output relations among programs. Technologies and research facilities common to several programs require identification; the operational content of each program must be described at length so that experts evaluating the relative importance of programs are aware of exactly what occurs in each.

As designed to this point, the hierarchy of figure 5.1 evaluates relative merit of alternative programs and technologies. It is thus a hierarchy of benefits that can be expected to accrue to each program area. Because it is constructed for three decades, it will be used to discount those benefits—and thereby direct current investment in R&D—over XYZRI's planning horizon. The next step is to elicit expert opinion to compare the elements of each level pairwise with respect to relevant elements on the superior level as a criterion. We note that in this application we quantify and examine funding practices. However, we do not pursue the programmatic decomposition of XYZRI's activities down to the level of selection among alternative projects designed to achieve the same goal. Yet we expect that this illustration makes evident to the R&D planner how such a process can be continued to produce definite results at a detailed level. Thus, for example, every component of level E in figure 5.1 could be further sub-

given year is crucial to its contribution to the industry. Of interest here is the potential availability, given efforts to develop the source and to bring the relevant technologies on line.

A second "virtue"—which may also appear as a problem area—is reliability of a mode of power generation. A technology that suffers from frequent stoppages or an otherwise constrained rate of production will be, ceteris paribus, less preferable than one that enjoys continuous operations.

Efficiency of performance is a third element that ought to govern preference of mode of generation. By efficiency we mean the rate of conversion of raw material into electric power relative to the theoretical efficiencies for competing technologies. This criterion is obviously more relevant to modes that consume nonreplaceable fossil fuels.

The profitability of a generating mode incorporates considerations of relative reliability and efficiency vis-à-vis the price and accessibility of fuel and the cost of capital investment for generation and related functions.

Finally, environmental effects must be minimized: this element introduces nonmarket costs into the determination of preferences for modes of electric power generation. Safeguarding the environment will be of varying difficulty and expense depending on the source of power used. In this category we ask the expert to consider the end processes of waste processing and disposal but not the environmental effects of mining the fuel initially. Although our analysis is subsequently biased in favor of the use of fuels that have environmental costs at the extractive stage—such as strip-mined coal—against those with costs at the disposal stage—such as spent nuclear fuels and radioactive wastes—we feel that XYZRI's responsibilities have typically been skewed more in the direction of containing wastes and by-products. That the electric power industry is held more accountable for radiation leakages than for mine disasters is a somewhat artificial compromise of the principle of systemic analysis.

Elements of "virtue" (see figure 5.1, level C) may also be considered as obstacles. We ask the expert to evaluate the relative severity of challenges posed to the industry's operation by the prospect of inadequate availability, inadequate reliability, inadequate efficiency, and so on. The intent is to identify problem areas to which R&D funds should be directed. Because we undertake the hierarchical analysis for each decade to 2000, in effect we endeavor to anticipate problems rather than to extrapolate trends.

Having identified problem areas, the next level of the hierarchy (level D) appraises facets of the industry's operations in terms of their relative susceptibility to the problems. Thus, for example, generation, transmission/distribution, and forecasting and analysis will typically differ in the degree to which their availability for a given year is problematic. One might think that adequate generative capacity is less likely to be available in 1990 than sufficient fore-

Figure 5.1. Hierarchy of XYZRI's R&D Program

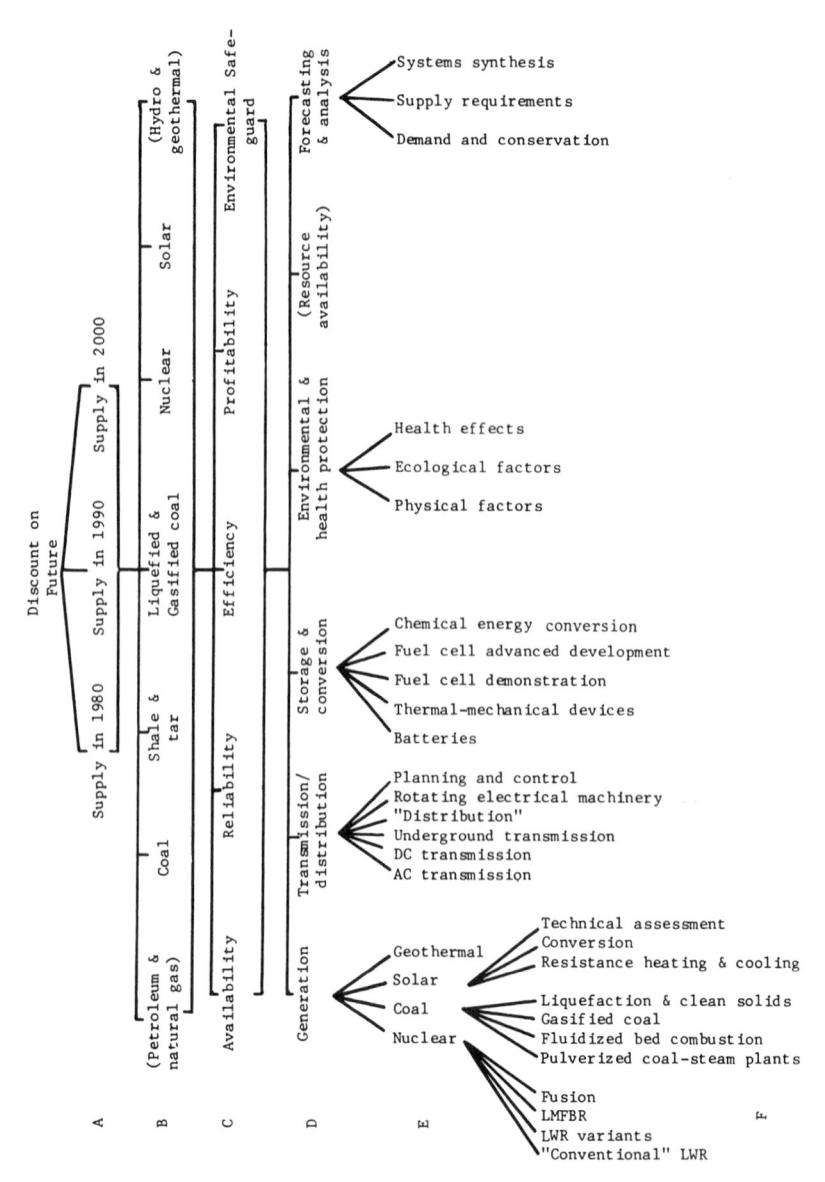

A. Discount on Future

B. Supply in 1980 | Supply in 1990 | Supply in 2000

- (Petroleum & natural gas)
- Coal
- Shale & tar
- Liquefied & Gasified coal
- Nuclear
- Solar
- (Hydro & geothermal)

C. Availability | Reliability | Efficiency | Profitability | Environmental Safeguard

D.
- Generation
- Transmission/distribution
- Storage & conversion
- Environmental & health protection
- (Resource availability)
- Forecasting & analysis

E.
- Forecasting & analysis
  - Systems synthesis
  - Supply requirements
  - Demand and conservation
- Environmental & health protection
  - Health effects
  - Ecological factors
  - Physical factors
- Storage & conversion
  - Chemical energy conversion
  - Fuel cell advanced development
  - Fuel cell demonstration
  - Thermal-mechanical devices
  - Batteries
- Transmission/distribution
  - Planning and control
  - Rotating electrical machinery
  - "Distribution"
  - Underground transmission
  - DC transmission
  - AC transmission
- Generation
  - Geothermal
  - Solar
  - Coal
  - Nuclear

F.
- Geothermal:
  - Technical assessment
  - Conversion
  - Resistance heating & cooling
- Coal:
  - Liquefaction & clean solids
  - Gasified coal
  - Fluidized bed combustion
  - Pulverized coal-steam plants
- Nuclear:
  - Fusion
  - LMFBR
  - LWR variants
  - "Conventional" LWR

to ensure that particular technologies are available when required. This means we are essentially problem oriented: first, attention is given to requirements and anticipated obstacles, and only subsequently are resources marginally reallocated to exploit particular technological possibilities.

As the point of departure we take XYZRI's discount rate of return on technological development. Greater emphasis is given to projects that come to fruition before 1985, slightly less emphasis to those maturing up to 2000, and only marginal importance to projects that have long gestation periods. In constructing the hierarchy we shall accordingly do three analyses—one for each of three years, say 1980, 1990, and 2000 (not later, because we wish to make judgments as definite as possible). Finally, after all three analyses are completed, we may weight them differentially. The formula 50-40-10 is suggested as a compromise between XYZRI's formula for discounting and our three-decade horizon. XYZRI's rate of discount was slightly adapted from 50 percent (to 1985), 45 percent (to 2000), and 5 percent (beyond 2000), to adjust for the three decades we used.

After a temporal weighting is determined, we identify the major force shaping the electric power industry's performance as the kind of fuel used. In this level, rather than rely on judgments, we used projections made by XYZRI supplemented by estimates supplied by the Exxon Corporation's Public Affairs Department to accord with XYZRI's aggregate rate of growth of demand. Most facets of the industry's operations will be designed to conform to opportunities and costs of raw materials used as fuels, whether depletable fossil fuels, nuclear sources, or "soft" sources. Because we are interested in meeting requirements for supply in the future, we take the determination of fuel sources of supply to best characterize XYZRI requirements. In figure 5.1 level B enumerates the elements of supply.

We have not pursued the developmental implications of electricity generation by petroleum and natural gas because its future is too constrained to justify appreciable R&D. Hydro- and geothermal sources—the former because opportunities for expansion in the United States are severely limited, and the latter because it appears to be geographically localized and to require expertise for its assessment, which we lack—are similarly left undeveloped. In other words, the R&D programs that we shall elaborate at subordinate levels of the hierarchy are limited to exploiting coal, shale and tar, liquefied and gasified coal, nuclear, and solar electricity generation. This plan differs from XYZRI's actual program mainly by the exclusion of geothermal R&D, which is a relatively small portion of the budget.

After sources of power are identified, one is required to seek obstacles to their utilization in a timely and economical manner. Here we incorporate several "virtues." It is apparent that the availability of a source of electric power in a

Other uncertainties play important roles. Fundamentally, the political climate, especially as it rewards investment in utilities, is uncertain. However, to a large measure, pressures on the electric power industry resemble positive feedback: if adequate supply is maintained at affordable prices, there is far less likelihood of government-created economic disincentives to invest than in a situation of inadequate performance that encourages increased governmental intervention. This, too, encourages a loss function that justifies planning for excess performance characteristics, not only in terms of aggregate demand. Basic to the public's evaluation of the electric power industry's performance will be the assessment of its efficiency and, broadly construed, its safety.

Heavily qualified, our response to the first question must be that planning under a variety of uncertainties is possible and economically rewarding if undertaken carefully and in detail. However, the magnitude of benefits from such efforts decisively outweighs any alternatives, such as trying somehow to control the environmental uncertainties. In short we have no choice but to incorporate uncertainties in our analysis.

We integrate three kinds of uncertainties in the analysis undertaken below. First, there is a discount rate implicit in any R&D program. This reflects the lag between investment in improving the electric power system and the time of anticipated return in the form of increased efficiencies, improved reliabilities, cheaper and cleaner fuels, and so on.

The second type of uncertainty arises from the need for flexibility in allocating resources to individual projects. R&D progress does not always proceed as planned. It is necessary to reevaluate projects prior to their completion and perhaps to reallocate the resources committed to them.

The third type of uncertainty deals with planning to minimize the expected cost of possible failures in R&D progress. This planning centers on XYZRI's notion of prudence. One approach is to compute loss functions, such as for over- and underproduction as discussed above. We indicate in the analytic hierarchy how this can be integrated into resource allocation, given a rough knowledge of the costs involved. A second, complementary approach places greatest redundancy on projects that fall into an R&D program and analyzes the impact on their priorities of wide changes in the uncertain parameters. The way to deal with this approach is to perform sensitivity analyses of project priorities for variations in the parameters.

XYZRI'S HIERARCHY OF R&D ALLOCATIONS

In designing a hierarchy, we wish to direct funds to the areas of research and development most in need and, at the same time, to roughly schedule the funds

cessful in its separate parts, will aggregate to a coherent system a quarter of a century hence?
3. How can XYZRI, given a qualitative selection of programs that will emerge from our analysis in response to the second question, allocate resources in a cost-effective manner so that the benefits of investment in technology made today accrue on schedule?

XYZRI's projections of the demand for electricity recognize that the bounds of uncertainty are larger than the demand for energy. This fact results largely from substitution effects and from potential technological developments that may electrify a larger portion of the heating and transportation aspects of American life. XYZRI projects a relatively high growth of demand—5.6 percent, bounded by high and low estimates of 4.1 percent and 6.5 percent, respectively. However, the costs of being wrong on the side of insufficient supply (including as they do political consequences of increased restriction and possibly centralized planning) are significantly greater than the costs of being wrong on the side of excess supply (including basically only excessive capital investment amortized until growth of demand catches up). A study by members of XYZRI concludes that the loss function justifies planning for perhaps more capacity than will be required.

There is less uncertainty about other facets of the demand for electricity. The geographic distribution of demand can be well constrained on demographic and mobility patterns. The magnitude of demand obviated by conservation efforts can also be bounded closely, largely on the basis of structural rigidities in the production processes of American industry and the limited possibilities for resource-conserving investment even where the adequate technologies are known.

More problematic are peak-load problems. They will be the more severe the more (1) "soft" energy sources supplant fossil fuels in a climate-dependent role; (2) transportation, including public transit, turns to electricity for power; and (3) pricing policies fail to grant enough encouragement to cause staggered work schedules, conservation measures, and acquisition of sufficient storage capacity in both utilities and private hands. Estimation of a loss function about peak loading suggests that in this case it is very much worse to underestimate the demand for storage than to overestimate it. Underestimation places excessive demands on generating capacity, reduces the efficiency of the overall electric power system, and threatens extensive time-related bottlenecks, such as brown-outs. Excess storage capacity, on the other hand, means at worst that petroleum will rarely have to be used as an expensive fuel to cover peaks. Further, there are likely to be useful spinoffs from large-scale storage advances supported by XYZRI to small-scale applications such as in private transportation.

5 XYZ RESEARCH INSTITUTE:
Planning Resource Allocation under Uncertainty

Planning for research and development is basically a process of prescribing commitments to particular technologies in the future by making resource allocations now. It intrinsically involves tradeoffs among "goods" or "virtues." It also confronts risks induced by a variety of uncertainties. R&D planning is especially problematic because the time horizon is longer than in most corporate planning of the public and private sectors, and the uncertainties are consequently that much greater.

To a technologist "risk" is to be minimized. To a planner "risk" is not directly manipulable. Risk is inherent in every course of action—the problem is to choose the right risks. This is true also of uncertainty: in planning we cannot remove it; instead we narrow its bounds and accurately estimate them. We thus think of placing estimates of cost on ranges of plausible but relatively undesirable outcomes around the preferred outcome. Loss functions are central to assessing the expected value of outcomes under uncertainties.

Three broad questions are raised in this application:

1. How can the XYZ Research Institute (XYZRI) plan for research and development under a variety of uncertainties?
2. How can XYZRI design and implement an R&D program that, if suc-

This chapter was prepared by T.L. Saaty and J.P. Bennett, 1977.

REFERENCES

Denison, E.F. 1974. *Accounting for United States Economic Growth, 1929-1969.* Washington, D.C.: Brookings Institution.

Grilliches, Z. 1960. "Hybrid Corn and the Economics of Innovation." *Science* 29 (July):275-80.

Jones, G. 1971. *The Role of Science and Technology in Developing Countries.* Oxford: Oxford University Press.

Kimenta, J. 1967. "Economic Theory and Transfer of Technology," In D.L. Spencer and A. Woroniak, eds., *The Transfer of Technology to Developing Countries.* New York: Praeger.

Mansfield, E.I. 1961. "Technical Change and the Rate of Imitation." *Econometrika* 29 (October):741-66.

Organization for Economic Cooperation and Development (OECD). 1972. *Analytical Methods in Government Science Policy.* Paris.

Rogers, E.M. 1962. *The Diffusion of Innovations.* New York: Free Press.

Rosenberg, N. 1972. *Technological Change and Economic Growth.* New York: Harper & Row.

Saaty, T.L., and L.G. Vargas, 1979. "Estimating Technological Coefficients by the Analytic Hierarchy Process." *Socioeconomic Planning Sciences* 13:333-36.

Schumacher, E.F. 1975. *Small Is Beautiful.* New York: Harper & Row.

Solo, R.A., and E.M. Rogers, eds. 1971. *Inducing Technological Change for Economic Growth and Development.* East Lansing: Michigan State University Press.

Solow, R.M. 1957. "Technical Change and the Aggregate Production Function." *Review of Economics and Statistics* 39 (August):312-20.

Spencer, D.L., and A. Woroniak, eds. 1967. *The Transfer of Technology to Developing Countries.* New York: Praeger.

Vernon, R. 1966. "International Investment and International Trade in the Product Life Cycle." *Quarterly Journal of Economics* 80 (May):190-207.

COSTS HIERARCHY

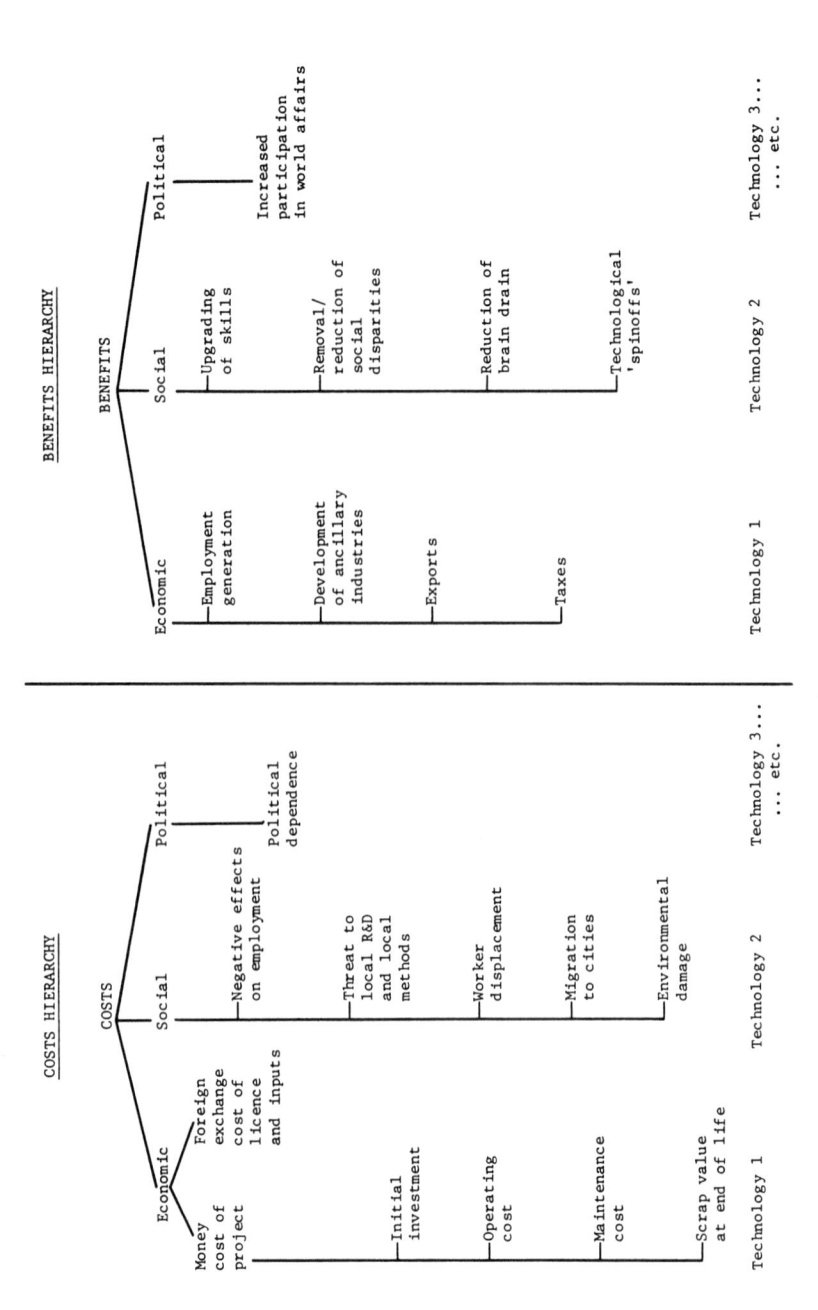

- Economic
  - Money cost of project
  - Foreign exchange cost of licence and inputs
  - Initial investment
  - Operating cost
  - Maintenance cost
  - Scrap value at end of life
- Social
  - Negative effects on employment
  - Threat to local R&D and local methods
  - Worker displacement
  - Migration to cities
  - Environmental damage
- Political
  - Political dependence

Technology 1   Technology 2   Technology 3... ... etc.

BENEFITS HIERARCHY

- Economic
  - Employment generation
  - Development of ancillary industries
  - Exports
  - Taxes
- Social
  - Upgrading of skills
  - Removal/reduction of social disparities
  - Reduction of brain drain
  - Technological 'spinoffs'
- Political
  - Increased participation in world affairs

Technology 1   Technology 2   Technology 3... ... etc.

Figure 4.4. Detailed Cost/Benefit Analysis Using the AHP

weight it obtains with respect to ease of adaptability to a rural economy and the absence of any conceivable second-order consequences associated with this technology.

Despite the high need for satellite television for rural education, it is perceived by the analyst to be a potentially dysfunctional technology in the sense of distracting the masses rather than really educating them. Similarly the high need score for oil exploration is counterbalanced by problems in adapting the technology to local situations, obsolescence risk, and possible second-order consequences like pollution of the coastal area. Nuclear energy gains on account of its relatively easy adaptability and the fact that the technology is a rather stable one less prone to obsolescence.

It is clear from this example that the AHP permits quantification of the relative priorities of various technological options. The rankings obtained here reflect the values, opinions, and judgments of a particular rater. But if the prioritization is done in a group setting, then debate can be generated and judgments made on the basis of consensus. The purpose of the example is to illustrate the application of the AHP rather than to suggest any particular prioritization of technologies for any particular LDC.

After the potentially most useful or desirable technologies are identified on the basis of the four key criteria, conventional approaches such as cost/benefit analysis can then be used to select from among the short-listed candidate technologies.

Figure 4.4 suggests a cost/benefit approach using the AHP. We construct separate cost and benefit hierarchies and use the final cost and benefit weights to derive cost/benefit ratios for the technologies under consideration. Thus we obtain an ordering of the technologies in terms of their cost/benefit ratios.

COMMENTS

Hierarchical analysis can be applied at many levels of policy making—global, national, sectoral, or specific technological levels. The process can be iterated, thereby changing the structure of the hierarchies or the judgments inputted into the pairwise comparison matrices. The need to deal with the explicit and implicit relationships between the levels of the hierarchy and the clusters at any particular level in a combinatorial fashion can stimulate inquiry along many focused channels and avoid sidetracking into irrelevant issues.

In the next chapter the AHP is used to select projects in research and development areas. This application involves the allocation of resources to different technologies to generate electric power. It is also a good example of how priorities are used to discount the future to ensure continuity of operations in an organization.

Solar energy technology is believed by the analyst to be most easily adaptable, followed by rural education through satellite television, and then by flood control. Nuclear energy, being more automated, scores higher on adaptability, whereas the need for trained and skilled personnel is higher for both coal gasification and oil exploration technologies, which makes them more difficult to adapt.

With respect to no risk of obsolescence, the relative standing of the candidate technologies is as follows:

	SOL	CG	RUR	FC	OIL	COMP	NUCL
Weight:	.155	.030	.135	.357	.058	.097	.168

C.I. = 0.20

Finally, the criterion of *no undesirable second-order consequences* led to the following prioritization:

	SOL	CG	RUR	FC	OIL	COMP	NUCL
Weight:	.457	.043	.172	.167	.043	.099	.018

C.I. = 0.11

The weights obtained for each technology under each criterion are then weighted by the criteria weights and summed to get the overall technology weights:

Solar energy: 0.259;
Coal gasification: 0.039;
Rural education: 0.243;
Flood control: 0.211;
Oil exploration: 0.109;
Computerized information bank: 0.062;
Nuclear energy: 0.077.

The overall weighted priorities suggest that solar energy should receive maximum emphasis, followed by satellite television, flood control, oil exploration, nuclear energy, computerized information bank, and coal gasification, in that order. The high weight for solar energy is principally due to the high

2. Coal gasification plants (CG) to utilize an abundantly available national mineral resource;
3. Satellite television for extending primary and secondary education to the rural areas (RUR);
4. Flood control techniques (FC) to avoid massive national losses due to floods;
5. Offshore oil exploration (OIL) to minimize dependence on foreign oil;
6. A computerized national information bank (COMP) to facilitate national- and state-level planning;
7. Nuclear energy (NUCL) for electricity generation.

These technologies are now compared to each other with respect to each of the assessment criteria. Application of the pairwise comparison procedure yields the following weights with regard to *need* for the different candidate technologies:

	SOL	CG	RUR	FC	OIL	COMP	NUCL
Weight:	.112	.027	.341	.179	.258	.058	.024

C.I. = 0.18

In the opinion of the analyst who provided the judgments in this matrix, rural education (a long-term, low-risk project) and oil exploration (a short-to-medium-term, high-risk project) are the major national needs. Flood control and solar energy are believed to be the next most important technologies from the point of view of addressing national needs most directly. The consistency index of 0.18 is rather high, even for a 7 × 7 judgment matrix. To some extent this happens because of the broad types of comparison involved. In real life, one would be more specific by clustering technologies so that they are more comparable.

Next, with respect to *ease of adaptability*, the relative standing of the candidate technologies is as follows:

	SOL	CG	RUR	FC	OIL	COMP	NUCL
Weight:	.381	.054	.263	.158	.034	.021	.090

C.I. = 0.13

TECHNOLOGICAL CHOICE IN LESS DEVELOPED COUNTRIES 77

Modern communications technologies are high technologies characterized by high obsolescence risk. LDC concern with obsolescence risk is reflected by the high weight attached to that factor in this sector. Criteria weights in the remaining sectors are obtained similarly.

Transportation and Distribution

	N	A	R	S	Weight
N	1	1/3	1/5	1	0.096
A	3	1	1/3	3	0.249
R	5	3	1	5	0.558
S	1	1/3	1/5	1	0.096

C.I. = 0.020

R&D and Institution Building

	N	A	R	S	Weight
N	1	5	1	3	0.397
A	1/5	1	1/5	1	0.090
R	1	5	1	3	0.397
S	1/3	1	1/3	1	0.116

C.I. = 0.010

Now these sectorwise criteria weights are adjusted for the sector priorities to get the overall criteria weights for the particular LDC:

Need: 0.302;
Ease of adaptability: 0.314;
No risk of obsolescence: 0.230;
No undersirable second-order consequences: 0.154.

Assessment of Candidate Technologies

It is now possible to apply these overall weights to candidate technologies. Let us assume that this LDC is considering inducting the following seven candidate technologies (all "mass" technologies, some of which have direct and potential impacts in many sectors):

1. Solar energy development (SOL) for rural power and irrigation;

Industry

	N	A	R	S	Weight
N	1	1/3	1	1/3	0.132
A	3	1	3	1	0.395
R	1	1/3	1	1	0.173
S	3	1	1	1	0.300

C.I. = 0.050

The high weight assigned to adaptability and second-order consequences is self-explanatory in this sector. Whereas in agriculture the problem of adaptability may be related to the ability or willingness to adapt, in manufacturing there may be infrastructural barriers to adaptation, such as lack of skilled manpower, local suppliers of spare parts, repair facilities, and the like. The size of the market might dictate scaled-down plants, which could create operating problems.

Education and Training

	N	A	R	S	Weight
N	1	5	9	3	0.587
A	1/5	1	5	1	0.172
R	1/9	1/5	1	1/5	0.044
S	1/3	1	5	1	0.196

C.I. = 0.033

The need for the particular type of educational technology is important, but education that raises levels of aspiration can be dysfunctional if there are no simultaneous increases in available opportunities. Hence a high score is obtained on undesirable consequences of rapid education.

Communications

	N	A	R	S	Weight
N	1	5	1/5	1	0.169
A	1/5	1	1/7	1	0.047
R	5	7	1	5	0.615
S	1	1	1/5	1	0.169

C.I. = 0.070

This matrix emphasizes that in the agricultural sector, the prime consideration for introducing an imported technology is adaptability. Risk of obsolescence and undesirable second-order consequences play relatively less important roles. These judgments, of course, are those of a particular analyst who provided the pairwise ratings shown in the matrix. Typically the entries of the matrix would be obtained after considerable debate and ultimate convergence by consensus among the members concerned.

Mining and Extractive Industries

	N	A	R	S	Weight
N	1	3	3	1	0.395
A	1/3	1	1	1/3	0.132
R	1/3	1	1	1	0.173
S	1	3	1	1	0.300

C.I. = 0.052

In this sector, in contrast to agriculture, need for the particular technology is felt to be the dominant criterion. "No undesirable second-order consequences" ranks second. Adaptability and risk of obsolescence are relatively less important, presumably owing to the state of development of this sector in the particular LDC.

Health

	N	A	R	S	Weight
N	1	1	3	7	0.402
A	1	1	3	7	0.402
R	1/3	1/3	1	3	0.143
S	1/7	1/7	1/3	1	0.217

C.I. = 0.002

These final priorities are again easy to interpret. The health needs of LDCs are widely different from those of the more advanced nations. Hence need and adaptability dominate here.

AN EXAMPLE: TECHNOLOGY TRANSFER USING THE AHP

In this example, which illustrates the approach described above, the sectoral priorities are assumed to be determined exogenously and given. In the context of a particular LDC, let us say the following are the sector priority weights:

Agriculture:	0.25;
Mining and extractive industries:	0.08;
Health:	0.12;
Industry:	0.15;
Education and training:	0.12;
Communications:	0.15;
Transportation and distribution:	0.06;
Research and development:	0.07.

Prioritizing the Assessment Criteria within Sectors

As already discussed, the assessment criteria do not play the same role in all the sectors. They are prioritized within each sector in the following pairwise comparison matrices:

Agriculture

	Need (N)	Ease of Adapt-ability (A)	No Risk of Obsoles-cence (R)	No Undesirable Second-Order Consequences (S)	Weight
Need (N)	1	1/3	7	5	0.292
Ease of Adapt-ability (A)	3	1	9	7	0.587
No Risk of Obso-lescence (R)	1/7	1/9	1	1	0.056
No Undesirable Second-Order Consequences (S)	1/5	1/7	1	1	0.065

Consistency Index (C.I.) = 0.031

CHOICE OF TECHNOLOGY

SECTOR PRIORITIES: S1, S2, S3, S4, S5, S6, S7

ASSESSMENT CRITERIA: CR1, CR2, CR3, CR4

CANDIDATE TECHNOLOGIES: T1, T2, T3, T4, T5, T6, T7

SECTORS

S1 = Agriculture
S2 = Mining and Extractive Industries
S3 = Manufacturing
S4 = Health and Welfare
S5 = Education and training
S6 = Transportation and distribution
S7 = Research and development and Institution building

ASSESSMENT CRITERIA

CR1 = Need
CR2 = Adaptability
CR3 = No risk of obsolescence
CR4 = No undesirable second order consequences

CANDIDATE TECHNOLOGIES (EXAMPLES)

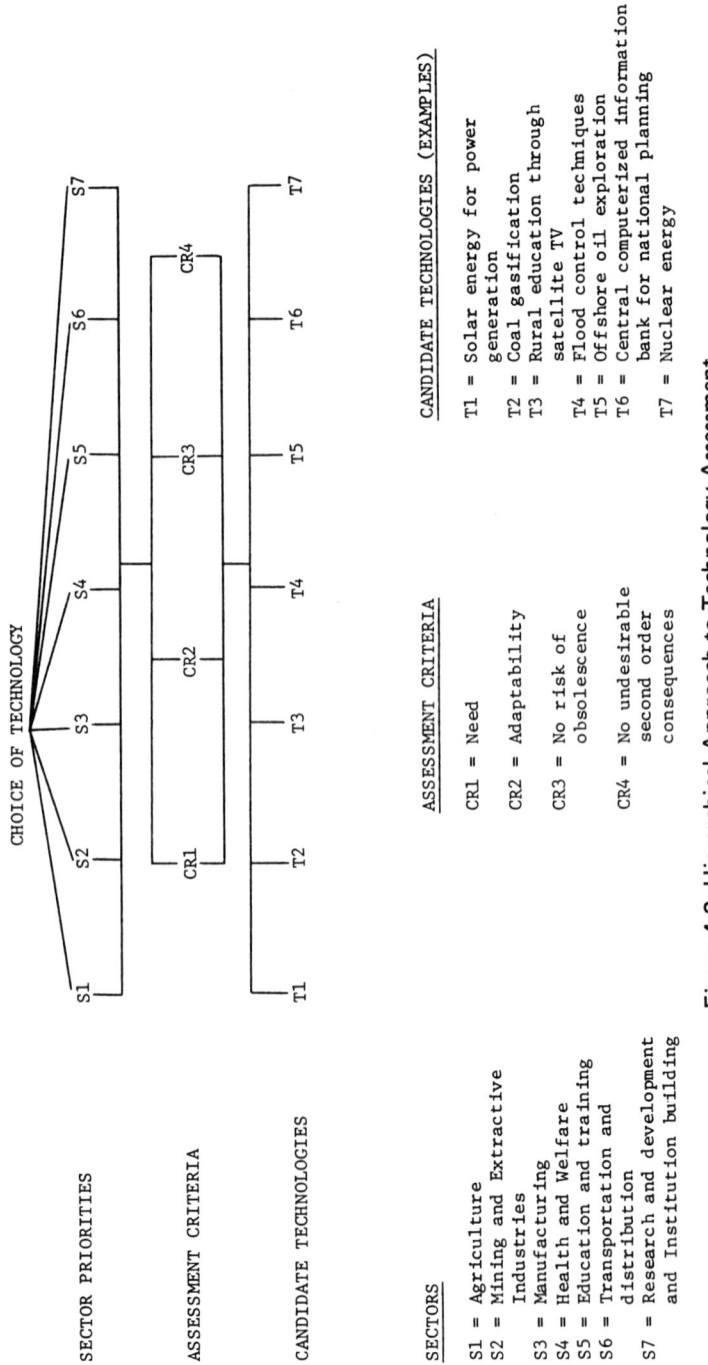

T1 = Solar energy for power generation
T2 = Coal gasification
T3 = Rural education through satellite TV
T4 = Flood control techniques
T5 = Offshore oil exploration
T6 = Central computerized information bank for national planning
T7 = Nuclear energy

Figure 4.3. Hierarchical Approach to Technology Assessment

INTERNAL/EXTERNAL CONSTRAINTS

PLANNING TIME FRAME

FACTORS INFLUENCING IMPORTANCE OF SECTORS

SECTOR PRIORITIES

INTERNAL/EXTERNAL CONSTRAINTS

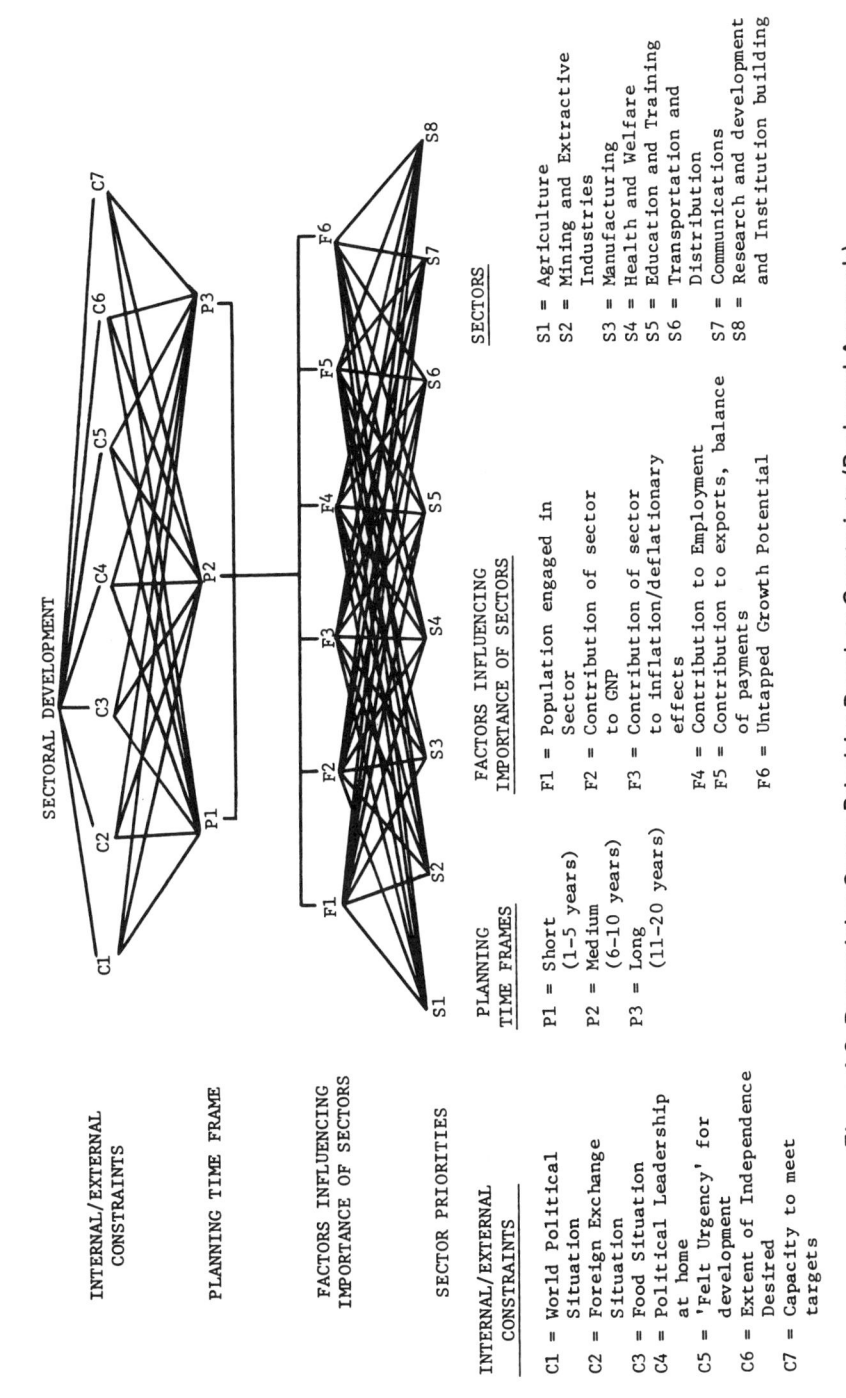

C1 = World Political Situation
C2 = Foreign Exchange Situation
C3 = Food Situation
C4 = Political Leadership at home
C5 = 'Felt Urgency' for development
C6 = Extent of Independence Desired
C7 = Capacity to meet targets

PLANNING TIME FRAMES

P1 = Short (1-5 years)
P2 = Medium (6-10 years)
P3 = Long (11-20 years)

FACTORS INFLUENCING IMPORTANCE OF SECTORS

F1 = Population engaged in Sector
F2 = Contribution of sector to GNP
F3 = Contribution of sector to inflation/deflationary effects
F4 = Contribution to Employment
F5 = Contribution to exports, balance of payments
F6 = Untapped Growth Potential

SECTORS

S1 = Agriculture
S2 = Mining and Extractive Industries
S3 = Manufacturing
S4 = Health and Welfare
S5 = Education and Training
S6 = Transportation and Distribution
S7 = Communications
S8 = Research and development and Institution building

Figure 4.2. Determining Sector Priorities Based on Constraints (Backward Approach)

the negative effects of certain types of technology. Impact analysis must be an integral part of any attempt to evaluate technologies for importation.

In general the needs for technology are influenced by sectoral priorities. Also, each of the preliminary assessment criteria listed above will be emphasized differently in the various economic sectors. For example, adaptability might be stressed in agriculture, which is a more traditional sector than manufacturing in most LDCs, whereas obsolescence risk might be underscored in manufacturing (see Saaty and Vargas, 1979).

Sectoral priorities may be taken as "given" if they are based on planning exercises done outside the context of technology assessment, which is likely to be the case in many LDCs. However, the sectoral priorities themselves can be hierarchically determined. Two approaches are possible: a forward approach that starts with a level of national objectives and works down toward the desired sectoral priorities, and a backward approach that begins with constraints in both the internal and external environment of the LDC and converges on the feasible sectoral priorities, given the constraints. (A more detailed explanation of the two approaches is given in chapter 6 of this book.) Figure 4.2 illustrates the backward approach.

Returning to the problem of technology assessment (figure 4.3), we then have sector priorities at level 1, assessment criteria at level 2, and candidate technologies at level 3. Two assumptions are made in this particular construction of the hierarchy. First, technologies may or may not be sector-specific; some can be of general applicability or may impact across many or all of the sectors—for example, transportation or communication technologies. Second, the importance of the assessment criteria varies across sectors, as mentioned earlier. Hence we prioritize the criteria by sector and weight the priorities of the criteria by sector weights to generate composite weighted criteria that can be applied uniformly to candidate technologies, after the technologies have been prioritized by criteria. A centralized technology evaluation organization would find this approach attractive from an administrative point of view and in the preparation of suitable guidelines.

To generate the criteria weights by sector, we pose, as before, a series of questions of the following type: For agricultural technologies (or manufacturing technologies, and so on), what is the relative importance of "need," "adaptability," "freedom from obsolescence risk," and "no undesirable second-order consequences"? This procedure entails pairwise comparison of each of the criteria with the others within a given sector.

It is thus possible to do a preliminary screening of many candidate technologies on the basis of the four key criteria and the sector weights of the country. This would result in a subject of the original list of candidate technologies that can be taken up for more detailed analysis.

in this way, we apply the weights of actor influence to these objectives to obtain a set of weighted objectives. The process is continued by comparing the scenarios with respect to their relative contribution to the achievement of each objective and by weighting the scenario priorities by the weighted objectives. This results in an index of the overall likelihood or importance of each scenario.

For the purpose of illustration, we have limited the hierarchy to only three levels. The richness of the hierarchy can be extended as desired by adding more levels and more elements within each level. For instance, a level of actor policies could be interposed between the objectives and scenarios, which might relate to taxation, imports and exports, degree of foreign ownership of capital encouraged, preferential treatments accorded to countries as sources of supply of goods and technologies, and so on.

Let us now see how this approach can be used to enable planners of an LDC to make technological choices. A survey of the literature suggests that the following criteria are paramount in technology transfer:

1. *Need:* Technology has to be tailored to the needs of the country. Need can be defined in terms of *suitability* and *urgency*. A technology might be considered suitable if it is proven to meet similar needs in other contexts. Needs will be influenced by overall national sectoral priorities.

2. *Adaptability:* It must be possible to adapt the technology to the local environment. Two considerations determining adaptability are the *ability* and the *willingness* to adapt. The lack of a sufficient science and technology base in terms of the availability of skilled manpower, maintenance facilities, materials in needed quantity and quality, presence of facilitating institutions and change agents, and the like, affects the ability to adapt. The willingness to adapt depends on the strength of custom, tradition, power relationships within the society, and similar social, cultural, and political considerations.

3. *Relative freedom from the risk of obsolescence:* In this chapter our attention is focused on what may be termed "mass" technologies – technologies whose interface with the eventual user is close and extensive. Many of these technologies are certain to involve substantial investment. In the context of an LDC, the technology transferred must be capable of being supported throughout its useful life; that is, some insulation from the risk of obsolescence must be available. The most modern technology available may be difficult to adapt, whereas an obsolete technology may at a later date leave the LDC without adequate support. Thus a careful tradeoff has to be made as to the nature of the technology to acquire.

4. *No undesirable second-order consequences:* If the LDCs have any advantage as latecomers in the process of technological development, it is the opportunity to profit from the lessons learned by the advanced countries as to

INTERNATIONAL TRANSFERS OF TECHNOLOGY

ACTORS A1 A2 A3 A4 A5 A6 A7

ACTOR OBJECTIVES O1 O2 O3 O4 O5 O6 O7 O8 O9 O10

SCENARIOS S1 S2 S3

ACTORS

- A1 = Governments of the developed countries
- A2 = LDC governments
- A3 = UN agencies (UNDP, UNCTAD, etc.)
- A4 = USSR and Eastern Bloc Nations
- A5 = Multinational Corporations
- A6 = Small and big businesses in the LDCs
- A7 = Labor unions

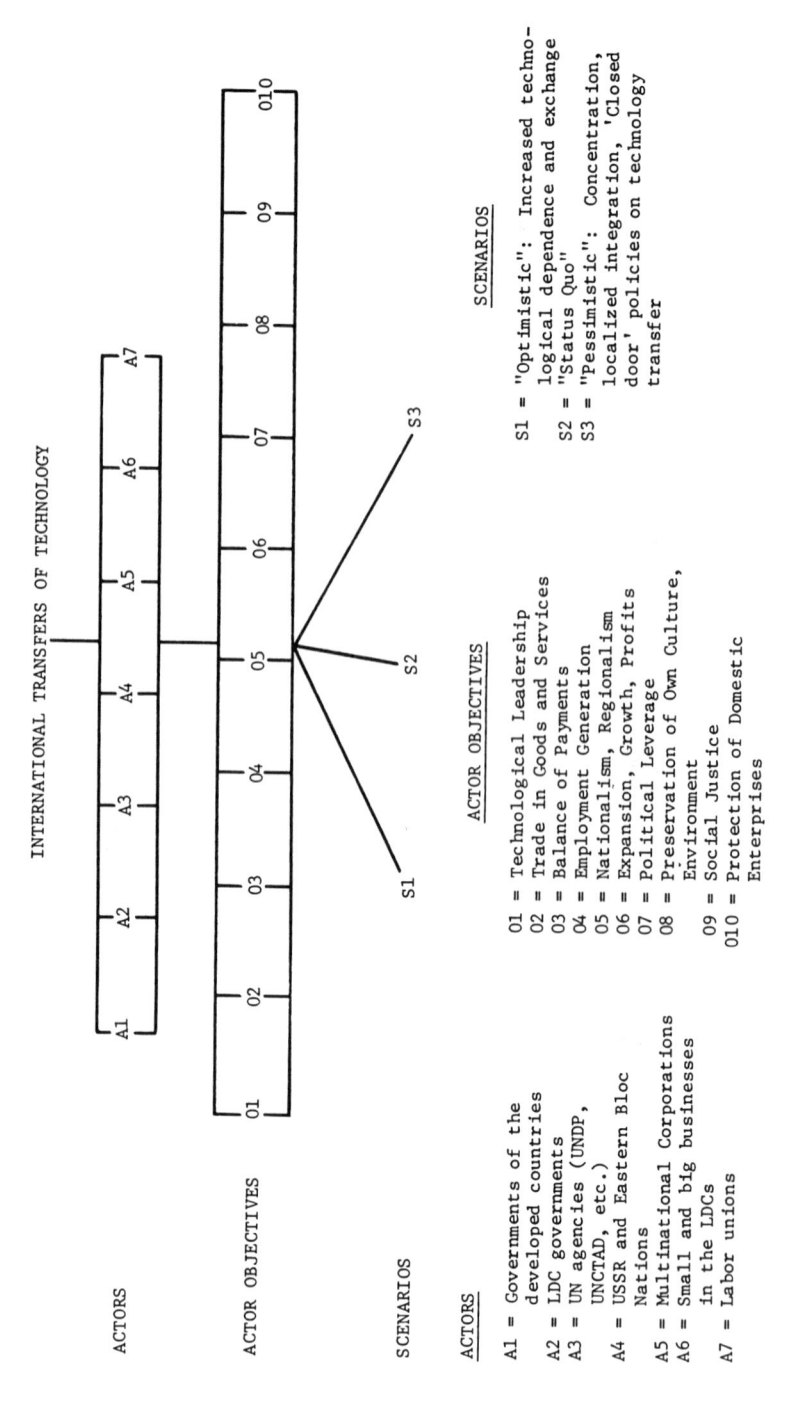

ACTOR OBJECTIVES

- O1 = Technological Leadership
- O2 = Trade in Goods and Services
- O3 = Balance of Payments
- O4 = Employment Generation
- O5 = Nationalism, Regionalism
- O6 = Expansion, Growth, Profits
- O7 = Political Leverage
- O8 = Preservation of Own Culture, Environment
- O9 = Social Justice
- O10 = Protection of Domestic Enterprises

SCENARIOS

- S1 = "Optimistic": Increased technological dependence and exchange
- S2 = "Status Quo"
- S3 = "Pessimistic": Concentration, localized integration, 'Closed door' policies on technology transfer

Figure 4.1. Future Course of Technology Transfers to LDCs

approach to technological assessment, choice, and transfer and analyze its possible impacts on the sectors of the economy of LDCs. After the potentially most useful technologies are identified, a benefit/cost framework is developed to also consider nontechnological factors that may influence economic development.

APPLICATIONS TO TECHNOLOGY TRANSFER

In dealing with the problem of technology transfer, the AHP can be applied at several levels. At a global level, one might be interested in predicting the future course of technology transfers to the LDCs in general terms. A hierarchical representation of this problem is depicted in figure 4.1. At the first level of the hierarchy, we list the following *actors* who might be expected to play some role in determining the future course of technology transfers: the governments of the developed nations; the governments of the LDCs; "neutral" third parties such as the many United Nations organizations involved in technology transfer issues; the USSR and Eastern bloc nations; multinational corporations; the private sector, represented by big and small businesses; and labor unions. Each actor pursues a set of objectives vis-à-vis technology transfer — for example, technological leadership, trade, balance of payments, employment generation, economic expansion, and so on. These objectives, spelled out in greater detail in figure 4.1, constitute the second level of the hierarchy. At the third level we indicate the future scenarios: an optimistic scenario that envisages increased flow of technology to the LDCs and among world nations in general, a scenario that is merely the extension of the status quo into the future, and a pessimistic scenario that foresees substantial reduction in the overall volume of trade in technology. Increased flow of technology could occur if, for instance, the much debated code of conduct for technology transfer and the international economic order should become realities. The pulls and hauls of the different actors and the strength with which they pursue current policies could result in indefinite extension of the status quo. Or the continued impasse over technology transfer issues could deflect the LDCs toward policies of self-reliance and regional cooperation, thereby reducing the flow of technology from the advanced to the less developed countries.

To estimate the likelihood of the three scenarios, we first make a pairwise comparison of the relative influence of the different actors, which yields a set of weights for this factor. Next the objectives of each actor are compared in pairwise fashion in terms of their importance to the concerned actor. We pose questions such as: "How important is objective O1 relative to objective O2, O3, and so on, for actor A1?" Having prioritized the objectives of each actor

from a number of different perspectives, with contributions from economists, sociologists, anthropologists, political scientists, and technical professionals. Some are concerned with the "how to" of technology transfer; that is, with the mechanisms and methods of transfer. Some describe the process of technology transfer and diffusion. Yet others critically assess the consequences of transferring advanced technology to less developed countries and appear to be voicing concern with a rather fundamental question: the "why" of technology transfer. These varied disciplinary approaches indicate the complexity of factors impinging on technological choice in the LDCs.

The field is rich in conceptualizations and historical accounts of the ways in which technology has been transferred among today's advanced countries. With respect to theories, one can mention the notion of the "technology gap" (Kimenta, 1967); the product life cycle hypothesis (Vernon, 1966); and the depiction of the diffusion process as a logistic or S-shaped curve (Rogers, 1962), which has stood empirical validation in economic studies (Grilliches, 1960; Mansfield, 1961). These theories have yet to be integrated into an overall framework that can offer some guidance to planners involved in technology transfer. All are vulnerable to the attack of being rather limited in scope. A recent body of literature views technology transfer as a bargaining process between economically unmatched participants in an imperfect market. Prescriptions for the LDCs range from moving toward an alternative model of development that emphasizes the small and the human (Schumacher, 1975) to a more "pragmatic" emphasis on developing integrated science and technology policies based on needs and goals, building up local research and development capabilities to better assimilate imported technologies as well as develop indigenous ones, and exploring avenues for regional economic and technological cooperation with other LDCs.

Two dominant and somewhat opposed themes emerge from a survey of the literature on international transfers of technology to the LDCs. One regards technology transfer as essentially a process of imitation, while the other considers technological change as predicated on sociocultural change. It asserts that unless a revolution occurs whereby social attitudes and values are rapidly transformed, externally introduced technologies cannot operate optimally in the social environment of the LDCs. It is possible to take a balanced approach, one that acknowledges the importance of imitation as well as the sociocultural barriers to it but allows that both can proceed simultaneously instead of sequentially in view of their obvious interdependence.

Most discussions of technology transfer have paid little attention to methodologies for the assessment of technology. The available ones (OECD, 1972) do not appear well suited to the needs of LDCs because most have as their aim the prediction of technological futures. In this chapter we present an integrated

4 TECHNOLOGICAL CHOICE IN LESS DEVELOPED COUNTRIES

It is widely held that the economic situation of less developed countries (LDCs) can be greatly improved by conscious and judicious application of science and technology to the solution of their many problems. This belief is well supported by evidence attributing the rapid economic growth achieved by industrially advanced countries to the technology factor (Solow, 1957; Denison, 1974). Early economic theorists noted that the level of savings and investment in the LDCs was low. They recommended transfusion of capital to spur investment and capital formation; but beginning with the late fifties the emphasis shifted to transfusion of technology rather than capital. However, the collective experience of the LDCs with imported technology over the past three decades has been far from encouraging, as is apparent from the growing discontent voiced by the "Group of 77."

A substantial literature attempts to grapple with the problem of transferring technology effectively to the LDCs (for example, Spencer and Woroniak, 1967; Jones, 1971; Rosenberg, 1972; Solo and Rogers, 1971). This literature represents a significant part of the scholarly output in the broader area of technology transfer and technological innovation. We make no attempt here to survey the literature on technology transfer in general, or even international technology transfer in particular, but will merely note that the problem has been approached

This chapter was written by V. Ramanujam and T.L. Saaty; previously published in *Technological Forecasting and Social Change* 19 (1981):81-98.

cludes studies, infrastructural projects, and commercial agricultural projects, stands at about KD 1.8 billion. The first plan, which covers the period to 1980, has a cost of KD 780 million.

The ADAR study (see Appendix A for full reference) was instrumental in the development of the agricultural program in the following aspects:

a. The econometric model developed by the study was the basis of the macroeconomic analysis that offered the framework within which the program was conceived.
b. The projections of agricultural commodities production and consumption offered a base line from which new projections, based on more recent information, were developed.
c. The transportation component of the agricultural program was entirely based on the ADAR study. The same methodology used in the study was used to forecast physical flows of commodities. Many of the projects identified by the study were included in the program. Minor adjustment, of specifications and/or costs, had, of course, to be made. The total cost of the transportation component of the program is estimated at KD 474 million, of which the first phase is KD 150 million.

The World Bank is investing in rail and in the improvement of the facilities of Port Sudan. Following the priorities of the study, the Saudi government is financing road and communication projects and electronic equipment for airports. A contract has been signed jointly by the Sudan and Egypt with a French firm to build the Jonglei Canal (160 miles long) to shore up the giant swamp at Sudd.

The Kuwait Fund is financing high-priority projects in the railway and in roads, such as connections between Sennar and Ed Damazine, Nyala and Zalingei, and rehabilitation and maintenance of the railway. The Kuwait Fund has also said that the study has helped them avoid supporting projects of low priority.

COMMENTS

The basic idea behind this study is the concept of planning by the backward process, presented in more detail in chapter 6. This process starts by identifying the possible futures (scenarios) of a system (for example, an economy or an organization) and ends by providing priorities for policies that could bring about the desired future. In the case of the Sudan, these policies were projects to be implemented to meet the demand for transportation.

The next chapter illustrates another situation where prioritization is important — the transfer of technology to less developed countries.

cent, 6 percent, and 7.3 percent GNP annual growth rates. (These figures give costs of projects and fleet except for trucks, buses, and air transport. They also do not include operating costs.) The corresponding total investment at 1974 price levels are 4,257.50 million dollars at the 6 percent GNP growth rate and 3,525 million dollars at the 4.3 percent GNP growth rate.

SOME MANAGEMENT STRATEGIES

Sudan transport has an interesting system of government corporations. For example, there is the Sudan Railway Corporation and the Sudan Airways Corporation. They are fairly autonomous; as the ministers tend to come and go with changes in administration, they sometimes find it difficult to control and maintain channels of communication with these groups, which are supposed to report to them. The management part of the study suggests, in some detail, setting up a technical office to assist the minister by acting as a coordinating body. Its primary functions would cover research, information planning, coordination, follow-up, and evaluation. Recommendations were also made concerning the internal organization of each corporation. The corporations have tended to become elitist, offering attractive career opportunities. But there is rivalry and lack of coordination among them. Both the technical office and the reorganization of the corporations are being implemented, and a consultant has been retained to assist in this process. We also felt it was essential to set up management information systems and have worked out the details of the kind of data base that should be maintained.

IMPLEMENTATION

Implementation of the Sudan Transport Study has been methodical and far reaching. It has enabled the Sudan to obtain funds for agriculture and transport from lenders and investors on a massive scale. Of course, not all investment in the Sudan is a direct consequence of this study, but much of it is. With regard to its influence on agriculture and associated transportation, the Arab Fund has noted:

> The ADAR Transportation Study was an important basis for the formulation of the Sudan's Basic Program for the Development of the Agriculture Sector. This program was developed by the Arab Fund, and a new entity "Arab Authority for Agricultural Investment Development" was created to take charge of its implementation. The capital of this Authority is KD [Kuwait Dinar = $3.40] 150 million, while the total cost of the program, which in-

THE SUDAN TRANSPORT STUDY   63

thing seemed to be needed: many rail lines would have to be double-tracked and ballasted, roads proliferated everywhere, and so on. The cost was so high that the Sudan would be committing its future for 100 years to pay for it, even if funds had been available, which they were not.

We went back to the 4.3 percent, the present growth rate, and found that most of the current facilities with the prevailing level of efficiency would be crammed to their limit. Obviously a compromise with a rational justification for growth had to be made somewhere between these two extremes. When we examined the 6 percent GNP growth rate, found feasible by the econometric analysis, it provided excellent guidelines for those projects that were found to be needed at 4.3 percent and remained invariant with high priority at 7.3 percent. These were mostly the projects we recommended for implementation.

SECTORAL INVESTMENT STRATEGIES

Policy variables were identified from the composite scenario and translated to exogenous variables of the econometric model (parameterized at different GNP growth rates) to obtain the investment share for the different sectors.

Total investment requirements to achieve the composite scenario projected growth of real GNP at 4.3 percent, 6 percent, and 7.3 percent per year are given in table 3.4. For example, at 7.3 percent they are estimated to be approximately 5,105 million dollars at 1974 price levels, or 7,647 million dollars at current price levels (considering inflation between 1974 and 1985). The latter figure represents approximately 10 percent of the GNP each year over the planning period 1972–1985. This will be divided among the major sectors as shown.

In terms of 1974 prices, the investments in transport are as follows: 655.80, 1,333.90 and 1,905.80 million dollars corresponding respectively at 4.3 per-

Table 3.4. Dollars (Millions), Current Prices

	4.3%	*6%*	*7.3%*
Transport	978.33	1,789.88	2,899.96
Agriculture	1,372.75	1,695.53	2,183.30
Industry	588.28	963.33	1,456.08
Services	1,307.35	1,194.58	1,107.20
Total	4,246.71	5,643.32	7,646.54

Table 3.3. Transportation Development Plan: Phase I (1974 Price Level in LS 000,000; 6% Growth Rate)

Projects	Distance (km.)	Priority	Class GNP Rates 4.3% L	4.3% H	6.0% L	6.0% H	7.3% L	7.3% H	Cost A	Cost B	Cost C	Recommended Class	Main Reason Flow	Main Reason Other	Committed Financing / in Progress	Cost Total	Cost Foreign Currency	Cost Local Currency
Rail																		
Port Sudan-Haiya	203	4.724	A	B	A	B	A	B	9.10	7.10	—	A	X			9.10	4.55	4.55
Haiya-Athara	271	3.455	B	B	B	B	A	B	12.20	9.50	—	B	X			9.50	6.30	3.20
Athara-Khartoum	313	8.443	B	B	B	B	A	B	14.10	11.00	—	B	X			11.00	7.30	3.70
El Rahad-Babanusa	363	1.005	B	B	B	B	B	B	—	12.70	—	B	X			12.70	8.50	4.20
Fleet (6% GNP)																10.90	40.90	—
Maintenance facilities																2.00	1.00	1.00
Road																		
Wad Medani-Gedaref	231	2.840	A	A	A	A	A	A	23.90	—	—	A	X		X	23.90	16.70	7.20
Gedaref-Kassala	218	0.872	A	A	A	A	A	A	14.20	—	—	A	X		X	14.20	9.90	4.30
Kassala-Haiya-Port Sudan	625	2.229	A	A	A	A	A	A	50.00	—	—	A	X		X	50.00	35.00	15.00
Wad Medani-Sennar	100	0.526	A	A	A	A	A	A	14.90	—	—	A	X		X	14.90	10.40	4.50
Sennar-Kosti	110	0.345	A	A	A	A	A	A	7.20	—	—	A	X		X	7.20	5.00	2.20
Sennar-Es Suki	47	0.546	A	A	A	A	A	A	7.00	—	—	A	X			7.00	4.90	2.10
Ed Dubeibat-Kadugli	137	1.253	C	C	C	C	B	C	—	12.30	8.80	B	X		X	12.30	7.40	4.90
Kadugli-Talodi	100	0.266	—	—	B	C	B	—	—	6.60	—	—						
Nyala-Kass-Zalingei	210	0.951	C	C	B	C	B	—	—	11.30	7.40	B	X	High-cost alternative provided		11.30	6.80	4.50
Jebel Al Aulia-Kostia	300	1.567	B	B	B	B	A	B	44.70	29.70	—	—	X	Together with alternate, high priority				
Juba-Nimuli	190	0.329	C	C	C	C	B	C	—	8.70	5.30	C	X			5.30	1.60	3.70
Juba-Amadi-Rumbek-Wau	725	0.494	C	C	C	C	C	C	—	—	20.30	C	X					
Fleet																20.80	20.80	

Note: This table is the first of nine; three in each phase.

aThe priority rating of this project is based mostly on potential rather than present development. In view of its high cost relative to other road projects, it has been omitted. It is recommended that it be given urgent consideration in the following planning period.

for the impact of the regions. Now the projects, the fourth level of the hierarchy, were compared pairwise in twelve matrices according to their impact on the regions to which they physically belonged. A project may belong to several regions, and this had to be considered. The resulting matrix of eigenvectors was again weighted by the vector of regional weights to obtain a measure of the overall impact of each project on the future.

The priorities of the projects could have been judged separately according to economic, social, and political impacts. However, these attributes were considered jointly in the judgment debate. A number of refinements of the approach along these lines are possible for future revisions of the plan. The results of prioritization showed not only the relative importance of the regions (see table 3.2) for possible investment purposes, but also those of the projects with respect to which of the three phases of implementation they should belong: the first phase—to remove bottlenecks; the second phase—to open up the agricultural areas and ship goods to the outside world; and the third phase—to encourage balanced regional growth and transport between regions whose contribution to the composite scenario is not as visibly urgent as those of other regions and, hence, will probably receive less of the overall investment.

Table 3.3 provides a sample of the recommendations for project implementation. A useful column, not included here, measures the cost/benefit of each project, which is obtained by dividing the priority of each project by its cost. The result is a ranking of the projects according to their overall feasibility and desirability. Implementation will proceed by focusing on the highest ranked projects constrained by the total amount of resources available for investment. Note that a project, such as a road, may be implemented with different grades of sophistication, and the cost of each of these was estimated. It was now far easier to see what needed to be implemented, what could simply be improved or upgraded, and what gaps had to be filled by new projects.

We found that at a 7.3 percent growth rate, which we assumed first, every-

Table 3.2. Priority Weights of Regions (Percent)

Bahr El Ghazal	Blue Nile	Darfur	East Equatoria	Gezira	Kassala	Khartoum	Kordofan	Northern	Red Sea	Upper Nile	West Equatoria
3.14	6.55	5.37	1.70	12.41	5.25	21.40	5.96	2.94	22.54	3.37	9.39

funding and continuous rechanneling of internal resources by the Sudanese government will provide sufficient resources to allow much of the regional economic development of scenario III. This scenario depicts a 1985 in which all regions are progressing at plausible accelerated rates. It uses population projections that foresee success in halting runaway migration to the urban areas through the government's regional development policies.

The composite scenario contemplates an annual rate of increase in GNP of 6 percent during the decade 1975–1985, nearly one-and-a-half times that of the reference projection. Total production per capita will rise. Internal consumption as a percentage of output will decline considerably, as one would expect under a policy that gives high priority to agricultural exports. By 1985, considerable industrial development will have taken place under this scenario. Food processing industries, as in scenario II, will be active. Most of the processing will be located in Khartoum and in other cities in the Northeast. Exports will greatly increase, but the regional emphasis will be maintained so that the Southeast no longer so dominates both the agricultural export sector and the economy at large.

The importance of transport in the projected development implies a large investment in capital goods for the rail system, such as rolling stock and communication equipment. An extensive portion of the main line will be doubletracked, and a new western spur line constructed. Much of the road system will be well developed, all-weather roads will connect the major cities, and the highway to Port Sudan will be in operation. Many feeder roads to the railway will be built throughout the agricultural areas. In general, it will be possible to reach the transport objectives of both scenarios II and III as far as the highway system is concerned. The Nile waterway will be improved and will be navigated by a modern fleet, backed up by excellent maintenance and docking facilities. The airway system will accommodate scenario II, with an operating air freight export service. Most air traffic and all international traffic will use the Khartoum airport. The secondary port at Suakin will be open and connected to the rail and road systems.

PRIORITIES OF REGIONS AND PROJECTS

The Sudan has twelve regions whose individual economic and geographic identity more or less justifies political division into distinct entities. The regions were compared pairwise in separate matrices according to their impact on each of the scenarios. They comprise the third hierarchy level. The resulting eigenvectors were used as the columns of a matrix that, when multiplied by the eigenvector of weights or priorities of the scenarios, gave a weighted average

THE SUDAN TRANSPORT STUDY 59

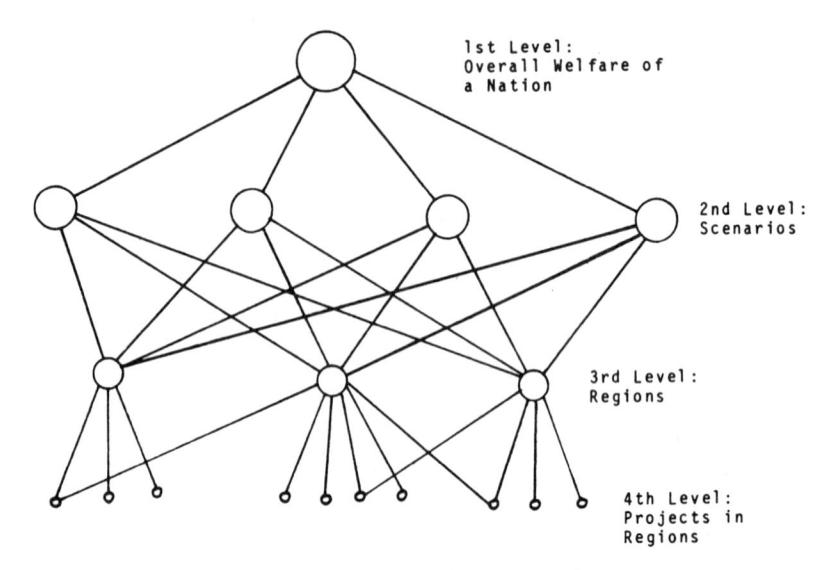

Figure 3.6. Hierarchy for Prioritizing Projects

1st Level: Overall Welfare of a Nation
2nd Level: Scenarios
3rd Level: Regions
4th Level: Projects in Regions

Table 3.1. Priorities of the Scenarios

		I	II	III	IV
Status quo	I	1	1/7	1/5	1/3
Agricultural export	II	7	1	5	5
Balanced regional growth	III	5	1/5	1	5
Arab-African regional expansion	IV	3	1/5	1/5	1

scenario II, the future given by far the highest priority, and is enlarged and balanced with certain elements from scenarios III and IV. This composition indicates the likelihood of a synergistic amplification of individual features.

THE COMPOSITE SCENARIO

The central theme of the composite scenario is agricultural production for export, which is the theme of scenario II with all that it implies for growth in the Northeast, the transport funnel to the outside world. But the massive initial

may be an attractive investment for surplus Arab funds presently in the world marketplace.

PRIORITIES OF THE SCENARIOS

Figure 3.5 shows a detailed elaboration of the first chart to illustrate how prioritization fits in the planning process. The hierarchy used to prioritize the projects in the regions is given in figure 3.6. The principle of hierarchic composition yields the impact of the projects on the overall welfare of the nation.

Pairwise comparison of the four scenarios according to their feasibility and desirability by 1985 (revision of the plan could separate these two criteria) gave rise to the matrix presented in table 3.1.

The priorities of the scenarios in the order they are listed are: 0.05, 0.61, 0.25, 0.09. As can be seen, scenario II dominates, with scenario III next in importance. Since the future is likely to be neither one nor the other, but rather a combination of these scenarios—with emphasis indicated by the priorities—this information was used to construct a composite scenario of the Sudan of 1985, described below. The composite scenario is the anticipated actual state of the future, as it is a proportionate mix of the forces that make up the four scenarios described above. The composite scenario takes the main thrust of

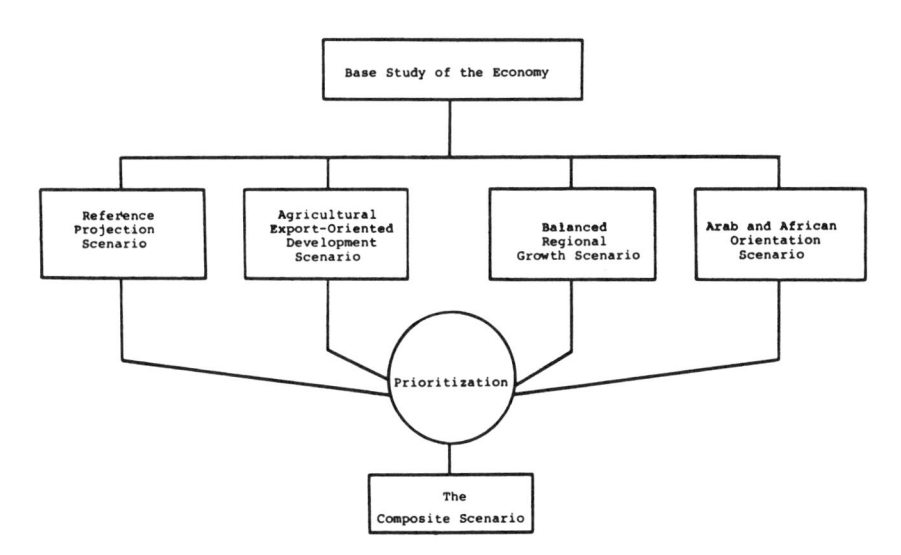

Figure 3.5. Formulation of a Desirable Future: The Scenarios

the interregional connections within the Sudan. This scenario depicts the greatest national economic gains over the decade 1975-1985.

Scenario III: Balanced Regional Growth

This scenario recognizes that the unequal development of the several regions of the Sudan is a source of some social strain and is a resource waste as well. Certain of the Sudan's less developed regions have tremendous potential for agriculture. This scenario presupposes calculated intervention into the processes of the reference projection of scenario I for the purpose of stimulating growth. This policy is primarily based on increased agricultural production and aimed at raising the level of economic activity in the poorly developed regions to a point where it is somewhat similar to that of the better developed regions. The policy also aims at self-sufficiency by 1985 in terms of internal consumption of food and clothing.

In this scenario, the major transportation emphasis is placed on the creation of a limited number of efficient corridors connecting the various regions. With its accent on regional balance, this scenario implies less rapid overall economic progress than does scenario II.

Scenario IV: Arab and African Orientation

This scenario is based on the Sudan's possible interest in serving as a link between the Arab and African worlds. This interest arises naturally since the Sudan has long been associated with both worlds in a cultural and a political sense. Sudan's geographic position makes its proposed interface role a natural one.

The scenario supports the transfer of Arab assistance and trade to African countries east, west, and south of the Sudan. It assumes that production and transport planning will attract Arab investment and promote economic transfer through the Sudan in its role as interface. More emphasis will be placed on other intermediate activities than in the other scenarios. In transport, the scenario presupposes the opening of new transport links to Egypt and other neighbors. Consequently, it entails by far the most ambitious transport plan of any scenario.

This is perhaps the boldest of the scenarios in that it proposes very large initial investments, generated externally for payoffs, some of which are social and political rather than economic and some of which depend on new markets whose existence may be speculative. It contains the idea that the Sudan

1985. New possibilities such as industrialization or a service-oriented economy, which do not seem feasible at this time, may be incorporated in a revision. All the scenarios are based, in part, on information derived from the agricultural survey, the econometric study, and estimations of present and projected production and consumption patterns. Hence the scenarios are all considered feasible on the basis of currently available information. The attainment of any one scenario will depend on the policies adopted by the government and the availability of the indicated resources. Summaries of the scenarios and their transport implications follow:

Scenario I: Reference Projection

The reference projection describes the likely state of the Sudanese economy and transport system in 1985 if no purposeful intervention takes place at present. We assume that the factors governing the evolution of the Sudan over the next few years are similar to those that have influenced the country's development in the recent past. The main characteristic of the reference projection is a conservative 3.5 percent annual expansion rate of the economy. The economy will remain centered on agriculture, and the crops and methods of farming will not change very much. Since production for export will not have increased greatly, the Sudan will suffer from a lack of foreign exchange and, consequently, from a shortage of imports needed for mechanization and modernization. This scenario makes the smallest contribution to the all-important composite scenario.

Scenario II: Agricultural Export-Oriented Development

In this scenario, the Sudan's development is oriented through government policy toward greatly strengthening the agricultural sector for export. In the short run, other requirements, such as capital goods, technological inputs, and most consumer goods unrelated to agriculture, will be satisfied through imports. This scenario shows a considerable strengthening of the Sudan's hard currency position and a resulting stimulation of the entire economy.

The scenario visualizes an annual growth of from 7 percent to 8 percent over the next several years. This implies a more rapid development of all sectors of the economy by 1985 than would take place under the first scenario. Under this scenario, the emphasis in transportation planning will be toward increasing the capacity of the transportation system as it exists today rather than improving an econometric model. Could the tools, methods, and applications of econometric model building be transplanted from the developed market economy countries to the developing world? WEFA's experience gained in such work for individual countries in Latin America and for the United Nations, the World Bank, and other international organizations bolstered the view that an econometric approach to the analysis of the economy of the Sudan could be fruitful.

There are many differences between forecasting for developed countries and for developing ones. Essentially they are: (1) economic activities structure, (2) weakness of the data base in developing countries, (3) size of the structural samples of available data, and (4) prevalence of structural change for the developing states. These differences were recognized and dealt with in the case of the Sudan. Fortunately, the British have established in the Sudan a mechanism for data collection and record keeping.

This part of the planning effort resulted in the construction of an overall model and sectoral models as analytical tools for describing the economy, for forecasting, and for providing a basis for policy analysis. Together with a traditional input-output model, these models form a balanced array with which to study particular problems of economic development. The group of models provided a great deal of structural information and insight into the workings of the Sudanese economy. Even though the main purpose of the work was not concerned with methodology, the process of model building for the Sudan did succeed in generating a useful and substantive methodological contribution in this field.

The macroeconomic model, solved by itself or in full linkage with the agricultural and transport models, points out the likelihood of a good growth economy in the Sudan during the coming decade, with real production expanding at a rate of about 6 percent annually. The prospects for cotton exports, both in volume and price, are good; this will provide an important driving force in the expansion of the economy as a whole.

SCENARIOS OF THE SUDAN'S FUTURE

In planning alternative strategies for the future of the Sudan's transport system, the method of anticipatory scenario construction was used (see chapter 5).

First a reference scenario of the state of the Sudan was constructed to include all major economic, political, social, and transport parameters. The other scenarios comprise variations in the values of these parameters (some of which were given in qualitative terms). Thus, diagnosis of the resource endowment as well as of social and political factors, their potentialities, and their organizational structure led to the development of four plausible scenarios for the Sudan of

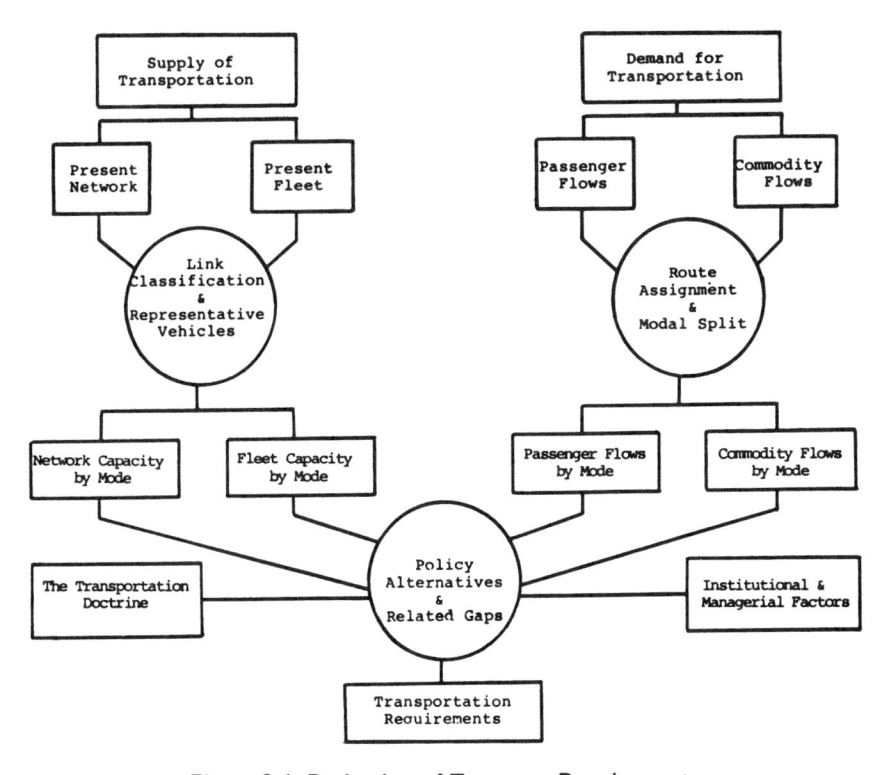

Figure 3.4. Derivation of Transport Requirements

coincide rather closely with what had been regarded of great importance in the Five-Year Plan for the Sudan, which preceded the study by a few years. Figure 3.4 shows the detailed flow chart of the transportation selection of the study.

ECONOMETRIC MODELS

Econometric models have come into their own in the last twenty-five years. They usually contain demand equations, production relationships, and equations for macroeconomic considerations; they estimate numerical parameter values (within some range of error) based on these equations. The highly regarded Wharton Econometric Forecasting Associates (WEFA), who participated in the study, maintains a check on the pulse of the American economy with just such

THE SUDAN TRANSPORT STUDY

```
                    ┌─────────────────────────────┐
                    │   BASE STUDY OF THE ECONOMY │
                    └─────────────────────────────┘
                            │
               ┌────────────┼──────────────┐
               │    ┌───────┴───┐  ┌───────┴───┐
               │    │Econometric│  │ Composite │
               │    │   Model   │  │  Scenario │
               │    └───────┬───┘  └───────┬───┘
               │            │              │
               │    ┌───────┴───┐  ┌───────┴───┐
               │    │ Exogenous │  │  Policy   │
               │    │ Variables │  │Implications│
               │    └───────┬───┘  └───────┬───┘
               │            └──────┬───────┘
               │                (Macro
               │                Analysis)
               │                   │
               │         ┌─────────┴────────┐
         ┌─────┴──────┐              ┌──────┴─────┐
         │Demographic │              │  Economic  │
         │  Patterns  │              │ Indicators │
         └─────┬──────┘              └──────┬─────┘
               └────────(Projection)────────┘
                             │
          ┌──────────────────┼──────────────────┐
   ┌──────┴─────┐    ┌───────┴────┐    ┌────────┴───┐
   │ Population │    │ Consumption│    │ Production │
   └────────────┘    └────────────┘    └────────────┘
```

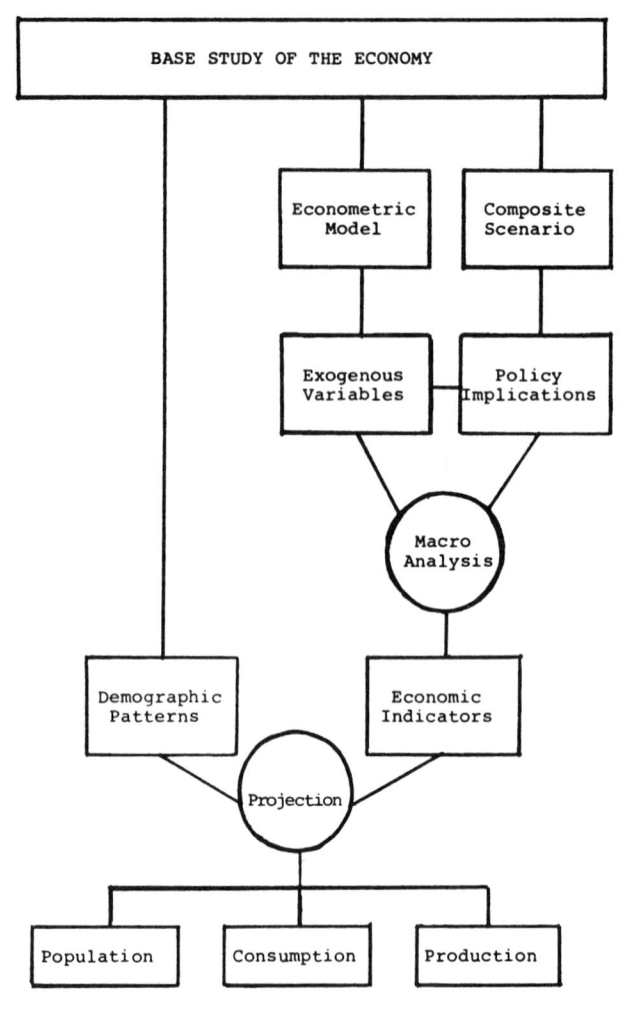

Figure 3.3. Identification and Projection of Economic Activities

social, and political development of the regions in which they fell. Their costs were computed for implementation at the three different assumed growth rates. The priority of each project was divided by its cost, thereby yielding a measure of the effectiveness of investment.

The set of projects was grouped essentially according to priority into three time phases for implementation. By way of validation, priorities tended to

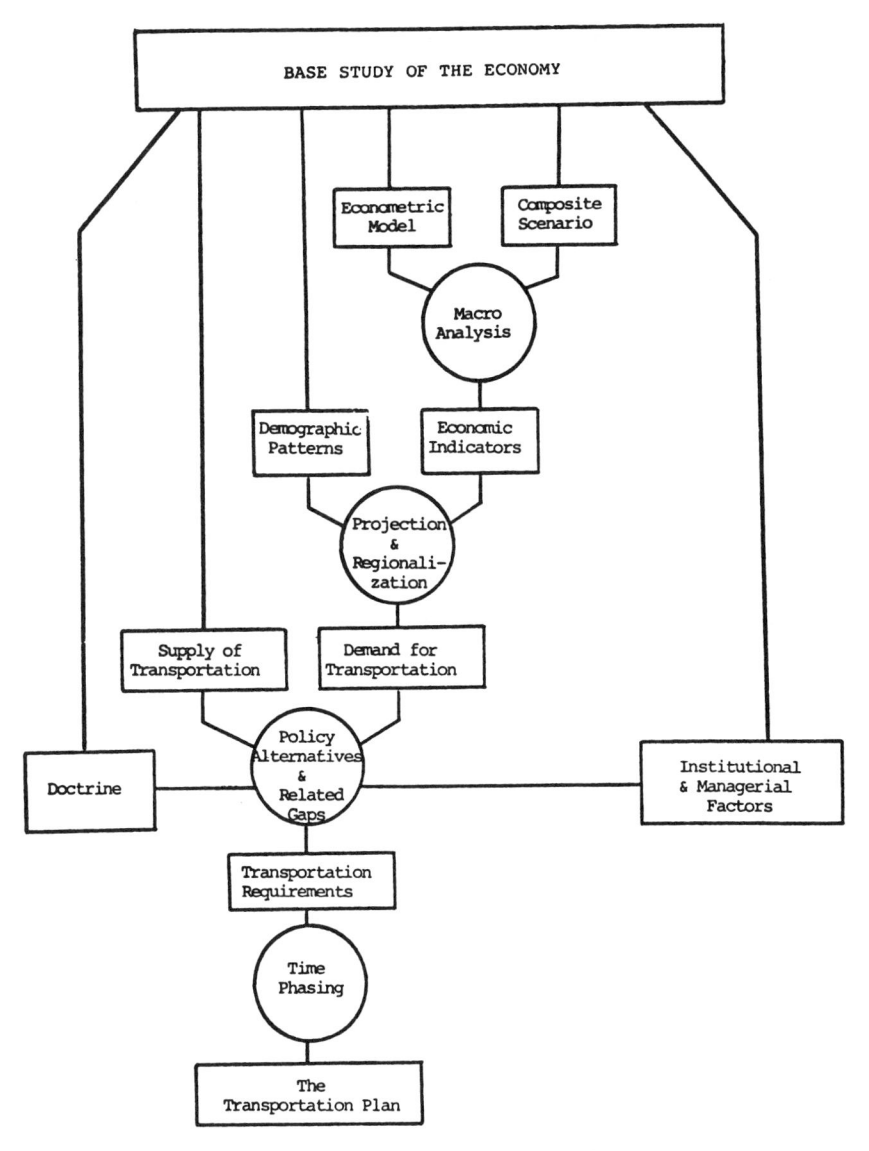

Figure 3.2. Transportation Planning Process

The Sudan has many distinct tribes, particularly in the West, that require social, political, and economic integration. One study has noted that 85 percent of the Sudanese population is not integrated in the economic structure. It is these tribes in the West, in Darfur Province, who produce the cattle, one of Sudan's major prospective activities for food export. Delivering cattle on the hoof for meat, as it is done in Sudan, toughens the product. Sudan now exports meat whose quality could be improved by using modern ranching methods.

BRIEF ACCOUNT OF THE STUDY

Figure 3.2 illustrates how the different elements of the study fit together. The planning began along two parallel lines: (1) the estimation of economic activities through econometric modeling and (2) the blending of social, political, and economic futures through scenario construction, both looking ahead to 1985. The contrasting scenarios of the future of the Sudan took into consideration detailed information regarding its agriculture, industry, politics, and transportation. The basic set of four scenarios, which we felt covered the spectrum of possible futures, were: (1) the reference projection, (2) agriculture for export, (3) balanced regional growth, and (4) Arab and African interface. Based on the idea of hierarchical prioritization applied to the scenarios with regard to their feasibility and desirability, a composite scenario was constructed reflecting the weights of the individual scenarios. The priorities of the important regions of the Sudan were then studied according to their potential contributions to that scenario. An overview of the interaction between econometric modeling and the composite scenario is brought out in figure 3.3.

We first had to identify the existing transport system, its capacities and demands. We then estimated requirements for new transportation connections and vehicles from econometric estimates of what would happen in the composite scenario under 4.3 percent, 6 percent, or 7.3 percent GNP growth rates. Since there are several modes of transport, such as river, rail, road, and air, commodities had to be divided into different priority classes based on factors such as bulk, importance, perishability, and cost of transport. The projects needed for each mode were identified with the use of a linear programming model, based on both passenger and commodity flows. Actually, for the Sudan, the regions were aggregated into nine central nodes among which the movement was assumed to take place. Later the links between the nodes were disaggregated by mode to accommodate connections between cities in the regions, because it is not known exactly where the activities of agriculture and industry would grow. The capacity and efficiency of the existing system were taken into consideration and allowed for in calculating additional needs. The projects thus identified were prioritized according to their contribution to the economic,

Avoiding the pipeline would have necessitated rapid improvement in equipment and in management practices and efficiency, and it could not be done soon enough to convince the government that it was a practical solution to this annoying and embarrassing problem for the capital.

Another debate has raged for some time in the Sudan. Should Khartoum, the capital, have a new airport, in view of the fact that the city had so grown as to surround the existing international airport, now considered a total nuisance by the city dwellers? But an airport costs tens of millions of dollars and, at least until the Sudan reaches the economic takeoff point, perhaps sometime in the late 1980s, the present Khartoum International Airport is serviceable despite its undesirable location and does not get so much traffic to justify, in purely economic terms, building a new one. However, an international airport is a status symbol for an emerging country with bright prospects; so even today the question of whether or not to build a new airport is a political issue.

Air connections are important for administering a far-flung country with extremely poor transportation and communication connections. Traveling by the Nile or by rail from Khartoum to the south, southwest or even to the west takes several days. Most of the provincial capitals have airports that can accommodate small aircraft for a few passengers. They have been operating rather satisfactorily in good weather. In bad weather, landings and takeoffs are risky. The fleet requires navigational aids, and the airports need runway renovation augmented by improvements both to instrument flight rules (IFR) and to visual flight rules (VFR). Should these take priority over other transport investments? For governance, for medical emergencies, and for quick business management trips, they are rather more important than they seem at first glance.

Yet another pressing problem is how to connect the Sudan with its neighbors for substantial trade purposes. The British had built the Egyptian rail south and the Sudan rail north. However, they are separated by about a 200-mile gap, connected by a dirt road, and the gauges are different. Even though the Egyptians are experienced farmers who can lend a hand to a country with limited population and vast agricultural potential like the Sudan, the Sudanese, for political reasons, are not anxious to make it easy for Egyptians to migrate south.

Apart from a two-and-a-half-hour flight from Cairo to Khartoum, there is no other way to travel between the two countries. Major exports have to go by sea. Cataracts and now the Aswan Dam make the prospects of using the river for transport to Egypt even less likely. What should be done about this problem and about improving transportation to Ethiopia and to the southern neighbors: Kenya (whose port of Mombassa is a more rapid and more convenient way of bringing imports to Juba than by the northern Sudanese route) to Uganda, Zaire, and so on? The connection here is by low-quality dirt roads. Again there are political considerations that affect the South's integration with the North if communication with southern neighbors becomes too open.

THE SUDAN TRANSPORT STUDY 49

In this area, much Nile water is lost through evaporation. One of the projects considered was the building of the Jonglei Canal to bypass the Sudd (cost estimated at .5 billion dollars). The Egyptians are participating in this project, which would bring more Nile water to Egypt. A major problem in the Nile is the growth of water hyacinths, which interfere with traffic by winding around the propellers of boats. The British used to maintain a program for continuous cleaning of the river; however, the cleaning has ceased in recent years due to lack of equipment. This problem is not as acute during the high-water season.

The 3,000-mile railroad network in the Sudan is of the old-fashioned narrow gauge (3 ft. 6 in.) single-track variety, built in the late nineteenth century by the British, flat on the desert or other grounds, with no built-up bed and mostly with no gravel. It carries the bulk of both passenger and commodity movements. During the rainy season from May through September, the rail lines are flooded and the sections washed out. The question at the beginning of the study was whether to change to standard gauge, to ballast, or to raise the bed and double-track, each of which would be a relatively costly operation for a poor country. In addition, there were those who felt that the power of the railway made it such a great and inefficient monopoly that roads, of which there are 12,000 miles, were now a desirable alternative. Roads are less useful for large haulage than rail, both because of lack of vehicles and because of higher ton-mileage costs. At present, only a few hundred miles of road are paved and a third are gravel surfaced; the rest are earth tracks, impassable in bad weather. However, building a highway is very costly even in the Sudan and many, many roads of varying quality are needed, so where does one begin? Is it really better over the short run to improve the rail, to upgrade the roads, or to do both—and to what extent? What about long-range planning and the effect of rising fuel costs?

In any case, the Sudan needs a system of feeder roads from the expanding agricultural areas primarily to the railway junctions and, more recently, to the nearly 1,000-mile highway from Khartoum to Port Sudan (the major outlet to the Red Sea), which curves around the Gezira agricultural region. It has been built segment by segment by the Americans, the Chinese, and the Italians; perhaps others will be involved for the unfinished half. Feeder roads have a high priority if agricultural exports are to support the development of the country.

In Khartoum, the shortage of gasoline brought by rail from Port Sudan, where it arrives by ships from Saudi Arabia, has become increasingly noticeable. (Since Port Sudan has become overloaded, another port a little to the south was considered, although one of the potential funding agencies suggested a delay on this decision.) This shortage has been due mainly to poor scheduling and other rail problems and to lack of storage facilities. At times there was rationing to about a gallon a day, if one was lucky enough to get it. Finally., it was decided to build a relatively expensive pipeline to solve this problem once and for all.

portant objective of the study was to *involve the Sudanese* in every phase of the planning so that after the study was completed they themselves would be doing the planning.

The demand for transport in the future depends strongly on how fast the economy and the population grow. Assuming a 6 percent GNP growth rate per annum, the investment in transport needs to be about 1.8 billion dollars between now and 1985 to keep pace mainly with growth in agriculture, which accounts for 55 percent of the GNP and provides an occupation for 75 percent of the people, and with opening up the country and satisfying the rising passenger demand.

PROBLEM AREAS RELATING TO THE PLAN

For a better appreciation of a transport plan for a nation, one needs certain background material about the needs of that nation. This is done below to give the reader a richer appreciation of the complexities that led to the research that was undertaken. As we shall see, we had to consider not only direct physical, economic, and trade requirements for transportation, but major political and social needs as well.

On January 1, 1956, the Sudan became an independent republic, ending over a half-century of government under the Anglo-Egyptian Condominium (1899-1955). The years following independence have been marked by a major sixteen-year civil war between the North and the South. The parts of Africa included in the colony called Sudan were of many origins and tribal affiliations and religions. However, the Sudan has two basically distinct cultures: the predominantly Arabic (Islamic) North and the Nilotic (animistic) black South. The South wanted independence as an African nation. The war ended in 1972, after 500,000 deaths and substantial destruction of the South. Considerable reconstruction is now taking place in the South. Although the economic viability of the South does not justify heavy expenditures, strong political considerations require that substantial funds be allocated both to the economic development of the South and to its integration with the North by effective transportation and communication systems. There has been relative stability in the Sudan since 1969. President Nimeiry has worked hard as a moderator to end the civil war and to heal the wounds through pacification of the opposing factions.

Access from Khartoum to Juba, the capital of the South, is by air in small craft; by rail to Wau in the southwest and then by a long dirt road to Juba; or by the Nile (a distance of 1,085 miles), which is the traditional route for carrying cargo to and from the South. It is also the "romantic" passenger route, requiring nine days and passing through the famous Sudd, the largest swamp in the world (estimated at 150,000 sq. mi.), which interrupts the flow of the Nile.

the Sudan's major urban centers, its location with respect to its African neighbors, and its need for new transportation projects. Some of these projects are improvements on existing facilities.

The far north is an uninhabited desert with virtually zero rainfall per annum. Only along the banks of the Nile, which flows through its center, is this pattern broken. Two feet of rain fall in the central portion, without which the land would be barren. Six feet of rain fall in the south, which is a rain-band forest. In its central part, the Sudan has an estimated 200 million acres of agriculturally useful land; at least 120 million acres suitable for cultivation, of which 17 million are now cultivated; and 80 million for grazing. This is nearly 30 percent of the total area. Another 19 percent is taken up by forests, 46 percent by deserts and swamps, and 5 percent by inland water. The drought of recent years has hurt some of the areas in the east but did not present the major problem in the Sudan that it did in the more arid countries of Central Africa.

Much of the waters of the Sudan come from the two Niles. The White Nile, which originates in Lake Victoria in Uganda to the south of Sudan, winds its way for over 2,000 miles north through the center of the country to Egypt. Actually, because of the High Aswan Dam in Egypt, Lake Nasser is formed by the Nile and backs up into Sudan. The White Nile is joined at the capital city of Khartoum by the Blue Nile, originating in Ethiopia. The two Niles and their tributaries are a major source of water for agriculture and for transportation. The Nile is dotted with nine cataracts, several of which are impassable north of Khartoum. Even though studied at some length, the White Nile cannot at present be turned into a Danube or a Rhine for the Sudan without considerable cost. Today it is the Blue Nile, with its irrigation schemes, that provides the waters of the fertile agricultural land of the Gezira Province.

BACKGROUND AND PURPOSE OF THE PLAN

Early in 1973 the government of the Sudan and the Kuwait Fund for Arab Economic Development felt that it would be useful to do a *comprehensive prefeasibility study for the transport sector of the Sudan of 1985.* The Kuwait Fund for Arab Economic Development, an agency of the Kuwait government, provided the funds for the fifteen-month study, and the government of Sudan cooperated by furnishing data and transport experts from their country.

The main purpose of our study was to design a transport plan for the Sudan and prioritize the transportation projects to relieve the present problems and to meet the rising demand of an expanding economy. Our plan was to determine the projects and the order in which they are to be implemented through the year 1985 in a way that *assists the government in securing investment funds* of the order of billions of dollars from outside sources. Perhaps the most im-

river, and air. These modes are combined together to provide a sparse and far-flung transportation infrastructure. The air network is centered at Khartoum, and the rail and road systems are oriented for export through Port Sudan. The country is characterized by low transport connectivity. Figure 3.1 identifies

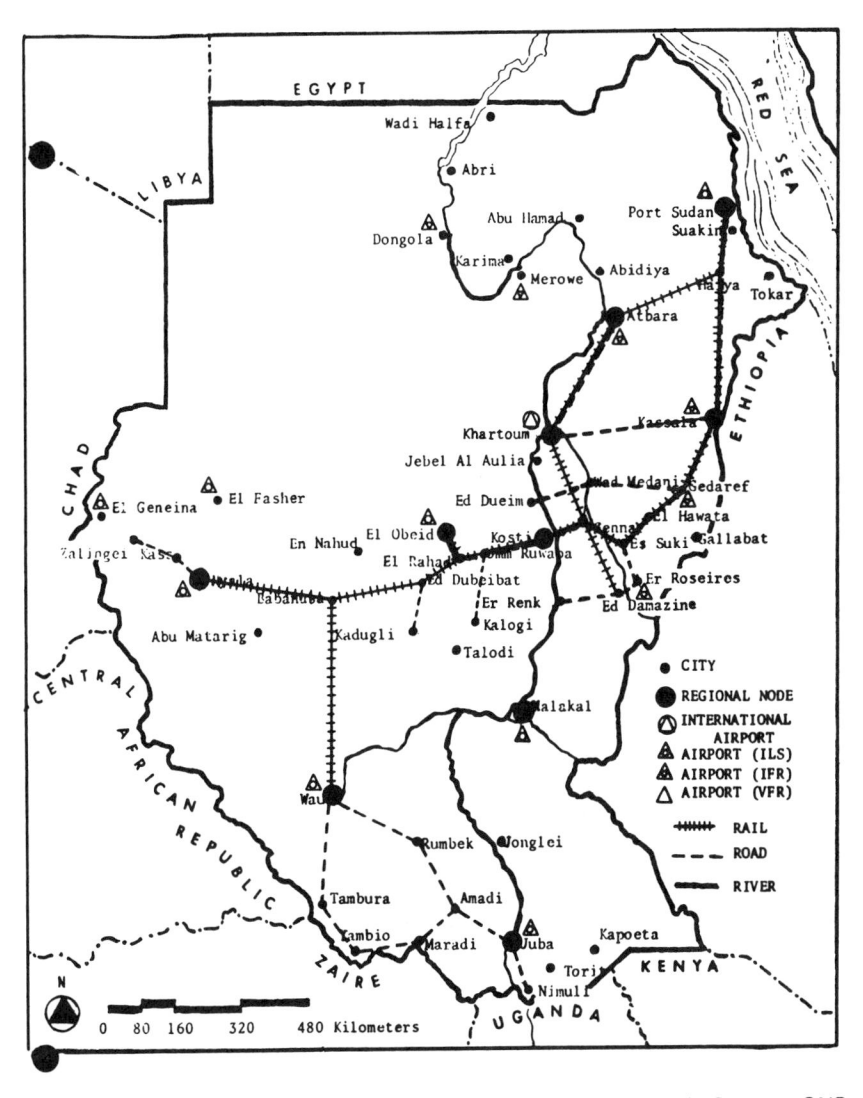

Figure 3.1. Sudan Transportation System Envisioned for 1985 (6 Percent GNP Growth Rate)

3 THE SUDAN TRANSPORT STUDY

We begin our applications with the Sudan Transport Study, in which a plan was developed to improve the Sudanese economy. (This study won an award from the Institute of Management Studies for being one of the best applied studies in 1977.)

THE SUDAN

Against a background of great potential agricultural riches, the Sudan, the largest country in Africa (967,491 sq. mi.), but with a population of only 18.4 million, is today a poor country with a GDP of about 6.15 billion dollars. Oil countries in the Middle East and international agencies, including the World Bank, recognize the capacity of the Sudan as a major provider of food for Africa and the Middle East and have been investing in its development.

The Sudan is serviced by four major modes of transportation: rail, road,

---

This chapter is based on an article of the same title by T.L. Saaty (*Interfaces* 8 [1977]: 37-57). It also draws on Saaty, "Scenarios and Priorities in Transport Planning: Application to the Sudan" (*Transportation Research* 11 [1977]:343-50), and on the ADAR Corporation's 1975 *Sudan Transport Study* (see Appendix A).

II APPLICATIONS OF PRIORITIZATION

largest corporations, to assisting developing nations to deal effectively with their many problems and limited resources.

REFERENCES

Brookings Institution. 1968. *Agenda for the Nation*. Washington, D.C.

Bunge, M. 1969. "The Metaphysics, Epistemology, and Methodology of Levels." In L.L. Whyte, A.G. Wilson, and D. Wilson, eds., *Hierarchical Structures*. New York: Elsevier.

Koopmans, T.C. 1969. "Note on a Social System Composed of Hierarchies with Overlapping Personnel." Cowles Foundation for Research in Economics at Yale University, Paper No. 302.

Miller, G.A. 1956. "The Magical Number Seven Plus or Minus Two: Some Limits on Our Capacity for Processing Information." *Psychological Review* 13:81-97.

Saaty, T.L. 1976. "Interaction and Impacts in Hierarchical Systems." Proceedings of the workshop, Decision Information for Tactical Command and Control, Airlie House, Airlie, Va., September 22-25. Also in C.P. Tsokos and R.M. Thrall, eds., *Decision Information*. New York: Academic Press, 1979.

———. 1977. "A Scaling Method for Priorities in Hierarchical Structures." *Journal of Mathematical Psychology* 15:234-81.

———. 1980. *The Analytic Hierarchy Process: Planning, Priority Setting, Resource Allocation*. New York: McGraw-Hill.

Since $n_1^2 + n_2^2 = n^2 - 2n_1n_2$, we have:

$$\frac{n^2 - n - 2n_1n_2}{2} + 1 = \frac{n(n-1)}{2} - (n_1n_2 - 1) < \frac{n(n-1)}{2}.$$

If we wish to compare objects that do not fall within the range of the scale, then clustering provides a way of introducing accuracy and decreasing the fuzziness involved in the comparison of small objects with large ones.

Examples of clustering required because of the large number of elements can be seen in chapter 13, in the discussion on corporate portfolio selection. Clustering due to different orders of magnitude can be seen in Appendix A at the end of the book.

To summarize these points, we note that clustering a complex problem into hierarchical form has two advantages: (1) great efficiency in making pairwise comparisons, and (2) greater consistency under the assumption of a limited capacity of the mind to compare more than seven plus or minus two elements simultaneously. Saaty (1977) shows that consistency decreases below the 10 percent level when more than five objects are compared at one time. Thus, when clustering, one would recommend that the size of clusters be kept small to attain greater efficiency in the process.

COMMENTS

In this chapter we have introduced the underlying theory of the Analytic Hierarchy Process. We gave a brief introduction to ratio scale measurement and the scale used. Formal hierarchies were then introduced, and we analyzed the idea of consistency for a hierarchy as a measure of how far our judgments are from being randomly provided. Methods of estimating the vector of priorities were introduced along with clustering analysis to make the process more efficient and consistent.

There are also a number of questions that come to mind in using the AHP. They range from ones concerning the interaction of people and how to obtain consensus or take geometric averages over the judgments, to time-dependent judgments, interdependence among the factors, and the possibility of feedback (see Saaty, 1980).

If the hierarchy, as it seems, is a faithful model of how our mind thinks, we must adapt it to deal with complex problems. It is not merely another technique but appears to be an effective vehicle for studying benefits and costs and doing planning. We have applied it in a wide diversity of areas ranging from private individual decisions, to setting priorities and allocating resources in some of the

THE BASIC APPROACH

If the matrix A is consistent, the three methods reproduce the original vector of priorities. However, in the inconsistent case ANC is more accurate than the other two methods. The NGM method provides a good estimate of the priorities if accuracy is not of extreme importance. These results can be used as a first approximation to the final results, which must be obtained by computer for solving the eigenvalue problem. Other ways of approximating the vector of priorities are discussed in Saaty (1980, p. 234).

Finally, to conclude the basic approach we must answer the following questions: What do we do if some elements in the levels of a hierarchy are not of the same order of magnitude as others? How can the one-to-nine scale be stretched so that any two elements can be compared regardless of their magnitude? How can we cope with large numbers of elements in a hierarchical level? The answer to these questions lies with clustering analysis.

One would like to have a scale extend as far out as possible. On the other hand, a scale must be finite to exemplify how large relative measurement can get. Also, if a scale is not finite, mental comparisons of disparate objects, such as an atom and a star, could not be made with satisfactory accuracy. To make comparisons of these types, we insert between these extremes objects that become progressively larger, enabling us to appreciate the transition in the magnitudes of measurement. Such a transition is made possible by dividing the objects into clusters where the elements in a cluster are within the range of the scale, and the largest object in a group is used as the smallest one in the next order-of-magnitude cluster. This enables us to continue the measurement from one cluster to the next one, and so on.

To decompose a hierarchy into clusters, we must decide which elements to group together in each cluster. This is generally done according to the similarity of the extent to which the elements of the hierarchy perform a function or share a property. We then conduct comparisons on the clusters and the subclusters and decompose the clusters to obtain the overall priorities. The clustering can be validated by comparing its results with the outcome if there were no decomposition.

The advantages of clustering are, of course, different depending on the type of problem at hand. If the problem is one of handling a large number of elements within a hierarchy, then clustering diminishes dramatically the number of pairwise comparisons otherwise required.

For example, let us assume that we have n elements to be compared among themselves. The total number of comparisons required is $[n(n - 1)]/2$. Now let us assume that n is partitioned into two clusters consisting of n_1 and n_2 elements each, and $n_1 + n_2 = n$. The number of comparisons required is:

$$\frac{2(2-1)}{2} + \frac{n_1(n_1 - 1)}{2} + \frac{n_2(n_2 - 1)}{2} = \frac{n_1^2 + n_2^2 - n}{2} + 1.$$

METHODS OF ESTIMATING THE VECTOR OF PRIORITIES AND CLUSTERING SCHEMES

Earlier we described in some detail how to obtain vectors of priorities as solutions of the eigenvalue problem:

$$Aw = \lambda_{max} w.$$

In Saaty (1980, p. 176) it can be seen that the eigenvector associated with the principal eigenvalue of A can be obtained as:

$$\lim_{k \to \infty} \frac{A^k e}{e^T A^k e} = Cw$$

where e is the column vector unity, e^T its transpose, and C a positive constant. This result allows us to approximate λ_{max} and w as accurately as desired but within computational capabilities.

In situations in which accuracy is not the most important factor, the vector of priorities can be approximated by one of three methods: (a) average of normalized columns (ANC), (b) normalization of row averages (NRA), and (c) normalization of the geometric mean of the rows (NGM).

Let $\hat{w}_i$ be the priority estimate of the ith activity. According to the first method we have:

$$\hat{w}_i (\text{ANC}) = \frac{1}{n} \sum_{j=1}^{n} \frac{a_{ij}}{\sum_{k=1}^{n} a_{kj}}.$$

The second method yields:

$$\hat{w}_i (\text{NRA}) = \sum_{j=1}^{n} a_{ij} / \sum_{i,j=1}^{n} a_{ij},$$

and

$$\hat{w}_i (\text{NGM}) = \left(\prod_{j=1}^{n} a_{ij} \right)^{\frac{1}{n}} / \sum_{k=1}^{n} \left(\prod_{j=1}^{n} a_{kj} \right)^{\frac{1}{n}}$$

is the estimate of w by the third procedure.

THE BASIC APPROACH

wise comparison matrix by the priority of the property with respect to which the comparison is made and add all the results for the entire hierarchy. This sum is then compared with the corresponding index obtained by taking randomly generated indices, weighting them by the priorities, and adding.

Let $n_j, j = 1, 2, \ldots, h$ be the number of elements in the jth level of the hierarchy. Let w_{ij} be the composite weight of the ith activity of the jth level, and let $\mu_{i,j+1}$ be the consistency index of all elements in the $(j + 1)$st level compared with respect to the ith activity of the jth level.

The consistency index of a hierarchy is defined by:

$$C_H = \sum_{j=1}^{h} \sum_{i=1}^{n_{i_j}} w_{ij} \mu_{i,j+1}$$

where $w_{ij} = 1$ for $j = 1$, and n_{i_j} is the number of elements of the jth level with respect to which the activities of the $(j + 1)$st level are compared.

Applying the index to the vacation site selection example, we have:

Second level priority vector: (.22, .19, .03, .07, .13, .36);
Second level μ_2: $\mu_{1,2} = (6.475 - 6)/5 = .095$;
Third level vector of μ's: $\mu_3 = (.091, .148, .185, .059, .104, .104)$,

where, for example, $\mu_{4,3} = .059$.
Hence, we have:

$$C_H = .095 + (.22, .19, .03, .07, .13, .36) \begin{Bmatrix} .091 \\ .148 \\ .185 \\ .059 \\ .104 \\ .104 \end{Bmatrix} = .185,$$

and using the corresponding random indices we have:

$$\bar{C}_H = 1.24 + (.22, .19, .03, .07, .13, .36) \begin{Bmatrix} .58 \\ .58 \\ .58 \\ .58 \\ .58 \\ .58 \end{Bmatrix} = 1.82.$$

The consistency ratio of the hierarchy is therefore $C_H/\bar{C}_H = .10$, which is within the 10 percent consistency range required.

Table 2.6. Comparison of Sites with Respect to the Six Characteristics

Minimal Driving Time	SSR	MC	VR	Convenient Facilities	SSR	MC	VR
SSR	1	1/7	1/5	SSR	1	9	5
MC	7	1	5	MC	1/9	1	1/9
VR	5	1/5	1	VR	1/5	9	1

New Acquaintances	SSR	MC	VR	Relaxed Environment	SSR	MC	VR
SSR	1	9	7	SSR	1	1/5	5
MC	1/9	1	1/9	MC	5	1	9
VR	1/7	9	1	VR	1/5	1/9	1

Children's Activities	SSR	MC	VR	Cost	SSR	MC	VR
SSR	1	9	5	SSR	1	1/7	1/9
MC	1/9	1	1/7	MC	7	1	1/5
VR	1/5	7	1	VR	9	5	1

Table 2.7. The Eigenvalues and Eigenvectors

	Minimal Driving Time	Convenient Facilities	New Acquaintances	Relaxed Environment	Children's Activities	Cost
SSR	.0668	.7107	.7511	.2067	.7219	.0510
MC	.7147	.0462	.0436	.7352	.0510	.2271
VR	.2185	.2431	.2053	.0581	.2271	.7219
	$\lambda = 3.183$	$\lambda = 3.295$	$\lambda = 3.436$	$\lambda = 3.117$	$\lambda = 3.208$	$\lambda = 3.208$

THE CONSISTENCY OF A HIERARCHY

In this section we generalize the measurement of consistency to an entire hierarchy. What we do is to multiply the index of consistency obtained from a pair-

THE BASIC APPROACH

SATISFACTION
WITH
VACATION

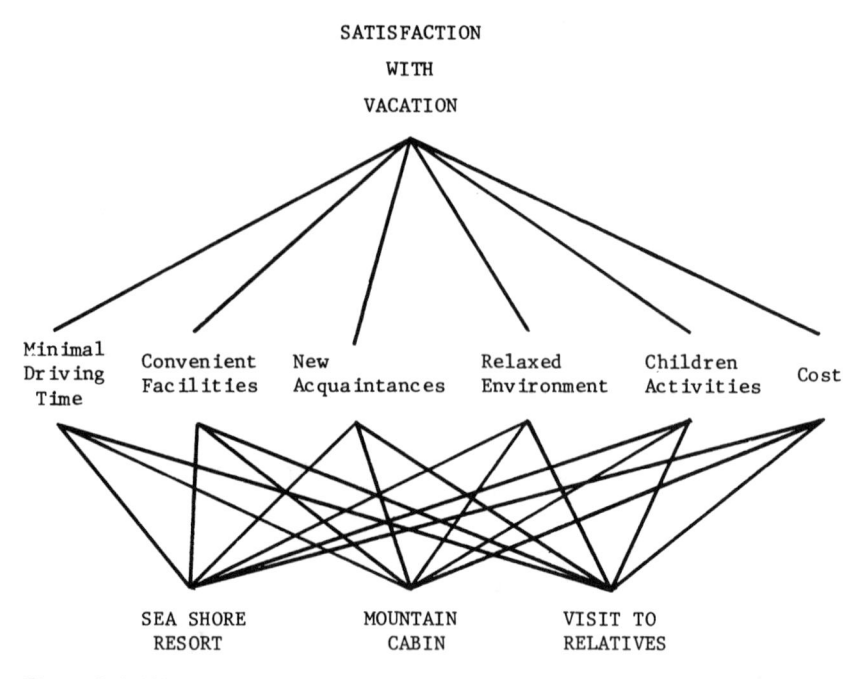

Figure 2.1. Hierarchy for Vacation Site Selection

Table 2.5. Comparison of Characteristics with Respect to Overall Satisfaction with Site

	MDT	CF	NA	RFE	CA	C
MDT	1	1	7	5	3	1/3
CF	1	1	5	3	1	1
NA	1/7	1/5	1	1/3	1/7	1/9
RFE	1/5	1/3	3	1	1/3	1/3
CA	1/3	1	7	3	1	1/5
C	3	1	9	3	5	1

The vacation site that this analysis indicates as the most preferred by the family is a visit with relatives.

So far we have mentioned consistency of judgments at each stage of the process. However, we have not aggregated each consistency value to provide an overall consistency measure for the overall process.

20, 5). These clusters may be regarded as two boulders broken into stones. The relative weights of the clusters are (.75, .25). The relative weights of the stones within the first cluster are (.667, .333), and within the second (.5, .4, .1). In order to obtain the relative weights of all five stones, we multiply each subset by the weights of its corresponding cluster. We get:

$$.75 \times (.667, .333) = (.5, .25)$$

and

$$.25 \times (.5, .4, .1) = (.125, .1, .025),$$

which is the desired set of weights.

AN EXAMPLE: VACATION SITE SELECTION

In a typical family of four, there will be a range of desires and pleasures to be derived from a vacation. The biased judgment of each family member will motivate the family to select a site. It is understood that the selection will hopefully satisfy the desires and pleasures that are considered most important to each individual.

The vacation site selection process begins by identifying the objective of a vacation and the desires held by each family member. Such a list may consist of the following characteristics: minimal amount of driving time to get to the desired place (MDT); convenient facilities for eating out and shopping (CF); making new acquaintances (NA); relaxed, carefree environment (RFE); activities for children (CA); and cost of the trip (C).

The family may identify three potential sites: a seashore resort (SSR), a cabin in the mountains (MC), and a visit to a favorite set of relatives (VR). The hierarchy is shown in figure 2.1. The pairwise comparison matrices developed in this example are shown in tables 2.5 and 2.6. The eigenvector of the first matrix (table 2.5) is (.22, .19, .03, .07, .13, .36), and its corresponding eigenvalue is $\lambda = 6.475$, which is not too far from the consistent value 6. Otherwise, one would have to revise the judgments. The eigenvalues and eigenvectors of the other six matrices are shown in table 2.7. To obtain the overall ranking of the sites, we multiply the last matrix on the right by the transpose of the vector of weights of the characteristics. This yields:

Seashore resort = .30;
Mountain cabin = .31;
Relatives = .39.

THE BASIC APPROACH

consider the priority functions:

$$w_z: Y \to [0,1] \text{ and } w_{y_j}: X \to [0,1] \; j = 1, \ldots, n_{k+1}.$$

We construct the "priority function of the elements in X with respect to z," denoted w, $w: X \to [0,1]$, by:

$$w(x_i) = \sum_{j=1}^{n_k} w_{y_j}(x_i) w_z(y_j), \quad i = 1, \ldots, n_{k+1}.$$

It is obvious that this is no more than the process of weighting the influence of the element y_j on the priority of x_i by multiplying it with the importance of y_j with respect to z.

The algorithms involved will be simplified if we combine the $w_{y_j}(x_i)$ into a matrix B by setting $b_{ij} = w_{y_j}(x_i)$. If we further set $w_i = w(x_i)$ and $w'_j = w_z(y_j)$, then the above formula becomes:

$$w_i = \sum_{j=1}^{n_k} b_{ij} w'_j \quad i = 1, \ldots, n_{k+1}.$$

Thus we may speak of the *priority vector* w and, indeed, of the *priority matrix* B of the $(k+1)$st level; this gives the final formulation:

$$w = Bw'.$$

The theorem that follows is easy to prove:

THEOREM *(principle of hierarchic composition)*. Let H be a complete hierarchy with largest element b and h levels. Let B_k be the priority matrix of the kth level, $k = 1, \ldots, h$. If w' is the priority vector of the pth level with respect to some element z in the $(p-1)$st level, then the priority vector w of the qth level $(p < q)$ with respect to z is given by:

$$w = B_q B_{q-1} \cdots B_{p+1} w'.$$

Thus the priority vector of the lowest level with respect to the element b is given by:

$$w = B_h B_{h-1} \cdots B_2 b_1$$

if L_1 has a single element, $b_1 = 1$. Otherwise b_1 is a prescribed vector.

An intuitive justification of this principle is as follows: Consider a set of five stones whose weights in pounds are 100, 50, 25, 20, and 5. Their relative weights are .5, .25, .125, .10, and .025, respectively. Let us consider two clusters, one consisting of the first two stones (100, 50), and the second of the last three (25,

given activity, including himself. This type of hierarchy satisfies one of the following properties:

1. Given two members of the hierarchy b_1 and b_2, one is supervisor of the other, that is, $b_1 \, D \, b_2$ or $b_2 \, D \, b_1$.
2. Neither member is a supervisor. Then there exists a unique supervisor b_3 such that $b_3 \, D \, b_1$ and $b_3 \, D \, b_2$; there also exists no supervisor b_4 for which $b_3 \, D \, b_4 \, D \, b_1$ and $b_4 \, D \, b_2$.

The supervision relation is defined on the Cartesian product of the set of activities and the set of people engaged in some of them. This binary relation satisfies the following properties:

1. Each person engaged in an activity has at most one supervisor in that activity.
2. No one is his own superior in any activity. A superior is obtained through the iterative application of the supervision rule. Thus the first superior of a person is his supervisor.

This concept of hierarchy can be extended to a set of activities. A hierarchy for a set of activities is the union of all hierarchies, one for each activity, all having the same head.

These two definitions of hierarchies are more restrictive than the one given in definition 4. Bunge's definition assumes that the dominance relation is transitive, a condition not required by our developments. Koopmans's definition of hierarchies refers to what we call incomplete hierarchies; that is, Koopmans deals only with tree-like hierarchic structures.

DEFINITION 5. A hierarchy is *complete* if, for all $x \in L_k$, $x^+ = L_{k-1}$, for $k = 2, \ldots, h$. Otherwise it is an incomplete hierarchy. We can state the central question as follows:

Basic problem. Given any element $x \in L_\alpha$ and subset $S \subset L_\beta$ ($\alpha < \beta$), how do we define a function $w_{x,S}: S \to [0,1]$ that reflects the properties of the priority functions w_y on the levels $L_k, k = \alpha, \ldots, \beta-1$? Specifically, what is the function $w_{b,b_h}: L_h \to [0,1]$?

In less technical terms, this can be paraphrased thus: Given a social (or economic) system with a major objective b and the set L_h of basic activities, such that the system can be modeled as a hierarchy with largest element b and lowest level L_h, what are the priorities of elements of L_h with respect to b? Our method to solve the basic problem is as follows:

Assume that $Y = \{y_1, \ldots, y_{n_k}\} \subset L_k$ and that $X = \{x_1, \ldots, x_{n_{k+1}}\} \subset L_{k+1}$. Also assume that there is an element $z \in L_{k-1}$, such that $y \in z^-$. We then

THE BASIC APPROACH

such that $u_1 \leq u$ for all $u \in U$. The element u_1 is unique and is called the supremum of E in S. The symbol sup is used to represent a supremum. (For finite sets largest elements and upper bounds are the same.)

Similar definitions may be given for sets bounded from below, a *lower bound* and *infimum*. The symbol inf is used.

There are many ways of defining a hierarchy. The one that suits our needs best is the following:

We use the notation $x^- = \{y | x \text{ covers } y\}$ and
$$x^+ = \{y | y \text{ covers } x\}, \text{ for any element } x \text{ in an ordered set.}$$

DEFINITION 4. Let H be a finite partially ordered set with largest element b. H is a *hierarchy* if it satisfies the following conditions:

1. There is a partition of H into sets $L_k, k = 1, \ldots, h$ where $L_1 = \{b\}$.
2. $x \in L_k$ implies $x^- \subset L_{k+1} \quad k = 1, \ldots, h - 1$.
3. $x \in L_k$ implies $x^+ \subset L_{k-1} \quad k = 2, \ldots, h$

For each $x \in H$, there is a suitable weighting function (whose nature depends on the phenomenon being hierarchically structured):

$$w_x : x^- \to [0, 1] \text{ such that } \sum_{y \in x^-} w_x(y) = 1.$$

The sets L_i are the *levels* of the hierarchy, and the function w_x is the *priority function* of the elements in one level with respect to the objective x. We observe that even if $x^- \neq L_k$ (for some level L_k), w_x may be defined for all of L_k by setting it equal to zero for all elements in L_k not in x^-.

The weighting function, we believe, is a significant contribution toward the application of hierarchy theory.

A number of definitions of a hierarchy have appeared in the literature. Although the above definition was developed without particular knowledge of these and differs substantially from any of them, we have selected two—one by Mario Bunge (1969) and one by the Nobel Laureate Tjalling C. Koopmans (1969)—to illustrate how other people conceive of a hierarchy.

Bunge defines a hierarchy as a triple consisting of a nonempty set S, a distinguished element b of the set called the "single beginner," and a binary relation D indicating dominance that is antisymmetric and transitive. The element b stands in some power of D to every member of S, and for any $y \in S, y \neq b$, there is exactly one $x \in S$ such that xDy.

Koopmans defines a hierarchy for a single activity headed by a subject, the supervisor, as the set of all persons to whom the supervisor is superior for the

The results produced the same ordinal ranking of the factors:

perseverance > hard work > productivity > intelligence.

This suggests that intelligence may not be the factor that contributes the most to the success of a person in a university position. This could be explained if one believes that intelligence is part of the learning process.

FORMAL HIERARCHIES

The laws characterizing different levels of a hierarchy are generally different; the levels differ both in structure and in function. The proper functioning of a higher level depends on the proper functioning of the lower levels. The basic problem with a hierarchy is to seek understanding at the highest levels from interactions of the various levels of the hierarchy rather than directly from elements of the levels. At this stage of development of the theory, the choice of levels in a hierarchy generally depends on the knowledge and interpretation of the observer. Rigorous methods for structuring systems into hierarchies are gradually emerging in the many areas of the natural and social sciences and, in particular, in general systems theory as it relates to the planning and design of social systems.

DEFINITION 1. An ordered set is any set S with a binary relation $\leq$ that satisfies the reflexive, antisymmetric, and transitive laws:

Reflexive: For all x, $x \leq x$;
Antisymmetric: If $x \leq y$ and $y \leq x$, then $x = y$;
Transitive: If $x \leq y$ and $y \leq z$, then $x \leq z$.

For any relation $x \leq y$ (read: y includes x) of this type, we may define $x < y$ to mean that $x \leq y$ and $x \neq y$. y is said to cover (dominate) x if $x < y$ and if $x < t < y$ is possible for no t.

Ordered sets with a finite number of elements can be conveniently represented by a directed graph. Each element of the system is represented by a vertex so that an arc is directed from a to b if $b < a$.

DEFINITION 2. A simply or totally ordered set (also called a chain) is an ordered set with the additional property that if $x, y \in S$, then either $x \leq y$ or $y \leq x$.

DEFINITION 3. A subset E of an ordered set S is said to be bounded from above if there is an element $s \in S$ such that $x \leq s$ for every $x \in E$. The element s is called an *upper bound* of E. We say E has a *supremum* or least upper bound in S if E has upper bounds and if the set of upper bounds U has an element u_1

THE BASIC APPROACH

	HW	PR	I	PE	Independence Priorities
HW	.0000	.3325	.2000	.2583	.062
PR	.4545	.0000	.6000	.6370	.550
I	.0909	.1396	.0000	.1047	.173
PE	.4545	.5278	.2000	.0000	.215

Now, each column of the matrix must be weighted by the priority of the factor obtained as if they were independent and the rows added. The result is the final priorities that reflect the interdependence among factors.

In our example, we have:

	HW	PR	I	PE			Dependence Priorities
HW	.000	.183	.035	.056	Adding by	HW	.213
PR	.028	.000	.104	.137	→	PR	.269
I	.006	.077	.000	.023	rows	I	.105
PE	.028	.290	.035	.000		PE	.353

The judgments used in this example were those of the authors. We asked a third person to provide judgments for the same problem and obtained the following priorities, which differ from ours. We often find a need to discuss judgments to produce greater convergence. There was none in this case.

	Dependence Priorities
HW	.311
PR	.168
I	.059
PE	.462

hard work – then we would obtain four matrices that describe the contributions of the different factors to each one. The following matrix summarizes the information of these four matrices. In it, the first set of numbers assesses the influence of all factors but *HW* on *HW;* the second set, on *PR;* the third set, on *I;* and the fourth set, on *PE*.

	HW	*PR*	*I*	*PE*
HW	1	$\left(x,x,\frac{1}{3},\frac{1}{3}\right)$	$(x,3,x,3)$	$(x,\frac{1}{2},1,x)$
PR	$(x,x,3,3)$	1	$(5,x,x,5)$	$(1,x,3,x)$
I	$\left(x,\frac{1}{3},x,\frac{1}{3}\right)$	$\frac{1}{5},x,x,\frac{1}{5}$	1	$\left(\frac{1}{5},3,x,x\right)$
PE	$(x,2,1,x)$	$\left(1,x,\frac{1}{3},x\right)$	$\left(5,\frac{1}{3},x,x\right)$	1

An x in this matrix means that a factor in the left-hand side does not contribute to the factor under which the x is located. Thus, for example, we compare productivity, intelligence, and perseverance with respect to their contribution to hard work. The resulting matrix of judgments is:

HW	*PR*	*I*	*PE*
PR	1	5	1
I	1/5	1	1/5
PE	1	5	1

The judgments have been obtained by deleting the column and the row corresponding to hard work from the matrix given above and selecting the first number of each 4-tuple. The resulting priorities are:

Table 2.4. Impact of Forces in U.S. Economy

	Economic	Social	Political	Ideological	Technological	Eigenvector
Economic	1	7	3	7	3	.45
Social	1/7	1	1/3	7	1/6	.09
Political	1/3	3	1	7	1/2	.17
Ideological	1/7	1/7	1/7	1	1/8	.03
Technological	1/3	6	2	8	1	.26

omists concentrate on the highest priority area, and they have ways to do cardinal measurement, we still need quantification of the other areas to obtain a 70 percent efficient explanation of what affects the economy.

Dependence versus Independence

An important issue is whether or not the elements of a level are independent of each other. If they are independent, the approach is straightforward as we have described it so far. However, if some interdependence exists among the activities of a level, we must assess it and consider it when computing the final priorities. Let us illustrate this with a two-level hierarchy.

Assume that the success of a person in a university position is characterized by (a) hard work (HW), (b) productivity (PR), (c) intelligence (I), and (d) perseverance (PE). If we consider them independent, we have

	HW	PR	I	PE	Priorities
HW	1	1/6	1/3	1/5	.062
PR	6	1	4	3	.550
I	3	1/4	1	1	.173
PE	5	1/3	1	1	.215

If, on the other hand, we detect some dependence and assume that each factor does not contribute to itself—for example, that hard work does not influence

Table 2.3. Real and Estimated Distances

City	Distance to Philadelphia in Miles	Normalized Distance	Eigenvector
Cairo	5,729	.278	.263
Tokyo	7,449	.361	.397
Chicago	660	.032	.033
San Francisco	2,732	.132	.116
London	3,658	.177	.164
Montreal	400	.019	.027

$$\lambda_{max} \cong 6.45$$

$$C.I. = \frac{6.45 - 6}{6 - 1} \cong .09$$

$$C.R. = \frac{.09}{1.24} \cong .07$$

those nearest to Philadelphia: Montreal and Chicago; those at an intermediate distance: San Francisco and London; and those farthest away: Cairo and Tokyo. The latter, because of relatively large value due to errors of uncertainty, cause the values of the others to be perturbed from where we want them to be. Thus if their eigenvector components change comparatively slightly and the increment is distributed among the others, the relative values of these can be altered considerably.

The Impact of Economics

The values in table 2.4 suggest that economic forecasting can at best account for only a part of the forces that shape the economy.

If economic forecasting were done perfectly and if we were to pool together economic and technological forces as part of an economic model, we obtain .71 for these two factors. Let us assume 70 percent efficiency (some may think that this is too high) in economic forecasting—including the right number of variables, relating them correctly, and using good data. Then the overall effectiveness of economic modeling is explaining how to manipulate economic and technological factors to change the economy is about 50 percent. This is encouraging but falls far short of an effective explanation. Although it is true that econ-

THE BASIC APPROACH 25

If we divide C.I. by the random consistency number for the same size matrix, we obtain the consistency ratio (C.R.). The value of C.R. should be around 10 percent or less to be acceptable.

To illustrate the theory we have seen so far, we give two examples below. These examples are hierarchies consisting of a level of alternatives and a single overall objective. This is the case when several activities are compared with respect to a given common property.

ILLUSTRATIVE EXAMPLES

Distance Estimation through Air Travel Experiences

The method was used to estimate the relative distance of six cities from Philadelphia by making pairwise comparisons between them as to how strongly farther each was from Philadelphia.

Table 2.2 gives numerical values to the perceived remoteness from Philadelphia for each pair of cities. The rows indicate the strength of dominance. The question to ask is: Given one city (on the left) and another (on top), how much farther is the first one from Philadelphia than the second? We then put the reciprocal value in the transpose position. Compare the solution of the eigenvalue problem with the actual result (table 2.3).

The problem may be reformulated by forming clusters of cities according to the order of magnitude of their perceived distance from Philadelphia. The elements in each cluster are first compared among themselves. Then the clusters are themselves compared to obtain the appropriate weights for each cluster. Finally the entire set of values is normalized. The cities cluster into three classes—

Table 2.2. Comparison of Distances from Philadelphia

Comparison of Distances of Cities from Philadelphia	Cairo	Tokyo	Chicago	San Francisco	London	Montreal
Cairo	1	1/3	8	3	3	7
Tokyo	3	1	9	3	3	9
Chicago	1/8	1/9	1	1/6	1/5	2
San Francisco	1/3	1/3	6	1	1/3	6
London	1/3	1/3	5	3	1	6
Montreal	1/7	1/9	1/2	1/6	1/6	1

than is B, or how much more does A benefit from X than does B? Here one may look at the elements in lower levels in terms of decomposition of higher-level elements.

The other category looks backward and asks: Given a cluster indicating a criterion X, and given elements A and B of the cluster, how much more important or representative is A than B with respect to X, or how much more does A affect or influence X than does B, or how much more does A contribute to X than does B?

When a group participates in the judgment process, the group may reach consensus on some issues after discussions about priorities; but when they differ, we take the geometric mean of their judgments. This is because the judgments themselves and their reciprocals must be viewed symmetrically. The reciprocal of the geometric mean of a set of judgments is the geometric mean of the reciprocals. This is not true of the arithmetic mean.

Considerable experimental data have been gathered to compare the one-to-nine scale with twenty-eight other different scales used within the eigenvalue formulation. Various statistical measures were calculated. The evidence strongly favors the use of the one-to-nine scale as a reflection of our mental ability to discriminate different degrees of strengths of dominance among a few objects. The complete comparative analysis of the scales can be seen in Saaty (1980, p. 53).

Now we compare the value of C.I. for what it would be if our numerical judgments were taken at random from the scale 1/9, 1/8, 1/7, . . . , 1/2, 1, 2, . . . , 9 (using a reciprocal matrix). A sample of size 500 was taken for matrices of order 1 to 10, and their eigenvalues were computed for matrices of each size. Matrices of order greater than 10 are rarely used because of the large number of comparisons required, that is, $(10 \times 9)/2 = 45$. Clustering is required in those cases (see chapter 13). Thus, we have for different-order random matrices and their average consistencies:

Size of Matrix	Random Consistency
1	.00
2	.00
3	.58
4	.90
5	1.12
6	1.24
7	1.32
8	1.41
9	1.45
10	1.49

Table 2.1. Intensity of Importance Scale

Intensity of Importance	Definition	Explanation
1[a]	Equal importance	Two activities contribute equally to the objective
3	Weak importance of one over another	Experience and judgment slightly favor one activity over another
5	Essential or strong importance	Experience and judgment strongly favor one activity over another
7	Demonstrated importance	An activity is strongly favored and its dominance demonstrated in practice
9	Absolute importance	The evidence favoring one activity over another is of the highest possible order of affirmation
2, 4, 6, 8	Intermediate values between the two adjacent judgments	When compromise is needed
Reciprocals of above nonzero numbers	If activity i has one of the above nonzero numbers assigned to it when compared with activity j, then j has the reciprocal value when compared with i	See note below
Rationals	Ratios arising from the scale	If consistency were to be forced by obtaining n numerical values to span the matrix

[a] On occasion in 2-by-2 problems, we have used $1 + \epsilon$, $0 < \epsilon \leq \frac{1}{2}$ to indicate very slight dominance between two nearly equal activities.

Our choice of scale hinges on the following observation. Roughly, the scale should satisfy the following requirements:

1. It should be possible to represent people's differences in feelings when they make comparisons. The scale should represent as much as possible all distinct shades of feeling that people have.
2. If we denote the scale values by $x_1, x_2, \ldots, x_p$, then it would be desirable that $x_{i+1} - x_i = 1, i = 1, \ldots, p-1$.

Since we require that the subject must be aware of all gradations at the same time, and we agree with the psychological experiments showing that an individual cannot simultaneously compare more than seven objects (plus or minus two) without being confused (Miller, 1956), we are led to choose $p = 7 + 2$. A unit difference between successive scale values is all that we allow; using the fact that $x_1 = 1$ for the identity comparison, it follows that the scale values will range from one to nine.

As a preliminary step toward the construction of an absolute intensity of importance scale for activities, we have broken down the importance ranks as shown in the scale in table 2.1. In using this scale, the reader should recall that we assume the individual providing the judgment has knowledge about the relative values of the elements being compared whose ratio is $\geqslant 1$, and that the numerical ratios formed are nearest-integer approximations scaled in such a way that the highest ratio corresponds to nine. We assume that an element with weight zero is eliminated from comparison. This, of course, need not imply that zero may not be used for pairwise comparison. Reciprocals of all scaled ratios that are $\geqslant 1$ are entered in the transposed positions (not taken as judgments).

Note that the eigenvector solution of the problem remains the same if we multiply the unit entries on the main diagonal, for example, by a constant greater than one. (If $w_i/w_j > 9$, one may need to embed the problem in a hierarchical framework to obtain reasonable answers.) In practice, one way or another, the numerical judgments will have to be approximations, but how accurate is the question at which our theory is aimed?

A typical question to ask in order to fill in the entries in a matrix of comparisons is: Consider two properties, i on the left side of the matrix and j on the top; which of the two has the property under discussion more, and how strongly more (using the scale values one to nine)? This gives us a_{ij}. The reciprocal value is then automatically entered for a_{ji}.

There are two categories of questions. The first has to do with prediction of issues (a forward kind of question) and asks: Given a property X and a pair of elements A and B, how much more likely or probable is it that A will be a consequence of X than will B, or how much more is A affected or influenced by X

THE BASIC APPROACH

of possible error the estimate has the observed value $(w_i/w_j)\epsilon_{ij}$ where $\epsilon_{ij} > 0$. Consistency can be looked at in two ways:

1. By identifying transitive preferences. For example, if apples are preferred to oranges, and oranges are preferred to bananas, then apples must be preferred to bananas.
2. By identifying a few relations that show the strength of preference and forcing these relations on all other comparisons. For example, if apples are preferred four times as much as oranges, and oranges are preferred twice as much as bananas, then apples must be preferred eight times as much as bananas.

This kind of relation cannot be expected to hold in general. Violating it leads to inconsistency. The question is, how damaging is such inconsistency to our understanding and control of the problems we face? To answer this question, we need to introduce the scale that we use throughout our applications.

THE SCALE

The judgments elicited from people to estimate w_i/w_j are taken qualitatively and numerical values assigned to them, until the participants learn to select the numbers themselves. In general, we do not expect "cardinal" consistency to hold everywhere in the matrix because people's feelings do not conform to an exact formula. Nor do we expect "ordinal" consistency, as people's judgments may not be transitive. However, to improve consistency in the numerical judgments, whatever value a_{ij} is assigned in comparing the ith activity with the jth one, the reciprocal value is assigned to a_{ji}. Thus we put $a_{ji} = 1/a_{ij}$. Usually we first record whichever value represents dominance greater than unity. Roughly speaking, if one activity is judged to be α times stronger than another, then we record the latter as only $1/\alpha$ times as strong as the former. It can easily be seen that when we have consistency, the matrix has unit rank and it is sufficient to know one row of the matrix to construct the remaining entries. For example, if we know the first row, then $a_{ij} = a_{1j}/a_{1i}$ (under the rational assumption, of course, that $a_{1i} \neq 0$ for all i).

Whatever problem we deal with, we must use numbers that are sensible. From these the eigenvalue process would provide a scale. The best argument in favor of a scale is that if it can be used to reproduce results already known in physics, economics, or another area, a ratio scale is already known.

Assume that each row of the matrix of pairwise comparisons is dominated by or dominates every other row, as the given activity ranks below or above according to that row in the rank order. Then the rank order is preserved in solving the eigenvalue problem since:

$$\lambda_{max} w_i = \sum_{k=1}^{n} a_{ik} w_k \geqslant \sum_{k=1}^{n} a_{jk} w_k = \lambda_{max} w_j.$$

This relationship holds when we have consistency and may or may not hold without it. From this, one can also show that ordinal consistency is preserved since $A_i \geqslant A_j$ (or $a_{ik} \geqslant a_{jk}, k = 1, 2, \ldots, n$) implies $w_i \geqslant w_j$.

Suppose now that a new activity is adjoined to the set. If its rank order is known in advance, its row must satisfy the same properties of dominance just mentioned. On the other hand, it is desired to determine its rank order from the comparisons. Then to preserve the previous order, one could compare it with one of the other activities, perhaps the one with strongest preference over it, and all other activity comparisons with it are made by forcing the numerical relations among the eigenvector components. Rank order would thus be preserved since the row of the new activity would be positioned between the other rows with appropriate dominance.

In case the inconsistency in comparisons leads to violation of dominance, and hence some elements in a row dominate and others are dominated, introducing a new activity may or may not violate the previous order even when it is done by attempting to preserve consistency in the new row. Rank order can no longer be taken for granted unless it is associated with consistency in making pairwise comparisons.

It is clear that in the inconsistent case rank order is preserved if row dominance is preserved. Thus to preserve rank order a certain degree of consistency is required. One goes from intuitive rank order to pairwise comparisons to test the consistency of the intuitive judgments. It appears that one should not order the activities prior to making the pairwise comparisons, as it may highlight inconsistencies and create concern.

We now establish:

$$\text{C.I.} = \mu \equiv \frac{\lambda_{max} - n}{n - 1} = \frac{-\sum_{i=2}^{n} \lambda_i}{n - 1} \quad \text{(the average of } \lambda_i \quad i = 2, \ldots, n\text{)}$$

as a measure of the consistency or reliability of judgments (supplied by an individual) whose true values are (w_i/w_j), $i, j = 1, 2, \ldots, n$. We assume that because

THE BASIC APPROACH

those of all other eigenvalues. The corresponding eigenvector solution has nonnegative entries and, when normalized, is unique. Some of the remaining eigenvalues may be complex.

Suppose then that we have a reciprocal matrix. What can we say about an overall estimate of inconsistency for both small and large perturbations of its entries? In other words, how close is λ_{max} to n and w' to w? If they are not close, we may either revise the estimates in the matrix or take several matrices from which the solution vector w' may be improved. Note that improving consistency does not mean getting an answer closer to the "real"-life solution. It only means that the ratio estimates in the matrix, as a sample collection, are closer to being logically related than to being randomly chosen. Thus consistency is a necessary condition for scaling activities with respect to some criterion to get valid results in the real world. However, it is not sufficient; one needs to validate results in practice. A perfectly consistent picture of a situation can be obtained from an individual who is removed from reality. But this picture may not have relevance to reality. However, a necessary step for anyone to obtain a valid picture is to be consistent.

From here on we shall use $A = (a_{ij})$ for the estimated matrix and w for the eigenvector. There should be no confusion in dropping the primes.

It appears that a reciprocal matrix A with positive entries is consistent if and only if $\lambda_{max} = n$. This can be seen by writing:

$$\lambda_{max} = \sum_{j=1}^{n} a_{ij}\frac{w_j}{w_i},$$

putting $a_{ji} = 1/a_{ij}$ and reducing this equation to the form:

$$(\lambda_{max} - 1) = \frac{1}{n} \sum_{1 \leq i < j \leq n} \left(y_{ij} + \frac{1}{y_{ij}}\right),$$

where $y_{ij} = (a_{ij})(w_j/w_i)$. Each term in parentheses has the minimum value 2 at $y_{ij} = 1$, and hence $\lambda_{max} \geq n$. If $\lambda_{max} = n$, it is easy to show that the sum in parentheses must attain its minimum at $y_{ij} = 1$, that is, $a_{ij} = w_i/w_j$, the consistent case. With inconsistency, $\lambda_{max} > n$ always.

Suppose we have a set of activities that have been rank-ordered in advance. How does the intuitive process of rank ordering according to a criterion survive the consistency question? What happens when a new activity is introduced? Does the pairwise comparison process preserve the order determined before its introduction? The subject can be approached from the general standpoint of consistency.

This matrix has positive entries everywhere and satisfies the reciprocal property $a_{ji} = 1/a_{ij}$. It is called a reciprocal matrix. We note that if we multiply this matrix by the column vector $(w_1, \ldots, w_n)$ we obtain the vector nw. That is:

$$Aw = nw.$$

We started out with the assumption that w was given. But if we only had A and wanted to recover w, we would have to solve the system $(A - nI)w = 0$ in the unknown w. This has a nonzero solution if, and only if, n is an eigenvalue of A, that is, it is a root of the characteristic equation of A. But A has unit rank since every row is a constant multiple of the first row. Thus all the eigenvalues λ_i, $i = 1, \ldots, n$ of A are zero except one. Also it is known that:

$$\sum_{i=1}^{n} \lambda_i = \text{tr}(A) \equiv \text{sum of the diagonal elements} = n.$$

Therefore only one of λ_i, we call it $\lambda_{\max}$, equals n, and:

$$\lambda_i = 0 \qquad \lambda_i \neq \lambda_{\max}.$$

The solution w of this problem is any column of A. These solutions differ by a multiplicative constant. However, it is desirable to have this solution normalized so that its components sum to unity. The result is a unique solution no matter which column is used. Thus we can recover the scale from the matrix of ratios by, for example, simply normalizing the first column.

The matrix A satisfies the "cardinal" consistency property $a_{ij}a_{jk} = a_{ik}$ and is called consistent. For example, if we are given any row of A, we can determine the rest of the entries from this relation. This also holds for any set of n entries, no two of which fall in the same row or column.

Now suppose that we are dealing with a situation in which the scale is not known, but we have estimates of the ratios in the matrix. In this case the cardinal consistency relation above need not hold, nor need an "ordinal" transitivity relation of the form: $A_i > A_j$, $A_j > A_k$ imply $A_i > A_k$ hold (where the A_i are rows of A).

As a realistic representation of the situation in preference comparisons, we wish to account for inconsistency in judgments because, despite their best efforts, people's feelings and preferences remain inconsistent and intransitive.

We can show that in a positive reciprocal matrix, small perturbations in the coefficients imply small perturbations in the eigenvalues. Hence the eigenvector is insensitive to small changes in judgment and is stable, relative to larger changes (see Saaty, 1980, p. 192). Thus the problem $Aw = nw$ becomes $A'w' = \lambda_{\max}w'$. We also know from the theorem of Perron-Frobenius that a matrix of positive entries has a real positive eigenvalue (of multiplicity 1) whose modulus exceeds

THE BASIC APPROACH

In the forward projection we analyze how well we would do with our present structure and resources. In the backward process we analyze where we would like to be in the future and work toward the present to identify the type of actions or policies that would help us attain the desired future. Thus, planning becomes a two-point boundary process—the forward projection takes us from the present to the future, and the backward process goes from the future to the present. Repetition of these two processes yields an analysis of the stable future.

These processes require in most cases the measurement of qualitative properties. Because there is no unified scale of measurement for these properties, and because fuzziness is involved, scientists have tried to assess their impact on the functioning of the system and to express them in monetary units. However, it is known that social illnesses are not correlated with the GNP (Brookings Institution, 1968). Thus, to use monetary units to measure all our actions could be right only if their consequences were solely economic. Nonetheless, we know that daily actions are a conglomerate of economic, social, political, and other dimensions. Tradeoffs among these dimensions must be made. The aforementioned process considers these tradeoffs without requiring the use of a unified scale for all the dimensions. This suggests that a new measurement framework should be used (Saaty, 1976, 1977, 1980).

RATIO SCALE MEASUREMENT

Suppose that we wish to compare a set of n objects in pairs according to their relative weights. Denote the objects by $A_1, \ldots, A_n$ and their weights by $w_1, \ldots, w_n$. The pairwise comparisons may be represented by a matrix of underlying ratios (assumed to exist) as follows:

$$A = \begin{array}{c|cccc} & A_1 & A_2 & \cdots & A_n \\ \hline A_1 & \dfrac{w_1}{w_1} & \dfrac{w_1}{w_2} & \cdots & \dfrac{w_1}{w_n} \\ A_2 & \dfrac{w_2}{w_1} & \dfrac{w_2}{w_2} & \cdots & \dfrac{w_2}{w_n} \\ \vdots & \vdots & \vdots & \ddots & \vdots \\ A_n & \dfrac{w_n}{w_1} & \dfrac{w_n}{w_2} & \cdots & \dfrac{w_n}{w_n} \end{array}$$

selected through the conscious choice of the actor who chooses alternatives he believes to be more beneficial to him. Thus the outcome of an event does not directly depend on the outcome of previous events, through a causal process, nor on attributes of the individual. The actor makes his choice of actions through his perception of the consequences that the outcomes will have for him.

The Analytic Hierarchy Process (AHP) synthesizes these two approaches by identifying the outcomes that are more beneficial to the actors and at the same time provides a way of assessing the factors (causes) that may have more to do with certain types of outcomes.

There are twelve types of problems to which the AHP can be applied:

1. Setting priorities;
2. Generating a set of alternatives;
3. Choosing a best policy alternative;
4. Determining requirements;
5. Allocating resources;
6. Predicting outcomes (time dependence) – risk assessment;
7. Measuring performance;
8. Designing a system;
9. Ensuring system stability;
10. Optimizing;
11. Planning;
12. Conflict resolution.

In general, we first determine the requirements of the system – what do we need to do? Second, we generate alternatives to satisfy those requirements – what are the possible courses of action? Third, we set priorities according to the importance of the requirements in order to implement the alternatives to attain some higher objective. Finally, we choose the best policy alternative or, in some cases, a mix of the best policy alternatives.

The alternatives depend on the overall objective we may have in mind. Thus we may either allocate resources, after assessing the risk of the allocations, or measure the level of performance of the system, analyze its stability, and possibly redesign the overall structure to fit the functions that must be performed to meet certain requirements. Whether we wish to change the structure or the function of a system, we must set goals and identify different types of futures that would help to attain these goals through the implementation of specific policies. Here the purposive and causal approaches can be clearly identified. On the one hand, we establish the purpose of the system; and on the other, we identify the possible forces (causes) that shape the future. To obtain a stable outcome, the planning process is decomposed into forward and backward projections, as will be shown in chapter 6.

THE BASIC APPROACH

In this chapter we show a method (the Analytic Hierarchy Process) for scaling the weights of the elements in each level of the hierarchy with respect to an element (criterion or objective) of the next higher level. We construct a matrix of pairwise comparisons of the activities whose entries indicate the strength with which one element dominates another vis-à-vis the criterion against which they are compared.

The Analytic Hierarchy Process is a theory for dealing with complex technological, economic, and sociopolitical problems. Its mathematical foundations are simple. Its purpose is to make a contribution toward unity in modeling real-world problems, away from the existing fragmentation where each problem tends to have its specialized model and terminology. Its major assumptions are that the methods we use to pursue knowledge, to predict, and to control our world are relative and that the goal that we seek — that is, knowledge — is itself relative. It all depends on what purpose motivates us to seek that knowledge at that specific time or, as is the case with the scientific method, what beliefs others have instilled in us about the world and how we should go about understanding it.

This process is intimately connected with the idea of consistency of thought. It admits inconsistency (lack of transitivity) and measures the effect of different levels of consistency on the results we seek. Also it avoids a priori assumptions and models and calls on the knowledge-seeking individual to construct the framework of that quest. The assumption here is that only by experience, reason, intuition, and other attributes of actually knowing can we know. The theory incorporates in its various processes judgments considered to be based on knowledge, whether derived from experience, from measurement, or from other models. The object is to fulfill as well as possible the purposes of the people concerned rather than to legislate an outcome based on principles set forth by outsiders to the problem. Thus, perceived constraints must be examined and not taken for granted — this is the only hope we have to plan our way out of difficult problems.

This new theory combines two well-known approaches: (a) causal processes and (b) purposive action processes. In the former an action is described as an event with particular outcomes. Thus the sequence is:

$$\text{Cause} \rightarrow \text{event (outcome)}.$$

The cause may be events either internal to the system or external. In purposive action processes the sequence is:

$$\text{Action} \rightarrow \text{event (outcome)} \rightarrow \text{consequence for the actors involved}.$$

In this type of process the actions are no longer identical with the events. Actions of the actor in the system control the outcome of events, and they are

2 THE BASIC APPROACH

A fundamental problem of decision theory is how to derive weights for a set of activities according to importance. Importance is usually judged by several criteria that may be shared by some or all of the activities. This weighting of activities with respect to importance is a process of multiple-criterion decision making, which we study here through a theory of measurement in a hierarchical structure.

The object of this approach is to use the weights, which we call priorities, to allocate a resource among the activities or, if precise weights cannot be obtained, to simply implement the most important activities by rank. The problem then is to find the relative strength or priority of each activity with respect to each objective and then compose the results to obtain a single overall priority for all the activities. Frequently the objectives themselves must be prioritized or ranked in terms of yet another set of higher-level objectives. These priorities are then used as weighting factors for the priorities derived for the activities. In many applications, we have noted that the process must be continued by comparing the higher-level objectives in terms of still higher ones and so on, up to a single overall objective. The arrangement of the activities—first set of objectives, second set, and so on to the single-element objective—defines a hierarchical structure.

not mere conventional representations of that reality. It is apparently this quality of the AHP that enables practitioners to assign numerical values to essentially abstract concepts and to deduce from those values decisions about the nature of a larger hierarchy.

The real power of the Analytic Hierarchy Process lies in the broad scope and varied types of problems to which it can be applied. In many ways the process may be considered an extension of our information-processing capacity and our thought processes. Unlike other mathematical techniques, the AHP assists in extending our ability to analyze multiple variables simultaneously. Problems, the issues surrounding problems, and the people affected by the problems no longer have to rely on techniques that arbitrarily narrow the scope of the problem.

The chemist-philosopher Michael Polanyi explains well the need for a methodology such as the one we present in this volume:

> To affirm anything implies . . . an appraisal of our own art of knowing, and the establishment of truth becomes decisively dependent on a set of personal criteria of our own which cannot be formally defined. If everywhere it is the inarticulate which has the last word, unspoken and yet decisive, then a corresponding abridgement of the status of spoken truth itself is inevitable. The ideal of an impersonally detached truth would have to be reinterpreted, to allow for the inherently personal character of the act by which truth is declared. [*Personal Knowledge* (Chicago: University of Chicago Press, 1958), p. 71]

worth keeping, which are worth expanding, and which new ones should be created. In the application of chapter 13, a benefit/cost framework is used to select businesses that provide large benefits at low costs. Here we note that benefits and costs need not be expressed in monetary terms. All benefits and all costs accrued by the corporation from businesses must be considered.

Finally, we illustrate how a portfolio of stocks can be selected. The approach considers three major categories of factors that influence the selection of stocks: (1) the inner strengths of the companies issuing the stocks, that is, the internal or intrinsic factors that characterize a company; (2) the external or environmental factors that influence the stock market and therefore the mind of the investor as to the type of transaction he or she may wish to make (for example, buy and hold, sell short, sell, and so on); and (3) the objectives of the investor and the risk that person is willing to take (that is, the investor may be a risk taker, may be neutral, or may be a risk averter). One's objectives and the risk category in which one can be classified play a minor role in the selection of stocks. Thus, for example, a risk averter may be interested in capital formation and therefore may wish to invest in highly stable stocks. A risk taker, in contrast, may be more interested in trading and will look for short-term profits rather than for capital formation; highly speculative stocks may be this investor's target.

COMMENTS AND CONCLUSIONS

The Analytic Hierarchy Process allows one to take a large set of complex issues that have an impact on a problem and to compare the importance of each issue relative to its impact on the solution of the problem. Management has traditionally relied on "gut-reaction" and similar techniques in assessing the relative impacts of various issues. When the number of issues is small (say, two or three), the relative weights can be readily assessed by the decisionmaker. However, in today's complex environment the number of issues surrounding problems has increased significantly in number and complexity. It is difficult if not impossible for individuals to rationally weight such a large number of issues simultaneously. Statistical techniques derived over the past to assist managers can fail because of the limited types and numbers of real-world problems to which they can be applied. The Analytic Hierarchy Process helps overcome these difficulties.

A basic premise of the AHP is its reliance on the concept that much of what we consider to be "knowledge" actually pertains to our instinctive sense of the way things really are. This would seem to be derived from the position of Descartes that the mind itself is the first knowable principle. The AHP therefore takes as its premise the idea that it is our conception of reality that is crucial,

INTRODUCTION

Chapter 11 deals with the estimation of future oil prices. First, forces widely believed to influence the price of oil are identified. These forces have different effects at different times. Several likelihoods or degrees of influence—for example, high, medium, and low—are assigned to them. Next, the levels of price increase are taken to range from very low (5 percent) to extremely high (160 percent). The problem is to assign priorities to these price increases through the forces that influence the price of oil. The process is carried out for different time horizons (such as 1985, 1990) so that price increases are assessed within the right time frame and adjusted for different rates of inflation.

A useful feature of the AHP is the opportunity it affords us to quantify intangibles, a concern that other methods seem to leave aside because they lack good procedures for measurement. Some people like to deal with intangibles in terms of probabilities when estimation is no easier, but is sometimes treated lightly because probability numbers are, after all, only estimates of a situation subject to randomness.

In chapter 12 intangible attributes are used to predict the outcome of competition in world chess championships. Here, psychological factors such as ego, gamesmanship, and personality play as significant a role as the technical factors of experience, preparation, technique, and the like. A combination of these two types of factors simplifies the task of predicting the outcome with surprising accuracy.

There are some basic differences between predicting oil prices and predicting the outcome of competitive games. Time is crucial for the former but not usually for the latter. Oil prices are determined by actors who are greatly influenced by outside forces, whereas competitive situations are usually much less influenced by the outside environment.

However, both predictions are based on the same idea: if the factors involved in any situation are properly assessed, many results that people consider uncertain could be predicted within a certain degree of assurance.

How should we act on our predictions? We have seen that when we select among alternatives, we may have to choose the single "best" alternative or we may select a mix of "best" alternatives. The second option is known to some as portfolio selection.

To illustrate how the AHP can be used to select portfolios of alternatives, three important and distinct examples have been chosen: marketing, corporations and conglomerates, and the stock market.

In marketing, the application shows how to generate and select new products that can be launched into the market, to identify and prioritize means of distributing the products most effectively, and to select the markets where they can be introduced.

For a corporation, portfolio selection is used to decide which businesses are

resources have been allocated first; that is, the resources are interdependent. What we need is a way of making tradeoffs among the various requirements by considering both costs and benefits of treatments. Thus we must first determine the needs of the community. These needs are then translated into amounts of resources required to satisfy them, such as doctors, nurses, and medical equipment, given hospital budgetary and space limitations.

A different situation arises when the requirements of a resource are fixed according to the activities needing it, but one must allocate a limited amount of that resource to the activities despite shortage. This is the subject of chapter 10. Electricity is rationed to industrial sectors according to their contribution to the well-being of a nation.

To obtain a balanced approach to rationing, we must compute priorities for all activities according to their impact on several objectives in changing the economy. However, many production activities are interrelated. Therefore, we need to establish interdependence constraints so that in making the allocation to maximize their contributions, we do not penalize high-priority activities that depend on low-priority ones for their survival when less energy is allocated to the low-priority ones.

The rationing problem of chapter 10 deals with the allocation of only one resource, electricity. A different and more complicated problem is that of allocating several resources. If these resources were independent of one another, we would have several independent problems in each of which a single resource would be allocated. However, if the resources themselves are not independent, relationships among them must be identified and incorporated into the resource allocation problem in the form of interdependence constraints.

So far, the summaries of the previous chapters have illustrated applications in which activities are prioritized, and the priorities are then used in planning to select "best" policies to attain desired futures, often by implementing them through appropriate resource allocation. Such entities are assumed to be known with a degree of certainty. Part V introduces the highly important element of uncertainty and risk in prediction.

PREDICTION

Whether we prioritize, plan, or allocate resources, we always seem to desire to deal with the future. The philosopher Arthur Singer has pointed out that the essential characteristic of humankind is desire. We also have the ability to satisfy desires — an ability that is greatly assisted by looking ahead to what we can expect. But, as a Chinese proverb cautions, "Prediction is difficult, especially where the future is concerned."

INTRODUCTION

Effective long-range planning must consider the capabilities and behavior of the actors, their objectives, their future strategies and the impact of these strategies on the outcome strategies that could lead to a desired future, and ways that could make that future attainable.

There is a difference in results when the process is applied to planning for the future of an organization or to resolving a conflict. In planning, after the policies have been formulated and tested for effectiveness to yield the desired future, resources can be appropriately allocated to implement these policies. In conflict resolution, it is difficult to allocate resources (except perhaps for mediation and arbitration effort) as a part of implementation, because the solution of the conflict depends on compromise between the parties in the conflict. Nonetheless, once accord is reached, implementation of its terms may involve some kind of resource allocation. This is the topic discussed through the examples of the next two chapters.

RESOURCE ALLOCATION

In general, distribution of resources is part of implementing a plan. In the case of projects in research and development, we must plan our activities ahead so that only projects most likely to produce satisfactory results receive the required share of the resources. Here, the available resources may be allocated in proportion to the contribution of each project to the goals. However, in the case of the Sudan Transport Study, for example, projects were allocated resources adequate for their completion according both to benefit priorities and to costs. Because of limited funds, not all the projects were recommended for implementation but only those with high benefit/cost ratios for which existing and potential funds were available. One does not allocate small amounts of money to many projects without ensuring the likelihood of their completion. The order in which projects are implemented should also be considered.

A more complicated situation occurs when the surrounding environment imposes constraints on the projects. In chapter 9 such a problem is illustrated in the setting of the U.S. health care system. In recent years the United States has ranked as low as nineteenth in the world in providing the care necessary to decrease mortality and morbidity rates. Countries such as Great Britain, with lower expenditure rates than that of the United States, provide higher-quality medical care. An acknowledged cause of inadequacies in the system is the faulty allocation of hospital resources. These resources should be distributed to different units of a hospital in response to community needs. Since we are dealing with several resources at a time, some needs of the units can often be satisfied by different resources, and some resources cannot be distributed unless other

level of personnel in an organization, and the plans developed at each level should be coupled with those of all other levels.

Finally, the principle of continuity in planning, which is concerned with the continuous change that organizations and their surrounding environments undergo, states that plans must be updated, extended, and corrected periodically. The actual performance of plans should be compared with their expected performance. If the actual and expected outcomes deviate significantly, actions are gradually taken to bring the actual outcome closer to the expected or desired one.

An approach to planning, consonant with these four principles, is discussed in chapter 6. It comprises three phases. The first involves an assessment of the outcome likely to occur if no active intervention were to take place. Here one attempts to answer the following question: Given the actors and their policies, what is the logical future that is likely to result from their actions? This process relates the present to the future and is known as the forward process. It deals with the "probable."

The second phase is concerned with the question: Given a desired future, what actions are necessary to attain that future? This process links the future to the present and is known as the backward process. It deals with the "possible."

The third phase consists of coupling the first two phases to evaluate the effectiveness of intervention. This is done by adding the new courses of action from the backward process to the old set of actions in the forward process and noting the change in projecting the likely futures. The third phase is applied iteratively to narrow the gap between the likely and the desired futures. An application of this three-phase process to conflict resolution is made in chapter 7.

Chapter 7 contains an analysis of the stability of the conflict in South Africa between the subordinated black majority and the ruling white minority. First, the outcome of the conflict is determined under the assumption that the current political situation remains unchanged. Next, possible solutions are identified and courses of action for the actors that may influence the outcome are generated. The two steps are then combined to compare the reality of the situation with several possible future alternatives. In this process one generates alternatives that could steer the situation toward a mutually agreeable solution. The problem is how to combine the different perspectives so that the alternatives generated provide a realistic solution to the conflict. The judgments used in the analysis were obtained from knowledgeable and responsible people.

A similar situation is studied in chapter 8. The conflict is between the United States and the Organization of Petroleum Exporting Countries over oil prices. Since the ideologies and politics of the actors involved in the international oil market are diverse, one cannot make accurate judgments without understanding the relationships among the actors and the factors that influence their behavior.

INTRODUCTION

should be continued or should be terminated because it appears unpromising. The question is: How does one plan such investment?

The application illustrated in chapter 5 deals with the allocation of funds to projects for the XYZ Research Institute (XYZRI). XYZRI gets its resources primarily from the electric power utilities to do research on alternative ways of generating electricity, distributing it, and storing it, as well as on other concerns such as environmental hazards. Thus, under each category there are many projects of importance to the utilities.

The problem calls for using three time horizons: 1980, 1990, and 2000. In each of these years one is concerned with the availability of resources; the reliability, efficiency, and profitability of these resources in producing electricity; and environmental safeguards. The funds are to be allocated to the projects by taking into account the time horizons, the type of resources, and the concerns mentioned above. The time horizons are used to ensure the continuity of XYZRI's operations. The priorities are assigned in the time horizons in a discounting process to allocate investment funds accordingly.

Using the Analytic Hierarchy Process (AHP), one first obtains the priorities of the projects. They represent the relative impacts of the projects on the criteria and, through the criteria, on the type of resources available in each of the three time horizons. By estimating the cost of the projects for the corresponding years and by combining them with their priorities in a benefit/cost approach, XYZRI can decide which projects to keep alive and cut off resources from others in which further investment appears counterproductive. This situation is a good example of planning activities for the future. Planning, the focus of Part III, is closely related in this case to the problem of assigning priorities to projects.

PLANNING

Planners have long recognized four principles that underlie the idea of planning: participation, coordination, integration, and continuity. The first principle maintains that the object of planning is not to produce plans for others to use but to engage the users in their formulation and application. Effective planning cannot be done for individuals or organizations; it must be done by them.

The coordination principle states that because activities are interdependent, they should all be considered in the plan. No activity can be planned for in an efficient manner if treated independently of other activities. Thus all activities must be dealt with simultaneously and interactively.

According to the principle of integration, planning should be done at every

Decisions as complicated as the above have parallels in the activities of individuals, groups, and nations. In these instances, too, a single benefit criterion such as economics may not be of sufficient scope to reflect the many factors involved. It is fashionable nowadays, because economics is thought to be a science, to constantly translate qualitative and intangible factors of social and political content into economic units. Nonetheless, using results obtained only from economics usually does not solve social and political problems but in fact often aggravates them. This observation is reinforced by the well-known fact that a country's GNP is not well correlated with its social and political health. Thus it does not follow that increasing the GNP necessarily ameliorates social and political problems. Tradeoffs must be made among all the dimensions involved in a decision. Such tradeoffs are crucial, particularly in situations such as the selection of an effective technology for less developed countries (LDCs).

A developing country can adopt a technology precisely as it is used in the developed countries, or it may adapt and change that technology to suit its society and culture. In chapter 4 a method is described for dealing with technology transfer as well as with social and cultural changes.

This balanced approach relies primarily on the identification of the parties involved in choosing the technology. LDCs usually rely on developed countries and international agencies to provide them with the know-how and necessary funds for development. On occasion, the supporting parties tend to force the LDCs into accepting the type of technology with which they themselves have had substantial experience. To avoid this situation, the balanced approach involves all interested parties that may benefit from the growth of the LDC in the process of choosing the technology. An interactive evaluation process is required so that judgments of both outside experts and national leaders and their advisers are considered in the selection of an appropriate and effective technology.

The idea of identifying the significant factors bearing on a problem, setting their priorities, and calculating tradeoffs among them has wider applicability than is illustrated by the Sudan and the technology transfer examples. In chapter 5 we show how the AHP can be applied to research and development.

Here one must make commitments to particular technologies by allocating a given resource (for example, a budget) to projects whose results may benefit individuals or organizations. In this case several projects usually need support at varying levels of intensity. The problem is to determine how much resource to keep investing in each in order to satisfy an overall objective. It is clear that one must take a long-range view of the problem, since only rarely would all the projects be successful. They should therefore be evaluated in the short and long run under various conditions of risk. Our task is to plan ahead to make sure that resources are allocated to each project until it is determined whether a project

INTRODUCTION 5

cations: prioritization, planning, resource allocation, and prediction. Because of the integrated nature of the subject, there is some overlap among these parts.

The object of this chapter is to introduce the material of the book through a brief discussion of the purpose of each study and of how the Analytic Hierarchy Process was used.

APPLICATIONS OF PRIORITIZATION

In Part II we discuss three situations for which setting priorities is the cornerstone upon which one can construct a solution to an important problem.

Several countries in Africa have a promising, bright future. The Sudan is one of them. Its potential agricultural riches are vast but need development together with an extensive transport network to carry food from the farmland to the export outlet on the Red Sea. This plan will require borrowing vast sums of money from the outside. In addition, the Sudan fought a bloody civil war after independence. That war created hostilities and suspicion between North and South. Here politics dilutes the effectiveness of economic commitment to developing the agricultural regions in the North.

A plan was needed to convince lenders that funds would be invested according to a rational scheme in which they could have confidence. The plan, as described in chapter 3, focused on the development of a transport network and resulted in a set of projects whose priorities were designed to meet the economic, social, and political needs of the Sudan around 1985.

Funds were allocated to projects according to the ratio of their benefits to their total estimated costs. These benefits were social and political as well as economic. The plan had to cope with the existing complexity of factors while averting major problems that could result from its implementation. For example, had the resources been allocated according to economic benefits alone, most of the projects would have been implemented in the agriculturally rich central regions. The tropical South would have felt deprived of its share of the benefits; civil strife, a pressing problem, could ensue, disrupting economic development, the major objective of the country. Hence tradeoffs and compromise among economic, social, and political factors had to be made.

Another important objective was to involve the Sudanese themselves in the development of the plan. This would have two benefits: first, they would continue the planning after the initial study was over; and second, their sensitivity to political nuances would help to strike a balance between investment in the North and in the South and would decrease the possibility of another major conflict.

To demonstrate the applicability of the method, we guide the reader through selected case histories in such areas as business, energy, health, transportation, and conflict resolution. We illustrate not only how to deal with a complex set of interacting factors but also how to allocate resources according to benefits and costs, how to combine projected and idealized planning in a unified framework, how to evaluate projects, and how to make effective decisions in the face of mounting complexity.

Chapter 2 contains a brief account of the Analytic Hierarchy Process. We show how it affords individuals and groups an opportunity to structure their understanding of a problem in a flexible manner instead of forcing them into a model that may be contrary to their judgment. They will be able to consider intangible as well as tangible factors within this structure, as the measurement process is indifferent to the concreteness of the model's elements.

The Analytic Hierarchy Process utilizes qualitative descriptions to define a problem and to represent the interactions of its parts. It also makes use of quantitative judgments to assess the strengths of these interactions. The decisionmaker first identifies his or her main purpose in solving a problem. Criteria are chosen and weighted according to the priority of their importance to the decisionmaker. The different alternatives are then evaluated in terms of these criteria, and a best one or best mix is chosen. The alternatives are then potential solutions to the problem.

The purpose of constructing hierarchies is to study, evaluate, and prioritize the influence (or impact) of the alternatives (or activities) on the criteria to attain or satisfy the overall objective. It is worth emphasizing that the criteria may be interpreted as the constituent parts of the overall objective or, conversely, that the overall objective is the satisfaction of a cluster of criteria with different weights. Measurement of the priorities of the alternatives' impact on the various criteria is carried out through a process explained in detail in chapter 2.

Briefly then, this approach elicits and synthesizes information from decisionmakers and other knowledgeable participants to identify problems and to agree on their structure. The participants refine the structure (by iteration), generate new courses of action, and evaluate the effectiveness of these courses. Tradeoffs in priorities are computed in the process, resulting in a portfolio of policies. Resource allocation can be made in terms of benefit/cost ratios computed through two different hierarchies. The process also measures inconsistencies that may reflect the quality of the knowledge, the content of the judgments, and the stability of the solution.

The book is divided into five parts. Part I, consisting of this chapter and the next, deals with background material. The remaining four parts deal with appli-

1 INTRODUCTION

Our minds have a limited capacity to assimilate and retain large amounts of information even for short periods of time. Because of such limitations, and because in many situations data are not available, we must base our decisions on the information at hand and on the experiences we have accumulated over the years. In today's complex world, no amount of information seems adequate to make objective decisions on multifaceted and controversial problems. No wonder individuals and even public and private enterprises often make decisions based on subjective knowledge rather than on a thorough and complete logical resolution of the issues – if that ever is a possibility.

In addition, complex decisions are usually characterized by a large number of interacting factors. The problem is how to properly assess the importance of these factors in order to make tradeoffs among them; how to derive a system of priorities that can guide us to make good decisions by choosing a best alternative. To answer this problem of decision making in the face of risk, uncertainty, diversity of factors, and varying opinions and judgments, a new approach has been developed by Thomas L. Saaty in recent years – the Analytic Hierarchy Process. The purpose of this book is to show the usefulness of this approach in complex decision-making problems. The value of the method will be better appreciated by examining its varied applications to current problem areas of significance to our world.

I PRIORITIZATION

here have involved the use of talent from many areas. The material should make readers aware of the complexity of problems to which the process has so far been extended and should bring to their attention different questions and issues that have been raised through implementation of the process. A detailed exposition of Saaty's theory is given in *The Analytic Hierarchy Process* (paperback, 1990 revised and extended edition, 412 pp., RWS Publications, Pittsburgh, PA (412) 621-4492. First edition published by McGraw-Hill International, New York, 1980.)

The book is intended for scientists in the areas of operations research and management science; for social, behavioral, and budding computer scientists; and, in general, for students and practitioners who would like to use a new approach for dealing with complexity. Here we show how to:

- Develop a framework for analyzing factors that affect the outcome of a complex decision;
- Do cost/benefit measurement and allocate resources accordingly;
- Do planning by iterative alignment of the priorities of projected and desired targets;
- Predict the value of an expected outcome, such as the expected price of a barrel of oil;
- Establish priorities for a set of activities and make a best choice or a mix of choices based on these priorities;
- Allocate resources according to the priorities;
- Measure consistency and how well relations are understood by the decisionmaker.

The Analytic Hierarchy Process is based on both absolute and relative measurement. The original theory was developed around the more important relative measurement and has been extended to deal with the normative absolute measurement. Material has been added in this 1990 printing in Appendix B to illustrate the ideas of absolute measurement.

Preface

This book presents applications of the Analytic Hierarchy Process developed by Thomas L. Saaty to deal with unstructured decision problems, together with case histories developed by him and in collaboration with others in areas of current societal concern. Its purpose is to provide the reader with examples of how to deal with unstructured problems, particularly ones involving socio-economic and political issues with qualitative and intangible factors.

These examples show how to use judgment and experience to analyze a complex decision problem by combining its qualitative and quantitative aspects in a single framework and generating a set of priorities for alternative courses of action. The process has inherent flexibilities in structuring a problem and in taking diverse judgments from people, whether singly, in a group working together, or by questionnaire. Decisionmakers will profit from this approach. It makes accessible to them a framework for understanding the complexity of the system they are in as it impinges on the surrounding environment.

To deal with complexity, we must first understand it. Systems thinking is necessary if all the important factors are to be considered. Complex systems problems can challenge and tax our logical capability to fully understand their causes and the consequences of any action we may take to solve them. Nevertheless, in time their effects on us tend to become better known than their causes. In addition, the causes may be many, and all interact in ways that defy understanding. In that case we must use our experience and feelings to assess the effects of a particular problem and to determine where, according to priority, we should apply our effort to deal with it. Because many people lack an adequate understanding of complexity but are nonetheless affected by it, we need dependable ways to combine our judgment and understanding to deal with complexity. That is what the Analytic Hierarchy Process, the subject of this book, is about; it integrates all valuable information - scientific, social, political, economic, - that has a bearing on the issues considered.

In this book applications of the Analytic Hierarchy Process are extended to problems in business, conflict resolution, energy, health, planning, prediction, technology transfer, and transportation. The first author has participated in and directed the development of all applications illustrated here.

The main purpose of the book is to present the practical facet of the Analytic Hierarchy Process developed by the first author early in the 1970's and to guide readers through selected applications. The examples developed

jointly prepared by both authors. Chapter 8 is our summary of a Ph.D. dissertation by Abdolhamid Gholamnezhad, written at the University of Pennsylvania under the supervision of the first author.

The following chapters were previously published elsewhere, and we wish to thank the various journals for their permission to reproduce the material here:

Chapter 3: Reprinted by permission of Thomas L. Saaty, "The Sudan Transport Study," *Interfaces,* Volume 8, No. 1, Part 2, Copyright 1977, The Institute of Management Sciences.

Chapter 4: Reprinted by permission of the publisher from "Technological Choices in Less Developed Countries," by Vasudevan Ramanujam, and Thomas L. Saaty, *Technological Forecasting and Social Change,* Volume 19 (1981):81-98. Copyright 1981 by Elsevier North-Holland, Inc.

Chapter 7: "The Conflict in South Africa: Directed or Chaotic?" by David S. Tarbell and Thomas L. Saaty, *Journal of Peace Science,* Volume 4, No. 2 (1980):151-68.

Chapter 10: "Rationing Energy to Industries: Priorities and Input-Output Dependence," by Thomas L. Saaty and Reynaldo S. Mariano, *Energy Systems and Policy,* Volume 3, No. 1 (1979), Crane, Russak & Company, Inc., New York.

Chapter 11: "Oil Prices: 1985 and 1990," by Thomas L. Saaty and Abdolhamid Gholamnezhad, *Energy Systems and Policy* (1981, forthcoming), Crane, Russak & Company, New York.

Chapter 12: "Hierarchical Analysis of Behavior in Competition: Prediction in Chess," by Thomas L. Saaty and Luis G. Vargas, reprinted from *Behavioral Science,* Volume 25, No. 3 (1980), by permission of James Grier Miller, M.D., Ph.D., Editor.

Chapter 13: Two papers are included in this chapter: reprinted by permission of Yoram Wind and Thomas L. Saaty, "Marketing Applications of the Analytic Hierarchy Process," *Management Science,* Volume 26, No. 7 (July 1980), Copyright 1980, The Institute of Management Sciences; reprinted from the *Journal of Portfolio Management,* "Portfolio Selection through Hierarchies," by Thomas L. Saaty, Paul C. Rogers, and Ricardo Pell, *Journal of Portfolio Management,* Spring Issue, No. 3 (1980):16-21.

Acknowledgments

We acknowledge with gratitude the contributions that our associates and colleagues have made to this book, which should be considered in every sense a joint effort rather than an individual accomplishment. In particular, we wish to thank the following individuals, who collaborated with the first author in the writing of various papers that form the background of a large portion of this book:

James P. Bennett (chapter 5)
John J. Dougherty, III (chapter 9)
James R. Emshoff (chapter 6)
Abdolhamid Gholamnezhad (chapter 11)
Reynaldo S. Mariano (chapter 10)
Ricardo Pell (chapter 13)
Vasudevan Ramanujam (chapter 4)
Paul C. Rogers (chapter 13)
David S. Tarbell (chapter 7)
Yoram Wind (chapter 13)

Chapters 2 and 3 are the work of the first author; chapters 1, 12, and 14 were

Concluding Remarks about Applications	278
References	278

Appendix A: Estimation of Input-Output Technological Coefficients ... 279
    Background ... 279
    Estimation of Input-Output Coefficients ... 281
    References ... 288

Appendix B: Absolute Measurement - Rating Alternatives One at a Time ... 290
    Absolute versus Relative Measurement ... 290
    Absolute Measurement and Ratings ... 292
    Using Ranges for Intensities ... 294
    Nonlinear Ranges ... 294
    Employee Evaluation ... 295

Index ... 298

		An Example	186
		Short-Term Rationing of Electricity to Industries	189
		Comments	192
		References	192

V PREDICTION

	11	**Oil Prices: 1985 and 1990**	**195**
		Factors Affecting Future World Oil Prices	197
		Estimation of Price Increases	201
		Computation of Oil Prices	202
		Comments	206
		References	206
	12	**Hierarchical Analysis of Behavior in Competition: Prediction in Chess**	**207**
		Relative Power of the Players: The Input	209
		Disposition of the Players toward the Game	213
		Predicting the Number of Games Played and Won	215
		Applications	216
		Parametric Analysis	224
		Comments	224
		References	225
	13	**Risk and Uncertainty in Portfolio Selection**	**227**
		Product Portfolio Selection	228
		Generation and Evaluation of New-Product Concepts	233
		Marketing Mix Determination	236
		Corporate Portfolio Selection	240
		Investment Portfolio Selection	247
		Comments	261
		References	263
	14	**Some Extensions in Application and Theory**	**264**
		Summary Outline of the Analytic Hierarchy Process and Extensions	265
		The Continuous Hierarchy	270
		The Stability of Hierarchies	272
		Application of the AHP to Some Problem Areas	275
		Group Judgments by Questionnaire	276

		Application: A Case Study	108
		Assessment of Forward and Backward Processes	114
		Comments	116
		References	116
	7	**The Conflict in South Africa**	**118**
		The Conflict Hierarchy	120
		First Forward Process	123
		First Backward Process	125
		Second Forward Process	128
		Second Backward Process	128
		Third Forward Process	129
		State Variables	130
		Comments	134
		References	138
	8	**Critical Choices for OPEC Members and the United States: A Hierarchical Search for Their Desired Future**	**139**
		Actors in the International Oil Market	142
		The Basic Methodology	148
		The Backward Process	155
		Comments	157
		References	161
IV	**RESOURCE ALLOCATION**		
	9	**Optimum Determination of Hospital Requirements**	**165**
		Model for Hospital Requirements Determination	166
		Hospital Requirements Priority Determination	166
		Resource Constraint Matrix Development	172
		Resource Optimization and Sensitivity Analysis	177
		Comments	178
		References	180
	10	**Rationing Energy to Industries: Priorities and Input-Output Dependence**	**182**
		Rationing Energy through Prioritization	184
		Classification of Energy Users by Industry	185
		Criteria Used to Evaluate Energy Users	185

	The Consistency of a Hierarchy	36
	Methods of Estimating the Vector of Priorities and Clustering Schemes	38
	Comments	40
	References	41

II APPLICATIONS OF PRIORITIZATION

3 The Sudan Transport Study 45
  The Sudan 45
  Background and Purpose of the Plan 47
  Problem Areas Relating to the Plan 48
  Brief Account of the Study 51
  Econometric Models 54
  Scenarios of the Sudan's Future 55
  Priorities of the Scenarios 58
  The Composite Scenario 59
  Priorities of Regions and Projects 60
  Sectoral Investment Strategies 63
  Some Management Strategies 64
  Implementation 64
  Comments 65

4 Technological Choice in Less Developed Countries 66
  Applications to Technology Transfer 68
  An Example: Technology Transfer Using the AHP 74
  Comments 80
  References 82

5 XYZ Research Institute: Planning Resource Allocation under Uncertainty 83
  XYZRI's Hierarchy of R&D Allocations 85
  Benefit/Cost Analysis of Programs 91
  Assuring Continuity of Operations 98
  Comments 98

III PLANNING

6 Planning: Forward and Backward Processes 101
  Forward and Backward Processes 103

Contents

Acknowledgments	xi
Preface	xiii

I PRIORITIZATION

1 Introduction	3
Applications of Prioritization	5
Planning	7
Resource Allocation	9
Prediction	10
Comments and Conclusions	12
2 The Basic Approach	14
Ratio Scale Measurement	17
The Scale	21
Illustrative Examples	25
Formal Hierarchies	30
An Example: Vacation Site Selection	34

First edition printed in 1982 by Kluwer-Nijhoff Publishing, Boston, under the title:

The Logic of Priorities
Applications in Business, Energy, Health, and Transportation
under the ISBN 0-89838-071-5 (hardcover)
and ISBN 0-89838-078-2 (paperback)
(Copyright © 1982 by Kluwer Boston)

Copyright © 1991 by T.L. Saaty and L.G. Vargas

Reprinted in paperback, 1991, by RWS Publications

ISBN 0-9620317-3-9

RWS Publications
Decision Making using the AHP
4922 Ellsworth Avenue
Pittsburgh, PA 15213
Phone: (412) 621-4492
FAX: (412) 682-3844

The Logic of Priorities

Applications in Business, Energy, Health, and Transportation

Thomas L. Saaty
Luis G. Vargas
University of Pittsburgh

Volume III

The Analytic Hierarchy Process Series

To Order RWS Publications' Books: Call, Write or Fax

RWS PUBLICATIONS
Decision Making Using the AHP
4922 Ellsworth Avenue
Pittsburgh, PA 15213 USA

Phone (412) 621-4492   FAX (412) 682-3844

The Logic of Priorities

Special Issues of Journals Devoted to the Analytic Hierarchy Process

Socio-Economic Planning Sciences, Guest editor: Patrick T. Harker, Volume 20, Number 6, 1986.

Communications of the Operations Research Society of Japan, Volume 31, Number 8, 1986

Mathematical Modelling: An International Journal, Guest editors: L.G. Vargas & R.W. Saaty, Volume 9, Number 3-5, 1987.

Proceedings of the First International Symposium on the Analytic Hierarchy Process, Tianjin University, Tianjin, China, September 6-9, 1988.

Communications of the Operations Research Society of Japan, Volume 34, Number 4, 1989.

European Journal of Operational Research; Decision Making by the Analytic Hierarchy Process: Theory and Applications. Guest editors: L.G. ᵛ R.W. Whittaker, Volume 48, Number 1, September 5, 1990.

Proceedings of the Second International Symposium on the Analytic F Process, University of Pittsburgh, Pittsburgh, Pennsylvania, USA, A 14, 1991.

Socio-Economic Planning Sciences, Guest editors: Bruce Golden & Wasil, Forthcoming, 1991.

Mathematical Modelling: An International Journal, Guest editoɪ Vargas & F. Zahedi, Forthcoming, 1992.

Books on the Analytic Hierarchy Process in other Languages

CHINESE

Analytic Hierarchy Process: Applications to Resource Allocation, Management, and Conflict Resolution, Thomas L. Saaty, translated by Shubo Xu, 1989, Press of Coal Industry, China.

Applied Decision Making Methods: Analytic Hierarchy Process, Shubo Xu, 1988, Press of Tianjin University, Tianjin, China.

FRENCH

La prise de décision en management, D. Merunka, 1987, Vuibert Gestion, 63 Bd. St. Germain, Paris.

Décider face à la complexité, Thomas L. Saaty, 1984, Enterprise moderne d'edition, 17 Rue Viete, 75017 Paris.

GERMAN

Haben Sie heute richtig ent-schieden?, Knut Richter and Gisela Reinhardt, 1990, Verlag Die Wirtschaft Berlin.

JAPANESE

The AHP: An Easy to Understand Model, Eizo Kinoshita, 1990.

The Analytic Hierarchy Process: Decision Making, Kaoru Tone, 1986, Japanese Scientific and Technical Press, Tokyo.

AHP Applications, Kaoru Tone and Ryutaro Manabe, June 1990, Japanese Science and Technology Press, Tokyo.

RUSSIAN

Analytical Planning: The Organization of Systems, Kevin P. Kearns and Thomas L. Saaty, translated by Revaz Vachnadze, 1990, Radio Moscow, Moscow.

The Analytic Hierarchy Process, Thomas L. Saaty, translated by Revaz Vachnadze, 1990, Radio Moscow, Moscow.

Books on the Analytic Hierarchy Process Available from RWS Publications

Analytical Planning: The Organization of Systems, Thomas L. Saaty and Kevin P. Kearns, 208 pp., paperback edition, 1991.

Decision Making for Leaders, Thomas L. Saaty, paperback, 291 pp., 1990.

Multicriteria Decision Making: The Analytic Hierarchy Process, Thomas L. Saaty, paperback, 502 pp., extended edition, paperback, 1991.

The Logic of Priorities: Applications in Business, Energy, Health, and Transportation, Thomas L. Saaty and Luis G. Vargas, paperback, 299 pp., paperback edition, 1991.

Books on the Analytic Hierarchy Process Available from other Publishers

Marketing Decisions Using Expert Choice, R.F. Dyer, E.A. Forman, E.H. Forman, G. Jouflas, workbook, 201 pp., 1988, Expert Choice, Inc., Pittsburgh, Pennsylvania.

An Analytic Approach to Marketing Decisions, Robert F. Dyer & Ernest H. Forman, 367 pp., 1991, Prentice Hall, Inc.

The Analytic Hierarchy Process: Applications and Studies, Bruce L. Golden, Patrick T. Harker and Edward A. Wasil,(Eds.), 1989, Springer-Verlag, New York.

Conflict Resolution: The Analytic Hierarchy Approach, Thomas L. Saaty and Joyce M. Alexander, 1989, Praeger, New York.

Thinking with Models, Thomas L. Saaty and Joyce M. Alexander, 181 pp., 1981, Pergamon Press, Inc.

Prediction, Projection, and Forecasting, Thomas L. Saaty and Luis G. Vargas, 253 pp., 1991, Kluwer Academic Publishers.

To Order RWS Publications' Books: Call, Write or Fax

RWS PUBLICATIONS
Decision Making Using the AHP
4922 Ellsworth Avenue
Pittsburgh, PA 15213 USA

Phone: (412) 621-4492   FAX: (412) 682-3844